GEOGRAPHIES FOR ADVANCED STUDY
Edited by Professor S. H. Beaver ma

WEST AFRICA

CHURCH, R. J. Harrison. **West Africa; a Study of the Environment and of Man's Use of It. 6th ed. Wiley, 1968. 543p il map tab bibl (Geographies for Advanced Study) 68-9201. 8.95**
There were significant changes in the fourth edition (1963) of this classic geography of West Africa, the standard of which has hardly been reached by geography books on any other African region of comparable scope. Compared to the fifth (1966), this edition has additional recent bibliographic references, at times replacing older ones as is the case for Upper Volta. A new table showing annual rates of population increases has been inserted in the chapter on political divisions. About three pages have been rewritten for Nigeria with a map of oil fields and pipelines (replacing one of tin on the Jos plateau) and a new map of political divisions in Nigeria. Biafra is cursorily mentioned in the text, not in the index. Maps, diagrams, the whole index are identical with the fifth edition. Church's *West Africa* is a must for all libraries in 1969 but only the largest or those specializing in Africa need buy the sixth edition, smaller ones which have the fourth or fifth need not.

CHOICE   SEPT. '69
History, Geography &
Travel

Africa

GEOGRAPHIES FOR ADVANCED STUDY

EDITED BY PROFESSOR S. H. BEAVER MA

WEST AFRICA

*A Study of the Environment
and of Man's Use of it*

BY

R. J. HARRISON CHURCH

BScEcon PhD

*Professor of Geography in the
University of London
at the London School of Economics and Political Science.
Sometime French Government
Post-Graduate British Fellow at the Sorbonne (Paris)*

WITH NUMEROUS MAPS
AND ILLUSTRATIONS

LONGMANS

LONGMANS, GREEN AND CO LTD
London and Harlow
Associated companies, branches and representatives
throughout the world

New editions © *R. J. Harrison Church 1960, 1961, 1963, 1966*
Sixth edition © *Longmans, Green & Co Ltd 1968*

First published 1957
Second Edition 1960
Third Edition 1961
Fourth Edition 1963
Fifth Edition 1966
Sixth Edition 1968

Russian Edition 1959

Printed in Great Britain by Richard Clay (The Chaucer Press) Ltd
Bungay, Suffolk

*If this book be of sufficient merit,
it is dedicated to the peoples of
West Africa and to all who have their
welfare at heart*

PREFACE

WEST Africa has been in contact with the outside world longer than any other part of Africa south of the Sahara. No other area of Africa has undergone such profound political, economic and social changes as have taken place recently in West Africa. The world and West Africa are making a great impact upon each other.

No apology is necessary, therefore, for this attempt to provide a modern and comprehensive study of West Africa, based on seven years of wide reading in scattered literature in several languages, and on very extensive field work throughout the area. While it casts its net widely, it does not necessarily include all that might be regarded by some as geographical; nor is its scope confined to matters exclusively geographical. Nevertheless, material wholly germane to government, anthropology and economics is not discussed in detail. No person could rightly imagine from the text that such matters are unimportant, but their study requires other specialists and other books.

Part One deals with the natural conditions in West Africa and with some of the human problems which these present. Part Two analyses man's work in agriculture, livestock holding, mining and the provision of transport, as well as the distribution of man himself, which often but not always results from these activities. Part Three is an examination of the individual countries, after a general review of their contrasted character and situation.

There is some variation in the content of chapters on the several countries, which results from their varying character and the relative availability or reliability of the material. The regional approach has been adopted in almost all chapters because, contrary to widespread belief, there is much regional variety in West Africa, a fact well understood by its peoples. A further reason for the study of regions within the countries of West Africa is that they have been somewhat neglected, although they have now great and growing importance in development plans. Development will fail, as some wild schemes have already, unless it is based upon a regional appraisal of the physical, economic and human resources.

The reader will encounter a few personal views. These are clearly evident as such and are offered as considered interpretations.

My sincerest wish is that this book will contribute to the knowledge of a delightful part of a fascinating and developing continent. May it be read in the spirit of the dedication

R. J. HARRISON CHURCH

The London School of Economics
and Political Science,
April 1955

PREFACE TO SIXTH EDITION

THE creation of twelve states in place of the four regions of Nigeria is the outstanding event since the last edition. Maps and text have been revised to take account of this momentous change, whilst a new map of fuel and power in Nigeria has been included. Figures of the estimated population for each country in 1966 and, for the first time, annual rates of increase are given on page 178. Full account has been taken throughout the book of economic and other changes.

R. J. HARRISON CHURCH

April 1968

NOTE ON GEOGRAPHICAL NOMENCLATURE

THE spelling of African place and tribal names is in a confused state. The early European orthography of African names was often grossly inaccurate. Some names have since been officially changed and improved, while others have persisted in their unsatisfactory form. The author, though wishing to see a name properly recorded, must use the official style, so that the name may be located on a map. At the suggestion of Mr. M. Aurousseau, former Secretary of the Permanent Committee on Geographical Names for British Official Use, I have adopted the names used by the map-making authorities of each country, except where long-recognised English equivalents exist, e.g. Fernando Po, Timbuktu, etc. For tribal names, I hope that I have succeeded in using the names most widely used and generally accepted by British ethnographers.

As the former French Guinea has become the independent Republic of Guinea confusion might arise over such terms as Guinea coasts, Guinea coastlands, Guinea Highlands and Guinea Savannah. Except where these are mentioned in the chapter on Guinea, they should be understood as referring to natural features of wider occurrence. The first two concern fringes of the Gulf of Guinea.

TEMPERATURE CONVERSION TABLE

FAHRENHEIT TO CENTIGRADE

°F	°C	°F	°C	°F	°C	°F	°C
112·0	44·4	96·0	35·6	80·5	26·9	65·0	18·3
111·5	44·2	95·5	35·3	80·0	26·7	64·5	18·1
111·0	43·9	95·0	35·0	79·5	26·4	64·0	17·8
110·5	43·6	94·5	34·7	79·0	26·1	63·5	17·5
110·0	43·3	94·0	34·5	78·5	25·8	63·0	17·2
109·5	43·1	93·5	34·2	78·0	25·5	62·5	16·9
109·0	42·8	93·0	33·9	77·5	25·3	62·0	16·7
108·5	42·5	92·5	33·6	77·0	25·0	61·5	16·4
108·0	42·2	92·0	33·4	76·5	24·7	61·0	16·1
107·5	41·9	91·5	33·1	76·0	24·5	60·5	15·8
107·0	41·7	91·0	32·8	75·5	24·2	60·0	15·5
106·5	41·4	90·5	32·5	75·0	23·9	59·5	15·3
106·0	41·1	90·0	32·2	74·5	23·6	59·0	15·0
105·5	40·8	89·5	31·9	74·0	23·4	58·5	14·7
105·0	40·6	89·0	31·7	73·5	23·1	58·0	14·4
104·5	40·3	88·5	31·4	73·0	22·8	57·5	14·2
104·0	40·0	88·0	31·1	72·5	22·5	57·0	13·9
103·5	39·7	87·5	30·8	72·0	22·2	56·5	13·6
103·0	39·4	87·0	30·5	71·5	21·9	56·0	13·3
102·5	39·2	86·5	30·3	71·0	21·7	55·5	13·1
102·0	38·9	86·0	30·0	70·5	21·4	55·0	12·8
101·5	38·6	85·5	29·7	70·0	21·1	54·5	12·5
101·0	38·3	85·0	29·5	69·5	20·8	54·0	12·2
100·5	38·1	84·5	29·2	69·0	20·6	53·5	11·9
100	37·8	84·0	28·9	68·5	20·3	53·0	11·7
99·5	37·5	83·5	28·6	68·0	20·0	52·5	11·4
99·0	37·2	83·0	28·3	67·5	19·7	52·0	11·2
98·5	36·9	82·5	28·1	67·0	19·4	51·5	10·9
98·0	36·7	82·0	27·8	66·5	19·2	51·0	10·6
97·5	36·4	81·5	27·5	66·0	18·9	50·5	10·3
97·0	36·1	81·0	27·2	65·5	18·6	50·0	10·0
96·5	35·9						

ACKNOWLEDGEMENTS

Thanks to the efforts of my former colleague Mr. R. E. Wraith, the Training Department of the Colonial Office gave me a grant from the Devonshire Courses Vote in 1949. I am much indebted to Mr. Wraith and to Mrs. Katherine Beamish, then of that Department, for their interest and help, and to the governments of Sierra Leone, the Gold Coast and Nigeria.

In the following years, the Federal Government of French West Africa, the governments of its component territories, the Institut Français d'Afrique Noire (I.F.A.N.), and the Government of Spanish Guinea all gave me immediate and most generous help, as they did on later tours in 1959 and 1964. I also enjoyed financial support from the Wenner-Gren Fund, from the Compagnie Fabre Frasinnet of Marseilles which gave me reduced fares on their ships, and from my college. The latter also gave me the services of two research assistants, who helped me with climatic and other maps. Nor could I ever forget the outstanding patience and hospitality shown me by administrative and technical officers, merchants, missionaries and private people—African, European and Lebanese —on countless occasions.

The initial idea for this book came from Professor Sir Dudley Stamp, C.B.E., D.Sc., D.Lit., LL.D. He encouraged me in the initial period of frustration and prodded me when necessary later on. Professor S. H. Beaver, M.A., has been a most assiduous and helpful editor. Miss Ursula M. E. Rodd, B.Sc.(Econ.), Mr. John Callow, B.A., Mrs. Christodoulou and Miss Sheila Chantler drew my maps with skill and patience, often helping me to know what I wanted. Miss B. G. Atkinson, B.A., and Mrs. O. J. Bird, B.A., typed my sometimes difficult manuscripts with speed and good grace.

Almost all of my chapters have been read by experts and, for this, my thanks are recorded in footnotes. I thank them all most sincerely again here, for they have added greatly to the value of this book. The chapter on Portuguese Guinea is by Professor Orlando Ribeiro and that on São Tomé and Príncipe by Mr. Francisco Tenreiro. I am most grateful to both of them for their contributions. I am also much indebted to my colleague Mr. R. Chapman, M.A., to Mr. J. Barnett, M.A., and especially to Miss Elizabeth Maxwell, B.A., and Mr. C. P. Hill, M.A., for reading my chapters; and to my wife for her checking and patience. Mrs. Judith Johnsrud, M.A., and Miss Alison Lathbury, M.A., M.S., read most of the proofs and made many improvements.

Considerable time and thought have been expended in finding and arranging suitable illustrations. As the numbers of these must be limited, I have included none of Vegetation; excellent photographs of this may be seen in the references listed in Chapter 4. I am most grateful to those who have provided illustrations without fee and to authors, editors and publishers who have permitted me to use certain maps.

Much effort has been expended by myself and my helpers in verifying facts and conclusions but West Africa is changing rapidly. Matters now true may cease to be and some mistakes may have slipped in. I should indeed be grateful to anyone who takes the trouble to tell me of any errors for which I take responsibility.

R. J. H. C.

CONTENTS

xv

MAPS AND DIAGRAMS

xvii

PLATES

Acknowledgements

For permission to reproduce photographs we are indebted to the following:
Ministère de la France d'Outre-Mer for Plates 1, 10; Caisse Centrale de la France d'Outre-Mer for Plate 39 supplied by Ministère de la France d'Outre-Mer; Information A.O.F. for Plate 43 supplied by Ministère de la France d'Outre-Mer; Ministère de la Cooperation for Plate 74; Agence Economique des Colonies, Paris, for Plates 3, 7, 8, 23, 41, 46, 48, 49, 50, 55, 60–64, 66, 91, 92; Etat-Major de l'Air for Plate 56; Ivory Coast Embassy for Plate 79; Liberian Information Service for Plate 78; Office du Niger for Plate 58; Ministry of Agriculture, Gold Coast, for Plate 19; Public Relations Dept, Government of Nigeria, for Plate 101; Gold Coast Information Services for Plate 20; Information Services Dept., Accra, for Plate 81 (Crown Copyright Reserved); Air Ministry for Plate 76 (Crown Copyright Reserved); United Africa Company (Timber) Ltd. for Plate 99; United Africa Company Ltd for Plates 12, 13, 14, 27, 28, 98; Aircraft Operating Co. for Plates 80, 95, 105; Amalgamated Tin Mines of Nigeria for Plate 106; Ashanti Gold-fields Corporation Ltd., for Plate 83; I.F.A.N. for Plates 9, 22, 37, 38, 42, 45, 71, 89, 90; Azur Ciné Photo for Plates 53, 54; West

African Photographic Services for Plates 11, 17, 21, 24, 84, 85, 86, 87, 104; the late Mr. J. Nicol and the West African Cocoa Research Institute for Plate 18; Prof. Boateng for Plate 82; Dr. S. Gregory for Plate 75; Prof. Orlando Ribeiro for Plates 67, 68, 110–114.

Plate 15 is Crown Copyright Reserved; Plates 93, 94, 97, 100 are Shell Photographs and Plates 2, 4–6, 16, 25, 26, 29, 30–36, 40, 44, 47, 51, 52, 57, 59, 65, 69, 70, 72, 77, 88, 96, 102, 103, 107–109 are from photographs by the author.

INTRODUCTION

LONG usage has given the term ' West Africa ' a fairly clear meaning; it is usage based upon a real physical separateness. West Africa is here taken as the area lying west of the boundary between Nigeria and Cameroon. The latter has close physical and human affinities with Central Africa. Thus, this study of West Africa covers the republics *d'expression française* including Togo and Guinea, Nigeria, Ghana, Liberia, Sierra Leone, Gambia, Portuguese Guinea and the islands of São Tomé and Príncipe, and the Spanish islands of Fernando Po and Annobon.

The distance between the extremities of West Africa is nearly equal to that between London and Moscow. The total area is 2·4 million square miles, or nearly five-sixths that of the United States. The population is over 100 million, being about one-half that of the United States, or the same as that of France and the United Kingdom. The republics *d'expression française* occupy three-quarters of the area; yet, largely because some of these republics include vast tracts of the Sahara, they have under one-third of the total population. Nigeria, one of the largest and most densely populated countries of the Commonwealth, has a population of about 59 million in an area four times that of the United Kingdom, and has well over one-half the population of West Africa and over twice that of the four times larger area of the republics *d'expression française*.

West Africa has for long been divided internally. Relief, climate, vegetation, soils and the responses in agriculture, livestock keeping, ethnic types, societies and religion, all tend to given an arrangement of east–west belts. The greatest and most fundamental division is between the south and the north. The former has a generally heavier rainfall, rather leached soils, was originally mostly forested, produces the oil palm and other useful tree crops, grows cassava, yams or rice for the main foods, is inhabited by purer negroes, was originally animist in religion and organised in small states or tribes. The latter has a lesser but more concentrated rainfall alternating with a long dry season, less leached soils, savannah woodland vegetation, produces guinea corn and millet as the main foodstuffs, is inhabited by fixed agricultural peoples or by nomadic pastoralists (particularly the Fulani), the dominant religion is Islam and the political organisation is often in larger units.

West Africa was possibly reached by Dieppe mariners in 1364; certainly by Portuguese ships from the fifteenth century onwards, particularly by those bound for Asia or Brazil. But the generally surf-bound coast, dense forest, trying climate and disease, all combined to restrict contact to the shipping of slaves, gold and other valuable commodities, such as ivory, pepper and gum.

Attention was concentrated on the Gold Coast, where many huge castle headquarters remain today; on the Slave Coast between the Volta and the Niger deltas, where Lagos Island and the Niger Delta afforded anchorages, and slaves were available from the prisoners of the states of Ashanti, Dahomey, Yorubaland and Benin; and on the coast between the Gambia and Sierra Leone, where estuary anchorages were available.

The slave trade provoked such hostility towards Europeans that they were not encouraged to penetrate inland, either by the ordinary Africans or by the slave-trade intermediaries, who were jealous of their position.

Slavery was not, of course, introduced to West Africa by Europeans. It had long been the practice of Arab peoples to take negro slaves; and for African rulers to use their political prisoners, criminals and prisoners of war for this purpose. But it was the Europeans who introduced the large-scale overseas slave trade.

This trade took African peoples, their gaiety and culture into the lands of North, Central and South America. In the Caribbean Isles they replaced the indigenous peoples. In the United States, the institution of slavery was a main cause of one of the most cruel and costly civil wars of all time; and the political, social and economic problems of the American negro are still grave. Negroes are, likewise, of great importance in Brazil, but there they have been more fully absorbed and prejudice has been largely overcome. The settlement of West

Africans in the New World remains one of West Africa's greatest contributions to world affairs.

After the abolition of the slave trade, West Africa declined for a time in economic importance. The Danes withdrew from the Gold Coast in 1850 and the Dutch in 1872. In 1866 the British Parliament gave serious thought to the idea of withdrawal.

There was soon to be quickened interest. France had never lost enthusiasm, especially in Senegal, and, after her defeat in the Franco–Prussian War, she was encouraged by Bismarck to seek compensation in the colonial field. Other powers were also impelled by the prestige which colonial possessions were thought to confer. Rapid industrialisation in Europe and rising populations required tropical raw materials, such as palm oil and rubber, as well as markets, which West Africa could supply. The Berlin Conference of 1884–5 enunciated the principle that title to territory could be maintained only by effective occupancy. In the resulting 'Scramble for Africa' the political map of West Africa was mostly filled in by 1890 and entirely so by 1904.

Unfortunately, too much 'development', by Africans and others, has been in the nature of 'robber economy', at the expense of the human and natural resources. This befell peoples and lands which, through earlier excessive isolation, have lagged behind in comparison with some parts of the world.

Recently there has been rather more rational development of mineral resources such as tin, diamonds, manganese, iron, phosphates, mineral oil and bauxite, as well as of gold mining. With this has gone the remarkable development of peasant-grown cash crops, such as cocoa and groundnuts, and of plantation crops in certain countries. Economic development is still uneven and depends upon available transport, rather than upon utilising the most suitable soils in the best climatic region. West Africa produces about three-quarters of the cocoa, groundnuts and palm kernels entering world trade, and one-quarter of the palm oil. West Africa also produces over 10% by weight of the diamonds, 10% of the iron ore, 5% of the tin and manganese, and 2% of the gold.

West Africa's position is also important strategically. During the Second World War the fine harbour of Dakar was denied to the Allies until 1943. The closing of the Mediterranean during much of the period from mid-1940 to 1942, and the long voyage round Africa to provision the British Eighth Army in North Africa, caused Takoradi (Ghana) to be used to

FIG. 1.—West Africa and the World.
(Based on a map in the author's *Modern Colonisation* by permission of Messrs. Hutchinson.)

receive supplies. These were then flown across to Egypt, a new network of aerodromes being built for this purpose in Ghana and Nigeria.

American troops landed in Liberia in October 1942, to establish air bases for Atlantic patrols and to safeguard, on this flank, the landings in North Africa. America later built a harbour at Monrovia and large amounts of American money have been spent in Liberia to develop rubber cultivation, iron mining, communications and other economic and social services. From 1941-2 the French pushed on with their long-discussed project for a trans-Saharan railway. They did not make much progress, but in any future conflict it may again be re-considered.[1]

European administration cut across the old physical and human divisions of West Africa, creating new political units often incorporating both savannah and forest lands. Europeans also introduced contrasting policies. The French tried to make African Frenchmen or French Africans, and replaced African chiefs by Direct Rule which until 1957 was, by British standards, highly centralised. The British retained and developed African institutions. Instruction was often given in African languages, whilst conscription was never applied for the Armed Forces.

In the early days the French policy seemed unduly harsh in its effects upon native life and institutions, but it may now prove to have been the means of unifying peoples previously very divided. By contrast, British policy which consistently sought to retain African society, may have been too conservative and may have made more arduous the creation of wider loyalties than those of tribes. But if greater unity can be attained it is likely to arise out of African life itself, rather than by merely copying European ideals and institutions.

[1] See the present author's essay ' The History of Projects for a Trans-Saharan Railway ', *London Essays in Geography*, edited by L. D. Stamp and S. W. Wooldridge, 1951, pp. 135–50.

I

THE PHYSICAL BASIS
OF WEST AFRICA

The following chapters relate to the whole of West Africa. Further details concerning matters discussed here may be found in the territorial chapters.

Chapter 1

GEOLOGY, COASTS AND SHORES[1]

GEOLOGY

THIS account is intended as an outline and aid to the explanation of surface forms, relief, drainage, soils, mineral deposits and the reactions of man.

Geological exploration of West Africa proceeds slowly because of the rarity of fossils and the common masking effect of lateritic and sand formations, overburden or dense vegetation. There are also few geologists in the field for such a large area; they have had to be trained outside West Africa, and climatic conditions are unkind to field work.

West Africa, like most of Africa, is largely composed of Pre-Cambrian rocks, which have been folded and are often aligned from north-east to south-west, as is reflected in much of the relief. They are exposed over about one-third of West Africa, or over two-thirds of the area south of 12° N., and are part of the vast continental platform of Africa, which in West Africa has an average elevation of about 1,300 feet. The oldest rocks may be about 3,000 million years old. Some are metamorphosed sedimentary rocks; others are ancient volcanics and intrusives.

Pre-Cambrian rocks have been variously sub-divided,[2] but their ages are uncertain, as radio-active dating methods are not reliable with metamorphic rocks. The oldest, or Lower Pre-Cambrian, probably comprises the Archaean (or Daho-meyan) and, probably, the Birrimian System.

[1] Dr. N. R. Junner, O.B.E., M.C., D.I.C., M.Instit.M.M., Director of the Gold Coast Geological Survey from 1930 to 1946, has given me most helpful criticism of this chapter. Professor C. A. Cotton, Professor of Geology at Victoria University College, Wellington, New Zealand, and Professor J. C. Pugh, M.A., formerly of University College, Ibadan, have also done likewise for the section on Coasts and Shores.

[2] N. R. Junner, 'Notes on the Classification of the Pre-Cambrian of West Africa', *Comptes Rendus de la 19ᵉ Session du Congrès Géologique International*, Algiers, 1952, Fasicule XX.

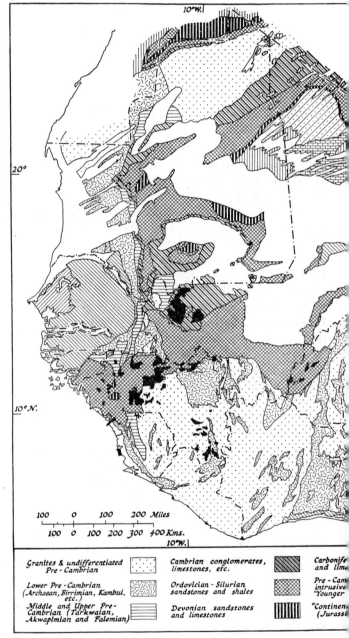

FIG. 2.—Geology.
(For names see Fig. 3.)

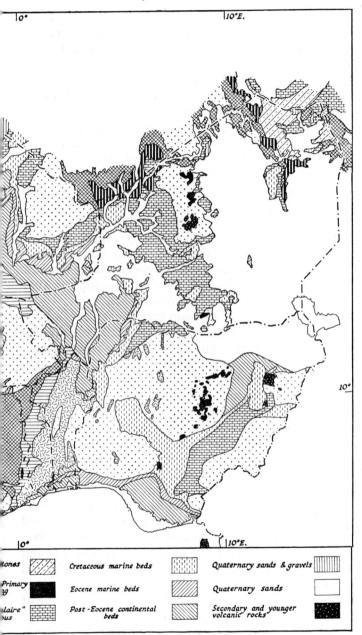

ones		*Cretaceous marine beds*		*Quaternary sands & gravels*		
Primary *g*		*Eocene marine beds*		*Quaternary sands*		
laire" *us*		*Post-Eocene continental beds*		*Secondary and younger volcanic rocks*		

The Archaean consists largely of highly metamorphosed rocks. Prevalent acidic types are mica schists, gneisses and quartzites. Most are the product of granitisation and metamorphism of original sediments. Basic rocks are garnetiferous gneisses and amphibolites. Gneisses of similar composition are found in the Kasila Series of Sierra Leone, and others are known in Mauritania and Nigeria.

The Birrimian System occurs in southern Ghana and Ivory Coast. It is divided into the Lower Birrimian, with folded and steeply dipping alternating greywackes and argillaceous beds, as well as some tuffs and lavas; and the Upper Birrimian (Greenstones) of mainly volcanic rocks. The Kambui and Marampa schists of Sierra Leone may also be Birrimian.

The Middle Pre-Cambrian probably includes the Akwapimian–Togo–Atacora Systems, and the possibly contemporaneous Tarkwaian System. Indeed, the Akwapimian may be a facies of the Tarkwaian. The Akwapimian System consists of quartzites, argillaceous sediments and silicified limestones. They were probably deposited on a continental shelf.

On the other hand, the Tarkwaian System consists of schists, quartzites and conglomerates (including auriferous conglomerates akin to those of the Witwatersrand), but no limestones. The sediments were probably originally deltaic or littoral, derived from nearby Birrimian mountains to the east or southeast. Thus, the gold occurs as fossil placers, derived from the destruction of original deposits in the Birrimian.

The Upper Pre-Cambrian probably includes the Falémian of Mauritania and eastern Senegal, the Rokel Series of Sierra Leone and the Buem Series of Ghana, Togo and Dahomey. It consists mainly of quartzites, phyllites and shales.

Diamonds, haematite iron ore, chrome and manganese ore occur in Pre-Cambrian rocks. Granite intrusions of at least three different ages are known, gold and tin being associated with some of them. Ultrabasic and basic intrusions of Pre-Cambrian age are found in the peninsulas behind Conakry and Freetown, and in Liberia at Cape Mount, Monrovia and Buchanan.

The trend lines of Pre-Cambrian folds run north-north-east to south-south-west in the interior massifs of Aïr and Adrar des Iforas, and in the eastern Guinea Coast lands. In Liberia they have an arc-like disposition from north-west to south-west; in Sierra Leone and farther north the directions are north-west to south-east, and north to south. There is a close connection between these trend lines and many relief features.

The eroded surface of one or other of the Pre-Cambrian groups provided a fairly level floor for the advance and retreat of shallow Palaeozoic (or Primary) seas. Little is known about the age of most of their deposits in West Africa. Basal-conglomerate beds, dolomitic limestones, sandstones and shales of Cambrian or Cambro-Silurian age are found in the western Sahara, associated with the great Taoudéni Syncline (see Fig. 2). They outcrop south-westward from Saharan Algeria along the northern and southern sides of the Eglab (or El Hank) Anticline, southward to the Senegal River (Tambaoura Scarp) and eastward into Mali. They reappear to form the vivid Bandiagara Scarp in the south-centre of the Niger Bend.

Above come Ordovician siliceous sandstones. These are found in the synclines of Tindouf (south of the Anti-Atlas) and Taoudéni; and covering shield rocks in the Fouta Djallon of Guinea, in the Mali Republic (Manding Mountains, Bandiagara and Hombori plateaux) and in the Upper Volta (Banfora).

The Ordovician sea retreated and was followed by the Silurian. Silurian shales indicate a deeper sea which lay over much of the Sahara and part of Guinea, into which great rivers brought much mud. Voltaian rocks of east-central Ghana are probably Ordovician or Silurian, but in the absence of fossils their precise age is unknown.

Following the Silurian there were alternating continental and marine phases in the Devonian. Deposits are found in the Tindouf and Taoudéni synclines of Mauritania, around the interior massifs of Adrar des Iforas and Ahaggar, in Guinea, and at Accra in Ghana—where the Devonian is marine in origin.

The Lower Carboniferous (Dinantian) sea succeeded the Devonian era. Its limestones are mainly restricted to the basins of Tindouf and Taoudéni. As this sea withdrew northwards, leaving gulfs and lagoons, it was replaced by continental conditions in Upper Carboniferous (Westphalian) times. Estuarine sediments of Carboniferous (or, perhaps, Upper Devonian) age occur between Cape Coast and Dixcove (Ghana).

In some cases Hercynian movements probably reinforced Pre-Cambrian trends, as in the Akwapim–Togo–Atacora range. Hercynian trends have two main directions: those of wide distribution but feeble strength of north-east to south-west direction; and those from north-west to south-east, which are limited practically to the borders of Senegal–Mali (Tambaoura), Fouta Djallon and Adrar (Mauritania).

Associated with and also subsequent to these Hercynian movements are many basic eruptive rocks comprising dolerite, basalt, gabbros and serpentine in dykes and sills. These outpourings are very important in the Fouta Djallon, e.g. northwest of Mamou, on Bintimani (Sierra Leone) and many peaks of the Guinea Highlands.

Apart from block faulting, uplifts and downwarps, and volcanic activity, the broad structure of most of the western Mali Republic, Guinea, Sierra Leone, Liberia, and almost all of the Ivory Coast and Ghana was determined by the end of Palaeozoic times. For the most part, these lands have almost certainly been above the sea continuously since then. The contrary is true of eastern West Africa. Nigeria was probably dry land from the Pre-Cambrian to the Lower Cretaceous, so that either Pre-Cambrian, Cretaceous or later rocks occur.

From Permian to Lower Cretaceous times there was a long period of elevation, denudation and re-deposition of the products of sub-aerial erosion, which Kilian called the 'Continental Intercalaire'. These deposits survive around Adrar des Iforas, Aïr and elsewhere. They consist of sandstones, conglomerates and variegated clays, containing fossilised wood and occasional remains of dinosaurs, reptiles and fishes. Their age is Jurassic to Lower Cretaceous.

Marine transgressions occurred in Cretaceous and Eocene times, entering in the east from the Gulf of Guinea and thence along the Benue, Gongola, Chad and Middle Niger basins. Shallow seas were connected, to the west of Adrar des Iforas and between the massifs of Aïr and Tibesti, with the Mediterranean, which then covered North Africa. Cenomanian deposits, important from Agadès southwards into Nigeria (where there are also Albian deposits), sometimes consist of siliceous and chalky limestones (forming plateaux and feeble scarps) or of thick clay deposits.   On the borders of these seas, the sandstone, shale and coal seams of Enugu (Nigeria) were laid down, and were followed by early Tertiary seas, lagoons, lakes or mud-flats.

Other Cretaceous–Tertiary gulfs occupied Senegal, the Gambia and north-western Portuguese Guinea; coastal Ivory Coast and the extreme south-west of Ghana; the Volta Delta, Togo, Dahomey and Nigeria.   Their deposits include gravels, clayey sands, shales, limestone, gypsum-bearing marl, ferruginous sandstone (Gambia and Senegal) and lignites (Nigeria).   Phosphates, salt, oil, gas and bituminous sands occur.

Continental conditions existed all over West Africa from Eocene or Oligocene times, except for a few places on the coast. In the far north stony wastes or *regs* and sand dunes or *ergs* were formed round the innermost massifs in the western Sahara, and frequently conceal a fossil relief underneath.   In late Tertiary and Quaternary times, the Middle Niger was a series of fresh-water lakes, but there was no Quaternary sea.

Volcanic outpourings occurred again in Cretaceous, Eocene, Miocene and Pliocene times, and were, in part, associated with the upward movement which also caused the retreat of the Eocene seas.[1]   Basement rocks in the Benue Valley were folded in with the Cretaceous sediments.   They were also often faulted, as in the Jos Plateau, Aïr and in the Fouta Djallon. All this was probably caused by the Alpine earth-storms in the north.   Volcanic flows are important in Aïr, south-west of and around Jos, in the Cameroon and Bamenda Highlands, west of Biu, and in the islands of Fernando Po, Príncipe, São Tomé and Annobon.   In Gorée and Cape Manuel (Dakar) there are Miocene basalt lava-flows and volcanic tuffs.

Volcanic activity was renewed in Quaternary times in Aïr, on Mount Cameroon (not yet extinct) and on Cape Verde (les Mamelles).   South of Kumasi, in Ghana, is Lake Bosumtwi, which occupies what some think is an explosive caldera but others consider a meteoric scar.

There was a maritime gulf in western Mauritania in early Quaternary times, but subsequently lacustrine or continental conditions became more general there and in western Senegal.

---

[1] For the effect of Miocene uplift on rivers, see pp. 17–20.

Freshwater limestones, clays and sands (some of the latter being æolian) remain as evidence of these conditions.

In the interior the main features of Quaternary age have been erosion and deposition caused by the oscillations of sea level, the evolution of the present drainage system and the formation of sand.

On the left bank of the Middle Niger are many virtually dry river valleys, such as the Tilemsi, Dallol Bosso, Azaouack and Dallol Maouri. Upstream there may have been others, but their courses have been obscured by wind-borne sands. There are similar relic valleys (Ferlo, Sine and upper Saloum) in Senegal. Urvoy [1] deduced three alternating wet and dry periods during Quaternary times, and considered that the Middle Niger is now in a relatively dry period.

These changes explain the existence of dry valleys and some river terraces; and are part of the explanation for the drying out of the lakes in the Middle Niger, upward movement of the land being a contributory factor.

During dry Quaternary periods there has been intensive weathering of sandstone formations, and wind has spread great sheets of coarse loose sand over vast areas north of an approximate line through Zaria, Ouagadougou, Bamako and Dakar. In wetter periods the rivers have spread out sheets of finer alluvium. These loose deposits smooth out many irregularities of relief.

West Africa is remarkable for its considerable geological variety—greater than in some other parts of Africa. Nevertheless, there is a great predominance of worn down Pre-Cambrian rocks, and widespread masking by sand in the interior, and by lateritic material in the south.

COASTS AND SHORES

The nature of any coast depends mainly on types and disposition of rocks, earth movements, relief, drainage and climate. The shoreline is more affected by winds, longshore drift, waves and tides. Both the coasts and shores of West Africa are difficult ones and their natures have profoundly affected West African development.

[1] Y. Urvoy, *Les Bassins du Niger*, Paris, 1942, p. 56.

Southward to the Saloum Estuary (north of the Gambia) north-east Marine Trade Winds, longshore drift and powerful waves, backed by the greatest fetch of open water, are smoothing a low shore. The Senegal and Saloum estuaries are seriously obstructed by variable sand-spits. Behind the dunes are relic lagoons (*niayes*), now mere pools or wet depressions.

From the Gambia to Cape St. Ann (southern Sierra Leone), the coast and river estuaries have been drowned, thus causing a ria coastline. Though the land has since gained upon the sea, there are no smoothed coasts. The explanation is that the continental shelf is comparatively wide, the tidal range is high for West Africa (13–17 feet and even 23 feet at Boké), tidal scour is strong, and south-west or north-east winds agitate the waters of a coast disposed directly across their path. Instead of sand-spits, mud-flats (with mangrove) form readily in the estuaries of Casamance (southern Senegal), Portuguese Guinea, Guinea and Sierra Leone.

The southern Sierra Leonean and Liberian shores are characterised by north-west trending sand-spits, which seem to be helped by a smaller tidal range than that found farther north.

The western shore of the Ivory Coast and the central part of Ghana have only moderate coastal accumulation. The change in coastal orientation in relation to waves of maximum fetch results in movement away from Cape Three Points, both to west and to east. Both coasts have occasional small but abrupt rocky promontories which, in the case of the Gold Coast, provided a little shelter for slave ships anchored east of them. On some promontories are the massive castles of the slaving and gold-trading era. The western Ivory Coast, however, was not attractive to traders, as there was no gold readily available and the people had a reputation as cannibals, causing the coast to be known as ' la Côte des Mal-Gens '. On the other hand, the relative dryness and low temperatures in July–September were added attractions of the Gold Coast shores.

From near Fresco (centre of the Ivory Coast shoreline) to Cape Three Points, and again from west of the Volta Delta to east of the Niger Delta, the coasts have suffered submergence. This may be the consequence of post-glacial rise in sea-level, but ' the known down-warped character of the coast, as attested by the altitude of sedimentary beds, suggests that the condition of partial drowning may have been repeated on a number of occasions, and that the last downward movement may have combined with the rise in sea-level in producing the present appearance '.[1]   These coasts have since been smoothed by continuous longshore drift under the action of heavy surf, and they often excel those of Mauritania and Senegal in sand-bar and lagoon formation.   Yet erosion is proceeding at Assinie (Ivory Coast), Keta (Ghana), Grand Popo (Dahomey) and, until defence works were built, at Victoria Beach (Lagos).

As an illustration of the forces to be met with along this coast, one may cite the silting, within a few months, of the badly located Abidjan canal of 1904–7.   Many years later, on October 4th, 1933, because of high flood-waters in the lagoon, a metre-wide ditch was cut through the old abandoned canal to release the flood.   In three days the ditch had a 100-metres-wide mouth, which in another five days had become 300 metres wide.   Yet after a week the flood exit had ceased, and six months later the outlet was fully blocked by the action of the sea.   A few miles along the coast at Grand Bassam, a high sand-pit at the western side of the Camoé estuary has grown two miles in fifty years.

The inland edges of lagoons in the Ivory Coast, Togo and Dahomey are often quite steep, and around Abidjan there are considerable cliffs.   Gautier[2] considered these to belong to an old shoreline; but though these cliffs are of loose sandy material, easily smoothed by wave action, they show no evidence of it.

West African coasts are mainly low, sandy and without natural harbours; except where a river and tidal range have kept an opening, as at Freetown, Lagos, precariously on certain inlets of the Niger Delta and at Calabar.   Even on the Niger inlets, the Escravos and Forcados bars threatened to kill the ports of Burutu, Warri, Koko and Sapele until a breakwater protecting the Escravos mouth was built.[3]   Almost everywhere the shore is dangerous to approach.   Ports have been enormously expensive to construct.   In only two respects is the

[1] J. C. Pugh, ' A Classification of the Nigerian Coastline ', *Journal of the West African Science Association*, Vol. 1, No. 1, pp. 3–12 at p. 4.

[2] E. F .Gautier, ' Les Côtes de l'Afrique Occidentale au Sud de Dakar ', *Annales de Géographie*, 1931, pp. 163–74.

[3] ' Forcados and Escravos Bars ', *Statistical and Economic Review*, United Africa Company Limited, September 1950, pp. 46–60.

West African coast relatively fortunate—in its lack of coral reefs and of violent storms.

BIBLIOGRAPHY

See references cited in footnotes.   Also:

R. Furon, *Geology of Africa*, Edinburgh, 1963.

L. Marvier, *Commentaire de la Carte Géologique d'Afrique Occidentale Française*, Bulletin 16, Direction des Mines, Dakar, 1953.

1 : 5 Million International Geological Map of Africa, 1938–52, and *Notice Explicative*, by R. Furon and G. Daumain, Paris, 1952.

Chapter 2

RELIEF AND DRAINAGE [1]

RELIEF

WEST AFRICA lies generally between 600 and 1,600 feet, and consists mainly of the worn, monotonous and fairly level surfaces of the platform of Pre-Cambrian rocks. Higher relief may occur where trends in the ancient rocks can still be traced—e.g. the north–south hills of the Sierra Leone interior. Residual granite domes are common, and the 'Younger Granites' are responsible for some bold relief—e.g. of the Jos Plateau of Nigeria. Certain series of the Pre-Cambrian give higher relief—e.g. the several Birrimian, Tarkwaian and Akwapim–Togo–Atacora ridges.

Gently folded or unfolded Primary rocks, which have been strongly dissected, are responsible for the impressive relief of much of the Fouta Djallon of Guinea, and for vivid erosion scarps—e.g. those of Mampong and Gambaga limiting the Voltaian sandstones of Ghana, the Banfora Scarp of the south-western Upper Volta and the Bandiagara Scarp of the Mali Republic. Others are partly along fault lines, such as the north–south scarps of the interior of the Fouta Djallon.

The generally low plains on Secondary or later sediments are also monotonous, though they may contain scarps such as the north–south Secondary and Tertiary ones in eastern Nigeria, or the Tertiary Thiès Scarp of Senegal.

Resistant basic intrusives formed the Sierra Leone (Colony) Mountains, Cape Mount (Liberia), etc. Intrusive dykes give

---

[1] Dr. N. R. Junner has also given me most helpful criticism of this chapter.

The best maps to use are either the 1 : 5 million sheet No. 5 of the *Europe et Afrique de Nord* series of the Institut Géographique National, the relief maps of West Africa in the *Atlas des Colonies Françaises* or the 1 : 10 million map of Africa published by J. Bartholomew and Son, Edinburgh.

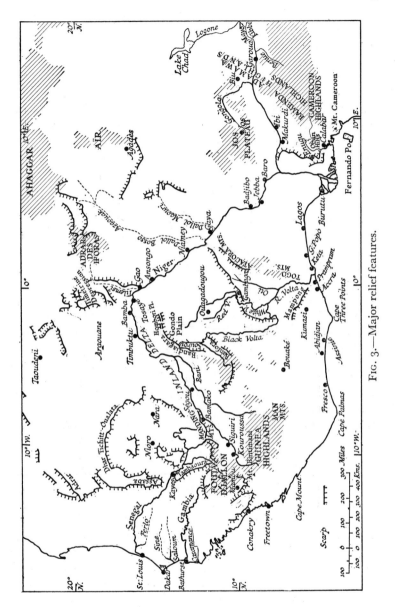

FIG. 3.—Major relief features.

many abrupt features in the Fouta Djallon, at Kakoulima near Conakry and at Siguiri, all in Guinea. A dolerite capping over granite has preserved Bintimani, 6,390 feet, in north-eastern Sierra Leone.

Cretaceous and later volcanic activity has been responsible for part of the highest relief of the Jos Plateau; for the Bamenda and Cameroon Highlands; Mt. Cameroon; the islands of Fernando Po, Príncipe, São Tomé and Annobon; and for Gorée and Cape Manuel at Dakar. The Mamelles of Cape Verde are Quaternary.

Important though these exceptions are locally, it remains true that relief is not a cause of great regional diversity. Nor does relief do much to upset the zonal arrangement of climatic and vegetational belts, except in the Fouta Djallon, the Guinea Highlands, on the Jos Plateau, the Adamawa, Bamenda and Cameroon Mountains, Mount Cameroon and the islands of the Bight of Biafra. Indeed, there is even a broad zonal arrangement of relief. In the south-west the ancient shield has been raised, and the south-flowing streams are now re-grading themselves across it. North of it is a wide central depression from Senegal to Lake Chad. Beyond, in the north-east, are the high massifs of Adrar des Iforas and Aïr.

Moreover, near the coast between Cape Palmas and Prampram there is a marine deep some 16,500–21,000 feet in depth, and aligned from west to east.[1] This section of the sea-bed (particularly near Accra) is steeper than that of any other part of the Atlantic coast of Africa. The 100-fathom isobath is 15 miles from Prampram, 19 miles from Accra and 45 miles from Takoradi. The 4,000-metre line is nearly parallel to and 60–70 miles from the coast between Cape Coast and Prampram, whilst the 5,000-metre isobath is about 145 miles out. With such slopes seismic conditions may be expected, and are the probable cause of earthquakes experienced in and around Accra. The Devonian, Carboniferous and Cretaceous rocks of Ghana all slope towards this deep, which may perhaps be correlated with the troughs of the lower Niger and Benue valleys. More certainly it may be associated with coastal submergence as discussed on p. 11.

[1] N. R. Junner and others, *The Accra Earthquake of 22 June, 1939*. *Gold Coast Geological Service Bulletin No. 13*, 1941, p. 31.

DRAINAGE

The drainage characteristics of West Africa may be sum-
marised as follows:

(a) Rapid run-off on crystalline rocks, especially on the south
or south-western Pre-Cambrian shield, where the rainfall
is particularly heavy.

(b) Behind the south-western and Guinea coasts, rivers are
cutting down to new base-levels, probably because of
Miocene and later uplifts, and inward tilting. Thus the
Volta and Benue rivers are gaining at the expense of
others. The Guinea coast rivers are frequently interrupted by rapids and deposit relatively little alluvium,
except close to the shoreline.

(c) Greater maturity and indeterminate courses of the rivers
of the sandy central lowland zone, compared with the
immaturity and vigour of the Guinea Coast rivers. The
Senegal and Upper Volta rivers have cut devious courses
from the central zone.

(d) Great seasonal variations in river-flow. Seasonal rains
cause extensive flooding—e.g. along the central Niger.
Tributaries frequently become distributaries—e.g. the
Sourou (see below). But much water is lost by intense
evaporation and percolation in the dry season.

Quaternary eustatic changes of sea level and alternation of
wet and dry climates have also been modifying factors. The
last of these is shown by the existence of dry river-courses on the
left bank of the Niger near Gao. Dry courses have likewise resulted from the deposition of dust by the Harmattan wind in the
beds of shrunken streams in the dry season. This feature is well
seen in the Inland Niger Delta of Mali.

Rainfall is heaviest and run-off most consistent in the Fouta
Djallon, the Guinea Highlands and Mount Cameroon. Short,
rapid streams descend from these direct to the sea. From the
inward side of the Fouta Djallon the head-waters of the Senegal, Gambia, Niger and many of their tributaries take their rise.

The Senegal began to define its present course in mid- to late-
Tertiary times, when the maritime gulf retreated from the

Senegal area. Recent and rapid accumulation of loose sand has obstructed its central and lower reaches, diverting it southward. Longshore drift and the Marine Trade winds are building a great sand-spit, *La Langue de Barbarie*, which ruins the estuary and has prevented St. Louis from developing into a good port. These various obstructions also cause widespread flooding when the river is full.

The Senegal is navigable [1] with difficulty in the rainy season (August to mid-October) for very small vessels as far as Kayes. After mid-October, navigation is limited to even smaller vessels and ceases lower down. The flow of the river varies greatly from year to year, and the railway now takes almost all the traffic. The estuary spit and bar are the main impediments to navigation with the sea.

The Gambia is a river, whose lower course has become a ria. It is navigable to the limit of the Gambia state and is the best river of western West Africa. Unfortunately, its value has been greatly compromised by the boundary, which has prevented it from serving its natural hinterland.

The Niger is some 2,600 miles long and passes through almost every climatic zone of West Africa. The Upper Niger is a mature river, with a well defined course, and which flowed into the various Secondary and Tertiary inland seas. In mid-Tertiary times, following upon the retreat of the Senegal gulf, the Upper Niger was captured by the Senegal River through the Nara-Nioro sill north-north-west of Ségou. When the climate became drier, sand wastes obstructed that outlet, and the Upper Niger then flowed into the Araouane Lake.

A return to more humid conditions in Quaternary times gave rise to many vigorous streams from Adrar des Iforas and Aïr which, flowing into one great stream around Gao, broke through the Badjibo sill (above Jebba, Nigeria) to join the head-waters of an existing stream, so forming the south-east flowing Lower Niger. Increasing sand accumulations in the Araouane Lake then caused that lake to sub-divide into several lakes, which over-spilled at Tosaye to join the Lower Niger.

Sand accumulations are still pushing the river southward at Timbuktu and obstructing its many channels. Yet in and after the rainy season the river floods areas between Ségou and Tim-

[1] For the navigable reaches of rivers, see Fig. 29.

buktu as extensive as England and Wales. This is because of the low-lying country and slight slope of the river. The lakes of this Inland Delta are reminders of former terminal lakes of the Upper Niger.

The Upper Niger is navigable from Kouroussa to Bamako between July and October. Below Bamako it is interrupted by rapids, caused by sandstone outcrops from the Manding Mountains, but the Middle Niger is navigable again from Koulikoro. Flood-waters are so delayed that although they are felt at Koulikoro in mid-July, they do not arrive at Timbuktu until about October.

The Inland Delta ends at Bamba, east of Timbuktu, and the Niger then passes through the Tosaye quartzite sill, cut in mid-Quaternary times, to link with the Lower Niger. It ceases to be navigable between Ansongo and Jebba, except for fairly short stretches—e.g. Niamey–Gaya. Between these places it has often cut down to the ancient basement rocks, whose outcrops cause the Fafa, Labbezenga and Bussa rapids. Moreover, half-way between Niamey and the Nigerian boundary it cuts through the end of the Atacora ridge by a series of cluses with sharp turns in the shape of a W.

From Jebba, and more easily from Baro, the river is navigable again. It has local high water from early August to mid-November. It again rises slightly from mid-February to mid-April, when the Upper Niger flood-waters, after their long journey and dispersion in the Inland Delta, arrive at last in the Lower Niger. Many of the Maritime Delta mouths are navigable for ocean vessels, and former mouths are often used by local streams.

The Benue is a vigorous river, unobstructed by severe rapids, whose course may possibly correspond to a major fault-line. Its valley has been a route-way for peoples coming from the east and north-east. The river may be navigated up to Makurdi between June and November, between Makurdi and Yola from July to early October, and between Yola and Garoua in the Republic of the Cameroon in August and September. When in flood, the Mayo Kebbi tributary often links the Benue with the Logone River, which otherwise flows north to Lake Chad. Since the Benue is a more powerful stream, a major capture is possible, which would deprive Lake

Chad of about two-fifths of its water supply. Despite the vigour of its head-waters, the Benue has many characteristics of a mature river. It has flat alluvial banks (so rare along African rivers), which are extensively flooded in the rainy season and offer possibilities for rice cultivation.

The Volta. Of the Guinea coast rivers, only the Volta demands special mention. The upper Black Volta flows first in a north-easterly direction, parallel to the Upper Niger, and, like it, is a mature stream that must have flowed via the Sourou into Secondary and Tertiary inland seas and an early Quaternary lake. The latter was presumably situated in the Gondo Plain, below the Bandiagara Scarp. In a wet climatic period the lake may have over-spilled, sending streams south-eastwards to join others farther south. The Sourou is now alternately a tributary and distributary of the upper Black Volta.

The White Volta is also a composite river which (with the Red Volta) has captured, or had directed to it, rivers which once drained northward. Similarly, the uppermost reach of the Oti was probably once a tributary of the Niger. The diversion, to vigorous Guinea Coast rivers, of streams from the great central depression is, indeed, a common phenomenon.

The lower Volta cuts through the Akwapim–Togo range by a gorge, wherein the Akosombo dam and a hydro-electric power station have been established (see pp. 409–11).

Lagoons are significant means of communication in the Ivory Coast, Togo, Dahomey, and especially in Nigeria.

Chapter 3

CLIMATE [1]

A. *CAUSATION*

Air Masses [2]

The fundamental cause of West African climates is the seasonal migration and pulsation of two air masses. The most widespread feature is the mass of Tropical Continental (cT) Air, warm and dusty, which extends from the Sahara, reaching its maximum southward extent in January between about 5° and 7° N. Alternating seasonally with it is the mass of Tropical (or Equatorial) Maritime (mT) Air, warm and humid, which trends inland in July or August to about 17° N. on the coast and to about 21° N. inland. Associated with Tropical Continental Air are dry north-easterly or easterly winds, and with Tropical Maritime Air wet south-westerly or westerly winds.

[1] Statistics used in this chapter are reproduced from information in the Meteorological Office, British Air Ministry; from the *Memento du Service Météorologique* (Dakar) for ex-French West Africa; from the Meteorological Departments of Ghana and Nigeria by courtesy of the Directors; from *Statistics illustrating the Climate of Sierra Leone*, Freetown, 1952, and various other official publications.

West African climatic statistics should be used with caution. Until 1938 most observations were made from instruments generally located in the grounds of agricultural or medical departments. Untrained observers are especially prone to errors in reading thermometers. Maximum and minimum thermometers are also liable to develop faults, which may not be noticed or corrected for considerable periods in the hands of inexperienced readers. Instruments were often badly sited and not always read regularly or sufficiently frequently, and their location within a given town has sometimes changed. More recently there has been great improvement, but upper air records are still few. Nor is it unknown for there to be interference with instruments, and rain-gauges are sometimes improperly used for the oddest purposes.

[2] I have profited from P. R. Crowe, 'The Seasonal Variation in the Strength of the Trades', *Transactions and Papers of the Institute of British Geographers*, 1950, pp. 25-47; 'The Trade Wind Circulation of the World' and 'Wind and Weather in the Equatorial Zone', ibid., 1949 and 1951. I am also deeply indebted to Professor Crowe for many helpful suggestions concerning this chapter. Miss Ursula M. E. Rodd and Mr. John Callow (see List of Acknowledgements) compiled and drew most of the maps in this chapter, for which I enjoyed a special research grant from the London School of Economics and Political Science.

Owing to differing densities of the two air masses, the front slopes upward towards the south, so that the Tropical Maritime Air forms a wedge under the Tropical Continental mass. The wedge penetrates northward as Tropical Maritime Air becomes predominant in and after May, retreating southward in August or September. Hence the depth of warm, moist air over any point increases and decreases, the rain-belt occurring where it is at least 3,000 feet deep and often at least 5,000 feet. The depth of warm, moist air also varies daily, and rain appears to be associated with such changes, as well as with seasonal advance and retreat.

Between these air masses is the Inter-tropical Front (or Inter-tropical Convergence Zone), which lies north of the Equator all the year. With the penetration inland of Tropical Maritime Air, the Front or Convergence Zone pushes north-westward; and with the retreat of Maritime Air, the Front returns south-eastward.

As dry air lies over moist, active weather does not occur at the point of contact of the Front with the earth's surface. Instead, there is usually a great width of persistent doldrums (or light winds) of 4–8 knots, with little or no low cloud and generally fine weather. The Front is thus a rain-screen rather than a rain-producer in West Africa.

Above both of these alternating surface air masses and wind systems come first the Equatorial Easterlies. These are related to the north-easterlies, but are humid, since they originate over the Indian Ocean. They fill the middle layers of the atmosphere over most of West Africa all the year round. These may, perhaps, play some part in line squalls at the change of season (see below); otherwise they are of importance only to air navigation. Above again are Westerlies, sometimes known as the Counter-Trades.

Relief

Once Tropical Maritime air has penetrated northward in sufficient depth, we should expect orographic rain wherever there are highland areas, particularly if they lie across the path of south-westerly rain-bearing winds. Such is the explanation of heavy rainfall in the Fouta Djallon of Guinea; the Guinea Highlands of Sierra Leone and Liberia; the Sierra

Leone Peninsula; to a lesser extent on the Mampong Scarp in Ghana; more so on the abrupt islands of Annobon, São Tomé, Príncipe and Fernando Po (particularly on the great wall of its southern coast); on the Cameroon and Bamenda Highlands; and outstandingly so on Mt. Cameroon. The average annual rainfall from 1941 to 1950 inclusive at Freetown (Hill Station), 820 feet above sea level, was 189·4 inches, and at Freetown (Falconbridge), 37 feet above sea level, 51 inches less.

These relief features (as well as others—e.g. the Jos Plateau) produce rain-shadow effects, local and farther afield. One explanation of the drier central sector of the Ivory Coast, and especially of eastern Ghana, Togo and Dahomey coastlines, is that rain-bearing south-westerlies lose moisture over the Guinea Highlands, Cape Three Points, the Mampong Scarp and the Akwapim–Togo Mountains, so becoming dry westerlies.

High relief also lowers temperatures and increases the diurnal range. In the cooler Fouta Djallon is Guinea's hill-station of Dalaba, 3,650 feet. Similarly, there is Hill Station above Freetown (Sierra Leone) at 820 feet, Jos in Nigeria at 4,100 feet, and the former German capital of the Cameroon at Buea, 3,000 feet. Below are described five relief climatic zones —Foutanian, Guinea Highland, Jos Plateau and the two Cameroon types.

Ocean Currents

These play a considerable part in climate. The cold southward-flowing Canary Current makes itself felt as far south as Cape Verde, where it is deflected oceanwards. It is responsible for occasional fogs and for low sea temperatures, which often cause persons returning to Europe by sea to catch cold. More happily, it cools coastal Senegal. Similarly, cold water of uncertain origin (but possibly an offshoot of the cold Benguela Current) upwells in the middle of the year off São Tomé, eastern Ghana, Togo and Dahomey. It cools sea and air temperatures and may play a part in causing dry weather, by restricting convectional conditions.[1]

[1] P. R. Crowe, op. cit., 1951, p. 33, quotes the following temperatures at the end of Lomé wharf (6° 08′ N., 1° 13′ E.) :

	Jan.	Feb.	Mar.	Apr.	May	June	July	Aug.	Sept.	Oct.	Nov.	Dec.
°F.	80	81	81	82	82	79	75	72	74	77·5	80	80

Between the cold Canary and Benguela Currents is the east-ward-flowing Guinea Current, which brings warm water to the Guinea Coast for the rest of the year, thereby reinforcing the effects of the already warm and moist south-westerly winds.

B. *CHARACTERISTICS AND CONSEQUENCES*

WINDS

(a) *The Trade Winds.* North of approximately the Gambia River, there is a seasonal alternation of Doldrum and Trade winds,[1] the rains being derived from squall-like disturbances moving westward along the doldrum zone, when it lies between approximately 10° and 20° N., from June to October.

In other months, dry North-east Trades prevail. The cool, or cold Canary Current produces, at about 2,000 feet, an inversion which may amount to 10° F. This stops vertical exchange and the making of rain.

The extraordinary strength of the Marine Trade winds of Senegal, especially across the exposed Cape Verde peninsula, is largely responsible for the remarkable contrast between the cooler temperatures of coastal Senegal, and the hotter ones of the interior.

(b) *The Harmattan.* Apart from the coastal fringe of Senegal, the warm and desiccating Harmattan north-easterly or easterly wind occurs during the dry season, when ordinary vegetative growth ceases. Clouds are absent, so that temperatures are relatively high during the day and low at night. Visibility is severely restricted, not by clouds, but by a haze of dust particles carried from the arid north. Even Mt. Cameroon, 13,350 feet high, may be invisible from nearby for many weeks.

Cold nights require people to have more blankets—a joy to Europeans and a trial to poor Africans. Low humidity dries up the mucous membrane of eyes, nose and throat. Lips, finger-nails and skin crack. Bare-footed Africans may find the skin of their feet so cracked as to make walking very painful. Epidemics of cerebrospinal meningitis are most prevalent at this season. The Harmattan also dries up plants and often coats

[1] P. R. Crowe, op. cit., 1951, p. 34.

them with dust particles. Dust is thickly deposited in houses and in such things as typewriters, radios, etc.

(c) '*Line Squalls*'. At the change of season with the north-ward or north-westward advance of the Inter-tropical Front, east to west or north-east to south-west thunderstorms or 'Line Squalls' occur, often misnamed tornadoes. It may be that with the change, from May to July and again in October, of the relative depths of the Harmattan and of the South-wester-lies, the Easterlies of the upper air levels descend to the surface. J. Navarro, however, has shown [1] that these storms are north-easterly rather than easterly, and have several routes towards the Guinea coast, ending in the regions of Mt. Cameroon, Cotonou, Abidjan and Tabou. These north-easterly 'Line Squalls' are, in fact, the partial cause of almost all rain received on the Guinea coast between May and July, and again from September to October. They are created under a long line of instability in upper layers, the humidity being supplied by South-westerlies.

'Line Squalls' are preceded by a day or two of high tempera-tures and oppressively still air. Finally, the sky darkens, there is vivid lightning and the noise of rushing wind. Behind the wind and swirling dust comes torrential rain, the lightning persisting. Winds become south-westerly and temperatures drop 10–20°. Heavy rain, of up to 2 inches in under an hour, then gives way to gentler rain without lightning. When the rain ceases, the clouds disappear and temperatures rise again. Such sudden and violent storms and rainfall encourage soil erosion and damage to crops, housing and communications; man and beasts may catch colds, pneumonia or worse. North of about 15° N. in the east and 17° N. in the west, these 'Line Squalls' are mainly dry storms or 'dust devils'—i.e. in Mauri-tania, Mali and the Niger.

(d) *South-westerlies*. Associated with moist Tropical Mari-time Air are south-westerly winds. They prevail all the year south of about 6° N., penetrating in July up the coast to about 17° N., and inland to about 21° N. in August. During their prevalence two or three days' continuous rain may occur at coastal places and for much longer on monsoon coasts (see

[1] J. Navarro, *Les grains du Nord Est et le régime des pluies sur la Côte du Golfe de Guinée*, 1950 (Duplicated MS.).

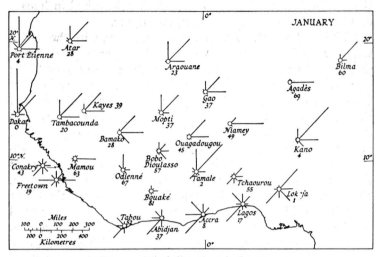

Fig. 4.—Wind directions in January.

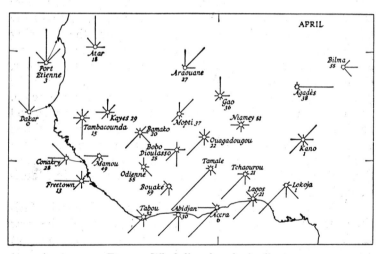

Fig. 5.—Wind directions in April.

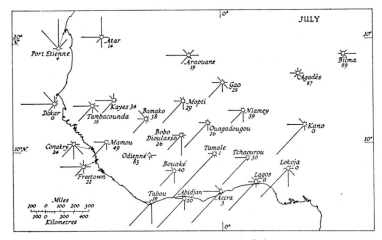

Fig. 6.—Wind directions in July.

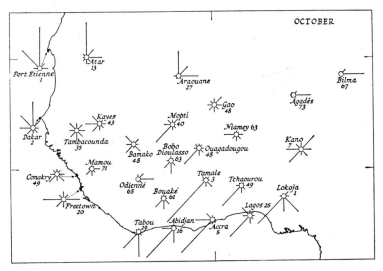

Fig. 7.—Wind directions in October.

The lines are proportional to the percentage of observed winds from each direction. Numbers give the percentage of observed calms. 28 stations.

later).   Continuous rain is rare inland, where it is generally heavy at first in late afternoon, becomes intermittent and accompanied by thunderstorms in the evening, and ceases as light rain early next morning.   This is especially so at the beginning and end of the rainy season.

Skies are frequently cloudy, and early morning mist is common, but otherwise visibility is good, except during actual rainfall.   The following figures illustrate some of these points.

Mean amount of cloud in tenths

Time	Jan.	Feb.	Mar.	Apr.	May	June	July	Aug.	Sept.	Oct.	Nov.	Dec.	Year
Enugu. (6° 27′ N., 7° 29′ E.) (Average 1943–7.)													
0900	4·6	4·9	7·0	8·1	8·3	8·6	8·9	8·8	9·1	8·7	7·1	5·4	7·4
1500	4·3	4·7	5·9	7·4	7·6	7·9	8·3	8·3	8·2	7·8	6·8	4·8	6·8

Mean number of days with less than 2·5 tenths average

Jan.	Feb.	Mar.	Apr.	May	June	July	Aug.	Sept.	Oct.	Nov.	Dec.	Year
Freetown. (8° 30′ N., 13° 14′ W.) (Average 1941–50.)												
12	12	10	3	1	0·2	0·1	0	0	0	1	7	46

Mean number of days with more than 7·5 tenths average

Jan.	Feb.	Mar.	Apr.	May	June	July	Aug.	Sept.	Oct.	Nov.	Dec.	Year
Freetown. (Average 1941–50.)												
2	2	3	7	12	16	26	28	23	17	12	7	155

Cloud-cover is intimately associated not only with south-westerly winds, but also with high humidity and low range of temperature.   And, although the rainy season may be long or short, fine weather often prevails for several or even many days.

As will be seen later, there are relatively few stations with a true equatorial climate.   The Guinea coastlands mostly have two rainfall maxima, the first and normally greater one being initiated by the Line Squalls discussed above.   These are followed by a relatively dry season from July to August, although cloud-cover and humidity remain high.   This little dry season is often explained as being due to the northward movement of the Inter-tropical Front or Convergence Zone, but Crowe[1] considers that ' the real key surely lies in the prevalence aloft

[1] P. R. Crowe, op. cit., 1951, p. 33.

of the marked inversion normally encountered in the south-east trades at about 3,000 feet. This is the season when the south-east trades are at their strongest and the waters beneath them are at their coolest. It is, therefore, in no way surprising that their normal inversion is not liquidated at the Equator but roofs over the whole strong southerly air stream. Such a 'roof' may be penetrated in three chief ways—(i) where a gigantic relief feature like Mt. Cameroon (13,350 feet) bodily protrudes through the inversion and stimulates convectional overturnings around its flanks; (ii) where more moderate elevations like the Fouta Djallon plateau are encountered by strong persistent winds; and (iii) by surface heating over a Continental interior. . . .' The latter exception explains Tropical rainfall, and the other two explain the Foutanian and Cameroon types.

(e) *On-shore and off-shore breezes.* Along the entire West African coastline and up to about 10 miles inland, sea and land breezes are important. The late afternoon on-shore (or sea) breeze results from the relative overheating of the land, compared with the sea. Conversely, there is a less powerful off-shore (or land) breeze during the night. Except where land descends sharply to the sea—e.g. at Freetown and around Mt. Cameroon—the sea breeze is usually the stronger. These breezes may partially divert the normal wind, as in Mauritania and Senegal, where the North-east Trades are more often north-north-west by day. They may even reverse it, as in Portuguese Guinea and Guinea, where in January a westerly wind frequently replaces the North-east Trades during the afternoon. Finally, they may reinforce the usual wind, as along the Guinea coast, where the South-westerlies are particularly strong in the afternoons.

In this section we have discussed the Senegal Marine Trade winds, the north-easterly Harmattan of the interior, the north-easterly or easterly 'Line Squalls' (also of the interior), the wet South-westerlies most prevalent in the mid-year months, and on-shore and off-shore breezes. Yet this variety is more apparent than real, and the prevailing winds are so overwhelmingly from the north-east or south-west, that a single runway oriented in these directions is sufficient in most West African aerodromes, unlike the runways in various directions found in lands of changeable winds.

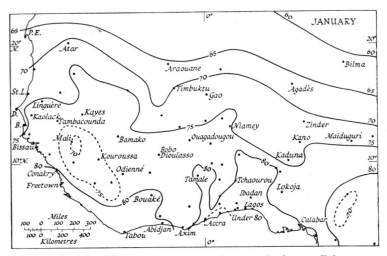

FIG. 8.—Mean daily temperatures in January, in degrees Fahrenheit, for 75 stations.

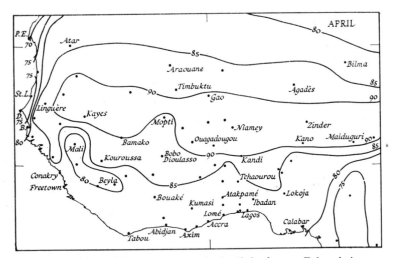

FIG. 9.—Mean daily temperatures in April, in degrees Fahrenheit, for 75 stations.

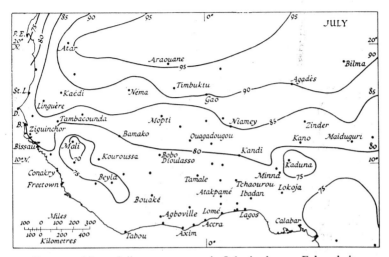

FIG. 10.—Mean daily temperatures in July, in degrees Fahrenheit, for 75 stations.

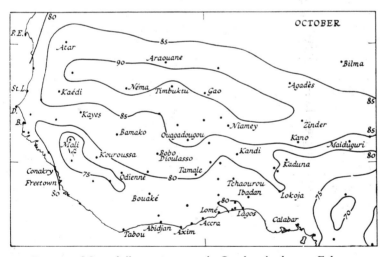

FIG. 11.—Mean daily temperatures in October, in degrees Fahrenheit, for 75 stations.

Broken lines on some of Figs. 8–18 indicate conditions below the norm for that latitude.

Seasonal winds, combined with the trend of the coast and degree of slope of the foreshore, account for the swell and surf of West African coasts. Swell is of relatively minor importance and is almost always from the north along the Mauritanian coast. Along the Senegal coast it is more southerly between June and September. On all other coasts, it is generally from the south and south-west. Surf, by contrast, is severe and hinders the establishment of ports. It helps to build up sand-bars, except from Cape St. Mary (Gambia) to Cape St. Ann (south of Freetown) where there is great tidal range.

TEMPERATURE

The common belief that West Africa is always exceedingly hot is exaggerated. The blanket is a much-used article, many of which are imported, and more (in delightful patterns and colourings) are made locally. The very high temperatures, so characteristic of many months in the lowland parts of similar latitudes in East Africa and India, are attained in West Africa only in or near the desert in summer. The writer has vivid recollections of sitting, swathed in a blanket, on a cool August evening, in an open-air Accra cinema, listening to the justified jeers of Ghanaians at the trailer of an American film asserting that the film it advertised brought ' the authentic atmosphere of the steaming hot jungles of Africa '.

West Africa has lower temperatures than world average for similar latitudes during the northern hemisphere winter in the dry far north, during the rains in the south, and almost all the year in highland areas and along the Senegal, eastern Ghana and Togo coastlines. On the other hand, temperatures are higher than world average for similar latitudes in April, July and October in much of the centre and north, especially in lowland areas. Fairly high temperatures are also common in the south at the end of the dry season.

High temperatures may cause a skin complaint popularly known as ' prickly heat '. Loose clothing should be worn, and the flowing robes of most northern people and their loose caps are very suitable. Thick-walled houses also help to withstand high temperatures.

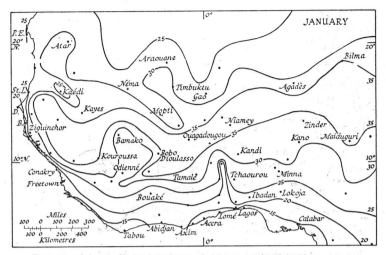

FIG. 12.—Mean diurnal range of temperature in January, in degrees Fahrenheit, for 75 stations.

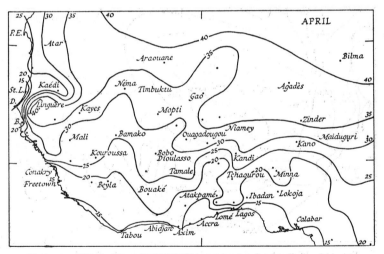

FIG. 13.—Mean diurnal range of temperature in April, in degrees Fahrenheit, for 75 stations.

C

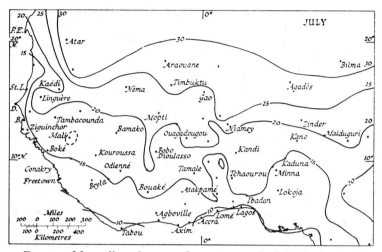

FIG. 14.—Mean diurnal range of temperature in July, in degrees
Fahrenheit, for 75 stations.

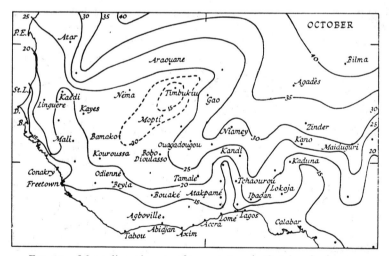

FIG. 15.—Mean diurnal range of temperature in October, in degrees
Fahrenheit, for 75 stations.

Yet the high temperatures by day of inland stations are rather offset by wider diurnal and seasonal range. Figs. 12–15 show the greater range of temperature to be in the centre, north-west, north and north-east. There is a gradually increasing range from the Guinea coast northwards, and a much sharper increase inland from the Senegal coast. The greatest ranges are found at the change of seasons.

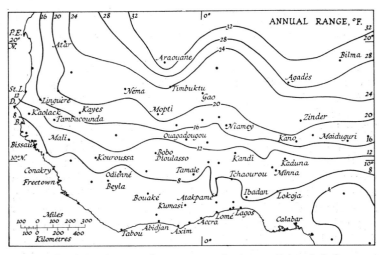

FIG. 16.—Annual range of temperature, in degrees Fahrenheit for 75 stations.

Fig. 16 summarises the general position for the whole year. Comparison with world averages for similar latitudes reveals that the Guinea coast has a little less than the annual average range for that latitude, an illustration of its somewhat op-pressive character. But the interior has more than the average, a well-known characteristic of the Sahara and its fringes.

SUNSHINE

Another fallacy concerning West Africa is that a supposedly pitiless sun shines ever fiercely. Such an idea is grossly in-accurate. As night and day are always almost equal, hours of sunshine can never exceed about twelve hours, as they may in summer in temperate lands. During the dry season the sun is often obscured by dust-haze; during the wet season, clouds as well as early morning mist often hide it. In consequence, the recorded sunshine is often remarkably little. The following figures of mean daily sunshine in hours are representative:

Jan.	Feb.	Mar.	Apr.	May	June	July	Aug.	Sept.	Oct.	Nov.	Dec.	Annual Mean
Freetown. (Average 1941–50.)												
8·1	8·2	7·7	7·0	6·3	5·3	2·8	2·2	4·0	6·2	6·6	7·0	5·9
					% of maximum possible.							
69	69	64	57	50	42	22	18	33	52	56	60	49
Kumasi. (6° 43′ N., 1° 37′ W.) Average of 9 years.												
3·9	4·3	4·8	5·0	3·7	2·0	1·1	0·9	2·3	3·9	4·6	3·9	3·4

Cloudiness (but not necessarily haze) diminishes inland, and is at a minimum near the tropic line.

After decades of devotion to topees or sun-helmets, white people in West Africa have realised that these are unnecessary. They have ceased to be worn by whites in ex-British West Africa, where they have sometimes passed to Africans, who use them more as a protection against rain. Oddly enough, in ex-French and other countries, where clothing habits of whites are otherwise often more sensible than in ex-British territories, sun-helmets died slower deaths. Even odder was the amazing spine-pad, deserving of a place as a museum piece. Against the relatively small amount of sunshine a soft panama or light cloth cap is ideal. Sun-glasses are very desirable, although there is a marked deficiency in blue and ultra-violet light, so that the value of the light is less than in temperate lands. It is for this reason that white people rarely get very tanned in West Africa, and that most photographs are under-exposed. Total solar radiation is also low, probably because of high water-vapour content, dust and bush-fire haze.[1]

RAINFALL

It should be obvious that, as elsewhere in the tropics, rainfall is the most vital element in the climate. Upon its amount (and especially its effectiveness), its degree of certainty, its length and how it falls, largely depend the natural vegetation, agriculture, mode of life and much else in West Africa. The association of rainfall with Line Squalls and south-westerly

[1] P. W. Richards, *The Tropical Rain Forest*, 1952, pp. 148–9.

winds is discussed above, and the various climatic types (which depend overwhelmingly on rainfall criteria) are outlined below.

Figs. 17–18 show the general picture of annual and monthly rainfall. The heavy monsoonal rainfall (May to October) of the south-western coast is evident, as well as the heavy rain of the Cameroon Highlands and Mt. Cameroon. The drier central parts of the Ivory Coast, and especially of eastern

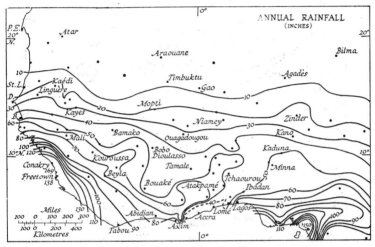

FIG. 17.—Annual rainfall in inches, for 95 stations.

Ghana and Togo, both annually and especially in August and September, are also clear. Otherwise, annual rainfall diminishes fairly regularly inland from the Guinea coast, both in amount and in duration. The advance and retreat of rainfall from south to north are likewise striking.

Where annual rainfall exceeds about 100 inches per annum, it may be regarded as dangerously excessive, especially if it falls in one sharp season. Such rain causes excessive leaf-growth and makes cereals (other than maize and rice) difficult or impossible to grow. Tubers such as cassava and cocoyams are hardier.

Heavy rain leaches out plant nutrients, erodes the soil and interrupts agricultural work and transport. Rain-water may drain away before it can be absorbed, so that increasing study is being made of rainfall effectiveness (residual or available rainfall).

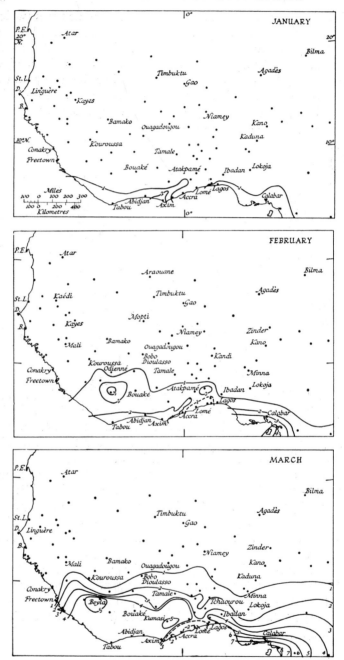

FIG. 18.—Monthly rainfall in inches, for 95 stations.

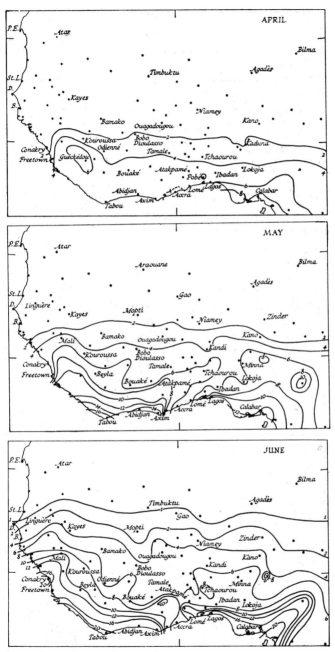

Fig. 18.—Monthly rainfall in inches, for 95 stations.

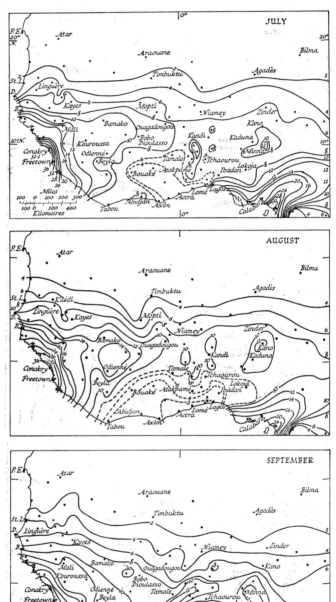

FIG. 18.—Monthly rainfall in inches, for 95 stations.

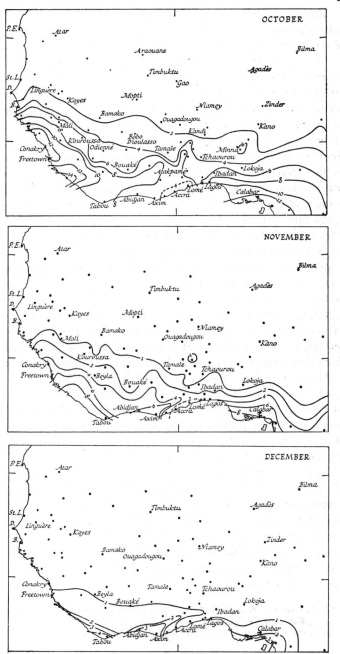

Fɪɢ. 18,—Monthly rainfall in inches, for 95 stations.

Thornthwaite's formula for computing potential evapotranspiration uses mean monthly temperatures and the latitude
of a given station.   Although a generally accurate indicator of
the latent heat of vaporization, it underestimates potential
evapotranspiration in the West African dry season and over-
estimates it during the wet one, because insufficient account is
taken of the attractive power of the atmosphere.   Garnier has
found that if figures for the mean daytime saturation deficit are
added to Thornthwaite's mean potential evapotranspiration
figures the values are increased in the dry season and reduced
in the wet, especially for interior states.   About 2,000 mm.
may be taken as the maximum mean annual potential evapotranspiration on Saharan fringes.   The minimum of under
1,000 mm. occurs in high parts near the coast.   Most of West
Africa has between 1,000 and 1,900 mm.   South of latitude
10°N coastal lowlands and areas above 1,600 feet have under
1,300 mm.   Senegalese and Mauritanian coasts have some
400 mm. less than nearby inland stations.   Mean annual
water surplus is substantial in the Guineas, Sierra Leone,
Liberia, coastal Ivory Coast and south-eastern Nigeria.
Water deficit corresponds closely with the length of the dry
season, but every place has a seasonal water deficit, and the
dry Ghana coast a exceptional annual one of 250–500 mm.[1]

About 4 inches (100 mm.) rainfall per month is often regarded as the minimum for full agricultural needs, and three
to four months of rainfall is the minimum for growing the
quick maturing millets on the outer fringes of the cropping
zone.   Where rainfall is fairly evenly distributed throughout
the year, about 50 inches annual rainfall seems to be ideal.

Apart from the amount of rain and its effectiveness, the length
of rainy season is obviously important in influencing which
crops may be grown.   Kontagora and Abeokuta (Nigeria)
have the same average total rainfall, but rainy seasons of about
seven and ten months respectively.   Where there is a double
maximum of rainfall, the short (or middle) dry period, if long
enough, provides another harvest time, and so more varied
crops may be grown.

[1] B. J. Garnier, ' A method of computing potential evapotranspiration in West
Africa ', *Bulletin de l'I.F.A.M.*, T. XVIII, Series A, 1956, pp. 665–76, and ' Maps
of the Water Balance in West Africa ', idem., T. XXII, Series A, 1960, pp. 709–22.

Lastly, tropical rainfall is extremely variable in amount, in time of onset and cessation, and in régime. Fig. 20 shows variability at certain stations in Ghana. Not only is there a high degree of general variability, but also variation between different districts in the same year.

In the interior and towards the northern limit of adequate rainfall, where water is precious, variability is greatest.

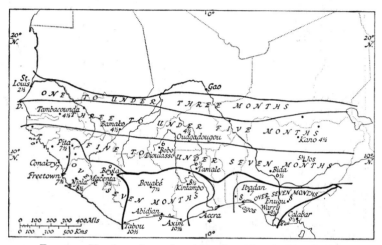

FIG. 19.—Number of months with at least four inches of rain.

Four inches monthly rainfall is sufficient for most plant growth. It is also the figure at about which precipitation and evaporation are generally in equilibrium. The heavy line is the northern limit of the double maximum of rainfall. Based on readings from 44 stations.

Average figures should be used only in the knowledge that in any year the actual rainfall may be about one-half greater or smaller, and that this may happen for several years on end. Thus, between 1901 and 1918, rainfall at Bathurst (13° 27′ N., 16° 35′ W.) in inches was:

1901	.	.	45·3	1907	.	.	34·0	1913	.	.	23·7
1902	.	.	29·4	1908	.	.	43·5	1914	.	.	48·9
1903	.	.	57·1	1909	.	.	56·6	1915	.	.	47·6
1904	.	.	38·0	1910	.	.	44·0	1916	.	.	38·0
1905	.	.	66·1	1911	.	.	28·1	1917	.	.	37·7
1906	.	.	64·4	1912	.	.	34·0	1918	.	.	54·0

The average was 43·9 inches. Rainfall in May varied between nil and 1·9 inches, in June from 2·2 to 12·3 inches and in October from 0·2 to 9·1 inches.

Fig. 21 shows for Zungeru (Nigeria, 9° 48′ N., 6° 09′ W.) the typical variation over five years in the amount of monthly rain and, particularly, in its distribution. Although

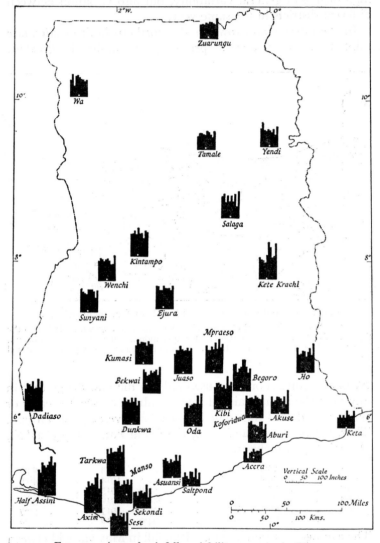

FIG. 20.—Annual rainfall variability 1924–33 in Ghana.

(Based on figures from *Gold Coast Handbook*, 1937. Each column represents one year.)

average figures show Zungeru with a single rainfall maximum, there was no such neat pattern for any one of the years 1907–11.

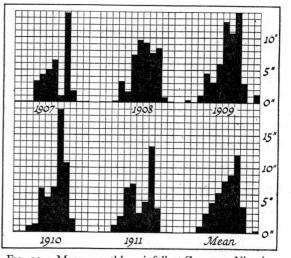

FIG. 21.—Mean monthly rainfall at Zungeru, Nigeria.

(From R. Miller 'The Climate of Nigeria', *Geography*, 1952 by kind permission of the author and editor.)

RELATIVE HUMIDITY

It is this factor, more than any other, which has given the West African climates a bad name. Yet high humidity is confined to the rainy areas and rainy seasons, especially in the early morning. During the dry season it is normal to sigh for greater humidity. The following figures are typical:

Mean Percentage of Relative Humidity

	January a.m.	January p.m.	July a.m.	July p.m.
Monsoon and Guinea Coasts				
Conakry (9° 31′ N., 13° 43′ W.) .	85	71	92	85
Accra (5° 31′ N., 0° 12′ W.) .	82	84	85	85
Porto-Novo (6° 30′ N., 2° 37′ W.)	90	77	89	85
Interior				
Timbuktu (16° 47′ N., 3° W.) .	39	29	68	46
Bamako (12° 39′ N., 7° 58′ W.) .	50	27	89	71
Beyla (8° 41′ N., 8° 39′ W.) .	68	31	94	84
Natitingou (10° 16′ N., 1° 23′ E.) .	43	22	81	75

High relative humidity and heavy rainfall allow dense and rank vegetation to flourish, insects to breed profusely and so spread disease, and the formation of mould and fungi on such things as leather and films. These articles should be kept in airtight tins, clothing in warmed airing cupboards, and machinery should be oiled frequently. Electric cables need far more insulation than in temperate lands. To man, high relative humidity by day generally causes lassitude; by night there may be a sensation of cold, even though temperatures are high. The writer recalls going to bed one night in the rainy season at Bouaflé (Ivory Coast) under three blankets, although the thermometer registered 74° F. In the dry season, when humidity is low, wood dries up and furniture comes apart. Leather, paper and plastics become brittle.

C. CLIMATES OF WEST AFRICA [1]

The Climates of West Africa may be classified as follows:

MONSOONAL
Dry Season followed by a long and very wet one:

South-west Coast Monsoonal
Liberian
Interior Sierra Leonean
Foutanian
Guinea Foothills
Guinea Highlands

EQUATORIAL
Rain in every month, with two maxima.

SEMI-EQUATORIAL
Up to four dry months, or low total rainfall, but with two maxima:

Semi-seasonal Equatorial
Seasonal Equatorial
Accra–Togo Dry Coastal

MONSOONAL-EQUATORIAL or CAMEROON
Rain in every month, variable number of maxima and a very high total rainfall.

[1] Local details of many climates may also be found in the section on climate in certain territorial chapters. In the following tables, temperatures (T) are means of daily maxima and minima, in degrees Fahrenheit, for each month. Rainfall (R) is in inches. After these letters are figures indicating the number of years to which the readings refer. Figures in feet refer to altitude.

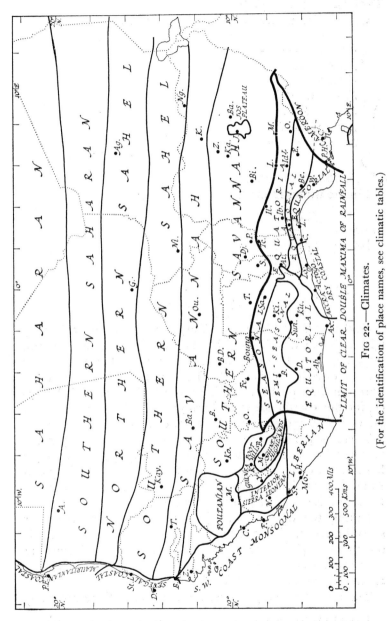

Fig 22.—Climates.

(For the identification of place names, see climatic tables.)

TROPICAL (SUDANESE)
One rainfall maximum, becoming shorter inland.

> *Southern Savannah*
> *Jos Plateau*
> *Savannah*
> *Senegal Coastal*
> *Southern Sahel*
> *Northern Sahel*
> *Southern Saharan*

MAURITANIAN COASTAL
Minute winter rainfall.

SAHARAN
No regular rain.

MONSOONAL

South-west Coast Monsoonal. This corresponds approximately with Hubert's *Casamancien*,[1] but that name is unduly localised, implying that the climate coincides with the Casamance district of southern Senegal. In fact, that district is at the northern limit of this climatic zone, which more typically includes the coastal areas of Portuguese Guinea and Guinea, Sierra Leone and the southern coast of Fernando Po.

There is a hot dry season, somewhat tempered by moist marine winds and quite high relative humidity; and a rather less hot wet one. The monsoon is at a maximum in July and August, has a high persistence, a median speed of about twelve knots and is sometimes 10,000 feet deep.

During the dry season, vegetative growth may cease for several months. Then the violent and continuous rains impair soil structure and cause severe leaching. All these factors are further deterrents to rich forest development, so that this is the realm of the Casamance Woodland.

The main food crop is rice, the more so as there are many

---

[1] Text by H. Hubert, in G. Grandidier, *Atlas des Colonies Françaises*, 1934.

coastal and inland swamps. Tree crops are also well suited here. In general, however, there is less variety of food crops than elsewhere. Some assert that the heavy rainfall and high relative humidity impair man's efficiency in this zone and slow down economic development.

	Jan.	Feb.	Mar.	Apr.	May	June	July	Aug.	Sept.	Oct.	Nov.	Dec.	Year
Ziguinchor (Casamance, Senegal).			18 ft.	12° 35′ N.,	16° 16′ W.								
T5	90·6	94·1	95·6	95·8	95·0	91·6	87·6	85·1	87·3	88·6	89·6	87·3	90·8
	62·1	63·2	66·6	67·5	72·0	75·4	74·2	74·0	73·8	74·0	70·6	65·0	69·8
R10	0	0·1	0	0	0·5	5·6	16·0	22·0	13·3	6·3	0·3	0	64·0
Conakry (Guinea).			16 ft.	9° 31′ N.,	13° 43′ W.								
T5	88·4	89·0	89·5	89·8	89·0	86·8	83·4	82·1	84·4	86·2	87·3	88·4	87·0
	72·6	74·2	75·2	75·6	76·1	74·6	73·4	73·4	74·0	73·8	75·4	74·6	74·4
R10	0·1	0·1	0·4	0·9	6·2	22·0	51·1	41·5	26·9	14·7	4·8	0·4	169·0
Freetown (Sierra Leone).			37 ft.	8° 30′ N.,	13° 14′ W.								
T10	84·9	85·9	86·4	86·5	86·3	85·6	82·9	81·6	83·1	84·8	85·3	84·7	84·8
R10	75·3	77·1	76·7	77·5	76·7	74·8	73·8	73·6	74·0	73·8	75·4	76·0	75·3
	0·2	0·1	0·6	2·5	5·9	12·4	37·6	35·9	25·6	10·6	5·4	1·6	138·2

Liberian. Like the Guinea Highlands climate, the Liberian type is transitional between the South-west Coast Monsoonal and the Equatorial climates. Compared with the former, there is generally less rain in the Liberian type, though it is much more evenly distributed.

The main characteristic is a drier period from about the last week of July to mid-August, well known in Liberia as ' the middle drys '. Although facilitating transport, these drier days are not sufficient to make harvesting of a cereal possible. The period is often too brief and too irregular in incidence to be recognisable in average monthly rainfall statistics.

	Jan.	Feb.	Mar.	Apr.	May	June	July	Aug.	Sept.	Oct.	Nov.	Dec.	Year
Harbel [1] (Liberia).			100 ft.	6° 24′ N.,	10° 25′ W.								
T18	88·3	89·5	90·0	89·6	87·5	84·3	81·0	80·2	82·2	85·2	86·6	86·9	85·9
R18	68·7	70·0	70·5	70·9	71·1	70·8	69·9	70·0	70·6	70·7	70·5	69·4	70·3
	1·0	1·7	4·6	6·2	11·7	16·3	18·4	20·2	24·5	14·6	7·4	2·9	129·4

[1] Botanical Research Station 9½ miles N. of Harbel and 5 miles further inland. Average annual rainfall at Harbel is 152 in.

Interior Sierra Leonean. This is a drier variant (in similar latitudes) of the South-west Coast Monsoonal climate. It occurs not only in Sierra Leone but also in north-western Liberia.

Rainfall régime is akin to the Foutanian type (see below) but temperatures are higher and diurnal variation less, whilst annual rainfall is usually heavier.

	Jan.	Feb.	Mar.	Apr.	May	June	July	Aug.	Sept.	Oct.	Nov.	Dec.	Year
Njala (Sierra Leone). 167 ft. 8° 06′ N., 12° 06′ W.													
T10	89·3	93·1	94·3	92·8	90·2	87·0	83·1	82·2	84·9	87·7	87·8	87·3	88·3
	67·4	68·7	70·4	71·4	71·9	71·2	70·9	70·9	71·1	70·5	70·2	68·2	70·2
R25	0·3	0·7	3·0	5·1	9·9	14·5	16·0	21·1	16·5	12·8	6·7	1·5	108·0

Foutanian. This is a highland variant, within the Fouta Djallon, of the South-west Coast Monsoonal type and is transitional in character between it and the Southern Savannah climate.

Rainfall is much less than in the South-west Coast Monsoonal climate, averaging between 60 and 80 inches, but the rainy season is up to two months longer. There are sharp variations with aspect and altitude, the south and west being wettest. Rain often comes in violent storms which cause severe erosion of the thin soils. Rainfall is less reliable than on the coast, but is steadier at higher elevations. Although mountain mists moderate the aridity of the dry months, relative humidity is lower (annual average 66%) than on the coast, because the Harmattan is the commonest wind.

Temperatures, particularly minima, are markedly low, especially from December to February. Daily variation is far greater, being 30–36° F. in the dry season.

	Jan.	Feb.	Mar.	Apr.	May	June	July	Aug.	Sept.	Oct.	Nov.	Dec.	Year
Mamou (Guinea). 2,440 ft. 10° 22′ N., 12° 05′ W.													
T5	90·6	92·8	94·1	92·8	87·6	84·1	80·0	79·2	81·6	83·0	85·5	87·8	86·6
	54·4	58·8	64·2	66·1	67·1	64·8	65·4	65·2	65·2	64·2	61·8	56·0	62·7
R10	0·3	0·4	1·8	5·0	8·0	10·1	13·2	15·8	13·4	8·0	2·4	0·3	78·9

Guinea Foothills.[1] This occurs between the Fouta Djallon and the Guinea Highlands, in nòrth-eastern Sierra Leone (Kabala) and south-eastern Guinea.

Total rainfall is about the same as in the Foutanian, but is less than in the Guinea Highlands type found at higher altitudes,

[1] A. Aubréville, *Climats, Forêts et Désertification de l'Afrique Tropicale*, pp. 110, 119 and 122, calls this the *Kissien* type, after the Kissidougou area. This book is a major source of reference.

or in the Interior Sierra Leonean and South-west Coast Monsoonal types found at lower altitudes. The rainfall régime is transitional between all these climates and the Southern Savannah. Relative humidity is also intermediate in character between the almost constantly humid Guinea Highlands and the more variable conditions of adjacent areas.

Temperatures vary little compared with the Foutanian or Southern Savannah climates, and are almost as equable as in the Guinea Highlands. Lowest means of daily minima are found in December–January and lowest means of daily maxima in June–August, when rainfall lowers afternoon readings.

	Jan.	Feb.	Mar.	Apr.	May	June	July	Aug.	Sept.	Oct.	Nov.	Dec.	Year
Beyla (Guinea). 2,218 ft. 8° 41' N., 8° 39' W.													
T5	87·6	89·3	89·1	86·2	83·8	82·4	78·8	80·3	83·0	84·0	85·0	87·8	84·8
	58·8	65·4	67·1	67·1	66·2	65·6	64·4	64·8	65·8	65·0	65·0	59·0	64·6
R10	0·3	1·6	5·2	5·9	6·9	8·6	9·6	10·4	11·5	5·6	3·5	0·9	69·8

Guinea Highlands [1]. Like the Foutanian, the Guinea Highlands type is a mountain modification of the South-west Coast Monsoonal type and is found in the Guinea–Sierra Leone–Liberia borderlands and in the Man Massif of the Ivory Coast.

There is more rain than in the Foutanian, but less than in similar latitudes on the coast. Equatorial influences are evident in that there is only one, or sometimes two dry months, and two rainfall maxima occur in some years. Relative humidity is high, except in January, and mists are common. At high altitudes temperatures are remarkably equable for such an inland and mountainous region—a further illustration of Equatorial influences.

	Jan.	Feb.	Mar.	Apr.	May	June	July	Aug.	Sept.	Oct.	Nov.	Dec.	Year
Macenta (Guinea). 2,015 ft. 8° 34' N., 9° 28' W.													
R5	0·4	1·9	5·8	6·6	7·7	10·3	19·9	23·1	16·1	10·0	8·0	2·1	111·9
Yengema (Sierra Leone). 1,270 ft. 8° 37' N., 11° 03' W.													
T10	90·4	93·9	94·2	92·9	91·0	88·9	84·7	83·9	87·5	89·1	88·9	88·4	89·5
	57·8	61·6	67·0	68·5	69·3	68·4	68·6	68·3	68·4	67·6	66·8	62·9	66·3
R15	0·4	0·8	3·8	6·3	9·0	11·1	10·6	16·2	15·8	11·5	5·7	1·6	92·7

[1] Hubert includes this area under his Foutanian, whilst Aubréville distinguishes it as the *Tomien*.

EQUATORIAL

The true extent of this type has been frequently exaggerated. Like Hubert's *Attiéen*, it includes the southern Ivory Coast, south-western and south-central Ghana and coastal Nigeria.

Temperatures may show diurnal and annual variation. between about 71° and 88°. There is constantly high humidity (at least 77%, except around mid-day), mostly convectional rainfall of at least 1 inch in each month, and 60 inches annually with two maxima. Consequently, plant-growth never ceases, and this is the ideal habitat of the Lowland Rain Forest.

Total rainfall is almost always less and rainfall is more evenly distributed through the year than in Monsoonal types. Less erosion and leaching occur, and the drier period between the two rainfall maxima permits the first of two or more harvests. It also facilitates travel and commerce at that time. Winds are gentle and doldrums frequent.

	Jan.	Feb.	Mar.	Apr.	May	June	July	Aug.	Sept.	Oct.	Nov.	Dec.	Year
Warri (Nigeria). 20 ft. 5° 31′ N., 5° 44′ E.													
T_5	88·4	90·8	91·1	90·8	88·6	86·1	82·6	83·1	83·9	86·0	88·8	88·6	87·4
	71·4	72·1	73·7	73·9	73·1	72·4	72·0	73·2	71·9	71·9	72·4	72·0	74·4
R_{46}	1·3	2·1	5·3	9·0	10·8	14·9	15·4	11·8	17·1	12·7	4·4	1·4	106·2
Lagos (Nigeria). 10 ft. 6° 27′ N., 3° 24′ E.													
T_5	90·5	91·0	91·5	90·5	87·9	84·2	82·2	81·7	83·9	85·7	89·3	89·3	87·3
	69·8	72·6	73·1	71·7	72·1	71·2	70·0	69·7	70·5	71·0	71·7	70·9	71·2
R_{55}	1·0	1·5	3·9	5·5	10·9	17·3	10·9	2·7	5·6	7·9	2·8	1·0	71·0
Axim (Ghana). 75 ft. 4° 51′ N., 2° 15′ W.													
T_{35}	85·9	86·8	87·1	87·6	86·1	83·9	82·9	81·9	82·6	83·7	84·9	85·8	84·9
	71·8	73·5	73·3	73·0	72·8	71·9	71·5	70·9	71·0	71·3	71·8	72·1	72·1
R_{33}	2·3	2·4	4·8	5·6	15·9	19·5	6·6	2·3	3·3	7·4	7·7	3·9	81·5
Abidjan (Ivory Coast). 65 ft. 5° 19′ N., 4° 01′ W.													
T_5	89·3	91·1	91·1	90·4	88·6	85·1	82·8	82·0	83·2	85·5	87·3	88·6	87·1
	72·8	75·0	75·4	75·2	74·6	73·1	72·0	71·3	72·6	73·8	73·6	73·6	73·5
R_{10}	1·6	2·1	3·9	4·9	14·2	19·5	8·4	2·2	2·8	6·6	7·9	3·1	77·1
Tabou (Ivory Coast). 13 ft. 4° 25′ N., 7° 22′ W.													
T_5	86·6	87·3	88·0	88·6	86·4	83·6	82·0	81·2	82·1	83·8	85·5	86·2	85·1
	73·4	73·8	74·0	74·2	74·0	73·8	73·2	71·8	72·4	73·4	74·2	73·6	73·4
R_{10}	1·5	2·7	3·9	4·6	16·4	22·8	6·9	3·9	7·8	8·7	8·7	4·6	92·5

SEMI-EQUATORIAL

Semi-seasonal Equatorial. This mainly corresponds with Hubert's *Baouléen* sub-type of the Equatorial. The name is not retained here, because it is restricted to the south-central

Ivory Coast; this climatic zone also extends through northern Ashanti, southern Togo, Dahomey and Nigeria.

Temperatures are similar to those of true Equatorial stations, although diurnal and annual range are greater. The main difference is the lower rainfall, especially in December and January, when vegetative growth may be halted.

	Jan.	Feb.	Mar.	Apr.	May	June	July	Aug.	Sept.	Oct.	Nov.	Dec.	Year
Bouaké (Ivory Coast). 1,110 ft. 7° 41′ N., 5° 02′ W.													
T5	92·2	94·3	95·4	94·6	91·0	87·3	85·0	83·6	85·5	88·0	89·6	91·0	89·7
	68·8	71·1	71·3	71·1	71·0	70·0	69·0	68·6	69·1	69·5	69·3	69·1	70·8
R10	0·4	1·5	4·1	5·8	5·3	6·0	3·2	4·6	8·2	5·2	1·5	1·0	46·7
Kintampo (Ghana). 1,211 ft. 8° 02′ N., 1° 52′ W.													
T21	90·8	94·3	94·3	91·8	90·3	86·9	84·8	83·8	85·2	88·0	89·9	89·7	89·2
	66·8	69·8	71·3	71·2	70·3	69·9	68·7	68·3	69·0	68·7	68·9	67·3	69·2
R21	0·4	1·7	4·3	6·2	8·2	10·2	6·9	5·2	13·0	9·0	3·3	0·4	68·8
Enugu (Nigeria). 745 ft. 6° 27′ N., 7° 29′ E.													
T5	89·7	92·1	92·7	91·1	88·1	85·1	82·9	83·0	84·5	86·5	89·2	89·3	87·8
	72·2	73·3	75·0	74·8	72·9	71·6	71·5	71·1	70·8	71·0	72·6	72·1	72·4
R35	0·7	1·0	2·6	5·7	10·4	11·2	7·7	6·9	12·7	9·8	2·1	0·5	71·3

Seasonal Equatorial. This was not distinguished by Hubert. It is drier and has a greater range of temperatures than his *Baouléen* or Semi-seasonal Equatorial. There are still two rainfall maxima, but there are three or four dry months. Vegetative growth is thoroughly halted, so that the natural forest was frail and is now rare.

	Jan.	Feb.	Mar.	Apr.	May	June	July	Aug.	Sept.	Oct.	Nov.	Dec.	Year
Salaga (Ghana). 593 ft. 8° 30′ N., 0° 30′ W.													
T27	95·5	97·2	98·5	96·9	93·8	91·4	89·1	88·1	90·0	91·7	94·8	95·0	93·5
	72·9	73·6	76·5	75·8	74·3	73·0	72·5	72·1	72·5	72·7	72·9	72·0	73·4
R27	0·5	0·8	2·7	4·7	5·7	6·6	5·6	7·2	9·9	5·9	1·4	0·5	41·4
Tchaourou (Dahomey). 1,071 ft. 8° 54′ N., 2° 36′ E.													
T4	94·1	98·5	98·1	95·2	91·6	88·0	84·8	84·1	85·5	88·4	92·2	94·3	91·2
	66·2	69·0	71·0	71·6	71·1	69·0	69·0	68·2	69·0	69·0	67·0	64·6	68·7
R4	0	0·6	1·9	3·5	6·4	8·9	4·3	6·9	8·5	3·1	0·4	0·2	44·7
Ibadan (Nigeria). 745 ft. 7° 26′ N., 3° 54′ E.													
T5	91·2	93·5	93·9	92·4	88·8	85·6	82·2	82·1	84·7	86·7	89·5	90·3	88·5
	69·2	70·5	72·7	72·5	71·9	71·0	70·0	70·0	70·0	69·7	69·9	69·2	70·5
R48	0·4	0·9	3·5	5·4	5·9	7·4	6·3	3·3	7·0	6·1	1·8	0·4	48·4

São Tomé, latitude 0° 20′ N., on the island of the same name, also has four drier months but from June to September. It is thus an example of southern hemisphere conditions just within the northern hemisphere during mid-year. The Benguela Current, which also affects Annobon at this time, helps to produce these conditions. (Cp. Accra–Togo Dry Coastal Zone.)

Accra–Togo Dry Coastal. This mainly corresponds with Hubert's *Beninien* sub-type of the Equatorial, but his misleading name is rejected. If named after the Bight of Benin, it gives the erroneous impression that all the shores of the Bight are within this dry zone; in fact those of Cameroon are among the wettest in the world. And if British readers should think the name is taken from the city of Benin, that again would be misleading, since it has the Semi-seasonal Equatorial climate.

South of a line beginning near Takoradi, passing through Nsawam, thence near the southern border of the Togo Mountains south of Palimé and Atakpamé in Togo, and into Dahomey through Savalou and Pobé to the coast west of Cotonou, has less than 45 inches of annual rain. The coastal fringe between Elmina and Grand Popo has under 35 inches. The rainfall pattern is equatorial, but the yearly and monthly totals are very low. Days of rain are also few. There are only two or three months with over 4 inches of rain, whereas in the Seasonal Equatorial type there are at least four and in the Semi-seasonal and Equatorial climates there are at least six months. Relative humidity is a little less than in the Equatorial zone. Temperatures are a little higher, except from July to September when they are much cooler.

The relative dryness and sparse vegetation were added attractions for the early European traders in gold and slaves. Of forty-five coastal forts, thirty-seven were built within this dry belt and near gold occurrences.

Some have explained the relative aridity of this area by invoking the direction of the coast as being the same as that of the rain-bearing winds. This is an insufficient explanation, since not all rain-bearing winds are south-westerly. Moreover, other parts of the Guinea Coast (e.g. around Lagos and Sassandra), though similarly aligned, are not so dry. Furthermore, temperature contrasts over land and sea tend to be more powerful when winds are parallel to the coast, thus making afternoon rain probable. Land and sea breezes and natural variation in winds also make 'parallelism' ephemeral.

Others have alluded to the proved occurrence of cold water off the Ghana Coast from July to September. Cool off-shore

Waters certainly explain the lower temperatures of July and August,[1] which also restrict the conditions favourable to convectional rainfall.

Another explanation is that the south-westerly winds which bring so much rain to Guinea, Sierra Leone, Liberia and to the projecting Cape Three Points region, are naturally deviated as westerlies over the land, especially in August. Hence they are drier in the central Ivory Coast, and especially over the central and eastern Ghana, Togo and Dahomey coastlines somewhat sheltered by the Togo Mountains.

Finally, this dry anomaly has been explained as a consequence of the northward curve of this coast, which thereby facilitates penetration of Harmattan influences.

	Jan.	Feb.	Mar.	Apr.	May	June	July	Aug.	Sept.	Oct.	Nov.	Dec.	Year
Accra (Ghana). 20 ft. 5° 31' N., 0° 12' W.													
T39	87·5	87·9	88·3	88·0	86·7	84·1	81·7	80·8	82·4	84·9	87·1	87·5	85·6
29	73·6	74·9	75·6	75·5	74·6	73·5	72·5	71·4	72·3	73·3	74·2	74·2	73·8
R47	0·7	1·5	2·2	3·0	5·0	7·5	2·0	0·6	1·5	2·3	1·4	1·0	28·6
Lomé (Togo). 34 ft. 6° 08' N., 1° 13' E.													
T5	85·1	86·7	87·9	86·2	85·5	82·8	79·7	78·8	80·2	83·3	85·5	85·3	83·8
	72·2	73·9	74·3	73·9	73·9	72·7	71·4	70·9	71·6	72·5	72·5	71·8	72·5
R15	0·6	0·9	1·8	4·6	5·7	8·8	2·8	0·3	1·4	2·4	1·1	0·4	30·8

Monsoonal Equatorial or Cameroon

This is Hubert's *Camerounien* sub-type of the Equatorial climate. It is also broadly coincident with his limits and includes, below 3,000 feet or less, the Bamenda and Cameroon Highlands, Mt. Cameroon, the Cross River and environs, and Fernando Po (except its southern quarter—see p. 522). Above 3,000 feet are montane micro-climates. In the Bamenda Highlands is a sub-type where rainfall is under about 110 inches annually, and temperatures lower but more variable than on the coast.

The Cameroon type results from the addition of a monsoonal effect to the Equatorial régime. Temperature and humidity

[1] J. H. Hubbard, ' A Note on the Rainfall of Accra, Gold Coast ', *Geographical Studies*, Vol. I, No. 1, 1954, pp. 69–75, and C. G. Wise, ' Climatic Anomalies on the Accra Plain ', *Geography*, 1944, pp. 35–38. See also J. H. Hubbard, ' Daily weather at Achimota, near Accra, Gold Coast ', *Geographical Studies*, Vol. III, No. 1, 1956, pp. 56–63.

conditions of the latter persist, but rainfall totals and high wind velocities in the wet season are akin to monsoonal conditions. The heavy rain may come in several maxima, though, broadly speaking, there is one great upsurge. There are no dry months, as there are in pure monsoonal conditions.

	Jan.	Feb.	Mar.	Apr.	May	June	July	Aug.	Sept.	Oct.	Nov.	Dec.	Year
Debundscha (W. Cameroon). 30 ft. 4° 07′ N., 8° 58′ E.													
R27	*9·3*	*10·4*	*21·0*	*19·4*	*30·0*	*47·0*	*55·5*	*53·2*	*60·9*	*45·2*	*25·5*	*14·7*	*392·1*
Victoria (W. Cameroon). 10 ft. 4° 00′ N., 9° 13′ E.													
T5	85·6	86·8	86·8	86·5	85·5	82·7	79·4	79·7	81·1	82·9	84·5	85·1	83·9
	70·8	71·3	72·7	72·4	72·1	72·2	71·6	71·5	71·6	71·3	71·5	71·4	71·7
R30	*1·7*	*2·7*	*6·1*	*8·3*	*13·3*	*25·1*	*38·8*	*31·7*	*16·9*	*10·2*	*4·1*	*1·5*	*160·4*
Calabar (Nigeria). 170 ft. 4° 58′ N., 8° 20′ E.													
T5	86·7	89·4	89·4	88·6	87·1	86·6	81·6	82·6	83·7	85·1	86·4	86·9	86·2
	73·0	73·4	74·5	74·2	74·5	73·3	72·6	72·3	72·7	72·5	73·0	73·3	73·3
R47	*1·7*	*3·0*	*6·0*	*8·4*	*12·3*	*16·0*	*17·7*	*16·0*	*16·8*	*12·2*	*7·5*	*1·7*	*119·3*

TROPICAL

Southern Savannah. This corresponds approximately with Hubert's *Soudanien-sud*. The name 'Sudan' is misleading to British readers, but there is no simple alternative. A vegetational name has disadvantages, but the advantages are sufficient to allow the name to be adopted.

This type largely coincides with the poor 'Middle Belt' of West Africa, between 7½–8° N. and about 11° N. in Nigeria, 12° N. in the Upper Volta and 13° N. in the west. It includes the upper Niger lands of Guinea (but not the Fouta Djallon), the northern Ivory Coast, southern Mali Republic, south-western Upper Volta, the Ghana Northern and Upper Regions, central and northern Togo, Dahomey and the Middle Belt of Nigeria around the rivers Niger and Benue. This climatic zone is roughly coincident with the Guinea Savannah.

There is a wide diurnal range of temperature in the dry season. There follows a seven to eight months rainy season, with lower temperatures and less variation. Variability of rainfall is greater than in climates already considered but less than in more northerly ones. Relative humidity varies between about 50 and 80% but in the dry season is under 70% at 9 a.m. It is this (rather than rainfall total) which is the vital factor.

	Jan.	Feb.	Mar.	Apr.	May	June	July	Aug.	Sept.	Oct.	Nov.	Dec.	Year
Kouroussa (Guinea). 1,247 ft. 10° 39′ N., 9° 53′ W.													
T5	92·4	96·5	99·0	98·5	94·3	89·1	86·2	85·1	86·8	89·5	91·2	90·8	91·6
	56·8	62·8	71·0	73·4	73·1	70·8	69·6	69·6	69·5	69·1	66·0	58·0	67·3
R10	0·4	0·3	0·9	2·8	5·3	9·7	11·7	13·6	13·4	6·6	1·3	0·4	66·3
Bobo Dioulasso (U. Volta). 1,421 ft. 11° 12′ N., 4° 17′ W.													
T5	93·6	98·0	100·8	100·8	96·3	92·1	87·0	87·8	93·0	95·2	94·6		93·6
	60·3	62·1	69·5	72·2	70·6	71·0	69·6	69·3	68·8	69·3	66·8	62·0	67·6
R10	0·1	0·2	1·1	2·1	4·6	4·8	9·8	12·0	8·5	2·5	0·7	0	46·4
Tamale (Ghana N.R.). 637 ft. 9° 24′ N., 0° 53′ W.													
T34	96·3	100·3	101·1	98·3	94·2	90·2	87·1	86·1	87·5	91·8	95·3	93·2	93·5
	66·4	70·4	74·0	73·8	72·7	70·8	70·9	69·8	69·7	70·5	69·6	69·5	70·7
R38	0·1	0·3	2·2	3·2	4·7	5·5	5·5	8·1	8·9	3·7	0·7	0·2	42·9
Bida (Nigeria). 605 ft. 9° 04′ N., 5° 59′ E.													
T5	93·8	97·0	98·3	98·1	93·3	88·0	85·7	84·3	86·1	89·8	94·6	94·0	92·0
	70·0	73·4	76·0	77·3	74·2	72·7	72·1	71·8	71·5	71·6	71·1	68·5	72·5
R25	0·1	0·3	1·0	3·0	6·0	7·7	7·6	8·4	10·2	3·8	0·3	0	48·5

Jos Plateau.[1] This is a highland variant of the Southern Savannah, so that temperatures are much lower. The rainfall régime is similar, but at exposed places on and near the south-western edge of the plateau annual rainfall may be higher.

Some authorities include this area in the Foutanian type, but temperatures on the Jos Plateau are more equable than in the Fouta Djallon. Moreover, rainfall is hardly monsoonal in character and is certainly less in yearly and in most monthly totals.

	Jan.	Feb.	Mar.	Apr.	May	June	July	Aug.	Sept.	Oct.	Nov.	Dec.	Year
Jos (Nigeria). 4,230 ft. 9° 52′ N., 8° 54′ E.													
T5	82·1	85·6	87·2	88·5	85·0	80·9	76·4	74·9	78·6	82·2	83·4	82·4	82·2
	57·0	59·3	64·1	66·3	65·4	63·4	62·7	62·3	62·2	62·2	60·3	57·2	61·9
R31	0·1	0·1	1·1	3·4	8·0	8·9	13·0	11·5	8·4	1·6	0·1	0·1	56·3

Savannah. In the main this coincides with Hubert's *Soudanien-nord* and extends between approximately 11°–13° N. in the south and 12°–14° N. in the north. It includes the southern interior of Senegal, interior Gambia, central Mali, most of the Upper Volta and part of northern Nigeria.

Compared with the Southern Savannah, rainfall is less and the rainy season is only five to six months in length. Variability of rainfall and range of temperatures are greater.

[1] Hubert did not recognise the Jos type, as he was primarily concerned with French West Africa.

	Jan.	Feb.	Mar.	Apr.	May	June	July	Aug.	Sept.	Oct.	Nov.	Dec.	Year
Tambacounda (Senegal). 187 ft. 13° 46′ N., 13° 11′ W.													
T 5	94·8	99·0	102·1	105·8	103·3	97·0	90·0	87·3	88·8	90·0	95·2	93·0	95·7
	58·8	*61·0*	*67·1*	*70·2*	*75·6*	*73·6*	*71·5*	*71·5*	*72·2*	*71·5*	*63·4*	*59·4*	*67·9*
R10	*0*	*0*	*0*	*0·1*	*1·1*	*6·9*	*7·6*	*12·0*	*8·5*	*3·2*	*0·1*	*0*	*39·6*
Bamako (Mali). 1,076 ft. 12° 39′ N., 7° 58′ W.													
T5	92·0	96·8	101·4	103·3	100·8	94·3	87·6	85·6	88·2	92·0	94·0	91·0	94·0
	63·0	*67·0*	*73·6*	*76·6*	*77·8*	*74·2*	*72·0*	*71·1*	*71·3*	*71·6*	*67·0*	*63·8*	*70·8*
R10	*0*	*0*	*0·1*	*0·6*	*2·9*	*5·3*	*11·0*	*13·7*	*8·1*	*1·7*	*0·6*	*0*	*44·0*
Ouagadougou (Upper Volta). 991 ft. 12° 22′ N., 1° 31′ W.													
T5	97·0	101·6	106·0	107·0	102·6	97·4	92·6	89·3	92·4	100·1	101·8	97·6	98·7
	57·6	*61·0*	*69·6*	*75·8*	*76·8*	*73·6*	*71·8*	*70·4*	*70·0*	*71·6*	*66·2*	*59·6*	*68·7*
R10	*0*	*0·1*	*0·6*	*0·8*	*2·9*	*4·9*	*8·4*	*10·4*	*5·6*	*0·9*	*0*	*0*	*34·7*
Kano (Nigeria). 1,549 ft. 12° 02′ N., 8° 32′ E.													
T5	85·6	89·9	95·7	100·8	99·3	94·5	87·2	85·1	88·0	93·5	92·5	87·1	91·6
	56·1	*59·5*	*65·9*	*72·4*	*74·6*	*73·9*	*71·1*	*69·6*	*69·4*	*68·1*	*61·6*	*56·9*	*66·6*
R48	*0*	*0*	*0·1*	*0·3*	*2·7*	*4·5*	*8·0*	*12·4*	*5·1*	*0·5*	*0*	*0*	*33·6*

Senegal Coastal.   More restricted in area than Hubert's *Sub-canarien sud*, this type is found in a narrow band from north of St. Louis southward as far as the Gambia estuary.

Rainfall is lower and comes in a shorter rainy season than in the adjacent Savannah or Southern Sahel zones (see Tambacounda and Kayes).   On the other hand, relative humidity is much higher in the dry season and less variable annually on the coast, because of the prevalence of moist northerly Marine Trade winds, in contrast to dry north-easterly or easterly winds at interior stations.

Maximum temperatures are not at the end of the dry season, but during the wet one.   This is because the Marine Trade winds have moved away north and the stimulus to coastal upwelling of cold water has come to an end.   This more than neutralises the effects of greater cloudiness in the rainy season.

Temperatures are more even and lower than inland, so that the climate is more pleasant, especially as coastal breezes are very strong over Cape Verde and Dakar streets are well aligned to catch them.

	Jan.	Feb.	Mar.	Apr.	May	June	July	Aug.	Sept.	Oct.	Nov.	Dec.	Year
Dakar (Senegal). 105 ft. 14° 39′ N., 17° 25′ W.													
T5	82·0	82·8	82·0	80·0	82·4	87·5	87·6	86·8	87·8	88·0	87·1	83·4	84·8
	64·8	*64·2*	*64·8*	*65·0*	*68·0*	*74·4*	*76·5*	*76·0*	*76·5*	*76·3*	*73·0*	*68·0*	*70·6*
R10	*0*	*0*	*0*	*0*	*0*	*1·2*	*3·5*	*10·4*	*5·7*	*1·7*	*0·2*	*0·0*	*22·7*

Southern Sahel.   This is found between 12–14° N. and 15–17° N., thereby comprising the northern interior of Senegal, southern

Mauritania, the southern Niger Bend country of the Mali Republic, the southern part of Niger Republic, and the northern fringes of Nigeria.

Rainfall is 20–30 inches annually, the rainy season is about three to five months in length but is often erratic, and there is a high range of temperature. This corresponds with the Sahel Savannah and is important cattle country. It is the most northern zone for regular cultivation without irrigation or the use of ground water.

	Jan.	Feb.	Mar.	Apr.	May	June	July	Aug.	Sept.	Oct.	Nov.	Dec.	Year
Kayes (Mali). 183 ft. 14° 24′ N., 11° 26′ W.													
T5	95·4	100·8	105·6	111·2	110·2	104·0	94·3	90·2	92·2	95·1	99·6	94·0	99·4
	62·1	66·0	71·6	77·0	81·8	78·6	75·1	73·1	73·2	74·0	68·4	64·1	72·1
R5	0·1	0	0	0	1·0	3·8	6·3	9·5	7·4	1·7	0	0	29·8
Niamey (Niger). 709 ft. 13° 31′ N., 2° 06′ E.													
T5	93·8	99·0	105·1	109·6	107·1	102·4	95·6	91·4	94·1	101·6	101·6	96·3	99·9
	56·8	60·0	68·2	75·4	80·3	76·6	74·2	72·2	73·1	72·6	64·1	58·6	69·3
R10	0	0	0·2	0·3	1·3	2·8	5·2	7·4	3·7	0·5	0	0	21·6
Nguru (Nigeria). 1,100 ft. 12° 51′ N., 10° 28′ E.													
T5	87·8	91·8	98·0	103·6	101·7	100·2	92·3	87·3	91·0	97·0	95·8	90·2	94·7
	53·8	57·8	63·6	69·3	72·6	74·3	73·1	71·4	70·9	66·5	59·1	54·7	65·6
R11	0	0	0	0·1	1·1	1·5	4·9	9·3	4·3	0·2	0	0	21·4

Northern Sahel. This is found between about 15–17° N. and 17–18° N. in central Mauritania, central Mali Republic and the Niger Republic. Rainfall averages under 16 inches per annum and in most cases is under 10 inches. It comes in about three months, but is highly erratic, and even quick-maturing millets often fail. Thorn Scrub is discontinuous, yet nomadic cattle are numerous.

'Winter' becomes an admissible term, since in this zone and at some stations in the Southern Sahel the lowest means of daily maximum temperatures are in the winter months. Rains are insufficient and rainstorms of too short a duration to reduce the very high 'summer' temperatures to the lowest for the year, although there is a lowering of over 10% because

	Jan.	Feb.	Mar.	Apr.	May	June	July	Aug.	Sept.	Oct.	Nov.	Dec.	Year
Gao (Mali). 876 ft. 16° 18′ N., 0° 08′ W.													
T5	87·3	91·2	99·2	106·6	110·0	108·2	101·8	96·3	100·6	104·2	96·0	89·0	99·2
	58·5	61·0	69·3	73·6	79·8	81·8	78·1	75·8	77·6	76·6	71·3	61·8	72·1
R9	0	0	0·1	0·1	0·3	1·2	2·9	3·6	1·0	0·1	0	0	9·3
Agadès (Niger). 1,706 ft. 16° 59′ N., 7° 56′ E.													
T5	82·4	91·6	100·6	107·6	112·0	111·2	105·6	101·6	105·8	105·0	94·3	90·2	100·6
	50·2	53·0	61·2	68·8	76·6	76·5	73·8	72·8	72·6	67·6	59·2	53·3	65·5
R10	0	0	0	0	0·2	0·3	1·9	3·7	0·7	0	0	0	6·9

of cloud. Yearly and diurnal ranges of temperature are very high. In the Aïr Mountains, daily minimum temperatures are even lower, e.g. at Agadès, and frost may occur.

Southern Saharan. This is found between 17–18° N. and 21° N. in north-central Mauritania, Mali Republic and the Niger Republic. Slight rain comes in most years for about six weeks, mostly from South-westerlies. There are occasional tufts of grass and sage bush, and cattle are still encountered in or around oases. As in the Northern Sahel, the lowest means of daily maximum temperatures are in winter. Lower temperatures occur in Adrar des Iforas and the Aïr massifs.

	Jan.	Feb.	Mar.	Apr.	May	June	July	Aug.	Sept.	Oct.	Nov.	Dec.	Year
Atar (Mauritania).	758 ft.	20° 31′ N., 13° 04′ W.											
T5	86·8	91·0	93·0	101·6	103·5	108·2	109·8	107·8	107·6	101·0	91·6	85·1	98·9
	53·8	55·2	62·3	67·1	71·3	80·1	77·2	78·6	78·8	73·6	62·5	56·0	68·0
R10	0·1	0	0	0	0	0·1	0·3	1·2	1·1	0·1	0·1	0	3·0

Araouane (Mali Republic) (935 feet, 18° 54′ N., 3° 33′ W.) and Bilma (Niger) (1,171 feet, 18° 43′ N., 12° 56′ E.) give very similar figures, except that as one proceeds eastward (as in other west to east climatic zones) rainfall diminishes, the percentage of calm winds doubles and the range of temperature increases by some ten per cent.

MAURITANIAN COASTAL

This has a more southerly extension than Hubert's *Sub-canarien-nord.* It is restricted to a narrow coastal band in northern Mauritania and Rio de Oro. The minute rainfall comes mostly in winter months, so that this might be regarded as an extreme southerly extension of the Mediterranean rainfall régime.

Like the Senegal Coastal type, relative humidity is again consistently high, north or north-westerly winds always predominating. Consequently, temperatures are also exceptionally low and equable for such a high latitude.

	Jan.	Feb.	Mar.	Apr.	May	June	July	Aug.	Sept.	Oct.	Nov.	Dec.	Year
Port Etienne (Mauritania).	23 ft.	20° 56′ N., 17° 03′ W.											
T5	79·4	82·2	81·4	81·2	82·8	85·8	80·8	85·3	90·8	86·6	83·6	77·8	83·2
	54·0	54·8	57·2	58·0	58·8	60·6	63·8	67·8	69·3	65·4	61·6	58·1	60·7
R10	0·1	0	0	0	0	0	0	0	0·3	0·5	0·1	0·4	1·5

SAHARAN

This is found north of about 21° N., i.e. a smaller extent than often suggested. Rain may fall in some years in any month. Vegetation and livestock are rare and restricted to oases. Temperatures are higher in summer than in the Southern Saharan zone but their yearly pattern is similar. ' The daily range in the heart of the desert is as much as 50° to 60° F.; the highest recorded temperatures on the surface of the earth are claimed by the Sahara. Shade recordings of 136° F. are said to have been made ; the surface of the ground frequently exceeds 170° F. . . . The annual range is between 30 and 40° F.' [1]

D. *CONCLUSION*

West Africa manifestly has many varieties of climate. Except towards the Sahara it does not have excessively high temperatures. The unwarranted bad reputation of its climates is a carry-over from the days when malaria was associated with bad air from swamps (hence the name), tropical medicine was unborn and the real cause of diseases unknown. Misapprehensions continue, especially since so many films trade on popular misconceptions. Moreover, people working in West Africa tend—consciously or unconsciously—to emphasise the discomforts, as this arouses sympathy. That the climate is supportable, is demonstrated by many missionaries who, although living under spartan conditions that officials and merchants would never endure, have quite often lived in West Africa without any home leave for some twenty years.

Those who perspire readily, feel fittest in the tropics. Exercise or moderate manual labour is not merely desirable but essential. The idea that manual labour should not be undertaken by non-Africans is absolutely false, as shown by many Italians and French. But hard manual labour over long hours in a strict routine is very bad—for Africans as well as for non-Africans. Eating and drinking habits need to be different from those prevailing in temperate lands. Less protein and carbohydrate are required, but more vitamins and salts in the

[1] L. D. Stamp, *Africa—A Study in Tropical Development*, 1964, p. 77.

form of fruit and vegetables.   If the right food is bought, prepared and served thoroughly clean and fresh, water boiled
and filtered, insects kept out of houses, the usual prophylactics
and daily exercise taken, sensible light clothes worn and strong
alcohol avoided or drunk in moderation, then anyone with
normal blood-pressure should keep very fit.

BIBLIOGRAPHY

General

Maurice A. Garbell, *Tropical and Equatorial Meteorology*, 1947.
B. Haurwitz and J. M. Austin, *Climatology*, New York, 1944.
W. G. Kendrew, *The Climates of the Continents*, 1957.
Thomas F. Malone, *Compendium of Meteorology*, American Meteorological
    Society, Boston, Mass., 1951.
C. Palmer, ' Tropical Meteorology ', *Quarterly Journal of the Royal Meteoro-
    logical Society*, Vol. 78 (1952), pp. 126–64.
Herbert Riehl, *Tropical Meteorology*, New York, 1954.

West African

    See references cited in footnotes.   Also:

A Pilot's Primer of West African Weather, Meteorological Office, 469, 1944.
*Weather on the West Coast of Tropical Africa from latitude 20° N. to 20° S.,
    including the Atlantic Ocean to 25° W.*, Meteorological Office, 492, 1954.
D. J. Bargman, ed., *Tropical Meteorology in Africa*, Munitalp Foundation,
    Nairobi, 1960.
Douglas B. Carter, ' Climates of Africa and India according to Thorn-
    thwaite's 1948 Classification ', The Johns Hopkins University Labora-
    tory of Climatology, *Publications in Climatology*, Vol. VII, No. 4, 1954.
R. H. Eldridge, ' A synoptic study of West African Disturbance Lines ',
    Quarterly Journal of the Royal Meteorological Society, Vol. 83, 1957, pp.
    303–14, and Vol. 84, 1958, pp. 468–9.
H. Germain, ' Synoptic Analysis for West Africa and the Southern Part of
    the Atlantic Ocean ', *Final Report of the Caribbean Hurricane Seminar*,
    Ciudad Trujillo, 1956, pp. 173–86.
R. A. Hamilton and J. W. Archbold, ' Meteorology of Nigeria and ad-
    jacent territory ', *Quarterly Journal of the Royal Meteorological Society*,
    Vol. 71, 1945, pp. 231–64.
P. Moral, ' Essai sur les régions pluviométriques de l'Afrique de l'Ouest ',
    Annales de Géographie, Novembre–Decembre 1964, pp. 660–86.
G. T. Trewartha, ' The Sahara, Sudan and Guinea Coast ', Chapter 7,
    The Earth's Problem Climates, University of Wisconsin Press, 1961.

Chapter 4

VEGETATION [1]

As in other parts of the world, the distribution and character of vegetation result from the interplay of climatic, edaphic (soils and soil water) and biotic influences (animals, especially man, and plants).

In West Africa man has been a ruthless modifier or destroyer of the natural vegetation and fauna. Edaphic factors are often extremely significant or even over-riding, especially near climatic margins and where lateritic crusts, saline or water-logged soils occur.

Of the climatic factors, rainfall and relative humidity normally exert the most powerful influences upon vegetation. Very important factors are the number of months with less than one inch of rain (see Fig. 24) and the minimum relative humidity, which is given approximately by the values at 1–3 p.m. (rarely recorded). The duration and frequency of low humidities are very significant. The minimum saturation deficit, which gives a measure of the evaporating power of the air independent of temperature, is even more useful, but rarely available.

There are about 6,000 flowering species belonging to over 180 families and some 1,500 genera in West Africa. Although

[1] I have drawn upon P. W. Richards, *The Tropical Rain Forest*, 1952; A. Aubréville, *Climats, Forêts et Désertification de L'Afrique Tropicale*, 1949; R. W. J. Keay, *An Outline of Nigerian Vegetation*, Lagos (2nd edit.), 1953, and unpublished material by the same author; D. R. Rosevear, ' Vegetation ', *The Nigerian Handbook*, 1953, pp. 139–73; J. Trochain, *La Végétation du Sénégal*, I.F.A.N., Dakar, 1940, and R. Schnell, *Contribution à une étude phyto-sociologique et phyto-géographique de l'Afrique Occidentale: les groupements et les unités géobotaniques de la région guinéenne*, I.F.A.N., Dakar, 1952. All these references contain maps and extensive bibliographies.

I am most grateful to Professor Richards and Dr. Keay for giving me criticism and much valuable help with this chapter. Botanical names are, as far as possible, in accord with R. W. J. Keay's revised edition of J. Hutchinson and J. M. Dalziel, *Flora of West Tropical Africa*, 1953 onwards.

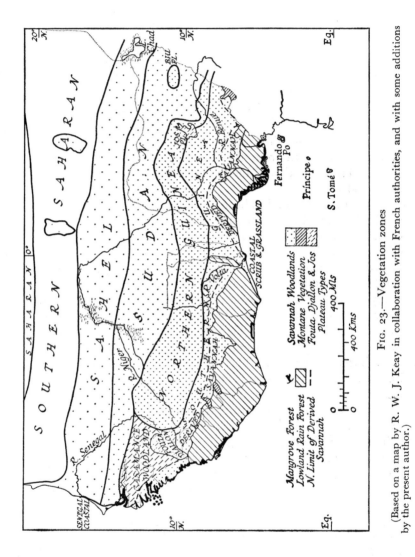

FIG. 23.—Vegetation zones

(Based on a map by R. W. J. Keay in collaboration with French authorities, and with some additions by the present author.)

1. A reg or stony desert, north of Kidal, Mali. Sand dunes or *erg* appear in the distance.

2. Much water is lost by intense evaporation and percolation in the dry season in the Savannah lands. Artificial storage for man and animals is being developed. The photograph was taken in the far north of Ghana.

3. The Niger in "the double V" between Say and Gaya, halfway between Niamey and the Nigerian boundary

SOIL EROSION
(Chapter 5)

4. Gully erosion started from th‹ Ouagadougou—Bobo Dioulasso roa‹ in the Upper Volta. Rainwater flowe‹ down the shiny surface of the road t‹ a corner behind the trees. There th‹ slope carried the water off the road t‹ start the gully, which was enlargin‹ rapidly.

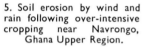

5. Soil erosion by wind and rain following over-intensive cropping near Navrongo, Ghana Upper Region.

6. Loose and degraded ‹ impoverished by continu‹ over-cultivation of ground‹ in the past, near Da‹ Senegal. The water-table ‹ also been lowered by h‹ demands for water in the ‹ and port. In an already ‹ environment the soils h‹ become even drier and poo‹

these figures may seem large, they are smaller than for tropical America or Indo-Malaya.

It is not intended to give here a systematic account of all the species occurring in each vegetational zone. Rather, the aim is to show the outstanding types, characteristics and aspect of the vegetation, where they occur, their relationships with other aspects of the environment—physical and human.—the value of certain species and some of the problems which arise.

STRAND AND SANDBANK VEGETATION

This is found on more or less pure sand, just above high water. It may be showered by sea-spray and is always enveloped in

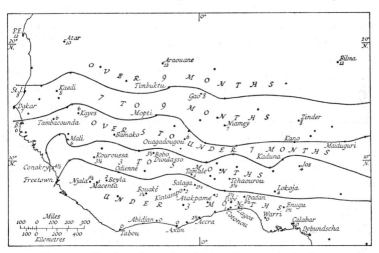

FIG. 24.—Number of months with less than one inch of rain.
This figure is critical for tree growth. (Based on readings from 103 stations.)

moist, salt-laden air. Strand and Sandbank vegetation is well developed on the sand-bar or sand-spit coasts of Senegal and the Gulf of Guinea.

Herbs, shrubs and grasses are common but discontinuous. Stunted bushes occur more rarely. On inward margins poor trees are seen.

THE FOREST REGIONS (HIGH FOREST)

Mangrove Forest. This occurs in muddy sheltered creeks, deltas and lagoons, wherever the water is brackish and strongly

D

tidal. Mangrove is best developed in the South-west Coast Monsoonal, Liberian, Equatorial and Cameroon climatic regions, but occurs as far north as the Senegal River. West African mangroves are of precisely the same species as those found along the east coast of America, but differ from those of East Africa and Indo-Malaya. Mangrove rootlets tend to hold loose, soft mud. As alluvium becomes consolidated, young healthy mangrove gives place, on the landward margin, to older mangrove and then to Fresh-water Swamp Forest or to Rain Forest.

Rhizophora racemosa (Red Mangrove) is overwhelmingly the commonest species. This has the famous ' stilt roots ', which do not penetrate the soil, but divide into innumerable rootlets, so making a felt-like underwater raft. Trees commonly reach 50 feet or more in height. Indeed, they are often far higher in the Niger Delta, where they are only occasionally invaded by very salt water. The trees are evergreen and make a dense canopy, which is the more impressive because of the dark, prop-like roots. *R. harrisonii* is dominant in the middle areas and is smaller. *R. mangle* is found only on the drier inner limit and is again smaller.

Mangrove bark has a high tannin and cutch content. The wood is excellent small constructional timber, and is also used in Nigeria for pit-props. It has a high calorific value as fuel, especially as charcoal.

Living mangrove assists land reclamation from the sea. Elimination of mangrove, with protective bunds against the ingress of salt water, often enables rice cultivation, as in the least saline areas of Sierra Leone and Nigeria, where the heavy rainfall and river-water can be used to flush salt out of the soil. On the Gambia River conditions are less favourable, as salt impregnation is greater and rainfall lower.

Fresh-water Swamp Forest. This is widespread in the Niger Delta, along fresh-water lagoons, rivers and in inland swamps. There is an outer fringe of ' sudd ' or ' floating grass ', papyrus swamps being a striking feature of Nigerian and some other creeks. Inward, are fixed grasses, shrubs or ferns, beyond which are species of Raphia and other palms. This fringing vegetation rarely exceeds 40 feet in height.

Inland comes the true Fresh-water Swamp Forest, which

may attain 100 feet, many trees having stilt roots. Diameters of the boles are less than those of the biggest trees of the Lowland Rain Forest and most species are different. The canopy is rather open and, in the gaps, tangled shrubs and lianes form a denser undergrowth. Climbing palms with hooked spines, related to the rattans of Asia, are characteristic. Useful trees are the Abura or Uwen (*Mitragyna ciliata*), *Pandanus candelabrum* (whose leaves are used for making mats and baskets), and species of Raphia such as *Raphia vinifera* and *Raphia hookeri*, used for roof-matting, rafters, piassava for brooms, and for wine. The mahogany *Khaya ivorensis* grows on the drier margin of swamps and is a valuable timber.

Lowland Rain Forest. This is the equivalent of Richards' *Tropical Rain Forest* and of Rübel's *Pluvisilva*. The West African forests lie on the north-western edge of the greater Congo Lowland Rain Forests. Its flora is the richest in West Africa, though poorer than similar forests in South America and Asia.

Separation of the western sector (see Fig. 23) of the forest is due mainly to lower rainfall in the gap and to the action of man.

The northward limit of Lowland Rain Forest may once have approximated to a line joining all stations with at least 45 inches annual rainfall, a minimum mean monthly relative humidity at 1 p.m. of at least 40%, and not more than three months with less than 1 inch of rain (see Fig. 24). Although annual rainfall may often be higher north of this line, the dry season is longer and critical afternoon relative humidities are lower.

Lowland Rain Forest is dense and the highest trees sometimes reach about 200 feet. Yet they do not rival the taller Californian redwoods or the Australian gums. Trees of the Lowland Rain Forest are highly varied in species, height, girth and age. Girths of over a yard are common and the trees are typically straight and slender, with few or no branches below the crown. Most barks are thin and smooth. A large proportion of the trees have buttresses extending outwards, sometimes many feet from the base of the trunk. The variety of species is the main difficulty in commercial forestry.

Oddly enough, the Lowland Rain Forest gives an impression of sombre uniformity. This is because many of the different trees have such superficially similar trunks, branches and leaves. But there are at least three tiers or layers of this forest with trees up to 60 feet, between 60 and 120 feet, and between 120 and 200 feet approximately. The uppermost tier usually has a discontinuous canopy but the lowest a more or less continuous one.

Undergrowth, woody climbers and epiphytes are characteristic, the climbers hanging above in great lengths, loops or festoons. Epiphytes (woody and herbaceous), mosses and lichens are numerous and luxuriant. Ground herbs may also be found.

Sunlight penetrates here and there. There is rarely much accumulation of rotting vegetation because of rapid decomposition. Mature forest on level, well-drained ground is easy to walk through and bare rock outcrops are often seen.

This forest has been reduced by one-half or more in the last century. In another century only scattered forest reserves may remain. Yet it is from this zone that so many famous woods are cut in the Ivory Coast, Ghana and Nigeria. It is also the zone of cultivation of the oil palm, cocoa, coffee, bananas and rubber. Among the best known timbers are certain mahoganies (*Khaya ivorensis* and *K. anthotheca*), Sapele (*Entandrophragma cylindricum*), Guarea (*Guarea cedrata*), Makoré (*Mimusops heckelii*), African Walnut (*Lovoa trichilioides*) and Dahoma or Ekhimi (*Piptadeniastrum africanum*).

Variations within the Lowland Rain Forest are caused mainly by biotic disturbance (see below) or by differences of relief, soil, slope, drainage, rock outcrops and parent materials.

It seems that the Cross River valley is the western limit of many plants and animals common in Central Africa which rarely, if ever, extend farther into West Africa.[1] Forests east of the Cross River, growing in an area of very heavy well-distributed rainfall and on soils derived from volcanic or Pre-Cambrian rocks, are the most completely evergreen and least non-seasonal forest type in West Africa. These forests may have been cut considerably in the past by intensive slave-raiding, and the resulting low population have allowed long and almost unchecked re-growth.

By contrast, the irregular forests of Benin grow mainly on

---

[1] D. R. Rosevear, op. cit., p. 150.

highly porous sands. They contain many mahoganies and a ground flora of wiry creepers. Most Ondo forests grow on soils from crystalline rocks and have two species entirely absent from Benin, namely, *Nesogordonia papaverifera* and *Mansonia altissima*. The undergrowth is also more shrubby. The Ijebu forests differ again in their poverty of useful trees and in their wide-spacing, sparse understory beneath the emergents, and a poor shrubby and herbaceous undergrowth. This may be ancient Fresh-water Swamp Forest developed in turn from mangrove.[1]

A frequent division is made by the separation of *Mixed* or *Semi-Deciduous* or *Dry Forest* (once used by Keay but now dropped by him) or *La Forêt Mesophile* (Aubréville, Mangenot, Schnell, Emberger) or of *Der Subxerophiler Tropenwald* (Milbraed). The present British tendency seems to be to merge this type within the Lowland Rain Forest. In the Equatorial Semi-seasonal or Seasonal climatic zones (see Fig. 27), where there are up to four months with less than 1 inch of rain (see Fig. 29), lower relative humidities and drier soils, the forest may contain rather more deciduous trees, though it is not transitional to Woodland or Savannah, and is not fire resistant. Although the flora and its physiognomy are similar to the rest of the Lowland Rain Forest, species are fewer and canopies may be more open. Deciduous [2] trees may predominate only in the upper storey, although there are also evergreens. Shrubs and smaller trees, making a strong woody undergrowth, are mainly evergreen. It is for these reasons that botanists dislike the term ' Mixed Deciduous Forest '. There are certainly not enough mature deciduous trees to justify the term ' Monsoon Forest '.

Obeche, Wawa or Samba (*Triplochiton scleroxylon*) may represent up to 20% of all dominants. Others of that family are Danta (*Nesogordonia papaverifera*) and *Hildegardia barteri*, which are absent from the wetter forest, *Mansonia altissima* and *Cola gigantea*. Other species are Iroko (*Chlorophora excelsa*), a mahogany, *Khaya grandifoliola* (but not *K. ivorensis* or *K. anthotheca* of wetter forests, or *K. senegalensis* of drier regions), Utile,

---

[1] D. R. Rosevear, op. cit., pp. 151–2.

[2] Individual trees are bare of leaves for several weeks annually, but since many trees are evergreen, the forest still presents an evergreen appearance.

Sipo or Assie (*Entandrophragma utile*), Albizia (*A. ferruginea*) and Afara (*Terminalia superba*). Those with popular names are cut for timber, and many of the trees also occur in Secondary and Depleted Forests. There are often more useful but less valuable trees than in other parts of the Lowland Rain Forest.

Other than the trees, this zone has some tuber geophytes which perennate during dry months, forming underground corms and tubers. Epiphytes are fewer—another indication of seasonal dryness—as is also the fact that herbaceous undergrowth may die down in the dry month or months.

Biotic Modifications of the Lowland Rain Forest

Depleted Forests. Wherever there is or has been selective felling of certain species only, the gaps may be colonised by Secondary Forest species. Often there is a patch-work arrangement of Primary and Secondary species. Depleted forests are characteristic of Benin and Ondo Provinces of Nigeria, and of the timber-producing areas of the Ivory Coast. In Ghana, however, all trees are generally cut, as the land is being taken over for food farms.

Secondary Forest. This results from the cutting and burning of the forest for periodic cultivation. Large trees may be left because they defy primitive methods of clearing, useful ones may be retained for their produce, and others for religious reasons.

The farmed patch is generally abandoned to forest re-growth only when fertility is exhausted. The soils are not only impoverished chemically but also physically, since their humus content and water-holding properties are impaired. The canopy has been broken and the sun's rays may now reach the ground. Consequently, soil temperatures are higher, rainfall more immediate in its action and relative humidity is lower.

These conditions are unfavourable to complete regeneration for a long time—perhaps for centuries. New plant-growth is, however, very rapid, and at first is generally by weeds and seedlings of trees and shrubs. These are quickly succeeded by climbers, such as species of *Combretum*, whose roots generally survive in the ground and which need much light. Lianes and a more or less impenetrable undergrowth are also typical of young secondary growth.

The first new trees are the more tolerant and less valuable, fast-growing, soft wood, low-density species. Floristic variety is far less than in the original forest, although *Acanthaceae* and *Zingiberaceae*, less common in natural forest, are numerous in young Secondary Forest. The Umbrella or Parasol Tree (*Musanga cercropioides*) is often an early dominant, but does not reproduce itself, since it will not tolerate shade. It dies within fifteen to twenty years and its fellows within thirty years, thus completing the first stage of regrowth. During this stage, trees are much smaller, thinner and more uniform than in ' Primary Forest ', except for more diverse leaf structure and colour.

Thereafter more variety is seen. Other trees become evident and many are tall, large, light-demanding and useful, such as Samba (*Triplochiton scleroxylon*), Iroko (*Chlorophora excelsa*) and Afara (*Terminalia superba*). The oil palm will often survive from farming days until the forest is high and dense again, when it will be stifled. It is never found in virgin forest.

Derived Savannah. If Secondary Forest is frequently cut and burned, or if the original period of cultivation is long and the soil poor, grass progressively invades the cut-over area, and annual fires (intentional or otherwise) gradually kill remaining trees. Fire-tolerant savannah trees may colonise these grasslands, and so there will be Derived Savannah, typical of the inner fringes of the Lowland Rain Forest (see Fig. 23) and of certain places within it—e.g. the Sobo Plains in southern Benin or of the Ivory Coast near Jacqueville. Forest patches found in Derived Savannah are remnants of the formerly more extensive Lowland Rain Forest.

CASAMANCE WOODLAND

Coinciding partly with the South-west Coast Monsoonal climatic zone, this occurs in the Casamance district of Senegal, Portuguese Guinea and lowland parts of Guinea.

Though the Casamance Woodland might be thought of as akin to Lowland Rain Forest, it is a woodland, with its own very individual physiognomy and composition. Because of the long dry season it was originally poorer floristically and has also been heavily cut by man, as shown by the widespread occurrence of the oil palm.

Originally, and now in a few relicts, it has only two stories.

The upper storey, 50–70 feet high, consists overwhelmingly of only four species: *Parinari excelsa*, *Erythrophleum guineense*, *Detarium senegalense* and *Afzelia africana*. With them are generally many lianes. The trees are strikingly different from those of the Lowland Rain Forest, because they are low-branching and spreading. The lower canopy, at 10–20 feet, of bushes, lianes and herbaceous plants, is likewise deciduous and thick.

On the northern fringes of the Fouta Djallon, where there are poor lateritic outcrops, the undergrowth is mostly of bamboo and the large trees are more varied. On sandstone edges and near streams in lowland Guinea, *Guibourtia copallifera* (gum copal) and *Coffea stenophylla* are much found, and on the northern boundary of the zone *Khaya senegalensis* is common.

FOUTA DJALLON

The mean altitude of the Fouta Djallon is between 2,600 and 3,250 feet, the highest point near the town of Mali reaching about 4,925 feet. No clear altitudinal gradations of vegetation occur, nor is there true Montane vegetation.

Originally, this region may have been the extreme northwestern limit of the Lowland Rain Forest. If so, it must always have been exceedingly frail, owing to the marginal position in latitude and altitude of the Fouta Djallon in relation to the main forests. Moreover, the sandstone weathers to an exceedingly infertile soil, or even to a lateritic crust; and there is a four-month dry season, only partly moderated by dew.

It is also possible and, perhaps, likely that the Fouta Djallon was originally covered mainly by Casamance Woodland, with some Lowland Rain Forest additions. The dominant was *Parinari excelsa*, which now survives only in tiny patches on crests, but is typical of the Casamance Woodland.

The original vegetation has been eliminated in the last century and a half, since the immigration of the Fulani. Fire has caused the advent of some species found in Secondary Forest or in Derived Savannah, and of a sparse herbaceous and semi-shrubby flora. The sedge, *Trilepis pilosa*, grows in tufts of fine wire-like leaves on almost bare rock, but itself makes a humus. Nevertheless, the Fouta Djallon is notorious for its *bowé* (sing. *bowal*), or lateritic exposures, almost bare of soil or vegetation.

SAVANNAH WOODLAND

The present line between Lowland Rain Forest and Savannah Woodland is one of the world's clearest boundaries, but is rarely, if ever, a natural one. It results from persistent cutting and burning of the vegetation by man.

Savannah is not a climatic climax but a biotic one. But for constant burning, Lowland Rain Forest would change gradually to Woodland in areas of lower relative humidity. Grass has entered because its roots survive frequent burning. Thus grass is a fire-climax not a natural climax.

Regular firing (to hunt out animals or to clear land for cultivation) has not only admitted grass and eliminated all trees which will not tolerate fire, but has allowed the advent of those species of trees which are fire resistant, especially the common Red Ironwood tree, *Lophira lanceolata* (not to be confused with *L. alata* of the Lowland Rain Forest which is not fire-resistant), popularly known as the Meni oil tree or False Shea butter tree, whose stems are chewed to clean teeth.

Although grass and other species are connected with the occurrence of fire, they may also be encouraged by edaphic factors, such as the occurrence of lateritic crusts with little soil, like the *bowé*, or by the alternation of flood and drought, as in the Afram Plains of Ghana.

Savannah Woodlands are sub-divided on grounds of physiognomy, as well as on botanical differences. Differentiating factors include density of plant cover, height, amount of grass and its character, and whether the plant or tree is deciduous or not in the dry season. Woodlands were less rich floristically than Rain Forests and stands are sometimes very uniform.

Ghana Coastal Scrub and Grassland. Although yearly rainfall is low, the relative humidity is high, so that the original vegetation was probably a mixture of Woodland and Forest species. The heavy hand of man, over some three centuries or so, has degraded the natural vegetation to dense scrub without grass west of Accra, and to grassland with few trees and patches of scrub east of Accra. The scrub vegetation is still a mixture of Forest and Woodland species. East of the Volta is Secondary Lowland Rain Forest (Oil palm Forest) or Derived Savannah, and north of it is Guinea Savannah.

Guinea Savannah.   This is found between about 8° and 13° N. and coincides roughly with the Southern Savannah climatic zone described in Chapter 3, and with the poor ' Middle Belt '. Rainfall averages 40–55 inches annually, there are four to five months with less than 1 inch of rain (Fig. 24), and critical relative humidity may drop to 14 per cent.

(a) *Southern Guinea sub-zone.*   On the margins of the Rain Forest this zone has grass averaging 5 to 10 feet or more in height.   The broad-leaved deciduous trees have short boles, are mostly 40–50 feet high and occur in clumps.   *Anogeissus leiocarpus* and *Lophira lanceolata* are common, as well as *Terminalia glaucescens, Daniellia oliveri, Hymenocardia acida, Vitex doniana, Detarium microcarpum* and *Afzelia africana.*   All are fire-resistant, but as they are burned year after year, they usually have twisted gnarled stems and corky bark, and so are useless for timber.   The tall, tussocky grasses are mainly species of *Andropogon, Hyparrhenia* and *Pennisetum.*

In swamp areas, grass is more dominant and trees are scattered, the Fan Palm (*Borassus aethiopum*) being common. On still moist but better drained slopes, and along rivers, there are outliers of Lowland Rain Forest.   On river banks are swamp species.

Leafing and flowering occur commonly at the end of the dry season, well before the first rains.   Leafing can be hastened by firing, which is, in consequence, generally done at the end of the dry season.   The leaves which soon appear (often with the help of dew and atmospheric moisture) are a wonderful help to starved cattle after the long drought and lack of pastures.   But fires at the end of the dry season are naturally fierce and cause much more damage than if started earlier.

(b) *Northern Guinea sub-zone.*   This is not normally found in contact with Lowland Rain Forest, of which there are only rare outliers.   This sub-zone is also poorer and distinct in its species, although the physiognomy is similar to the Southern Guinea one.

The Northern Guinea sub-zone is found in the Niger Valley lands of Guinea (Kouroussa) ;   along the borders of the Ivory Coast and Upper Volta (Odienné and Ferkessédougou) ; in the southern part of the Mali Republic (Bougouni) ;   in central Togo (Sokodé and Bassari), Dahomey (Djougou, Parakou, Bembéréké) and in Nigeria (Zaria).

The original climax vegetation of this sub-zone probably resembled the great ' Miombo woodlands' of East, Central and South Tropical Africa. It is poorer in species than are those areas, the trees are also smaller, fewer and with less development of branches. All this may result from climatic variation in past eras, and from drier winds and more intensive burning in West Africa.

Where there is not too much firing, dominant species are *Isoberlinia doka*, and *I. dalzielii*, *Monotes kerstingii* and *Uapaca togoensis* (syn. *U. somon*). But *Brachystegia*, so thoroughly typical of this vegetational belt in East and Central Africa, is not found in this zone in West Africa. Moreover, several genera which have many species in Southern and East Africa are represented by very few in West Africa.

This savannah woodland is about 20–40 feet high and, where the canopy is closed, grass is absent. Where the canopy is open, grass is dominant, though shorter than in the Southern Guinea zone. Shrubs are common.

Useful trees such as the Shea butter or Karité (*Butyrospermum parkii*), Tamarind (*Tamarindus indica*), Locust Bean tree, *Parkia spp.*, *Vitex doniana*, *Afzelia africana*, *Daniellia oliveri* and the rubber climber (*Landolphia heudelotii*) are generally preserved.

(c) *Jos Plateau sub-zone.* Keay and others use the old term ' Bauchi Plateau ', though they do not extend their vegetational type to include Bauchi town. For reasons of relief, morphology and vegetation, the term ' Jos Plateau ' is preferable.

The plateau averages 4,000 feet, and rises to just over 6,000 feet in places. Though at such altitudes montane vegetation might be expected, Keay considers that the vegetation of the plateau is not montane, though there are many plants which show affinities with plants of East and Southern Africa. Many others are identical with plants in those areas. Most species of the Northern Guinea sub-zone are found on the plateau, and Keay [1] has concluded that originally Northern Guinea vegetation once covered it, with the special additions just mentioned. Monod [2] considers that the original woodland

---

[1] Keay, op. cit., pp. 29–30.
[2] Th. Monod, ' Notes sur la flore du Plateau Bautchi', *Mélanges Botaniques*, I.F.A.N.-Dakar, 1952, pp. 11–37.

was more montane, and that the present examples of Northern Guinea vegetation are not relicts, but advents to the plateau. Ingress to the plateau on the north-eastern side is easy because of lower altitudes, gentler slopes and interdigitation of plain and plateau.

Whether the original woodland was Montane or Northern Guinea in character, it has been so thoroughly destroyed that most accessible areas are almost treeless and are under grass, which is heavily farmed and grazed. Tin and colombite mining have also greatly impaired the vegetation and drainage. The present plant-cover is a highly degraded form of Northern Guinea vegetation, with montane additions.

Sudan Savannah.   This is found in a belt some 120–240 miles wide, from Senegal to Nigeria and beyond, north of the Guinea Savannah.

In the Sudan Savannah annual rainfall averages about 22–40 inches, there are seven almost rainless months, and relative humidity in early afternoons of the dry season may drop to 8%. It may be regarded as the most typical of all Savannahs and occurs roughly in the climatic belt of that name.

It is one of the clearest climatic, vegetational and human zones, yet one of the most affected by man. It is often densely inhabited—e.g. in northern Nigeria, the Upper Volta and western Senegal—so that there is much secondary vegetation. There has also been some spreading of species from the south, and from the north—particularly of acacias. Consequently, the vegetation of this zone is difficult to define.

Trees, which almost always occur singly, average 25–50 feet in height and have wide-spreading crowns. The Dum Palm (*Hyphaene thebaica*), *Sclerocarya birrea*, *Balanites aegyptiaca* and Baobab (*Adansonia digitata*) are common, the latter especially in the west. The last two, as well as the locust bean (*Parkia spp.*), shea-butter tree (*Butyrospermum parkii*), *Acacia albida*, *Tamarindus indica* and Kapok (*Ceiba pentandra*), are all protected because of their value. There are also smaller trees, 10–20 feet high, such as the acacias. Lower again is the bush or shrub of 6–20 feet, in which climbers (e.g. *Combretum micranthum*) are represented, being very common on rocky hills or lateritic outcrops.

Most trees have small leaves, to prevent excessive transpiration, though there are a few broad-leaved ones. As one proceeds northward through the zone these disappear, but those with thorns (for example, the acacias) become more common. Most trees lose all their leaves in the dry season, but *Acacia albida* is a most useful exception.

In this zone, grass shoots up only just before the rains. It is also shorter (3–5 feet), less tussocky but more feathery than in the zones to the south. Consequently, it is very useful for grazing and is less deliberately burnt, so that fires are not so violent. It is a most interesting fact that moderate grazing, by keeping the grass short, can arrest fires and so allow greater tree growth and regeneration.

The original climax (xerothermic) may perhaps still be seen on isolated or inaccessible rocky slopes, or along water-courses. It is thought to be similar to vegetation still seen in south-western areas of Northern Rhodesia.

Senegal Coastal Vegetation. This coincides with the equally narrow climatic zone fringing the coast in Senegal to a depth never exceeding 30 miles. Greater atmospheric humidity, together with the higher water-table in the *niayes* of Senegal (pp. 192–3) and even in some *aftouts* of Mauritania, permit a naturally more luxuriant vegetation than in the drier interior.

Around the *niayes* and, to a much lesser extent, the *aftouts*, are trees and plants of the Guinea Savannah, together with poor looking oil palms and the *Borassus aethiopum* palm. Away from these clay depressions, drier vegetation of the Sudan Savannah and Sahel Savannah, is seen. The baobab is fairly frequent.

Sahel Savannah. This occurs in southern Mauritania, north-central Senegal, in much of the Niger Bend country of Mali, in the southern Niger, in the extreme north-east of Nigeria, and it has at least eight dry months.

The original climax was probably Thorn Woodland. This has now become more open, so that it is easy to drive a jeep between the trees. These average 15–30 feet in height, are deciduous, and finely divided in their leaf structure. They have very spreading and deeply penetrating roots, which fix the loose sand. The trees also have thorns.

The many acacias, with their light foliage and thorns, are

always regarded as characteristic. The *Acacia seyal*, 6–12 feet in height, prefers clay depressions, where there are often dense stands. It is most frequently seen in the Mali Republic and to the west thereof. *A. raddiana* is taller, very common and typical of this zone, and prefers light dry sandy soils. *A. senegal, A. laeta* and *A. ehrenbergiana* and *A. nilotica* are the sources of gum and grow well on fixed dunes in Mauritania, Mali Republic and the Niger Republic. *A. nilotica* (with several varieties) is found in profusion in the flood-plain of the Senegal River and, together with *A. sieberiana*, along most streams. These last are up to 40 feet in height.

Thorn shrubs, forming tree-steppe, are also characteristic. One is *Commiphora africana*, or African myrrh, some 10–16 feet tall, with a short conical stem and swollen base divided, near the ground, into rigid spreading branches. These branches are straight rigid thorns. Leaves are shed in October, and soon after there are red flowers. It grows in sandy and rocky places, and is particularly common in the Niger. Other shrubs are *Balanites aegyptiaca*, with small leathery leaves, and *Euphorbia balsamifera*, which is a fleshy spurge found in rocky environments. Grasses are short, discontinuous, wiry and tussocky, but much used by cattle and sheep. There are no real gallery or fringing forests, only riparian woodland of certain acacias mentioned above.

Fires are far less serious than farther south, because there is neither the density of trees nor height and cover of grass to warrant them, nor such density of population to start them. Soil and water supply exert powerful influence or control.

FOREST OUTLIERS, FRINGING FORESTS AND RIPARIAN WOODLAND

These extensions of the forest occur along streams, in swamps, ravines, on hillsides and other favourable sites in the Savannah Woodlands. They depend upon edaphic moisture, rather than upon the low or seasonal rainfall.

Adjacent to rivers in the Guinea Savannah are specifically riverine species, such as *Brachystegia eurycoma*, whose brilliant red leaves show up the courses of the rivers. Beyond is a dense understorey of evergreen shrubs and climbers, with widely spaced emergents above, some 40–60 feet high.

In flatter and poorly drained outer margins of a valley, there may be Raphia Palms with tall dense grass. Even farther out are Borassus Palms and bamboo.

Farther north, in the Sudan Savannah, Riparian Woodland occurs, with dense deciduous climbers and shrubs, alternating with tall grass and isolated trees.

In the Sahel Savannah, Riparian Woodland consists mainly of the more moisture-loving acacias of the same zone and of the Sudan Savannah.

Semi-saharan and Saharan Vegetation

Southern Saharan. After the small summer rains, grasses and annuals appear. Certain other plants may be sustained by winter dew. Many of the acacias and other trees or shrubs of the Sahel Savannah persist. Woody species are mostly Tropical but the herbs are mostly Mediterranean. Grasses grow in very isolated tufts.

In the less arid and cooler Adras des Iforas and Aïr massifs, there is Sahel Savannah vegetation.

Saharan. In most places there is a very dispersed permanent vegetation of tiny scrubby plants and bushes, with trees in favoured sites. Permanent vegetation here and in the Southern Saharan zone depends upon underground water and the nature of the sub-soil, rather than upon rain, but seasonal herbs (*acheb*) spring up only after rains and soon mature.

In saline areas there are often chenopods which can provide camel forage. Another fodder plant and fuel provider is Had or *Cornulaca monacantha*. In oases, outliers of the Sahel Savannah appear.

Montane Vegetation

Montane Rain Forest. Altitude may modify vegetation because of increased and more constant humidity and cloudiness, less sunlight, lower temperatures and less evaporation. Consequently, above about 3,000 feet in the Cameroon and Bamenda Highlands, Mt. Cameroon, the islands of the Bight of Biafra and in the Guinea Highlands, there is a tall canopied Montane Rain Forest. Lianes are scarce (except, apparently on São Tomé), but bryophytes (mosses), tree-ferns (*Cyathea spp.*), epiphytes (orchids and begonias) and lichens are abundant. Species with temperate affinities also occur.

Above about 4,550–4,880 feet, trees are smaller and less varied but temperate species are quite common. This zone alone, or this and the previous one, are often termed ' Mist Forest ', since it is usually saturated in mist. At its upper margin, ferns, mosses and epiphytes become less conspicuous than white lichens on trees. The mist zone ceases at about 6,000 feet.

Forest is not usually found above about 4,500 feet in the Cameroon and Bamenda Highlands, except as tongues up to about 7,800 feet. On Mt. Cameroon it ceases at about 5,000 feet on the north side, and at about 8,000 feet on the south-west, varying because of soil, slope, drainage, exposure and fire. Lesser interference by man has enabled forest in the Guinea Highlands to survive fairly well.

Montane Woodland. This occurs on the upper edge of the Montane Forest and is a drier type with abundant grass. It is easily degraded or destroyed by fire and, for this reason, is poorly represented on Mt. Cameroon. There, it often gives place to grassland, except near the forest and in protected gullies. It is better represented in the Cameroon Highlands, and especially in the Bamenda Highlands. Bamboo brakes occur in parts of the Bamenda Highlands above about 7,000 feet, but are unknown on Mt. Cameroon or Fernando Po. Only on the peaks of the Guinea Highlands (highest is Mt. Nimba 6,026 feet) does *Parinari excelsa* occur as in the Casamance Woodland.

Montane Tall Grassland. This is probably derived from Montane Woodland as the result of frequent burning. Grasses are about 2–3 feet high, and there are isolated trees. It occurs in the Cameroon and Bamenda Highlands and in the Loma Mountains of Sierra Leone. Large herds of Fulani cattle are kept in this zone in the Bamenda Highlands.

Montane Short Grassland. This is found above about 7,800 feet in the Cameroon and Bamenda Highlands, and above 10,000 feet on Mt. Cameroon. Grasses are shorter and more compact, with narrower leaves, and with moss between the tussocks. A heath *Blaeria mannii* is very characteristic but trees are absent. Plants of European affinity are common and tall lobelia occur.

On Mt. Cameroon, above about 12,000 feet, the cinder-like lava is sparsely covered by very short tufts of grass, and by moss and grey lichens.

VEGETATION AND THE NEEDS OF MAN

Though Rain Forests may be the origin of all flora, their survival beyond another century seems doubtful. They are being felled to provide space for food crops to feed the rapidly rising populations, and for profitable cash or export crops such as kola nuts, citrus fruit, bananas, coffee, rubber and cocoa. These pressing claims against the Rain Forests have arisen in the last half-century, though shifting agriculture had, over a far longer period, already converted much virgin forest into secondary bush.

In the past, timber exploitation consisted of the highly selective felling of mahoganies and a few other species. A much wider range of timbers is now exported, and much of the ' useless ' timber is used for making fibre-board, etc. Nevertheless, timber is a relatively minor export. Only the Ivory Coast, Ghana and Nigeria export any significant amount of timber and in all of them, at the best, it only reaches a very poor fourth place in order of value. Rain Forests are falling not so much at the demand of the timber merchant, but far more to that of the villager avid for more land.

Another acute problem is the almost entire disappearance or degradation of Woodlands, and their replacement by Savannah. It is generally agreed that forest and woodland are the only natural climaxes as far as very roughly 15° N.

Bush firing was recorded at the time of Hanno's voyage, nearly 2,500 years ago. It was accentuated by the Ghana, Mali, Songhai and other empires, whose domains lay around the middle Niger up to more than a thousand years ago. A vicious circle of fire leading to grass leading to fiercer fire, has for centuries been shrivelling the life out of the Woodlands between about 8° and 15° N. These were originally the most extensive vegetation in West Africa but, because they were frailer and have been the longest attacked, they have largely succumbed to firing by man and to the advent of grass.

North of the 20–28-inch isohyets, natural vegetation is generally of the Sahel type. This is more than holding its own and acacias are increasing within it. The short grass does not permit violent fires, the population is slight and possibilities of cultivation are so restricted that there is no pressure on these lands adjacent to the Sahara.

Far from the Sahara encroaching as Stebbing [1] so stoutly maintained, it is now regarded as fairly stable. The relative stability of the Sahel vegetation and of its northern margin seems to confirm this. An Anglo-French Commission, which investigated the matter in 1937, found no instance of live sand dunes along the Nigeria–Niger boundary, no universal lowering of the water-table by natural causes, and no rapid drying out of Lake Chad. They did, however, find deterioration by wind and water through the action of man, and urged protection of head-waters, the reservation of forests and contour farming. Many such measures have been undertaken.

Over geological time, it is certainly true that the Sahara was less extensive. It is equally true that it was, at times, more extensive. We are now in a phase of moderate Saharan extension. Whatever the phase, we could do little or nothing to alter it. But as the real trouble is man-made and farther south, we may perhaps do something.

Contrary to Stebbing's belief, the desperate modern problem concerns not so much the margins of the Sahara, but the realm of the Woodlands, which is ever ceding territory to grass. It is all-important to control bush-firing internationally either by preventing it, or by limiting its range, or by insisting upon firing early in the dry season before vegetation is too dry. This last proposal would, of course, defeat the whole aim of many pastoralists, who fire vegetation to get earlier leafing of trees and herbage for cattle at the end of the long dry season, when cattle desperately need fodder.

[1] E. P. Stebbing, *The Forests of West Africa and the Sahara*, 1937, and 'The Threat of the Sahara', *Journal of the R. African Soc.*, Vol. 36, supplement. For a summary and reply see L. D. Stamp, 'The Southern Margin of the Sahara: Comments on some recent studies on the question of Desiccation', *Geographical Review*, 1940, pp. 297–300 and Aubréville, op. cit., pp. 309–44.

The Rain Forests must also be defended. In temperate lands, where temperatures and rainfall are lower, removal of large blocks of forest (which is also so much lower and less vigorous in temperate countries) probably has little or no climatic effect. In the tropics, however, temperatures on bare land are obviously higher than in a shaded forest. When the tremendous transpiration from a Rain Forest and its cooling effect on clouds is eliminated, significant contributions to relative humidity and rainfall disappear.

Aubréville[1] considers that the Rain Forests of West Africa are responsible for replenishing the south-westerly winds with moisture, without which the Savannahs would have less rain, lower relative humidity and a shorter rainy season.

Each inroad into frailer parts of the Rain Forest gives a freer path to the desiccating Harmattan. This has happened in the Fouta Djallon, in the V-shaped bend of the Ivory Coast Rain Forest south of Bouaké, in the Ghana Coastal Scrub, on the Jos Plateau and along the Benue valley, all now open to this drying wind.

Removal of forests also greatly affects the drainage pattern. Soils around river sources need tree cover and the binding effect of roots to hold them. Streams often run in forests, even in the dry season, because trees by their cool surfaces induce dew and condensation. Remove the forests and the streams dry up. Cutting of forest often means removal of soil and the clogging of rivers.

Cutting of any Woodland frequently leads to soil erosion by wind in the dry season. Cutting of Rain Forest on steep slopes may assist gully erosion; and cutting on level land may induce sheet erosion and the laying bare of underlying lateritic concretions, like the *bowé* of the Fouta Djallon of Guinea.

Removal of natural vegetation, followed by prolonged over-farming, has impoverished many areas. Such is the case between Dakar and St. Louis in Senegal, southern Sierra Leone (where the Secondary Forest is remarkably poor), near Koforidua in Ghana, and in heavily populated parts of Onitsha and Owerri Provinces in Nigeria.

[1] Op. cit., pp. 333–8. Richards, op. cit., p. 405, lists authorities on this controversial matter. See also J. N. Oliphant, ' *The Land-Use Movement in West Africa* ', Imperial Forestry Bureau, 1943.

Only the restriction of bush-firing and the control of grazing can revive the Woodland zone. The Rain Forest zone, though less severely degraded, also needs selective protection. Building needs will require wood, and fuel supplies must be assured. But what of the urgent need of land to feed more people and grow more export crops? Better farming on existing land must provide most of the answer. Bush fallowing may suffice and not unduly damage the natural vegetation when the population is small. Increasing land pressure with the same agricultural system must ruin the forest and, in the end, the soils and the people as well. It is not forest reservation but bush fallowing which is so wasteful. Permanent cropping is essential everywhere if the remaining vegetation, the soils and man himself are to survive. Steep slopes and all land not suitable for farming should be retained or replanted as permanent forests. Defence of forest and woodland is one of the outstandingly urgent tasks in West Africa to-day, for on it depends the very continuance of agriculture—the basis of West African economy.

BIBLIOGRAPHY

See footnote near beginning of chapter. Also:

Vegetation map of Africa, Oxford University Press, 1959.
S. HADEN GUEST, J. K. WRIGHT and E. M. TECLAFF (eds.), *A World Geography of Food Resources*, 1956, Chapter 16.
G. W. LAWSON, *Plant Life in West Africa*, 1966.
Commonwealth Forestry Handbook (Annual) for nomenclature of timbers.
Timbers of West Africa, Timber Development Association Ltd., London.

and sections on Forestry in chapters on the Ivory Coast, Ghana and Nigeria in this present book.

Chapter 5

SOILS, THEIR PROCESSES AND THEIR PROCESS PROTECTION [1]

In general, the study of soils has lagged behind the other physical sciences, so that it is not surprising that relatively little study has been made of the soils of West Africa.

Heavier rainfall and higher temperatures permit far greater chemical decomposition of rock and soil than in temperate lands, especially on exposed upper slopes. In conditions of good drainage, silicates of acid igneous rocks weather to kaolin and iron oxides; and silicates of basic igneous rocks weather to bauxite and iron oxides. These changes are most evident in rocks having little silica (e.g. dolerite) but are less obvious in schists. Quartzites and sandstones hardly weather at all, as quartz is extremely stable.

Erosion of the top soil may expose these end products, or laterite. This substance hardens irreversibly on exposure to air and is insoluble. It occurs primarily as a cap on Miocene and Pliocene surfaces, into which the rivers are cuttng, so letting the laterite fall down the slopes.

Laterite may be defined as a ferruginous or aluminous crust, or a material heavily indurated with iron oxides. It may be present either as nodules, as massive ironstone or bauxite, or as a soft subsoil material that hardens on exposure to air. It is a rock rather than a soil. A ferruginous conglomerate may also be formed anywhere after transport (e.g. by past or present rivers or by downwash) of ferruginous gravels, which become concreted together. Long alternation of wet and dry seasons can cause the beginnings of laterite at the present day.[2]

[1] Dr. E. W. Russell, formerly Director of the East African Agriculture and Forestry Research Organisation and of the Soil Science Laboratory of the Department of Agriculture, University of Oxford, has given me much help with this chapter.
[2] On laterite see J. A. Prescott and R. L. Pendleton, *Laterite and Lateritic Soils*, Commonwealth Bureau of Soil Science, Technical Communication No. 47, 1952.

Long erosion from upper slopes to lower ones, in gently undulating country, gives a sequence known as a ' catena '. Near the crests are red soils, but farther down the soils are less red. Lower still are grey or black soils, of fine texture and with more silica. These are more fertile, but are heavier to work and are often little used because of the danger of fly. The others are poorer, readily eroded but easier and healthier to work.

Soils may be classified in many ways.   An important classi-fication is by physical structure or ' feel ' of the soil; hence such terms as sand, sandy loam and clay.   Another is by colour, and is frequently used in association with the first method.   Most well-drained tropical soils are red if they contain any iron, because of the inevitable formation of iron oxides.

We now distinguish Red Loams from Red Earths by feel. The Red Earth is a freely drained, free working, erosion resis-tant soil, typically very deep.   The Red Loam is more plastic when wet, often shallower and not so well drained, and hence is more liable to erosion.

Richard-Molard [1] distinguished other West African soils by physical character thus:

Loose sands of aeolian, riverine, lacustrine or marine origin.
Alluvial soils in which silica and alkalis are constantly renewed by erosion from upper slopes, but which are restricted in area and often fly infested.
Poto-Poto muds of the tidal mangroves.
Tanns of Senegal, where the short wet season is insufficient to remove salt accumulation.
Bowal and Lateritic soils.

Sampson and Crowther,[2] after giving types corresponding to certain of those above, add two others which are not well drained and so differ radically from the red soils, though they can occur in close juxtaposition to them on the same parent material. *Grey Earth* occurs in badly drained depressions. It is a fine particled indurated clay which is absolutely im-pervious. *Black Earth*, known as *Firki* in northern Nigeria,

[1] J. Richard-Molard, *Afrique Occidentale Française*, 1949, pp. 29–30.
[2] H. C. Sampson and E. M. Crowther, *The West Africa Commission*, 1938–39, Technical Report 1, The Leverhulme Trust, p. 11.

occurs in very dry areas, is heavy and impossible to work when wet and cracks deeply as it dries. This type generally contains concretions of calcium carbonate and may be alkaline as a result of the accumulation of sodium in association with the clay. It occurs in depressions of dry regions around Lake Chad, and even in the Accra Plains of Ghana.

Because of the relative lack of limestones (and of their associated clays and sands), lime is very scarce. Leaching by heavy rain soon washes out the lime and soils tend to be acidic. ' The general shortage of lime in West African soils and crops is reflected in many ways. Almost all household waters are soft. . . . Medical men know that much of their work arises from calcium deficiency among a people who do not drink milk and whose vegetable food is low in calcium. It is possible that many native food practices, e.g. the use of a variety of leafy plants as ' spinach ' and of baobab and other leaves in soups, go some way to meet the body's need for calcium as well as for vitamins.' [1]

Most West African soils are deficient in plant nutrients. Consequently, the crops, plant litter and humus formed from the litter are all low in nutrients. If the crops are fed to animals, the manure they make is also of little value. Substantial renewal of plant nutrients from animal manure is not possible in the forest zone, as the tsetse fly so far prohibits the keeping of large animals. Moreover, animals would compete with existing crops for space and with man for food. Artificial fertilisers are not made cheaply within West Africa, and imported ones are costly. Unless subsidised, most farmers are unable to afford them and are not very familiar with their use.

High temperatures so hasten decomposition by insect and bacterial growth, that wood-bark and dead leaves are rapidly converted into humus, and then into carbon dioxide, water and soluble chemicals. Those vital to plant growth (other than calcium or lime discussed above) are potassium, phosphorus and nitrogen. The latter is easily washed out, and nitrogen starvation is one of the most important factors limiting plant growth. Much phosphorus and nitrogen are absorbed by cereals, cotton and groundnut crops, the produce of which

[1] H. C. Sampson and E. M. Crowther, *The West African Commission*, 1938–39, Technical Report I, The Leverhulme Trust, pp. 12–13.

is either eaten or exported. Much of the phosphorus and nitrogen from West African farms find their way to European farms, through cattle-cake made from groundnut or cotton-seed residue being eaten by cattle and turned out in manure. Nigeria's normal annual export of 300,000 tons of groundnuts involves an annual loss of phosphates from Nigerian soils equal to that contained in 17,000 tons of superphosphate.[1]

The semblance of fertility given to some West African soils by luxuriant vegetation is generally highly misleading. The dense vegetation (much less dense than many non-Africans believe) is greatly encouraged by high temperatures and rain-fall, rather than by propitious soils. The forest provides its own nourishment from decaying organic matter in thin top soil. Wherever the forest is absent and rainfall exceeds about 100 inches per year, most soils are infertile, because they are heavily leached of plant nutrients and are acidic.

As mineral and animal fertilisers are scarce, it is vital to get as much chemical enrichment as possible from vegetation. Trees should be retained as far as possible, since temperatures are lower under them and decomposition, bacterial activity and evaporation are less. Trees also lessen the rate of per-colation and leaching because they use water and plant nutrients. Surface mulches also seem to be very useful.

Yet it is obvious that with increasing populations and the need to produce more crops, vast areas of forest cannot be re-served. Land fertility must be retained and improved by better farming and by overcoming the high cost of imported fertilisers.

SOIL CONSERVATION

Soil conservation aims at achieving two things—the reten-tion of soil fertility (chemical conservation), and the retention of proper soil structure and siting (physical conservation). These aims are difficult to achieve in areas of high temperature and rainfall, where accelerated erosion by man ('soil erosion' as distinct from natural 'erosion') must be restrained. Often

[1] Sir E. John Russell, *World Population and World Food Supplies*, 1954, p. 289, referring to M. Greenwood in *Empire Journal of Experimental Agriculture*, Vol. 19, pp. 225–42.

the most important thing to conserve is water, which automatically conserves the soil. On the other hand, in high rainfall areas the problem is to get rid of unwanted water quickly with the minimum loss of soil.

Savannah country, with its sudden and torrential rainfall after a dry season, is very subject to erosion. Although trees on hill slopes give no absolute protection against gullying, they can be very useful where there is no level land above the slope, since they prevent sheet erosion. They also help to hold the soil on watersheds and around river sources.

African practices of placing straw or stones on yam mounds, intercropping and the retention of stumps of felled trees also hold the soil.

European intervention in West Africa, by stopping tribal warfare and by introducing health measures and a higher standard of living, has caused a great increase in the human and animal population. This population has to be fed with more food crops, land has also to be devoted to cash crops, and there is population pressure in some areas (see Chapter 10).

Increased pressure on the land causes greater deforestation, shortened bush fallows and more soil exposure. Steep slopes tend to be farmed where they should not be, and soils are washed down by heavy rain. Roads and footpaths, especially on water-sheds, can also cause gully erosion by rapid run-off of water.

In savannah areas, soil erosion is caused in similar ways, but overstocking of animals is an additional problem. ' Pastures ' are often grazed bare and the soils both cut and compacted by cattle-hooves. Severe soil-wash may then result during the infrequent but heavy storms, so revealing bare rock. This is a major problem in the over-populated parts of the extreme north of the Ghana Upper Region, in the Upper Volta, Mali and in northern Nigeria.

As a first effort to improve soil productivity, deep ploughing was tried, but with most unfortunate results. Later efforts aimed at producing a green manure (clover, pea or bean) which would keep the soil covered and which, when turned in, would provide nitrogen and humus. Mucuna or Bengal Bean (*Styzolobium aterrium*) was tried at Ibadan, Nigeria, and elsewhere, but it did not increase the organic-matter content of the soil.[1]   Green manuring is a method that all theoretical people think must be good and nearly all practical people find of little or no economic value.   Green manure crops usually have larger phosphate and calcium demands than the local food crops.   Thus, if they are to improve the next crop, they must usually be manured with phosphates, lime and sometimes potash.   Their benefit to that crop then corresponds to about 1–2 cwt. per acre of sulphate of ammonia, which could more easily be applied to the crop direct.   Green manure crops thus require additional expense in use of land, labour and money, they may produce no more food crops or cash return, and they compete for space with well-tried crops.

Mechanised farming, with proper safeguards such as contouring and rotation with grass leys, may enable more land to be cultivated.   Thus it may be economically more advantageous than the present wastefully small and scattered patches of African farms, but would be politically and socially possible only in areas of low population, where there would be little or no disturbance to existing farmers.

Meanwhile, individual farmers are encouraged to farm around contours leaving occasional ridges, to keep soil covered and to have a sound rotation.   Various improvement schemes incorporating these, and with control of forest cutting and of head-waters, have been initiated in the Ghana Upper Region near Navrongo and Bawku, in northern Nigeria (e.g. near Kano), in Guinea around the Bafing source, and elsewhere.

BIBLIOGRAPHY

See references cited above and Chapter 6, pp. 93–7.   Also:

Proceedings of the First Commonwealth Conference on Tropical and Sub-Tropical Soils, 1948.   Commonwealth Bureau of Soil Science, Harpenden.
P. VAGELER, *An Introduction to Tropical Soils*, trans. by E. Greene, 1933.
G. W. ROBINSON, *Soils, Their Origin, Constitution and Classification*, 1949.
H. VINE, ' Is the lack of fertility of tropical African soils exaggerated? ', *Proceedings 2nd Inter-African Soils Conference*, 1954, pp. 389–412.
A. PITOT, ' L'Homme et les Sols dans les Steppes et Savanes de l'Afrique Occidentale Française ', *Les Cahiers d'Outre Mer*, 1952, pp. 215–40.

---

[1] P. H. Nye, ' Recent Progress in Work on the Fertility of West African Soils ', *Journal of the West African Science Association*, 1954, pp. 18–25 at p. 23 (includes a bibliography).

2

THE RESOURCES AND
THEIR DEVELOPMENT

*The following chapters relate to the whole of
West Africa. Further details concerning
matters discussed here may be found in the
territorial chapters.*

Chapter 6

AGRICULTURE [1]

A. *GENERAL CONSIDERATIONS* [2]

AGRICULTURAL pursuits are the basis of almost all West African life. As in any part of the world, important determinants of crop distributions are climate and soils. In the tropics, rainfall (especially its seasonal distribution) is especially significant. Thus the kola nut tree requires a fairly heavy annual rainfall of at least 50 inches. The coconut palm and the groundnut legume must be grown in sandy soils; maize needs at least 30 inches annual rainfall and soils of more than average richness.

Biological factors also affect rural economy. Thus, the tsetse fly severely restricts the areas within which large cattle may be kept. Consequently, mixed farming and the renewal of soil fertility are not easy where the tsetse fly occurs and only the small resistant *Ndama* cattle survive. In the Sudan and Sahel Savannahs, the tsetse fly is more or less absent and larger humped cattle may be kept, the land is easily cleared and prepared, and mixed farming is possible. Nevertheless, it is not common, because animals are kept mainly by nomads.

In the Forest, crops have to be raised from small plots won from the forest by periodic cutting and burning. Soils are soon exhausted (see Chapter 5) and, as there is very little

[1] I am much indebted to the late Dr. F. R. Irvine and to Mr. T. A. Russell, formerly Senior Botanist to the Department of Agriculture, Nigeria, and now at the Royal Botanic Gardens, Kew, for their most valuable criticisms of this chapter.

[2] Allusion can only be made to a few general aspects. Others are mentioned in the chapter on Soils and in the regional chapters. See also Bruce F. Johnston, *The Staple Food Economies of Western Tropical Africa*, Stanford University Press, 1958; John de Wilde and others, *Agricultural Development in Tropical Africa*, 2 Vols., Johns Hopkins Press, 1967; J. Papadakis, *Crop Ecologic Survey in West Africa*, 2 Vols., F.A.O., 1965; R. Schnell, *Plantes alimentaires et vie agricole de l'Afrique Noire*, 1958; F. R. Irvine, *A Text-Book of West African Agriculture*, 1953, Part I.

animal manure, and artificials are expensive and difficult to use satisfactorily in the tropics, there is no simple alternative to a long fallow period. Thus the forest farmer generally expends much energy per acre. Yet he is more than compensated by the growth of permanent tree crops such as the oil palm, cocoa, kola and coffee; and by wild or semi-wild forest materials—such as timber and minor forest products. With heavier and more evenly distributed rain, he is also less restricted in his farming calendar.

By contrast, Savannah farms are generally larger, less varied and the shorter growing period restricts the farmer to one main crop in each season for each field. Nevertheless, 'when the amount and distribution of the rainfall render crop production certain, the standard tends to be lower than when the rains are apt to disappoint and where there is only one season for crop production.' [1] Population pressure may also induce better farming, e.g. among the Kabrai of Togo, the Hausa around Kano, and others.

The social organisation of West African peoples, and their conception of the place of women, greatly affect agricultural methods and the crops grown, especially in the Forest. The area of land farmed may be limited by the amount which a man can cut from the forest, and which the women can then cultivate. Yams are generally planted by men, the women then planting and cultivating vegetables on the yam mounds. The income from the vegetables belongs to the women.

Inter- or double-cropping is very common in West Africa. Although this method may seem inefficient and looks a muddle, it saves labour and land, and limits soil erosion by keeping the ground covered. Moreover, some plants may benefit from inter-cropping. On the other hand, mixed cropping may necessitate the use of crop varieties suited to this system. The cotton grown in southern Nigeria is of vigorous robust growth, and will flourish although inter-planted among other crops, where a cotton of less robust growth, such as the more valuable Allen type of the north, would fail through competition.

Again, a new process may unduly complicate the farming community by upsetting the relative proportions of men and

---

[1] Pim, op. cit., p. 133.

women's incomes. The income from the cracking of palm nuts belongs to women. Nut-cracking machines are more efficient, but are somewhat expensive for Africans, and difficult for women to operate. If they are bought and used by men, social conflict may result.

Not only is there division of cropping on a sexual basis among some peoples, but also there is a tradition for or against certain crops. Thus benniseed is especially grown by the Tiv in Nigeria, and the Fulani cattle-keeping people are averse to fixed agriculture. Miège [1] has shown that the relative spheres of rice and yam cultivation corresponded originally to two great cultural groupings of peoples in West Africa—those of the West Atlantic group (rice growing) and those of the East Atlantic group (yam growing). The boundary between them, in the Ivory Coast, is a major ethnic and crop divide.

Communal or group ownership of land, though now undergoing many changes, is also a restrictive factor in the rational development of crops, especially when farm-plots are small and scattered. Co-operative methods may be a solution.

There have been many external factors affecting West African agriculture. Portuguese slave-traders found difficulty in feeding captives on the long voyage to the New World, because most indigenous West African produce from the forest—mainly fruits, insects, rodents, Monitor lizards and fish —would not store for long periods. Among introductions from America for this purpose, and later for other reasons including sheer accident,[2] have been cassava, sweet potatoes, groundnuts, maize, lima beans, chillies, tomatoes, papaw, guavas, pineapple, tobacco and American cotton. Muslim pilgrims returning overland from Asia via the Sudan, or the Portuguese bringing them from Asia, are believed to have introduced Indian cottons, certain yams, the cocoyam, aubergines, citrus fruits, mangoes, bananas (later sent on to the New World), certain peas and beans and sugar cane. Some recent introductions are swamp rices from Asia, sisal and cocoa from America. Cocoa was first introduced to São Tomé and

[1] J. Miège, 'Les Cultures Vivrières en Afrique Occidentale', *Les Cahiers d'Outre-Mer*, 1954, pp. 25–50.
[2] For introduced crops and plants see H. Labouret, *Les Paysans d'Afrique Occidentale*, 1946, pp. 182–8 and G. Howard Jones, op. cit., Chapter 2.

Fernando Po, and from the latter to the mainland. Many of these crops are now vital foodstuffs. Unfortunately, less skilled cultivation than that found in South-east Asia and, in the past, lack of selection, have sometimes resulted in crops of poor quality.

Governments have sought, in diverse ways, to encourage certain crops. The extreme form of this was in the Ivory Coast after 1912 when, under Governor Angoulvent, there was compulsory cultivation of cocoa and of certain foodstuffs. Export crops were often unduly encouraged, e.g. by allocating agricultural research funds almost exclusively to them, rather than to food crops. Former French territories, with small populations, were the first to modify this position.

Overseas export crops are rather more restricted than food crops, both in variety and in distribution. The success of an export crop depends not only upon physical factors such as soil and climate and upon economic criteria, but also (and often much more) upon such things as whether a given people is willing to try a crop, and whether it can be fitted into its farming methods. The distribution of export crops is sometimes irrational and incomplete, and West Africa is littered with unsuccessful attempts to introduce all kinds of crops.

More purely economic factors also affect crop distributions. Many African crops can be grown for export only if there is bulk transport. Groundnuts, shelled or unshelled, depend upon railways for their cheap carriage over great distances. Cocoa, being of greater value by weight, can be sent by road. Proximity to transport is a powerful determinant of the extent of cash crop cultivation.

Some produce is still largely obtained by simple collection, such as piassava and raphia fibre, but most produce comes from subsistence farmers growing small amounts of diverse crops. Some peasant farmers have specialised (e.g. on cocoa or groundnuts), and then crop limits may be more accurately defined by geographical and economic criteria.

Crops grown for a standardised article, or which need processing, such as fruits for canning, are best grown on plantations. But in British West Africa before independence non-Africans were not normally allowed to establish plantations, and plantation crops were practically absent from British

Riverside swamp rice cultivation at Oussouye, Casamance (Southern Senegal). The rice is grown on land formerly occupied by Mangrove, some remaining stumps of which may be seen. Behind are oil palms in their ideal habitat of swamp. Typical of swamp areas in Casamance, Portuguese Guinea, Guinea and Sierra Leone.

CROPS

8. Cassava at a research station in Mali.

Cassava tubers. The photograph was taken in Senegal, an indication of dispersion of this basic food crop.

10. Oil palm forest in swampy Rain Forest near Sassandra, Ivory Coast

11. With a climbing loop, the harvester clim oil palm tree which, outside plantations, may sixty feet in height. The leaves are cleared a the fruit bunches, which are then cut and low by rope.

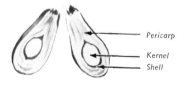

12. Bunches of oil palm fruit. African grown palm fruit (*left*) usually has a thin pericarp and thick kernel shell. Plantation fruit (*right*) has a thicker pericarp and the kernel is thin shelled.

THE OIL PALM

territories, though in Guinea, the Ivory Coast, and the Bight of Biafra islands plantations have for long been very important. Africans could establish them, and have done so in some places, but few possess the capital or technical knowledge. Similarly, rubber is grown for export in Liberia, not only because of suitable climatic and soil conditions, but especially because the Firestone Rubber Company could obtain large concessions. Since just before independence, Nigeria, Ghana and Sierra Leone have shown interest in establishing plantations, usually under the auspices of state or partly state organisations.

World shortage of certain foods led to trials of mechanised farming, with traditional land-ownership in ex-British territories,[1] and with or without it in ex-French ones. Groundnuts were cultivated mechanically with both systems near Kaffrine and Sédhiou in Senegal. In the Inland Niger Delta of the Mali Republic rice and other crops are being produced by mechanical methods, and at Sokoto in Nigeria with traditional landholding. Mechanical cultivation may so reduce labour that cultivable areas can be extended, but yields usually fall.

There are, moreover, social agricultural and economic limitations to mechanisation. Areas most suitable for it are moderately or thinly populated Savannah areas, where present productivity of the land is limited by the amount of hoe cultivation possible during the short rainy season. Yet it must be remembered that the African hoe, with its blade set acutely to the handle for light soils and nearer to a right angle for heavy soils, though laborious to use and capable of cultivating only a small area, is well adapted to African soils, as it works only the richer top layer. Deep ploughing is dangerous because it brings up poorer soils and greatly loosens the ground. Then on dry level lands wind erosion may follow and, after heavy rainfall on steep slopes, there may be gully erosion.

Before considering the geographical distribution of collected produce and crops, it is convenient to make a rough classification. First in fame and in daily significance are the oily fruits, especially the oil palm, but also the coconut, sheanut and benniseed. Then there are the cereals—rice, maize, guinea corn, millet and minor cereals. Roots are important in forest

[1] See *Report of a Survey of Problems in the Mechanisation of Native Agriculture in Tropical African Colonies*, H.M.S.O., 1950.

E

areas, especially cassava and yams. Lesser roots are cocoyams, sweet potato, ginger and tiger 'nuts'. Edible fruits are widespread, such as the tree fruits—mango, papaw, orange, lime, grapefruit, banana, plantain and pineapple; in Guinea and the Ivory Coast fruits are grown commercially on a large scale, and on a much smaller but increasing scale in Ghana and Nigeria. The tree fruits of cocoa and coffee have an indirect use and are very important cash crops. Another large group are the legumes, especially the so-called ground-'nut' (used as an oil seed), peas and beans. There are many vegetables, such as onions, shallots, okro, African spinach, peppers, chillies, tomatoes, cucumbers, gourds, pumpkins, melons, aubergines, etc. Other significant products are rubber, sugar cane and tobacco.

B. *MAIN CROPS*

The South-Western Rice and Tree Crops Zone

In Casamance (or southern Senegal), Portuguese Guinea, Guinea, Sierra Leone, Liberia and the Ivory Coast west

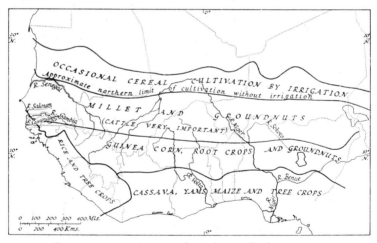

FIG. 25.—Approximate and very generalised crop belts.

Root crops are mainly grown where there is no long dry season. Cereals (except maize) are mainly grown where there is a considerable dry season. Most crops grow in several zones.

of the Bandama River (except for Tabou District), the dominant food crop is generally rice, as it also is of the floodplains of the Senegal, Saloum, Gambia, Niger, Kaduna, Sokoto and, locally, elsewhere.

Rice is much appreciated in West Africa and its cultivation is extending rapidly, in this zone and elsewhere. It is a high yielder, its taste is much liked, it keeps well, and may be transported for sale far away. It is extremely easy to prepare and cook, compared with most African foods. But its cultivation requires care and skill, so that often it is the more alert peoples who cultivate it. Thus in Senegal the Serer grow it successfully, but the Wolof generally do not.[1]

Before 1939 large quantities of rice were imported into British West Africa from Burma and Malaya, and into French West Africa from Indo-China. These imports totalled about 250,000 tons per annum. After the war such quantities could not be imported, particularly from those countries, yet demand for rice increased because of higher standards of living, increased urbanisation, and because many British Africans developed the taste for rice while serving with the army in Burma. Rice cultivation had to be increased in West Africa and, so long as it is not grown ' dry ' on hillsides, is a good crop to grow. It will tolerate compact and acidic soils, will grow in otherwise useless swamps and, as it needs little or no fallow, it does not upset farming routine, as would the introduction of another tuber crop.

Another species, *Oryza glaberrima*, a ' red rice ', may have been grown for some 3,500 years in Africa.[2] It probably originated in the Inland Niger Delta or Upper Senegal, whence it was taken to the south-west coasts, via the Gambia and Casamance Rivers.

These rices, and particularly *O. sativa*, are often grown ' dry ' on hillsides, and in light soils wherever the rainfall is at least 35 inches in the growing season. Dry rice is inter-cropped or grown in rotation with cassava, cotton, guinea corn, millet and maize. All the crops of the Cassava Zone are also grown.

Swamp-rices are being increasingly cultivated in former

[1] J. Dresch, ' La Riziculture en Afrique Occidentale ', *Annales de Géographie*, 1949, pp. 295–312.
[2] R. Porterès, ' Vieilles agricultures de l'Afrique inter-tropical ', *L'Agronomie tropicale*, 1950.

mangrove swamps of the Gambia, Portuguese Guinea, Guinea, and Sierra Leone. Swamp-rices are also grown in inland swamps, in river flood plains and in the south-west corner of Ghana. As inland and coastal swamps are being planted for rice, so dry upland rice cultivation can be reduced, thereby lessening soil erosion. Some think it would also help to distribute improved upland rice seed, so increasing yields and enabling a reduction of areas planted.

West African Rice Production [1]

	Area in thousand hectares	Thousands of metric tons
		Paddy
	1965	1965
Gambia . .	27	37
Guinea . . .	250	300
Ivory Coast . .	261	240
Mali . . .	140	150
Niger . . .	9	11
Nigeria . . .	235	350
Senegal . . .	85	110
Sierra Leone . .	255	310

[1] *Production Yearbook*, 1966, Vol. 20, F.A.O., Rome, 1967.

' Hungry Rice ', ' Acha Grass ' (Hausa) or ' Fundi ' (Temne, Sierra Leone) is *Digitaria exilis*. It is grown in uplands above about 2,500 feet as a substitute for rice. It is extremely tolerant of rainfall, as well as of variety and depth of soil. It is much grown on the Jos Plateau, in Bornu and in the Fouta Djallon, as is another variety, *Digitaria iburu*.

Citrus Fruits are best grown in upland areas of this zone, where the relative humidity is high, and in areas of high rainfall near the coast in the Cassava, Yams, Maize and Tree Crops Zone. Planters have developed an export from Guinea.

Sweet Orange (Citrus sinensis) grows well on the edge of the forest away from the sea, where soils are not sandy. These oranges often remain green when ripe, an impediment to their export, except as juice.

The skins have a high oil content. In Guinea around

Kindia, Mamou and Labé, oil is produced by Africans. A better oil is extracted from the Bitter Orange (*Citrus aurantium*), which is grown on European plantations near Labé.

Limes (*Citrus aurantifolia*) grow in the same conditions as oranges, but at lower altitudes. They are much grown near Cape Coast (Ghana) and near most African villages.

Lemons (*Citrus limon*) and *Grape Fruit* are grown on plantations in Guinea and the Ivory Coast for export and are found scattered elsewhere.

Avocado Pear (*Persea americana*), an introduction from Central America, likewise thrives in moist forested country. It has an extremely high food value.

Turkish Tobacco (*Nicotiana rustica*) is grown in the higher open parts of this zone, often after rice or hungry rice.

Melegueta Pepper or *Grains of Paradises* (*Aframomum melegueta*) belongs to the ginger family (see under Sierra Leone and Nigeria). The tiny seeds account for the old name ' Grain Coast ' (Liberia), from where they were exported in the past for medicine and spice. They are now used a little in veterinary medicines.

THE CASSAVA, YAMS, MAIZE AND TREE CROPS ZONE

This zone includes areas of former or actual Rain Forest with over 45 inches of rainfall annually, and occupies the Guinea Coastlands.

Forest is periodically cut and burnt to provide tiny patches for growing cassava, some yams (see below) and cocoyams; beans and peas, okro, tomatoes, chillies, fluted pumpkins and other vegetables; fruits such as plantains, bananas and pineapples; sugar-cane and tobacco; and cereals such as maize and rice. Useful trees, which are generally planted and safeguarded, are the oil palm, coconut palm, the kola, papaw, breadfruit, avocado pear, citrus fruits, etc. Some of these are also export crops, cocoa, rubber, coffee and ginger almost exclusively so. Other valuable products are piassava and raphia (see pp. 67, 314 and 508).

Cassava or **Manioc**, *Manihot utilissima* or *esculenta*, is a native of South America. It has many varieties, varying in their content of prussic acid. Those which tend to have little are sometimes classed as ' sweet ', those with more as ' bitter '.

This tuber withstands considerable drought, is unaffected by migratory locusts and, if left in the ground after ripening, is not attacked by insects. Though it does best in well-drained loams, it will grow on almost any soil. For this reason and because it exhausts the soil, it is normally the last crop in a rotation. Extensive cultivation of cassava near towns (e.g. Accra) has exhaused great areas, and it suffers widely from a virus disease known as leaf mosaic.

Cassava prefers a moderate annual rainfall of 30–40 inches (760–1,015 mm.) so that tubers are produced rather than too many leaves. Thus it is often grown under the shade of trees in areas of heavier rainfall. It thrives especially in south-east Ghana, southern Togo (where there is an exportable surplus of flour and tapioca), southern Dahomey and Nigeria, where it is spreading in the north.

Cassava is a perennial which grows to about 6 feet and produces clusters of long, rather narrow tubers. These are peeled, soaked or boiled to remove the prussic acid, and then pounded and made into a kind of dumpling ('fufu'), which takes the place of bread or potatoes. The tuber can also be boiled or fried (after initial peeling or soaking), or dried and later grated into flour. The moist pulp may be warmed slowly to produce 'gari' meal. Starch is also made and if this is dropped on to heated plates, tapioca is produced.[1]

The *Yam* is a fundamental food in the Guinea Coast territories, especially in the 'Middle Belt' or Southern Guinea Savannah Zone. Of the many edible types, some are indigenous (the white and yellow), but many others have been introduced, probably by the Portuguese from Asia. Like cassava, it is a tuber, though larger and with a better flavour. Because of this and its greater weight, the need for rich loamy soils (not clay or sand), intolerance of shade and consequently more restricted cultivation, it commands a higher price. Thus it is more of a luxury than cassava and is the subject of much commerce. Yams are generally the first crop in a rotation, as they require much nitrogen and potash.

Holes up to 2 feet deep and wide are dug and manured, and

---

[1] On cassava see W. O. Jones, *Manioc in Africa*, Stanford, 1959, and 'A Map of Manioc in Africa', *Geographical Review*, 1953, pp. 112–14.

separate mounds or continuous ridges are then generally made at least 3 feet in height. The seed-yams are pushed into the hills at ground level, which are then capped by dried grass and soil or stones. Moisture is thereby retained, temperatures are more even, a mulch is available for the growing vine and erosion is prevented. Maize and upland rice are often sown between the mounds, and women generally sow vegetables on them. Yam vines are trained along a pole, or dried stalks.[1]

The *White Yam* (*Dioscorea rotundata*) and the *Yellow Yam* (*D. cayenensis*) produce long tubers and prefer drier areas. The *Water Yam* (*D. alata*) is spherical, larger, originates from South-east Asia and prefers wetter places. This water yam is softer, exudes water when cut, does not keep well and is inferior in taste. But it will grow on poorer soils.

The *Chinese Yam* (*D. esculenta*) produces many small tubers and, like the water yam, thrives in wetter areas, where rainfall exceeds about 70 inches per annum, humidity is constantly high and dry months few. There are other lesser varieties.

Maize or *Corn* (*Zea mays*), of disputed introduction,[2] is—outside the rice areas—the chief cereal of forest and savannah lands with 30–60 inches annual rainfall, or near rivers. It does best on sandy loam or loamy soils rich in humus; like the yam and sweet potato, it dislikes shade. Two harvests can be secured where there are two rainy seasons, and it is often the first food crop to be harvested.

Oil palm (*Elaeis guineensis*) is indigenous to the swampy parts of West African forests and occurs as far south as those of the Congo. The densest stands are not necessarily where the climatic and soil conditions are most favourable, but where population is or was greatest, and where there has been long contacts with Europeans. Thus, there are many oil palms in south-eastern Sierra Leone but fewer in Liberia; more originally (before cocoa became more profitable) in the Ivory Coast and in Ghana; in Dahomey (planted by prisoners of King Guezo from 1839, when their disposal as slaves had become practically impossible); and west and especially east of the

[1] For a description of yam cultivation, see C. Daryll Forde, ' Land and Labour in a Cross River Village ', *Geographical Journal*, Vol. XC, pp. 24–51.
[2] M. D. W. Jeffreys, ' How ancient is West African maize? ', *Africa*, 1963, pp. 115–31.

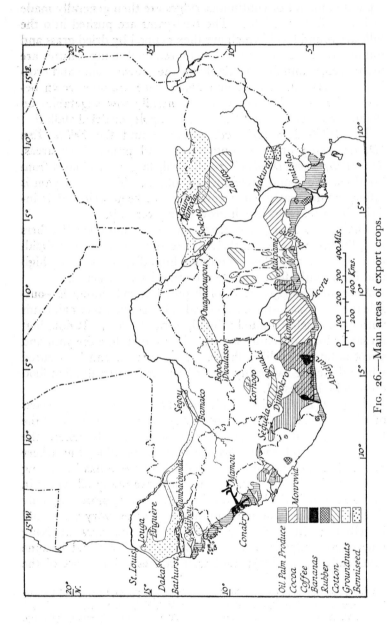

Fig. 26.—Main areas of export crops.

Niger and its delta, which, like the Congo, was long visited by slave ships.

The oil palm is not common in high forest but, when the forest is disturbed and habitations are built, the oil palm follows. The connexion with man is reinforced, as it is the source of West Africa's best vegetable oil, used in cooking, for illumination, in the making of soap, and in many other ways in everyday African life. Palm kernels and oil are also important exports. About one-eighth of Nigeria's exports by value are palm kernels and oil, which comprise about one half of the exports of Dahomey. In 1965 West Africa supplied over 25% of the palm oil exports and over 85% of the palm kernel exports of the world.

Palm plantations around Abomey in Dahomey were planted at the suggestion of the slave traders looking for new articles of commerce. European-owned plantations were few, having been refused (except for experimentation) in British colonies. Being less remunerative than cocoa, coffee or banana cultivation, oil palm plantations were also few in non-British territories. However, a number of plantations have now been established as a means of agricultural diversification.

The oil palm ideally requires a minimum rainfall of about 80 inches, distributed over at least eight months of the year, but it can survive with as little as 50 inches, if that amount is evenly distributed. Thus it reacts badly to a pronounced dry season. It also needs much sunlight; one of the advantages of Sumatra for the oil palm being rainy nights but sunny days.

In its soil requirements, however, the oil palm is more tolerant; the dense stands in Ibo country of eastern Nigeria and in Benin Province demonstrate that it will grow on sandy soils where cocoa will not flourish. Nevertheless, it does much better on moist, deep rich loamy or alluvial soils.

Generally, palms are planted near roads or compounds and are given little or no attention. Tapping for palm wine (the sap) reduces bunch yields. For this and other reasons detailed below, the quality of the semi-wild palm is rather poor.

By contrast, that from plantations in West Africa, Congo, Malaya and Sumatra is superior. Yields of fruit per acre are some ten times higher, the amount of oil in the fruit is also much greater, more of this increased amount of available oil is extracted, and its quality is superior, as it contains less free fatty acid (a noxious ingredient resulting from fermentation of over-ripe fruit). The superior oil can be used in margarine and tinplate manufacture, and yields more glycerine when used for soap. The poorer oil is used in making soap, paint, candles, and as a lubricant.

In 1900 Nigeria produced almost all the world supply of palm oil, which then represented 88% of her exports. In 1938 she exported 110,000 tons, which represented 10% of her exports, but her plantation rivals exported 344,000 tons. During and after the Second World War production in Malaya and Indonesia fell away, but Nigerian output increased to around 200,000 tons and improved in quality.

Exports from the Congo began in 1915, from Sumatra in 1919 and from Malaya in 1926. From South-East Asia both oil and kernels[1] are available, since less oil is used locally. In West Africa only the thinly populated areas are able to export both oil and kernels, the heavily populated areas having only a surplus of kernels.

Because of the spontaneous growth of palms and their struggle for light in West Africa, they grow taller than in Asiatic plantations, often reaching 60 feet. The palm bears fruit only after a longer period. The tree has to be climbed, a skilled, distasteful and dangerous task. The fruits are orange-red, tinged with black, and are produced in clusters weighing some 50 lb. Two to twelve clusters are produced each year, according to the age of the palm. The weight of each bunch increases up to the eighth year of the tree. Beneath the skin of the fruit is the fibrous pericarp, which yields palm (pericarp) oil. Unfortunately, this pericarp is often thin in West African palms.

Africans extract the oil by boiling, pounding, re-heating and skimming in the 'soft-oil' process. It is tedious and yields 55% of the total oil, which is of average free fatty acid content. Alternatively, men generally ferment the fruit, trample it, pour boiling water over it and skim off the oil. This 'hard-oil' process (it produces oil which only melts at a higher temperature) is quicker, yields 65% of the oil, but gives a high free fatty acid content. It is the more common process

---

[1] Asiatic kernels are so small, however, that they were but little used until after 1945.

where water is available. When the oil is extracted, the nuts
are the women's perquisite. They crack them and sell the
kernels.

A hand-press can extract 65% of the oil, which may have
less than 2% f.f.a. if the fruit is fresh. The machine is expensive for Africans, but saves much time. It is, however,
difficult for women to work.

Another improved method of oil extraction is in small
' Pioneer ' mills, which extract up to 85% of good oil from fresh
fruit, and which may crack or return the nuts to the women.
The much larger factory mills established on plantations, not
only extract 90% or more of the oil, but extract the kernel oil
as well.

Pioneer mills are numerous in Nigeria and Sierra Leone.
There are a few large factory mills in the Ivory Coast, Togo
and Dahomey, and one near Sapele in Nigeria, but difficulties
are experienced in getting fresh fruit. It is sometimes said
that the bulk of the world's palm oil must come from plantations and large factory mills, but Pioneer mills in Nigeria,
where suitably placed, are doing well (see pp. 493–4), while a
hydraulic hand press can give good oil. With improvements
in the oil palms and in oil extraction, the West African peasant
should be able to supply a product acceptable to the world
market, and at lower prices than the plantation and factory
mill product, with its higher cost.

Palm kernels are milled commercially in Europe or America
and, until 1939, practically exclusively so.[1] They contain
half their weight in oil, which is used in making margarine,
cooking oils, soap, toilet creams, glycerine and paints. The
pulp residue is combined with sweeter materials to make an
excellent cattle-food. In Africa, kernel oil for domestic
needs is obtained either by roasting or soaking the kernels, and
then pounding and soaking them in warm water. The oil is
used as skin or hair oil, or as cooking fat.

At the several national and regional oil palm research stations, valuable work is being done in improving cultivation of
the oil palm and in selecting and distributing better palms.
In this work, use is being made of improved material (e.g.

[1] Palm kernel crushing mills have been established since then in the Congo
on plantations, but hardly at all in West Africa until the French started in 1950.

the *Deli* variety), as well as of high yielding local palms. But with few plantations in West Africa, it is difficult to introduce improved varieties rapidly. Cutting out of poor palms and replanting have not been very successful, because of the prejudice of chiefs who dislike the spread of private ownership of the land, which such planting involves.

Palm Oil—Exports from Principal Countries

Country	Hundred metric tons				Percentages			
	1909–13	1924–28	1934–38	1965	1909–13	1924–28	1934–38	1965
Nigeria . .	819	1,281	1,370	1,524	67·7	59·5	29·7	27·6
Ex-Fr. W. Africa .	192	241	212	145	15·9	11·2	4·6	2·6
Congo (L) . .	21	192	603	658	1·7	8·9	13·1	11·9
Others . .	178	173	250	354	14·7	8·1	5·4	6·4
Total Africa .	1,210	1,887	2,435	2,681	100·0	87·7	52·8	48·6
Indonesia . .	—	253	1,709	1,258	—	11·8	37·1	22·8
Malaysia . .	—	13	341	1,404	—	0·6	7·4	25·5
Total Asia . .	—	266	2,050	2,663	—	12·4	44·4	48·3
Grand Total .	1,210	2,152	4,612	5,514	100	100	100	100

Palm Kernels—Exports from Principal Countries

Country	Hundred metric tons				Percentages			
	1909–13	1924–28	1934–38	1965	1909–13	1924–28	1934–38	1965
Nigeria . .	1,763	2,491	3,329	4,222	53·8	46·3	45·5	64·9
Ex-Fr. W. Africa .	523	700	815	474	16·0	13·0	11·1	7·3
Sierra Leone .	465	654	755	501	14·2	12·2	10·3	7·7
Congo (L) . .	65	677	782	n.a.	2·0	12·6	10·7	—
Others . .	458	824	1,019	847	14·0	15·3	14·0	13·0
Total Africa .	3,274	5,346	6,700	6,044	100·0	99·5	91·5	93·9
Indonesia . .	—	29	363	274	—	0·5	5·0	4·2
Malaysia . .	—	—	58	126	—	—	0·8	1·9
Total Asia . .	—	29	421	402	—	0·5	5·7	6·2
Grand Total .	3,274	5,375	7,320	6,504	100	100	100	100

Figures from C. Leubuscher, *The Processing of Copra, Oil Palm Products and Groundnuts*, 1949, H.M.S.O., and for 1934–38 and 1965 from *Trade Yearbook*, 1966, Vol. 20, F.A.O., Rome, 1967.

Cocoa[1] (*Theobroma cacao*) is perhaps the most famous and valuable crop of West Africa, it being grown entirely for export. Indeed, West Africa produces three-quarters of the world's cocoa. Cocoa accounts for about two-thirds by value of the exports of Ghana, São Tomé and Príncipe, and Fernando Po; for about one-quarter of those of Togo; for one-tenth of those of Nigeria; and for one-fifth of those of the Ivory Coast.

The tree is indigenous to the Amazon basin, the name being an Aztec one. Cocoa was introduced by the Portuguese to the island of São Tomé in 1822, and unsuccessful attempts were made to grow it in what was then the Gold Coast early in the nineteenth century. But in 1879 it was re-introduced by Tetteh Quashie of Mampong (Akwapim), who, on returning from the Fernando Po plantations, took back six beans to his village. The plant was also taken to Nigeria, and from there the first export from the mainland (of 121 lb.) took place in 1885. The first export (of 80 lb.) from the Gold Coast was in 1891, and record exports of over 400,000 tons were achieved there in recent years.

In Ghana and Nigeria all cocoa is grown on African farms averaging about 1¼ acres. This is also the case in the small cocoa area of Sierra Leone (developed since 1938), east-south-east of Kenema, and of Togo. But in the Ivory Coast there are a few European and Lebanese plantations in newer areas in the centre and west. Non-African plantations are also found in north-central Liberia, on Fernando Po, São Tomé and Príncipe. The last five are on rich volcanic soils. São Tomé was the major West African producer until 1910, when British cocoa firms withdrew their custom, following revelations of slave-like labour conditions on the plantations.

Cocoa requires deep soils of heavy loam or light clay, rich in potash, and especially those derived from granites, diorites, schists and gneiss. It will not grow on light sandy soils, so that it fails on such soils in eastern Nigeria, although the rainfall is adequate. Undulating country, like that of southern Ashanti, gives the best drainage. Irrigation, to compensate

---

[1] For world-wide studies of cocoa, see D. H. Urquhart, *Cocoa* (2nd edit.), 1961, and G. Viers, ' Le Cacao dans le Monde ', *Les Cahiers d'Outre-Mer*, 1953, pp. 297–351.

for a dry season, may lower fertility and yields, as in São Tomé.

Cocoa also dislikes drying winds, so that it must be protected from the desiccating Harmattan. It also requires a gradually developing, long and steady wet season of at least nine months, and an annual rainfall preferably of around 60 inches (1,525 mm.) per annum. It is grown in shaded clearings of the denser forest, as in Ghana; or in close plantings to make its own shade, as in parts of Nigeria. This keeps the soil moist, provides leaf enrichment, reduces erosion and, above all, protects the shallow roots. The rainfall of Western Nigeria is only just sufficient for cocoa, and the short but pronounced dry season is bad for it (Ibadan 1·4 inches or 35 mm. from December to February; Tafo, Ghana, 7·5 inches or 190 mm.). In Sierra Leone and Liberia the dry season is too severe, and the rainy season develops too fast and brings rain even into the harvesting months of August and September.

The tree begins bearing economically in the fifth to seventh years and reaches maximum yields when about twenty-five years old. A main crop is secured between October and March and a minor one from May to August. Large yellow, red or brown pods, each up to about 10 inches long, are formed on short stalks hanging mainly from the trunk. These pods are opened and the 30–40 white beans with adhering sticky pulp are then fermented and dried to their chocolate colour, the pulp then being removed.

The United States is the largest market. To eliminate excessive numbers of middlemen, there are marketing boards in most countries, which buy at a fixed price and, with accumulated profits, keep funds to stabilise the income of farmers when prices fall, and to aid cocoa research and education.

Despite the great place of West Africa, and especially of Ghana, in the world cocoa trade, the cultivation of the tree is beset with many problems. Soils are somewhat exhausted in south-eastern Ghana and in the former cocoa area south of Abeokuta (Nigeria). African farmers have taken to cocoa cultivation so whole-heartedly that they have often neglected to grow valuable food crops. Food is imported at needlessly high prices and rural indebtedness may

Exports of Cocoa Beans[1]

Country	Metric tons						Percentages of total cocoa exports					
	1898	1908	1918	1928	1938	1965	1898	1908	1918	1928	1938	1965
Ghana	188	12,946	67,404	223,339	261,557	501,920	0·2	6·7	24·6	43·5	37·0	38·3
Nigeria	35	1,388	10,383	49,950	97,542	305,560	0·0	0·7	3·8	9·7	13·8	23·3
Ivory Coast	—	3	420	14,515	52,719	126,410	—	0·0	0·2	2·8	7·5	9·6
Togo	—	84	1,576	6,317	7,628	17,150	—	0·0	0·6	1·2	1·0	1·3
São Tomé and Principe	9,945	28,560	17,332	14,638	12,729	8,850	11·5	14·8	6·3	2·9	1·8	0·7
Fernando Po and Rio Muni	800	2,267	4,220	8,664	12,212	29,060	0·9	1·2	1·6	1·7	1·7	2·2
Cameroon and Rest of Africa	311	3,181	3,699	8,478	24,965	90,400	0·4	1·7	1·2	1·4	3·6	6·9
Africa	11,279	48,429	105,034	325,901	469,352	1,079,350	13·0	25·1	38·3	63·2	66·4	82·3
Central and S. America and W. Indies	72,070	138,600	162,792	181,264	229,450	200,740	83·2	72·1	59·4	35·4	32·5	15·3
Asia and Pacific	3,451	5,468	6,374	7,234	8,094	27,710	3·8	2·8	2·3	1·4	1·1	2·1
Grand Total	86,800	192,497	274,200	514,399	706,896	1,311,550	100	100	100	100	100	100·0

[1] Figures from *Gordian*, April 25, 1939, pp. 186-87, and for 1965 from *Trade Yearbook* 1956, Vol. 20, F.A.O., Rome 1967. The diminishing proportion occupied by Central and South American and West Indies supplies is striking, though Brazilian production has maintained its proportion. Within West Africa, the decline of São Tomé is striking, as is the meteoric rise of Ghana.

be a problem.[1]   The attraction of the cocoa areas in Ghana and the Ivory Coast is seen in the yearly movement of thousands of labourers from the Upper and Northern Regions and the Upper Volta.

Cocoa is a delicate plant and easily degenerates.   Severe threats are the virus disease of Swollen Shoot, the fungus disease of Black Pod and the attacks of Capsid insects.   It is an unpleasant fact that cocoa has been subject to severe disease or pests in one producing country after another.

' Swollen Shoot ' is a virus disease of which the cocoa tree, the silk cotton tree (*Ceiba pentandra*) and the wild kola (*Cola chlamydantha*) and other trees are hosts.   The virus is carried by the mealy bug (*Pseudococcus spp.*).   This is protected by the Crematogaster ant, which feeds on the honey-dew secretion of the mealy bug.   No cure has been found for this insidious disease, which kills cocoa trees slowly but surely.   Each year the harvest is poorer, the pods more rounded and smaller, young shoots become swollen and the leaves mottled.   If the disease were left unchecked, cocoa might be exterminated in Ghana.   The only checks are the cutting out of infected trees, or the spreading around the roots of a poison, which, when absorbed by the tree, is transmitted to the mealy bug when it sucks the sap.   The disadvantages of the first method are its cost and the natural unwillingness of farmers to see such a method applied to trees which, though diseased and bearing ever-smaller harvests, are still alive.   The disadvantage of applying poison is that it is impossible to grow food crops nearby, or to keep animals, and it is not certain that the poison may not affect the cocoa bean.   What is desperately needed is a simple cure for Swollen Shoot, rather than difficult methods of controlling its spread.   Meanwhile, Swollen Shoot occurs in Sierra Leone, the Ivory Coast, in south-east Ghana (Koforidua and environs) and east of Ibadan in Nigeria.   Although Swollen Shoot is serious, Black Pod and Capsids are more widespread, and are often greater menaces.

The   former   West   African   Cocoa   Research   Institute

---

[1] W. H. Beckett, *Akokoaso—A Gold Coast Village*, 1944.   For a less pessimistic view, see Polly Hill, ' The Mortgaging of Gold Coast Cocoa Farms, 1900–54 ', *Report of Fourth Annual Conference of the West African Institute of Social and Economic Research*, 1955.

PALM OIL EXTRACTION

A hand-press at work. Note kerosene tin for collecting oil.

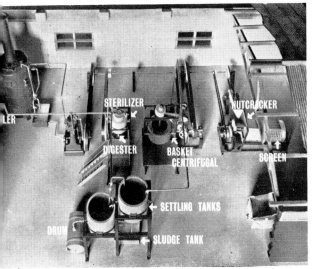

LER
STERILIZER
NUTCRACKER
DIGESTER
BASKET CENTRIFUGAL
SCREEN
← SETTLING TANKS
DRUM
← SLUDGE TANK

14. Interior of model of early Pioneer oil mill, with roof cut away

16. Interior of a larger factory-type mill, as found in Dahomey and the Ivory Coast

Exterior of a typical Pioneer oil mill, Amuro, Nigeria

17. Pods on trunks of cocoa trees. The photograph shows the slender girth of the trees, forked trunks, close planting and the dark interior of a cocoa farm.

19. Normal pod (*above*). Swollen Shoot po rounded, mottled and smaller (*below*).

COCOA

18. Adults and nymphs of the mealybug, *Pseudococcus njalensis*

20. Typical swellings produced by Swollen Shoot virus

21. Kola nuts. The right-hand child is wearing indigo-dyed cloth, with a pattern made by tying pebbles into the cloth before dyeing (see p. 510).

22. Cocoyam. corms on sale in the Ivory Coast

CROPS

23. Guinea corn intercropped with cotton

Picking groundnuts off the stems

25. Dwarf Lagoon and Ndama cattle by the sea in Dahomey. Note sizes in relation to men.

26. A herd of large and varied Zebu cattle, on the north-eastern boundary of Ghana, near Bawku. Note the large humps. Despite the rainy season, these cattle were already in poor condition and had several hundred miles farther to travel.

27. Typical sheep of northern Nigeria.

28. Typical Sokoto goat

(W.A.C.R.I.) at New Tafo, Ghana, did research for all British West Africa but is now a Ghana institute. Co-operative societies are also helping to improve methods of cultivation, fermentation of beans and marketing.

Coffee is indigenous to Africa and has many varieties, each with rather different climatic or altitude requirements. Like cocoa, it needs fertile, well-drained, undulating yet sheltered environments. Compared, however, with cocoa, coffee requires lighter soils and matures more rapidly. It grows in the Rain Forest zone to about 8° N., where these conditions are fulfilled, and where there are roads.

Arabica, which originated in Ethiopia, is the best quality. It must be grown at about 2,000 feet or over, which limits it to the Cameroon and Guinea Highlands, especially the N'Zérékoré area. *Stenophylla* grows wild, and is also cultivated in Sierra Leone east of Kenema, and in the *arabica* regions just mentioned. *Liberica* is indigenous to Liberia, is hardy and widely grown, but poorer in quality. *Gros indénié* is indigenous to the Ivory Coast, where it is grown especially in the west-centre. *Excelsa* and *Canephora* (with its varieties of *robusta*, *kouilou* and *petit indénié*), indigenous to Central Africa, are of superior quality to *liberica*, and mature early. *Robusta* is extending rapidly in the Ivory Coast, as *kouilou* and *indénié* are much afflicted with disease.

Coffee requires machinery for proper preparation, so that African farmers may need financial help or co-operatives, if they are to succeed. Alternatively, coffee is well suited to larger plantations.

The Ivory Coast is the largest producer, and coffee is its greatest export by value as it was in Guinea in the last years of French rule. Small producers are Sierra Leone, Liberia, Togo, Fernando Po, São Tomé and Príncipe. Ex-French lands had a protected market in France until 1964.

Kola (*Cola acuminata*, *Cola nitida*, etc.). The second species of kola, indigenous to Ashanti, the Ivory Coast and Sierra Leone, but also cultivated extensively in Nigeria, is the chief kola of trade. The first species is native to Nigeria, the Gabon and Congo Basin, but is less cultivated. The trees grow to a height of about 50 feet and do not bear a useful crop until about ten years old.

The kola tree has been cultivated in West Africa for a very long time, and trade in its nuts was widespread even before the arrival of Islam.   It was almost certainly this trade (as well as that in salt, slaves and gold) which occupied merchants of the Mali Empire in the thirteenth century, and which led to the foundation of colonies of Dioula (Dan) peoples in Guinea, Liberia and the Ivory Coast.   Indeed, Beyla in Guinea was founded by Dioula in 1230, as a centre for the slaves and kola nut trades.[1]

Within the areas of at least 50 inches rainfall and the Rain-forest, the main producing districts are the coast lands and south-eastern interior of Guinea (Kissi country); south-central Sierra Leone; the northern fringes of the Ivory Coast between 6° 30' and 7° 30' N.; southern Ashanti; southern Dahomey, especially around Adjara and Domé; and the Agege–Abeokuta–Benin belt of Nigeria.   In several areas (e.g. in the Abeokuta District) it has taken the place of cocoa, where the soil has proved insufficiently good to support that crop.

The green, wrinkled pods contain about six to ten nuts, claret, pink or white.   The latter colours are rarer but more valued for their sweeter taste, colour and higher caffeine content.   Although produced in the forest zone, the nuts are mostly consumed in Savannah lands by Muslims.   The nuts contain caffeine, kolatine and theobromine, and have a very astringent taste.   The effect of chewing them is somewhat similar to that of drinking coffee or tea; namely, a stimulating or sustaining effect.   They are often chewed by Africans doing heavy manual work or on long marches.   The white nuts are a symbol of friendship, but the red ones may be emblems of enmity.   Kola nuts also have religious (white nuts only) and legal significance.   Many Africans consume some 700 nuts per year, or about 22 lb.   A red dye can also be made from them.

Rubber exports from indigenous trees such as *Funtumia elastica*, and from vines such as *Landolphia heudelotii* and *L. owariensis*, were important from Rain Forests up to and during the First World War.   The development of plantations of *Hevea*

[1] See M. H. LeLong, ' La Route du Kola ', *Revue de Géographie Humaine et d'Ethnologie*, No. 4, pp. 35–40.

brasiliensis in South-east Asia practically killed West African wild rubber exports, except during the Second World War. *Heva brasiliensis* was little grown in West Africa until the Firestone Rubber Company began planting in Liberia. Their success has probably been due to the high rainfall (average 129 inches—3 m. 275 mm.), rational methods and great capital expenditure. Until 1951 rubber accounted for about 90% by value of Liberian exports. There are several African plantations and many peasant producers in Liberia and near Benin in Nigeria, and a few European-directed ones in the Ivory Coast and Nigeria.

Coconut (*Cocus nucifera*) must have sandy or very well drained loamy soils with, preferably, about 70 inches (1,780 mm.) annual rain, or equivalent irrigation, and high relative humidity. It is a typical sight on coasts, and there are plantations in Togo, Dahomey, São Tomé and Príncipe. Copra is produced and the leaves are used as thatching material but many trees are diseased. Elsewhere, coconuts have only local significance as a food crop, though their cultivation could be extended along the Ivory Coast, Ghana and the south-western Nigerian coasts.

Plantain (*Musa paradisiaca*) is another important foodstuff brought from Asia at an early date. It is taller than the banana plant, and the fruit is longer and straighter. On the stems, too, these fruits are more out-spread and fewer. It takes twelve to fifteen months to mature and should be grown in rich, damp soils.

The green fruit is roasted, boiled or fried in oil. It may also be sliced, dried and then ground into meal or flour. The skins are burned and the ashes mixed with palm oil to make soap. Fibre from the stalk is used for scouring pots, and as a sponge.

Bananas are more systematically grown in Guinea and the Ivory Coast than in the ex-British countries, because the French permitted non-African plantations and provided a large market at high prices. Yet on climatic grounds Sierra Leone and, to a lesser extent, Ghana and Nigeria offer excellent possibilities for Africans to develop the crop, if banana boats could be induced to call, and if these countries could compete with the Caribbean and Canary Islands.

Bananas are often grown in valleys, or round the sides of swamps (thus bananas are often seen near rice), especially where the dry season is pronounced, as in Guinea. There they are grown on small co-operative plantations and smaller private African ones; the most successful are nearest the coast. The first variety grown was akin to the Canary banana. Small, sweet and fragile, it required wrapping for export, but was suited to mediocre soils, and had a fine flavour. The *Gros Michel* variety, introduced from Jamaica to Sierra Leone and Western Cameroon when under United Kingdom Trusteeship and the *Cavendish* or *Poyo* variety used in the Ivory Coast since 1956, require richer soils (or more fertilisers), but produce more, larger and less fragile fruit.

Bananas and plantains require deep, rich, loamy soils and 40–100 inches annual rainfall, or irrigation. Because of their fragility, bananas are grown for export near good communications, e.g. on the rich volcanic and alluvial soils of and near Mt. Cameroon (Cameroon Republic), on the fairly rich soils of the central Ivory Coast (especially near Abidjan and Agboville on the railway), in valleys near Kindia and Mamou in the Fouta Djallon of Guinea and on its coast near Forécariah and Benty.

Bananas are also grown for everyday food and to shield coconut, oil palm, cocoa or coffee seedlings.

Cocoyam (*Colocasia esculenta*), indigenous to the South Sea Islands, was formerly much grown in the wettest forest areas, e.g. in the Ivory Coast and in eastern Nigeria. An improved Cocoyam (*Xanthosoma sagittifolium*), or ' tannia ', was introduced to the Gold Coast in 1843 from the West Indies, and is now much commoner there and elsewhere than the other species.

Cocoyams grow easily and provide shade and conserve dampness for cocoa seedlings. The corm, or underground stem, is round with lesser cormels around it. These are prepared like cassava, and the leaves and stalks are also eaten.

Pineapple (*Ananas comosus*), from Central America, has many varieties and prefers sandy-loam soil of low elevation, preferably near the sea and with moderate rainfall. A small export is carried on from Guinea and Ivory Coast plantations, where there is some canning of juice and fruit.

Sugar Cane (*Saccharum officinarum*) is being increasingly grown on the riverine soils of the *fadamas* of northern Nigeria and with irrigation near Jebba, as also at Komenda (Ghana Coast).

Tobacco (*Nicotiana tabacum*) is widely grown around compounds, especially in this zone. American tobacco is grown in the south-central Ivory Coast, Ghana and especially in Nigeria.

Okro or *Gombo* (*Hibiscus esculentus*) is indigenous to West Africa and is much grown, the fruit and leaves being used as vegetables. It does well even in sand. *Sorrel* (*H. sabdariffa*) is grown for its leaves, fibre and oil from the seeds. *Kenaf* (*H. cannabinus*), indigenous to India, provides good rope and material for bags, and the leaves are eaten.

Fluted Pumpkin (*Telfairia occidentalis*) is much grown with cassava in eastern Nigeria. The shoots, leaves and seeds are edible. The *Edible Pumpkin* (*Cucurbita pepo*) and small tomatoes are widespread.

Lima or *Butter Beans* (*Phaseolus lunatus*) is important in humid areas. *Haricot Beans* are extensively grown in ex-French lands, especially Dahomey.

Yam Bean (*Sphenostylis stenocarpa*), so called because it has a tuber, is much grown in Ibo country, Benin and southern Ashanti, wherever there is at least 35 inches annual rain. Most of the peas and beans listed in the Guinea Corn Zone are also grown.

THE GUINEA CORN, ROOT CROPS AND GROUNDNUT ZONE

This corresponds roughly with the Guinea Savannah. Other important crops are millet,[1] oil seeds and nuts, sweet potatoes and cotton. The main source of vegetable oil is the shea butter tree. Fruits, other than the mango and cucurbits, are few. Almost the same vegetables are grown as in the forest, especially peas.

This is the most southerly zone in which cattle are numerous. They may be either the small resistant breeds, or the large non-resistant *Zebu* type, or crosses of these.

[1] For millet and groundnuts, see next zone, and for root crops, the previous zone,

Guinea Corn, Giant Millet or **Sorghum** has many varieties and its origin is uncertain, but is Ethiopian according to Sauer.[1] Some regard it as the most important cereal in West Africa.

The Grass and Sweet Sorghums are used for fodder, but Grain Sorghums are grown for man and animals. The most important of these are ' Durra ' (*Sorghum durra*), ' Maskwari ' (Fulani name) or ' Mazakwa ' (Hausa name) which is *S. cernuum*, and true Guinea Corn (*S. guineense*). All are grown where it is too dry for maize or unirrigated rice, and either where there is an annual rainfall, ideally, of 32–40 inches, or where there are annual floods and after retreat of the water. It does best where there is only one clear rainy season of five months. It likes the same heavier soils as maize, but *S. cernuum* needs alluvial soils. Guinea corn is grown as an annual or perennial crop for up to three years, interplanted with Bulrush millet.

The plant generally grows up to 12 feet high and has abundant small grains in loose flowering-heads on the end of a stem. Guinea corn is an excellent human food, and intoxicating drinks are also made from it. The grain is marketed over considerable distances. A red-seeded variety provides a medicine and (from the stems) a red dye for cloth, leather and fibre. Bran and the leaves from mature plants are fed to animals. The stems are also used for fencing, fuel, mats, thatch and as poles. *Sorghum dochna, var. technicum*, is grown for broom-making.

Shea Butter Tree (*Butyrospermum parkii*)—French Karité—is the only source of domestic oil in the Guinea Corn and Millet Zones. It is widely distributed between 10° and 14° N., but seldom in great density. It requires moderate rainfall of about 35–50 inches per annum, and is tolerant of damp land and sea air. When damaged by annual bush fires it averages about 20 feet. If not so damaged, it grows much taller—e.g. near compounds.

Because of its dispersion, the problems of collecting fresh fruit and of making an oil (or ' butter ') low in free-fatty acid content are even greater than with the oil palm. Moreover, the oil has a distinctly rancid flavour. For this reason, but

[1] Carl O. Sauer, *Agricultural Origins and Dispersals*, 1952, pp. 76–7.

especially because of the low density of trees, the low human population and the remoteness of many producing areas, the product is mostly used locally.   Nevertheless, there is a small export from Mali, Upper Volta and Dahomey.   It is the kernels which are used, and there is quite an extensive internal commerce in the oil.

Benniseed, Sesame, Tilseed or ***Gingelly*** (*Sesamum orientale*) is indigenous to West Africa, from where it was introduced to India.   It is an annual, and the seeds have a higher oil content than groundnuts, though the yield per acre is much less.   Most of the West African exports come from Nigeria, where it is largely grown by the Tiv of Benue Province.   It is also grown in Dagomba country of Ghana, in the Upper Volta, Guinea, Mali and Sierra Leone.   The seeds yield more oil if the plant is grown as the last crop on exhausted sandy loam or loamy soils, with plenty of moisture for two months only.

The oil is used outside Africa as a substitute for olive oil, in confectionery, margarine, cooking fats and soap.   In Africa, the seeds are used for a kind of porridge and in soup, and the leaves are put in soup.   The crop can be used as an excellent green manure.   A poorer variety is *S. radiatum.*

Sweet Potato (*Ipomoea batatas*), an introduction from South America, grows where there is 30–50 inches (760–1,270 mm.) annual rainfall, or in very sandy soils with heavier rainfall. It is important in Guinea, in Mali—Upper Volta—Ivory Coast borderlands, in the curious coastal savannah of the Ivory Coast, in the Volta Delta, in southern Senegal and in northern Nigeria.   Like yams, it is grown in mounds or ridges and is a creeper.   The tubers are small and numerous, and the leaves can be eaten by man as a spinach, or raw by animals.   It should be noted that in the United States, sweet potatoes are sometimes called ' yams '.

Cotton (*Gossypium sp.*) is an ancient crop in almost all parts of West Africa, except in the densest forest, but it is most success-ful wherever the dry and wet seasons are sharply defined.   In the south, cotton is generally inter-cropped with maize or yams; in the north, it is inter-cropped or rotated with ground-nuts or guinea corn.   Thus it is a crop which is spread through several climate and crop belts and, though mainly grown for local cloth, some is exported.

American Allen cotton (*Gossypium hirsutum*) is suited to the north, where there are fewer crops to grow and space can be found for single cropping, which this cotton demands. In several provinces of Northern Nigeria, it is grown partly for export. In the Mali Inland Niger Delta, rice cultivation competes with cotton. Moreover, in competition with ground-nuts, cotton is generally uneconomic and more difficult to grow, except on heavier soils.

In the south, where the rainfall is heavier, cotton is much grown, but almost entirely for domestic purposes. There are two varieties of *Gossypium barbadense*: ' Ishan ', which gives a tough fibre, and ' Meko ', a poorer variety.

In the Middle Belt, neither Allen cotton of the north nor the varieties of the south do well, and there is no good local variety.

Production of Ginned Cotton[1]

Country	Thousands of metric tons	
	1934–8	1965
Ex-French West Africa . .	6	31
Nigeria	10	44

[1] About one-half is used within ex-French West Africa, and two-thirds within Nigeria. Figures from *Production Yearbook*, 1966, Vol. 20, F.A.O., Rome, 1967. Nigerian figures are Marketing Board purchases.

Indigo (*Indigofera arrecta*), indigenous to East and South Africa, is a shrub of about 4 feet, whose leaves are used for the dye. It requires rich soils and about 30 inches (760 mm.) annual rainfall. In the south, the dye is produced from a wild plant, the Yoruba or West African Indigo (*Lonchocarpus cyanescens*). Indigo dye is still used extensively in Nigeria and Sierra Leone. *Henna* is also grown for its dye.

Garden Egg (*Solarnum melongena*), known also as Asiatic auber-gines, does well with moderate rainfall, as do the peppers (*Capsicum annuum* and *C. frutescens*).

Mango (*Mangifera indica*) is a native of southern Asia, but is found throughout West Africa, especially in the Middle Belt. The West African unimproved variety has small fruit not always of good flavour. The trees are excellent for shade along roads, provide tanning used for leather, and a fairly hard wood.

Pigeon or *Congo Pea* (*Cajanus cajan*), introduced from India, requires good soils and dry conditions. *Cow Pea* (*Vigna unguiculata*) should have good soils and at least 25 inches annual rain, but will grow in poor sandy soils. Both peas and pods may be eaten. The leaves provide a spinach, and the Cow Pea is also a green manure crop.

Sword Bean (*Canavalia ensiformis*) is much grown on the Jos Plateau.

Locust Bean (*Parkia biglobosa* and *clappertoniana*) is valued for its seeds, which are boiled, pounded, fermented and then made into balls and sold as *daudawa*, a product rather like cheese. The pulp in the pods is used for soup.

Onions are extensively grown in northern Nigeria and in the dry coastal areas of Ghana.

Calabashes are widely grown for making utensils.

THE MILLET AND GROUNDNUT ZONE

This is the most northerly agricultural zone, and roughly corresponds with the Sudan and Sahel Savannahs. With millet are found the lesser millets and all the crops of the previous zone, except yams, the shea butter tree and fruits, though cucurbits are grown. This is the ideal region for Zebu cattle, which are often kept even farther north, where permanent cultivation is impossible.

Millet (*Pennisetum typhoideum*), known also as Bulrush Millet or Pearl Millet and in Hausa as ' Gero ', is almost certainly indigenous. It grows about 6 feet high, and at the head of the spike is a compact, rod-like concentration of grey grains; hence the popular names. One variety matures in two months, another in three months, and a third in four to five months. Their distribution is a reflection of the length of the rainy season.

Millet grows best in light loamy or sandy soils rather lacking in humus, and requires under 28 inches (700 mm.) annual rainfall. Indeed, it is generally grown with 11–16 inches (275–400 mm.). It benefits from clear skies, low humidity and considerable diurnal temperature variation.

The plant is used in the same way as guinea corn. It is the main cereal of the Niger Republic, central Mali and northern Upper Volta, Senegal, Mauritania and of the driest areas of Guinea, Togo, Dahomey and Nigeria. *Tamba* (*Eleusine coracana*) is a poor type of finger millet, used for food and for beer. *Hungry Rice* and *Iburu* are also much grown. (See p. 100.)

Groundnut (*Arachis hypogoea*) is probably native to South America, and is also known as the peanut or monkey nut. It is an important African food in most places, but does best between 8° and 14° N. (especially between 11° and 13° N.), in rich but sandy soils. The latter are essential, as the pod matures in the soil. Rainfall must be at least 14 inches (355 mm.) per annum in the humid atmosphere of coastal Senegal, or 25–35 inches (635–890 mm.) in the drier interior lands. If two light rainy seasons occur, two crops can generally be grown.

There are two types of plant—the ' spreading ' or ' running ', and the ' bunched ' or ' erect '. Both are annuals, and the runner is the more common and better yielder. On the other hand, the erect is more suitable for inter-cropping and for the heavier red-clay soils of Zaria (northern Nigeria), where the rainfall is greater. The crop is grown in rotation or inter-cropped with millet, guinea corn or cotton. Groundnuts, however, need much lighter soils than cotton. To work such soils, the French developed a very suitable hoe known as the ' hilaire ', after Hilaire Maurel, who was associated with the early development of Senegal.

Until about 1950 the crop was grown exclusively by African peasants, but there is some not very economic mechanised production at Kaffrine and Sédhiou (Senegal). Other such schemes have failed. In Senegal there are some 450,000 peasant farmers using about 2·3 million acres. In addition, some 70,000 casual labourers or ' navétanes ' migrate from the poorer districts of Mali, Portuguese Guinea and Guinea into either Senegal or the Gambia (according to which offers the highest prices) as squatters or harvest labourers. In northern Nigeria the average size of farms is 3–4 acres.

Export entirely depends upon cheap bulk transport, so that commercial cultivation is intensive in physically suitable areas

on or near lines of communication in Senegal, the Gambia, in
northern Nigeria roughly north of an east–west line through
Zaria, and in the Niger near to the boundary with Nigeria.
With the new railway to Maiduguri (northern Nigeria),
cultivation may extend there.

The groundnut is not a nut, but a bean.   Inside each pod are
two seeds which, when crushed, give an oil highly valued for
cooking and as a substitute for olive oil, as well as being used in
the manufacture of margarine and soap.   The outside shell
yields a little poorer oil.   The nuts are mostly shelled or decorticated locally, to economise transport costs, but some oil is
thereby lost and the end products are less valuable.   The

Groundnut Production[1]

Country	Thousands of metric tons	
	1934–8	1965
Ex-French West Africa	920	1,742
Gambia	Not available	144
Nigeria	550	1,542

Groundnut Exports[2]

Country	Thousands of metric tons	
	1934–8	1965
Ex-French West Africa, In Shell . .	301·1	—
,, ,, ,, Shelled . .	116·2	331·7
Gambia, In Shell	39·8	—
,, Shelled	0·3	33·7
Nigeria, Shelled	234·4	457·2

Groundnut Oil Exports[2]

Country	Metric tons	
	1934–8	1965
Ex-French West Africa	2,685	147,484
Nigeria	Nil	92,208
Gambia	Nil	13,032

[1] *Production Yearbook*, 1966, Vol. 20, F.A.O., Rome, 1967.
[2] *Trade Yearbook*, 1966, Vol. 20, F.A.O., Rome, 1967.

residue of the crushed nuts gives an excellent cattle-cake. After the fall of France in 1940, groundnut oil came to be extracted in Senegal on a much larger scale than before. Between 1940 and 1943 the French even used the oil in West Africa as a costly substitute for diesel oil, and in recent years a textile fibre has been made from groundnut meal.

The first shipment of groundnuts from West Africa was from Rufisque (Senegal) to Rouen in 1840, and annual shipments started in 1845. Intensive cultivation followed the opening of the Dakar–St. Louis line in 1885, the Kaolack branch in 1911, the completion of the Thiès–Niger railway in 1923, two branch railways in 1931, and the many roads. Continuous cropping led to soil exhaustion, and cultivated areas are now mainly in south-central Senegal.

Senegal is the nearest groundnut producer to Europe. Groundnuts and derivatives (especially oils) are about 94% of Senegal's exports. Mali and Niger export much smaller quantities but the crop is vital to them. In the Gambia groundnuts are even more vital. They are almost the only cash crop and constitute about 98% of the exports. Nuts pass across the Senegal–Gambia border according to relative prices. In Portuguese Guinea, groundnuts comprise over half the exports by value.

In Northern Nigeria the most important areas are in Kano and Katsina Provinces, but the crop is significant south to Zaria, east to Maiduguri, west to Sokoto and north into the Niger. Again it was the opening of the railway to Kano in 1912, the branch from Zaria to Gusau in 1927 and on to Kaura Namoda in 1929, and the extension of the main line from Kano to Nguru also in 1929, that made possible such a vast cash crop. It accounts for about a quarter of the Nigerian railway tonage and of Nigerian exports by value. Kano station deals with about one-fifth of all groundnuts grown anywhere in West Africa for export.

An excessive amount of labour is at present used in cultivation. High prices for groundnuts have made worthwhile the use of artificial fertilisers, which are sometimes put in with the seed. The farmer can expect up to a four-fold return for his outlay on fertiliser.[1]

---

[1] A useful study is *The Cultivation of Groundnuts in West Africa*, O.E.E.C., Paris, 1953.

Water Melon (Citrullus vulgaris), indigenous to Africa, requires high temperatures, light soils and water at the beginning of growth. It is much cultivated near the desert by irrigation, especially from the Niger and Senegal Rivers. The kernels of the seeds are used in soups and sauces. The melon grown in southern Nigeria has flesh unfit for eating, and is grown for the seeds ' egusi ', from which a good oil is pressed, much used in cooking.

BIBLIOGRAPHY

See references cited at the beginning of the chapter and in the text.

Also, H. R. JARRETT, ' The Present Setting of the Oil-Palm Industry with special reference to West Africa ', *The Journal of Tropical Geography*, Vol. 11, 1958, pp. 59–69.

A. B. MOUNTJOY, ' Vegetable Oils and Oilseeds ', *Geography*, Vol. XLII, pp. 37–49.

Chapter 7

LIVESTOCK AND FISHERIES [1]

LIVESTOCK

As with crops, there are clearly defined livestock (especially cattle) zones. These are determined by the tsetse fly, which, so far, has made it impossible to keep Zebu cattle in the south. Thus this zone has been unable to develop mixed farming, though its heavily leached soils would benefit much from manure enrichment. The north, being freer from the tsetse fly, is the great cattle zone, from which there is a considerable trade in cattle to the south. Cattle-rearing could be greatly increased there if more water were available during the long dry season, and if pastures and feeding were improved.

Moreover, if the tsetse fly danger of the wet season could be overcome, cattle movements should no longer be necessary, and the Fulani and other nomads might eventually be persuaded to become settled and to take up crop-farming. Sedentary crop-farmers might also take more readily to cattle-keeping. Such revolutions would enrich both soil and man, and would extend the cultivated area.

Ethidium bromide and related drugs, together with the Antrycide salts, have proved highly active against *Trypanosoma congolense* and *T. vivax*, carried by the tsetse fly and the causes of trypanosomiasis in cattle. But the prophylaxis seems uncertain after some time, and it is difficult to carry out periodic treatments on nomadic animals. Their greatest value may be to enable cattle to travel safely through a fly area on their way to consuming areas for slaughter, as has been shown so successfully in Nigeria.

[1] I am very indebted to Mr. I. L. Mason, of the Institute of Animal Genetics, Edinburgh, for valuable comments on the section on Livestock, and to Dr. C. F. Hickling, Fisheries Adviser, Colonial Office, for his review of the Fisheries section.

Cattle. South of about latitude 10° N. only small, humpless cattle are found permanently, and they are relatively tolerant of the trypanosome. Their small stature may possibly be connected with calcium deficiency of soils and herbage in the forest zone. If so, it is by a mechanism of natural selection towards the optimum size to suit this poor environment. As rainfall decreases to the north-east, leaching becomes less severe, so that calcium content increases and animals are certainly larger. But they are also larger in the north because they are mostly more vigorous breeds which, however, are not immune to trypanosomiasis. Indigenous cattle in the south have achieved immunity at the price of severe debility, which is partly shown in their small size.

There are three main types of humpless cattle, the most famous being the small *Ndama* found especially in the Fouta Djallon and Guinea Highlands. It has a short, large head, and fawn or brownish-red colouring. It is the main source of meat for Guinea, Sierra Leone and Liberia.

The second or *Dwarf Shorthorn* (*Muturu* in Nigeria), is very small (weighing only about 220 lb.), stocky and dark or piebald. Sub-types of this are the *Lagoon*, *Somba*, etc.

On the inner fringes of the forest are types intermediate between the *Ndama* and *Dwarf*, such as the *Baoulé* (Ivory Coast) and most Ghana cattle.

The third type is the large *Chad* (or *Kuri*), found on the shores and islands of Lake Chad, especially in the Niger Republic. This has huge stump horns, a much larger body than the *Ndama*, is whitish-grey in colour and, despite its geographical location far inland, is humpless.

All these types of humpless cattle probably originated from Asia and North-east Africa in the distant past.[1] Before the later arrival of the Fulani people, humpless cattle were found all over West Africa. They yield up to only 55% by weight of meat and very little milk.

Cattle become much more significant between 9–10° N. and

---

[1] A. G. Doherty, 'Live Stock Problems', *West Africa Commission*, 1938–39, Leverhulme Trust 1943, p. 63, para 297, however, puts forward the interesting idea that European cattle might have been introduced by the slavers to their coastal forts and that the present cattle, which have European colourings and form, are their degenerate descendants. His survey has much to say of the problems of livestock in West Africa.

12–14° N.; they are still humpless and are mainly crosses between the *Ndama* and the larger humped *Zebu*. They have an incomplete resistance to fly. Included in this cross-type are the *Djakoré* of Senegal, the *Bambara* or *Méré* of Mali, the mis-named *Sanga* of Ghana, the *Borgu* in Dahomey and Nigeria, and the *Biu* of Nigeria. This intermediate zone may offer opportunities for mixed farming.

North of 12–14° N. are found the humped Zebu cattle intro-duced from Asia perhaps as early as the sixteenth century B.C. With them were introduced to West Africa some of the bare rudiments of cattle-keeping. Most cattle are owned by no-mads, are not immune to trypanosomiasis, and before the rains they endure some three months of starvation. During the rains they are better fed, although dispersed from rivers and the tsetse fly. Transhumance of these cattle is inevitably extensive. It is difficult to say whether this is the cause of Fulani nomadism, or whether the Fulani and other nomads took to cattle-keeping because it fitted their ways.

Migrations by the Fulani in West Africa since the seventh century, together with yearly transhumance, have led to many types of Zebu cattle. These are taller than the humpless ones (except the Chad), with the longer legs necessary for trans-humance. They are generally light in colour—white or grey with black extremities; they may also be black, fawn, red or piebald. They will support much more work and give more milk than the humpless variety, but only the same percentage of meat to total weight. Moreover, zebus take up to six years to mature, and often calve only in alternate years.

The main varieties are the shorthorn *Maure*, *Tuareg*, *Azaouak*, *Fellata* and *Sokoto* (*Gudale*), all used for transport, milk and meat. They have remained fairly pure because of relative isolation. There are also the medium-horned *Diali* and *Adamawa*. The lyre-horned white or grey *Fulani* cattle occur in Senegal, Mali, Niger and Nigeria, are much affected by movement and crossing with humpless cattle, and are good meat-yielders. Rather similar are the large, red *Bororo*, with long-lyre horns, and known as *Rahaza* in Nigeria.

The following table shows average weights, to the nearest 50 lb., of certain breeds, according to three authorities. With-in each breed the actual weights of animals vary according to

TRANSPORT

29 and 30. To replace ferries on wide rivers by bridges such as that *above* at Kankan (Guinea) across the Milo, tributary of the Niger River, may be very costly. It is sometimes possible to adopt a seasonal alternative of a drift or submersible causeway such as that *below* across the Niger River, between Bamako and Koulikoro (Mali). It crosses the rocky sill which prevents river navigation here, but the causeway is submerged for about five months. A road bridge was opened at Bamako in 1960. In the distance are the Manding Mountains (see p. 241).

31 and 32. Lorries are usually overloaded with goods, or with passengers taking voluminous heavy baggage, or by both. The average life of a lorry used in this way may be as short as a year. If coach services are to be developed, the bus must be capable of carrying heavy loads easily loaded and unloaded. Both photographs were taken in Guinea, but the left one might have been taken anywhere in Tropical Africa.

TRANSPORT

33. French West African Railways progressively introduced diesel locomotives from 1948. The first diesel locomotive on a British West African railway appeared in 1954. This is one of the first diesel locomotives on the Dakar-Niger Railway.

34. Ferries on wide deep rivers are major impediments to speedy lorry transport. When this photograph was taken seven vehicles were waiting on one bank and five on the other.

sex, age, area, feeding and condition. The order of decreasing size is the humpless *Chad*, the humped *Bororo* and *Zebus*, followed by the humpless *Ndama* and *Dwarf Shorthorns*. Nigerian figures are, in all cases, higher than those for French West Africa, probably because Gates is quoting figures from Government farms and Doutressoulle those for ordinary stock.

	Doutressoulle (1947)		Gates (1952) (Nigeria only)		Mason (1951)
	Adult cow	Adult bull	Adult cow	Adult bull	
Humpless					
Chad (Kuri)	900–1,100	—	—	1,200	1,050
Ndama	—	550–650	—	750	550–750
Dwarf Shorthorn	250	300	(400)	500	250
Humped					
Fulani and Shorthorn Zebus	550–650	650–900	700	1,000–1,100	550–900
Red Bororo	550–650	650–900	—	1,200–1,300	750–1,000

Nomadic peoples are sometimes ready to learn improved methods, so that veterinary officers have successfully inoculated against rinderpest, pleuro-pneumonia and other diseases. But a vast amount needs to be done in the improvement of breeds. Crosses with temperate cattle have mainly been unsatisfactory, except in the Cameroon Highlands, and upgrading can best be achieved by selective breeding of indigenous stock.[1] Other difficulties are that most Africans will not feed, water or house their animals, and want an all-purpose beast.[2]

[1] See D. E. Faulkner and J. D. Brown, *The Improvement of Cattle in British Colonial Territories in Africa*, H.M.S.O., 1953.

[2] G. Doutressoulle, in his comprehensive *L'Elevage en Afrique Occidentale Française*, 1947, gives the following figures (p. 287), which demonstrate the consequences:

	Average yield of meat per animal		Annual production	
	Beef cattle	Sheep	Wool per sheep	Milk per cow
France	350 kg.	17½ kg.	6 kg.	2,000 litres
French West Africa . .	130 ,,	12½ ,,	0·6 ,,	500 ,,

F

The Fulani keeps his animals less for commercial profit, than for subsistence and as a sign of social status. He does little or no selective breeding, keeps as many animals as possible, and sells only when he needs ready cash or finds particular animals useless to him. It is reckoned that only 13% of the cattle and 8% of the sheep and goats of West Africa are sold for meat. Thus the whole conception of cattle-rearing and sale is fundamentally different in West Africa from the commercial cattle-rearing countries of the world. This must always be borne in mind, especially when considering cattle areas and trade routes.

Fig. 27 shows the main concentrations of cattle. Total figures are approximately as follows [1]:

Senegal	1,920,000
Gambia	185,000
Mauritania	2,000,000
Mali	4,640,000
Upper Volta	2,000,000
Niger	3,900,000
Portuguese Guinea	230,000
Guinea	1,800,000
Sierra Leone	200,000
Liberia	28,000
Ivory Coast	350,000
Ghana	505,000
Togo	166,000
Dahomey	393,000
Nigeria	7,500,000

Despite the possessive attitude of the Fulani towards his cattle, several hundreds of thousand head of cattle are exported annually from the republics of the Niger, Mali, Upper Volta and Mauritania to the coastal countries, particularly Ghana. Although northern Nigeria is an importer, she is also an exporter via Lagos to Ghana.

Cattle provide food for the Fulani and other cattle-keeping peoples, for Europeans, and for better-off Africans. As wage-

[1] Figures for 1964-5 from *Production Yearbook*, 1966, Vol. 20, F.A.O., Rome, 1967.

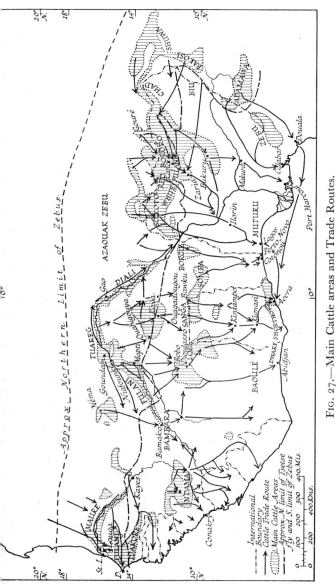

FIG. 27.—Main Cattle areas and Trade Routes.

(Based upon maps by F. Bonnet Dupeyron *Densité et répartition du Cheptel and Commerce du Bétail*, 1945, *and Cartes d'Elevage du Sénégal et de la Mauritanie*, 1950, Office de la Recherche Scientifique d'Outre-Mer; G. I. Jones, 'The Beef Cattle Trade in Nigeria,' *Africa*, 1946; *Atlas of the Gold Coast*, 1949; G. Doutressoulle, *L'Elevage en Afrique Occidentale Française*, 1947 and I. L. Mason, *The Classification of West African Livestock*, 1951.)

earning and cash crops develop, and railway and droving facilities improve, so the demand for meat increases. Army service by Africans likewise increases their appreciation of meat. About 350,000 cattle are killed for meat annually within ex-French West Africa (population 25 million). About one million are slaughtered annually in Nigeria (population 59 million and plainly of higher meat purchasing power), of which 150,000 come from ex-French territories.

Ghana is easily the greatest *per capita* consumer of meat in all West Africa. Annual consumption there is about 200,000 head, coming partly from between Niafunké and Gao in the Mali Republic, and partly from local sources. Thus Ghana, with about 7 million people, used over half the amount of meat consumed by ex-French West Africa's 28 million people, who also live in more predominantly cattle country.

Kano (northern Nigeria) is the greatest commercial cattle centre in West Africa. Several cattle-trains are despatched each week to Lagos; the journey takes forty hours and the animals arrive in poor condition. Many more are driven south on foot, taking about three months. Some are lost and the survivors likewise arrive in as bad a condition as those sent by railway.

If rail charges were lower and refrigerator vans were provided, more cattle could be slaughtered in the north in better condition, and meat sent south, rather than live animals. Meanwhile, several governments have provided pens along the cattle routes, pasturages have been improved, e.g. at Ilorin, and rest camps established for the drovers. Large modern abattoirs exist at Bamako and Zuarungu (Ghana), and others are projected at Ouagadougou, Ibadan, Kano, etc. Some meat is carried south regularly by air, from Bamako, Ouagadougou, and Niamey.

Kano has also long been a great leather and skin centre. After the opening of the railway to Lagos in 1912, overseas trade in these products was developed by European firms, which have made notable improvements in methods of preparation.

Zebu cattle are relatively poor milk-yielders and dairy produce is made only by the Fulani. Most Africans buy little; Europeans used tinned imports. But owing to the difficulty of obtaining such supplies between 1939 and 1945, small butter and cheese factories were established in the larger towns of most territories. Clarified butter-fat is made in Nigeria for cooking and for export, and separated milk is fed to pigs kept increasingly by Lebanese in several towns in Nigeria and other countries.

Sheep. The large sheep is kept by nomads in the Sahel, where there are at least 10 million sheep, as many goats, but only 1 million people. Sheep are hairy, large and long-legged; they commonly move in great flocks. Most of them are kept for meat, although the uncommon long-haired *Maure* variety of Mauritania and Mali is used more for its skin and fleece. The *Tuareg* type, found generally east of Timbuktu, is good for meat and milk. The *Fulani* type, farther south, are better meat animals but poorer milkers.

About one million *Macina* sheep are found in large flocks, mainly in the Inland Niger Delta between 14 and 17° N. and, to a much lesser extent, in Mauritania and the Niger, wherever the rainfall does not exceed 24 inches (610 mm.). These sheep are probably of North African origin, medium in build and with an open fleece. This is of high value, being elastic, light and durable. About 700 tons are produced annually, of which some 400 tons are used in France in the manufacture of sports cloth, mattress-covers and felts. In Mauritania, Mali and Niger the fleece is used for blankets and clothing. The meat and milk are poor. These sheep are kept by settled Fulani, whose shepherds (former captives) move with the sheep to the outer dry fringes of the Inland Delta during the rains and floods.

A degenerate variety of the *Macina*, known as the *Goundoum*, is found in small flocks along the banks and on the islands of the Niger River, between Timbuktu and Niamey. During the floods they are on the higher right bank (Gourma), after which they occupy the islands until the grass is too poor. They are then taken to the low left bank.

Small, short-legged, hairy sheep are found south of 14° N., and are kept in very small flocks by sedentary farmers. They are generally white and black, or white and red in colour, and are significant only for their hairy wool. When crossed with merinos, the wool is good. There are probably about 6 million of them.

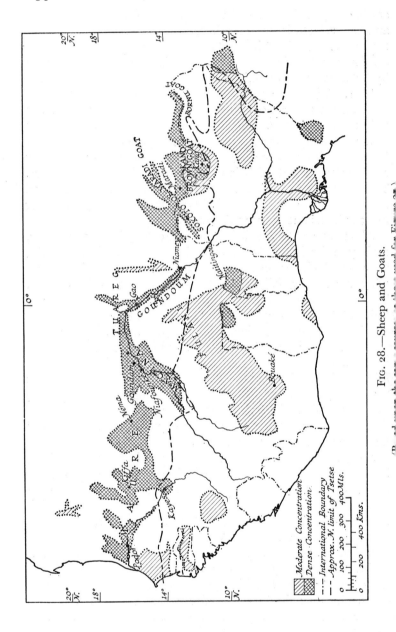

FIG. 28.—Sheep and Goats.

Goats. Goats look remarkably like sheep in Africa and they are generally kept together. Goats are easily reared, endure a long dry season without undue ill-effect and also withstand the humidity of the south much better than sheep. Weight for weight, goats give more meat than any other animal in West Africa. Goat meat is consumed in greater quantities than any other.

As with cattle and sheep, there is the same contrast between on the one hand the large type north of 14° N., kept by Fulani, Maure and Tuareg, which originated in North-east Africa or Asia, giving much milk and good meat from the female, but very susceptible to the tsetse, and on the other hand the smaller goat south of 14° N., resistant to fly, prolific and giving good meat from the male. The northern type number about 17 million, and the southern about 6 million.

Specially renowned goats are the intermediate sized *Sokoto Red* or *Maradi*, and the *Kano Brown* or *Zinder Brown*. These are sources of coloured glacé kid leather, a valuable export from Nigeria and the Niger. The goat is small to medium in size, very prolific indeed and gives good meat and milk. *Bornu* goat-skin is also valuable for suede leather.

Goats and sheep are fundamental to nomadic peoples, as their skins are used for making water-containers, bellows, belts, cords, cushions, saddlery, bags, mats, sandals, etc. Demand is insistent, and made greater by rapid wear resulting from poor preparation.

Pigs. The African black long-snout pig, probably introduced at an early date by the Portuguese, lives in an even wilder state than the other domestic animals. Pigs are limited to non-Muslim peoples, and are mainly found in the southern parts of Nigeria and Dahomey, southern and central Ivory Coast, the Casamance area of Senegal, and around Dakar and other towns.

Berkshires and Yorkshires have been introduced into most West African countries. Many Lebanese have piggeries to produce bacon and ham. Where water, skimmed milk from the dairies (mentioned earlier in this chapter) and labour are available, the prospects for development are good. The Middle Belt deserves especial consideration for piggeries, as it is centrally sited for varied fattening foodstuffs, such as groundnut cake, millet, benniseed, sweet potatoes and palm kernel waste.

Camels. These live in the Sahara and its immediate confines, mainly beyond even the Millet Zone. They are practically restricted, therefore, to Mauritania, Mali and Niger.

In Mauritania they are especially important in the centre (Trarza and Tagant), east (Hodh), and north (Adrar); in the Mali Republic in Timetrine and Kidal regions north of Timbuktu, Bamba and Bourem, and down the Niger to Gao; and in the Niger around Tahoua, Agadès and the oases. In all there are about 200,000, over a third being in Mauritania.

In the past these animals linked West Africa to the Arab World and so helped the spread of Islam. But the advent of Europeans, the turning of trade southward and the pacification of the Sahara, have greatly reduced their value and the variety of breeds required. Instead of being vital in the Sahara in war and peace, camels are now required which are capable of carrying heavy loads through the desert fringes—e.g. groundnuts from the Niger into Nigeria.

Horses. Some authorities have thought that the ponies of Baol (Senegal), of Bobo Dioulasso (Upper Volta), and especially the *Coto-Coli* of Atacora country (northern Dahomey and Togo) are indigenous, as such types are not found in North Africa or the Nile Valley. Yet it is difficult to be sure they are indigenous, as no fossil remains or cave-drawings of horses have ever been found in West Africa.

Most, if not all, horses seem to have been introduced from the seventh to the thirteenth centuries, as a result of the Arab invasions of North Africa. Thus there are the Arab-Barbary types found in the high areas of Mali and the Niger, and progressively poorer varieties of these southward into the basins of the upper Senegal and Niger. Another type was introduced by Arabs from the Upper Nile towards the end of the thirteenth century. It is now found in Sokoto, Katsina, Kano and Bornu Emirates, with poorer varieties to the north as far as Agadès, Niger, as well as astride the Niger River from Say to below Niamey.

Most horses live immediately south of the camels. Horses succumb quickly to the tsetse fly, whose outposts are the horse's southern limits, roughly along a line through Kaolack, Tambacounda, Kita, Bamako, Sikasso, Bobo Dioulasso, Tenkodogo, Nikki, Bida and Maiduguri. Horses are found mainly in western Senegal near the sea, in Mali (especially in Hodh and around Ségou and Mopti) and in the Niger and Northern Nigeria. In West Africa horses are used essentially for ceremonies and sport.

Donkeys (Asses). These are more acclimatised and tougher, and during the dry season they are used quite far south. Their normal regions are western Senegal; the Trarza and Assaba districts of Mauritania; around Mopti, Timbuktu and Gao in Mali; in the Niger southwards into Nigeria as far south as Bida; and in the Upper Volta around Ouagadougou. There are probably nearly three-quarters of a million in all—two and a half times as many as the horses—and they are used by the Fulani and other peoples for cattle-droving, for ceremonies and especially for transport.

Mules. Most African tribes refuse to rear these, except the Hausa, who rear many, especially around Sokoto.

Chickens. These are ubiquitous, small, and give only about 60 tiny eggs a year. In most parts they are given no attention, and some tribes refuse, or once refused, to eat eggs—e.g. the Mende of Sierra Leone. But in northern Nigeria the Hausa sell several million surplus eggs each year for despatch southwards, and the Mossi of the Upper Volta also keep many poultry. The Gambia Poultry Scheme failed in 1951 owing to fowl pest (Newcastle disease), the insufficiency of local feeding stuffs, and their deficiency in vitamin B_1 (causing low egg yield). Its lessons have been learned, so that day-old chicks are flown in and inoculated, while feed is balanced with imported vitamin-enriched feeding stuffs. In most countries more poultry are now raised by battery and open-house methods but eggs and especially poultry are still too expensive for most Africans.

Guinea Fowl. These are widespread in the Savannah zones and are much appreciated.

Ducks. Barbary or Muscovy ducks are numerous along the Senegal, Gambia and Niger Rivers, and in the Rain Forest Zone. They give about double the amount of meat of chickens or guinea-fowl.

Turkeys. These were first introduced by the Portuguese and are numerous in the drier areas of the Guinea Coast.

Rabbits. These are caught almost everywhere, practically entirely for Europeans.

Bees. These are valued by Savannah peoples, and wild honey is sold in markets. Beeswax is collected for export, especially in Senegal and the Gambia.

Snails. A giant variety is an important source of protein to forest peoples.

BIBLIOGRAPHY

See footnotes cited above, especially

G. DOUTRESSOULLE, *L'Elévage en Afrique Occidentale Française*, Paris, 1947.

Also:

I. L. MASON, *The Classification of West African Livestock*, Commonwealth Agricultural Bureaux, Farnham Royal, Bucks, 1951.

Rapport zur L'Elevage en Afrique Occidentale Française, *Conference on Stock-rearing in regions of tropical and sub-tropical climates*, Lucknow, 1950 (F.A.O.).

W. DESHLER, 'Cattle in Africa: Distribution, Types, and Problems', (with large map), *Geographical Review*, 1963, pp. 52–8.

P. VEYRET, 'L'Elevage dans la Zone Tropical', *Les Cahiers d'Outre-Mer*, 1952, pp. 70–83.

FISHERIES

Sea Fishing. Sea fishing by Africans was restricted in the past by the economic state of the countries, by insufficient capital and inability to build anything larger than elaborate canoes. Fishing with canoes means inshore fishing, by daylight, mainly in the dry season; it means also small returns per canoe. Yet anyone who has watched tiny canoes thrusting through the violent surf and venturing miles out to sea, can only be amazed at African endurance. Dried fish play a considerable part in trade, as meat is generally expensive south of 10° N., where the tsetse fly prevents the keeping of large cattle.

Fishing is most important off Mauritania, Senegal, Ghana and Togo, which account for about three-quarters of fish caught in West African waters. Other countries are developing fishing, especially Nigeria. Mauritanian waters supply much of the Senegal total of over 160,000 tons annually; they are also visited by trawlers from Europe, Japan and the Canary Islands, which return thence with their catch, or land part of it for drying at Port Etienne.

Fish processing depots in Senegal at St. Louis, Dakar, M'Bour, Joal and Sangomar, as well as in Mauritania at Port Etienne, treat sharks, dry white fish and do a little canning. Total exports of fish from Mauritania and Senegal are about 5,000 tons per annum, mainly dried fish, but also some tuna.

In the Gulf of Guinea most of the fishing is done by Fanti, not only from their own Ghana villages,[1] but also far to the west, east and south. There are, for example, important Fanti fishing villages at Monrovia, Lagos, in Cameroon and Angola. Annual consumption of all fish in Ghana is probably about 115,000 tons, of which about 85,000 tons are caught off-shore. Tuna fishing and processing has started there.

Russian and Japanese trawlers come with factory ships, and these dispose of the cheaper fish at most West African ports. This and locally caught fish are distributed in refrigerated containers by lorries.

Lagoon Fishing. The extensive lagoons of the Guinea Coast are rich in small fish. These are mostly caught by cast nets but some peoples build elaborate mazes of wicker, which extend over considerable areas of the lagoons, especially in Dahomey. About 20,000 tons of fish are sold here annually.

Fresh-water Fishing. The extent of such fishing varies between peoples and rivers. Rivers most intensively fished are the Senegal and the great bend of the Niger. Many of the riverine peoples of the Niger and its nearby lakes are more concerned with fishing than with cropping or livestock rearing. Lake Chad is also a considerable source of fish. About 60,000 tons of dried and smoked fish are sold annually from the Middle Niger, often far afield.

In recent years a few fish farms have been started. Some of them are in pools behind minor barrages built for water supplies, or for swamp rice cultivation. Other fish farms are in specially constructed fish ponds, e.g. at Panyam, sixty miles south-west of Jos, Nigeria. Fish can also be kept in swamp rice fields under certain circumstances and they may increase the rice yield by about ten per cent, according to experience in Indonesia.

[1] See p. 400.

BIBLIOGRAPHY
(For Livestock see p. 138.)

G. A. STEVEN, *Report on the Sea Fisheries of Sierra Leone*, Freetown, 1945.

F. R. IRVINE, *The Fishes and Fisheries of the Gold Coast*, Crown Agents for the Colonies, 1947.

Chapter 8

MINERALS AND POWER [1]

GENERAL

GOLD has been mined in West Africa for at least a thousand years. The Empire of Ghana, whose zenith was in A.D. 1000, obtained gold from the Falémé River and the adjacent Bambouk Mountains. The Manding or Mali Empire, which had its zenith in A.D. 1332, probably sent its merchants into what are now the Ivory Coast and modern Ghana to buy gold, kola nuts and slaves. Tin was worked on the Jos Plateau long before the advent of Europeans, as was lead at Abakaliki in Ogoja Province, Nigeria. Salt-digging in the Sahara, and the exchange of salt and cattle for kolas and gold, are ancient trades in West Africa.

Gold brought Europeans to West Africa. The Portuguese landed at Shama, at the mouth of the Pra river, in 1471, and in that year made the first recorded direct export of gold to Europe. Gold was also exported down the Senegal and Gambia rivers from the Falémé Basin. Gold, gum, spices, ivory and slaves were staple exports for centuries.

Several metals were smelted and worked into objects of everyday use. In Ashanti and the Baoulé countries, brass weights were used to weigh gold. These small weights were delightfully shaped to represent animals, birds, fish, reptiles, insects and allegorical figures. Gold itself was used for ceremonial or ornamental objects such as stools, bowls, staff heads, chains, rings and bracelets. Another famous metal industry was brass and bronze founding at Benin, which may antedate the Portuguese. But if this was so, it is difficult to see how the copper, and especially the zinc, were obtained, though the tin could have come from the Jos Plateau. Tin articles were made

[1] Mr. G. E. Howling, formerly Director of the Mineral Resources Division of the Overseas Geological Surveys, has given me valuable criticism of this chapter.

in the Naraguta area (Nigeria) at least from the eighteenth century. Iron has long been smelted in small bloomeries almost throughout West Africa, generally for making cooking-vessels, hoes, matchets and such articles.

European exploitation of minerals dates from 1878, when, on the initiative of a Frenchman, Pierre Bonnat, mining began on the banket reefs of Tarkwa, Ghana. It was hampered by the difficulties of transporting heavy equipment and by poor labour. Gold-mining needs were, in fact, responsible for opening the Ghana Railway from Sekondi to Tarkwa in 1901, its extension to Obuasi in 1902, and for a branch to Prestea in 1912. The need for bauxite caused the opening of the Awaso branch in 1944. In Nigeria the Bauchi Light Railway was opened in 1914 for the needs of tin-mining, and the Nigerian Eastern Railway to Enugu in 1916 for coal-mining. It was extended to Jos in 1927 to serve the tin-fields directly. Mineral lines were opened in Liberia from Monrovia to the Bomi Hills in 1951, to the Mano River 1961, and the Bong Mountain in 1965 to facilitate iron-working, as was that from Buchanan to Mt. Nimba in 1963, and from Pepel to Marampa in Sierra Leone in 1933. Many existing railways made possible later mining developments.

Mining plays quite a part in West African economy, and has a major share in the total capital invested (and sometimes lost). It pays considerable amounts in wages, whilst mineral traffic is an important element in certain railway revenues. Mining companies often provide housing and free medical attention not only for their employees but also for dependants and friends. The only minerals worked by government corporations are Nigerian coal, some of Ghana's gold, and Guinea's diamonds. Mining royalties and taxation are significant revenues to the governments of Mauritania, Guinea, Sierra Leone, Liberia, the Ivory Coast, Ghana and Nigeria. Development of oil in Nigeria and of iron in Mauritania and Liberia are revolutionising the fortunes of those countries, whilst potential power and bauxite reserves may industrialise Guinea and Ghana.

Minerals form a considerable part of the total exports of Mauritania, Guinea, Sierra Leone, Liberia, Ghana and Nigeria. They are important, too, in diversifying economies.

Mining was less important in non-British territories, though many important developments have taken place since 1947 (iron ore in Liberia, Mauritania and Guinea, bauxite in Guinea, phosphates in Senegal and Togo, manganese and diamonds in the Ivory Coast). More are in progress, particularly of copper in Mauritania and more iron in Liberia.

In the past, ex-French West Africa was less intensively prospected for economic minerals than ex-British West Africa, but this situation changed after 1945. Though ex-French West Africa is probably poorer in minerals than ex-British West Africa, it is by no means deficient. Some minerals are remotely sited, and the lack of real ports in the Ivory Coast (until 1950), Togo and Dahomey (until 1965), has been an obstacle. French capital has often seemed hesitant to invest in mining overseas. Many enterprises were partly non-French, e.g. African for gold, British for iron and diamonds, Canadian for bauxite, to take examples from ex-French Guinea. So far, that country has more mineral workings than any other part of former French West Africa.

IMPORTANT MINERALS WORKED

It is intended here to give a general survey of each mineral. Fuller details may be found in the regional chapters.

Gold. The Ghana workings are the only important ones. Gold occurs in:

1. Birrimian (Pre-Cambrian) quartz reefs, or lodes, with some free gold.
2. Tarkwaian (Pre-Cambrian) banket or conglomerate reefs, rather akin to those of the Witwatersrand.
3. Oxidised ores of the above series, worked open-cast.
4. Alluvial deposits, worked by dredges.

During the present century nearly 70% of the production has been from quartz reefs, and almost exclusively from Ashanti and the Western Region. The Ashanti Goldfields Corporation mine at Obuasi is probably the richest large goldmine in the world. Its output for the past forty years has averaged about one ounce of gold per ton of ore.

In Guinea, gold occurs in alluvial and residual placer deposits in the Bouré and Tinkisso rivers, north and north-west of Siguiri. This area is intermittently worked by African miners. Minor workings in ex-French West Africa are also generally alluvial.

In Nigeria, gold-mining has been erratic and indifferently organised; production was mainly from alluvial and small lode deposits in the Ilesha area of Oyo Province. Alluvial workings in Sierra Leone have also dwindled. A little alluvial gold is won in Liberia.

The following table shows how gold exports have declined in the whole area, except from Ghana.

Production of Gold in West Africa
In thousands of troy ounces—fine gold

Country	1938	1965
Ghana	677·5	760·2
Ex-French West Africa . .	118·0	34·5
Sierra Leone	31·5	Nil
Nigeria	25·0	0·6
Liberia	2·0	1·7

Diamonds. All West African production is from alluvial sources. By weight of output, West Africa is far ahead of South Africa, but well behind in value.

Ghana is the largest producer, the diamonds being small and mainly of industrial quality. Mechanised production began in the Birrim Basin in 1920. Africans work on their own account in the Bonsa Basin.

Larger, and occasionally very large diamonds (such as one of 770 carats) are found in Sierra Leone, where a company works some eight areas at Yengema and Tongo. There are many dispersed and very prolific African 'diggings'.

Production near Kissidougou, in south-eastern Guinea, began in 1936 and has also developed west of Beyla. The

Diamond Production in Thousand Metric Carats

Country	1965
Guinea	72
Sierra Leone	1,525
Ivory Coast	198
Ghana	2,273
Liberia	539

Ivory Coast has become a significant producer and quickly outdistanced the output from Guinea, both in respect of quantity and quality.

Iron Ore. Before the Second World War, the only iron ore worked on a large scale in West Africa was in Sierra Leone, but other very rich deposits are now quarried in Mauritania and Liberia.

Hæmatite occurs in highly metamorphosed Birrimian rocks at Marampa-Lunsar in Sierra Leone. Similar deposits, not worked, occur farther inland around Tonkolili, and near Fort Gouraud in northern Mauritania. At the latter some six million tons are mined annually, being 64% *Fe*.

The Bomi Hills deposit, 50 miles from Monrovia, Liberia, is a massive magnetite of 65% *Fe*. It is now being intensively worked. Even larger deposits on Mt. Nimba, in the Bong Hills and near the western border are being developed by Swedish, American, German, Liberian and other capital.

Ferruginous laterite is widespread, but rarely of sufficient iron content to be worked for large-scale iron industries. However, deposits of limonite-rich lateritised basic rocks, containing up to 51·5% iron ore, were worked open-cast about 5 miles from Conakry in Guinea between 1953 and 1965. The ore proved difficult to sell because of its high chrome content, and because of competition from Liberian and other hæmatites. Poorer deposits at Mt. Patti near Lokoja, Nigeria, are fairly well sited for use in a proposed iron and steel industry.

Large iron or steel industries are unlikely to be established in West Africa. Nigerian coal is not well suited to iron smelting; and there are very few other coal deposits, none of which is worked, nor likely to be. Electric steel production on a large scale is unlikely. All capital, machinery and most skilled labour would have to be imported. Nevertheless, small plants are being built for semi-political reasons.

Iron Ore Production (Thousand Metric Tons)

Country	1965
Mauritania	5,965
Guinea	300
Sierra Leone	1,400
Liberia	10,270

Bauxite. Workable deposits of the tropical lateritic type of bauxite, the ore of aluminium, have so far been found only in Ghana, Sierra Leone and Guinea, though occurrences have been noted elsewhere.

Quarrying really began in Ghana during the Second World War at Awaso, south-west of Kumasi, and at Mount Ejuanema, near Mpraeso. Awaso alone continued production after the war. Peacetime development of the other deposits, especially at Yenahin and Kibi, depend upon the second phase of the Volta Hydro-Electric Power Project for the local reduction of the ore. The Sierra Leone deposit was opened in 1964.

Large deposits occur east of Boké, near Dabola, and north-west of Kindia. At the latter, some 1,000 million tons have been proved, and there is a project for a hydro-electric power station on the Konkouré River, with an aluminium works to produce 100,000 tons a year. Meanwhile, alumina is being produced at Fria.

There are also small deposits on the Los Islands, off Conakry. Working began on Kassa Island in 1952, and will last about twenty years. The bauxite was first shipped to Canada, later to Poland and other countries.

Manganese. Several deposits of manganese ore occur as surface concentrations from the weathering of manganese-rich Birrimian rocks in Ghana. The main deposit worked is at Nsuta, 34 miles from Takoradi and alongside the existing railway. Ghana is generally the seventh world producer.

A smaller deposit is worked near Grand Lahou in the Ivory Coast.

Tin. Tin ore is derived from granite and pegmatite. It was washed out from the parent rock by ancient and existing rivers, in whose gravels it now occurs on the Jos Plateau. Some of the ancient river-courses and their gravels were later covered by volcanic lava.

Tin ore not so covered was first worked by Africans and later by Europeans. At the present rate of working, such deposits in Nigeria may soon be exhausted. To reach further supplies, it will be necessary to sink shafts through the basalt to get at the deep deposits. This will change not only the style of mining, but also its capitalisation. Tin prices then prevailing will determine whether such profound technical and financial re-organisation is worth-while. All the ore is smelted in the mining area.

Columbite. This was formerly a waste product of tin-mining in Nigeria, but the metal it contains is now highly valued for the production of certain classes of stainless steel and other alloys, for jet engines and gas turbines. Nigeria is the main world producer, but production has varied greatly according to needs in the U.S.A.

Ilmenite, Zircon and Titanium. The world's largest known deposit of rutile (titanium dioxide) is worked by means of a floating suction dredge north of the Sherbro Estuary in Sierra Leone, which should become the leading world producer. Ilmenite and zircon were obtained from Senegal's Petite Côte beaches from 1922 to 1964, and from Sanyang beach in the Gambia from 1956–8. These operations became uneconomic in competition with Australian and Malaysian producers who, in turn, may be undercut by the Sierra Leone firm. Unworked deposits occur in the Casamance (Senegal); at York and Hastings near Freetown, Sierra Leone; and in the Ivory Coast and Dahomey. Ilmenite is used mainly for titanium paints. Zircon is used in refractories and in the manufacture of zircon alloys.

Oil. Intensive prospecting has been undertaken in Nigeria, especially around the lower Niger. Production and export began in 1957–8 from wells at Oloibiri and Afam; from these and other fields pipelines lead mainly to Port Harcourt and to a terminal at Bonny for export. Development is difficult in the delta but production has increased rapidly, including off-shore, and a refinery has been installed. Oil is Nigeria's leading export, while natural gas is being used in local industry and for electrical generation. Export in liquid form is in prospect.

Phosphates. Calcium phosphate at Lam-Lam and aluminium phosphate at Pallo, both near Thiès, Senegal, were first quarried in 1950 from Lower Eocene strata. Some 45,000 tons of the former and 52,000 tons of the latter were produced in 1953, when the Lam-Lam quarry proved uneconomic and was closed. Exploitation has since been concentrated on the much larger deposit of aluminium phosphate, from which some 100,000 tons are produced annually for fertilisers. A nearby deposit of calcium phosphate is being developed by another company at Tivaouane.

A deposit near Anécho, Togo, yields 1¼ million tons a year, and its exploitation is very easy.   Other deposits are known at Cive (near Matam) on the Senegal River, in the basin of the Lama River in Dahomey, at Abeokuta in Nigeria, and in the dry valley of the Tilemsi 78 miles north of Gao, Mali.

Limestone.   Limestone, in forms suitable for cement manufacture or for building stone, is relatively rare in West Africa. Yet cement is in great demand and is expensive, especially far from a port.   Marly limestone, at the junction of Cretaceous and Eocene series, is worked at Rufisque (Senegal), which has West Africa's earliest cement factory.   There are some six factories in Nigeria, each Region having been anxious to have at least one.

Salt.   This has been worked for centuries in the Sahara at Trarza and Idjil in Mauritania, and at Taoudéni in Mali. Saline earths are dug at Kaolack and St. Louis (Senegal) and at Bilma (Niger), and salt is obtained from saline springs at Daboya, Ghana.   Sea water is evaporated at Ada, Keta, Accra and many other places on the coast.

The Saharan deposits were the source of ancient exchange with kola nuts from the south.   Movement of salt has been completely changed in direction by large imports of cheap European salt through the ports, and by the output from the factory at Kaolack, Senegal.

MINERALS AT PRESENT OF LESSER IMPORTANCE

Chromite.   Chromite occurs in lenses in some serpentine rock, and in talc schists.   The only deposit ever worked is at Hangha, Sierra Leone.   The ore is not of the highest grade, and production ceased in 1964.   There are unexploited deposits in Togo and Dahomey.

Coal and Lignite.   The Enugu coalfield in eastern Nigeria is the only one in West Africa.   The coal is obtained from adit mines, is sub-bituminous, and of Cretaceous age.   Production is low at approximately 500,000 tons per annum.   The field extends well to the north and north-west, but probable reserves are only some 150 million tons—much less than a year's output in the United Kingdom.   Nigerian coal is used on the railway and for electricity production, but is better suited to gas production and the manufacture of chemical by-products.   Its combustible character makes export difficult but this has been more hampered by labour difficulties in the mines and on the railway, by cheaper and better South African coal and by competition from Nigerian and other oil. Lignite occurs near the coal, in the vicinity of the Niger River, and proposals have been made for its use as a source of oil and chemicals.

Uranium. Reserves are being developed at Arlit, near Agadès, in the Aïr Massif of Niger by a company in which the French Government has a 45% holding, private French companies 40%, and the Niger Government 15%. Uranium ores also occur in the Jos Plateau of Nigeria.

Silver–Lead–Zinc. These occur in the Lower Cretaceous rocks of Eastern Nigeria. At Ameri-Nyeba and Abakaliki in Ogoja Province, lead was extracted by the Portuguese or by Africans. After centuries of disuse, the deposits were reworked from 1925 to 1929, and again in 1949. Similar deposits at Zurak, in the east of Plateau Province, also have an ancient history, and were re-worked from 1930–7 and again about 1950. Extensive re-development is proceeding at Ameri.

Tungsten. Ores of tungsten have been or are being worked a little in Nigeria, and in the Niger.

Platinum. Platinum has sometimes been worked at York and Hastings, near Freetown, Sierra Leone.

Copper. A copper deposit at Akjoujt, Mauritania, is reported to contain 500,000 tons of metal. There has been a small production at Gaoua in the Ivory Coast.

HYDRO-ELECTRIC POWER

There are many possible sites on the Senegal, Niger, Volta, Konkouré and other rivers, but development for power is likely only in a few places. West African rivers are so seasonal that large dams are necessary to create the necessary storage and head of water. Insulation of electric cables is expensive in areas of high humidity, so that transmission is costly. Disturbance in electrical storms is also a practical and economic difficulty. Nevertheless, there is a great need for electrical power in West Africa for industries, mines and mineral processing, railways and towns.

Significant hydro-electric power generation was for long limited to plants on the southern edge of the Jos Plateau, which together have a capacity of about 20,000 Kw and whose output is used in the tin-fields; and to the Grandes Chutes station in Guinea, inaugurated in 1954, with a capacity of 9,500 Kw. There are very small plants on Fernando Po, and on the main Firestone Rubber Concession in Liberia.

The great Volta River Project in Ghana began producing power in 1965. Over half of the available 564,000 Kw will be used in a smelter at Tema, which should make Ghana a major producer of aluminium. Mines, towns and existing industries will also receive power, and another dam could be built in north-western Ghana at Bui. The Volta River Project will greatly diversify and strengthen Ghana's economy. At Kainji, in northern Nigeria, the first of three dams to be built under the Niger Dams Project came into operation in 1968. The initial capacity will be 320,000 Kw but will later be raised to 960,000 Kw. This power will be used for general domestic and industrial purposes in Nigeria. A second dam will be built about 1980 some 64 miles farther down the Niger at Jebba, with a capacity of 500,000 Kw. By 1984 a third should be started in the Shiroro Gorge of the Kaduna River, with a 480,000 Kw capacity. These three dams will get the best from different river régimes, and will also be integrated with electrical production using natural gas which started at Afam, eastern Nigeria in 1963. (See also pages 409–11, 502 and 507–8.)

BIBLIOGRAPHY

See under MINERALS in the chapters of Part III. Also:

References in *Bulletin of the Imperial Institute* (up to 1948), in *Colonial Geology and Mineral Resources* (1950 onwards) and in *La Chronique des Mines Coloniales* (Paris).

M. G. ARNAUD, *Les Ressources Minières de l'Afrique Occidentale, Bulletin No. 8 de la Direction des Mines*, Dakar, 1945.

Chapter 9

TRANSPORT[1]

AFTER the eighth century there were frequent journeys across the Sahara to the relatively fly-free interior lands of West Africa. The spread there of Islam is a vivid result of these contacts; in the reverse direction, leather, taken from what are now the northern states of Nigeria, was sold in Europe as ' Moroccan leather '. The fringes of the Sahara were linked by Arab traders, and by Islam, but to the south lay the repellent forest. Though trans-Saharan traffic was considerable, it was often interrupted and was very difficult in the dry season.

After the Turks had barred North Africa, European contact with West Africa was necessarily by sea. But the West African forest repelled Europeans, just as it had the Arabs. To the difficulties of penetrating the forest were added those of an inhospitable coast, difficult to approach and to land upon. Beyond lay the fly-ridden forest, where animals could not be kept and the wheel was unknown. While other inter-tropical regions were easier of access (though often more remote), more inviting, healthier and more advanced, it was natural that European attention should be mainly concentrated in the Americas, in India and the Indies.

Early European interest in West Africa was in relation to those areas. Thus, Senegal was sometimes thought of as a landfall on the way to India, but even then as an inferior one to Algoa Bay, Mauritius or Cape Town. The greatest significance of West Africa was as the source of slaves for the American plantations. By the Treaty of Tordesillas, 1494, the Pope

[1] The author has based this chapter largely upon an essay written by him for inclusion in a work entitled *Geographical Essays on British Tropical Lands*, to be published by George Philip & Son, Ltd. His thanks are due to the Editors and to the Publishers for permission to make use of it in this work.

allotted West Africa as a Portuguese sphere, so that the slave trade was at first mainly in Portuguese hands for predominantly Spanish markets. The only other West African products which were sufficiently valuable to withstand difficult and costly transport were Melegueta pepper, ivory and gold. They gave their names to various parts of the coast—the Grain Coast ('the Grains of Paradise'—Pepper), Ivory Coast (nineteenth-century name), Gold Coast, Slave Coast—though most parts of the coast traded in several commodities.

From the fifteenth century the various trading nations or companies established forts, particularly along the central and eastern Gold Coast shoreline, where there was a little more protection, the rainfall was low, the forest in consequence less dense, and where all the above-mentioned produce was available. The slaves were brought in on foot and the produce by slave-porters. Transport to the coast presented no great problem but one aspect of transport to the new world did, namely, how to feed the slaves on their long voyage? The wild fruits then available in West Africa were unsuitable for storage, and so the Portuguese, in particular, introduced new crops [1] to provide food for the long sea voyage.

The creation of British interests in India, Dutch and then British occupation of the Cape, the abolition of the slave trade and the independence of Central and South America, all induced decay in the old trades in West Africa. Some competitors had come and gone earlier, and there was a general lack of British interest in West Africa during the second and third quarters of the nineteenth century. Not so among the French, who had been allowed to retain their ancient bases, despite their loss of them in most Anglo-French struggles.

That the French kept their interest in West Africa was a reflection of the fact that inland from St. Louis and Gorée lay no forest. After the establishment of St. Louis in 1659, the French made regular expeditions up the Senegal River, and they were the only power which penetrated inland to any extent in West Africa for nearly two centuries. Their later advance into Algeria, Tunisia and Morocco made them heirs of the old trans-Saharan trade.

In the last quarter of the nineteenth century there was a

[1] See p. 95.

general revival of European interest in the West African forest lands. Rapid industrialisation and rising populations in Europe needed supplies of vegetable oils and certain minerals which this region could supply, in return for cheap manufactured goods. These new needs led to a scramble inland to control the sources of supply, and at the Berlin Conference of 1884–5 it was decided that title to colonies could be maintained only by effective occupancy. Powers which still retained coastal stations, such as France and Britain, pushed their political influence inland; a newcomer, Germany, secured a foothold. On the other hand, Denmark and the Netherlands had sold their coastal holdings in 1850 and 1872 respectively, at the time of the decay of the old economic régime and before the new large-scale palm oil trade. This added its nomenclature to the coast with the Oil Rivers Protectorate, proclaimed in 1885 over that area in and around the Niger delta which, in 1900, produced 88% of the world's palm produce.

At first, head porterage had to be used for carrying imports; and palm oil was sent to the coast by the curious and expensive method of barrel-rolling. Porterage was a social evil, a political danger and an economic waste. Although railways were frequently constructed under harsh conditions of labour, they were (the few navigable rivers excepted) the first alternative to porterage. Labour was released for agriculture, mining and other activities, which made possible a cash economy.

River Transport.[1] Political control over new and undeveloped territory, and the need to carry cheaply low value materials in bulk over great distances, even in the rainy season, made railway construction vital to progress almost everywhere. Rivers might have served had they been better graded, less seasonal and with more direct courses. As it was, they were and are of significance only in Nigeria and the Gambia. Yet the excellent Gambia River has been severely restricted in its use by the odd political boundary; and private shallow-draught steamer services on both the Benue and Niger Rivers depend economically upon a public branch railway to the Niger at Baro.

Rail Transport. Whether a railway is built depends first

[1] See also Chapter 2.

upon physical considerations, such as relief and the nature of the terrain, presence of navigable rivers, availability of ballast and, until recently, of water. Secondly, there were political factors, such as the need for effective military control and efficient administration. Thirdly, there are economic considerations, such as the availability of labour and capital, and the prospects of economic return. All these have weighed in varying degrees in different places, but it is important to realise that railways—as also roads and aerodromes—were sometimes built in West Africa for political purposes, rather than as the result of precise economic consideration.

Hurried construction of railways through little-known country, difficult to survey, together with the vital need to keep down costs, meant that gradients were severe, curvature acute, the track devious and often economically ill-placed. In consequence, capacity and speeds are low, and journey times excessively long. This is especially true of the Sierra Leone Government Railway, which has the added disadvantage of being only 2 feet 6 inches in gauge. It is to overcome these difficulties for passenger traffic that the French early initiated the use of diesel traction. In 1949 the express from Dakar to Bamako, hauled by a diesel locomotive, covered the 769 miles in twenty-nine hours, and was rarely late. The express from Lagos to Kano, hauled by a steam engine, covered the 700 miles in forty-three hours, and was very frequently late, though gradients and curvature are no greater than on the French line. The first diesel locomotives for British West Africa came only in 1954.

Until the First World War, railways were unrivalled as means of political and economic progress. Thereafter they were sharply challenged by lorry transport, which took away much shorter distance traffic in valuable produce and passengers. Internal air services have also taken much first-class passenger traffic. Yet railways are generally vital to carry heavy mining machinery, minerals, timber, live cattle and such exports as groundnuts from far inland, and even to distribute petroleum and aviation spirit for road and air competitors.

Railway construction in West Africa was undertaken in the face of every possible difficulty. The Sahara, too great an obstacle for early railway engineers because of the lack of water, is too expensive to cross with a modern railway, which could never pay. Therefore, almost all lines have been built from the generally inhospitable coastline. In the early days equipment had often to be off-loaded into surf-boats. Skilled labour had to be imported at much expense in money and lives, in the infancy of tropical medicine and hygiene. Heavy rainfall necessitates good ballasting, yet ballast material was generally lacking near the coast, precisely where it was most needed. Track maintenance is difficult and expensive in a primitive country, where rainfall can cause many washouts. Bridging has almost everywhere been considerable and expensive—i.e. across large rivers, like the Niger at Kouroussa and at Jebba, and the Benue at Makurdi; across small ones, like the many torrential streams immediately east of Freetown; and across lagoons and inland swamps, as in Dahomey. River valleys can rarely be followed because of danger from flood and disease carrying mosquitoes and flies.

The most general physical difficulty presented to railway engineers was the forest, where surveying and construction were especially difficult. As immediate economy was essential, few earthworks were constructed. Some lines, like the Ghana railway from Sekondi to Kumasi, have been realigned at greater cost than that of their original construction. Railways were the first means of liberating many forest peoples from isolation, of bringing them into touch with savannah peoples, and of linking both of them with the outside world.

Long railways pushing north from the Guinea Coast have central sections largely unproductive of traffic and crossing thinly peopled country. Thus on the Lagos–Nguru railway, there is very little goods and not much passenger traffic from stations between Oshogbo, 182 miles from Lagos, and Zaria, 617 miles; and between Enugu, 151 miles from Port Harcourt, and Kafanchan Junction, at 459 miles, there is normally almost no traffic at all. These unproductive sections lie in the poor ' Middle Belt ', with its low population density, and in which the difficulties of both forest and savannah lands are present, but few of their resources. The paucity of traffic from these long sections is a major economic and operational problem.

Another was West Africa's deficiency in coal. Until 1915

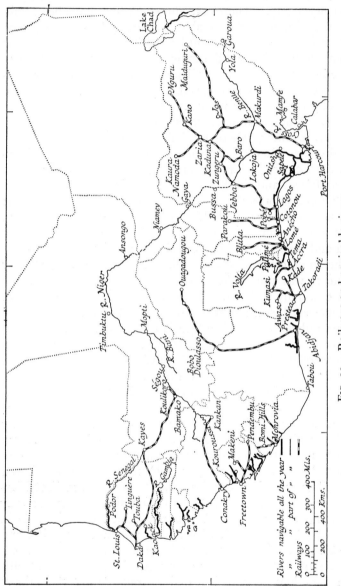

FIG. 29.—Railways and navigable rivers.
(For greater detail see maps of individual territories.)

all coal was imported, but thereafter the mines at Enugu were been able to supply railway coal to Nigeria and sometimes to Ghana. In French West Africa, wood was often used, though it is inefficient as fuel, and timber-cutting has caused severe soil erosion, e.g. in Guinea. During the Second World War experiments were made in French West Africa in the use of groundnut oil for diesel-electric traction, but it was not a commercial proposition. Diesel-electric coaches and loco-motives require costly imported heavy oils (except in Nigeria); nevertheless, greater efficiency of working has been achieved.

Railways were, indeed, the means of creating new horizons socially, politically and economically. They introduced many West Africans to wage-earning and mechanical skills. They united lands which had never before been one, and from that union nationalism arose. A wider economy was created, and new towns depending upon the railways developed, such as Kafanchan in northern Nigeria. Housing materials and foodstuffs could be widely distributed. Meat was introduced extensively into the forest zone; dried fish, kola nuts and European goods could be distributed in the interior.

Lines in ex-French and British West Africa have evolved in different ways as the result of contrasted historical, geographical and political circumstances. The French had penetrated eastwards up the Senegal and down the Niger Rivers. They were ultimately in possession of continuous territory, in which movement was relatively easy. Their railways were planned to supplement the navigable sections of the Senegal and Niger Rivers, and to link these lands with the Atlantic and Guinea coasts. The systems are officially known as the Dakar–Niger, Conakry–Niger,[1] Abidjan–Niger and Benin–Niger, even though the latter two do not reach the Niger River. Most lines have been built for local development and as parts of a general plan for economic integration within the former Federation of French West Africa.

By contrast, British West African railways were all built from the coast, within isolated colonies, as economic or political need arose. Much impetus for railway construction came from the Liverpool, Manchester and London Chambers of Commerce and from that vigorous and far-seeing Colonial Secretary,

[1] Now the railway of the Republic of Guinea.

Joseph Chamberlain. The common denominator in both French and British colonies was to secure effective political control of the interior, and to develop and retain within one's own colony as much trade as possible.

Provision of Railways and Railway Traffic in West Africa

Country	Length of railways in km.	Population per km. of track	Area in square km. per km. of track	Millions of net ton-kms. 1965	Millions of Passenger-kms. 1962
Senegal	992	3,276	299	302	291
Guinea	662	4,380	371	44 (1959)	46 (1959)
Sierra Leone	498	4,383	145	16 (1964)	43 (1964)
Ivory Coast	625	5,850	516	325	507
Ghana	963	6,985	247	353	498
Togo.	443	3,535	128	7	73
Dahomey	579	3,800	199	44	78
Nigeria	3,475	15,328	254	1,987	859

Road Transport. Roads were no alternative to railways until cheap and efficient lorries became available after the First World War. Even now road transport is complementary to rather than competitive with rail transport. Roads are costly to build and often more expensive to maintain than railways; and road transport may be interrupted in the wet season. Time-devouring ferries also often hinder road transport. It cannot compete with railways for all-season economic carriage of large low-value loads over great distances. Since this is the nature of most haulage in West Africa, road transport is best suited either to shorter hauls from door to door, to cross-

Provision of Roads in certain West African countries

Country	Total length of roads in kilometres	Population per km. of road	Area in square km. per km. of road
Mali	13,000	315	93
Upper Volta	16,662	275	16
Guinea	10,500	276	23
Sierra Leone	6,360	343	11
Liberia	2,720	371	41
Ivory Coast	28,000	131	12
Ghana	8,634	779	28
Togo	2,946	538	20
Dahomey	5,886	374	20
Nigeria	73,600	756	13

country routes, or to carriage in areas without railways. Most passengers prefer road transport because of its flexibility. Lorry transport is one of the most important private enterprises in West Africa, especially among Africans and Lebanese. Roads have been most developed in western Senegal, southern Ivory Coast, southern Ghana and in southern Nigeria.[1]

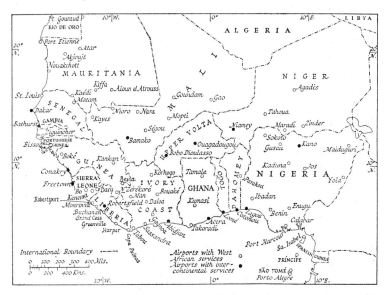

FIG. 30.—Airports with Inter-Continental or local West African services. Air routes are not shown, as these change frequently.

Air Transport. Until the Second World War air transport had hardly touched West Africa, but then the loss of the Mediterranean–Suez routeway, and the campaigns in North Africa, put West Africa on a new and vital supply air route. Airports such as Yundum (Bathurst), Hastings, Wellington and Lungi (all three near Freetown), Takoradi, Accra, Apapa (Lagos), Kano and Maiduguri were vastly improved, or built from nothing, as were many subsidiary airstrips in Ghana and Nigeria. That French West Africa was faithful to Vichy until early 1943 was a further incentive to the air defence of British West Africa. Only after French West Africa joined the

[1] For an excellent road map of West Africa, see *Michelin, Map*, No. 182.

Allies did much construction of airports take place there. The fine Dakar airport at Yoff dates from the end of the war, and was built with American aid.

War and peace needs do not necessarily coincide. Dakar, Accra and Kano benefited permanently and are West Africa's busiest airports. Yundum (Bathurst), the British strategic equivalent to Yoff, cannot rival it in peace. Again, the several Freetown airfields were vital to the defence of the naval base and Atlantic convoys, especially when Dakar was unfriendly, but all these airfields are unnecessary in peacetime. Lungi has alone been retained because it is away from the dangerous mountains behind Freetown, and its runway is the longest and firmest, but it suffers from being on the opposite side of the estuary from Freetown and has to be reached by a half-hour's launch journey from the city, or by light aircraft from Hastings, south-east of Freetown. Monrovia's intercontinental airport, built by the Americans after 1942, is fifty-five miles from the city. Another at Fisherman's Lake was discarded in peacetime, as was Apapa (Lagos).

Some twenty national airlines now serve West Africa, putting it within a day of Europe, Asia, North or South America, and South Africa. Passenger traffic is being increasingly taken by airlines, especially to and from Nigeria, which is at the far end of the sea-route, but at the nearer end of the air services. The same is true of ex-French West Africa, where the ships are particularly slow because of their many ports of call. Ships are patronised mainly by leisured passengers, cargo and second-class mail.

Internal air-services have developed remarkably. Major towns are linked by weekly or more frequent services. Air passages are sometimes cheaper than by rail or road, especially on cross-country routes. From Kano to Jos by train takes over twenty hours, but under an hour by air.

Climatic factors influence air services in several ways. The rainy season makes air navigation more difficult and dangerous, though accidents are very rare. However, this is also the season when less air services are required, as fewer Europeans are then in West Africa, and commodity trading is at a minimum. Where there are only grass runways, rain may put them out of action by waterlogging. Since prevailing winds are mainly

. The Fouta, or left bank
od plain of the Senegal
ver. Vegetation has to be
sistant to periodic flooding
lowed by drought. The
ht or Mauritanian flood
in is known as the Chemama.

36. On the left the Fort of St.
Louis, which changed hands so
often in Franco-British wars.
It is now a library. At the end
is a hotel, and on the right a
typical balconied house.

Cayor fishing village, with
oes and backed by sand
es, on the smooth sandy
t 38 miles north-east of
Cape Verde

38. Sahel Thorn Shrub on loose, saline, sandy soil at Richard Toll, before the irrigation scheme. Irrigation works here and in Mali have led to conflict between herdsmen, who can no longer pasture their herds as shown above, and the new farmers.

SENEGAL

39. The first 1,500 irrigated acres at Richard Toll. The town is on the left, by the Senegal River. Beyond the town is the Taouey River and Barrage.

40. The Barrage on t[h]e Taouey tributary of t[he] Senegal River. When t[he] Senegal floods, its wate[r] surge up this tributary a[nd] the sluice gates are open[ed] —generally from mid-Ju[ne] to mid-November. Ther[e] after they are closed [to] prevent the inlet of bracki[sh] tidal water.

either north-east or south-west, it is unnecessary to have run-ways in many directions.   Unfortunately behind the coast low clouds are common in early morning, so that aerodromes should be adjacent to the sea, where this phenomenon is at a minimum. An otherwise much more convenient site at Cotonou (Dahomey) had to be abandoned for this reason, and Ikeja airport, 12 miles north of Lagos, is from this point of view, less satisfactory than the earlier one at Apapa, although Ikeja has a longer runway.

Railways were pre-eminent as transport media in West Africa until about 1930, when the full challenge of road trans-port was evident.   That from air services became severe about 1950.

It is important that wise road, rail, river and air policies be pursued without harmful overlapping, restriction or subsidy, but with impartial co-ordination.

Backward areas of potential value can develop rapidly under the influence of efficient road services, especially when linked with railways or good rivers.   All populated and developed areas obviously need roads.   Air services are most helpful for the development of quick cross-country routes for passengers. Nevertheless, railways and rivers (where available) can carry heavy and bulky commodities most economically over great distances in all seasons.   Bulk transport is the basic require-ment for West African trade.   These considerations point to the need for a transport plan for each area, worked out in relation to its physical, social and economic geography.

BIBLIOGRAPHY

R. J. HARRISON CHURCH, 'The Pattern of Transport in British West Africa', in *Geographical Essays on British Tropical Lands*, Philip, 1956; 'The Evolution of Railways in French and British West Africa', *Compte Rendu du XVIe Congrès International de Géographie*, Lisbon, 1949, Tome IV, pp. 95–114; 'Trans-Saharan Railway Projects' in *London Essays in Geography*, edited by L. D. Stamp and S. W. Wooldridge, 1951; and 'Geographical Factors in the Development of Transport in Africa', *United Nations Transport and Communications Review*, Vol. 2, No. 3, 1949, pp. 3–11.

P. R. GOULD, *The Development of the Transportation Pattern in Ghana*, Depart-ment of Geography, Northwestern University, 1960.

E. K. HAWKINS, *Road Transport in Nigeria*, 1958.

G

E. J. TAAFFE, R. L. MORRILL and P. R. GOULD, 'Transport Expansion in Underdeveloped Countries: A Comparative Analysis', *Geographical Review*, 1963, pp. 503–29.

B. E. THOMAS, 'Railways and Ports in French West Africa', *Economic Geography*, 1957, pp. 1–15, and *Transport and Physical Geography in West Africa*, National Academy of Sciences, Washington, 1960.

H. P. WHITE, 'The Ports of West Africa—some geographical considerations', *Tijdschrift voor Economische en Sociale Geografie*, 1959, pp. 1–8.

GILBERT WALKER, *Traffic and Transport in Nigeria: the example of an underdeveloped tropical territory*, Colonial Research Studies No. 27, U.K. Colonial Office, 1959.

Statistical and Economic Review, United Africa Company, September 1954, March 1955 and March 1961.

Chapter 10

POPULATION DISTRIBUTION AND MOVEMENTS [1]

THE population of West Africa is here examined from the geographer's viewpoint: namely, distribution and spatial movements, and their correlation with the physical and economic environments. R. R. Kuczynski, *A Demographic Survey of the British Colonial Empire*, Vol. 1, *British West Africa*, 1948, is an encyclopædic source concerning the reliability of censuses. The ethnographic aspects are dealt with in studies of the major peoples published by the International African Institute (London), and in other studies. Maps on the 1/1 million scale of tribal distributions and population density have been published by the Institut Français d'Afrique Noire (Dakar). J. Richard-Molard in his *L'Afrique Occidentale Française*, Chapter II, gives short accounts of the various races, languages, religions, ethnic groups, their past history and present modes of life in that area.

Census figures are unreliable for Africa because of widespread illiteracy and dispersion of the population. When censuses are taken, people often fear heavier taxation or have a superstitious dread of counting, and methods of enumeration have often been bad. The figures for French West Africa probably have a higher degree of reliability, as censuses are taken every five years. Conscription and Direct Rule also lead to fuller demographic information.

Areal Distribution. West Africa has the highest average population density in Tropical Africa, yet its population pattern has no simple explanation. Population distribution is not, as in Europe, the result of long trial and error over many centuries by advanced peoples, in each type of environment.

[1] For the population by political divisions, see Chapter 11 and subsequent chapters.

Tradition is stronger in West Africa than in most temperate regions. Attachment to the soil, even in poor areas, and dislike of nearby fertile but non-traditional areas, are important factors. Thus the Ibo of south-eastern Nigeria are densely concentrated in a mediocre environment, but to the east are richer and thinly peopled lands. The same is true of fairly heavy concentrations on infertile *bowé* around Labé in Guinea, of the Mossi concentration in the Upper Volta, of the Kabrai in the Atacora Mountains of northern Togo, and many more.

Fertile areas were often left unpeopled or only thinly occupied, either because of slave raiding or the fear of it, e.g. in the Bole region of north-western Ghana. Tribal conflict also has depopulated many areas; hence the thinly peopled ' no-man's land ' or ' shatter-zones ' between the well-populated old Dahomey state and Yorubaland, between the latter and Benin, between Kano and Bornu, and many more.

Once the population is reduced by these or other factors to about 12 per square mile in country of few streams, or nearer 70 per square mile where there are many streams, tsetse fly infestation often becomes so severe as to make the area uninhabitable. A certain minimum population is required to control fly and make habitation possible.

Most Africans live near the soil, so that the correlation between water supplies and population is sometimes close. Thus there are the peopled valleys of the Senegal, Niger and Sokoto, where tsetse are few. But elsewhere dwelling in such areas has often meant danger from mosquitoes, simulium and tsetse flies, as well as from floods. Ibo country again provides a paradox, of a densely peopled area with very poor water supplies (see p. 444).

Defence considerations, important in the siting of settlements everywhere in the world at one time or another, have been very significant in West Africa. This was especially true in the days of inter-tribal warfare, but tradition is so strong that most peoples remain loyal to the ancient nuclei, though the original siting reasons have passed away. Ibadan arose as the Yoruba war camp around Mapo Hill, from which there are excellent views. The Somba live in the poor hill-country of the Atacora Mountains in Dahomey, the Dan and the Labe

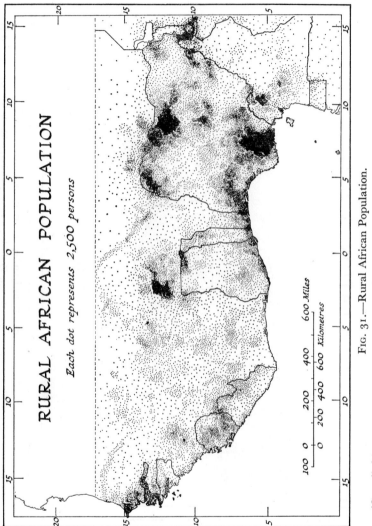

RURAL AFRICAN POPULATION

Each dot represents 2,500 persons

FIG. 31.—Rural African Population.

(Compiled by Glenn. T. Trewartha and Wilbur Zelinsky, and reproduced with their kind permission.)

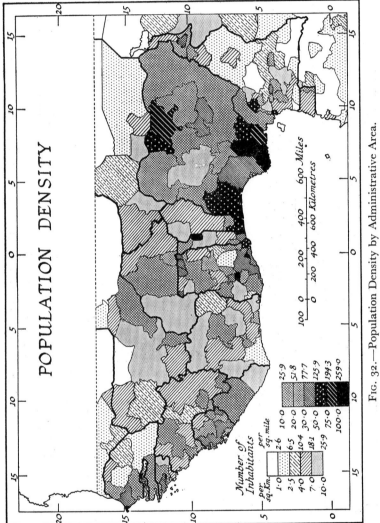

Fig. 32.—Population Density by Administrative Area.

(Compiled by Glenn T. Trewartha and Wilbur Zelinsky, and reproduced with their kind permission.)

in the scarp fastnesses of Bandiagara, and the primitive Birom were pushed on to the agriculturally poor Jos Plateau. The intense peopling of the Fouta Djallon by the Fulani may be partly explicable in terms of easier defence, healthier conditions and the chance to remain cattle-keepers, though settled ones, with Ndama cattle rather than with their traditional Zebu humped cattle.

In other places the defence factor, though real and fundamental, is less obvious. Many settlements were established close to look-outs, to which retreat could be made if necessary, as at Savalou and Savé in Dahomey. Likewise the Somono and Sorko first lived near the Niger River, to use it for escape if attacked; and the lagoons of the Ivory Coast, Togo and Dahomey have been favoured by some peoples for the same reason.

The varying abilities of peoples in the organisation of their political, social and economic affairs have also been important factors. Thus the Kano area is densely peopled because first the Hausa rulers, then the Fulani Emirs, and later the British, provided settled government. With this fundamental prerequisite, the alert Hausa farmer has made much of available water and of the fairly fertile light soils, farming them more intensively than in any other large region in West Africa. The other Emirates of Nigeria generally have more than the average population density of that latitude, for the same reasons of defence and settled government. They have, however, less than for Kano because of poorer water supplies, except along the Sokoto River.

Traditional attachment to a state, like that already alluded to for towns, is also strong. Thus New Juaben, formed by Ashanti people outside Ashanti, is a small state around Koforidua. It has the highest rural density of population in Ghana —671 per square mile. Had the state been larger, the density of population would have been far less.

One of the most arresting features of the West African population map is the existence of the poorly peopled Middle Belt, on the outer fringes of the forest, a belt which may be followed from the upper Niger eastwards through all the Guinea Coast lands, roughly between $7\frac{1}{2}°$ N. and $10°$ N. This belt, which has few natural resources and produces no considerable exports, suffered from slave-raiding from the north and from the south, and has all the diseases and difficulties of forest and savannah, with no compensating advantages.

Efforts have been made to re-populate this zone, notably with Mossi in the central Ivory Coast and with Kabrai in central Togo. Roads and railways have also done something to even out or relocate population, but no major alteration has taken place; nor is this likely for a long time.

Population Pressure on the Land. A matter of increasing urgency in some areas is pressure of population on the land, which European intervention has tended to increase, often through specifically humanitarian work. Tribal wars have ended, many tropical diseases have ceased to take great toll of life, modern communications bring in relief supplies if famine occurs, and infantile mortality has diminished, so that populations are increasing. At the same time the land, which formerly had to produce only subsistence crops, must now carry export crops as well. The fallow period has been drastically shortened, land area per head is less, and soil erosion has greatly increased. Land pressure and soil erosion will increase until improved methods of farming are found which Africans can and will accept.

Population pressure may exist in Ibo and Tiv areas of eastern and northern Nigeria respectively, in the Mossi country of the Upper Volta and around Zuarungu in the north-eastern corner of Ghana.

Labour Routes. The advent of Europeans has profoundly affected population distribution, by re-directing trade to and from the Atlantic and Guinea Coasts. Previously, economic activation had been by the Arabs from the Sahara towards the forest fringes, and by the states of the Niger Valley into the forest, e.g. for Ashanti and Baoulé gold. The new importance of the European coastal trading points ultimately led to dense new clusters of very mixed population in more or less new settlements, such as St. Louis, Dakar, Freetown and Accra.

More influential has been the cultivation of cash crops and the development of mining, with consequent new clusters of population, e.g. in the groundnut districts of Senegambia and the mining towns of Ghana. From poorer areas of the Mali Republic, Portuguese Guinea and Guinea 'navé-tanes' or 'strange farmers' move annually into Senegal or the Gambia to grow their own groundnuts, or to harvest those of resident farmers. Likewise, cocoa and coffee cultivation in the Ivory Coast, cocoa cultivation and gold mining in Ghana, and tin mining in Nigeria, have given rise to well-defined labour routes, especially from the poor and densely peopled Mossi country of the Upper Volta and other poor areas. In Ghana there are 350–400,000 migrant workers.

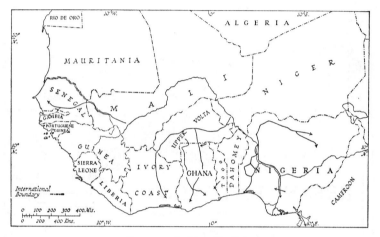

FIG. 33.—Labour Routes.

They are attracted by wages to provide bride money, by lower prices, simpler administration, the love of adventure and the mark of distinction which travel confers. Most of the movement is temporary, but some is permanent. There is little outward movement from Ghana and Nigeria, though some 20,000 Ibo work on plantations in Fernando Po, and others in Continental Spanish Guinea and Gabon. Kru from Liberia, Sierra Leone and the Ivory Coast are found working on ships in the West African trade.

Towns. Because of inter-tribal wars in the past and the occurrence of fly and disease, trade routes were much more sharply restricted in location than they are now. Many towns owe their origin partly or entirely to being well-defended halting places on these routes, e.g. Kano adjacent to its two

prominent hills used as look-outs.   Other examples are Zinder
and Agadès.

Caravan halts were especially important if they were also
the place for change of mode of transport, e.g. from camel to
donkeys, horses or men—as at Kano—or were at the junction
of varied regions, e.g. Bouaké.   Some are now much less
significant, such as Odienné, because of the decay of an old

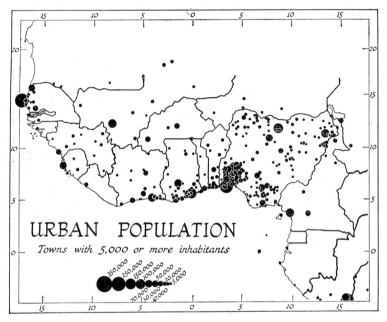

FIG. 34.—Urban Population.

(Compiled by Glenn T. Trewartha and Wilbur Zelinsky, and reproduced with
their kind permission.)

trade route, just as some former Roman towns have decayed in
Britain or France.

Religious centres are sometimes significant, especially in
Muslim areas.   Such is the case with Djenné and Mopti.
Many towns were state capitals, such as Gao, Ségou, Ouaga-
dougou, Kumasi, Abomey, Kano and Benin.

European conquests led to many new towns, resulting from
the new political and economic order.   Administrative towns
were established, such as Kaduna, Buea, Bingerville and, later,

Abidjan. New significance was given to small centres by the system of ' District ' or ' Cercle ' administration. Hill stations for European officials were established at Dalaba (Guinea), Hill Station (Freetown), Jos (Nigeria), and Moka (Fernando Po).

Early European trading-points and forts such as Elmina and Gorée, and gum ' escales ' like Dagana along the Senegal, are not always of great significance now. They have given place to countless new trading centres. There are important ports, such as Dakar, Conakry, Freetown, Takoradi, Cotonou and Port Harcourt; or new inland centres like Nsawam or New Tafo in Ghana. Railways have led to the creation of new towns, as at Baro on the Niger River and Kafanchan in Nigeria, Kindia and Mamou (Guinea). Riverside settlements (some being ports) have also arisen because of new trade, such as Lokoja, Koulikoro and Kayes. Possibly the most striking examples of new towns are those which depend mainly upon mining, such as Jos and Bukuru (tin— Nigeria), Prestea (gold—Ghana) and Nsuta (manganese— Ghana). As industrial developments increase, so this process will speed up, often with attendant housing and social difficulties.

There were more towns in West Africa in pre-colonial days than anywhere else in Tropical Africa. To the old towns of the dry savannahs and Yorubaland have been added the numerous towns which have developed elsewhere from colonial and other contact. In the larger ones there is often severe congestion, as well as poor and insanitary housing, and long journeys to work are necessary. This is especially the case in Lagos. On the other hand, the new town of Tema in Ghana has been built on garden city lines, and is a notable example of a spacious layout within which there will soon be well over 100,000 people, mostly well housed, and living near their work and close to varied facilities. Such concepts have also been applied to some new or replanned districts of Ibadan, Lagos, Kumasi, Abidjan, Freetown, Dakar and other towns. There is now a need to encourage the location of industry in some of the smaller towns, so enlarging their populations and stemming the flow of people to the congested urban clusters.

Non-African Population. African education was more generally developed in the ex-British lands, so that more Africans were in senior posts. European administrators have been replaced by Africans in almost all government departments, except in the Ivory Coast, and non-Africans are now mainly technical advisers, business executives, teachers and missionaries. They are least numerous in the radical rates of Guinea and Mali, and most numerous in the conservative Ivory Coast.

Non-Africans could not own land in British West Africa, but were permitted to do so in other countries (except Liberia), where planters sometimes established themselves. They still have some importance in the Ivory Coast, and especially on the islands of the Bight of Biafra. In Senegal and the Ivory Coast Europeans continue to own or manage many hotels, cafés, shops, business and industrial enterprises to an extent unknown in British West Africa even in colonial days.

In most countries the non-African population has become far more varied since independence. It is no longer dominantly from the former colonial power, but usually includes experts from many other European countries, Russia, China or Taiwan, Israel and America. Newly independent countries are keen to use the experience of countries which have themselves faced formidable problems and adopted new methods or techniques in solving them. Advice and help have also been sought from United Nations agencies, so that experts from many countries now make short visits to West African states. These and other visitors have stimulated a notable development of hotels in the major towns.

The ' Syrians ', as they are almost always called, are, in fact, predominantly Lebanese, and number 31,000. They are mainly the small traders and shopkeepers of West Africa, particularly up-country, although some have built up large and varied enterprises in the major cities. Indian merchants are also to be found in ex-British states and in Portuguese provinces.

BIBLIOGRAPHY

Other than works cited above, see:

Cartes Ethno-Démographiques de l'Afrique Occidentale, I.F.A.N., Dakar, 1 : 1 million scale, with text.

GLENN T. TREWARTHA and WILBUR ZELINSKY, ' Population Patterns in Tropical Africa ', *Annals of the Association of American Geographers*, Vol.

XLIV, 1954, pp. 135–62, from which most of my maps have been taken and which has an exhaustive bibliography.
K. M. BARBOUR and R. M. PROTHERO, *Essays on African Population*, 1961.
R. MANSELL PROTHERO, *Migrants and Malaria*, 1965.
R. MANSELL PROTHERO, ' Migratory Labour from North-Western Nigeria ', *Africa*, Vol. 27, 1957, pp. 251–61.
J. ROUCH, ' Migrations from French Territories into Ghana ', *Africa*, Vol. 28, 1958, pp. 156–9.
Y. URVOY, *Petit Atlas Ethno-Démographique du Soudan entre Sénégal et Tchad*, I.F.A.N., Paris, 1942. Maps 1 : 5,500,000 with text.
Special Number on Urbanism in West Africa, *The Sociological Review*, Vol. 7, No. 1, July 1959.

For material on or maps of population in the individual lands of West Africa, see Chapters 12–28 inclusive.

3

THE POLITICAL DIVISIONS

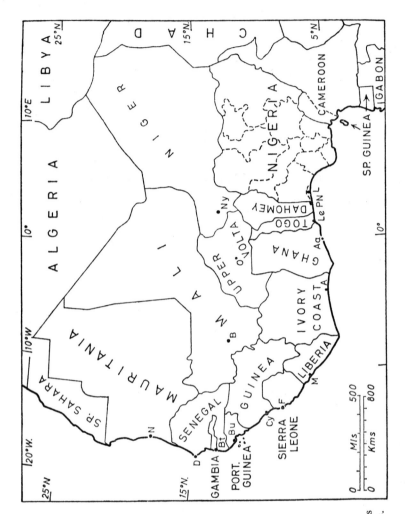

Fig. 35.—Political divisions and their capitals.

Chapter 11

GENERAL INTRODUCTION TO THE POLITICAL DIVISIONS [1]

Nature's divisions in West Africa trend mainly west–east, so that contrasts occur in a south–north direction. Economic activities and social and political organisation are frequently in close accord with natural regions.

By contrast, most political boundaries were hastily drawn between 1885 and 1919, with scant regard for natural and human patterns. Almost all boundaries are highly artificial geometric lines, or follow rivers or watersheds or other divides which are rarely ethnic.

Boundaries often reflect the limit of military penetration, e.g. the northern boundary of Ghana. Many are the result of compromise, such as the north-western boundary of Nigeria. Others are the consequence of exchange, such as the British cession of the Los Islands, off Conakry, Guinea, in exchange for the present north-western Sierra Leone boundary.

Rarely have international lines been drawn to respect the unity of African peoples. Thus the Niger Republic–Nigeria boundary divides the Hausa people. Even more cynical was the deliberate partition of the Kru people by the Ivory Coast–Liberia boundary, so that French West Africa might secure some of these sea-loving people, so useful on West African ships.[2] Less deliberate but more drastic was the partition of the Ewe between Togo under French Mandate and Togo under British Mandate in 1919, and continued as Trusteeships from 1946 until 1960 and 1957 respectively.[3]

The already unsatisfactory Niger Republic–Nigeria boundary

---

[1] See Fig. 33, p. 169.
[2] Sir Harry Johnston, *Liberia*, 1906, Vol. 1, pp. 280–96, and R. Earle Anderson, *Liberia—America's African Friend*, pp. 83–95.
[3] See Chapter 24, pp. 417–19.

also bisects ancient natural trade routes. Far more serious in this respect is the highly artificial Gambian boundary composed of arcs and straight lines, which shuts off the Gambia River from its natural hinterland.[1] The fine lagoon waterway between Porto-Novo, the capital of Dahomey, and Lagos, the Nigerian Federal capital,[2] is crossed by the Dahomey–Nigeria boundary.

The mainly irrational boundaries limit the following political divisions: [3]

Country	Capital	Area in sq. miles	Population	Ann. rate of increase, 1958–66	Density per sq. m.
SENEGAL	Dakar	76,104	3,580,000	2·4	47·0
GAMBIA	Bathurst	4,008	336,000	1·9	83·8
MAURITANIA . . .	Nouakchott	419,121	1,070,000	1·6	2·6
MALI	Bamako	464,752	4,654,000	2·2	10·0
UPPER VOLTA . . .	Ouagadougou	105,811	4,955,000	2·4	46·8
NIGER	Niamey	458,874	3,433,000	3·2	7·5
PORTUGUESE GUINEA .	Bissau	13,948	529,000	0·2	37·9
GUINEA	Conakry	94,926	3,608,000	2·8	38·0
SIERRA LEONE . . .	Freetown	27,925	2,403,000	1·2	86·1
LIBERIA	Monrovia	43,000	1,090,000	1·6	25·4
IVORY COAST . . .	Abidjan	124,471	3,920,000	3·0	31·5
GHANA	Accra	92,100	7,945,000	2·7	86·3
TOGO	Lomé	22,002	1,680,000	2·7	76·4
DAHOMEY	Porto-Novo	44,684	2,410,000	2·7	53·9
FEDERATION OF NIGERIA .	Lagos	356,669	58,600,000	2·0	164·3
FERNANDO PO and ANNOBON .	Santa Isabel	786	74,000	3·2	94·2
SÃO TOMÉ and PRÍNCIPE .	São Tomé	372	61,000	-0·4	164·0
TOTAL WEST AFRICA .		2,349,553	100,348,000	2·2	42·7

From 1904–1958 French West Africa was the largest political unit of West Africa and of the French Union. The Federation broke up in 1958–9 with the independence of Guinea and the later decision of the other seven members to become independent republics, some linked by a Customs Union. Ghana, Guinea and Mali formed a ' Union ', whilst the Ivory Coast, Upper Volta, Niger and Dahomey created the Benin-Sahel Entente, which Togo joined in late 1965.

The oldest French settlements are the islets of Gorée (off Dakar) and St. Louis (Senegal Estuary), which were founded in 1659. From them the French later penetrated up the

---

[1] See Chapter 13, p. 216; and the present author's *Modern Colonization*, pp. 112–15.

[2] See Chapter 25, p. 433; and the present author's *Modern Colonization*, p. 116.

[3] Statistics are from the United Nations *Demographic Yearbook*, 1967. Population totals are estimates for 1966.

Senegal and down the Niger Rivers. These provided west–east routeways; and the Sahel zone, through which they partly flow, is one which facilitates movement and has fewer hazards from disease than many others.

French ingress from the Guinea Coast was subsidiary to the greater line of movement from west to east, and to British lines of advance from that coast. Consequently, French West Africa had its main axis and extent in poor Saharan, Sahel and Savannah lands, with lesser projections to the richer forested Guinea Coast. French West Africa thus had long lines of communication in relatively unproductive country, and was very continental, with a high proportion of land to coastline. Indeed, Mali, the Upper Volta and the Niger Republic are land-locked states.

Ex-British West Africa, a mere expression covering four separate countries, developed from the richer forested lands. The politically and economically diverse and generally richer lands of ex-British West Africa need much shorter lines of communication, and have relatively greater coast lines, far greater populations and overseas trade.

The ex-French lands are rather over dependent upon a few products. The dry zone countries of Senegal, Mauritania, Mali, Upper Volta and the Niger Republic depend overwhelmingly upon groundnuts and livestock, except for Mauritania's iron ore and Senegal's phosphates. Dahomey relies upon oil palm produce. Only the Ivory Coast and Guinea have more varied economies, the former with coffee, cocoa, bananas, timber and diamonds, the latter with coffee, bananas, bauxite, alumina and diamonds. These two countries have good potentials.

Contrasted political organisation and economic regulation have led to differing economies. Thus, plantations established by non-Africans have been permitted and encouraged outside of ex-British territories. Plantation-produced bananas and other fruits are significant exports from Guinea and the Ivory Coast, but are unimportant exports from the non-plantation lands of ex-British Nigeria, Ghana and Sierra Leone. Cocoa and coffee are also partly produced on non-African plantations in the Ivory Coast. Cocoa, the chief export of Spanish Fernando Po and of Portuguese São Tomé and Príncipe, also comes

almost entirely from large non-African plantations, as does
rubber (the main agricultural export of Liberia) from the vast
Firestone Company plantations.   Independence is encouraging
African plantations.

Mineral production was slight in French West Africa until
1953, largely because of the unwillingness of private French
capital to invest in such enterprise.   Even now, iron, bauxite
and diamonds are won in the successor republics largely with
foreign capital, often aided by French public rather than
private capital.

Political independence, nationalisation in Guinea, and fears
of possible nationalisation in Ghana and Mali, are said to have
caused some hesitancy among private investors towards new developments in those lands.   Yet before it broke up French West
Africa had received some ' refugee ' capital from France sent to
an area reckoned as safer financially than the mother country.

The economic development of Liberia, Portuguese and
Spanish territories suffered in the past from shortage of capital,
as well as from traditionalist methods or narrow conceptions of
the means of development.

The economies of ex-French West Africa, and of the Portuguese and Spanish territories, were far more closely integrated
with their metropolitan countries than was that of ex-British
West Africa with the United Kingdom.   Production has been
heavily subsidised, prices were frequently far above world levels,
and exports were commonly directed to protected markets in
the metropolitan country or its dependent territories.   Such
was the case with groundnut oil extracted and refined in
Senegal, which enjoyed, like other crops, a protected market in
France and the Community.   Cocoa from Fernando Po is
heavily protected in Spain, whilst banana exports from Fernando
Po were once prohibited in favour of Canary Island production.

British West Africa was not free from restrictions, but those
that prevailed resulted from the decisions of the African peoples
themselves, rather than from those of the British Government
in London.   Economic regulations in British territories proceeded from the bottom upwards.   In non-British territories,
control is still tighter, and proceeds from the top downwards.
In consequence, economies are often less rational, and *per capita*
commerce and income are lower.

British political aims in West Africa were in complete contrast to those pursued by Spain, Portugal and France until 1955. These three powers sought to attach their territories in a close political and economic union with the mother country. Portuguese territories are Provinces of Overseas Portugal, but the French ones are now free republics. The culture and outlook of these mother countries were diffused widely, so that as many Africans as possible should become assimilated or at least closely associated and identified with the protecting power. African customs and institutions were given little or no encouragement, and African languages but little used in education. These policies have tended to produce an African élite sometimes sympathetic to the governing or former power but divorced from African life; the majority of the populations have had limited initiative.

British policy, by contrast, was directed to achieving the political and economic independence of overseas territories. Political and economic links with the United Kingdom were of the loosest kind, diverse and constantly changing. Political, social and economic power rested with African elected Legislative Councils and with generally wholly African Executive Councils drawn from the dominant African political party. Needless to say, the aim of such bodies was to develop African culture, institutions and languages; but this was equally British policy. The élite in British territories have sometimes been unsympathetic to Britain until self-government was achieved, but it is an élite far less divorced, or not divorced at all, from African life.[1]

Contrasted political aims and methods make international political co-operation difficult. But international technical co-operation has grown enormously since the Second World War in such matters as communications, customs control, labour, trade and the control of human, animal and plant pests. International conferences in West Africa on such matters of common concern are happily frequent.

In the following chapters, the countries are analysed as they

[1] For a fuller discussion of political policies, see Chapter 33, ' Policies and Problems in Africa ', by the present author, in W. G. East and A. E. Moodie (Editors), *The Changing World*, 1956. Chapters 30 and 31 are analyses of the history and boundaries of Africa.

occur geographically. Thus, there are first the relatively dry lands of Senegal, the Gambia (so much an enclave of Senegal), Mauritania, Mali, the Upper Volta and the Niger. Then follows the wetter country of Portuguese Guinea and the other countries to the south-east.

BIBLIOGRAPHY

See references cited in footnotes above:

R. J. HARRISON CHURCH, *Environment and Policies in West Africa*, 1963.

On ex-French West Africa (A.O.F.) see:
A. SECK and R. MONDJANNAGNI, *L'Afrique Occidentale*, 1967.
VIRGINIA THOMPSON and RICHARD ADLOFF, *French West Africa*, 1958.
J. RICHARD-MOLARD, *L'Afrique Occidentale Française*, 1956.
G. CAPOT-REY, *Le Sahara Français*, 1956.

All the above have extensive bibliographies. Also see references in the following territorial chapters.

Also *Bulletin du Comité d'Etudes Historiques et Scientifiques de L'A.O.F.*, and, since 1939, the *Bulletin, Mémoires, Notes* and *Annales Africaines* published by the Institut Français d'Afrique Noire, Dakar.

Also *Rapport Annuel sur l'A.O.F. aux Nations Unies, Annuaire Statistique de l'A.O.F.* and *Tableaux Economiques*.

MAPS

G. GRANDIDIER, *Atlas des Colonies Françaises*, 1934.

The following maps are all published by the Institut Géographique National or the Service Géographique de l'A.O.F., unless otherwise stated.
Topographic:
  1 : 7,500,000, 1 : 5,000,000, 1 : 2,500,000 and 1 : 1,000,000 in various
    styles and colours. French West Africa on one sheet, 1947–59.
  1 : 500,000 covers almost all French West Africa. Improved versions
    are appearing.
  1 : 200,000 is the best map.
  1 : 100,000, 1 : 50,000, 1 : 20,000 and 1 : 10,000 available for some areas.

Vertical Air Photographs:
    1 : 5,000, 1 : 10,000, 1 : 15,000, 1 : 20,000 or 1 : 25,000.   Available for
    major towns.

Geological:
    All by Service des Mines, Dakar.
    1 : 1,000,000, 1 : 500,000, 1 : 200,000 and 1 : 20,000 (Dakar).   Each
    with a memoir.   Cover rather scattered areas.

Vegetation:
    1 : 200,000.   Several sheets.   Office de la Recherche Scientifique Outre-
    Mer, 1951.

Livestock:
    1 : 5,000,000 Six maps—Eleveurs, Densité des Bovins, Densité des ovins
    et caprins, Viande consommable, Commerce du Bétail, Zones
    d'Elevage.   Office de la Recherche Scientifique Outre-Mer, 1945.
    Also 1 : 5,000,000 map of Trypanosomes pathogènes by Laboratoire
    Central de l'Elevage, Dakar, 1952.
    1 : 3,000,000 maps of Tsetse flies, 1949.

Population:
    1 : 5,000,000 Density of Population.   Office de la Recherche Scientifique
    Outre-Mer, 1944.
    1 : 1,000,000 Six Ethnic sheets and Six Density sheets, of which some have
    appeared.   Institut Français d'Afrique Noire, Dakar.   Y. Urvoy,
    Petit Atlas ethno-démographique du Soudan, 1942.

Communications:
    1 : 3,000,000 Michelin Map No. 182.   An excellent general motoring
    map.

See also under individual territories.

Chapter 12

SENEGAL—THE ANCIENT BASE[1]

THIS state, with an area of 76,104 square miles and a population in 1966 of 3,580,000, is appropriate as the first ex-French area to be analysed. It has fewer people and a lower density of population than some other parts of former French West Africa, but is still outstanding in some ways.

The islands of St. Louis in the Senegal Estuary and of Gorée off modern Dakar were the first areas in West Africa to be colonised by the French. From the Senegal River, the upper Niger was reached, and the French Sudan and Niger lands were conquered.

Senegal is a leading world commercial producer of groundnuts and has large groundnut oil factories. These products are still the largest export from Senegal, despite the development of phosphates, tuna fishing, and considerable industry especially near Dakar. While the search for oil has so far been unrewarding, small amounts of natural gas have been found which may be used industrially. Dakar is one of the finest ports of Africa and is of importance, too, in world strategy. It was the federal capital from 1904 until 1959, but is now the capital only of Senegal.

Nevertheless, this country is potentially less rich than the Ivory Coast, which has outstripped Senegal in all but strategic supremacy. Much of central and eastern Senegal is semi-desert, where water may be found only expensively at great depths. Even in the settled zones, water is often very scarce in the dry season. There has been severe degradation of the soils first tilled for groundnut export between St. Louis and Dakar; but for this these lands might more readily have been developed as a source of vegetables and fruit during the European winter, in competition with North African supplies.

[1] M. Paul Pélissier, formerly of the University of Dakar, who guided me in most of Senegal, has also made most valuable suggestions concerning this chapter.

CLIMATE [1]

Senegal has sharply contrasted coastal and interior climates, well shown in the figures for Dakar, Ziguinchor, Tambacounda and Kayes, given in Chapter 4.

The Casamance coast has a South-west Coast Monsoonal Climate; its hinterland has the Southern Savannah type.

The rest of the coast is exceptionally equable, not only for the normal reasons of proximity to water, and the usual after-noon sea breezes and nocturnal land ones, but also because

(a) the north-north-easterly Marine Trade winds bring a refreshing coolness and greater humidity during the dry season;

(b) the land breeze, vigorous in the dry season, strengthens the Marine Trade winds by night;

(c) the exceptionally cool waters of the Canary Current also lower temperatures.

Although rainfall may be low, effective humidity is high. Temperatures are much lower than in the interior, the daily and annual range are less, and there is more movement in the air. Thus the Senegal Coastal Climate is much more easily tolerated by Europeans than are most West African climates.

By contrast, interior Senegal has the Southern Savannah, Savannah or Southern Sahel climates; and is subjected to the usual alternation of intensely desiccating north-easterly Harmattan winds, with a short season of wet south-westerly ones. There is the usual diminution in rainfall, thinning of vegetation and lowering of the water-table from south to north.

Like all areas near the northern limit of the South-westerlies, Senegal suffers from extremely variable rainfall. St. Louis had 5 inches of rain in 1903 and 26 inches in 1912. Dakar had 15 inches in 1937 and 27 inches the following year. Further-more, while rainfall for a year may seem normal in amount, it varies greatly in its onset and termination, especially in central and northern Senegal. Finally, if the rains cease early the groundnut may fail to secure its necessary 110–25 growing days.

[1] A detailed work of reference on climate, geology, soils and vegetation is J. Trochain, *La Végétation du Sénégal*, Institut Français d'Afrique Noire, 1940.

GEOLOGY AND RELIEF [1]

Though Senegal is bordered on the east and south-east by Pre-Cambrian and Primary rocks which give higher and bolder relief, most of the territory was occupied by Upper Cretaceous and later seas, until their withdrawal at the end of the Eocene period. These and later deposits floor the monotonous plains which rarely rise above 200 feet. Earth movement and possible faulting caused the higher relief of the Thiès Plateau and its scarp, and the shallow synclines of Cayor, Baol and Sine-Saloum.

Retreat of these seas coincided with Tertiary volcanic activity at Cape Manuel and Gorée. The elegant 'plateau' residential area of Dakar is situated on basalt rocks and these also protect the harbour, constructed on the adjacent flat and soft Quaternary sands.

In Quaternary times, upward movement has been responsible for raised beaches. More volcanic activity took place in the Cape Verde Peninsula, this time at the Mamelles. Their rounded form (the name means breasts), and the fact that lava from them is found over fossilised laterite, proves their youth.

A former wetter climate was undoubtedly responsible for relic valleys found in the Ferlo, for considerable erosion in the plains of western Senegal, and for the transport and deposition of clay in the Sine-Saloum Delta.

Following that wetter period, there was a vast carpeting of loose wind-borne sands in north-east–south-west trending dunes in western Senegal, which thus has a gently undulating surface. Tertiary and Cretaceous deposits are rarely visible except where they outcrop in cliffs, e.g. at Cape Naze and Cape Rouge, south-east of Dakar, or in the Thiès scarp and in the lower valley of the Ferlo.

The only other relief features are the live coastal dunes, extending north-east from Cape Verde. They also trend south-west to north-east, and are often interspersed by clay

---

[1] Consult topographic maps on scales of 1 : 100,000 or 1 : 200,000 of *Service Géographique de l'Afrique Occidentale Française* ; 1 : 1,000,000 geological maps and accompanying *Notices Explicatives* of the Service des Mines, and the *Atlas des Colonies Françaises*.

depressions with generally fresh water lakes or *niayes*, fringed by quite luxuriant vegetation.

MAJOR REGIONS

THE FOUTA is the left bank flood-plain of the Senegal River, between Bakel and Dagana, known on the Mauritanian bank as the Chemama (p. 231).

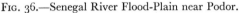

FIG. 36.—Senegal River Flood-Plain near Podor.

Heights in metres.   Intermittent streams shown by dotted lines.   (From Podor sheet of Carte Régulière d'A.O.F., 1940.)

The Senegal Valley (see Fig. 36) is 6–12 miles wide and often contains several streams.   The Senegal River also divides, e.g. to enclose the Ile à Morfil (Fig. 39), which averages 300 by 8 miles.

The Fouta has grey loamy soils, unlike the sand of adjacent regions, and a greater cover of Sahel Savannah.   Upon the retreat of the annual floods, it is fairly intensively cultivated for millet by the sedentary Toucouleur, as well as by sedentary Fulani. At the end of the cropping season, cattle are brought in by nomadic Fulani and by Maure, until the floods return. Thus, this region is important to nomadic and fixed peoples, and is sharply distinguished from neighbouring regions.

Towns such as Dagana, Podor and Matam are markets for millet, groundnuts and gum, though gum from the Sudan has killed much of the latter ancient trade.

Several points along the river are the scenes of experiment by the *Mission d'Amenagement du Sénégal*. At Guédé, 80 miles upstream from Richard Toll, is an irrigation scheme of some 2,500 acres on the edge of the flood-plain. A 6 mile long embankment surrounds the project and water is pumped into 12 miles of canals. A thousand acres are planned for irrigated rice. Of the lower areas, 625 acres produce two food crops annually—rice and millet, and 875 acres are given over to dry season crops or drainage works. These 1,500 acres are irrigated by gravity. This scheme provides African colonists with huts, rations, cloth and tools. Again, in the Ile à Morfil, immediately south-west of Boghé, flood waters are controlled for millet cultivation.

THE OUALO (SENEGAL DELTA). At Richard Toll ('the garden of Richard', Governor 1822–6), the head of the delta, the Senegal breaks up into several distributaries, especially when in flood. In the Oualo there are also innumerable intermittent or abandoned courses or *marigots*, relic dunes and swamps. To the west these are saline, and about 5,000 tons of salt are exploited annually at Gandiole (Fig. 37) near the Senegal Estuary for use by St. Louis fishermen.

Powerful longshore drift, the north-east Marine Trades and strong waves, backed by the greatest fetch of open water, combine to turn the mouth of the Senegal southward and to maintain its ever-changing sandspit, the *Langue de Barbarie*, now some 15 miles long but with an average breadth of under 100 yards.

The estuary of the Senegal has always been dangerous because of the variable end of this sandspit, and a bar across the river mouth, yet St. Louis has existed in its present site since 1659.

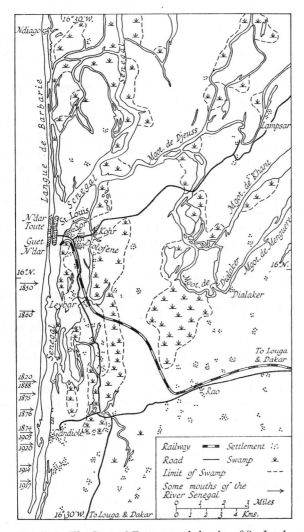

FIG. 37.—The Senegal Estuary and the site of St. Louis.

(Based on the 1 : 200,000 St. Louis sheet of the Service Géographique de l'A.O.F., 1943 and map in *Géographie Universelle*, Vol. XI, 2e partie, p. 453.)

St. Louis lies on an islet, 2,400 yards by 350 yards, which was easily defended, and though within the difficult Senegal Estuary, was sheltered and adjacent to the trade route round Africa. Up-river were to be found slaves, gum and gold (from the Faléme tributary). The Gambia River would have been preferred by the French, but it was in the hands of the British; so the inferior Senegal River became the means of French penetration into West Africa from St. Louis.

The difficulties of St. Louis as a port helped the development of Dakar after 1857, and the opening in 1885 of the first railway in West Africa, between these towns. Though supplanted as a port, St. Louis remained the capital of Senegal (and of Mauritania) until 1958, when that of Senegal was transferred to Dakar and that of Mauritania began transfer to Nouakchott. The population of St. Louis doubled between 1940 and 1951 because of the development of Government services. In the latter year it was 62,200, including 1,840 non-Africans but was only 39,800 in 1954.

The island is the administrative and commercial centre, and has an attractive sleepy air, reminiscent of small towns of southern France. Its buildings are solid and of stone, have a European as well as a Creole style, and are lived in by all races. There is a small trade in groundnuts, skins, gums and imported goods on the river. Quays are mainly on the east side of the island.

The town spread early on to the sandspit, where the northern settlement N'Dar Toute, had Mauritania's administrative offices. The southern settlement of Guet N'Dar has mainly Lébou and Wolof fishermen. It is one of the largest fishing centres in West Africa, fish being prepared by Africans and several European firms. About 2,000 tons officially pass through its markets each year. On the mainland are Sor, with the railway station and European residences including modern flats, and African Diolofene farther south-east.

The so-called *Delta Irrigation Scheme* was begun in 1947 because of the urgent need for locally grown rice, to overcome the requirement for expensive and uncertain imports. These averaged 55,000 tons a year from 1931–40 and some 60,000 tons are now required. By mechanical cultivation and irrigation 13,500 acres produced 13,800 tons of paddy in 1961, immediately south-west of Richard Toll, near the head of the delta.

This development has disturbed only a few nomads, and the level character, virtual lack of vegetation, the clayey soils, and the possibility of using Lake Guiers as a natural reservoir were attractive features.   Yet the area is infertile so that heavy applications of artificial fertilisers are necessary each year, whilst the soils also have a high salinity.   Irrigation must also be by the expensive method of pumping, and there are problems of preventing sheet erosion by wind during the dry season,

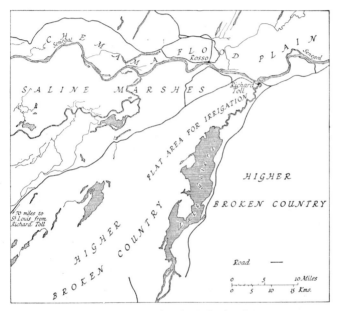

FIG. 38.—The Senegal Delta Irrigation Scheme.

and of prodigious losses at harvest time from Queleas birds and, to a lesser extent, from ducks and grasshoppers.   Wild rice is another nuisance.   Although originally 15,000 acres were to be irrigated, no extensions are being made.   Capital costs have had to be written off, and current costs are not always covered.

To provide the necessary water, a barrage was built in 1948 across the Taouey, which connects Lake Guiers to the Senegal. This was necessary because the Senegal River has so gentle a gradient and so small a discharge in the dry season, that salt water penetrates not only upstream, but even up tributaries.

To prevent it entering Lake Guiers, local people had built a
new earth barrage across the Taouey each year.   They thus
retained fresh water within the lake for use during each dry
season, but the ensuing floods destroyed the earth barrage.
Now the sluice gates are opened during flood-water and closed
as the floods fall around November 15th.

DIANDER (CAYOR COASTLANDS).   The same factors which
are responsible for diverting the Senegal River mouth, and for

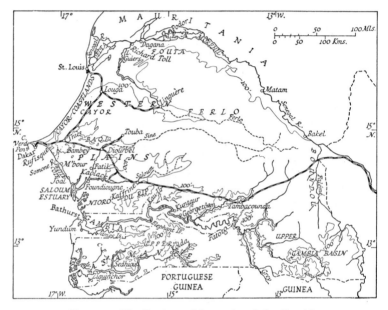

FIG. 39.—The Regions of Senegal and the Gambia.

making an unstable sandspit, have made the smooth coastline
of Cayor.   Dunes rise to over 130 feet, often being covered with
scrub, resulting from the higher humidity and more moderate
temperatures of this Senegal coast.   The dune belt extends up
to 15 miles inland and is used by Fulani and Maure herdsmen.

In the north, there are marshy depressions or *niayes* (meaning
' clumps of oil palms ') between the dunes, and parallel with
the coast.   Dew and intermittent streams provide water for the
niayes and around their edges is luxuriant vegetation.   European vegetables and sweet potatoes are grown for the St. Louis
and Dakar markets, by men who also fish off-shore.   Dwarf

Gorée. Note the Miocene volcanic ...ck visible at the farther end, and in the cliffs.

42. Cape Verde lighthouse and the Quaternary volcanoes known as *Les Mamelles* ('breasts'), west of Dakar and almost at the most westerly point of Africa. Behind them is Yoff Airport.

DAKAR

3. N.E. across Dakar Harbour. In the foreground are basaltic cliffs of Bel-Air, the Commercial ...nd part of the Residential and Administrative Quarters. The passenger pier is on the right, ...he Naval Dockyard on the left, the groundnut and groundnut oil wharves are in the inner far ...orner, and the fuel pier on the farther breakwater closing the harbour. Beyond is a Naval Air ...ase. In the far distance is the narrowest part of the peninsula behind Hann and, to the left of it, the developing industrial estate.

44. Central Dakar and the harbour

45. Avenue Pasteur, on the Miocene lava plateau.

47. Ultra-modern housing at Fann. The houses on the left made up of circular rooms built by pouring quicksetting cem over a balloon frame. The projection on the more conventic house is to increase ventilation.

46. Thirteen storey block of apartments

DAKAR

48. Groundnut oil mi

bananas and coconuts give quite a Guinea-like atmosphere to these valuable freshwater depressions.

By contrast, in the south and extending into the Cape Verde Peninsula, some lakes are saline and frequently invaded by the sea, e.g. Lake Retba. The sand is also less consolidated and younger.

Cayor deep may be a drowned river valley connected with the same postulated fault that may explain the Thiès scarp. The deep is an important fishing ground for fishermen using canoes (some having light engines), and the daily turnover of fish on Cayor beach may reach £2,500, representing 140 metric tons. An ice factory there packs at least five tons of fish per day. Some seventy lorries transport fish and vegetables from Cayor alone. Along the whole of the Senegal coast there are about 5,000 canoes and 20,000 fishermen, and some 30,000 tons of fish are landed annually. The Wolof often work full-time but the Lébou and Serer fish only in the dry season.

CAPE VERDE PENINSULA.[1] The eastern limits of this peninsula are often taken to be the Thiès Lower Eocene scarp, yet west of this lies the Cretaceous area around Rufisque. The true peninsula or tombolo was formed west of this latter area, beginning with the volcanism of Cape Manuel.

Immediately south of Dakar are the Miocene basalts of Cape Manuel, Gorée and the Madeleine Islets. Farther west, and constituting Cape Verde, are the two Quaternary volcanoes of the Mamelles. Laterite occurs on top of the Miocene volcanic rocks and underneath lavas from the Mamelles, so dating the laterite as Pliocene. Basalts from the Mamelles form Almadi Point and its reefs—Africa's most westerly point.

Along an otherwise dry, sandy coast, early navigators found the green hills of the Cape Verde Mamelles—green because their

[1] An encyclopædic reference is *La Presqu'île du Cap Vert*, I.F.A.N., Dakar, 1949. See also 1 : 10,000 'Environs de Dakar' maps of *Service Géographique de l'A.O.F.* On Dakar the main references are D. Whittlesey, 'Dakar and the other Cape Verde Settlements', *Geographical Review*, 1941, pp. 609–38, and 'Dakar Revisited', Idem, 1948, 626–32; Léon Coursin, 'Dakar: Port Atlantique', *Les Cahiers d'Outre-Mer*, 1948, pp. 275–85; J. Dresch, 'Les Villes d'Afrique Occidentale', Idem, 1950, pp. 217–22; *L'Agglomeration Dakaroise, Etudes Sénégalaises, No. 5*, I.F.A.N. (St. Louis), 1955; Ch. Toupet, 'Dakar', *Tijdschrift voor Economische en Sociale Geografie*, Feb. 1958, pp. 35–40; and A. Seck, 'Dakar', *Les Cahiers d'Outre-Mer*, 1961, pp. 372–92; Richard J. Peterec, *Dakar and West African Economic Development*, 1967.

H

projecting rounded forms catch extra humidity. The older basalts of Cape Manuel gave shelter to the equally basaltic

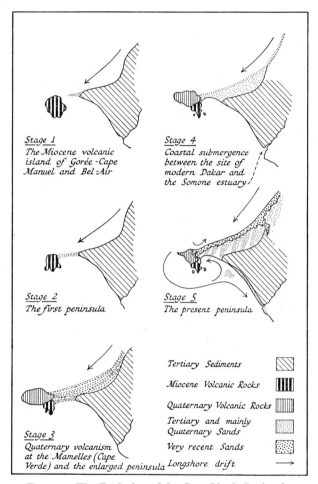

Stage 1
The Miocene volcanic island of Gorée-Cape Manuel and Bel-Air

Stage 4
Coastal submergence between the site of modern Dakar and the Somone estuary

Stage 2
The first peninsula

Stage 5
The present peninsula

Stage 3
Quaternary volcanism at the Mamelles (Cape Verde) and the enlarged peninsula

Tertiary Sediments

Miocene Volcanic Rocks

Quaternary Volcanic Rocks

Tertiary and mainly Quaternary Sands

Very recent Sands

Longshore drift

FIG. 40.—The Evolution of the Cape Verde Peninsula.
(From Diagrams by J. Richard-Molard in *La Presqu'île du Cap Vert*, 1949, p. 15, and redrawn.)

Gorée Islet, occupied from the fifteenth century by Europeans (from the seventeenth by the French), the embryo of modern Dakar and—with St. Louis—of French West Africa.

Dakar. Dakar was first occupied permanently in 1857—just

after the Crimean War had revealed the need for greater attention to strategy. Work was begun in 1861 on the first pier, which is about 650 feet in length, and is now incorporated in the southern jetty. A second, longer jetty proved successful in 1866, and the *Messageries Impériales* (now the *Messageries Maritimes*) transferred its calling point, on the route from France

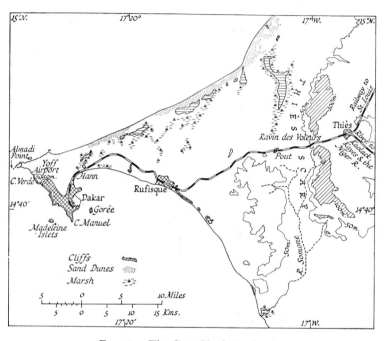

FIG. 41.—The Cape Verde Peninsula.
(Heights in metres.)

to South America, from St. Vincent to Dakar. But by 1878, Dakar's population was still only 1,556.

For the next quarter of a century development was steady. In 1885 West Africa's first railway was opened between St. Louis and Dakar, to obviate navigation of the difficult Senegal estuary. Thereafter, Dakar attracted most of the traffic to and from the Senegal Valley, and St. Louis decayed as a port. The new railway achieved even more by stimulating the cultivation of groundnuts along its route. By 1891 the population was

8,737. In 1892 the southern jetty was extended another 650 feet and a breakwater of 910 feet built on to it.

The next great impetus came as a result of the decision taken in 1898, at the time of Anglo-French differences and of British troubles in South Africa, to make Dakar into an important naval base. The northern breakwater was built, thus creating a true harbour with depths averaging nearly 30 feet.

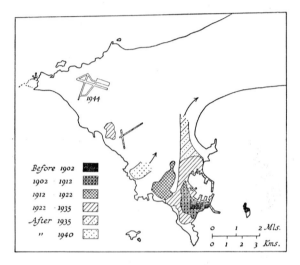

FIG. 42.—The Historical Development of Dakar.

The southern jetty was again extended and a dry dock built in the western harbour. Shortly after, between 1904 and 1910, great improvements were again made in the south by the construction of Piers (Fr. Moles) 1 and 2, more dredging, and by the provision of better loading and storing facilities. In 1904 the population had risen to 18,477 and Dakar became the federal capital.

These naval and civil developments made Dakar into a true port and town, and brought about its rational layout immediately south of the harbour. By 1914 its population was 23,833, still less than one-tenth of the present total; 2,772 were non-African civilians and 1,242 non-African army and navy men.

The 1914–18 war brought a great increase of traffic to Dakar, the tonnage of shipping cleared trebling between 1911 and 1918. But a more lasting development was the opening of the through railway from Dakar to Bamako on the Niger River in 1923. Thereafter, Dakar was not only the main port for Senegal and Mauritania, but also for the French Sudan, and its trade became more diversified. Although Kaolack (linked by railway in 1911) ultimately excelled Dakar in groundnut exports, the latter has benefited enormously from this trade and the processing of groundnut oil.

Between 1926 and 1933 new port works were again undertaken, this time in the northern sector of the port. Pier 8 was built for the efficient refuelling of ships. The groundnut storage yard was laid out and Piers 5 and 6 built for groundnut export and, later, for shipping groundnut oil by pipeline. These improvements killed Rufisque as a groundnut port. Before the works were undertaken, the population of Dakar in 1924 was around 40,000, but by 1931 it was 53,982, and in 1936 was 92,634, all figures including Gorée and nearby mainland villages.

Just before the Second World War, the northern jetty was equipped for the discharge of tankers and Pier 3 was constructed near the end of the southern jetty. Loading and storage facilities and depths of water were also greatly improved. Pier 4 has since been built for groundnuts, Pier 1 and the northern jetty have been extended, and a vast cold store has been completed to help the local fishing industry and the importation of European perishable foodstuffs.

Dakar city has been booming since the war, as the result of money and new labour being put into overseas development, of ' refugee ' capital being removed from France to establish new commercial and industrial undertakings, of the great increase in local groundnut oil extraction, and of the development of the city as an air centre of world significance. The population, which had doubled between 1926 and 1936, again doubled between 1936 and 1946. In 1955 the population was 230,579 including suburban villages and Gorée. In 1961 the figure was 374,700.

Water and housing have been scarce, and the cost of living high. The residential development of Dakar has been restricted by several factors. Lébou land rights have held up

re-development in the centre, and the African Médina has been
a problem on the north-west.   The French Forces occupied
an inordinate amount of land, especially on Cape Manuel.
To these specific difficulties have been added those of scarcity
and high cost of imported materials, shortage and poor
quality of labour.   Nevertheless, apartments with up to seven-
teen stories have been erected in central Dakar; while a fine
suburb of villas, with striking styles of architecture, has been
built at Fann, overlooking Madeleines Bay.

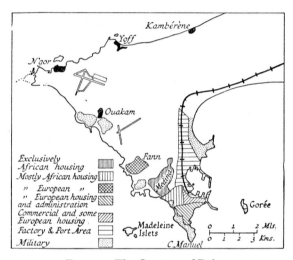

FIG. 43.—The Quarters of Dakar.
(Villages in black.)

Further water supplies have been obtained by deep borings;
there is now an elaborate system of distribution and vast
quantities of water are taken on by calling ships.   On the
other hand, the water table shows signs of being lowered and
certainly the vegetation around Dakar has been degraded—
perhaps by this, but undoubtedly more by over-farming on the
doorsteps of such an attractive market.

Dakar is a considerable industrial centre.   Its industries are
mainly located along the railway and road leading out of the
peninsula, between Hann (not to be confused with residential
Fann to the north-west) and Tiaroye, on former sandy wastes.
The three groundnut oil refineries (two producing 30,000 tons

each per annum), soap, sack, shoe, cotton drill and soft drink factories, a brickworks and a fish cannery are based essentially upon the processing of local raw materials. Mercantile and naval ship repairing, the brewery, match and cigarette factories, oil refinery, truck assembly, and the flour mill depend mainly upon imported materials. Paper wrapping, metal, furniture and clothing factories make up entirely imported materials. Local exports are groundnut products, especially groundnut cake and oil.

The port has 540 acres of protected waters, 100 acres of which have dredged depths of $32\frac{1}{2}$ feet. There are 2,530 yards of commercial quays with these depths, and 3,204 yards with depths of 26 feet or more. In all, there are 4 miles of quays, at which some forty ships can be accommodated and from which 4,400 ships are cleared annually. On the basis of tonnage cleared, Dakar is the third port of France and the French Community, following only Marseilles and Le Havre and exceeding all overseas ports. This demonstrates its major rôle—that of a calling port, especially on South American, West and South African routes, of French and other European (but not British) passenger ships.

Dakar has taken the place of St. Vincent (Cape Verde Islands), but Las Palmas still attracts British ships. Petroleum companies furnish oil at cheaper rates there than at Dakar, the shipping lines find useful freight in fruit and vegetables from the Canary Islands to Britain, and the stop is popular for its tourist attraction. But if Dakar could compete with Las Palmas in price of fuel oil, it might attract outward bound British ships. More recent harbour works include the construction of Pier 7 and improvements elsewhere, especially for phosphates and groundnut oil storage and loading. These could double the pre-war traffic.

By its strategic position adjacent to the most westerly point of Africa and at the nearest point to South America, Dakar has been able to attract the ever-increasing air traffic on the Europe–South America and North America–South Africa routes. It is also the centre of some West African services and is touched by other African systems. The superb airport was built after 1943 and is served by almost all European air corporations and by several others, there being at least a dozen inward and a dozen outward services a day. About 250,000 passengers pass through Yoff airport annually and 4,500 tons of freight.

Given the strategic position of the general site, the development of the town has been greatly favoured by the Miocene basalts of Cape Manuel, and the Eocene limestone plateau with superficial laterite. This fairly level plateau, with an average height of about 100 feet, is excellent for residences and for federal government buildings. North and north-east of it are loose Quaternary sands, easy to excavate for port works. Dakar harbour is always easy to enter, since there is no current or drift, the tidal range averages only 16 inches, it is naturally sheltered from the north-north-easterly and westerly winds, and harbour works have provided shelter from the south-westerly ones.

For its residents, especially for its Europeans, Dakar has the advantage of a far more pleasant climate than almost any other part of West Africa except, perhaps, Accra. Temperatures are very moderate. Daily maxima are 88° F. from June to October and daily minima are 65° F. from January to April. Daily range varies from 9° to 17° F. during the year. Its rainfall of nearly 23 inches comes mostly in four months. Not only does it have the usual on-shore and offshore breezes of all coastal stations but the narrowness, digitated nature, and planned road alignment of the peninsula ensure that all these breezes have their maximum effect. Furthermore, it enjoys for nearly nine months the north-north-east Marine Trade winds, not the over-dry and dusty Harmattan of interior Senegal.

Strategy has made the general site important, and the detailed site factors have helped the development of a great city of over a quarter of a million people concerned in its functions as the Senegal capital, leading port, major commercial and industrial centre of ex-French West Africa, and a great calling point on inter-continental air and sea routes.

Outstanding general and specific advantages of site, a good climate, the diverse functions of Dakar and the nature of French colonial theory, have combined to make Dakar a European, as well as an African city. Indeed, it might be regarded as the last European city on the route to South

America. French people live in Dakar exactly as they do in France, with cafés, restaurants, multi-racial schools and many-storied offices and apartment blocks. Because of its situation as a calling place on world trade routes, and its considerable European market, it can command an import of temperate fruits and vegetables (often from Morocco) far cheaper and in greater quantities than can other West African towns. Again, because of its large European population and its more fixed character, general imports are much more varied than through other West African ports.

Dakar is unique in West Africa. It forms a vivid contrast to Lagos and Accra where no Europeans live permanently. Many children have their secondary and university education in Dakar with Africans. The plateau is thoroughly European in aspect and more beautiful than many cities in Europe of equivalent size.

The Rufisque Cretaceous Region lies east of the Cape Verde Peninsula and the Dakar industrial belt, with which it is frequently considered. Geologically it antedates the formation of the peninsula, and the limestone (Cretaceous-Eocene) of Rufisque contrasts with the loose sand, basalt and laterite of the peninsula. Limestone rocks also outcrop south of the Somone Estuary and extend inland to Diourbel and Gaouane.

Rufisque, population (1962 est.) 50,000, antedates Dakar by several centuries and was first named Rio Fresco by the Portuguese, who stopped regularly for fresh water, obtained from seepages in the fixed dunes. Rufisque was for long the main exporter of groundnuts until Dakar and Kaolack replaced it. Between the two wars it was quite moribund, but has revived as an industrial town with groundnut-oil refineries, a cretonne cotton factory, a tannery and shoe factory, pharmaceutical works, engineering assembly shops and, nearby at Bargny, West Africa's first cement factory, which produces about 180,000 tons a year.

On the edge of this region lies the clay marshland of Pout, which belongs to the Cayor Coastlands or to the Cape Verde Peninsula. Pout is significant for its brickworks, capable of making fifty tons or 20,000 bricks per day.

The Southern or 'Petite Côte'. Beyond Rufisque are cliffs formed of Eocene deposits and laterite, followed by cliffs of Cretaceous rocks beyond the Somone River (see Figure 39). It is, therefore, unlike any other part of the Senegal coast. Popenguin, Portudal and Joal were early European points of contact, probably because the area had more fresh water seepages, a denser vegetation, is more sheltered, and has less swell and surf than the northern coast. But these roadsteads were supplanted first by Rufisque and later by Dakar and Kaolack.

The modern significance of this coast has also declined because of the cessation in 1964 of the extraction of titanium and zircon ores from its beaches and those of the Sangomar Peninsula. First worked in 1922 these ores were for long the only significant Senegalese minerals. Concentration of the first ore by electro-magnets and of zircon by mechanical means was effected at Djifère, in the Saloum Estuary. These operations became uneconomic in competition with large Australian, Malaysian and Sierra Leone producers, and because of the difficulties of navigating the Saloum Estuary.

Fishing is still important here. Main catches are of white fish (Yaboys, Cobos and false cod). Fish is sent dried or fresh to Dakar, Rufisque, Thiès and Kaolack. Joal has firms drying and canning fish, but the catching and preparation of sharks for skins, fins, liver oil, meat and fertiliser failed. Oysters are also found, especially around the Somone outlet. The pastures of la Petite Côte are visited in the dry season by Fulani herdsman.

SALOUM ESTUARY. South of Joal commences the long sand-spit of Sangomar. The spit is an analogue of the *Langue de Barbarie*, and diverts the Saloum southward, though, like the Senegal, it occasionally flows across the spit.

A ria coast commences here and continues southward into Sierra Leone. The Saloum estuary or ria was probably formed from the drowning of a very shallow relic valley. The land has since gained, and the estuary is clogged by much silt. Around the many channels are salt flats or *tannes*, which, if only they could be desalted, would be valuable rice-lands. Dykes with flap-valves are being built, especially near Fatick, to keep out salt water and to retain fresh flood-waters until a certain height is reached. Then the valves let out the fresh water, without admitting salt water. Behind the *tannes* are areas cultivated for rice, millet and groundnuts.

Despite a bar at its entrance and a meandering course, the Saloum is navigable to Kaolack, 73 miles, for ocean vessels of about 4,000–6,000 tons and not drawing over 11 feet.

Koalack, population (1962 est.) over 70,000, has become Senegal's main groundnut port, owing to its proximity by rail and road to the main areas of cultivation in the Western Plains. There is also a large modern salt works producing some 55,000 tons per year and provisioning almost all parts of French West Africa.

Downstream at Lyndiane is a groundnut processing works and the port is of growing significance, whilst Foundiougne has declined as a port. Small ocean vessels can reach Fatick on the Sine tributary.

THE WESTERN PLAINS. These extend from just west of the St. Louis–Dakar railway eastward and also southward into the Gambia, where they are known as the Sandhills region. On the south-west they terminate in the Thiès Scarp (Fig. 41), which is about 200 feet high, and a vivid feature of the landscape. Its altitude, like that of the Mamelles of Cape Verde, is sufficient to cause heavier rainfall (about 3 inches more at Thiès than at Dakar) and the so-called ' Forest ' of Thiès.

Most of this slightly undulating plain is under 130 feet, and consists of lacustrine and continental Mio-Pliocene argillaceous sandstones which cover Eocene and earlier formations. In many places there are relic dunes, aligned from north-east to south-west, which give a pronounced ' grain ' to the country. Superficial sand is absent only in parts of the Ferlo Valley and along the coast around M'Bour. This deep blanket of sand has so choked the valleys that, for example, the Sine Valley above Diourbel is scarcely evident, except for a band of denser vegetation.

The northern part (north of 15° N.) of this large region, known as the *Cayor*, has a deficient rainfall (10–16 inches), so that it has Sahel Savannah, and crop lands are not continuous. The naturally sparse vegetation has been much devastated by fire, over-pasturing, and felling of gum-acacias by the Wolof whose farming practices are destructive.

Louga is an important town lying on the northern edge of this region, in contact with the coastal dune region, and where pastoral Fulani nomads meet sedentary Wolof groundnut farmers.   Formerly a great Muslim religious centre, it is now the leading cattle market in Senegal, being admirably situated between the main cattle rearing regions to the north and the meat consuming towns of St. Louis, Kaolack, Thiès and Dakar.   Louga has been served by a railway since 1885, and in 1931 became a junction with the opening of the Linguère branch.   Though many of the surrounding groundnut lands are now largely exhausted, Louga is an important groundnut, millet and gum marketing centre, and has a groundnut oil refinery and associated soap works.

Thiès,[1] with an estimated population in 1962 of 70,000, is the main centre of the Western Plains.   It has been connected by rail with Dakar since 1885, and from 1923 has been a junction for the St. Louis and Niger lines.   A double track exists to Dakar, and Thiès is a notable road centre.

Communications have helped to encourage its groundnut market.   Industry started with the large railway workshops, which employ some 3,000 men.   Nearby are the large Pout brickworks, and a phosphate refinery, using material from the Pallo quarries nearby.   These produce 300,000 tons of aluminium phosphate rock annually.   This is found at a depth of 6 feet, the beds being 16–26 feet thick.   More important deposits of calcium phosphate are worked at Tivaouane, north-west of Pallo, production being over 1 million tons.   The phosphates are of great significance, in that they lie near farming lands in desperate need of fertiliser.   Considerable exports are being developed.

The *Baol*, which lies south of Cayor and north of the Saloum River, has Sudan Savannah vegetation.   Between Fatik and Bambey the country is inhabited by the Serer people, who conserve the useful trees even to the extent of putting thorn branches round them in the dry season to ward off livestock. The Serer are also most unusual in that, as well as growing crops, they keep cattle and fertilise their farms with manure. Fields are hedged with thorn bush to restrict the movement of cattle.   Such conservation practices and mixed farming are still very exceptional among West African peoples.

---

[1] See also G. Savonnet, ' Une ville neuve du Sénégal: Thiès,' *Les Cahiers d'Outre-Mer*, 1956, pp. 70–93 and *La Ville de Thiès: étude de géographie urbaine*, I.F.A.N., St. Louis, Senegal, 1955.

They are certainly in very marked contrast to those of their neighbours, the Wolof of Cayor and Nioro du Rip.

Wherever the Serer live, the Baol has the appearance of a well-kept park or orchard, with many baobab, acacia and mango trees. Groundnuts and millet are the main crops, with beans and cotton as lesser ones. The Serer country of Baol is the most peopled and socially knit part of Senegal.[1]

The *Nioro du Rip* country lies south of the Saloum River and is peopled by Wolof. Lying in a zone of heavier rainfall it was naturally more wooded, and this characteristic has been retained as it has a smaller population and is less farmed.

THE FERLO PLATEAU. Central Senegal is a little higher (130 feet or over) and far drier than the Western Plains, but is otherwise similar, except that its sandstone is more ferruginous. It extends into the Gambia, particularly in North Bank, MacCarthy and Upper River Provinces, where it is termed ' Sandstone Plateau '.

In the Ferlo, villages are practically confined to relic river valleys, where water may be found near the surface. Elsewhere, water is so deep that vegetation is Sahel Savannah and the area is almost uninhabited, except for Fulani nomads who, until recently, have tried to retain the Ferlo for their exclusive use. Water from deep borings (160–260 feet) has begun to change the vegetation, and Wolof are entering to grow groundnuts.

On the eastern fringes is a sub-region where the argillaceous sandstones thin out in contact with the metamorphic rim. Again there is an almost complete mask of sands, clays and laterites, but the rivers are incised and bordered by borassus palms. On the southern margins, near to and south of the railway, are important groundnut lands and some fixed Fulani herdsmen.

THE BOUNDOU. This is the rim of Pre-Cambrian schists, quartzites and sandstones. Hills rise abruptly to nearly 600 feet and there is evidence of erosion surfaces.

The region is crossed by the Dakar–Niger Railway, but is only poor seasonal pasture land, though in past centuries alluvial gold was of great importance from the Falémé Basin.

[1] P. Pélissier, ' Les Paysans Sérères ', *Les Cahiers d'Outre-Mer*, 1953, pp. 105-27.

NIOKOLO (UPPER GAMBIA). This is an undulating plain, averaging about 300 feet, with occasional higher plateaux and hills, e.g. around Mako, which attain nearly 1,300 feet. These are either fragments of the Pre-Cambrian eastern rim, or of the Palæozic sandstones and the Pre-Cambrian quartzites of the Fouta Djallon in the south-east, or formed from eruptive rocks. Apart from these, there is a general cover of superficial deposits, either of sand, clays or laterite in the area which largely account for the very poor vegetation and bare uninhabited countryside. Only the hills and river courses are slightly more fertile.

CASAMANCE. This territory lies south of the Gambia, so that it was somewhat isolated from the rest of Senegal, especially until the Trans-Gambian road was built by the French across the Gambia.

Because of its southerly position, Casamance has Monsoonal conditions and more vegetation than other parts of Senegal. Ziguinchor has nearly three times as much rain as Dakar, and twice as many rain-days. Rice is the dominant food crop.

The river and its tributaries are bordered, in tidal areas (as far as 75 miles up river), by fairly thick mangroves, behind which marshes have often been reclaimed for rice cultivation. Raphia and oil palms, bamboos, teak and silk-cotton trees are all found. Argillaceous sandstones cover the whole area, with much alluvium along the rivers and in the estuaries. Titaniferous sands occur on estuary beaches.

Three sub-regions are distinguishable:

(a) *Fogni* (*Lower Casamance*)[1] from the ocean to Ziguinchor. Here there is a succession of low marshy areas deeply penetrated by tidal arms. As in Portuguese Guinea, mangrove or rice fields are backed by valuable stands of oil palms. *Ziguinchor* (population about 30,000), head-quarters of Casamance, stands on the left bank of the river, 42 miles upstream, on the first considerable piece of firm ground. It can be reached by boats of about 800 tons, and there are river jetties. It is also served by air.

(b) *Central Casamance* lies beyond Ziguinchor, and produces

[1] See P. Pélissier, 'Les Diola: étude sur l'habitat des riziculteurs de Basse-Casamance', *Les Cahiers d'Outre-Mer*, 1958.

more groundnuts than the previous region. Even more might be grown but for tsetse fly infestation of great areas believed to be suitable for cultivation. In 1949 an experimental mass-production groundnut scheme, using mechanical cultivation, was begun (see p. 210) near *Sédhiou*. This town is 110 miles up the Casamance River, and is reached by ships of five feet draught.[1]

(c) *Yassine, Pakao, Fouladou* (*Upper Casamance*) are higher and drier. There are abrupt edges to the river valleys, succeeded by considerable expanses of bare *bowal* (laterite surfaced country) suitable only for intermittent pastures. In the better areas, groundnuts are grown. *Kolda* is the main regional centre. This country merges into the Upper Gambia region.

ECONOMIC RESOURCES

AGRICULTURE

Millet is overwhelmingly the main foodstuff and is grown in rotation with groundnuts, the virtually exclusive cash crop. In 1965 there were about 2·7 million acres under millet and some 600,000 tons were produced. There were about 2,600,000 acres under groundnuts, tilled by 400,000 growers. Groundnut production averages 1·1 million tons, of which approximately 100,000 tons are retained for seed and 150,000 tons for local food.

Other than millet and groundnuts, significant food crops are rice, about 110,000 tons annually, from river valleys, especially the Casamance; cassava, about 170,000 tons annually, mainly from the Louga, Thiès and Kaolack districts; sweet potatoes, 7,000 tons, principally from Casamance and Thiès; beans, 15,000 tons, mostly intercropped with millet, and so in rotation with groundnuts; and maize, 30,000 tons from the river valleys.

Food crops (other than millet grown in rotation with groundnuts) have declined in favour of the export crop of groundnuts, but this dangerous tendency is now being countered.

[1] See also A. Seck, ' La Moyenne Casamance ', *Revue de Géographie Alpine*, XLIII, No. 4.

Groundnuts are the very life-blood of Senegal, which is the fourth largest world producer, the second cash producer, and the nearest one to Europe. Groundnuts and groundnut products (mainly groundnut oil and cake) account for almost all the exports of Senegal. Until recently, outside Dakar and St. Louis, there was almost no other economic activity. Senegal and the Gambia are outstanding examples of cash monocultures.

The texture of Senegal soils is ideal for groundnuts. Most soils average 3·4% only of clay, the ideal percentage being between 2% and 5%. Nevertheless, because of over-cultivation, the chemical and humus contents of soils in the older areas of cultivation between St. Louis and Dakar have greatly deteriorated from even their natural mediocrity. The Wolof have impoverished their central and northern region by over-cutting and firing the natural vegetation. On the other hand, the Serer, who live mainly in the naturally wooded Sine–Saloum area, have protected the vegetation and manured the soils. In view of the poverty of Senegalese soils and their increasing exhaustion by man, locally produced phosphates from the groundnut region itself are of great significance.

Groundnuts have been a peasant subsistence and export crop for a long time. Exports date back to 1840; they were encouraged, as in the Gambia, by the needs of French soap manufacturers and by the lack of a French import duty on groundnuts.

The earliest cropped areas were around Podor, Matam and Bakel in or near the Senegal valley, near St. Louis, and in and near the Cape Verde Peninsula. The soils of all these areas are now largely exhausted.

A great impetus to production and switch in producing areas came with the opening of the St. Louis to Dakar railway in 1885, along which lands were soon given over—all too exclusively and intensively—to groundnut cultivation. Also Hilaire Maurel had devised an improved hoe to increase yields; this hoe, now used throughout Senegal, is known as a ' hilaire '.

The second impulse and change came with the building of the railway eastward from Thiès. It reached Diourbel in 1908, Guinguinéo in 1910, Kaolack (by a branch) in 1911, Koussanar in 1913, Tambacounda in 1914, and the through route was opened to the Niger in 1923. Groundnut cultivation spread in the Baol, especially as far east as Koussanar, where the climate is far more suitable and the soils richer than between St. Louis and Dakar.   In 1931 branch railways were opened, one from Diourbel to Touba, and the other to Linguère from Louga (on the St. Louis to Dakar line).

More significant than these branches was the construction of roads, mainly after 1923, and especially in the later thirties. Roads have extended cultivation far beyond the railways.   Yet rail transport still canalises much of the export trade towards Kaolack, in the heart of the main producing area.

The Kaolack district accounts for almost half the area under groundnuts in Senegal and for nearly half the production and sales.   The next most important producers are the Thiès and Diourbel districts, which each account for about 15% of the cultivated area, and nearly the same percentage of production and sales.   The lowest yields are in the old and dry areas of Louga and Linguère.   The best yields are obtained from the youngest and relatively small districts of Tambacounda and Ziguinchor (Casamance), the latter having a high percentage of its crop for sale.   These last two areas have soils of better texture, more humus and chemical nutrients than those to the north.

Senegal is an important focus for seasonal labour for the cultivation and harvesting of groundnuts.   Some 35,000 *navé-tanes* arrive annually in Senegal, of whom three-quarters go to the Kaolack District.   Another 10,000–20,000 go to the Gambia.   Before the Second World War, these seasonal labourers came mostly from the French Sudan.   Now, despite free rail transport, these are much less numerous and more come from Guinea on foot to Tambacounda, and then by rail free of charge.

Mechanical cultivation of groundnuts is being tried at Boulel, 12 miles north of Kaffrine.   The soils are very suitable and the area was uninhabited, but water is now available and the Department of Agriculture is in charge.   Some 8,000 acres have been cleared.   There, and at Guédé near Touba, at Baïla near Taïf, and at Tif south-east of Kael, agriculture has been encouraged by marabouts of the Mouridism Islamic movement. At these places smaller but still large-scale clearing has gone on, partly for community cultivation of groundnuts.   Modern economic and technical methods have been interwoven with an Islamic community and sect of feudal character.[1]

At Séfa, 8 miles up the Casamance river from Sédhiou, is a much larger scheme run by the Compagnie Générale des Oléagineux Tropicaux. Some 15,000 acres have been cleared, but, as in Tanganyika, roots have been difficult to clear. Lateritic pans are near the surface and rains are variable, especially in June–July. After a first year of failure through weed infestation, the weeds are now ploughed in before sowing. One and a half metric tons of nuts were obtained per hectare as an average of 1,700 hectares (4,250 acres) mechanically cultivated in 1953. There were also 1,125 acres of mechanically tilled but peasant cropped lands, with rather better yields.

Towards the end of the First World War, the local shelling of some groundnuts was undertaken to save cargo space. This led later to the establishment of small oil-extraction works at Kaolack, Diourbel, Ziguinchor and Louga. The first one at Dakar was opened in 1924, and groundnut oil was first exported from Senegal in 1927. Until 1937–8 exports were limited to 5,500 tons of groundnut oil per annum, because extractors in France had become so alarmed at this competition. During the war the limit was raised to 12,000 tons and then to 45,000 tons annually.

The Second World War gave an enormous impetus to Senegal oil extraction. After the fall of France, Senegal could neither export groundnuts, nor import fuel oil. So in 1941 a large-scale extraction plant (Lésieur-Afrique) was opened in Dakar (by a Dunkirk firm whose factory was overrun by the Germans), with a capacity of 20,000 tons of crude oil per annum. It has a pipeline to the nearby pier, and the oil was at first used in North and West Africa as an uneconomic substitute for diesel fuel oil. Since then it has been exported to Casablanca or Algiers for final refining, and domestic use in the formerly protected Algerian market.

Two other factories in Dakar carry out complete refining of groundnut and other vegetable oils. Their annual production is about 18,000 tons of oil, 24,000 tons of crushed seeds, 4,000 tons of soap and 1,000 tons of cattle food.

[1] On this and on cultivation of Senegalese groundnuts generally see P. Pélissier, ' L'Arachide au Sénégal ', *Les Cahiers d'Outre-Mer*, 1951.

Outside Dakar, complete refineries are located at Lyndiane (near Kaolack) and Louga, both with a capacity of 6,000 tons per annum of refined oil. Crude-oil refineries are located at Rufisque, Kaolack, Diourbel and Ziguinchor, whose oil is finally refined at Dakar.

Senegal refineries have the capacity to deal annually with almost the entire annual cash crop. So far, however, about 460,000 tons of groundnuts in shell are crushed locally to yield about 150,000 tons of oil, three-quarters of which are crude oil and the rest refined oil. Crude oil is exported for final refining in North Africa or France. About 200,000 tons of residue are produced and 25,000 tons of soap. Oil production is equal to about two-thirds the needs of France. Groundnut-oil storage tanks, at the north end of Dakar harbour, have a capacity of 5,000 tons, and tankers can be loaded with 300 tons of oil per hour. Exports of shelled nuts are about 225,000 tons, representing some 330,000 tons in shell. Exports in shell are only about 18,000 tons.

The use of most of the Senegal crop for local oil extraction is in striking contrast to the Gambia, where little oil is produced by modern methods; and to Nigeria, where oil was first extracted locally by machinery in a very small Kano factory only in 1949, twenty-eight years after the first mill in Senegal, and in the face of governmental indifference.

Local processing reduces transport of material and the acid content of the oil. It provides a valuable fuel from shell waste, local employment and revenue. On the other hand, oil-tankers have to return to Dakar in ballast, and the now large-scale oil industry in Nigeria has never enjoyed a large protected market, as did the Senegal crushers until 1965.[1]

---

[1] See P. H. Mensier, ' Les Huileries au Sénégal ', *Revue internationale des produits coloniaux et du matériel colonial*, 1948, p. 27; J. Suret-Canale, ' L'Industrie des oléagineux en A.O.F.', *Les Cahiers d'Outre-Mer*, 1950, pp. 280–8; *Les Cahiers Hebdomadaires de l'A.O.F.*, No. 20, 1953 (no author given). For a general study of groundnut cultivation in modern Senegal see J. Suret-Canale, ' Quelques Aspects de la Géographie Agraire au Sénégal ', *Les Cahiers d'Outre-Mer*, 1948, pp. 348–67. For the problems of local crushing see J. C. Gardiner, *Oilseed Processing in Nigeria*, 1953; *The Cultivation of Groundnuts in West Africa*, O.E.E.C., 1953, pp. 39–41.

LIVESTOCK [1]

Senegal has only moderate numbers of livestock, most of its needs in meat being met by cattle driven south-westward from Mauritania towards towns on the Senegal, Gambia and Casamance rivers, railways or main roads.

The fact that the Serer people are cattle-keepers as well as crop-farmers accounts for the greatest concentration of local cattle south-west of Diourbel and around Kaolack. Sheep and goats are likewise important south-west of Diourbel, but also near M'Pal (east of St. Louis) and Mekhé. By relating the density of the livestock population to the human population, however, northern Senegal is shown to have many herds, kept mostly by nomadic or semi-nomadic Fulani. (For Fishing, see Chapter 7, p. 138.)

MINERALS

Mineral working is necessarily restricted in range and is recent in its development. The oldest worked mineral is salt from marine-salt evaporation works on the Saloum Estuary opposite Kaolack (p. 203). Phosphates near Thiès (p. 204) and limestone for cement manufacture near Rufisque (p. 201) are more recent. Basalt and laterite are quarried for road making.

COMMUNICATIONS

Rivers. The Senegal was the earliest means of French ingress into the interior. Its place has now been taken by the railway, but a little local traffic remains on the river. Small ships can reach Podor (177 miles from St. Louis) all the year; between July and January boats can reach Matam (400 miles from St. Louis); and in August and September Kayes is the limit—603 miles from St. Louis, and within Mali. For the Saloum and Sine rivers see p. 202 and for the Casamance p. 206.

Railways. The St. Louis–Dakar line was the first in West Africa. Though built to overcome the insufficiency of St. Louis as a port, the line was even more successful in developing

---

[1] See maps by F. Bonnet-Dupeyron published 1950 by the *Office de la Recherche Scientifique Outre-Mer* (O.R.S.O.M.), 20 rue Monsieur, Paris, 7.

groundnut cultivation along its route. There is considerable passenger traffic, eighteen diesel-electric trains running weekly in each direction.

The through route from Dakar to Bamako and Koulikoro, on separate navigable reaches of the Niger River, was opened in 1923. The link between the Senegal and Niger Rivers had been finished in 1904 and projections into the gap from Thiès and from Kayes were started in 1907. The important branch to Kaolack was completed in 1911, and the lesser one from Diourbel to Touba in 1931, as was the branch from the St. Louis–Dakar line from Louga to Linguère. The through railway provided an efficient life-line for the French Sudan, and replaced through transport on the poor and seasonal Senegal River. It also serves the main groundnut areas of western and south-central Senegal and halted the major diversion of trade to the British Gambia. Normally there are three through passenger trains weekly in each direction between Dakar and Bamako, 769 miles, covering the journey in twenty-six hours, the trains being drawn by diesel-electric locomotives. There are diesel rail cars three times a week in each direction between Dakar and Kaolack.

Roads. These were somewhat neglected until recently, in defence of the railways. However, there are tarred roads from Dakar to beyond Thiès and across the Gambian borders to Ziguinchor. Yet the road into Mali is frequently interrupted because of its bad surface.

Air. Apart from the international services passing through Dakar, there are local services between Dakar, St. Louis and Ziguinchor.

Conclusion

Despite its northerly latitude, Senegal has a relatively cool and humid coastline, compared with the interior. Dakar may be said to enjoy an almost semi-tropical climate of remarkable freshness, whilst in the centre of Senegal are barren, dry wastes.

Senegal is largely summed up in two words—Dakar and groundnuts. Dakar is the most developed of all West African towns and is a calling-point of major significance. Groundnuts are the only cash crop, and there seems to be no foreseeable alternative to this apparently soil-exhausting crop.

BIBLIOGRAPHY

See footnotes cited above.   Also:

J. L. BOUTILLIER, et al., *La moyenne vallée du Sénégal*, 1962.

R. J. HARRISON CHURCH, 'Senegal', *Focus*, American Geographical Society, September 1964.

H. DESCHAMPS, *Le Sénégal et la Gambie*, *Que sais-Je?*, Paris, 1964.

ARMAND LUNEL, *Sénégal*, Lausanne, 1967.

PAUL PÉLISSIER, *Les Paysans du Sénégal; les civilisations agraires du Cayor à la Casamance*, 1966.

E. SÉRÉ DE RIVIÈRES, *Le Sénégal et Dakar*, Paris, 1953.   (Includes a long bibliography.)

Etudes Sénégalaises published by Centre I.F.A.N., St. Louis, Senegal, and *Travaux du Département de Géographie de l'Université de Dakar*.

MAPS

See p. 183.   Also:

Topographic:

    1 : 5,000 Dakar and St. Louis.   I.G.N.   1945.

    1 : 10,000 Presqu'île du Cap-Vert.   I.G.N.   1947–52.

               Dakar.   S.G./A.O.F.   1946.

               Rufisque.   I.G.N.   1946.

    1 : 20,000 Rufisque, Thiès and small coastal areas.   I.G.N.   1949–52.

    1 : 50,000 St. Louis, Lampsar and Presqu'île du Cap-Vert.   S.G./A.O.F. 1950.

    1 : 100,000 Senegal.   S.G.A. and S.G./A.O.F. 1941.

Geological:

    1 : 20,000 Presqu'île du Cap-Vert.   Service des Mines de l'A.O.F.   1948.

Vegetation:

    1 : 200,000 Thiès O.R.S.O.M. 1950.

Livestock:

    1 : 500,000—1 : 5M Series of maps showing density and movement of livestock,   meat   consumption,   breeds,   transhumance,   etc. O.R.S.O.M. 1950.

Population:

    1 : 1,000,000 Demographic map.   O.R.S.O.M. 1950.

    1 : 2,000,000 Tribal Map.   O.R.S.O.M. 1950.

Administrative:

1 : 2,000,000 S.G.A. 1960.

Chapter 13

THE GAMBIA—A RIVERINE ENCLAVE[1]

THE Gambia has an area of 4,008 square miles and a population of 336,000 in 1966. By far the smallest state in Africa, and with much water and swamp, it is entirely surrounded by Senegal, except for the short coastline. Common policies and shared services are being developed between the two countries, but complete integration is unlikely in view of their very different systems.

HISTORICAL OUTLINE [2]

The first European to describe a voyage up the Gambia River was Alvise da Ca'da Mosto, a Venetian, who sailed up it in 1455. Soon afterwards, by the Treaty of Tordesillas of 1494, the Portuguese secured exclusive rights of trade on the West Coast.

In 1588 a claimant to the throne of Portugal granted the right to trade along the Gambia River to certain London and Exeter merchants. These grants were later transferred to other merchants, after being confirmed by Queen Elizabeth I.

About 1651 James, Duke of Courland, erected a fort on an island 16 miles up-river. It was captured by an English fleet in 1661, renamed James Fort, and thereafter used by successive English trading companies.

In 1765 James Fort and other settlements were taken over by the Crown and administered as part of Senegambia, with its capital at the captured French town of St. Louis on the Senegal River. But in 1783 Senegambia ceased to exist, as Senegal was

---

[1] Dr. H. R. Jarrett, formerly resident in the Gambia, has very kindly read this chapter.

[2] For historical studies see Harry A. Gailey, *A History of the Gambia*, 1964, J. M. Gray, *A History of the Gambia*, 1940, and Lady Southorn, *The Gambia*, 1952. The latter also surveys, in a popular way, many aspects of the Gambia.

returned to the French, and the Gambia reverted to the Africa Company until 1821, when Crown rule was established.

In 1857, in exchange for the renunciation by the British Government of their gum rights at Portendik (Mauritanian Coast), the French ceded their remaining rights at Albreda, on the north bank of the Gambia.

The present state averages only some 15 miles in width (30 miles near the coast) and extends along either bank for 292 miles to the tidal limit of one of the finest navigable rivers of Africa. Such excellent rivers are rare, but its usefulness has been greatly reduced by the political boundary.

If the French had possessed this fine waterway, it is likely that they would have used it rather than the Senegal River as their main way into the interior. In the event, however, their first base was at St. Louis, in the dangerous Senegal Estuary; otherwise both town and river would have been of local rather than of territorial significance. 'Dakar' might have developed on the Gambia River, and a shorter and more direct railway could have been built from it to the Niger. Money thus saved might have been put to better use in developing western Senegal. It is possible to argue that this alternative site for Dakar would have been less suitable strategically and less healthy than present-day Dakar. Again, though ground-nut cultivation might have been less developed without the above-mentioned railways, a shorter railway from the present Mali to Kuntaur, at the limit of ocean navigation on the Gambia, would have hastened development of that poor inland country.

A fine waterway has been divorced from its natural hinterland and rational economic development of Senegambia gravely compromised. Political ruination of a natural waterway, and the division of Senegal into two limbs, could be ended by association with Senegal. A short railway link might then be made to Tambacounda on the Dakar–Niger Railway.

THE RIVER

In the dry season, the Gambia River is navigable only in the Gambia, but in the wet season launches may reach the Grey River. Ocean vessels up to 19 feet draught can always reach Kuntaur, 150 miles from Bathurst, and even George-town, 176 miles, if of lesser draught. Vessels not exceeding 6 feet 6 inches in draught can go on to Fatoto, 288 miles from Bathurst, the last wharf for regular steamers. Launches and canoes can reach Koina, 292 miles, the last village in the Gambia, where the tidal range is still 2 feet. There are thirty-three wharf towns at which Government steamers call.

Kuntaur is the most important groundnut centre on the river and also grows much rice.[1] Above Kuntaur floods are more significant than tides to navigators and riverside dwellers, especially if they are rice farmers. Floods can cause rises of up to 30 feet on certain parts of the river.

The estuary is generally considered to commence at Elephant Island, 93 miles upstream, where the river is 1 mile wide. This is the wet season limit of salt water, and of fringing mangroves, but in the dry season salt water penetrates to about 137 miles upstream. There are depths of 30 feet at the estuary mouth. The mile wide navigable channel to Bathurst has two sharp turns, and there is a bar which ships of over 21,000 tons cannot cross.

CLIMATE

The rains arrive first in the interior, which they reach in April, and they end there in September. On the coast they begin only in June or July, but last until October. August is normally the rainiest month everywhere. During the wet season, 30–45 inches of rain may be expected.

On and near the estuary, as in coastal Senegal, the intensity of the dry season is lessened by heavy dew, by high relative humidity, lower temperatures, and by sea breezes—though these are less strong than at Dakar. Marine Trade winds account for 43% of the average readings at Bathurst, the Har-mattan for 17%, and the rain-bearing westerlies or north-westerlies for 18%, the rest being calms. The fact that even the rain comes predominantly from the north-west is interest-ing. Upriver, where the Savannah Climate prevails, the Harmattan accounts for some 60% or more of the readings.

[1] See F. Huxley, ' Exploration in Gambia ', *Geographical Magazine*, Vol. 22, pp. 270–77, and E. Gordon, ' A Land Use Map of Kuntaur in the Gambia ', *Geographical Journal*, Vol. 116, pp. 216–17, for detailed land use and soil maps.

MAJOR REGIONS [1]

THE COASTAL REGION.   This is a flat and monotonous area of unconsolidated marine and aeolian sands, low dunes being typical, as in Senegal.   Some ten feet below the level surface is Tertiary ferruginous sandstone, which occasionally forms cliffs up to sixty feet high, as at Cape St. Mary.

As in western Senegal, the soil is light in colour and texture, originally low in chemical nutrients and very infertile.   The *niayes*, or wet hollows, so typical and useful there, are not found here.   The oil palm provides the only significant resource.

St. Mary's Island, $3\frac{1}{2} \times 1\frac{1}{4}$ miles, separated from the mainland by Oyster Creek, is really a sandbank.   It ends eastward and southward in a sandspit, occupied by a once insalubrious part of Bathurst, known ominously and—until recently—correctly as Half Die.

Bathurst.[2]   After Gorée Islet (off Dakar) was returned to the French in 1816, another base was required to suppress the slave trade on the Gambia River.   So a fort was established on Banjol(a) Island, which was soon renamed St. Mary's Island. The town developed as merchants and missionaries settled round the fort.   It was named Bathurst, after Earl Bathurst, then Secretary of State for the Colonies.   A district of Bathurst is known as Portuguese Town, and it has some evidence of Portuguese influence (probably from Brazilians), but it is doubtful if there was a Portuguese settlement here in the fifteenth or sixteenth centuries.

The nineteenth century establishment was undoubtedly fixed for strategic reasons at the constriction point on the river, where it is only 2 miles wide; otherwise, the site is exceedingly bad.   Bathurst is situated on two sand dunes about 6 and 8 feet high, separated by a depression at water level, and adjacent to a river subject to yearly floods.

Until the bund from Half Die was completed in 1949, annual floods caused Bathurst to be likened by a distinguished surgeon to ' a water-logged sponge, floating in a sea of its own

[1] See H. R. Jarrett, ' Major Natural Regions of the Gambia ', *Scottish Geographical Magazine*, Vol. 65, pp. 140–4, and ' Geographical Regions of the Gambia ', Vol. 66, pp. 163–9.

[2] See H. R. Jarrett, ' Bathurst—Port of the Gambia River ', *Geography*, 1951, pp. 98–107, and *West African Review*, 1948, pp. 633–6.

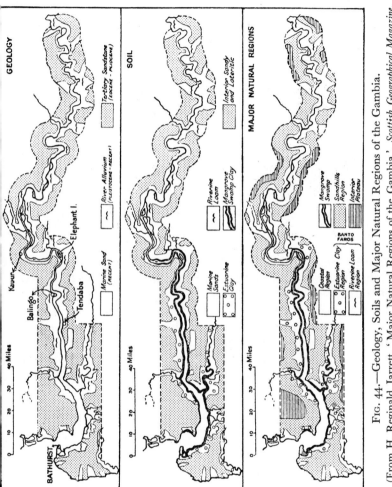
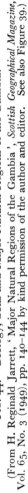

Fig. 44.—Geology, Soils and Major Natural Regions of the Gambia.

(From H. Reginald Jarrett, 'Major Natural Regions of the Gambia', *Scottish Geographical Magazine*, Vol. 65, No. 3 (1949), pp. 140–144 by kind permission of the author and editor. See also Figure 39.)

excreta' .[1] Especially was this so in Half Die and other reclaimed parts. Despite the town's broad streets, regular plan and at least one large open space, Bathurst was until then aptly described by President Roosevelt to Mr. Churchill as ' that hell-hole of yours '.[2] Malaria and yellow fever were formerly

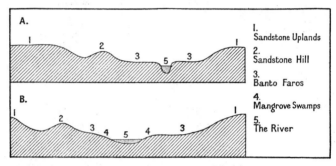

FIG. 45.—Profile of Major Natural Regions of the Gambia.

(From H. R. Jarrett, *A Geography of Sierra Leone and Gambia*, 1954, by kind permission of the author.)

severe, and the infantile mortality rate from dysentery and allied diseases exceeded 250 per thousand until 1938. President Roosevelt caught fever here in 1943, hence his remark.

The problem of re-developing Bathurst is made more acute by shortage of space and overcrowding. In 1942, 10% of the population regularly slept in the streets. One typical compound of three two-roomed houses and five one-roomed huts housed sixty people. The population has grown recently as follows:

	Total	African	Non-African
1911 . . .	7,700	7,470	230
1921 . . .	9,227	8,962	265
1931 . . .	14,370	14,185	185
1944 . . .	21,152	20,278	274
1951 . . .	19,602	Not available	
1965 . . .	29,780	,,	,,

The *Development and Welfare in the Gambia Report*, 1943, suggested reducing the population to a maximum of 8,000 people

[1] Warrington Yorke, ' The Problem of Bathurst ', *West African Review*, March 1937, p. 7.
[2] Quoted in Sir Winston S. Churchill, *The Second World War*, Vol. 4, *The Hinge of Fate*, p. 662.

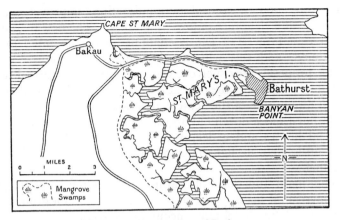

FIG. 46.—The position of Bathurst.
(From H. R. Jarrett, *A Geography of Sierra Leone and Gambia*, 1954, by kind permission of the author.)

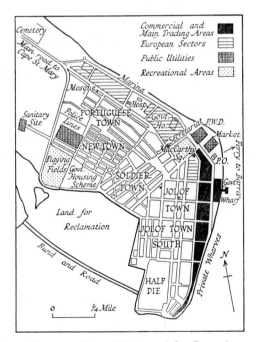

FIG. 47.—Plan of Bathurst (after Jarrett)

and 1,600 houses, control of immigration, improvement of drainage and clearance of low-lying areas. The new road and bund west from Half Die is enabling $3\frac{1}{2}$ square miles to be reclaimed, and this will greatly reduce congestion. A far better proposal, now shelved, was to build a new capital near Sukuta, leaving only the port at Bathurst. Meanwhile, there is much diminution of the acute war-time congestion.

Bathurst has a dozen old and small wharves owned by commercial houses and a deep-water one of 27 feet. Ships are also off-loaded to lighters and anchor in the 9–14 fathom channel.

The main functions of Bathurst are administrative and commercial, it being particularly a control point for groundnut exports. A fine hotel may encourage tourism.

Before and during the Second World War, Bathurst was a flying-boat base and a strategic counter to Dakar, unfriendly to the Allies from 1940 to 1943. But since the building of the fine airport at Yoff for Dakar, only one inter-continental service passes through Yundum (Bathurst), which could not equal Yoff in strategic position, facilities or health. Yundum is also used by West African services.

MANGROVE SWAMPS. The soils of the estuary and lower river fringes are of clayey alluvium, heavily impregnated with salt. This makes them very costly to reclaim.

Man avoids them, except for obtaining wood or capturing wild fowl. Even if a suitable rice could be found for these saline soils, removal of the mangrove would make wash-outs a danger.

BANTO FAROS. These are Manding words meaning ' beyond swamp '. They are grasslands which are submerged in the flood season but are above water in the dry season, when their coarse grasses wither. The Raphia palm provides piassava for local use, and might be more exploited.

Soils in this riverine ribbon are of lighter alluvium, and more fertile than those of the previous region. But below Kau-ur, where the Gambia River commences its great southward turn, the soils are saline and of little use.

Above Kau-ur, however, salt does not occur, and the ' banto faros ' of the Gambia River and its tributaries in MacCarthy and Upper River Provinces are fairly intensively used for rice cultivation by the women.   The men are mainly engaged in growing groundnuts for sale, millet and guinea corn.

THE SANDHILLS REGION.   This is underlain by light Tertiary sands and sandstone, and is well—even too well—drained. Low hills alternate with shallow valleys.   Much laterite or ferruginous crust is encountered, and the area is very infertile. Above Niankwi Tenda this zone is very narrow.   Below that point it averages 3 miles on either side.   Tall grass alternates with baobab, locust bean and kapok trees.

It was in this region, south of Bathurst and of Yundum airport, that the Colonial Development Corporation's ill-fated Mass-Production Poultry Scheme was sited.   Operations began in 1948, directed by an American with no African experience. In 1950 fowl typhoid killed 30,000 out of 80,000 birds, and it proved impossible to produce the necessary feeding-stuffs locally, upon which the scheme depended.   It was unpopular in the Gambia, where food was already short and made scarcer by the scheme.   The project was abandoned in 1951 at a loss of about £628,000.   If the sum expended in the Gambia had been used in Britain, 72 million eggs could have been produced. Only 38,520 eggs reached Britain, valued at £576, but produced at a cost of £20 15s. 7d. per egg.   This appalling failure well illustrates the poverty of the soil and the endemic fowl diseases of the area.

THE SANDSTONE (INTERIOR) PLATEAU.   This level area, which has an average altitude of 100 feet in the west, 120 feet in the middle river and 150–160 feet in the upper river, is an extension of the Eocene–Pliocene Ferlo Plateau of Senegal. Except in its flatness and slightly higher altitude, it resembles the Sandhills Region.   Ferruginous or lateritic outcrops are frequent and the Gambia River has cut a gorge in these between Niankwi Tenda and Fatoto.   At the latter point the cliffs are 150 feet high.

These last two regions are well populated because they are beyond danger of flood, are healthier and more useful.   Though infertile, the sandy soil is light and suited to the groundnut, which has long accounted for at least 95% by value of Gambia's exports.

Most Gambian villages stand on the dry, quickly-drained,

sandy soils adjacent to groundnut patches and to ' banto faros '
suitable for rice. As the latter cannot be easily grown in the
lower river because of mangrove and saline soils, truly rural
population tends to be greater up-river.[1]

ECONOMIC RESOURCES

AGRICULTURE

Groundnuts are the only major cash crop, and occupy two
thirds of the cultivated ' uplands '. The crop is grown entirely
by African farmers on some 210,000 acres, helped by 10,000–
20,000 seasonal workers. Average yields are low, and a unit
of the Medical Research Council found the soils to be extremely
deficient in magnesium, copper and boron. Improved varieties
of groundnuts and better farming methods are also required.

Groundnuts were first exported from the Gambia in 1830
and have been the leading export since 1845. Average exports
have been as follows:

	Tons.				Tons.
1840–49 .	. . . 10,000	1910–19 .	.	.	. 50,000
1850–89 .	. . . 20,000	1920–39 .	.	.	. 60,000
1890–99 .	. . . 27,000	1950–59 .	.	.	. 60,600[2]
1900–09 .	. . . 40,000	1960–65 .	.	.	. 59,360

The seasonal or ' strange farmers ', who in some years take
part in groundnut production in the Gambia, come (like the
similar *navétanes* who migrate to western Senegal) from the
Mali Republic, Portuguese Guinea and Guinea. They help
with cultivation and harvesting, and also farm their own
allotted patches.

This seasonal migration has been going on for at least a
century. In 1852 Governor MacDonnell stated that ' at least
one-third of the produce exported is from groundnuts grown
by strange farmers, who come from the interior and stay two
or three years '. This seasonal immigration, now much greater
to Senegal, is among the best known labour movements in
West Africa.

[1] H. R. Jarrett, 'Population and Settlement in the Gambia', *Geographical Review*, Vol. 38, pp. 633–6.
[2] Decorticated nuts were first exported in 1954 and almost exclusively so since 1956. They have been reckoned in terms of unshelled nuts.

SENEGAL

49. The Saloum River port of Kaolack

50. Salt works at Kaolack. Natural *tannes*, or salt marshes, are evident around.

51. Groundnut lands being prepared after the first rains near Bambey

Brushwood protection of the ful mango tree and of a village. typical scene in the better oded Serer country between Dakar-Niger Railway and the Saloum River.

53. Working face of iron-ore mine in Kédia d'Idjil, east of Fort Gouraud.

MAURITANIA

54. Mineral pier, dump and marshalling yards at Port Etienne.

Jarrett has shown[1] that there is no close correlation between the number of strange farmers in any particular year and either the volume of groundnuts exported after harvesting or the price payable to the farmer for the crop. The universal African desire to travel and escape for a while from family ties, and to earn cash for a bride price, debt redemption or capital equipment, are probably the main incentives. A poor season, however, acts as a disincentive in the following one.

That the Gambia is excessively dependent upon groundnuts is all too evident, yet it is not easy to find alternative exports. The most promising development may be increased rice cultivation, since imported rice often costs three times as much per ton as exported groundnuts.

Rice, the favourite though not the main foodstuff, is of ever-increasing importance. There has been some remarkable clearance of mangrove swamp in the lower river, and of fresh-water swamp in the upper river, by farmers for rice cultivation, so that the area under that crop (65,000 acres in 1964) doubled in sixteen years. The potential rice area is estimated at 200,000 acres. A large-scale mechanised scheme failed in the fifties.

Millet, locally known as *Koos*, is the basic food. It is grown in rotation, or inter-cropped with groundnuts. It is said that by inter-cropping, the extensive roots of millet dry out the soil and hasten the maturing of the groundnuts. Millet does not flourish in the poor upland soils, though it is the basic food.

Lesser food crops are maize, guinea corn, cassava, hungry rice, sweet potatoes, other vegetables, the oil palm and the coconut—the last two mainly in the coastlands.

Apart from groundnuts, the only agricultural products exported are palm kernels, hides, skins and beeswax. The first of these accounts for some 1–2% of exports only. The others are insignificant, though beeswax was the main export up to 1830, when groundnuts supplanted it. Cotton is grown, especially in North Bank Province, for local cloth.

Minerals

Ilmenite, with a high titanium dioxide content, was located in 1953 at Sanyang, 30 miles south-west of Bathurst. The ore

[1] H. R. Jarrett, ' The Strange Farmers of the Gambia ', *Geographical Review*, 1949, pp. 649–57.

is found on raised beaches along the Atlantic coast and extends from the surface downwards about 8 or 9 feet. These deposits were worked from 1956–8 but were then abandoned owing to unfavourable prices.

CONCLUSION

The Gambia River has been prevented from serving its proper hinterland, and the tiny Gambia has suffered severely from the disadvantages of a one-crop economy. Increased rice cultivation can do much to alter this.

Although the country is an enclave, no advantage has been taken of this fact, e.g. the Gambia might have developed many oil factories to attract Senegal groundnuts. Trade from across the frontier in hides and skins might also have been encouraged. Bathurst could have been developed as a free port, like Monrovia, Liberia. The future may lay in integration with Senegal. The Gambia River would then be available to cheapen the transport costs of groundnuts and other goods from a vast hinterland, and the river towns and Bathurst should prosper.

BIBLIOGRAPHY

See footnotes cited above. Also:

BURTON BENEDICT (ed.), *Problems of smaller territories*, 1967.

H. DESCHAMPS, *Le Sénégal et la Gambie*, *Que sais-Je?*, Paris, 1964.

M. R. HASWELL, *Economics of Agriculture in a Savannah Village*, Colonial Research Studies, No. 8, H.M.S.O., 1953.

D. A. R. RICHARDSON, ' Private Enterprise on the River Gambia ', *Progress*, 1966, pp. 229–38.

Statistical and Economic Review, United Africa Company, March 1953.

MAPS

Topographic:

    1 : 10,000 Directorate of Overseas Surveys, 1948.

    1 : 50,000   ,,   ,,   ,,   ,,

    1 : 125,000   ,,   ,,   ,,   1956.

    1 : 200,000 Service Géographique de l'Afrique Occidentale Française.

    1 : 250,000 G.S.G.S. 1949.

    1 : 500,000   ,,   1948.

    1 : 1,000,000   ,,   1948.

Special:

    1 : 25,000 Land Use. Directorate of Overseas Surveys, 1958.

Chapter 14

MAURITANIA—THE LINK WITH NORTH AFRICA[1]

ALTHOUGH the Mali and Niger Republics also adjoin North African lands in the Sahara, Mauritania is the truest link with North Africa, particularly Morocco. Contacts between peoples are of long standing, and the predominant inhabitants of present-day Mauritania are known in French literature as *Maures*. These people call themselves *Bidanes* ('whites') and have Berber and Arab blood, with some Negro admixture. They are often light in colour and dress in blue robes in order, it is said, to accentuate their pale colouring. They are of medium height, spare in build, with wavy black hair, and are predominantly nomadic keepers of livestock. The few agriculturalists are generally their semi-slaves or descendants of slaves. The Moors are well known for their hospitality and are great drinkers of sweet green tea, said to have been introduced about a century ago from Morocco. Their way of life derives from their nomadic existence and Islamic faith.

HISTORICAL OUTLINE

Despite its name, modern Mauritania does not coincide with the former Roman Province of *Mauretania Tingitana*, whose limits did not extend beyond the Draa River, far to the north. Indeed, it was in the period after the decay of the Roman Empire and at the height of the Arab conquests, that contacts between the areas now occupied by Mauritania and Morocco were closest.

As with most other parts of West Africa, the first European contacts were in the fifteenth century by Portuguese who came

[1] I am indebted to Monsieur G. J. Duchemin, Director of the Senegal-Mauritania Centre of the Institut Français d'Afrique Noire, for his valuable comments on this chapter and for guiding me in Mauritania.

227

for the slave trade.   They established a fort on Arguin Island,
which was later captured by the Dutch and English.   Probably because of the sparse population, the slave trade soon gave
way to that in gum arabic, over which there was intense rivalry

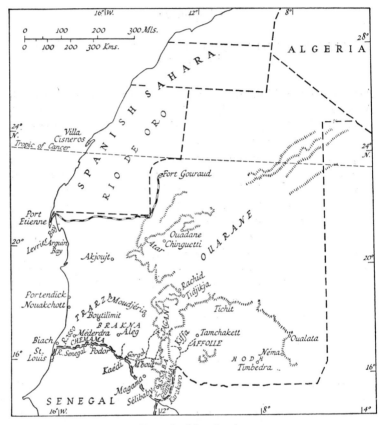

FIG. 48—Mauritania.

between the Dutch and French, until the Dutch finally withdrew from the coast in 1727.   Thereafter, the rivalry was between the French and British, until the British withdrew in
1857, against French cession of Albreda on the Gambia River.
However, the trade in gum declined in the twentieth century,
in face of competition from the Sudan.

Most of modern Mauritania, as distinct from points on the

coast, was occupied between 1902 and 1914. It became a colony in 1920 and an independent republic in 1960.

The present-day country extends north and north-eastward from the Senegal River ultimately into pure desert. Its area of 419,121 square miles makes it the third largest state of West Africa and twice the size of France. It is larger than Nigeria, yet the measure of the aridity of Mauritania is the population of only 1,070,000 in 1966. Only six towns have over 3,000 people—Port Etienne, Nouakchott, Kaédi, Tidjika, Atar and Aioun.

With by far the lowest density of population in West Africa— indeed one of the lowest in Africa—the land is indeed one of difficulty. Until 1958 its political capital lay outside the country at St. Louis, Senegal. It is now at Nouakchott.

Despite its relatively long coastline, Mauritania has only one port, Port Etienne, on the boundary with Rio de Oro.

CLIMATE
(See also Chapter 3)

The outstanding features of the climate of this territory are the persistence in the interior of the Harmattan winds, the consequent aridity, and the great variation between day and night temperatures.

Humid Marine Trade winds are felt along the coast, but they bring little rain, and that mostly in ' winter '. The wet South-westerlies reach as far as the centre or north between August and October, but to a very variable extent and inten-sity. In the extreme south-east of the territory, where the Southern Sahel climate prevails, the annual rainfall is about 18 inches at Kaédi and 26 inches at Sélibaby. At Rosso it averages nearly 12 inches. North of Rosso the Northern Sahel climate is found.

In the north-centre about 3 inches annual rain occurs in the Southern Saharan climate, e.g. at Atar. Although the rain-fall is so small, the cooling effect may be significant and wel-come. Heavy dew at night throughout the territory provides some vital moisture. North of 20–21° N. rain is rare and Saharan conditions prevail.

So far as temperature is concerned, the diurnal variations

exceed the annual ones. As a rough average, the diurnal range is 20–30° F. on the coast and 30–35° F. inland.

WATER RESOURCES

It is obvious from the above that water is a fundamental factor in Mauritanian life and development. It is generally found at great depths in the north and often so even in the south.

Water is most readily available in the Chemama or Senegal Valley; in clay depressions in the south, where it can generally be found not deeper than 60 feet; and at the base of large dunes where, however, it may be as much as 300 feet deep.

In the region limited by Aleg, Podor and Kaédi, there is much water available at 130–195 feet in depth, but it can be tapped extensively only with costly equipment. To the west, in Trarza, the water table is nearer the surface and is already reached by the local people. Its exploitation has been greatly improved by the French. Originally, there were only a few earth barrages in Mauritania, which often lasted no longer than a year. There are now modern ones at Aneikat-Gaoua (Brakna), which permit the cultivation of 5,000 acres, a similar one at Mokta Sfera, 25 miles east of Kiffa, and some ten others. So far some 30,000 acres have been brought under cultivation with water from French constructed dams. More are needed, however, especially along regular cattle routes.

GEOLOGY AND NATURAL REGIONS

Pre-Cambrian rocks are present in Mauritania, but they are generally covered by other series. In western Mauritania they are obscured by great accumulations of Quaternary sands, which occur in north-east to south-west trending dunes, some being live and some fixed.

Central Mauritania sees the thinning of these sands. Cretaceous and Post-Eocene rocks occur in Trarza and Brakna; to the north and east pre-Cambrian rocks outcrop or are near the surface.

In eastern Mauritania Ordovician, Silurian and—to a lesser extent—Devonian sandstones give rise to magnificent scarps which can be traced through the country from near Sélibaby to far beyond Atar. (See Fig. 48.)

THE COASTAL ZONE. There are the same smooth shore and mobile dunes as in Senegal, but with two significant differences. First, a few capes and islands break the coastline as at Arguin, and these were used as slave depots and, for much longer, as gum-trading points. Secondly, instead of the always fresh-water *niayes* of Senegal, with their luxuriant vegetation, there is, in the north, a succession of salt encrusted mud-flats (*sebkhas*), marshy only after rare rains, which are remnants of former lagoons. South of Nouakchott, is the Aftout-es-Saheli clay depression, which is almost always marshy in character. In the far south is a former Senegel outlet, and beyond this marsh is a long spit upon which, within Senegal, at St. Louis, were the government offices of Mauritania from 1920 to 1960.

The coast has shifting sandbanks, e.g. at Portendik and Arguin, and the action of the dry winds on loose sands often causes sandstorms; whilst the waters of the cold Canary Current, in contact with warm air, produce fog and mist. These and the smooth shoreline add to its dangerous character. Yet there is a considerable continental shelf with much plankton, so that ships from Europe and the Canaries, sometimes based on Port Etienne, fish for varied fish and crustacea.

Port Etienne lies on the east side of the Cape Blanco Peninsula (the western half of which is Spanish) and on the west side of the sheltered Lévrier Bay. It exports iron ore brought by mineral line from near Fort Gourand, and has fish-drying and freezing factories. Dried fish are mostly exported to Cameroon and Equatorial Africa. The railway also brings in water, and some is condensed from sea water.

Nouakchott is the Mauritanian capital and has a small pier.

THE CHEMAMA. This is the Mauritanian part of the Senegal River flood-plain, is Mauritania's only large area of arable land, and is mostly cultivated by the Toucouleur. From it comes much of the millet consumed in Mauritania. *Kaédi* and *Rosso* are important river trading points.

PLAINS OF SOUTHERN TRARZA AND BRAKNA. These lie south of the Méderdra–Aleg–Moudjéria line. The country is composed of clayey plains (*aftouts*) and of intervening north-east–south-west trending stable dunes (*sbar*). The latter are infertile, but the former can be used as water becomes available. These plains are covered by fairly dense Sahel Savannah.

In the short rainy season there are many shallow meres and water-courses, and even some flooding. Modern barrages are being constructed. Trarza is the leading gum area, followed by Brakna. *Méderdra* is a gum-collecting centre and has artisans who make cushions and decorated coffers.

CENTRAL PLAINS OF NORTHERN TRARZA, NORTHERN BRAKNA AND AKJOUJT. These lie north of about 17° N. and are also known locally as the Sahel. Dunes are progressively barer and more mobile, and north of about 18½° N. Sahel Savannah gives way to Southern Saharan vegetation. Hills have spurges, but acacias and useful grasses occur only in damp depressions.

South-west of Akjoujt, there is an *aftout*, some 30 miles wide, which reaches the coast. Copper occurs in basal rocks near the same settlement (see below).

THE GRANITE MASS OF ZEMMOUR. This is situated in the north-west, astride the Rio de Oro boundary. Its greater height and impervious rocks enable acacias and other dwarf trees, shrubs and grasses to survive to a surprising extent. Camels are extensively raised here.

GUIDIMAKA. This lies around Sélibaby, in the extreme south-east of Mauritania. It is similar to the Bondou region of Senegal, except that Guidimaka also has steep-edged mesas, which are outliers of the Primary sandstone scarp of Assaba. The sub-region of Douaich is entirely composed of such outliers. The seasonal Gorgol streams provide opportunities for cropping and intermittent pasturing; tamarisks, acacias and small palms are common.

THE SANDSTONE PLATEAUX. These occupy almost all eastern Mauritania. South of the scarp running north-east-wards from Atar, the plateaux are of Ordovician and Silurian sandstones and shales, probably similar to the Voltaian system of Ghana, and equally infertile. In Mauritania their barren character is heightened by aridity and masks of loose sand. In the far north the sandstones are of Devonian to Lower Carboni-ferous age, dip north and have east–west scarps. (See Fig. 48).

As in Ghana, the edges of the sandstone are impressive scarps. Continuing from the Mali Republic, they run east to west north of Tichit, north to south west of Kiffa and towards Sélibaby, south to north towards Rachid, north-westward to near Akjoujt, and then mostly north-eastward in several series. The scarps average two hundred feet in height, are sometimes broken into several mesas and etched by ravines. Indeed, south of Atar the scarp is eroded into a rather chaotic collection of valleys and flat-topped hills. Springs are fairly frequent along the scarps and have helped such settlements as Atar, Moudjéria, Kiffa and Tichit. Some seasonal torrents have been dammed to make possible the greater production of millet.

Fort Gouraud lies on the Moroccan road and is an important post near the Rio de Oro border. Eastward lies the Kédia d'Idjil hills whose north-eastern peaks have rich hæmatite iron ore, Mauritania's most important resource (p. 235). To the north-west lies the Sebkha of Idjil, once much exploited for salt, but now worked mainly for local sale to the nearest settlements.

Atar (see Fig. 48 and Plates 53-4) is an important military post and track centre, with a trade in dates. *Moudjéria* also trades in dates.

On the plateau the only settlements of note are the oases *Chinguetti*, *Ouadane* and *Tidjikja*. They all produce dates, the latter having some 50,000 palms.

ECONOMIC RESOURCES

AGRICULTURE

Both because of the nature of the country and the attitude of the people, agriculture is of minor importance. Real cropping is found only in the Chemama, in oases, along seasonal rivers such as the Gorgols and Karakoro (respectively west and east of Assaba), and adjacent to barrages. It is mostly done by descendants of former slaves of the Moors, by Wolof below Dagana, by Toucouleur from Dagana to Magama, and by Sarakollé above Magama. Millet is the main crop, with much smaller amounts of maize, rice and water melons. Rice is almost only grown towards M'Bout and in Guidimaka by the Sarakollé. Temperate cereals are grown in oases.

Dates are important near centres mentioned above. Unfortunately, they are not produced in sufficient quantity or of such quality as to be exported.

Gum Arabic is produced from the *Acacia senegal* and *A. arabica*, the first giving the harder and better gum. The gum is employed in pharmacy, in cooking, in textile industries and in the manufacture of dyestuffs. It first came to mediæval Europe from the ports of Asia Minor, whose merchants had obtained it from Arabs in Red Sea ports, who in turn had bought it from the areas that are now in the Sudan. Because of the trade being in the hands of Arabs, the gum came to be known as ' gum arabic '.

When Europeans went to the Mauritanian Coast, the gum trade soon predominated, and was the source of rivalry between the Dutch, French and British from the seventeenth to the nineteenth centuries.

France is the greatest consumer of gum arabic in the world, but important quantities are also used by the United Kingdom and the United States. In the last quarter of a century the Sudan has again been able to control the market by exporting gum of higher quality.

Gum is obtained by tearing strips of bark from the trees, which bear from their fourth or fifth year until their twentieth to twenty-fifth year. The tree also provides fibre for rope and nets. Most of the Mauritanian production comes from areas situated between 15° and 17° N. It is especially important in Trarza, which produces about 1,000 tons, and in Brakna. In Trarza the trees grow on the north-east to south-west trending sand dunes to the number of about 50–150 per acre, especially east of the road from Rosso to about 30 miles north of Méderdra. The dampness of sea-breezes and dew by night are important factors in the growth of trees in this area. In Brakna rainfall is greater and more certain, but the sandy-clay soils are less suitable than the dune soils of Trarza. Gum is generally sent down to the once-famous *escales* on the Senegal River, such as Dagana, Podor, Kaédi and Matam.

LIVESTOCK

Cattle are the traditional resource of this poor country[1] and are overwhelmingly of the *Maure* type of Zebu. Maure

[1] See also Chapter 7. There are excellent cattle maps of Mauritania and Senegal prepared by F. Bonnet-Dupeyron and published by the *Office de la Recherche Scientifique de la France d'Outre-Mer*. See also P. Prigent, P. Kane and B. Ka, L'élevage du boeuf en Mauritanie, *Bull. du Ser. Zootech. et Epizoot.*, de l'A.O.F., 5, pp. 235–41.

cattle are very hardy and weigh some 800 lb. on an average. Extensively used as beasts of burden, they will carry up to about 200 lb. each. Most cattle are found in the Hodh and near the seasonal Gorgol rivers. There is an abattoir and freezing plant at Kaédi, the main livestock centre. Livestock are also exported on the hoof to Senegal and the Gambia.

Sheep and goats are mainly concentrated in the coastlands, in Tidjikja, and especially around Tamchakett (E. Assaba). Lesser concentrations are in Brakna and Trarza. Mutton is a very important item in the diet of the Moors. Sheep and goat skins are used in making saddlery, cushions and much else. Only in the south are there sufficient skins for export.

Donkeys are important as beasts of burden in the better-watered areas, especially near the coast and in the south-east. Camels are important everywhere as beasts of burden and are extensively hired to Senegal merchants during the groundnut trading season. The main area for camels is around Akjoujt.

In the northern areas, livestock largely depend on seasonal pastures and on such plants as the Nitre bush (*Nitraria refusa*), the Had (*Cornulaca monocantha*), various grasses, annuals and chenopods, e.g. *Haloxylon tamariscifolium*. Rearing of cattle and sheep, transport, constructional work and commerce are the main source of income for the inhabitants of the north.

MINERALS

Mauritania is being transformed economically and socially by the opening of rich hæmatite iron ore deposits. These occur as thick cappings on the north-eastern peaks of the Kédia d'Idjil Hills, east of Fort Gouraud. There are at least 250 million tons of 63% iron content, half of which can be worked open cast, has few impurities, and is very dry. There is also much ore of lower iron content. A company with French, British, German and Italian capital is mining the deposit, and a 400-mile railway has been built to Port Etienne, the nearest deep-water port, whose natural depths of 44 feet alongside the mineral pier enable the loading of 65,000 ton ore carriers in calm water. A more direct route across Rio de Oro was ruled out in the face of onerous Spanish terms; nevertheless, a $1\frac{1}{4}$ mile tunnel through granite had to be built at a cost of £3 million to keep within Mauritania at the south-eastern corner of Rio de Oro. Nearby fixed sand dunes required spraying to secure a stable track, while nearer Port Etienne mobile dunes may require periodic realignment of the track. Townships were built at either end of the line in utter desert, and water is carried to Port Etienne from a well 75 miles along the railway.

A branch railway is to be built to permit working of copper ore (1·9–2·9% copper) near Akjoujt, where an annual output of 20,000 to 25,000 tons of blister copper and a little associated gold would be possible. There is also more iron near Atar. A little salt is still dug in the Sebkha d'Idjil, north west of Fort Gouraud, and in the Aftout-es-Sahéli, north of Nouakchott.

The metamorphosis of Mauritania from direst poverty to modest viability is akin to that of some oil-rich Arab sheikdoms.

BIBLIOGRAPHY

See references in above text. Also *Etudes Mauritaniennes* published by Centre I.F.A.N., St. Louis, Senegal, especially:

TIM BRIERLY, ' Mauritania ', *Geographical Magazine*, February 1965, pp. 754–65.

R. J. HARRISON CHURCH, ' Mauritania ', *Focus* (American Geographical Society), Vol. XII, November 1961; ' Problems and Development of the Dry Zone of West Africa ', *Geographical Journal*, cxxvii, pp. 187–204 and ' Port Etienne: A Mauritanian Pioneer Town ', *Geographical Journal*, cxxviii, pp. 498–504.

MOKHTAR OULD HAMIDOUN, *Précis sur la Mauritanie*, 1952, and PIERRE MUNIER, *L'Assaba*, 1952.

C. TOUPET, ' Orientation Bibliographique sur la Mauritanie ', *Bulletin de l'Institut Français d'Afrique Noire*, Dakar, Vol. XXI, pp. 201–39.

MAPS

See pp. 183 and 235. Also:

Topographic:

    1 : 20,000 Port Etienne and Kédia d'Idjil. S.G./A.O.F. 1957.

    1 : 100,000 Cap Blanc. 2 sheets. I.G.N. 1954.

    1 : 200,000 S.G./A.O.F. and I.G.N. Some 20 sheets.

    1 : 500,000 S.G./A.O.F. and I.G.N. 1966.

Transhumance:

    1 : 200,000 and 1 : 500,000 O.R.S.O.M. 1950.

Population:

    1 : 1,300,000 O.R.S.O.M. 1950.

    1 : 2,000,000 Tribal Map O.R.S.O.M. 1950.

Chapter 15

MALI—LAND OF LIVESTOCK AND
IRRIGATION WORKS[1]

THIS country of 464,752 square miles is some five times the size of Great Britain. Nevertheless, its population in 1966 was estimated at only 4,654,000, so that it has an average of about nine people per square mile. Over three million people are sedentary, especially the Bambara, Marka, Songhaï, Malinké, Dogon, Minianka and Senoufo. Most of the rest are nomads, especially the Fulani, Tuareg and Maure.

The territory is dry, even in its southern parts. The growing of crops, especially rice, depends almost entirely upon irrigation or flooding from the Niger River and its tributaries. The greatest resource, however, is livestock. One indication of poverty is that men migrate regularly from the Mali Republic to grow and harvest groundnuts in Senegal and the Gambia, to work on plantations in Guinea and the Ivory Coast, and in mines, on cocoa farms and in domestic service in Ghana.

HISTORICAL OUTLINE

It was in the lands that at present constitute the Mali Republic that the most famous ancient empires of West Africa were centred. The first of these was that of Ghana, which may have been established in the fourth century A.D., and is mentioned in Arab writings from the ninth century onwards. In the eleventh century it was probably at its zenith, but after 1076 was conquered by peoples from North Africa, and its rulers became converted to Islam. It finally declined after a

[1] M. Gérard Brasseur, formerly Directeur of the Institut Français d'Afrique Noire at Koulouba–Bamako, gave me most valuable criticism of this chapter.

237

second conquest in 1240.   Ruins of its capital exist at Koumbi Saleh, just over 200 miles north-north-east of Bamako.

Ghana was succeeded by the Mali (or Manding) Empire. This originated in the seventh century, was at its climax in the thirteenth to fourteenth centuries, and had its capital at Mali on the left bank of the Niger.   In the fifteenth century this empire declined at the hands of the Gao or Songhaï Empire, which likewise traced its origin to the seventh century.

The Songhaï Empire split up after 1591 and, until the arrival of the French at the end of the nineteenth century, there were a number of minor states under the Fulani and the Bambara.

The three empires of Ghana, Mali and Gao were quite highly organised and received considerable revenues from trans-Saharan trade.   The later period of the Ghana and the whole era of the Gao Empire were strongly influenced by peoples from North Africa, and there can be little doubt that even the Mali Empire, although indigenous, ultimately depended upon North Africa for its economic survival.

The most famous explorers of this area were the Arab Ibn Batuta in the fifteenth century ; Mungo Park who travelled down the Niger between 1795 and 1797 and again on his fatal journey in 1805; Réné Caillé, who visited the area in 1827; and Barth of 1850–55.

The routeway up the Senegal and down the Niger was an obvious one for European penetration, since it offered great stretches of river navigation with no major physical obstacles. The French established their first permanent fort on the upper Senegal as early as 1712.   Expeditions were sent to Bambouk (Falémé Valley) in search of gold in 1730–1, 1756 and 1824, though by the latter date gum was of greater importance.

Advance beyond the Senegal River was initiated by Faidherbe and by 1866 Ségou on the Niger had been reached. Forts between the Senegal and Niger Rivers were built between 1879 and 1881.   The railway was begun in the latter year, being opened to Koulikoro in 1904.   It linked the upper limit of navigation on the Senegal River with two navigable reaches of the Niger.   The through line to Dakar was opened in 1924.

The territory became a separate French colony from 1892–9, and again from 1904.   It has had its present name since independence in 1960; it is a reminder of the earlier empire.

CLIMATE AND VEGETATION
(See also Chapters 3 and 4.)

Typical average rainfall figures are Araouane 2 inches, Gao 9, Mopti 20, Kayes 30, Bamako 44 and Sikasso 55 inches. Most of the Mali Republic is dry; north of 19° N. there is

FIG. 49.—Mali.

M = Mopti, Bg = Bandiagara, Dj = Djenné, Di = Diafarabé, Sg = Sansanding, Ko = Koulikoro, S = Sikasso, Ba = Bafoulabé, Go = Gourma Rharous.

virtually no rain and Saharan conditions prevail. Even in the north-east in the mountainous Adrar des Iforas, there is less rainfall than in the Aïr Massif of the Niger Republic.

South of about 19° N. and extending nearly to Timbuktu, or farther south in the east and west, are Semi-Saharan conditions.

From about 17° to 15° N. in the Northern Sahel and Southern

Sahel climatic zones rainfall is light, variable and of short duration. Diurnal temperature ranges remain high, because of almost unimpeded insolation and the high degree of refraction. Evaporation is also intense, so that the human body can feel cold even when the temperatures are 60–70° F. In building reservoirs for watering the large numbers of livestock, account must be taken of this high evaporation. The Niger River and its tributaries may modify conditions by their flood or irrigation waters. Near the rivers are extensive swamps; Otherwise the vegetation is Sahel Savannah.

Between 15° and 12° N. the Savannah climate prevails and the vegetation is Sudan Savannah except, again, near the rivers.

South of about 12° N., in the extreme south-west, the Southern Savannah climate occurs and the wet season is longer. Because of the many ferruginous crusts, the rainfall is less effective than might be supposed and the vegetation is poor Northern Guinea Savannah.

Geology and Relief

Most of the Mali Republic is very flat. Yet it is well known for its vivid sandstone mountains and plateaux which are limited by steep scarps. The sandstones are probably Ordovician and Silurian in age, are flat-bedded, and lie unconformably on Pre-Cambrian schists and gneisses. In the sandstones are sheet intrusions of dolerite and gabbro. The most famous sandstone scarps are Tambaoura south of Kayes, that of the Manding Mountains, and the long and almost continuous scarp which extends from Banfora in the Upper Volta northwards to the magnificent Bandiagara Scarp south of the Niger Bend.

The other major relief feature is Adrar des Iforas, which consists of Pre-Cambrian schists and granitic intrusions.

The Niger River and its tributaries flow through the great depression which is so much a feature of West Africa between the ancient rocks of much of the Guinea Coast and the massifs of the Saharan interior. In this depression was a late Tertiary–Quaternary lake, which was drained by over-spilling into the Lower Niger, whose sources were then in Adrar des Iforas.

The western part of the Mali Republic benefits from the

55. Bamako and the Niger Plain from the Ordovician-Silurian escarpment, on which stands Koulouba—the administrative quarter.

MALI

56. Bamako Market in Neo-Sudan style. Note also the many commercial houses and the numerous trees of this city.

57. The Sansanding Barrage and Bridge.
Note one of three travelling arms for
adjustment of sluices.

58. Adjusting a sluice

59. Combine harvesting of paddy

Timbuktu, with mosques in the distance

The Bandiagara Ordovician Silurian scarp of levelded sandstone. Note the Sahel Savannah vegetation.

62. Village on the Bandiagara escarpment

Part of the Hombori Mountains

Sheep near the Niger River

NIGER REPUBLIC

66. The Tigueddi scarp, thirty-
eight miles south of Agades.

PORTUGUESE GUINEA

67. Bissau. Note the spac
roads of this capital, four
1941. The river mud flats s
the great tidal range along
south-western coast. At Biss
is about $17\frac{1}{2}$ feet.

68. Protective and dividing
bunds (or earth embankments)
in a swamp rice field

Senegal River, with which the Upper Niger River communi-
cated via the Nara–Nioro sill until the Tertiary inland lake
was formed.

MAJOR REGIONS

BAMBOUK AND THE MANDING MOUNTAINS. These mountains of Palæozoic sandstone are northern spurs of the Fouta
Djallon of Guinea. The Bambouk Mountains terminate
westward in the impressive Tambaoura Scarp, overlooking
the Falémé River. A rocky sill in the Senegal River, just
above Kayes, is an outlying remnant, and makes that town the
limit of seasonal navigation on the Senegal.

Kayes. Before the completion of the through Dakar–Niger
Railway, Kayes was a trans-shipment point between the Senegal
River and the railway to the Niger River. The town is a
major cattle and sheep market, dependent upon the export
trade in livestock to Senegal by rail and road. It also trades
in gum, hides and skins, and there is a local tannery. The
population in 1958 was 19,517.

The Manding Mountains lie east of the Bafing and end east
of Bamako, where their southern edge dominates the Niger
left bank and is occupied by Koulouba, the administrative
quarter of Bamako. These mountains are flat-topped and
often covered by laterite. As in the case of the Senegal River
at Kayes, there are outliers in the Niger below Bamako, so
making that city the lower limit of navigation of the Upper
Niger. (See photograph p. 128.)

Bamako. The capital of the Mali Republic was a mere village
when occupied by Borgis–Desbordes in 1883. It developed
rapidly, not so much as a result of the separation of the territory
from Senegal, but rather from the opening of the railway in
1904. In consequence of this, it became the capital, which
had previously been at Kayes. The greatest impetus, however,
came after 1924, when the through railway to Dakar was
opened, and trans-shipment at Kayes to the Senegal River ended.
The Niger bridge, opened 1960, will help develop the south bank.

The political departments are at Koulouba; the technical
departments, the railway, commercial and African quarters are
on the plain between the scarp and the river. The town has

been very well planned and varied trees line the roads. Some of the buildings are in an interesting neo-Sudan style.

Bamako is an important administrative and military centre, as well as one for railway, road, and local and international air communications. It is also a very important market, especially for cattle and for kola nuts. It has a famous school for training

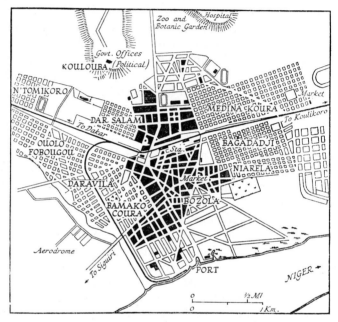

FIG. 50.—Bamako (after Dresch). A bridge across the Niger was opened in 1960.

African artisans, especially in gold and silver filigree-work, leather and ivory. These articles are exported in small amounts to neighbouring territories. There are minor industrial establishments, such as wood and metal furniture works. There is also an important abattoir from which meat is sent by air to Conakry, Abidjan, Lome and Cotonou. Near Bamako are small fruit (generally mango) plantations, which are almost the sole source of edible fruit in Mali.

Bamako has grown rapidly since the Second World War; the 1946 census recorded nearly 37,000 people, that of 1954 65,000, and the 1960 census 131,900.

Koulikoro. Just as Bamako owes some of its importance from being at the lower end of the navigable Upper Niger, so Koulikoro is significant as being at the commencement of the navigable Middle Niger. The railway joins the towns and the two navigable reaches of the river. Apart from its significance as a river port, Koulikoro has a groundnut oil factory, which also extracts shea butter oil. The Office du Niger has a rice mill, which hulls most of the rice which it sells outside the Mali Republic. Koulikoro is a collecting centre for goods railed westwards to the coast, and for the despatch of imported goods down the river. As a port it deals with about 60,000 tons of traffic.

Sahel. This is an area of sandy lowlands lying north-west and north of the Niger River, as far as Ségou and extending into Mauritania. It was through the Nara–Nioro sill that the Upper Niger once drained to the Senegal River, and present intermittent drainage is also in that direction.

In this region the Ghana Empire had its capital, but today the area is very dry. Nevertheless, it supports great numbers of livestock, especially sheep. The regional centres are Nioro and Nara.

Azaouak. This is the vast sandy plain and cattle country north of Timbuktu, drier than the Sahel but otherwise similar.

Tanezrouft. This is flat stony desert, while El Hank, in the far north, is broken desert country.

Timetrine, Terrecht and Adjouz. In these regions Tertiary limestones and arid erosion forms give broken country, with occasional scarps. Ouadis from Adrar des Iforas sometimes have water but, as their courses are often blocked by dunes, marshes tend to form. The eastern edge of Terrecht is known as the Kreb de Terrecht and adjoins the dry Tilemsi valley. All these lands are very dry.

Tilemsi Valley. A sandy trough, this averages 30 miles in width and some 170 miles in length. It is a magnificent example of a valley etched in a wetter period, when the Tilemsi was the upper part of the present-day Lower Middle Niger.

Tessalit lies above the eastern edge of the Tilemsi but below a great bluff some 300 feet high.

Adrar des Iforas. This great highland somewhat resembles the larger Aïr Massif and is an extension of the Ahaggar

Massif. Adrar des Iforas averages 2,000 feet above sea level and is drained westward to the Tilemsi. Archaean schists comprise most of the north, east and south; granite intrusions make up the western heights towards the Tilemsi. Quaternary rejuvenation has made the ouadis narrow and deep.

Broken and trenched, Adrar des Iforas is also barren. It is almost uninhabited, unlike Aïr, home of some Tuareg.

IOULLEMEDENE. Lying between Adrar des Iforas and the Niger River, and extending into the Niger Republic (see Djerma Ganda) and the Sokoto region of Nigeria, this area is very dry and eroded. The annual rainfall at Menaka is about 8 inches. Many mesas occur, and north of Menaka is a rather large group of hills which rise 300 feet above the plain.

THE NIGER VALLEY. The Niger and its tributaries are the life-givers of the Mali Republic. Water is used for rice cultivation, the rivers for navigation and for fishing; and it would appear that, in the Inland Delta region at least, rainfall is increased by the amount of water in the many channels of the river. Downstream, as far as the annually flooded areas (between Diafarabé and Timbuktu), the river plains are generally well peopled and sometimes cultivated with the plough in a system of simple mixed farming.

Although the annual floods of the Niger have long been utilised to grow millet, it is only since about 1940 that great efforts have been made to harness them to grow rice and cotton. There are two main methods of using flood waters:

(a) By canal irrigation fed from the great Sansanding Barrage, or from the minor Barrage des Aigrettes at Sotuba. For this the Office du Niger has had to undertake great engineering works on the Niger, build canals, level vast areas accurately and completely, and has had to attract its labour force and colonists. In return, water control is complete.

(b) By simple works undertaken by the Department of Agriculture, to modify flooding, especially at the beginning and end of seasonal floods. Little expense is incurred and, as the riverine lands are generally already used, the aims are to make better use of the water and to increase the cultivable area.

Cultivation results from the latter method are inferior, but the cost is far less, and the areas improved are many times greater. The Office du Niger has irrigated about 123,000 acres and the Department of Agriculture 500,000 acres, both having been in full operation for comparable periods.

Each year about 5,000 acres are additionally irrigated by the Office du Niger in what was previously waste or poor seasonal pastures, whilst the Department of Agriculture provides some 7,500 acres of richer riverine lands with controlled water supply.

The Niger Valley within the Mali Republic may be sub-divided as follows:

(i) *Upper Valley*. In both the Guinea and Mali Republics tributary rivulets are being harnessed by rough barrages near confluence points with the Niger. Canals direct water to farmers who thereby get their water earlier and in a gentler and more systematic way. The main stream is often paralleled by a tributary, and this may be used as a drainage canal, or as a reservoir.

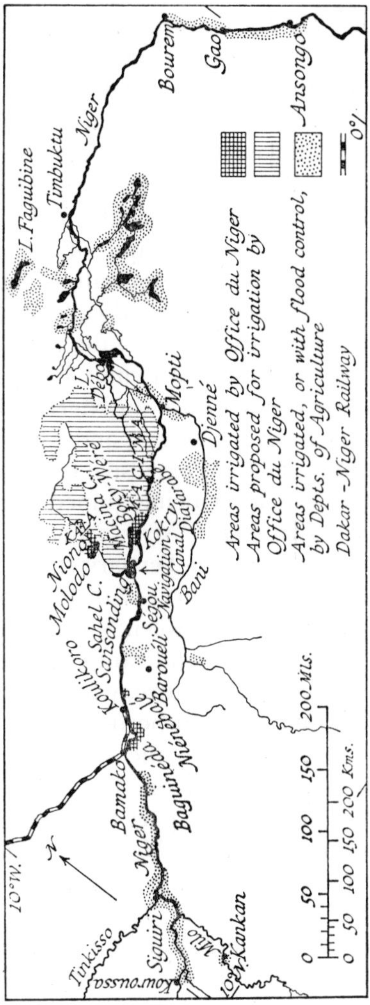

The Upper Niger is navigable from Kouroussa downstream

FIG. 51.—Irrigated areas in part of Guinea and Mali.

to Bamako and the Milo can be used from Kankan, but traffic on these is much less than on the Middle Niger, and is mostly concerned with provisioning the gold mining areas near Siguiri (Guinea).

(ii) *The Djoliba Sector from Koulikoro to Sansanding.* The river plains are intensively cultivated, but the river flows in a slightly incised and confined valley, so that annual flooding is restricted.

It was in this sector that the Office du Niger's predecessor made initial experiments at Niénébalé in 1922 and at Baguinéda in 1929, the latter being irrigated from the Barrage des Aigrettes at Sotuba. At Niénébalé and Baguinéda there are about 19,000 irrigated acres and some 5,500 colonists. (See Fig. 51.) The Department of Agriculture has also irrigated 32,000 acres by refilling an abandoned valley between Barouéli and Tamani. In all these areas, rice is the main crop.

Ségou, the Bambara capital from 1660 to 1861, is the head-quarters of the Office du Niger. Trade comes to its important market from the Niger, and by lorry from the Bani River at Douna. There is extensive trade in fish, cattle, hides, salt and cotton, the latter being ginned in the town.

(iii) *The Inland Niger Delta.* This area corresponds to a former lake of late-Tertiary times, which was drained when it overspilled to connect with the Lower Niger. In this former lacustrine area, between Sansanding and Timbuktu, the Niger has an almost insignificant gradient and is easily diverted into a more southerly course, whenever a valley becomes obstructed by Harmattan wind-borne sand. The Inland Delta area may be sub-divided into the dead delta from Sansanding to Diafarabé, and the live one from Diafarabé to Timbuktu.

It is in the dead part that the main works of the Office du Niger are located. Above Sansanding is a great barrage, 884 yards long, extended northward by an embankment to prevent lateral percolation. The barrage has 488 small sluice-gates, each adjustable like deck-chairs by means of three travelling lifting arms. There is a navigation canal, and over the barrage and the embankment (which together are a mile and three-quarters long) is a bridge, one of only six across the Niger. The Sansanding Barrage was begun in 1934 and completed in 1941, except that temporary wooden sluices were in position until 1947.

The immediate effect of the barrage was to raise the level of the Niger by some 14 feet. A feeder-canal leads water into the Sahel and Macina Canals, which have been cut through sand to unobstructed parts of former Niger thalwegs, now once again filled with water. Hence, the essential aim has been to revive the dead delta by sending water down abandoned valleys.

From the main canal, lesser ones send water to the mechanically levelled and prepared fields, excess water being led off by drains. The scheme has been in full operation only since 1947, and by 1963 about 100,000 acres had been irrigated here to support some 35,000 African colonists. These have come to settle in this former semi-desert from eastern and southern Mali and the Upper Volta.

Colonists are provided with huts, gardens, animals and simple equipment, which they retain as long as they remain; they also receive initial seed, food and training. Although the land is prepared mechanically, each family has its own leased holding. After paying annual dues, cultivators sell through the co-operative.

Originally the aim was to create a second Nile Valley, where vast quantities of cotton could be produced to free France from American supplies. But inexperienced farmers often allow the cotton to degenerate; the soils are seldom rich enough because the Niger has not deposited silt to anything like the depth found along the Nile; and cotton could not support the cost of haulage to France. So from 1941–60 the emphasis was on rice, which occupied at least 85% of the irrigated lands of the Inland Delta, against 15% or less by cotton.

The areas of Boky-Wéré and Kokry, fed by the Macina Canal, have been mainly concerned with rice cultivation, because of the more impermeable soils.

The Sahel Canal feeds the areas of Niono, Molodo and Kouroumari in the north. Originally intended for Egyptian cotton production in the north and for American cotton in the centre, these areas have been turned over to American cotton in the north and to American cotton and rice in the centre. There is mechanical production of rice at Molodo on over 18,000 acres with paid labour, and the latest aim is to increase mechanical cultivation in other sectors, return to an emphasis on cotton (for local manufacture), and to introduce sugar cane, etc.

Below Diafarabé is the live sector of the Inland Delta, as the Niger here sub-divides into the Diaka branch, which rejoins the main stream in Lake Débo. The Diaka and Niger have natural levées which are occasionally breached, and water control consists in modifying the gaps and strengthening the banks.

(iv) *The Lacustrine Sector.* This comprises the numerous channels and lakes, beginning with Lake Débo, and extending to Kabara—the ' port ' of Timbuktu. Lake Débo is an interior lake which, in the flood season, extends considerably in size and depth. It acts as a secondary regulator of floods to the Sansanding Barrage. Beyond Lake Débo the Niger flows in a vast network of streams, which has a slackening effect upon the current. These streams have also built their banks above the general level of the countryside, so that when lakes are eventually filled by floods, they do not empty into the river.

Millet and rice have always been grown around these lakes. Rice is first sown on the highest fringes, and then, as lake level declines by evaporation, the rice is transplanted two or three times to lower levels. Thus water-control schemes seek to equalise, for as long as possible during the year, the water entering the lakes, so that more land can be sown as the floods decline.

In both the Inland Delta and the lacustrine reaches of the river there are nutritious pastures, visited seasonally by large herds of cattle, which find here their richest sustenance. There is thus some conflict of interest between pastoralists and farmers, though in many cases it is people associated with the pastoralists who grow rice and millet, while they are near the river with the cattle.

A more acute problem is raised by irrigation schemes either on former pasture-lands (as along the Diaka) or cutting across transhumance routes (as with the Office du Niger works in the Macina). Traditional pastures should be respected, as also cattle routeways, for which canal bridges are necessary.

There is also the effect upon the Niger River of abstracting water for irrigation. Some fear that this will so impair its flow, that annual floods will no longer be strong enough to remove obstructing sand, deposited in the shrunken dry-season river by the north-eastern Harmattan wind. It has also been said that the lakes are no longer completely filled each year. This may or may not be due to removal upstream of irrigation water. If it is due to this, then it may be said that more land has been revived than has been destroyed. Another barrage near the downstream end of the lacustrine region would enable full water control to be provided for all the lakes.

Wherever floods are to be expected, permanent settlements are on higher ground. Such is the case with Macina, Nia-funké (famed for its camel and goat hair blankets) and Goundam, where there are hills 200–300 feet high.

Timbuktu has for centuries been an admirable example of a market at the meeting place of desert and water. Here, at the end of a trans-Saharan caravan route, produce from Europe and North Africa, desert salt, dates and tobacco, were bartered for slaves, kola nuts, gold, ivory, millet and rice.

The town originated under the Tuareg in the twelfth century. It was put by them in the charge of Buktu, a female slave: hence the name, meaning ' the place of Buktu '. It became part of the Mali Empire in 1325 and was re-occupied by the Tuareg in 1434. Prosperous and fairly well known, Timbuktu declined after capture by the Songhaï Empire in 1468. Later a ruler enabled it to attain great prosperity in the sixteenth century, but in 1591 the town was overwhelmed by an expedition from Morocco. It was governed by local pashas, again by Tuareg, Fulani, and others until the French captured it in 1894. From a population of 45,000 in the sixteenth century, it has declined to 7,000, and has lost all its importance, because of the decline of the desert caravans.

In the course of some eight centuries the Niger has moved 7 miles (flood limit 5 miles) south from the town, which is now served by Kabara or Korioume on the river. A flood-season tributary permits canoe traffic up to the town until February.

(v) *Post-deltaic Sector.* Below Kabara, the Niger is again one stream, and flows in a valley 6 or 7 miles wide. This is a semi-desert zone, and for irrigation it is necessary to construct dykes to retain water.

Gao was the Songhaï capital whose zenith passed with Moorish occupation in 1591. It lies on the left bank of the Niger and is an important road, river and air centre, with a market of moderate trade.

THE BANI PLAINS. The plains lying around this great Niger tributary often have expanses of bare laterite or ferruginous crust, giving rise to *bowal* wastes. To these bare, hot and secluded plains, the Bani brings a ribbon of fertile watered lands and a means of transport.

Djenné, a Songhaï town probably founded in the eighth century, was a centre for Koranic studies. It is now a market (especially for fish) and a centre for artisans making leather articles, cloth and blankets. But it has lost ground to Mopti and Ségou, better served by communications. Djenné has a huge mosque rebuilt by the French in 1907 in neo-Sudan style.

Above the town many acres of the Pondory Plain (see Fig. 51) have been irrigated. Water is admitted by canal from the Bani, 32 miles above Djenné, thereby watering higher land previously untouched by floods.

Mopti lies on the right bank of the Bani, just above its confluence with the Niger. It is a considerable fish and cattle market but, except by air, is rather isolated in the flood season.

THE MINA, SIKASSO, BANDIAGARA AND HOMBORI PLATEAUX AND SCARPLANDS. East of the Bani River, the land rises almost imperceptibly to the great east-facing scarp of Palæozoic sandstone, which extends into the Upper Volta as the Banfora Scarp. In Mali, the highest points are at 2,500 feet.

The most impressive and famous scarp is that of Bandiagara, which has an almost sheer drop of 800 feet. It is inhabited by the Dogon peoples, studied by Marcel Griaule. Settlements lie on the scree and spring line of the lower slopes, and terraces have been built to make fields often as small as a few square feet. A notable speciality is the cultivation of onions. In the Hombori Mountains, practically deserted by man, are some sheer drops of 2,000 feet (Plate 63).

In all this sandstone country water is scarce, and the annual rainfall is only 23 inches at Bandiagara, 19 at Mopti and rather less at Douetza. The main markets of this large region are Bougouni, Sikasso, and Koutiala.

THE NIGER BEND LANDS. South of the great loop of the Niger is a monotonous low and dry plateau. Pre-Cambrian gneisses and schists form low hills north-east of Hombori, through which the Niger cuts a gorge above Bourem. There are occasional tors and some laterite. As the rocks are impermeable, the region is marshy in the wet season (when water collects in hollows), but exceedingly dry for most of the year. There is extensive transhumance between these lands and the Niger River and lakes.

Immediately south of the Niger are the Takamadasset Hills, which are fixed dunes.

ECONOMIC RESOURCES

AGRICULTURE

Rice and Millet. Lands capable of being cropped more or less permanently are very restricted. Most of the country belongs to the Millet Zone, so that millet is the main food crop. Irrigation works have enabled large amounts of rice to be grown as well, so that the Mali Republic not only grows sufficient millet in most years, but is able to export rice, instead of importing it as was the case before the Second World War. Nevertheless, away from the rivers little rice can be grown because of aridity and the depth of the water-table.

The Mali Republic produces about 20,000 tons of rice annually, surplus to its needs. About 8,000 tons come from areas developed by the Department of Agriculture and about 12,000 from those of the Office du Niger. The areas developed by the Department of Agriculture produce much more rice, but most is used for subsistence. The Office du Niger lands have a surplus for sale, because their local needs are less, owing to the smaller population.[1]

The *Shea butter tree* occurs widely in the southern part of the Mali Republic but is seldom properly tended. Production of nuts is the highest of any ex-French West African republic, and most of the produce is used locally, as export is rarely economic over great distances. Such as does leave Mali goes generally to the Upper Volta.

Cotton production by irrigation was the original aim of the Office du Niger, but has proved difficult. Fully mechanised cultivation is being tried to supply the needs of local manufacture. Export is uneconomic in view of the difficulties of transport.

[1] On rice cultivation, see J. Dresch, 'La Riziculture en Afrique Occidentale', *Annales de Géographie*, 1949, pp. 295–312; P. Viguier, 'La Riziculture Indigène au Sudan Français', *L'Agronomie Tropicale*, Vol. IV, 1939, pp. 339–78; and Chapter 6 of this present book (section on rice).

Unirrigated cotton production is 50% more than irrigated in Mali—San, Koutiala and Sikasso districts being the main producers.

Groundnuts are grown where there are light soils and enough rain near the railway in the west, or close to roads not far from the railway. The Mali Republic is second to Senegal in cash production, and some 55,000 tons surplus to local needs are normally produced. But the haul of 750 miles is a great deterrent to extending cultivation for other than local needs.

The *Kapok tree* is found in the centre and southern parts— seeds, fibre and wood being used to some extent by the local populations. There is a small export of its fibre.

Gum arabic is collected especially in the Nioro and Timbuktu regions, but it has suffered the same decline in competition with the Sudan that has been experienced in Mauritania.

LIVESTOCK

Livestock are more important than in any other country in West Africa, except Nigeria. There are reckoned to be some 3,900,000 cattle and 7,000,000 sheep and goats.

Because of the Niger River, its tributaries and the occurrence near them of the tsetse, Ndama cattle occur in the Bamako area, and south and east of it; Zebu cattle are found north only of 15°–16° N. The increase of livestock is entirely dependent upon the provision of more wells or barrages. On the other hand, irrigated lands often conflict with transhumance routes. There is extensive transhumance between the pastures along the Niger and its tributaries (with the fine *gamarawel* grass), and the pasture lands of the north and north-west.

Apart from the usual varieties of sheep, there are Macina fleecy sheep found between Ségou and Timbuktu in the Inland Delta region. An attempt to cross Bokhara (Astrakhan) sheep with rather similar local breeds ended in failure.

There is considerable export of cattle towards Dakar, the Ivory Coast, Ghana and, to a lesser extent, to Liberia and Nigeria. At least 30,000 cattle and about 100,000 sheep and goats are sent annually to Nigeria, some 30,000 cattle and 90,000 sheep and goats to Ghana, and 14,000 cattle and 25,000 sheep and goats to the Ivory Coast. The great centres for the collection and despatch of hides and skins are Bamako and Kayes.[1]

Fish are of great significance to the peoples living along the Niger. The greatest market is at Mopti. Dried fish are the subject of extensive commerce, some 30,000 tons being sold annually, some as far afield as Ghana.

MINERALS

Gold. At the time of the Ghana, Mali and Songhaï Empires, gold was an important article of commerce. Most of it came from former workings along the Falémé tributary of the Senegal River. Gold also occurs on the Manding Plateau, but the bedrock has not been located.

Salt. Exploitation of salt has a long history and it was another staple commodity of commerce in past centuries. Salt was mined at Terhazza and was described by El Bekri in the eleventh century, but is no longer worked. At Taoudéni salt-rock is still cut in trenches, and brought by camel caravan to Gao and Timbuktu. Local production of salt in the Mali Republic now accounts for only about 4,500 tons out of the total consumption of 18,000 tons. The rest comes from Kaolack in Senegal, Mauritania and Europe.

Iron occurs as magnetite near Kayes, and as non-phosphoric hæmatite near the railway between Kayes and Bamako. These deposits may be worked in the future.

There are phosphates in the dead valley of the Tilemsi, 80 miles north of Gao, but their quality is poor and their location remote. Manganese, tin, lead and zinc also occur.

COMMUNICATIONS

The Middle Niger is a slow but fairly important means of transport from mid-July or August to mid-December or even March from Koulikoro to Gao. It is especially the means of distributing goods to and from riverine towns and the Office du Niger's irrigation works. From Bamako to Kouroussa the Upper Niger is navigable from July to December, but the Milo tributary is more used up to Kankan. The Bani is also navigable in the rainy season.

[1] G. Doutressoulle, *L'Elévage au Soudan français. Son économie.* Mortain, 1952.

Much traffic goes by roads which are mainly south of the Niger and Bani Rivers. But roads are sometimes interrupted during the wet season, and then the rivers are very useful.

The railway links the two navigable reaches of the Niger between Koulikoro and Bamako, as well as the upper Senegal, though navigation of the latter is of no consequence. But by providing a through route to Dakar, the railway is the obvious lifeline of Mali, just as the Niger River and roads are its prolongations as internal trunk routes. Air services serve Nioro, Nara, Bamako, Ségou, Mopti, Goundam and Gao. Bamako also has intercontinental traffic.

Conclusion

This republic has vast tracts of useless country, but if the Niger and other rivers can be fully harnessed, far more crops—especially rice—may be grown. Meanwhile, its main resource is still livestock. Cost of transport will always be a handicap to this land in the heart of West Africa.

BIBLIOGRAPHY

See references cited in footnotes. Also:

PAULE BRASSEUR, *Bibliographie Générale du Mali*, I.F.A.N., Dakar, 1964.
R. J. HARRISON CHURCH, ' Problems and Development of the Dry Zone of West Africa ', *Geographical Journal*, cxxvii, pp. 187–204.
RENÉ DUMONT, *Afrique Noire: Développement Agricole. Réconversion de l'économie agricole: Guinée, Côte d'Ivoire, Mali*, 1962.
P. HAMMOND, ' The Niger Project ' in W. H. LEWIS (ed.), *Emerging Africa*, Washington, 1963.
G. SPITZ, *Le Soudan Français*, Paris, 1955. (Includes a full bibliography.)
G. SPITZ, *Sansanding et les Irrigations du Niger*, Paris, 1950.
Y. URVOY, *Les Bassins du Niger, Etude de géographie physique et de paléographie*, Paris, 1942.
JOHN DE WILDE and others, *Agricultural Development in Tropical Africa*, 2 vols., Johns Hopkins Press, 1967.

MAPS

See p. 183. Also:

1 : 20,000 Bamako S.G./A.O.F. 1952.

Chapter 16

THE UPPER VOLTA—LAND OF THE MOSSI [1]

THE Upper Volta is far smaller than the other poor dry lands of Mauritania, Mali and the Niger. It is also considerably farther south, lying within both the Millet and Guinea Corn zones, so that most of its lands are capable of cultivation. There is no desert, though there are many unproductive areas.

Within its dry territory of 105,811 square miles there were, in 1966, as many as 4,955,000 inhabitants. Nevertheless, the Upper Volta is an exceedingly poor and relatively infertile country. Many areas are uninhabited, e.g. up to 12 miles either side of the three Volta rivers and the Bougouriba, where there is danger from floods and from sleeping sickness. In the Fada N'Gourma district there is a vast swampy area north of Pama, where the bite of the Simulium Fly may cause blindness (Onchocerciasis) by the larvæ entering the eye. South-east of Banfora there is another uninhabited area, empty for historical reasons, yet having fertile soils.

Consequently, a great problem of the Upper Volta is pressure of population in the centre of the country. The republic has many times more people per square mile than any other dry country in former French West Africa, and this in a land whose soils are thin, poor and eroded.

In the western sandstone country, water is deep because of rapid percolation, and in the rest of the republic it is difficult to find in wells in the Pre-Cambrian rocks because of rapid run-off. In general, rainfall may be collected only by constructing barrages in hollows, or on the intermittent rivers.

Unfortunately, there seems to be no easy means of diversifying or increasing production in the Upper Volta. As in the over-

[1] I am most grateful to M. le Moal, Director of the Institut Français d'Afrique Noire at Ouagadougou, who guided me in the Upper Volta and has given me most helpful advice on this chapter.

peopled parts of Ibo country in Eastern Nigeria, men must migrate temporarily for work. Some 150,000 go annually to the cocoa farms or mines of Ghana, or to the cocoa or coffee farms and plantations in the Ivory Coast. A few have settled permanently in the irrigated areas of the Inland Niger Delta. Economic reasons are not alone in causing this migration ; the love of adventure, freedom and the prestige of such a trip also play their part.

Another problem of the Upper Volta is that, like the Niger, it is obstructed from direct outlet to the sea by a foreign country. The Upper Volta is, in any case, very remote from external markets and sources of supply, being in the heart of West Africa, though the railway from Ouagadougou gives direct access to the deep-water port of Abidjan. Whilst this railway is of great value in cheapening and diversifying imports, it is unlikely to develop much export traffic, since the Upper Volta has so little of value to offer. The rail journey from Ouagadougou to Abidjan is 711 miles, a very great distance to carry any but valuable goods at a profitable rate. In 1953, the last year before the railway was fully open, 40% of the imports and nearly 90% of the exports passed through Ghana.

Many developments are going on but the real question is whether this poor country will eventually be able to support them.

HISTORICAL OUTLINE

Most of the country formed part of the main Mossi Empire, the present dynasty of which dates back to the early eleventh century. It has had its capital at Ouagadougou since the fifteenth century. The present population of this part of the country is about 1·6 million. The dynasty of the Mossi kingdom of Yatenga (capital Ouahigouya) dates back to the twelfth century.

Apart from the Mossi peoples, other more or less original inhabitants are the Bobo, Samo, Lobi, Gourounsi, Gourmantche and Dagari. These people are also non-Muslim and are almost entirely settled farmers.

The Muslim invaders number about 600,000 and are mostly pastoralists or in commerce. The pastoral groups are the

Fulani and the Tuareg; the commercial peoples are the Dioula.

This area was the scene of Binger's travels in 1898 and the French occupation dates from 1896 to 1901. A British column arrived at Ouagadougou one week after the French in 1896. The country first became a separate entity from 1919 to 1932 inclusive, and has again been one since 1948. It became an independent republic in 1960 and is closely associated with the Ivory Coast, Niger and Dahomey in the Benin–Sahel Entente.

CLIMATE
(See also Chapter 3)

Owing to its more southerly latitude than the other dry lands of Mauritania, Mali and the Niger, the Upper Volta

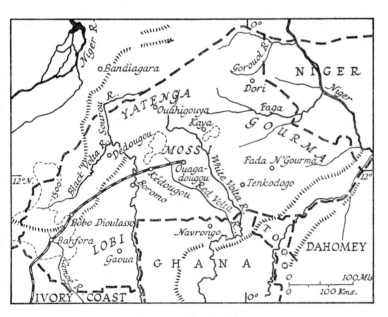

FIG. 52.—Upper Volta.

has more rain. In the Southern Savannah climatic zone, e.g. at Bobo Dioulasso, rains begin in May, extend to October, and average 46 inches. At Fada N'Gourma, which has the Savannah climate, they begin in May and extend to September,

K

averaging 33 inches. For the same period they average 29 inches at Ouahigouya. The northern limit of the country has the Southern Sahel climate.

Temperatures tend to be high at the end of the dry season, e.g. the mean of daily maxima in March and April at Ouagadougou is 106°, but temperatures are considerably lower in the south-west. At Ouagadougou, from January to March, relative humidity is exceptionally low, being 12–16% at 1 p.m.

Owing to the general thinness of the soils and the widespread occurrence of laterite, the countryside and its vegetation look even drier and poorer than the above rainfall figures suggest.

The south-western part of the country consists of Northern Guinea Savannah, with scattered trees or clumps; the rest of the country is Sudan Savannah, with infrequent trees. In the north, the paucity of trees is due to climate; in the heavily populated Mossi lands it is due to the intense population, since only the large and useful trees (especially the baobab) are kept.

GEOLOGY AND RELIEF

Most of the Upper Volta is composed of Pre-Cambrian rocks. There are some granite tors, but the country is mostly monotonously flat, with only a slight southward slope and occasional steps or edges. Laterite is frequent and the water-table is very deep.

Because of the impermeable nature of the rocks and rapid run-off, rivers are alternately dry or in sudden flood. Water shortage is made more acute by the high density of population.

The south-western borderlands, however, are composed of overlying Silurian sandstones, which give infertile flat country, comparable with that found in the Voltaian Basin of Ghana. The sandstone region of the Upper Volta is likewise limited by an impressive scarp, that of Banfora, some 500 feet high, which has its steep edge facing south-east.

The upper part of the Black Volta River drains the sandstone region and once flowed north along the course of its tributary, the Sourou, to the great central depression of West Africa. It has, however, been captured by the rejuvenated and, therefore, more vigorous Black Volta. The upper waters of the

Camoé drain the scarp in impressive falls. The other Volta streams follow the general trend of the ancient rocks of the rest of the country.

MAJOR REGIONS

YATENGA–MOSSI COUNTRY. This lies in the north-west of the country and is rather dry. Sand and lateritic or ferruginous crust ridges overlie the Archaean base. Both soil and vegetation are thin and poor, in part the result of the actions of the peoples of the ancient Yatenga Mossi Kingdom. There has been infiltration by Fulani pastoralists, as this area is practically free of tsetse.

GOURMA AND THE EASTERN FRINGES. Voltaian sandstone and more recent sands overlie part of the Archaean base, and the surface is heavily laterised. Seasonal rivers flow eastward to the Niger River in wide, shallow valleys. Broken country encloses the Gôrouol Valley.

The settled Gourmantche population is poor, as are the Fulani nomads, though there are many livestock. The population rapidly becomes less dense towards the south-east.

Fada N'Gourma lies on the Niger–Volta watershed, and is largely a French creation.

MOSSI LANDS OF THE SOUTH-CENTRE. These are geologically akin to Yatenga. Despite the thin soils and rather low rainfall (35 inches), they are the densely settled lands of the main Mossi kingdom of Ouagadougou. Vegetation is thin, the grass short and the trees are bushlike, except for the baobab and shea butter, which are safeguarded.

Ouagadougou, the capital, has been the Mossi capital for centuries and the French retained the Morho Naba in some semblance of his spiritual, though not political, authority. The town is a great missionary headquarters. In 1961 the population was 59,126.

Kédougou is an important market and has a shea butter mill and cotton ginnery. *Boromo* also has a shea butter mill.

LOBI AND GAOUA COUNTRY. This has the same Pre-Cambrian base and there are many granite tors. The Lobi and Bobo produce groundnuts, shea butter kernels and benniseed for export, as population pressure is less. It is possible that the population of this area may once have been greater and that it was reduced by sleeping sickness. In any case, it might well be increased once sleeping sickness has been eradicated. If the Mossi could be persuaded to move more readily in family units, this might become an area for their re-settlement. The Bobo are naturally not favourable to such resettlement schemes for their traditional rivals.

EASTERN EXTENSION OF THE SIKASSO PLATEAU. This is the Silurian sandstone plateau, which terminates in the eastward facing Banfora scarp. Geologically, this region is in contrast to all the rest of the Upper Volta. To some extent the porosity of its rocks is offset by the greater rainfall, and because of this and the better farming methods of the Bobo, the soils are less eroded. The region produces the same surplus commodities as the previous one.

Bobo Dioulasso, with 45,000 Africans and 1,550 non-Africans in 1959, is a pleasantly planned town situated just above and behind the scarp edge of the plateau. From 1934 to 1954 it was the terminus of the railway and completely over-shadowed Ouagadougou in economic importance. It is a collecting centre for cotton (some of which is ginned in the town), groundnuts, shea butter and cattle. There are sisal plantations nearby and it has a groundnut oil factory. Both it and Ouagadougou are served by air.

ECONOMIC RESOURCES

AGRICULTURE

The Upper Volta is within the Guinea Corn and Millet zones, the former corresponding roughly with Bobo country and the latter with Mossi country. Beans are often inter-cropped with guinea corn, millet or cotton.

The Mossi are so numerous and their soil so poor, that the maximum effort must be made to cultivate as intensively and continuously as possible. Because of land hunger, and the distance to ports, little can be produced for export. For the same reason, the Mossi attempt self-sufficiency and, conse-quently, they cultivate varied crops.

The Bobo seem to be better cultivators, but this may be

because they have less eroded soils and more certain rainfall. Population pressure is also much less severe among them.

Shea butter trees are densest in the south and south-west and provide the main source of oil, as well as a small export trade.

Groundnuts are grown most successfully in the south and south-west, where rainfall is more certain and where communications are better and shorter. About 4,000 tons of decorticated groundnuts are exported, and the through railway from Ouagadougou may make it possible to increase this figure. The Bobo Dioulasso groundnut oil mills treats much of the total cash crop. It may prove best to treat the whole of the export crop in this way, and overcome some of the difficulty of long rail haulage by selling the more valuable oil.

Sisal is grown on European plantations near Bobo Dioulasso, but its cost of production is high compared with that of plantations in East Africa.

Benniseed, grown at the end of the growing season, is produced on a small scale in excess of local demand.

Cotton has long been made up locally into the usual narrow strips and over 2,000 tons still find their way annually into the Ivory Coast and Ghana in this form. A semi-government company (Compagnie Française des Textiles) is encouraging cotton cultivation.

Livestock

The northern limit of the tsetse is roughly along a line from Ouahigouya to Kaya and Fada N'Gourma. Consequently, only the northern part of the country is free from this fly and has Zebu cattle. In the south the small Ndama and Lobi resistant cattle are found, the latter around the north-west corner of Ghana.

Sheep are of two kinds, the *Fulani* which has horns and the *Tuareg* of the Dori country in the east which has no horns.

About 30,000 cattle are exported annually from the Upper Volta (the territory's most valuable export), as well as many more in transit from Mali. Most go to Ghana and about a quarter to the Ivory Coast. A modern abattoir has been established at Ouagadougou.

MINERALS

Gold and manganese have been located, but nothing is worked on any considerable scale for the world market. There exist two famous native workings of iron, at Tourny near Banfora and at Ouahigouya, where there are small primitive iron furnaces. The smelted iron is used to make household and farming implements.

CONCLUSION

The Upper Volta is confounded by its remoteness, a dense population which is often undernourished, thin soils and water scarcity. Minerals seem few and would, in any case, be costly to work. There are hardly any surpluses of cash or other crops, so that transit trade between Mali, Ghana and the Ivory Coast, and remittances of Upper Volta labourers mainly in Ghana and the Ivory Coast are the main sources of income.

BIBLIOGRAPHY

S. Daveau, 'Les Plateaux du Sud-Ouest de la Haute-Volta. Etude géomorphologique', *Travaux du Dept. de Géographie de l'Université de Dakar*, No. 7, 1960.

S. Daveau, M. Lamotte and G. Rougerie, 'Cuirasses et chaînes birrimiennes en Haute Volta', *Annales de Géographie*, Vol. LXXI, pp. 460–82.

P. Delmont, 'Esquisse géographique du Gourma Central—le Cercle de Dori', *Notes Africaines*, I.F.A.N., 1949, pp. 57–60 and 86–89.

Y. Urvoy, *Les Bassins du Niger, Etude de géographie physique et de paléograqhie*, 1942.

John de Wilde and others, *Agricultural Development in Tropical Africa*, 2 vols., Johns Hopkins Press, 1967.

Etudes Voltaïques, Centre I.F.A.N., Ouagadougou.

Chapter 17

THE NIGER—A FINGER INTO THE DESERT[1]

THE Niger has an area of 458,874 square miles with a population in 1966 of 3,433,000. Nearly all its peoples live in the south, along the borders of Nigeria.

The Niger has an extreme width of nearly 1,000 miles, and from north to south averages some 650 miles. Its only cultivable area lies within the Millet Zone. Like the Upper Volta, the Niger is secluded from the sea by foreign countries.

HISTORICAL OUTLINE

The Tuareg (singular Targui), the most famous inhabitants, are Berbers and came to the Aïr Massif from Egypt, via the Fezzan. They obviously had considerable contact with the Romans, because they use Roman names for the months and for many other things. Although not Christian, they use many ornaments of cruciform pattern and, whilst professing Islam of a non-dogmatic kind, the men are veiled (for protection against the sand), but not the women.[2]

The Tuareg probably established themselves in the Aïr Massif in the eleventh century and their Sultanate of Agadès dates back at least to the fifteenth century. Its power was largely derived from its place on trans-Saharan caravan routes. In 1515 Agadès was captured by the Songhaï. In the seventeenth century trans-Saharan trade declined, though the trade with the south remained important and Agadès was supreme as a political centre until 1870. Meanwhile, Bornu had become

---

[1] I am indebted to M. Le Moal, Director of the Institut Français d'Afrique Noire at Ouagadougou, Upper Volta, for valuable criticism of this chapter.

[2] For an interesting, though old study of the Tuareg, see F. R. (now Lord Rennell of) Rodd, *People of the Veil*, 1926. Also A. Bernard, *Afrique Septentrionale et Occidentale*, 2ᵉ partie—*Sahara—Afrique Occidentale*, pp. 325–9.

significant as a semi-tributary state on the south, and was at its zenith from 1571 to 1603. It was conquered by the Fulani in 1808.

French occupation was effected between 1897 and 1900. The boundary with Nigeria, although according the French a well-watered road between the Niger River and Lake Chad, divides the Hausa people and cuts across north to south trade routes. Whenever the controlled prices for groundnuts in the Niger Republic and in Nigeria are different, there is some movement of groundnuts across the boundary, particularly from farmers living near it but remote from control posts on the roads. Many imported goods are brought across from Nigeria ; more would move if there were no boundary here.

The Niger was established in 1922, and the capital was moved from Zinder to Niamey in 1926. The present boundary with the Republic of Chad was fixed in 1929 and that with Libya in 1935.

The Hausa, who number about 1,125,000, are the largest group and are the sedentary people of the southern border, with close contacts with their kin in Nigeria. The Djerma and Songhaï (about 544,000) are the next largest group and are also sedentary people, but live in the south-west around the Niger River. They emigrate in considerable numbers to Ghana, where they engage in commerce. The almost wholly nomadic Fulani number about 414,000 and are mostly in the south; the Tuareg (about 250,000) are mainly in Aïr and its western and southern environs.

CLIMATE

(See also Chapter 3)

The climate of the Niger is similar to that of other hot, dry lands of West Africa. North of 20° N. there is normally no rain, except on high ground. Storms may appear but, because of the intense evaporation, rain rarely reaches the ground. Along the southern border, in the Southern Sahel climatic zone, about 22 inches annual rainfall occurs. Tahoua, on the northern border of this zone (lat. 15° N.), has 15 inches. Agadès (lat. 17° N. and alt. 1,719 feet), in the Northern Sahel climatic zone, has about 6 inches. At Bilma (lat. 19° N.) in the Southern Saharan type, 1 inch of rain may occur annually. As in all such lands, rainfall is highly variable from year to

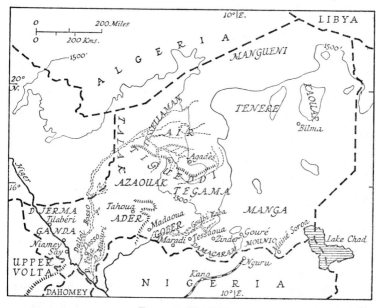

FIG. 53.—The Niger.

year. The diurnal and seasonal range of temperature is exceptionally high.

GEOLOGY AND RELIEF

Pre-Cambrian rocks appear significantly only round Zinder and in the Aïr massif. Elsewhere, they are mainly [1] covered by Secondary and Tertiary rocks in the western and central borderlands adjacent to Nigeria, and mainly by Quaternary sands elsewhere. It is unusual to find Secondary rocks over wide areas in West Africa, except here and in adjacent parts of Nigeria. In the Niger they are mostly sandstones, much affected by semi-arid erosion and by varying degrees of laterisation. Quaternary sands cover vast areas in the south-centre, east, north-east and north-west, thereby accentuating the great aridity.

[1] There is also an extension of Primary Voltaian sandstones to just within the extreme south-west corner.

MAJOR REGIONS

DJERMA GANDA.   Because of the distance of this part of the
Niger River from its sources and of the slackening of its flow
in the Inland Delta, floods come in mid-January, in the dry
season.   This is a very great help to the local farmers near the
river.

The lands on the left bank of the Niger River are composed
of Miocene and Pliocene continental soft sandstones and clays,
with some laterite.   These level plains (as well as southern
Azaouak) are crossed by wide and shallow yet sharply defined
relic river valleys, known as dallols.   In earlier Quaternary
times these were vigorous tributaries of the Niger River and
are evidence of former wetter conditions in this part of the
Sahara.   Along these old river beds water may still be found
near the surface, and acacias and borassus palms line their
banks.

Beyond the valleys these plains have acacias and African
Myrrh.   Water is generally to be found only at depths of
100–250 feet, except near the Niger River where the water
table is higher and the vegetation denser.   This whole region
ends northwards in the Adrar Aouelaouel and eastwards in the
Tahoua scarp.

Niamey, population 40,000, capital of the Niger, is on the
left bank of the Niger River and is an important centre for
river, road and air routes.   These have caused it to be preferred to Zinder as a capital, despite the fact that Niamey is
in the far west of the territory, and that Zinder is more central.

ADER.   This is a plateau of Eocene series, often capped with
laterite.   Rainfall averages about 15 inches, but percolation
is rapid, and Ader is drier than might be expected, being
covered by thin and small Thorn Bush.

Tahoua is a market for the produce of nomads and sedentary
peoples.

GOBER.   Sandy plains occur east of Madaoua and as far as
the road north from Tassaoua.   They are practically uninhabited, except near the intermittent Goulbi Kaba stream.
Vegetation is poor Thorn Bush.

Maradi was situated by a stream of the same name but disas-
trous floods in 1947 and 1950 caused it to be resited on higher

ground. It is a prosperous town, being a collecting point for groundnuts, cotton grown along the stream, Maradi Red Goat skins, hides and cattle. Groundnut oil is extracted in a local mill, and Maradi is also an important administrative centre. There are ties of kinship and trade with Katsina and Kano in northern Nigeria, though much trade is directed through Dahomey.

DAMAGARAM and MOUNIO. Granite tors appear here above a clay plain, where the water-table is much shallower. Moreover, the rainfall is greater, being 22 inches at Zinder, and seasonal lakes and semi-permanent rivers occur. This is the most important groundnut area, despite the fact that the soils are not so suitable as the sandy ones of Maradi. It also has the greatest density of gum trees, particularly in the Gouré and Maïné Soroa districts. If the price of gum became more favourable, more could be exported from this region, down the Nigerian railway from Nguru.

Zinder, population 16,500, was the Niger capital until 1926, and is still the commercial capital. It lies on a plateau between two ouadis and is really composed of three towns. It is a great groundnut, hide and skin market; has craftsmen making articles in skin and leather and blankets from camel, goathair and wool. It is a lesser Kano, with which it has close trading relations. There are several groundnut oil mills between Zinder and the border.

MANGA. This is the sandy semi-wasteland around Lake Chad. Although the rainfall may reach 18 inches or more a year, percolation is so rapid that the area is very dry. Pastures are found only near the lake.

TENERE and KAOUAR. This vast area along the eastern boundary is a continuation of Manga. There are sand dunes with occasional granite tors.

Bilma is an oasis on the edge of the desert. It has some trade and 4,000 tons of salt are produced annually nearby.

MANGUENI PLATEAU. This is a broken desert country of Archean schists and gneisses and Palæozoic sandstones, with superficial sand and gravel. Former rivers have caused great erosion, so that there are frequent outlying mesas.

AÏR. This vast and vivid relief feature of Pre-Cambrian gneisses and granites, together with some black volcanic lavas,

tuffs and ashes of Quaternary age, rises abruptly from the surrounding lands.   It extends for about 250 miles from north
to south and 150 miles from east to west.   Many subsidiary
massifs may be distinguished, and all lie between 3,500 and
5,000 feet above sea level.   The southern limit of Aïr is taken
to be at the Tigueddi Scarp.   There is a Tuareg saying that
' wherever there is stone it is Aïr; wherever there is sand it is
Tenéré '.

Rainfall is some 10 inches or more on the exposed parts,
despite the fact that much of Aïr lies north of 18° N.   Yet this
rainfall is highly erratic and almost all of it comes in thunderstorms which cause severe erosion.   Because of its dryness, and
the altitude which modifies the otherwise great heat and also
causes greater daily range of temperature, Aïr is exceptionally
healthy.   It is drained westward to the Tessellaman depression
by short rivers, whose deep valleys were cut by streams in a
wetter climate than now.   Their grasslands are of great value
to nomadic herdsmen.   Rich uranium deposits occur in the
massif, and their development will bring new life to Aïr.

Agadès, some 1,700 feet up, is the great centre of Aïr.   It
lies on a foothill, at the side of a ouadi in a Lower Cretaceous
clay plain like that of Tessellaman.   It had its most opulent
period in the sixteenth and seventeenth centuries.   After
subsequent decline it survived as a centre for herdsmen and
for craftsmen making saddles and sheaths.

Talak.   These plains lie west and south-west of Aïr, and
are composed of loose Quaternary sand over Cretaceous limestones.   Talak is almost pure desert and practically devoid of
population.

Tessellaman and Northern Azaouak.   This is an island
of rich pasture within the desert of Talak, extending from west
of Aïr to south-west of it, and is composed of Lower Cretaceous
clays.   Its pastures are nourished by streams draining the
western side of Aïr and collecting within this semi-swamp, of
great significance to nomadic cattle keepers, especially those
from Aïr.   The swamp has quite an extensive range of vegetation, particularly of grasses and acacias (especially *Acacia seyal*).

Tegama Plateau.   This vast plateau extends between Aïr
in the north and Damagaram in the south.   It has infertile
soils derived from flat Cretaceous or possibly Triassic sand-

stone, and the area is semi- or complete desert. The sand-stone has been considerably eroded by the Goulbi Kaba to expose underlying clays in wide valleys. Only in these is water available.

ECONOMIC RESOURCES

AGRICULTURE

Permanent cropping is almost confined to the lands near the Niger River, and eastward and northward from it to about 80 miles north of the Nigerian boundary. Northward for about another 100 miles there are rare and isolated patches of cultivation where water is available. Thus the distribution of crop land is similar to that in Mauritania, where the only important zone is along or near the Senegal River or its tributaries.

Again, the predominant cereals are various kinds of millet and—to a lesser extent—guinea corn in clay or other moist soils. Some Hungry Rice (Iburu or Fonio) is grown in dry areas. As in Guinea and the Mali Republic, there has been much development of improved rice cultivation in hollows of the Niger Valley, with controlled irrigation from the river. Cotton, indigo, temperate cereals and vegetables (especially beans and onions) are grown in gardens for local needs. Dates are grown in the northern oases.

The only considerable cash crop is the groundnut, grown between Maradi, Tessaoua, Zinder and the Nigerian boundary, and in the south-west, and which accounts for about one-half of the exports by value. Gum occurs in all the southern borderlands but because of transport difficulties only a little is exported from the Gouré and Mainé–Soroa areas.

LIVESTOCK

The effective northern limit of livestock rearing is generally 15° N., except for Aïr and its confines. Thus the areas suitable for livestock are far less extensive than in the Mali Republic. Moreover, the cattle keepers—even the true nomads—are very much concentrated in the western and southern regions. Extension of livestock rearing depends upon the provision of more water. Apart from that which may be found in the valleys of Aïr at depths of only 15–20 feet, most underground water is between 100 and 250 feet down, as in the Post-Eocene continental beds east of the Niger.

The curious large-horned humpless Chad cattle live near that lake; otherwise all cattle are Zebus. *Arab Zebu* are found east of Gouré and in the north. The *Azaouak Zebu* is short-horned, small and strong; the *Bororo Zebu* has large lyre-shaped horns.

It is estimated that 900,000 hides and skins to a total value of £280,000, 160,000 head of cattle and 470,000 sheep and goats valued at £3,800,000, are exported annually. The official trade figures only record about one-third of this traffic. Most of the cattle trade is with Sokoto, Katsina and Kano for sale to other parts of Nigeria.

Types of sheep tend to vary with each tribe. The *Tuareg* is good for meat and milk; the *Goundoum* kept by the Songhaï and more valued for its skin and wool, is a poor variety of the Macina and is found only along the banks of the Niger River.

Goats are very numerous and the *Maradi* is especially valued as a source of coloured glacé kid leather, being almost as valuable as the *Sokoto Red*.

Camels are relatively few in number but very important for trade between Aïr and Kano in the trading season. For the peoples along the borderlands, donkeys are the main beasts of burden.

Minerals

The most significant mineral is uranium, now being developed. Salt is still quarried near Bilma and at other places. Natron and sodium sulphate are also worked a little. Very small amounts of tin and wolfram are being obtained near Agadès. These are sent by lorry to Kano and then by rail to Lagos.

Communications

The shortest links of the Niger with the outside world are by road from Maradi to Katsina, or from Zinder to Kano. From Kano traffic passes along the 700-mile railway to the deep-water Nigerian port of Lagos. Alternatively, traffic passes through the port of Cotonou in Dahomey, by rail to

Parakou and on by road. This route was much developed for reasons of economic nationalism. Both routes are expensive because of the distances involved and breaks of bulk. From 1963–5 Niger and Dahomey were on such bad terms that an even longer route via Abidjan (Ivory Coast), the railway to Ouagadougou (Upper Volta) and road into Niger was used.

Some 20,000 camels are still used for transport of millet and imported goods (including kola nuts) to the northern oases, against dates and salt southward. There is also some trans-Saharan trade. Air services serve Niamey (including intercontinental), Tahoua, Agadès, Maradi and Zinder.

CONCLUSION

Within the vast Niger there is a great variety of relief and of human population, yet over the whole country lies the uniform problem of water supplies. All development depends upon securing more water, and the prospects are not good.

Meanwhile, the only relatively well-developed part of the territory is the south-centre, between Maradi and Zinder. Aïr, healthy and beautiful, is too far north and too remote to be capable of much development for stock-rearing or agriculture, even if more water could be obtained. On the other hand the uranium ores of Aïr may be the means of making Niger self-supporting.

The Niger is likely to remain poor, not only because of its poverty of resources and its aridity, but also because it is secluded north of Nigeria, far from overseas markets and sources of supplies.

BIBLIOGRAPHY

R. Capot-Rey, *Le Sahara Français*, 1952.
R. J. Harrison Church, ' Niger ', *Focus*, American Geographical Society, September 1965.
J. Robin, ' Description de la Province de Dosso ', *Bulletin de l'I.F.A.N.*, 1947, pp. 56–98.
E. Séré de Rivières, *Le Niger*, Paris, 1952.
Y. Urvoy, *Petit Atlas ethno-démographique du Soudan*, 1942.
Etudes Nigériennes, Centre I.F.A.N., Niamey.

MAPS

See p. 183. Also:

1 : 50,000. Certain towns. Institut Géographique National.

Chapter 18

THE PORTUGUESE PROVINCE OF GUINEA—
LAND OF ESTUARIES AND RIVERS [1]

THE Portuguese Province of Guinea or, more popularly, Portuguese Guinea, is about one half the size of Sierra Leone, or one-third that of Portugal. Like the islands of São Tomé and Príncipe, Portuguese Guinea is a reminder of the very early contacts of Portugal with West Africa.

After its discovery by Nuno Tristão in 1446, fortified posts were established for the trade in slaves, gold, ivory and European goods. But penetration of the interior was impossible, as the Mali and Wolof Islamised kingdoms, which had cavalry troops, were hostile.

As usual, slaves were obtained through African intermediaries. Some were sent to Bahia, one of the earliest points of colonisation in Brazil. In and around this town there is much evidence of cultural transfer from Portuguese Guinea. Slaves were also despatched to the Cape Verde Islands, where they were employed on plantations; their descendants form the Creole population of that archipelago. Trading posts and castles at various places on the Gulf of Guinea were first administered from the Cape Verde Islands; from the latter many Creoles have come to modern Portuguese Guinea to engage in agriculture and have brought with them their Portuguese Creole *lingua franca*.

In 1879 Portuguese Guinea was separated from the Cape Verde Islands administration. By then the French had occupied Ziguinchor (Casamance Senegal), which still retains some Portuguese features, and the British were at Bolama. So

---

[1] This chapter is based on material by Professor Orlando Ribeiro, Professor of Geography in the University of Lisbon. It has been translated from French and edited by the author, R. J. Harrison Church.

the first capital was established at Geba, at the limit of navigation on the Geba River.   Although unusually central for such
an early capital, it was in a swampy area where there was

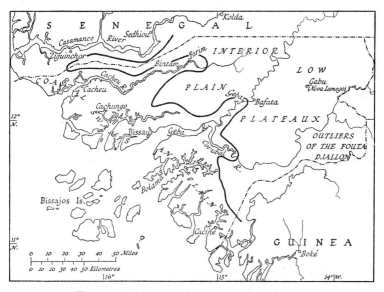

FIG. 54.—The Portuguese Province of Guinea.
The heavy line shows the tidal and mangrove limit.   It is also a great climatic,
vegetational and human divide.

much malaria.   Consequently, it was later abandoned in
favour of Bolama, after that island was ceded by the British in
1890.

In 1941 the capital was re-transferred to Bissau, in the Geba
Estuary, on a well populated island joined to the mainland by a
causeway, in the economic centre of the country, and with
depths of 36 feet at low water for anchorage and of 20 feet at
the quay.

The interior was only finally pacified in 1912.   At that time
Bissau was a fort surrounded by ramparts and palisades, with
a few houses belonging to Cape Verde people.   It is now a
well planned, flourishing town and port.

POPULATION

In an area of 13,948 square miles, Portuguese Guinea had a population of 529,000 in 1966, so that the average density per square mile was 38. It is highest in the coastal regions, and in the north, lower on the islands, in the south and the interior.

Of the 1950 total of 510,777, 503,935 were African, 4,568 were of mixed blood (many being Cape Verdians), 2,263 were White and 11 Indian. The 'civilised' population, which alone under Portuguese law has full citizenship, numbered 8,320. It comprised all Whites, Indians and those of mixed blood, but only 1,478 Christian Africans 'assimilated' to Portuguese culture. In and around the old towns of Farim, Cacheu, Geba, Bissau, Bolama, etc., Portuguese Creole is spoken and Portuguese rather than African names are common.

The towns of Farim, Cacheu and Cacine are in decline as the result of political and economic changes in recent decades; and the first capital of Geba is in ruins and invaded by bush. Bafata and Canchungo, on the contrary, are developing rapidly. Bissau, the young capital, and Bolama have three-quarters of the 'civilised' population and enjoy municipal status.

Human differences reinforce physical contrasts within Portuguese Guinea. As in other matters, the line of demarcation is approximately along the limit of tides and fringing mangroves (see Fig. 54).

Inland live the Manding and Fulani, the former numbering 64,000 and the latter 108,000. Both are Islamic and basically pastoral. Even where the Fulani have become semi-fixed, their huts resemble tents, in that the roofs reach almost to the ground. Moreover, settlements are always small and are abandoned frequently. Agriculture is rudimentary and shifting, being concerned mainly with millet and groundnut production.

The Manding are more fixed, have larger villages, and are often craftsmen, Islamic missionaries, smugglers, traders and, in the past, warriors. Although they cultivate groundnuts, cotton, vegetables and fruit gardens, they really disdain agriculture.

By contrast, in the coastal and estuarine swamps and plains live the animist, vigorous, expansionist but settled Balante, who number 154,000. This people, and the less numerous Floup of the extreme north-west, have been the great reclaimers of mangrove for swamp rice cultivation, using bunds for water control and applying manure. Their buildings are large and permanent and house families, animals, grain and all belongings. Settlement is in hamlets. Animals are kept mainly for manure and, in the wet season, are kept indoors, away from crops.

Most other peoples of the coast are culturally similar, but they also undertake fishing, navigation and coconut collection. Such are the 36,000 Papel of Bissau Island and the 72,000 Mandjac, who live west of Bissau. All the coastal peoples keep pigs and small cattle (although the Papel and Mandjac do not use manure). They collect and prepare the usual products from the coconut, oil and raphia palms.

CLIMATE AND VEGETATION

The coastal area has the South-west Coast Monsoonal climate (see pp. 48–9). In Portuguese Guinea there are five very wet months, in which the relative humidity often reaches saturation point, and violent storms are common. During the longer dry season, the Maritime Trades are far more common than the Harmattan, which appears only towards the close of the season. The interior, by contrast, has the Southern Savannah climate (see pp. 56–7).

The vegetation shows the same marked division. Along the coast and up the many wide and deeply penetrating estuaries mangroves grow luxuriantly, but have often been cleared for rice cultivation. Behind the mangroves comes much Fresh-water Swamp Forest and then Casamance Woodland. In the drier interior there is Guinea Savannah, with an exceptional amount of grass in the hills.

GEOLOGY, RELIEF AND MAJOR REGIONS

Portuguese Guinea is sharply divided on grounds of climate, vegetation, relief, human types and economy, between the flat Coastal Swamps and Plain on the one hand, and the Interior Plain, Low Plateaux and Fouta Djallon outliers on the other hand.

Recent marine transgression drowned the lowest reaches of the rivers, so creating ria estuaries, which are good waterways and are deep indentations of the coast. Off the coast are some sixty islands. Some of these adjoin the mainland, and are connected at low tide (tidal range is about 12 feet) by recently developed lateritic rock. The Bissajos Islands are farther out, but were doubtless separated in the same way. Drowning of rivers with such gentle gradients has contributed to the slackening of flow and silting of their lower courses.

The Coastal Plain and the Interior Plain both belong to the southern extremity of the great Senegal Basin, whose deposits are post-Eocene. Flat and monotonous, these plains are nearing the end of a cycle of erosion, the rivers making vast and numerous meanders and flooding severely in the wet season, or at high tides. Minor relief features result only from the outcrop of lateritic rocks, or occasional cliffs of up to 160 feet in height.

Behind the Coastal Plain and Interior Plain are the Low Plateaux of Pre-Cambrian rocks. One such plateau is that of Gabu-Bafata, with a clear western edge at the latter town and following, approximately, the line of the Geba River. The rivers are incised, and lateritic crusts are widespread.

In the extreme south-east, approximately south of the Upper Corubal River, are outliers of the Fouta Djallon. Valleys are separated by flat-topped interfluves, averaging 350–700 feet in height. These have widespread bleak exposures of older lateritic crusts practically bare of soil, and supporting only poor grass used by nomadic Fulani cattle keepers. These are the *bowé* of French writers (see p. 285).

ECONOMIC RESOURCES

Unlike the other Portuguese West African Province of São Tomé and Príncipe, Portuguese Guinea is a low-lying country. Plantations belonging to absentee landlords are almost unknown, and the economy is based on traditional farming and the collection of wild produce by Africans.

Rice is the basic food and the main crop in coastal, riverine and inland swamps. The Balante people are renowned in West Africa for the reclamation of mangrove for rice cultivation.

Oil palm produce is produced mainly in the same areas as swamp rice, especially along the coast and on the islands. Most of the oil is consumed locally, though a little is exported. Palm kernels are, however, the second export by value.

Groundnuts are the main export of Portuguese Guinea and leading cash crop of the plateaux, being especially important around Farim, Bafata and Gabu (Nova Lamego). As in Senegal and Nigeria, they are grown mainly by Muslim peoples who require considerable cash to buy their voluminous garments. The annual crop is about 90,000 tons, of which some 50% is exported. An increasing amount is being processed locally. There are three mills (two also process rice), and the oil cake is sent to Europe.

Oil seeds (groundnuts, cake and oil, palm kernels and oil, copra) account for about 90% of Portuguese Guinea exports. They are sent mainly to Portugal and there handled by a large company whose extensive works constitute the largest industrial concentration of the Portuguese capital.

COMMUNICATIONS

The three main rivers (Cacheu, Geba and Corubal) are each navigable for about 100 miles. They and coastal channels are cheap and important means of transport and make the construction of a railway unnecessary.

The rivers have been well supplemented by over 2,000 miles of earth roads, comprising an excellent network for this small country.

Bissau airport is served by a West African service giving inter-continental connexions. Bissau is also the main port but is supplemented by Bintam and Bolama.

CONCLUSION

Portuguese Guinea has developed rapidly since the thirties, particularly in the cultivation of rice. It would seem that much more can still be done to develop that crop and its internal and external markets. There is a less favourable prospect for the present leading export of groundnuts.

BIBLIOGRAPHY

A. Teixeira da Mota, *Guiné Portuguesa*, 2 vols. (*Monografias dos Territorias do Ultramar*), Agência Geral do Ultramar, Lisbon, 1954. Has English and French resumés.

F. Tenreiro, Bibliografia Geográfica da Guiné, *Garcia de Orta*, Vol. II, No. 1, 1953, pp. 97–134, lists 450 references.

O. Ribeiro, ' Sur quelques traits géographiques de la Guiné portugaise ', *C.I.A.O. de Bissau*, 1952.

A. Carvalho Guerra, ' Subsídios para o estudo do clima da Colónia da Guiné ', *Boletim Cultural da Guiné Portuguea*, Vol. II, No. 5.

J. Carrington da Costa, ' Fisiografia e Geologia da Província da Guiné ', *Boletim da Sociedade Geológica de Portugal*, Vol. 5, 1946.

O. Ribeiro, ' L'Aménagement du Terroir en Afrique Occidentale ', *Bulletin de la Société Royale de Géographie d'Egypte*, Vol. XXV, 1953, pp. 165–77.

F. Tenreiro, *Acerca da Casa e do Povoamento da Guiné Portuguesa*, Lisbon, 1950.

Boletim Cultural da Guiné Portuguesa, 1946 onwards, and the *Publicações do Centro de Estudos da Guiné Portuguesa* are valuable sources, particularly the articles in them by A. Teixeira da Mota.

MAPS

Atlas de Portugal Ultramarino, 1947.

1 : 50,000 Ministério do Ultramar, is an excellent series—the best of all Portuguese colonial maps.

1 : 500,000 is the largest scale covering the whole country.

Chapter 19

GUINEA—THE HIGHLAND WATERSHED [1]

THIS country, with an area of 94,926 square miles and a population in 1966 of 3,608,000 has an average density per square mile of 38. This is higher than that of many ex-French West African republics, but low compared with that of Sierra Leone or other ex-British West African lands. Seasonal migration of men for groundnut cultivation in Senegal and the Gambia even points to over-population in the northern Fouta Djallon.

Guinea is a land of more than ordinary interest. First, as with Casamance, Portuguese Guinea and northern Sierra Leone, but unlike the rest of West Africa, it has a recently submerged coast. More unusual are its highlands and the fact that in them were a number of non-African planters. Thirdly, as its abrupt mountains lie astride the south-westerly or westerly rain-bearing winds, it is not surprising that it has a very heavy rainfall. The country is further characterised by great expanses of laterite, and this induces rapid run-off of rainwater. The republic is the source of many famous rivers, such as the Bafing and Bakoy headwaters of the Senegal, the Gambia, the Niger and its tributaries the Milo and Sankarani. Many rivers also flow directly to the coast. The French often speak of Guinea as a ' château d'eau '.

On human grounds, too, Guinea is exceptional. Two-fifths of the African population are Fulani, many of whom are settled. Lastly, the socialist economy and varied and considerable potential of the country are exceptional. The more usual exports, such as palm produce, are less important, private and state plantation-grown coffee and fruits replacing

---

[1] M. M. Houis, formerly Director of the Institut Français d'Afrique Noire at Conakry, who accompanied me in much of Guinea at great trouble to himself, has further assisted me by his criticism of this chapter.

them.   Rice is the main food and may become a regular
export.   As in Sierra Leone, the development of minerals has
greatly helped Guinea.   Gold, almost wholly obtained by
African miners, was worked for centuries, but diamonds have
been exploited only since 1935, and bauxite and iron exported
systematically only since 1952–3.   Alumina has been produced
since 1960 and this and large bauxite reserves make her great
hydro-electric power potential even more important.   It is
likely, however, that if hydro-electric power is ever used locally
to make aluminium, it will be in connection with bauxite
deposits east of Boké, where a very large deposit is to be
worked.

HISTORICAL OUTLINE

French interests in this part of the coast date back to the
seventeenth century at least, but were in competition with the
Portuguese and the British.   The establishment of ' factories ',
however, does not date back earlier than the nineteenth century, when there were also Portuguese, British and German
ones.   At the beginning of that century this coast was also a
hide-out for slave-boats, still operating at the end of the slave
trade in defiance of British and other anti-slavery patrols.
British political interests in the coast were mainly centred in
the Los Islands, which remained British until 1904.

The first assumption of French sovereignty was in the Boké
region in 1849.   There was considerable advance after 1854,
when France was anxious to occupy the area before the British
could link the Gambia with Sierra Leone.   In 1868 there were
negotiations between Britain and France with the object of
exchanging the Gambia for a part of what is now Guinea.
But these parleys had no result, and the boundaries with
Sierra Leone were defined in 1882 and 1889.   German interests were eliminated in 1885.   The boundary with Portuguese Guinea was agreed in 1886 and that with Liberia in
1911.   In 1891 this territory, until then governed from Senegal,
became a separate colony and in 1893 was named French
Guinea.   It became the Republic of Guinea in 1958, when it,
alone of the French West African countries, voted for independence.   The French then withdrew most personnel and
equipment.

CLIMATE

Owing to the high relief and the south-east trending coast, there is considerable climatic variety. Climatic regions are determined by relief rather than by latitude.

As one would expect, rainfall is highest on the coast and on the western slopes of the Fouta Djallon. The rains start in

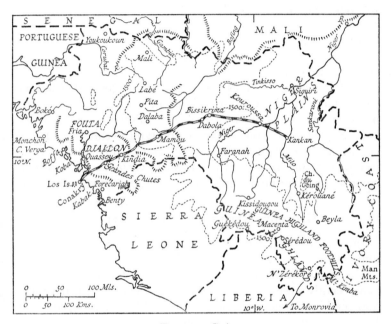

FIG. 55.—Guinea.

March in the south and reach Conakry in early May. They end in the north in November and in the south by December. July and August are everywhere the wettest months, and until October movement may be difficult, owing more to the floods than to heavy rain.

South-west Coast Monsoonal Zone. Here the rainfall is heavy, 169 inches (4,300 mm.) at Conakry and 111 inches (2,800 mm.) at Boké. Rain is regular from the end of June to early October and much of the rain comes at night. In July and August, and sometimes even in September, there may be rain for several days on end. Annual relative humidity averages 70–80%.

Days are hottest in April, reaching about 90° F. or 32° C. In August they are cooler because of rain, but nights tend to be oppressive.

Because of the high rainfall and humidity and small range of temperature, this climate is unhealthy. This, together with the treacherous estuaries and fly, may explain why this coast was relatively little visited between the fifteenth and nineteenth centuries and, until the mid-nineteenth century, less affected by the slave trade.

For the *Foutanian, Guinea Foothills* and *Guinea Highland* climates, see Chapter 3.

Southern Savannah. This is found in the Niger and tributary valley lands of the north-east, and in lowland areas on the northern and north-western border. Thus Kouroussa, Kankan, Siguiri and Youkounkoun are typical stations. Local conditions conform with those of the rest of this climatic zone (see p. 56), but rainfall is particularly variable. It tends to come in the afternoons as sharp storms, but rarely at night.

GEOLOGY, RELIEF AND MAJOR REGIONS

In Guinea differences of relief and geology powerfully determine the various regions.

COASTAL SWAMPS. As in Portuguese Guinea, the coast is a recently submerged one, the inlets being drowned valleys and the islands remnants of old hills. As there is no constant longshore drift, and the tidal range is high, sand-bars or lagoons do not readily form.

The estuaries are muddy and bordered by mangrove. There are two theories concerning this mud accumulation. The first is that mud-laden river water coming into contact with salt water drops mud particles. The second explanation is that near the shore-line there is a compensatory upward movement to balance coastal submergence, thus assisting mud accumulation.

The coast was so unhealthy in the past that slave traders hardly visited it until the nineteenth century. Then its tricky channels and dense vegetation provided hide-outs from British anti-slavery naval patrols operating from Freetown and from the Los Islands.

The Baga have long been renowned for rice cultivation in reclaimed mangrove swamps, protected by bunds. Ever greater efforts are being made to reclaim mangrove for rice cultivation.[1]

The muddy mangrove coastline and the coastal plain are broken at two points by rocky spurs—at Cape Verga and behind Conakry. The former consists of schists and quartzite and the latter of granite and ultra-basic eruptive rocks, found also in the Los Islands and in the Kakoulima area, north-east of Conakry.

Conakry, the capital of Guinea, lies on Tombo Island. This is a little over 2 miles long and 1 mile in width, and is

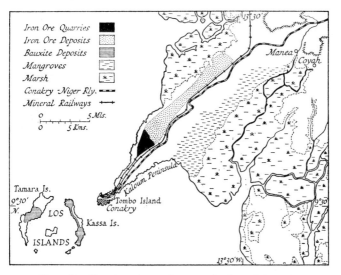

FIG. 56.—Conakry, its environs and mineral deposits.

connected by a causeway to the mainland. Conakry has deep water and no surf, though approach has to be from the south. The port is somewhat sheltered by the Los Islands and by breakwaters. Yet, despite natural advantages, Conakry remained a relatively minor port until 1952 (when iron ore

[1] See also under Agriculture, pp. 290-1.

began to be exported), largely because of the relative poverty of the territory and lack of capital.   Concrete wharves or piers are on the north-west side of the island and are equipped for handling passengers, iron ore (although export ceased in 1965), alumina and bananas.   Other important exports are palm produce, coffee, diamonds, groundnuts, pineapples and orange oil.

The population of Conakry grew from 13,600 in 1936 to 26,000 in 1946 and 109,500 in 1960.   About 45,000 of these live on the island.   Roughly speaking, the north-west sides of both Tombo Island and the peninsula have the administrative and good residential quarters, whilst the south-eastern side of the island is much overcrowded.   New quarters have been built on the mainland.

As more hydro-electric power is becoming available, so more industries are being established by state initiative and under state control.   Since independence a furniture works, a textile mill, and a large cigarette, tobacco and match factory have been built near Conakry.   Older concerns are soft-drinks and soap factories, fruit canneries, a paint and plastics works, and a mining explosives factory.

Benty is, so far, the only other true port of Guinea.   It is 10 miles from the sea, on the south bank of the Mellacorée River, where it widens out into a drowned estuary or arm of the sea.   It is adjacent to the Sierra Leone boundary, and was used first by the French Navy in 1867.   Economically, it is a most useful supplement to Conakry, as it is easily accessible to banana boats of up to about 8,000 tons and has no bar. Through it go most bananas exported from the southern coastlands.

THE COASTAL PLAIN.   Between the wide mangrove belt and the Fouta Djallon foothills is a coastal plain of sandstone gravels, washed down from the highlands, and overlying laterite and a substratum of granite and gneiss.   This gravel plain, 30–50 miles wide, narrowest in the north-west but wider and flatter in the south-east, is sheltered from coastal breezes by the broad mangrove but has a heavy rainfall, high humidity and temperatures.   It also suffers from waterlogging after heavy rain.

Nevertheless, villages are more numerous here than on the foothills or outlying mesas.   The villagers grow rice, hungry rice, maize, kola nuts and the oil palm, the latter being the main resource. Many of these villages have also reclaimed mangrove swamp for rice. There are banana plantations around the inland end of the Conakry (Kaloum) peninsula, near Forécariah and Benty. Pineapples are also grown at Benty and Ouassou (north-west of Dubréka).

THE FOUTA DJALLON. This great highland mass is mainly within Guinea. It rises on the west and north by a series of fault-steps, but the eastern slopes are gentler and their valleys shallower.

Some 5,000 square miles are above 3,000 feet. These figures might indicate rather unimpressive mountains but on the contrary they are majestic, because of intense dissection.

The Fouta Djallon consists mainly of level, westward-sloping siliceous Cambrian to Ordovician or Devonian sand-stones, which cover Birrimian rocks to a depth of some 2,500 feet. On the remarkably level plateaux, there are frequent expanses of bare hard impervious ferruginous crust or *bowal* (plural *bowé* = 'no trees'). These bowé are particularly bare in the extreme north and most extensive in the west.

Oddly enough, the highest areas are the most densely peopled by the Fulani, who were attracted by the healthy conditions and pastures. Nevertheless, they were forced to rear the small Ndama cattle and to become semi-fixed pastoralists. They retained former prisoners of war (who were allowed to free themselves) to grow their crops in the valleys, where the negro settlements are still found. The worse the bowal, the more captives were required to provide food; hence the coincidence of denser population in poor high parts used for wet-season pastures, and in valleys used for crops and dry-season pasturing.[1]

Basic eruptive gabbros and dolerite often occur in the sand-stone as sills or dykes, so causing some of the vivid rock edges, over which there are often impressive waterfalls, e.g. near Pita. Soils on these rocks tend to be richer; near Labé are plantations of bitter oranges grown for their oil, of jasmin for perfume, and of arabica coffee. On the western edge of the Fouta Djallon, gabbros often form the peaks, e.g. Mont Gangan (3,627 feet)

---

[1] J. Richard-Molard, ' Les densités de population au Fouta-Dialon et dans les régions environnantes ', *Compte Rendu du XV Congrès International de Géographie*, *1949*.

near Kindia, or the Kakoulima Massif (3,273 feet) north-east of Conakry.

The sandstone has been intensely and curiously dissected, either by Caledonian or Hercynian warpings or by fractures in the underlying Pre-Cambrian rocks, or as the result of tension during the Alpine earth movements. It may be along these lines of weakness that the still-youthful rivers have worked.

Evidence of rejuvenation (probably Miocene) is widespread. Uplift may still be continuing as the rivers, like many others in West Africa, show signs of youth in otherwise mature landscape.

Valleys are almost always narrow and deeply trenched, often in a north–south direction. Rivers frequently take right-angled turns through gorges to another valley, suggestive of capture. Thus the highland is cut up into a chequer-board pattern of blocks isolated by vast chasms. The most obvious north–south trench is that east of Kindia, which almost separates the Fouta Djallon into two parts. There is also a west–east trench partly followed by the railway and by the Tinkisso tributary of the Niger.

Upon this dissected and divided highland there falls heavy seasonal rainfall, so that mighty rivers take their rise here. The flora is special, because of the heavy rain and flooding followed by months of dryness, the frequence of ferruginous crusts or laterite, high relief and relative inaccessibility. Yet owing to the depredations of man, especially late bush firing to provide green shoots for cattle at the end of the dry season, the original forest rarely remains on the plateaux (see Chapter 4).

Soil conservation is vitally important in the Fouta Djallon, as so much soil has already been washed down the rivers. Moreover, the relatively dense population uses such thin soils that they are constantly loosened by heavy rain, as well as being thoroughly leached of their chemical nutrients.

Apart from subsistence crops, the keeping of livestock, orange, jasmin and coffee plantations, bananas are cultivated in damp valleys as far east as Mamou, though most plantations are nearer Kindia, e.g. in the Kolenté–Kakrima depression. Valley cultivation of bananas is essential to allow growth during the dry season, many planters having made their own reservoirs along the rivers. By contrast, pineapples and citrus fruits are grown on higher drier ground.

The main towns of Fouta Djallon are the old ones of Mali, Pita and Labé; Mamou and Kindia are creations of the railway. Timbo, the former capital of the Almanis of the Fouta Djallon state, is now a village, with neither economic nor political importance.

Kindia is an important railing point for bananas. Its main interest lies in the Pasteur Institute, five miles outside the town, established in 1925 to carry out medical experiments upon anthropoides in their natural environment. Since 1939 snakes have been kept there to prepare serum against snake bites and rabbits for anti-rabies serum.

Mamou is a great route centre. Especially significant is the road to Dalaba (a lovely hill station), Pita, Labé and on to Senegal.

Dabola lies on the railway at the contact of the Fouta Djallon with the Niger Plains.

GUINEA HIGHLANDS. Along the north-north-eastern part of the Sierra Leone–Guinea boundary, the mountains narrow and the mighty Niger takes its rise. Had it not been for the political boundary, this could have been an ideal crossing of the highland mass for a railway from the coast to the Upper Niger. It is also here that the flat sandstone cover and lateritic surfaces disappear south of about 9° N. and the Guinea Highlands begin.

The Guinea Highlands are, indeed, in great contrast to the Fouta Djallon. They are composed of granite, gneisses, schists and quartzites. It is a region of rounded forested hills, with some more or less bare dome-like summits, e.g. Mount Nimba, 5,695 feet. Although the Guinea Highlands trend north-west to south-east, dissection has cut them up into several north-east–south-west segments.

The heavy and well-distributed rainfall, the steep slopes and, until about 1948, relative inaccessibility have allowed the survival of some Rain Forest. The gneisses give fairly rich soil for rice, oil palm, maize, kola, cassava and cocoyam. There are important coffee plantations, and some experimental ones of tea at Macenta and of cinchona at Sérédou. Iron, graphite and other minerals occur and might be mined if communications improved, e.g. if the Liberian mineral railway to Mt. Nimba were extended here. Kola nuts have long been traded north.

N'Zérékoré is an important trading centre because of roads north to Kankan, south-east to the Ivory Coast and especially to the nearest deep-water port at Monrovia. About 20,000 tons pass along the Monrovia road, and the Guinea Government has a fleet of lorries. Palm kernels and coffee are increasingly exported by this route.

Macenta and *Guékédou* are other market centres in the forested hills. The latter has considerable trade with Sierra Leone. If the railway of that colony had a higher capacity it might help south-west Guinea to develop its external commerce.

GUINEA HIGHLAND FOOTHILLS. Although geologically similar, and sometimes as high, these are more dissected than the Guinea Highlands. Impressive foothills are the steep edge near Boola, the Pic du Tio north of Beyla, the Chaine du Gbing east of Kérouané and the Dongoroma Mountains to its west.

There are good Ndama cattle on these grassland foothills, which are more fertile than the Guinea Highlands, because of lesser leaching and deeper soils. Rice and tobacco are grown in excess of local needs.

The Rain Forest formerly extended here, but there are now few trees, except along streams. Diamonds are mined in this region (see under Minerals).

Beyla was probably founded by the Dioula around 1230, as a centre for the slave and kola nut trades. It is now a small market which has surpluses of rice, tobacco (burley) and cattle. *Kissidougou* and *Faranah* are other markets.

NIGER PLAINS. The eastern limit of the Fouta Djallon is clear orographically and geologically, the horizontal sandstones ending in a steep edge north and south of Bissikrima.

The plains are composed of the same rocks as the Guinea Highlands and Foothills, except that granite intrusions are commoner and that laterite is widespread—a grave disadvantage.

The average elevation of these plains is about 1,000 feet, but there are several upstanding relief features. These are either steep sandstone outliers of the Fouta Djallon, or rounded granite domes. Both are to be seen west of Siguiri, and the Pre-Cambrian rocks are also responsible for the rocky river sill at Kouroussa which ends navigation up the Niger, and for the

69. Western edge of Fouta Djallon, near Dubreka and Conakry, with irrigated bananas in near-by valley and dry rice on hillside. (See north of Fig. 56.)

0. The Fouta Djallon from ,india. Note the treeless almost evel plateau surface, and the trench-like valley.

71. Macenta, in a hollow of the rounded and forested Guinea Highlands. In the lower flatter areas is Derived Savannah.

72. Guinea Highland Foothills ear Boola, with Derived Savannah

73. The Fria plant, 90 miles north-north-east of Conakry, Guinea, which, alone in Africa, reduces bauxite to alumina.

74. Conakry harbour, Guinea. The passenger quay is just off the picture on the left, the first visible one being the general wharf. Beyond is the iron-ore terminal (disused since 1965), with a dump of dark iron ore behind. On the far right is a third pier for loading alumina

gold-bearing quartz veins and gravels so feverishly worked by African families.

Along the rivers, rice cultivation has been increased by flood control works (see Fig. 51). Elsewhere, Ndama cattle are kept, and crops of cassava, sweet potatoes, millet and groundnuts are grown. The shea butter tree is very evident. In general, crops are poor because of the laterite covering.

Kankan, the eastern terminus of the railway, is on the Milo tributary, easier to navigate than the Niger. It is a road, railway, river and air centre, a market for local produce (especially rice) and for produce from or going to the Guinea Highlands. In this latter trade about 300 lorries are engaged. In Kankan there are some 17,000 Africans and some Lebanese and Europeans. It boasts a fine hotel and river bridge. Otherwise it has rather the character of a huge village, with huts and crops along many roads.

Kouroussa, at the limit of Niger navigation and on the railway, is subsidiary to Kankan.

Siguiri, on the navigable Niger, is the market for food and other supplies for the goldfields.

SOIL CONSERVATION

Soil conservation is of vital importance in Guinea. If a land with similar soils existed in Europe, two-thirds of it would be regarded as unsuitable for agriculture or stock-rearing, and would be left as open space of forest. But in Guinea many of these poor sandy soils are quite intensively used because of pressure on the land. Rice and hungry rice are often sown in areas where there is less than 4 inches of soil, but where rainfall of up to 160 inches per year can come to wash it away.

It has been estimated that about 60% of the country ought not to be cultivated, but should be used for intermittent pasturage. About 30% could be used if proper cultivation and anti-erosion methods were employed. Only about 10% of the territory, mostly situated on the coast and in river valleys, is capable of being cultivated without particular precautions.

Guinea suffers not only from thin soils and devastatingly heavy rainfall, but also from severe bush firing by the

L

pastoral Fulani at the end of the long dry season.   As the source of so many great rivers, it is also more than usually subject to severe erosion.

An interesting scheme has been evolved to safeguard the source of the Bafing, or Upper Senegal.   The Departments of Agriculture, Animal Husbandry and Forestry have collaborated to control the use of 5,000 acres around the headwaters.   Some 400 people live in this area, though the vegetation and soils are extremely poor.   The departments are improving the soils, controlling the use of pastures and replanting trees and grasses. Such a scheme might well be copied in many other parts of Africa.

ECONOMIC RESOURCES

AGRICULTURE

As with all matters in Guinea, agricultural production is much determined by the sharply contrasted regions, though cassava is grown everywhere.   In general, the oil palm, rice, bananas, hungry rice, maize and kola nuts are the subsistence crops of the Coastal Plain and of the Guinea Highlands. In the former, rice and bananas (almost exclusively on plantations) are also grown as cash crops.   In the Guinea Highlands the main cash crop is coffee.

In the Fouta Djallon the subsistence crops are upland rice, a little swamp rice, fonio or hungry rice, maize, millet and bananas.   The export crops are bananas grown in the valleys, citrus fruits and pineapples grown on sloping ground, all mainly on plantations.

In the Niger Plains the subsistence crops are rice near the rivers, hungry rice, maize and millet elsewhere.   There is no important cash crop.

Rice has developed to such an extent in recent years in Guinea, that it is the main food in most areas.   In the past, relatively little rice was grown and all of it was upland, but the country now produces much rice from swamps, with a production of approximately 400,000 tons annually.   Nevertheless, rice is still a major import.

Along the coast there has been the same effort to reclaim

mangrove swamps for rice as in Portuguese Guinea and Sierra Leone. In the northern part of the Coastal Plain the Baga have long been skilled in reclaiming mangrove swamp and building polders. It is not certain whether they learned this skill from the Mali kingdom of the Middle Niger, from the early Portuguese, from the Portuguese via Africans, from Portuguese Guinea, or developed the skill themselves. They have reclaimed considerable areas in the north, where, so long as the water control is satisfactory, climate and soils seem good.

Large reclamation schemes have also been undertaken to permit mechanical cultivation of new areas. Thus the Government has tried to develop about 5,000 acres at Monchon, near Boffa, and 1,875 acres at Koba. Africans, with European help, have reclaimed 3,750 acres on Kabak Island (Forécariah District), at Dubréka, near Conakry, and at Bintimodia, south of Conakry.

When mangrove is cleared for rice cultivation, salt must be eliminated from the soils by flushing with fresh river water, and sea water must be excluded. At Monchon it was difficult to keep the fresh river water supply available to the lands, as the river is silting up.[1] In Portuguese Guinea, Guinea and Sierra Leone it has also been found that lands which appear to be free of salt often have toxic alkalis appearing in the soil, once rice cultivation has been started.

Also of significance has been the reclamation of inland and riverine swamps, most of them along the Niger and its tributaries. Water control is similar to that undertaken along the same rivers in Mali. The greatest project is that for the reclamation of 32,500 acres in the Siguiri area.

Bananas. As in the Ivory Coast, their cultivation at first depended upon a preferential tariff in France, and because of this help there was a flush of banana production here and in the French Community. Of the total production of about 300,000–400,000 metric tons, Guinea produced about one-fifth. Guinea's bananas were shut out of the saturated French market in 1959, so that markets have been sought in Western and Eastern Europe, in competition with bananas from the Canary Islands, the West Indies, the Ivory Coast and Cameroon. Export to Britain is said to be impossible

[1] See above, p. 282.

in view of strong competition.   Moreover the British are said
to dislike small sweet bananas.   Guinea has a production
climax between August and February, just when European
fruits are freely available.   It would be ideal if the flush were
from November to May.

The type grown has been evolved from the dwarf Chinese
banana, introduced in 1898 and similar to that grown in the
Canary Islands.   As the Guinea banana is delicate, it requires
expensive wrapping with polythene.

The following export figures illustrate the rapid growth of
production:

	Metric tons			Metric tons			Metric tons
1917	197	1925		1,534	1933		21,758
1918	188	1926		2,320	1934		26,075
1919	235	1927		3,041	1935		30,908
1920	266	1928		4,326	1936		45,054
1921	387	1929		6,110	1937		55,000
1922	671	1930		9,133	1938		54,765
1923	904	1931		11,000			
1924	982	1932		16,793			

During the war, exports were very restricted, being only
2,646 tons in 1944.   But in 1947 they were 26,000 tons, rising
to 32,515 tons in 1948 and to 54,000 tons in 1951.   Present
production is about 45,000 tons, plantation produced fruit
comprising 20%.   The fruit accounts for about 10% of Guinea
exports.

There are over 11,000 acres under bananas.   The main area
is within the Ouassou–Benty–Mamou triangle, wherever there
are flat, fertile, humid lands near railways or roads, but
especially near Forécariah.   Commercial production started
first in valleys in the Fouta Djallon, where bananas mature
more slowly and the fruit is stronger and drier than that grown
on the coast.   There were, until recently, fewer banana pests,
and the mountains are healthier for non-African planters.
On the other hand, cost of transport to port is higher, and the
nights are cold in the dry season, the aridity of which is
countered by costly irrigation.   The average plantation is
50–100 acres and the banana bunches average 35–40 lb. each.

By contrast, on the Coastal Plain, where conditions approximate to those in the Ivory Coast, water is more than sufficient
and flood control works are sometimes required.   Soils are

more leached, as the result of heavier rain, so that heavy expenditure on fertiliser is necessary. This is also the initial area of the banana-root borer (*Cosmopilites sordidus*), and of the fungus Cercosposiose (*Cercosposa musae*) which cause great havoc and require costly spraying with chemicals. But transport is quick and easy, and so new plantations are made here rather than in the highlands. The bunches are smaller in this zone, weighing between 25 and 30 lb.

Oranges and Orange Oil. These, and possibly other citrus fruits as well, were introduced by the Portuguese in the fifteenth century or thereabouts. Sweet oranges have long been grown haphazardly by Africans, mainly in the Fouta Djallon.

Guinea sweet oranges have thick and oily skins, which are scratched or scraped with a sharpened spoon or blunt knife. The oil is inevitably of poor quality, since the sweet (rather than the bitter) oranges are used. No plant selection or grafting is done and no care exercised in cultivation. Once the oil has been extracted, it is often adulterated.

By contrast, near Labé there are well organised plantations which have 1,250 acres and a distillery. They alone grow the bitter orange and, by scientific methods, produce high quality oil. The estate also extracts essence from orange leaves and from the flowers. Furthermore, it grows lemons, bergamots, lemon grass and jasmin for essence production, and is trying silkworm culture.

Pineapples. Cultivation of pineapples for export began in 1934, aided by French tariff preference. The fruit is grown on well drained slopes, mostly near Kindia, but some is produced on the Coastal Plain, near Forécariah, Benty and Ouassou in growing competition with bananas. Unfortunately, like bananas, pineapples have their main harvest at a time when they are in competition with temperate fruits. Ways of overcoming this difficulty are by canning, which deals with five-sixths of the harvest, and by trying to force the fruit to mature earlier.

Kola Nuts. Kola trees are fairly widespread in the Coastal Plain and in the Guinea Highlands. There is extensive trade in these, especially from the latter towards Kankan and the Mali Republic. Indeed, the roads which now lead northward from the Guinea Highlands have been made from the old trails followed by merchants taking kola nuts one way, and salt and cattle in the other direction.

Palm Kernels.   The construction of the road from N'Zérékoré to Monrovia (Liberia) made possible a vast increase in the export of kernels from the Guinea Highlands.   On the coast, large plantations at Yogoya and at Katako, in Bofa and Boké Districts respectively, are being regenerated.

Coffee.   This developed remarkably in the Guinea Highlands and accounted for about a third of Guinea's exports at independence.   Since then it has fallen to a very low figure because of the loss of the French market, smuggling into Liberia or the Ivory Coast, and through disease.

LIVESTOCK

There are about $1\frac{1}{2}$ million cattle in Guinea, almost all of them in the Fouta Djallon or in the Niger Plains.   All are of the small, humpless Ndama type kept by the Fulani—this being the only territory where the Fulani keep such cattle.

The most important cattle area is around Labé, and from there livestock are sent to the rest of Guinea, to Sierra Leone and to Liberia.   Although the cattle are small, the proportion of meat available per carcass is normally about 45% and in the richer pasture lands around Beyla may reach about 53%. The meat is also of higher quality than that normally obtained from average Zebu cattle.

MINERALS

The mining of gold has probably gone on for centuries in Guinea and is still mined a little by Africans.   Guinea has, however, undergone an economic revolution, because of the recent and far more valuable working of diamonds, bauxite and iron ore.

Gold.   Gold is mined along and near the Niger and its tributaries in the Siguiri area.   The bedrock consists of a decomposed schist, which is covered by clay, gravel, alluvial loam and, generally, some laterite.   Gold is obtained either by working veins in the bedrock, or by finding free gold in gravels near the present rivers, or in the river beds themselves.   In the latter two cases the origin of the gold is the Birrimian Series, west of Siguiri, where there are quartz lodes.

Since 1905 the area has been reserved exclusively for African working. The miners sink shafts of only 2 feet in diameter up to a maximum depth of some 60 feet. Shafts are often only 13–16 feet apart, and galleries are sometimes made from pit to pit. But galleries are never timbered, so that the mining is highly dangerous. Moreover, only about half the gold-bearing area can be exploited. While the men work down in the pits, the women pull up the gold-bearing gravels in calabashes, and then wash out the gold. All work is done on this family basis.

Mechanical gold mining is restricted to a little dredging in the Tinkisso River.

Diamonds. Commercial production of diamonds began in 1935. They occur in alluvial gravels of tributaries of the Makona River in the same way as in Sierra Leone, and the company which worked them until 1961 was connected with those in Sierra Leone and Ghana. The open-cast workings lie about 14 miles away from the road between Macenta and Kérouané. Another working is west of Beyla. Most of the diamonds are small, but some are gem stones, especially in two workings. The general quality is about equal to that in Sierra Leone.

There were illicit diggings, and part and then all of the concessions were nationalised. Thereafter diamond co-operatives were formed and illegal mining declined. The two European companies have been nationalised and, while their production had already declined since independence because of labour and political difficulties, it has fallen still lower under state direction.

Bauxite. (See Fig. 56.) The very large bauxite deposits of Guinea are typical of those in most tropical countries, in that they are trihydrates. The most important ones so far prospected are those at Boké, Dabola and Fria. The last two are served by road and railway and near falls which might be harnessed for hydro-electric power. As a first stage, bauxite is mined at Fria, 90 miles north-north-east of Conakry, by an international company. It runs a large and efficient alumina plant producing about half a million tons annually, which is sold to company participants in the United States, France, the United Kingdom, Switzerland and Germany, as well as other countries. Alumina now comprises over half of Guinea's exports. Power from the Kaleta Falls on the Konkouré River could be developed to enable smelting of the alumina to aluminium, but this would need much capital, and would compete with the large integrated plant being developed at Boké.

The development of the Los Islands deposits started systematically in 1950, and export began in 1952. The bauxite here derives from the laterisation of underlying syenite. The bauxite is cut out by electric or steam driven shovels, from concentrations in hollows, the methods being similar to those employed in British and Dutch Guiana.

The bauxite is crushed, washed to rid it of some impurities and dried to exclude moisture. A wharf has been built on the east side of Kassa Island to receive ships of up to 20,000 tons; these are quickly loaded with the pulverised dry bauxite, which is shipped overseas. The other island of Tamara is also being exploited, but crushing and washing is done on Kassa Island.

The working of bauxite is done with heavy equipment, organised in the most efficient way, and it is intended to scrape off all the available bauxite from these low islands, which after some twenty or thirty years may present a very different appearance. The annual production is about 300,000 tons, but has been much affected by disputes between the original operating company and the government. The latter has now nationalised the concession and mining is done by a Hungarian organisation. Mining will cease soon, as reserves are nearly exhausted.

Iron Ore. (See Fig. 56.) The Kaloum Peninsula deposits have been known since 1904, there being at least 200 million tons of roughly 51·5% iron content. The ore consists of an older basic eruptive type of ferruginous magnetite, which has laterised surfaces. It is low in phosphorus content, but high in chrome (1 to 3%), nickel (0·1%), alumina (10%) and water. These factors delayed its exploitation, and it was necessary to mix the iron ore with over three-fifths of other ores in a blast furnace, but the ore is no worse than that worked for some time in Cuba, Indonesia and the Philippine Islands.

The ore occurs in two layers: an upper hard one 6–20 feet thick, quarried from 1953–65, and a softer lower one of 25–80 feet in thickness. The concession covers some 42,500 acres, 5 miles east of the port of Conakry and production was highly mechanised. The beds slope upward with little overburden.

Exploitation was exceedingly simple. Charges were fired in the crust and giant diggers loaded the broken material into 25-ton lorries, which carried it to the crusher. The material was later screened and loaded into 65-ton railway wagons, with bottom doors. The rail haul was only 5 miles on a railway to a special wharf. There, belt conveyers filled a 12,000-ton ship in under twenty-four hours. It was hoped to achieve an annual export of about $1\frac{1}{2}$ million tons but it varied between $\frac{1}{3}$ and $\frac{3}{4}$ million tons. Because of competition from the richer and purer hæmatite ores of Mauritania and Liberia, and because of import restrictions affecting mechanical efficiency operations ceased in 1965. One-third of the capital invested in this undertaking was provided by the British Iron and Steel Corporation.

Hydro-electric Power

Because of the heavy rainfall, the many deep gorges in the Fouta Djallon and the level plateaux, there is a high potential for hydro-electric power. On the other hand, evaporation is high during the long dry season, the thin vegetation on the plateaux is unhelpful to water and soil conservation, and lakes are rare.

A great impetus to the development of hydro-electric power has been given by the development of iron and bauxite deposits. If vast quantities of cheap electricity can be produced at Kaleta on the Konkouré River, 90 miles north-east of Conakry, it might be possible to establish an aluminium industry there, alongside the existing alumina works. Such power would also be available for a similar purpose at the rich bauxite deposit at Boké. The power might further enable production of local iron and steel, and encourage many other industries.

Communications

In a territory with so much high country of a particularly dissected character, it is obvious that means of transport are of more than usual importance. Moreover, the highland mass obstructs communications between the coast and the Upper Niger and its various tributaries, which are valuable means of communication in the north-east.

At the end of the nineteenth century, when France and Britain were rivals in the area now occupied by Guinea and Sierra Leone, the interior could be pacified only by means of roads or, preferably, by railways. Thus, the Guinea and Sierra Leone railways were rival routes into the interior, and that in Guinea was built to prevent the British from reaching the lands of the Upper Niger. It also had the object of creating a hinterland for Conakry, at that time subsidiary commercially to Freetown.

Unfortunately, the narrowest part of the highland mass, the waist line between the Fouta Djallon and the Guinea Highlands, lies on the boundary with the north-eastern part of Sierra Leone. Had this not been so, this would have been the easiest route for a railway or road. The French railway was built in the face of appalling engineering difficulties, through precipitous country and at great cost in lives, material and money. As the boundary kept the British from the Upper Niger, the Sierra Leone Railway was built for the strictly local purpose of serving oil palm areas, and is too near the southern coast. Because of an unfortunate political boundary, both railways have unsatisfactory routes, were built at considerable cost and have only moderate traffic to offset high capital burdens.

The Guinea railway was begun in 1900, reached the Niger at Kouroussa in 1910, and the more easily navigated Milo tributary in 1914. It rises to 2,346 feet, but this figure gives little idea of the very frequent steep gradients and sharp curves on the railway, the lines of which are frequently on the narrow ledges of precipices. The scenery of this railway is magnificent and quite exceptional in West Africa. Until the development of banana exports on a large scale, the railway had little traffic and its importance was mainly administrative. Despite the mountainous country which it crosses, there were fast auto-railers which did the journey from Conakry to Kankan, 414 miles, in thirteen hours, but the railway is now in disrepair.

There are some good trunk roads, and the southern towns are linked with Monrovia (Liberia), their nearest port.

Conakry, Boké, Labé, N'Zérékoré, Beyla and Kankan are served by air.

CONCLUSION

Guinea has, for West Africa, exceptionally varied relief and economic resources. The low and rainy Coastal Plain is well suited to the production of oil palm produce and rice for all of which there is keen demand. The Fouta Djallon is suited to the growth of pineapples on its slopes and to banana cultivation in its valleys. Coffee in the Guinea Highlands developed very rapidly initially, and could be resuscitated. Rice cultivation in the Niger Plains can also be extended.

In addition to varied cash and food crops, mineral production is diverse but has been adversely affected by state interference and subsequent control. This is especially true of all diamond mining, and of the Boké bauxite deposit. Fear of expropriation delayed development at the latter, as a result of which the concession was cancelled and all work ceased for several years. Political fears have delayed the development of hydro-electric power, and so the possibility of an aluminium industry.

BIBLIOGRAPHY

See references cited in footnotes. Also:

BERNARD CHARLES, *Guinée*, Lausanne, 1963.
RENÉ DUMONT, *Afrique Noire: Développement Agricole. Réconversion de l'économie agricole: Guinée, Côte d'Ivoire, Mali,* 1962.
M. HOUIS, *La Guinée Française,* Paris, 1953. (Includes a bibliography.)
Etudes Guinéennes. Centre I.F.A.N. Conakry.

MAPS

See p. 183.
Topographic:
    1 : 50,000 I.G.N. 1957–

Chapter 20

SIERRA LEONE—
BRITAIN'S CONTRIBUTION TO THE
SETTLEMENT OF FREED SLAVES [1]

THERE is a legend that Hanno the Carthaginian watered his ship in the Freetown Estuary about 500 B.C. The first written reference appears in an account, written in 1462 by Pedro da Cintra, of a Portuguese voyage to the coast. To the rugged and high peninsula on which Freetown now stands he gave the name Sierra Leone or ' Lion Mountains ', either because of the frequent lion-like roar of thunderstorms over the peninsula, or because the shape of the mountains as seen from the sea reminded him of a lion. The name was later extended to the whole country.

From the sixteenth to the eighteenth centuries the Rokel Estuary was constantly visited by European slave traders. But at the end of the eighteenth century the mountainous peninsula became the scene of Britain's partial reparation for her part in the slave trade. With the support of the British Government and a few philanthropists, Granville Sharp assembled a pioneer party of 351 destitute ex-slaves. Some fifty white women of doubtful character came later.

These groups were joined by 1,131 former American slaves who had fought with the British in the War of American Independence. They had been assembled in Nova Scotia, whence they were taken for settlement at Freetown in 1792. Among many other early immigrants were about 800 Maroons from Jamaica, who arrived in 1800, though most of them and their descendants later migrated to the Gold Coast or returned to Jamaica.

This town of freed slaves, most of whom had not been born

[1] I am much indebted to Dr. H. R. Jarrett, formerly Senior Lecturer in Geography at Fourah Bay College, Freetown, for his criticism of this chapter. Certain maps are also his.

in Africa, endured hostility from the peoples of the interior, and attack from the sea by the French during the Revolutionary and Napoleonic Wars. In 1808 Britain took control of the new settlements, proclaiming the Sierra Leone Peninsula a Crown Colony and the slave trade illegal. From 1817 to 1819 several hundred discharged African soldiers were settled in Freetown, and in the appropriately named nearby villages of Waterloo and Wellington.

The British Navy played the major rôle in suppressing the slave trade by sea from West Africa. Freetown was the main naval base and, whenever between 1808 and 1854 slave ships were captured, freed slaves were resettled in and around Freetown, if their homeland could not be determined or reached. Up to 1833, 34,000 slaves had been liberated at sea and sent here, e.g. to such aptly named villages as Wilberforce, founded in 1811.[1]

Descendants of ex-slaves are generally known as Creoles. They are often characterised by their mixed blood, non-African culture and higher standards of education and literacy than most Africans of the interior. This was especially so in the past.

After the initial hostility of the local Africans, there was little advance beyond the peninsula. But, with the general ' Scramble for Africa ' in the last quarter of the nineteenth century, it became necessary to define the boundaries with Liberia and French Guinea, the latter having expanded around the north and eastern sides of Sierra Leone and hemmed it in. By 1898 the Protectorate had come into existence and all boundaries were defined, except for one sector with Liberia, finally agreed in 1911. Thus organisation of the Protectorate started a century after that of the Colony. The Protectorate was, in consequence, in contact with European ideas and methods for a relatively short while.

As Freetown was the main naval base and the senior British settlement, it was responsible, during much of the nineteenth century, for the government of other territories down the coast. Many Creoles were engaged in this service. Others were in business and in education, but as the other territories have developed their educational systems and become economically

---

[1] For the history see: C. Fyfe, *A History of Sierra Leone*, 1962; *Sierra Leone Inheritance*, 1964; A. J. Porter, *Creoledom*, Oxford, 1963; F. Harrison Rankin, *The White Man's Grave: A Visit to Sierra Leone in 1834*, 1836.

and politically more powerful than Sierra Leone, the Creoles no longer found their position so privileged. Moreover, the Protectorate peoples improved their social, political and educational status. Rivalry between these peoples has been an important obstacle to unity in Sierra Leone.

Although Sierra Leone has a longer history of education and social services than has any other territory, it has been overtaken in recent years by the larger lands of West Africa, where greater and more varied resources have brought larger revenues. Unlike Nigeria or Ghana, Sierra Leone began mineral workings only in 1929, but she is now an important producer of diamonds and iron.

Until the advent of the Colonial Development and Welfare Acts, Sierra Leone was one of those poor countries which became relatively poorer because of her inability to afford necessary expenditure upon such things as bridges and roads. She has also been retarded by the Colony–Protectorate division, but upon independence in 1961 this administrative division was eliminated.

POPULATION [1]

It is estimated that in the last century the population of Sierra Leone has increased by 80%. According to the 1963 Census the population was distributed in an area approximately the size of Scotland as follows:

	Area in square miles	Total population	Density per square mile
Western Area (partly ex-Colony) . .	327	195,000	596
Northern Province .	13,875	898,000	65
Southern Province .	7,660	542,000	71
Eastern Province .	6,063	548,000	90
Total Sierra Leone .	27,925	2,183,000	78

[1] For a study of the ethnographic and other aspects of the peoples, see K. L. Little, *The Mende People—a people in transition*, 1951, and M. McCulloch, *Peoples of the Sierra Leone Protectorate*, International African Institute, 1950.

The population of the two parts of the Western Area were:

Freetown 128,000
Rural Areas 67,000

The density of population in Sierra Leone is relatively high for Africa. A national average of 78 persons per square mile and of over 90 per square mile in the Eastern Province are high for a poor country, where shifting agriculture is widespread but land insufficient for it.

CLIMATE [1]

As in Guinea and Liberia, there is the same rapid onset of an exceedingly rainy and almost uninterrupted wet season, which generally lasts from May to October or November.

Along the Sierra Leonean coast, as far as Bonthe Island, the South-west Coast Monsoonal climate prevails. But at Sulima there is generally a short but clear break in the rains, so that town is the approximate western limit of the Liberian climate.

Unlike neighbouring lands, Sierra Leone has a range of mountains reaching the sea in a north-west to south-east trending peninsula. This lies across the path of rain-bearing winds and has a particularly heavy rainfall, amounting to over 230 inches (5,840 mm.) at the highest points and averaging 144 inches (3,360 mm.) at Freetown. However, as in most tropical lands, there is wide annual variation.

Unexpectedly, perhaps, the Interior Sierra Leonean climate (pp. 49–50) has more rain than the Fountanian of central Guinea, despite the lowland character of much of western Sierra Leone compared with the Fouta Djallon. The north-eastern mountainous border of Sierra Leone has the Guinea Foothills climate (p. 50-1), and the eastern upland border that of the Guinea Highlands.

Unfortunately, the heavy rainfall of Sierra Leone (and of its neighbours) causes run-off, soil-wash and severely leached soils. Heavy rain and high temperatures may have helped to produce

[1] See S. Gregory, *Rainfall over Sierra Leone*, Department of Geography, University of Liverpool Research Paper No. 2, which has a bibliography. Also *Atlas of Sierra Leone*, p. 5, and *Statistics illustrating the Climate of Sierra Leone*, Freetown, 1952.

lateritic soils. There are great areas of lateritic sand or gravel and sandy loam, upon which only poor grass will grow. The long dry season halts vegetative growth for several months annually, and this fact and the leached soils account for the naturally poorer forest, itself heavily degraded by man— especially in the north.

VEGETATION

The small size of trees and poor nature of the vegetation in this territory of high rainfall require explanation. In Guinea the vegetation is likewise poor in the mountains, but that can be attributed to infertile sandstone and lateritic coverings. But in the lower areas of Sierra Leone, where the rainfall is everywhere over about 90 inches a year, the vegetation should be richer. ' As it is, the vegetation has been so affected by farmers, that the once extensive areas of rain forest have now disappeared and there remain only islands of forest (less than 5% of the total area); the rest, owing to the degradations of shifting cultivation, has degenerated into areas of high bush, low bush and orchard bush. In addition . . . there are extensive swamp areas in the coastal zone . . . tidal mangrove forest near the sea coast, and flooded sedge and grass swamps behind. Sometimes scattered trees are present in the latter giving a park-like effect. These swamp types of vegetation have grown up on the more recent geological deposits and are not thought to be derived in any way from the degeneration of rain forests.

' There are many evidences that in the past the greater part of Sierra Leone was covered by Rain Forest but that, un-happily, is now far from being the case. The forests have gone down before agricultural demands and shifting cultivation. As these became progressively more intensive, owing to in-creasing population, forest was converted to high bush, high bush to low bush, and low bush to orchard bush with grass; while in isolated cases, where other conditions, such as drainage have not been propitious, the ultimate degradation to grass flats has been reached.' [1] Nearly one-third of Sierra Leone is

---

[1] F. J. Martin, *A Preliminary Survey of the Vegetation of Sierra Leone*, Freetown, Government Printer, 1938. Also *Soil Conservation and Land Use in Sierra Leone*, Freetown, Government Printer, 1951.

now covered by Savannah and grass and only one-twentieth is forest.

The proportions of the country under the various types of vegetation are roughly as follows:

Forest (excluding Mangrove) 3–5%—stable through forest reservation. Mainly on eastern ridges and in south-east.

High bush (Secondary Forest) 20–25%—rapidly decreasing. Found in south-east.

Low bush (poorer Sec. Forest) 20–25%—stable in area but decreasing in value. Found in south-centre.

Savannah and grasslands 35–45%—especially in north. Increasing in area and declining in value.

Swamps—all kinds 10–20%—see below.

Inland freshwater and coastal mangrove swamps are a feature of Sierra Leone. These are often suitable for wet-season cultivation of swamp rice, to replace upland rice, which tends to assist soil erosion. Upland soils are severely leached, and lateritic in nature, and increasing population has led to their over-intensive use. It is by better farming and swamp cultivation that degradation of soils can be halted, forests improved and the livelihood of man made more secure.

Geology and Physiographic Regions [1]

The Sierra Leone Peninsula. This north-west trending peninsula, at the northern end of which stands Freetown, is about 25 miles long from north-west to south-east and averages 10 miles across from south-west to north-east. Mountains rise steeply from the sea to Picket Hill, 2,912 feet, in the south-centre, and to the famous Sugar Loaf Mountain, 2,494 feet, behind Freetown. The mountains have erosion platforms, the more important being at 2,400, 1,800 and 1,300 feet. These vivid mountains are very different from the rest of Sierra Leone, and are composed of a varied and interesting complex of basic intrusive igneous rocks (gabbros, norites, etc.), in the form of a lopolith of uncertain age. The western part has foundered, hence the abrupt seaward face.[2]

---

[1] For available maps, see p. 329.

[2] J. D. Pollett, ' The Geology and Mineral Resources of Sierra Leone ', *Colonial Geology and Mineral Resources*, Vol. 2, No. 1, 1951.

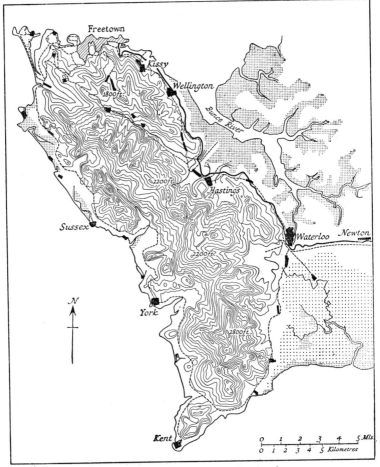

FIG. 57.—The Sierra Leone Peninsula.

The stippled areas indicate swamps.
(From H. R. Jarrett, *The Port and Town of Freetown, Geography*, April 1955, by
permission of the author and editor.)

At the base of the hills are flat expanses of lateritic pan,
and raised beaches resulting from isostatic compensation
when much of the lopolith foundered.

At the lowest levels mangrove occurs. The hills are now a
forest reserve, constituted to restore soil cover and, by restrain-
ing run-off, to protect water supplies both for present domestic
needs and future hydro-electric power development.

Around this peninsula are settled the Creoles who comprise part of the population of this province. Within the peninsula some 55,000 live in rural areas and some 65,000 in Freetown. Villages are mostly about 100 feet up, along the main road around the peninsula, and especially on the eastern side near the railway. Many of these Creole settlements, which have characteristic street plans and house types distinguishing them from tribal villages, are decaying. Creoles no longer have a privileged position in village commerce, and they are gradually moving to Freetown and its dormitory village suburbs. Moreover, the fertility of the soil has seriously declined in this area of long settlement, over-intensive farming of cassava, leaching and eroding rainfall.[1] Erosion has been halted by the forest reserve mentioned above, but the farming area is necessarily restricted and what remains tends to be overworked. Only in the small valley swamps is there systematic manuring of land, in this case for the production of vegetables. Farms and the marketing of produce are badly organised and villages now depend more upon fishing.

One logical re-development is the encouragement of tree crops. These hold the soil and provide humus from their leaves. These crops would be near the Freetown market and the port. Bananas and citrus fruits have been grown, but export can succeed only if they are cultivated on plantations and if fruit ships call. It is useless to export bananas as deck cargo but banana ships en route from Cameroon or the Ivory Coast might be encouraged to call.

Another promising activity, sponsored by the agricultural station at Newton (just east of the peninsula), is the improved rearing of pigs and chickens. This activity is limited by the availability of sufficient feeding stuffs from groundnut cake and palm kernel residue of oil extraction.

The first mineral won in Sierra Leone was alluvial platinum from the western side of the peninsula. Work commenced in 1929 in the Big Water, near York. Large returns were at first forthcoming, but these declined after 1935 and mining ceased in 1941, to be resumed again only from 1945 to 1949. The

[1] See *Land Utilisation in the Colony Peninsula*, Government Printer, Freetown, 1948; Roy Lewis, ' Creoledom revisited ', *Geographical Magazine*, May 1964, pp. 9–19.

alluvial nuggets were derived from lodes or bands of basic igneous rock, through which the streams have cut. Unfortunately, the parent rock has not been found.

Ilmenite is abundant in the rocks and streams near York, Hastings and Middle Town. It assays 47% to 53% titanium dioxide and contains appreciable quantities of platinum. Other minerals known to occur in the peninsula are felspar, hypersthere, diallage, olivine and titano-magnetite.

Freetown, capital of Sierra Leone, was founded in 1792 as an atonement for the evils and miseries of the slave trade. It was chosen as a well-known site, superior to most places on the Sierra Leone coastline. It has a hilly environment at the northern end of the peninsula, adjacent to which is a deep channel of the easily-entered, sheltered and large estuary. Pure water was also available. It was therefore ideal also as a naval base for suppressing the slave trade and, in times of war, has been important to the defence of the Atlantic and the protection of convoys.

Oddly enough, by comparison with the rest of the West African coastline, nature was here so lavish in her natural shelter, that man provided the 1,203-feet-long Queen Elizabeth II Quay only in 1953. Proposals for a deep-water quay were first made in 1910, sanctioned in 1913, but suspended in 1915 on account of the war and not pursued in 1921 for lack of money. Upstream at Pepel is a deep-water loading installation belonging to the Sierra Leone Development Company and used for shipping iron ore.

Freetown has been the subject of much unfavourable (if incidental) comment,[1] but like Monrovia it has much more character than most West African cities, especially other ports. Its older three storied white frame houses, with first floor balcony and third floor dormer windows, are copied from the American colonial style. As at Monrovia, it was the only style ex-slaves from America had known.

In 1799 a Royal Charter empowered the appointment of a Mayor and Corporation. Freetown has been a bishopric

[1] For example, Graham Greene, *The Heart of the Matter*, 1948. For scientific studies see H. R. Jarrett, ' The Port and Town of Freetown ', *Geography*, 1955, pp. 108–118; ' Recent Port and Harbour Developments at Freetown ', *Scottish Geographical Magazine*, 71, pp. 157–64 and ' Some aspects of the urban geography of Freetown, Sierra Leone ', *Geographical Review*, 1956, pp. 334–54.

since 1852 and was British West Africa's first diocese. It also had the first hospital and railway in British West Africa. Fourah Bay College, founded in 1827, has provided some university education for about a century, far longer than any other institution in all West Africa.

Like other West African cities it has distinctive quarters. There are the usual ones such as Kru Town, but also some more unusual sections. Thus (as also at Bathurst, Ouidah and Lagos) there are Portuguese Town, three-quarters of a mile south-east of Kru Bay, where lived ex-slaves who had returned from Brazil, and Maroon Town, on the east side of Kru Bay, where the Jamaican Maroons established themselves in the nineteenth century.

Behind the old lighter wharf the land rises steeply to Tower Hill. Not far from sea level, and at a break of slope, is a massive silk cotton tree, underneath which the first freed slaves and deported white women are said to have collected after disembarkation in 1787. Fort Thornton, on the gentle lower slopes of Tower Hill, was the first Government office, and the hill itself the early military headquarters. Between Fort Thornton (Government House—the Governor-General's residence) and the old wharf is the oldest part of the town containing the Law Courts, Secretariat, Post Office, Cathedral and commercial quarter. Residential quarters lie to the west and east. Farther east, the deep-water quay, the railway workshops, rice and groundnut mills in Cline Town form a second harbour zone. There is, as yet, little industry as the national market is so small. However, there is a small industrial estate farther out of Freetown.

Freetown had an early Hill Station, at first exclusively reserved for European officials. It lies south-west of and about 800 feet above Freetown, and was reached from 1904 to 1929 by an Emmett-like railway, which had its only distinction in being the steepest non-funicular railway in the world. Mount Aureol, on the south-east side of Freetown, is now occupied by Fourah Bay College.

In 1948 the Freetown population of 64,576, comprised 17,331 African non-natives (largely Creole), 46,081 African natives, 372 Europeans and 792 Asiatics (Lebanese and Indian). In 1966 the population was 148,000.

Freetown has the usual problem of replanning an old site, made more difficult by the hilly environment. This has also affected the location of the airport. At the end of the Second World War there were airfields at several places along the east coast of the peninsula, and at Lungi across the estuary. Only the latter can take large and fast planes, because of the dangers of the nearby mountains on the Freetown side. Consequently, a launch journey or extra flight is necessary between Freetown and Lungi.

COASTAL SWAMPS. The Coastal Swamps, which average some 20 miles in width, are well defined because of their liability to wet season flooding. They are mostly composed of Pleistocene sediments (Bullom Series), have special types of vegetation and land use, and are threaded by navigable, tidal waterways. Flooding occurs because of the heavy rainfall (over 125 inches), which falls on a flat and low lying area, where much of the sub-soil is clay or sand.

Pleistocene deposits are in sharp contrast to the ancient rocks found elsewhere in the interior. The Coastal Swamps have alternating bands of gravels, grits, sands and clays, with here and there a little lignite and pottery clay. Along the south coast are large areas of coarse marine sand ridges which are relic cliffs. Lacustrine, lagoon, estuarine, deltaic and marine conditions occurred widely here in recent geological times, as they do still on the fringes.

On the west coast, although there are some fine silts, most of the swamps consist of different kinds of clay, including pottery and brick clays. Lignite occurs near Newton, east of the Sierra Leone Peninsula. When this lignite is dried, cleaned, ground to powder and briquetted, it might be used as fuel, but its calorific value is only one quarter that of coal, and it has other disadvantages. Salt occurs north and south of the Scarcies Estuary; rutile, monazite and zircon are widely distributed and are heavily concentrated in the gravels of many rivers near tidal limits.

According to Martin,[1] there are four types of coastal swamp vegetation, namely:

Mangrove swamps, found at the mouths of most rivers. Mangrove has been cut to make room for swamp rice farms. The

[1] Op. cit., pp. 4–5.

clay soils are very suitable for holding water in rice fields but
salinity is a problem.

Sedge swamps, found behind the mangrove swamps of many
rivers. These are badly drained and are frequently flooded to
over 5 feet throughout the rainy season; by the end of the dry

FIG. 58.—Relief and Regions of Sierra Leone.
(Based on 1 : 500,000 maps, G.S.G.S. Map No. 3921.)

season all but the deepest parts are dry again. Soils are alluvial, deep and rich, though generally slightly saline near
mangrove swamps.

Flooded grasslands are found on the larger rivers above the
tidal zone. Soils are much lighter and flooded only when the
rivers are in spate.

Coastal parkland, Farm bush and *Scrub* are found in Pujehun and Bonthe Districts, wherever coarse marine sands occur. These are water-logged in the wet season and very dry in the dry season. Consequently, trees are stunted and widely spaced.

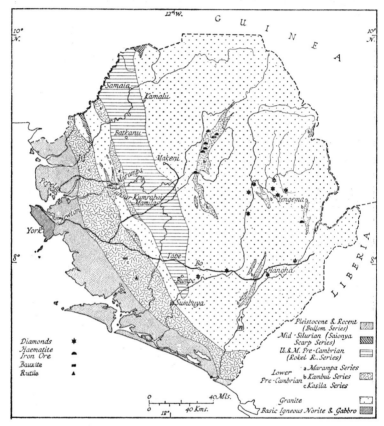

FIG. 59.—Geology and Minerals of Sierra Leone.
(Based on 1 : 1 million maps, Survey and Lands Dept., Freetown.)

It is only in inland and coastal swamps and fertile tidal areas that permanent cropping has so far succeeded. In cleared mangroves the elimination of salt in the soil, the prevention of toxic (ferrous sulphide) accumulations on empoldered lands, and defence works against tidal scour have sometimes proved problems. With Portuguese Guinea and Guinea, Sierra

Leone is famed for its mangrove clearance for rice cultivation. As swamp rice replaces upland rice production, so forest and soil degradation and erosion should diminish. Rice output will rise and the standard of living improve.

About 1896 it was discovered that the less saline mangrove swamps could be utilised for rice, and development accelerated after both wars. In eighty years 70,000 acres have been planted. By far the most important of the reclaimed mangrove areas are in the lower Great and Little Scarcies Rivers and around Port Loko, where over 50,000 acres are used for rice farming (see Fig. 60).

The average rice farm has three acres. Initial clearing and preparation is exceedingly arduous, but once cultivation can be started, annual work is easy. Fertility is maintained by the continual deposit of silt from river water, and weeds are checked by salt water floods. Near the sea, fields must be bunded to prevent deep flooding by saline water. Higher up, bunding is not essential and quick-growing (four-month) varieties are used. The main rice growing area starts about 6 miles from the sea and extends upstream for 15 miles. Wherever natural drainage is adequate, and the river water at high tide is fresh for at least five months, the salt deposited during the dry season will be cleared sufficiently by rain and fresh water floods. At Mambolo there is a rice mill, and the Rice Research Station at Rokupr.

In the south, clearing of mangrove has been done mainly since 1938. The south has been developed later for two main reasons. Although there are more extensive areas available than in the north-west, they are dispersed, being interrupted by unsuitable areas of coarse sand. Secondly, the area is more remote from the chief market of Freetown. There is only about one-third the acreage found in the Scarcies, and about two-thirds is mechanically ploughed. On both the south and west coasts there are still some 100,000 acres of undeveloped mangrove swamps, although those easiest to develop have mainly been cleared.

Behind the mangrove swamps are some 60,000 acres of virgin riverine grasslands on the southern littoral, and some 40,000 acres of swamp grasslands and sedge swamps in the Scarcies areas, some of which may be suitable for tractor cultivation.

Where flooding is deep, tall erect rices must be used. In still deeper water the so-called ' floating ' rices of Indo-China, such as are used in the Inland Niger Delta in the Mali Republic, are suitable. The strong root-system of sedges and grasses is a problem in these areas, entailing much preparation in the early years. Thereafter work is easier, and the soils have such a high content of organic material that they can be cropped with little or no fertiliser. In the drier parts, sweet potatoes and early cassava are grown in the dry season.

Piassava, the other important product of the Coastal Swamps, derives its name from a Brazilian word for the prepared fibres from the base of the leaf-stalks of the Raphia palms (*R. vinifera* and *R. gaertneri*), which grow in South American and West African swamps.

The world's best quality (Prime Sherbro) is mainly limited to the Bonthe District riverine areas, including Gbap, Taigbe and the Lake Kwarko area (see Fig. 64). The poorer Sulima quality comes from the Lakes Mabesi and Mape, and the Pujehun, Zimi and Sulima areas. The differences of quality result from better methods of preparation, rather than from the fact that *R. vinifera* predominates in Bonthe and *R. gaertneri* in Sulima areas. A large swamp on the north-west of Lake Kwarko produces the finest Prime Sherbro piassava, because retting is done by the local people in sunny stagnant water which, except for a brownish tinge, appears to be clear. In the Sulima area, however, retting is done in small pools in high forest. The water is cool and does not cover all the bundles. But some piassava produced around Lakes Mabesi and Mape, and at Zimi, is excellent when fully retted.

The first export was from Sulima in 1892. From this area, which still produces the bulk of Sierra Leone's piassava, production spread to the lake and riverine areas of Sherbro. Piassava exports go mainly to the United Kingdom, the U.S.A. and Western Europe. Piassava is used in the manufacture of strong brooms and scrubbing brushes. It is also used in removing air bubbles in the manufacture of steel castings, though here chemical silicones may replace it.

Bananas are grown widely but haphazardly in the Coastal Swamps in the areas just east of the Sierra Leone Peninsula and across the estuary in Lungi, near the airport. If there were plantations and more uniform fruit could be produced, a considerable export would be possible, provided that banana ships called regularly. Meanwhile, a Syrian has made a start near Songo and between the bananas has planted beans which, with unwanted bananas, are fed to bacon pigs.

The Coastal Swamps of Sierra Leone have an attractive future, so long as they are continuously developed for rice, and piassava is improved in quality and quantity. Considerable income could also come from systematic banana exports, and from the rearing of pigs for the Freetown market. Soil fertility in the mangrove and riverine swamps, initially greater than anywhere else in Sierra Leone, is being sustained. The agricultural potential of Sierra Leone lies in the Coastal Swamps.[1] Quarrying of bauxite and rutile (source of the metal titanium) and their local processing, have helped the poor and remote Moyamba and Bonthe Districts.

THE COASTAL PLAIN. Beginning behind the Coastal Swamps, this region extends inland up to about 100 miles from the coast, rising in gentle undulations to about 400 feet at the foot of the scarp marking the edge of the Interior Plateaux and Mountains. Above the plain are remnants of former plains at 450, 525 and 700 feet.

Underlying the lowland are north-west to south-east belts of metamorphic and other rocks of Pre-Cambrian (Birrimian) age. Immediately east of the Pleistocene deposits of the Coastal Swamps are the metamorphic Kasila Series, consisting of gneisses and granulites, which occur in a belt averaging twenty miles from west to east. The Moyamba Hills belong to this series. The area around Port Loko is singularly infertile, with only thin soil over a lateritic pan.

East of the Kasila Series are the scattered occurrences of metamorphic Marampa Schists, as well as granites. Marampa Schists, which occur around Marampa and northward across the boundary, consist of altered argillaceous and arenaceous Birrimian sediments, in which there is high grade but occasionally phosphoric hæmatite iron ore, containing 52–69% iron. The largest deposits and those of better physical condition and iron content are in the Sula Mountains, and may be worked

[1] H. D. Jordan, *Development of mangrove swamp areas in Sierra Leone*, Commission for Technical Cooperation in Africa south of the Sahara, 1963.

later. Probable reserves in Sierra Leone are given as 98 million tons.[1]

The more accessible iron occurrences at Lunsar were first worked in 1933, and occur in thick deposits caused by over-folding in two abrupt hills. The ore is simply scraped off the hills, one having been lowered 100 feet in thirty years of working. Most of the richer red hæmatite ore has been re-moved; washeries or concentrators now deal more with grey, soft, schistose powder ore of 45% iron, which they upgrade to 93% iron oxide.

The ore is loaded into wagons on the 3 feet 6 inches gauge mineral railway and taken to the private loading pier at Pepel, 55 miles away on the north-eastern side of the Rokel Estuary. The concession is owned by the Sierra Leone Develop-ment Company. About 2,000 workers are employed, and annual exports are some 2 million tons of ore, or about one-sixth of Sierra Leone exports by value, and the second most valuable item. The deposits are among the most accessible to Europe and America.

The Rokel Series extend from near Sumbuya in the south, to beyond Saionya on the north-central boundary, and average 20 miles in width. The series comprise sandstones, shales, conglomerates and some intrusive rocks. As the Rokel Series are less resistant than granite or the Marampa Schists, the re-sulting landscape is lowland, with savannah and rare forest patches, e.g. near Tabe and Bumpe in the south, Kumrabai Mamila in the centre, Batkanu and Samaia in the north. It is likely that this belt of sediments has never been thickly forested. In the rainy season the plain is often flooded, and swamp rice cultivation is being encouraged, but in the middle of the dry season all but the larger streams become intermittent. Villages are rare and there is a vivid contrast between the low population on the Rokel Series and the denser population on the granitic rocks found to the east, e.g. towards Makeni and Kamalu. Yet the sandstones of the Rokel Series hold water, which could be secured from wells and bore holes, so that more people could be sustained. No significant minerals have been found in the series.

[1] ' Steel in the Commonwealth ', *British Iron and Steel Federation Monthly Statistical Bulletin*, Vol. 28, June 1953.

It is generally the ancient volcanic rocks, associated with the Rokel Series, that form numerous abrupt and isolated hills, such as the Kasabere Hills near Yonibana, the Malal Hills east of Marampa, and ridges south-west of Batkanu. However, the steep Saionya Scarp, rising to 2,515 feet on the north-western boundary, is formed of flat bedded Silurian sandstones and shales, with intercalated sills of diorite, and is part of the Fouta Djallon.

Over the rocks of the Coastal Plain, laterite and lateritic gravel are widespread, with sandy patches in valleys. Another characteristic is the low, poor Secondary Forest, resulting from infertile soils and man's depredations. The crops, which resemble those in the next region, are considered in the section on Agriculture.

THE INTERIOR PLATEAUX AND MOUNTAINS. East of approximately the 400-foot contour is a plateau region belonging to the Guinea Highlands and mainly 1,000–2,000 feet above sea-level. Most of it is floored by granite with dolerite sills, but there are important occurrences of Kambui Schists, a highly metamorphosed and mineral bearing formation of the Birrimian Series.

The most important relief features are shown on Fig. 58. Many of them are series of scarps and plateaux. Some have residual domes, notably tooth-like Bintimani in the Loma Mountains. It rises to 6,390 feet and is capped with Palæozoic dolerite. The Sula Mountains, extensively surfaced by laterite, contain great unexploited reserves of rich hæmatite iron ore. The Kangari Mountains are severely dissected and thickly wooded.

There are many smaller hill masses, and bare granite domes and pinnacles are common. Otherwise, the surfaces of the plateaux are flat over considerable expanses, though trenched by deep V-shaped valleys to depths of 200–300 feet.

The Kambui Schists are important sources of minerals, especially of diamonds. These are alluvial and occur in gravel beds 8 to 20 inches deep, lying beneath an overburden of about 3 feet. The parent rock is not certain, but may be Kimberlite, as in South Africa, though some believe the diamonds originated in Palæozoic dolerites. The stones are larger than in Ghana; indeed, the largest gem stone ever found in an alluvial deposit in Africa was recovered from the Woyie River in 1945.[1]

A company with a former monopoly operates near Yengema, west of Sefadu, and at Tongo, south of Sefadu. In their highly mechanised mining the overburden is removed and the diamond-bearing gravels loaded into small wagons. The gravels are then washed, sorted and concentrated. The concentrate is passed over greased shaking tables, to which the diamonds adhere, while the heavier minerals pass on. Operation is simple and inexpensive, and yields are very high, such production being about half a million carats annually.

After widespread illicit diamond digging and smuggling in the late 'fifties the monopoly was ended, the company compensated, and restricted to their most profitable areas. Diggers were then licensed, and there are now over 2,000 licensees, each of which employs gangs of about four men. Although some system is being brought into their work, much ground is left unworked, and tiny diamonds fall through their sieves. While their production is currently very important, it could decline rapidly. All this output should pass through government buying offices. Diamonds account for over half of Sierra Leone exports.

From 1937 to 1964 some chromite was quarried and adit-mined near Hangha, 186 miles east of Freetown on the railway. The low grade ore occurs in lenses in serpentine and talc schists of the Kambui Hills. The operation was never very profitable.

In the southern part of the Interior Plateaux and Mountains, where the rainfall exceeds 100 inches, the vegetation is Secondary Forest. In the north where the rainfall is less, the vegetation is Guinea Savannah. Almost anywhere else in West Africa the rainfall would still permit Rain Forest, but the soils have been heavily leached by the torrential rainfall and impoverished by over-farming.

In the south and in the better areas of the north, farms are usually cultivated for one or two years only. But in the poorest areas of the north, where level farmland is scarce, it is usual to farm for two or even three years before reverting to the

---

[1] See J. D. Pollett, 'Diamond deposits of Sierra Leone', *Imperial Institute Bulletin*, 1937, and W. T. Gordon, 'Note on Large Diamonds recovered from gravels of the River Woyie, Sierra Leone,' *Idem*, 1945.

seven- to nine-year fallow.   Consequently, poor lands become poorer.

In the north and west, where land must be farmed for more than one year, rice is always the first crop after fallow.   The following year is used for pure or mixed crops of cotton, hungry rice, groundnuts, guinea corn, millet, cucurbits, benniseed and, to a lesser extent, sweet potatoes, cassava and peas.   In the south and east, where land is used only for about one year, subsidiary crops such as maize, cassava, sweet potatoes, yams and beans are always inter-cropped with the rice.   If the rice is grown in a swamp, other food crops are grown in the dry season and regular annual cultivation is generally possible.

Ginger, grown in Moyamba and Bo Districts, is the only crop grown purely for cash.   A special farm is cut from bush for it, and it takes the place of rice in rotation.   Other crops may be partly sold for cash, but are grown primarily for subsistence.   The oil palm, cocoa, coffee and kola nuts are also cash crops, but are not grown in the system of fallow farming. It is interesting that the Temne cultivate their soils much more deeply than do other peoples.

ECONOMIC RESOURCES

AGRICULTURE

Approximate figures for food production are:

	Area under cultivation (thousand acres)	Annual production (tons)
Upland Rice	594	} 394,000 (Paddy)
Swamp Rice	148	
Cassava	50	60,000
Sweet Potatoes	8	9,000
Fundi (*Digitaria exilis*) . .	15	4,500
Groundnuts	48	21,000

Sierra Leone's rainfall of 90–170 inches annually is the main factor in causing rice to be the greatest food crop.   It is the chief object of farming, except in a few areas of Temne country (north-west centre) and near towns where cassava may be more important, and in the north-east where millet is somewhat more significant.   With the oil palm and minerals, rice

is a major element in the country's economy.   Although all rice
grown is for home consumption, and there are heavy imports,
the drift away from rice cultivation to diamond mining may
soon be reversed if diamonds become more elusive.

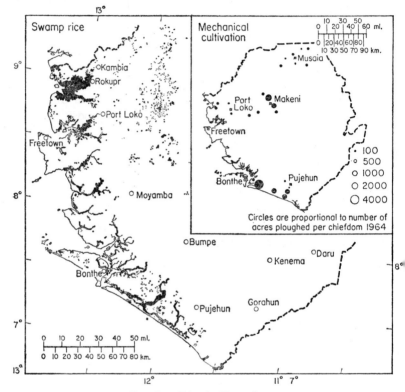

FIG. 60.—Rice in Sierra Leone.
(From a map compiled by D. V. Havapathirane and K. Swindell for *Sierra Leone
in Maps*, ed. J. I. Clarke, by permission of University of London Press.)

For centuries rice was grown almost entirely on upland
farms by the system of shifting farm patches, but since 1923
there has been a rapid increase in swamp cultivation, resulting
from the enthusiasm of agricultural officers.

Upland or dry rice production is considered deleterious,
not only because it accelerates erosion and prevents soil conservation and afforestation, but also because the increases in
population and in the percentage of non-farmers require

75. Freetown from the estuary.

76. Rice cultivation along the Great Scarcies River, north of Bumpe. Rokupr town is in the extreme right centre, the site of the West African Rice Research Station. Most of the farms have mature rice.

In the Interior Plateaux and Mountains on, on the edge of Forest and nnah at Bunumbu, looking to the Nimi Hills

78. The Bomi Hills iron-ore mine, Liberia.

THE IVORY COAST

79. From above Abidjan looking S.S.W. In the foreground is the Administrative Quarter, below which is the rail terminus and lighter wharves. Away to the left, commercial houses are just visible. The bridge connects Abidjan with the island of Petit Bassam and so with the African township and industrial quarter of Treichville. Another bridge was opened in 1967. Quays are on the bay to the right. At the top of the photograph is the sandbar and the Vridi Canal.

greater production and new areas of cultivation. It is doubtful whether primitive upland rice farming can support a population of more than sixty per square mile, which is below the average for Sierra Leone.

Many times that number may be supported by using inland, riverine and coastal swamps for rice production. Cultivation of inland swamps cannot cause erosion, but they are usually infertile and require fertiliser; mangrove swamp soils are generally quite rich and fallowing is not usually needed. Yields are therefore better, though inter-cropping is impossible; the work in swamps is unpleasant and may be unhealthy. There is also considerable prejudice against swamp rice among those accustomed to upland rice.

Of the swamp rice areas, the inland swamps (mainly in Bo, Makeni, Kenema and Kailahun Districts) are more extensive than the coastal ones. Inland swamps are easier to clear than mangroves, and are also more compact. Clearing of coastal swamps is a major operation, requiring hard work and skill. Their successful cultivation requires care and capital for drainage, and there has been considerable trouble with toxic accumulations in bunded fields. Meanwhile, Sierra Leone has been very successful in the reclamation of mangroves, though behind Portuguese Guinea in this respect. Production in the Coastal Swamps is described on pp. 312–14.

Oil Palm. Palm produce, a vital food, and once Sierra Leone's leading export, accounts for about one-tenth the exports. The oil palm is widely distributed, but the densest areas are around the Scarcies Rivers, along the branch railway and in the south-east.

There are a number of old and new plantations, but most palms are scattered on farms or in the bush, so that the fruit is often allowed to drop from the trees, so impairing the quality of the oil.

A major problem with Sierra Leone palm fruit is that it has a very narrow pericarp and a large nut. Consequently there is little available palm oil, and this is badly extracted. Communities have been helped to plant improved *Deli* and *Angola* palms, which have thicker pericarps containing more oil. Nut-cracking machinery has been distributed and some ten Pioneer oil mills have been established. These extract more

M

oil and secure a better quality, but operating costs have been high and they have not increased total output.

The annual production of palm oil is about 35,000 tons, most of which is consumed locally. Better extraction methods ought to bring larger quantities and better qualities for home

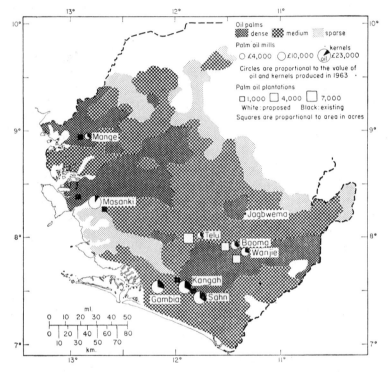

FIG. 61.—The Oil Palm in Sierra Leone.

(From a map compiled by K. Swindell for *Sierra Leone in Maps*, ed. J. I. Clarke, University of London Press.)

and export use. About 50,000 tons of kernels were exported annually until 1965, when a kernel crushing factory was opened at Wellington, capable of crushing this amount.

Piassava. See under Coastal Swamps.

Cocoa. Cultivation dates mainly from 1925, since when planting has been concentrated in the forest areas of Kenema, Segbwema and Kailahun. The long, intensely dry season can be tolerated by cocoa only where there are at least 100 inches annual rain. To the north-west the vegetation is too open, and towards the coast the soils are too poor for cocoa, or swamps forbid its cultivation. Little is grown towards the Gola Forest because of insufficient labour and poor

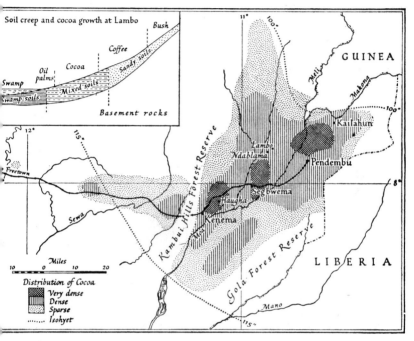

FIG. 62.—Cocoa in Sierra Leone.

(From G. T. Rimmington, ' Cocoa in South-Eastern Sierra Leone ', *Geog. Jour.*, 1961, p. 134.)

Reproduced by permission of the Royal Geographical Society.

communications. Present exports are about 3,000 tons annually.

Kola nuts. Being a tree crop, these are, like the oil palm, cocoa, coffee and other trees, admirably suited to soil conservation practices. Kola trees are most numerous in southern Kono, Moyamba and the Peninsula. Nuts are produced for local consumption and for export to other countries in West Africa. Most go to the Gambia, whence some pass to Mali.

The quality of the nuts is high and the varieties differ from those found in Ghana and Nigeria.

Ginger. This is grown on separate plots outside the usual rotation as a very minor export, the principal areas of production being in Bo, Moyamba and Bombali Districts. It is the

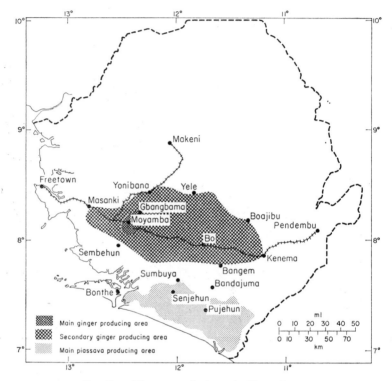

FIG. 63.—Piassava and ginger in Sierra Leone.

(From a map compiled by K. Swindell for *Sierra Leone in Maps*, ed. J. I. Clarke, University of London Press.)

main product of Moyamba District. Some areas are exclusively under ginger but the annual production is quite small. Sierra Leone ginger is used medicinally, and this restricted sale accounts for the low demand and output. This may be fortunate, because its cultivation on sloping farms induces soil erosion. But as the plots total only a quarter to half an acre each, the damage is very local.

Coffee. Coffee is grown mainly in the cocoa areas, but it also extends westward and especially northward, as it can withstand some drought. *Robusta* and *liberica* are grown. Exports are developing and, like cocoa, it accounts for about 2% of Sierra Leone exports.

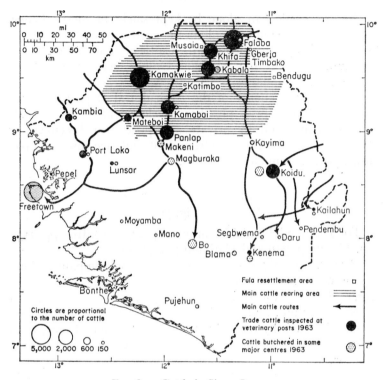

Fig. 64.—Cattle in Sierra Leone.
(From a map compiled by K. Swindell for *Sierra Leone in Maps*, ed. J. I. Clarke, University of London Press.)

Groundnuts and Benniseed. Both of these are important northern food crops. A groundnut mill at Freetown produces oil locally, so reducing imports. The principal groundnut areas are Kambia, Bombali and Koinadugu districts in Northern Province, and Kailahun in Eastern Province. In all, there are about 33,000 acres cultivated. As groundnuts are best grown in Sierra Leone on sandy sloping surfaces, their cultivation is not being encouraged because of the risk of soil erosion.

Bananas and citrus fruits have been discussed with the Sierra Leone Peninsula (p. 307).

LIVESTOCK

Ndama cattle can alone be kept safely in Sierra Leone. They are fairly common only in the north-east, where they are kept mainly by nomadic Fulani. Cattle number about 200,000 but more come in from Mali and Guinea, across the northern and eastern boundaries.

Through the energy of the Agricultural Department, the breeding of European pigs has developed at Newton, Njala and Kenema, and by private enterprise near Freetown, at Hangha, and elsewhere. Groundnut and rice mills at Freetown provide some feeding stuffs.

MINERALS AND POWER
(See Fig. 59)

For Diamonds[1] and Chromite see pp. 317–18, Iron pp. 315–16, Lignite p. 310 and Platinum pp. 307–8.

Bauxite. Mining began in 1964 by a Swiss company seeking a new supply. The deposit is a capping averaging 30 feet over some 18 miles of the Mokanji Hills. Production is 100–200,000 tons per annum, and washing and concentration are effected before despatch by road about 20 miles to Bagru Creek, from where lighters take the ore to ocean vessels which anchor near Bonthe.

Rutile. Near the bauxite working is one of rutile, possibly the largest by content in the world, and likely to replace Australia as the main producer. Rutile is a source of titanium, used in aircraft and missiles; and of titanium dioxide used in paint and other materials for whiteness and opacity.

Some geologists have taken a very optimistic view of hydro-electric power possibilities. The greatest difficulty is the highly seasonal rainfall. Yet if suitable barrage sites could be found it might be possible to smelt iron electrically.

[1] Kenneth Swindell, 'Diamond Mining in Sierra Leone', *Tjdschrift voor Economische en Sociale Geografie*, 1966, pp. 96–104.

Minerals represent over two-thirds of all Sierra Leone exports, though none were mined before 1930. In future, corundum, columbite, tantalite, ilmenite, titano-magnetite, ilmeno-rutile and molybdenite may be exploited.

COMMUNICATIONS

In the nineteenth century, when only the Sierra Leone Peninsula (ex-Colony area) was under British rule, head porterage and canoe transport sufficed. The south- and south-west-flowing rivers of the interior also came to be used and still have considerable local importance, especially in coastal areas and in the Western Plain. Some 500 miles of launch routes are still used.

The 310-mile-long Government Railway was opened in stages between 1899 and 1908, and the branch between 1908 and 1911. The main line was built mainly to serve the oil palm districts, but it cut across navigable waterways and for many years could not compete with water transport, or even with head porterage in some areas. The railway was built economically with the small gauge of 2 feet 6 inches, sharp curvature and steep gradients, all of which have reduced its capacity and speed.

Once suitable vehicles were available, roads were vital to hasten development, yet for many years they were very few and were disconnected 'feeders' to the poor and unremunerative railway. But by 1930 lorry competition had become severe for the railway, as road haulage was taking goods to and from the rivers. The Government restricted this competition by imposing tolls on certain roads.

It is only during and since the Second World War that the elements of a road network have been constructed. Freetown was connected with the interior by road only in 1941. Road transport, now unrestrained by tolls, is still handicapped by three ferries. As late as 1950 there were no government-organised ferries to make a connexion with Guinea, and it cost £5 to £6 to persuade local people to ferry cars across the Great Scarcies River at Kambia or the Moa River at Sanibalu. The road between Kabala and Faranah (Guinea) was opened only in 1950. In 1951 a grant of $210,000 of American aid was made towards the replacement of ten ferries by bridges.

After the Second World War the future of the low capacity and under-equipped railway was doubtful, but in 1949 and again in 1964 it was decided to retain and improve it. The track has been much improved, and diesel locomotives introduced. Reference has been made in the regional description to the Mountain Line operated to Hill Station from 1904 to 1929 and to the privately owned mineral line from Pepel to Marampa opened in 1933.

Sierra Leone is served through Lungi by a service from Britain and by local French and African air services linking with inter-continental services at Dakar or Accra, and also connecting Sierra Leone with almost all other West African countries. Internal services began in 1958.

CONCLUSION

Sierra Leone is a small country; much of it is mountainous and about two-fifths is very poor. Indeed, the coastal and inland swamps are the only fertile areas. Elsewhere the soils are very leached and soil erosion is acute on steep slopes.

Not only is the rain very heavy but the rainy season is followed by a sharp, dry one. Apart from the usual problem, which any dry season poses to the farmer, intense drought after severe rain gives a less vigorous vegetative cover to the soil, and inhibits the good growth of crops like cocoa. Nor is such violent seasonal alternation kind to man, and some have seen in this a partial explanation of slow economic progress in Sierra Leone and adjacent lands.

Due to the settlement in the eighteenth and nineteenth centuries of the Sierra Leone Peninsula by people who had lived in semi-temperate or temperate lands, fairly intensive farming was practised in the peninsula; and the educational and cultural level of the people was so high that they took posts in many other territories. The former Protectorate was organised a century later and its resources developed much more recently. The oil palm is the main vegetable resource, but poor varieties are dominant, and oil extraction has remained primitive. Cocoa, coffee, and other commodities have become significant relatively recently. Mineral development dates entirely from 1929, most of it from 1934 and now dominates the economy.

The fact that Sierra Leone was to some extent the Mother of Ghana and Nigeria for long caused it to rest on its laurels. Provincialism was noticeable and progress retarded by Colony–Protectorate rivalry. Now that Sierra Leone is independent, has widespread and highly profitable diamond mining and a deep-water wharf, trade has quickened. It has good prospects in its rice cultivation, iron ore reserves and, perhaps, in other minerals, but its small population hinders industrial development. An interesting development is the establishment of a small diamond cutting and polishing industry.

BIBLIOGRAPHY

See works cited in footnotes. Also:

J. I. CLARKE, *Sierra Leone in maps*, 1966.
S. GREGORY, ' The Raised Beaches of the Peninsula Area of Sierra Leone ', *Trans. Inst. Bri Geogs.*, 1962, pp. 15–22.
D. T. JACK, *Economic Survey of Sierra Leone*, Freetown, 1958.
H. L. VAN DER LAAN, *The Sierra Leone Diamonds*, 1965.
ROY LEWIS, *Sierra Leone*, H.M.S.O., 1954.
The Bulletin, The Journal of the Sierra Leone Geographical Association.
Sierra Leone Studies, Freetown.

MAPS

(All Survey and Lands Dept., Freetown, except when stated otherwise.)
Atlas of Sierra Leone, Freetown, 1953.

Topographic:

   1 : 6,250 Freetown.
   1 : 10,000 Colony and townships. D.O.S.
   1 : 62,500 Sierra Leone.
   1 : 63,360 Vicinity of Freetown. G.S.G.S.
   1 : 250,000 All Sierra Leone.
   1 : 500,000 Layer coloured—one sheet. G.S.G.S.

Cadastral:

   1 : 1,250 Town Plans.

Various:

   1 : 500,000 Chiefdom Boundaries, Agricultural Production and Trade.
   1 : 1,000,000 Administrative, Vegetation, Tribal, Geological, Soil, Population, Agricultural Products, Soil Conservation, Land Classification, Population and Fallows, Degraded Areas, Zones of Production, Forest Reserves, Mineral Deposits (D.O.S.), Navigable Waterways (Survey Department, Accra).

Chapter 21

LIBERIA[1]

'The Love of Liberty Brought us Here'

LIBERIA resulted from the efforts of the American Colonisation Society (founded in 1817 and still in existence) and other societies, to settle American ex-slaves in West Africa. Americans, with very varied motives, had been impressed by British efforts at the re-settlement of former slaves in and around Freetown in Sierra Leone.

The first and abortive effort by the American Colonisation Society was at Sherbro Island in Sierra Leone in 1820; the first permanent settlement was in 1822 on Providence Island at Monrovia. Many more parties arrived, there and elsewhere in subsequent years, including slaves freed by the American Navy. The American Colonisation Society had some responsibility for the government of their settlements until 1847, but in that year Liberia became an independent state and took as its motto the words quoted above. In 1857 the colony of 'Maryland in Liberia', with its capital at Harper, was admitted as a county of Liberia.

From the beginning Liberia had tremendous problems. The ex-slaves, who had come mainly from America, were generally several generations away from tribal life, and were more American than African. They also lacked techniques, experience and capital. It is true that the American Colonisation Society gave subsidies from year to year, but these did not enable them to acquire specific skills or to set up trades in their new home. Even if the former slaves had possessed technical training, they were anxious to forget their past and to live comfortably in the future.

[1] This chapter has been read by Professor P. W. Porter who carried out field work on population and land use in Liberia, and interpreted the air photo coverage of the country by Aero Service Inc. of Philadelphia.

It must also be remembered that these poor ex-slaves, with their sorrowful background, were landed on what is probably the worst part of West Africa. It has the heaviest rainfall, a very difficult shoreline and leached soils. From the first they encountered the hostility of the Africans; and European powers, especially the French and British, were unhelpful and, on several occasions, aggressive to the new state.

In recent years the Republic of Liberia has undergone rapid development and profound changes. Until 1926 it was chronically in debt and exported only small quantities of palm oil and kernels, piassava and coffee. But in 1924–6 the Firestone Rubber Company of America secured a concession to plant rubber, in return for which the Liberian Government was granted a new large loan and yearly revenue from various parts of the concession's activities.

The greatest impetus to advance has been since 1942 when the Americans secured the right to land troops in Liberia at a time when this area was of strategic importance in the Second World War. Since 1944 Liberia has had in President Tubman a most enlightened and energetic head of the state. The combination of his drive, American money, Firestone revenues and iron ore royalties have all helped. Liberia has two deep-water ports, a first-class airport and roads which, although insufficient, do include one through to Guinea bringing transit trade and links with Sierra Leone and the Ivory Coast. There have also been political reforms, whereby the Africans of the interior are associated with the government of the country. Until 1950 this was entirely in the hands of the Americo-Liberians—descendants of ex-slaves.

POPULATION

The area of Liberia is 43,000 square miles and the 1962 census found a population of 1,010,000. The Americo-Liberians number some 15,000 and live almost exclusively in coastal towns or in plantations along the St. Paul River, which enters the sea near Monrovia, the capital. There are about 50,000 westernised Africans and under 700,000 others.

There are some 22,000 foreigners in Liberia, of whom 7,000 are other Africans, especially Fanti fishermen from the Ghana coast. There are about 2,500 Americans, half of them being on the Firestone plantations. There are large numbers of Lebanese, Dutch, British, French, Germans and Spanish.

The average density of population is approximately twenty per square mile, but it varies greatly. The greatest densities of population are found immediately in and around Monrovia, on the Firestone and iron-ore concessions, up the St. Paul River, near the road from Monrovia to Guinea, towards Zorzor, Voinjama and Bolahun in the north-west, and through Sakripi, Gban and Tappita to the south-east. These densities are mostly of over 50 and some are of over 150 per square mile.

However, 25 per cent of the country has densities of only 4–15 per square mile, and another 35 per cent has a density of under 4 per square mile, large tracts being uninhabited. The lowest densities are in the extreme west-centre and in the eastern third of the country where there are large forests. Economic development of these areas may prove difficult because of the shortage of labour.

Climate

The coastal areas of Liberia have over 160 inches of rain annually in the north-west and 100 inches in the south-east, though high points like Cape Mount have up to 200 inches. The wet season lasts from late April or early May until October or November, with a secondary ' middle-dry season ' in July or August. This minor dry season is variable and erratic in its occurrence and extent, but it is this which distinguishes the Liberian climate from the South-west Coast Monsoonal type. Relative humidity is generally about 95% in the wet season and 82% in the dry season.

Average daily temperatures are 79° F. and rarely, if ever, exceed 92° or drop to under 55°. The average diurnal range is about 14° F.

In the interior conditions are considerably better because the rainfall is about one-half or less that on the coast and it falls in a shorter season, generally from June to October. Range of temperature is greater and relative humidity less.

Geology and Physiographic Regions

Most of Liberia is composed of Pre-Cambrian gneisses and schists. It lies mainly on the lower south-western slopes of the Guinea Highlands, whose outliers are in general accord with Huronian trend lines. Rivers flow rapidly over the bedrock with hardly any kind of true valley and have many rapids.

Pre-Cambrian intrusive rocks, such as massive granites, pegmatites and diorites, are also found. The latter mostly occur on the coast, where they give the relief features of Cape Mount (1,068 feet) at Robertsport, Cape Mesurado (290 feet) on which lies Monrovia, Grand Bassa, Baffu Point just east of the Sangwin, and Cape Palmas on which is Harper near the mouth of the Cavally River. These promontories are broadly similar to Cape Vergas and the Conakry (or Kaloum) peninsulas in Guinea, and the Sierra Leone Peninsula behind Freetown.

Frequently associated with the relief features of the Liberian coast, or with river estuaries, are north-west trending sandbars, which are being built by wave action. Behind the sandbars are lagoons, the largest being Fisherman's Lake at Robertsport. Mangrove is not very deep, extending inland only up creeks or the main rivers.

Coastal Plain. This is about 10–50 miles wide and has poor savannah or occasional swamp vegetation. The Americo-Liberians settled in various places along the coast; and to this area, like Europeans in their territories, they limited their government for a full half-century.

Monrovia, the capital of Liberia, was founded by ex-slaves from America in 1822. The Americo-Liberians ultimately established themselves on the upper part of the diorite ridge of Cape Mesurado and built a town, the style of which is very reminiscent of the Southern States of America. The foot of the ridge, and settlements on Bushrod Island are, by contrast, rather squalid, though no more so than similar quarters in other West African ports.

The deep-water harbour on Bushrod Island, just north of Cape Mesurado, built as an American Lend-Lease project between 1945 and 1948, and operated by a company, consists

of breakwaters 7,702 and 7,250 feet in length which approach
each other to give an entrance of 1,022 feet and a channel
of 600 feet.   The cost of this harbour was some $20 million,
and it was built in the face of great physical difficulties.   The

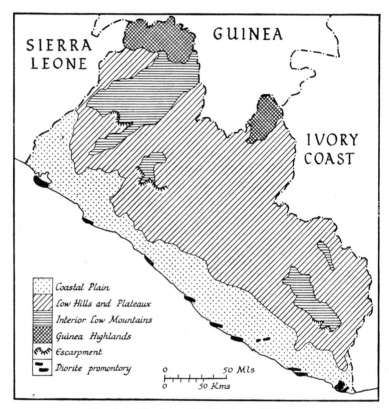

FIG. 65.—Physiographic Regions of Liberia.
(Based on a map by P. W. Porter in ' Liberia ', *Focus*, American Geographical
Society, September 1961.)

wharves and piers can accommodate seven ships of up to
28 feet draught.   Monrovia is a free port—the only one in
West Africa.   Within the free port area of 507 acres, foreign
merchandise may be unloaded, stored, mixed, repacked or
manufactured, and then forwarded by land or sea without
payment of duty.   Liberian products may even be taken into
the free area and brought back into customs territory without

the payment of any duty, even though they may have been combined with or made a part of other articles in the free area.

Rubber for export is brought by diesel lighters down the Farmington River and a short distance westward along the coast. Iron ore, from the Bomi Hills, Mano River and Bong Mountains, comes by mineral lines; goods in transit to and from Guinea travel via the Monrovia–N'Zérékoré road opened in 1947. There is also a shipping service between Monrovia and the other coastal settlements. Buchanan exports Mt. Nimba iron ore, Greenville takes ships of up to 6,000 tons, whilst Harper is a roadstead.

The inter-continental airport at Roberts Field, constructed in 1942, adjoins the Firestone Harbel Estate, 55 miles from Monrovia. An airport at Monrovia has West African services.

LOW HILLS AND PLATEAUX. These hills, considered as part of the Coastal Plain in Sierra Leone, are about 400–1,200 feet high. They are mainly under Rain Forest.

INTERIOR LOW MOUNTAINS. These are mainly in the Western Province, where several ranges trend north-east to south-west. They are again under Rain Forest and have a very thin population of generally under fifteen persons per square mile. Much of this country is virtually unexplored.

STEEP SCARPS. The southern edge of the mountains is limited by some vivid scarps, e.g. at Reputa on the Monrovia–Ganta road.

GUINEA HIGHLANDS. These are found along the northern border, and grassy dome-like crests of up to 4,500 feet occur in Liberia, especially on Mt. Nimba, rich in iron ore.

Except for the Coastal Plain, Liberia has a rather complex relief. In the lower parts there are often separate hilly masses, which may rise to 3,000 feet. The higher points are mostly in the north-west.

ECONOMIC RESOURCES

AGRICULTURE

Liberian soils are extremely leached, so that the most suitable crops are tree products. This may account for the success of the Firestone plantations, especially as rubber trees take little from the soil.

Most agriculture in interior Liberia is the customary subsistence farming. The following figures[1] give the approximate areas under various types of land use in Liberia:

Use	Area in thousand acres	% of total area
Farms in shifting cultivation . .	10,000	41·7
Commercial forest	7,500	31·1
Non-commercial forest . . .	4,000	16·7
Tree crops	200	0·8
Commercial rubber (mostly Firestone)	100	0·4
Other (wasteland and non-agricultural)	2,200	9·3

About one-half of Liberia is considered suitable for cultivation. It is estimated that some 2 million acres are capable of use for annual food crops and that about 5 million acres are adapted to tree crops or more extensive cultivation of annual crops. Another 5 million acres on gentle to rolling upper slopes and hills should be used only for tree crops.

Liberia is at the meeting place of the Rice and Cassava Zones (see Chapter 6), and the crops of these zones are its main foods. Most of the land is farmed only for one or two years and is then rested for between seven and fifteen years. Annual planting of 600,000 acres of rice and cassava involves the periodic use of about 10½ million acres of land. Unlike Portuguese Guinea, Guinea and Sierra Leone, there has so far been little development of swamp rice cultivation.

Rubber is overwhelmingly the most important cash crop. The earliest production of rubber in Liberia was from wild rubber on behalf of a British company in the early years of this century. But as early as 1907 some 2,000 acres were planted on Mount Barclay by Sir Harry Johnston's Liberian Rubber Company. This plantation was abandoned in 1920 because of poor prices.

When this low price had led to the Stevenson Plan to increase world prices by controlling exports, particularly from the Far East, an agent of the Firestone Rubber Company became interested in the abandoned British plantations and rented them in 1924. Although they were in a semi-derelict

---

[1] *Reconnaissance Soil Survey of Liberia*, U.S. Departments of Agriculture and State, June 1951, p. 33. This is a useful source of reference.

condition a small export of rubber was made to the U.S.A. in 1925.

After long and involved negotiations, the Firestone Rubber Company secured a concession in 1926 of up to a million acres. The Company has two estates: one very large at Harbel on the Farmington River, 15 miles from the sea, and

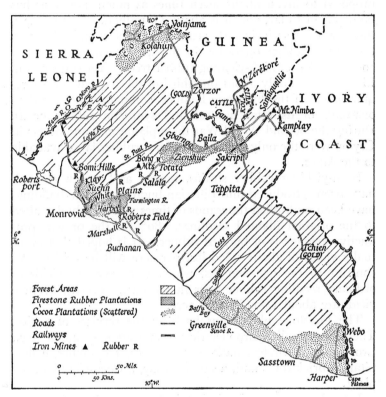

FIG. 66.—Economic Resources of Liberia.

another very much smaller 25 miles up the Cavally River on the eastern border. So far the company has leased 160,000 acres and has cleared and planted about 90,000 acres, on which there are some 10–11 million rubber trees, ranging in age up to nearly thirty years. Some 73,000 acres are in production, though a replanting programme was begun in 1952. Production is approximately 56,000 long tons annually.

Despite these impressive figures, the achievement is much less than the Firestone Company originally intended. It has only one-sixth of the planned area under lease and less than one-twelfth planted. Instead of employing the intended 350,000 workers, they employ about 22,000. The original production estimate was 200,000 tons of rubber, and it was proposed to invest about seven times as much money as has been put in so far, which is about £6 million. Nevertheless, these are the relatively early years of the project and it is by far the largest rubber operation in the world, with the greatest concentration of high-yielding rubber trees. Yet rubber from Liberia covers only about one-third of the natural rubber requirements of the Firestone Rubber Company, and less than one-sixth of its total natural and synthetic rubber needs. During the Second World War these plantations and others in Ceylon were the only sources of natural rubber latex available to the Allies.

High-yielding rubber strains, known as ' proven clones ', have been introduced into Liberian buddings. The buddings have been multiplied thousands of times and then bud-grafted to the original planted seedlings. 80% of the present productive acreage is of budded rubber. It is hoped that eventually yields of about 1,800 lbs. per acre will be achieved in contrast to the 350–500 lbs. which were average yields of ordinary seedling rubber trees in the past. Present average yields are about 1,000 lbs. per acre.

The Firestone plantations have all the services of a city. There is a small hydro-electric power station of 4,000 Kw., two powerful wireless stations, 21 schools, 4 churches, 2 hospitals, a brickworks and, needless to say, a Coca-Cola bottling plant.

It can be seen from all this that the Firestone plantations have had a very great influence on the economic development of Liberia, upon its exports and its national revenues, and upon the availability of natural rubber to the dollar area.

Moreover, there are many other rubber plantations—foreign and Liberian. There are six more ex-patriate plantations occupying some 50,000 acres. Two of these originally planted other crops such as bananas (at Greenville) or cocoa and coffee (between Ganta and Sakripi), but they changed to rubber when those crops failed. Some 4,000 Liberians have rubber farms occupying about 130,000 acres (one-third more than Firestone), one-half of which is mature but yielding poorly because of inefficient methods, despite the gift of over 10½ million seedlings and advice from Firestone, which will also buy their rubber.

There are, therefore, over a quarter of a million acres under rubber in Liberia. In 1945 this crop accounted for 96·6% of Liberian exports; the percentage has now dropped to around one-fifth because of the rapid development of iron mining. Until this occurred Liberia was dangerously dependent upon one crop, essentially upon one plantation. Even now, it is almost the only cash crop, and is not without some pressing problems. The mines, with their higher wages, are attracting labour, while Firestone must replant large acreages of old trees. For these and other reasons, their yields have fallen since 1958.

Coffee was the main export until about 1880, when Brazil began to dominate the market. Coffee again has some significance, especially in the well populated areas between Voinjama and Kolahun, along the trunk road between Gbarnga and Ganta, and to the south-east of that town. The principal varieties of coffee produced are *liberica* and *robusta*.

Cocoa was probably introduced about 1930 by labourers returning to Liberia from the plantations of Fernando Po.

So far, however, cocoa is of little importance. It may be that the dry season and its low relative humidity are disadvantageous to it, as in neighbouring Sierra Leone. There are a few plantations.

Kola nuts are mostly grown in the north-centre above about 800 feet. They are, in part, traded to Guinea.

Palm oil and kernel production is being developed, especially in the south-centre.

Sugar is grown rather more in Liberia than in adjacent territories. Most of it is grown in the better-populated areas where it is used for making rum.

Groundnuts and cotton have local significance in some parts of the interior and, as in other territories, country cloth is made from the cotton.

FORESTRY[1]

In the nineteenth century there was some export from Liberia of camwood, then in demand as a dyestuff. Since the cessation of that export because of the competition of synthetic dyes, there has not been much timber cut, though various companies or agencies have made surveys and small exports through Monrovia, Harper and Greenville.

It is reckoned that only about 31% of the total area has timbers useful for commercial exploitation. Most of these (60%) lie in the east, with smaller areas in the centre (15%) and west (25%). A large concession, mainly for timber, but also for palm produce and minerals, is held by a British company in the south-east. The large Gola Forest, astride the Sierra Leone boundary, gives Sierra Leone its only considerable area of useful timber. There are good stands of the best hardwoods, but both here and elsewhere extraction is difficult because of the paucity of roads and competition for labour with the mines.

LIVESTOCK

Liberia is more deficient in livestock than any other territory in West Africa, largely because of the very unfavourable environment. Nevertheless, more could be done to keep small cattle, goats and poultry. There is a fairly important trade in cattle from Mali and Guinea.

MINERALS

Iron ore quarrying began in 1951 in the Bomi Hills, 45 miles north-west of Monrovia, to which they are linked by a mineral line. The concession is held by an American company, and much of the ore goes to the U.S.A., where it fulfils about 1% of American needs. There are some 20 million tons of massive magnetite and hæmatite containing about 65% iron, and also about 100 million tons of itabirite containing 35–50% iron, all lying in a basin formation with projecting crags at the edges. A second mine was opened in 1961 on the Mano River, and

---

[1] *Forest Resources of Liberia*, 1951, published by U.S. Departments of Agriculture and State as *Agriculture Information Bulletin No. 67*.

linked by an extension to the Bomi Hills railway. Here there are reserves of about 100 million tons of red and black itabirite of 55% iron content.

The third mine on Mt. Nimba began operations in 1963 on its first ore body containing at least 300 million tons of 60–70% iron. An adjacent mountain has similar amounts of ore of up to 60% iron. Another large reserve a little south at Kitoma may be developed by another company. The Nimba deposit has been described as ' the greatest and richest iron ore reserve in the world '. There is almost no overburden, impurities are insignificant, and the ore can be used untreated. It is carried by Liberia's third mineral railway to her second deep-water harbour at Buchanan, which accommodates ore carriers of 65,000 tons.

The fourth mine is in the Bong Hills, 50 miles north-east of Monrovia, to which it is joined by another mineral railway. Here there are some 200–250 million tons of much poorer ore, averaging 38% iron, which is beneficiated to 65% iron. While all other mines are opencast, this one also has an adit. Mining began in 1965, but prospects are much less good than for Nimba.

Liberia suddenly became a major exporter of rich ore, exporting some 20–25 million tons annually. Several other areas are known to have rich ore and substantial reserves, so that long term prospects are bright. An iron and steel industry may be established at Buchanan, using coke brought as a return cargo. The Nimba railway will soon be used for general traffic as well, so opening new areas for timber, rubber, oil palm and other traffic from Liberia and, possibly, from Guinea.

Diamonds were first recorded in 1910 from alluvial flats along several rivers. There have for long been intermittent workings by individuals and companies on the Loffa River in its central and upper reaches, and diggings near Mt. Nimba. Exploration is active in these and other areas.

COMMUNICATIONS

The lack of communications has been a limiting factor in the development of Liberia. Until the early days of the Firestone

Concession, Liberia had no real roads, except in the immediate environs of Monrovia. Elsewhere the country was served by narrow trails—still the means of communication over much of the country. Goods are often carried by porterage.

Most rivers are obstructed by rapids. The St. Paul is navigable from its mouth at Monrovia to White Plains, a distance of 15 miles.

Much of the recent renaissance in Liberia stems from the development of communications. The deep-water harbour at Monrovia has the added merit of being a free port, and coastal steamers link up the main settlements with this port. Ports are developing at Buchanan for the export of iron ore from Mt. Nimba and for general trade, and at Harper for timber.

Roads have been built, not only by the Firestone Rubber Company and by the Liberia Mining Company (which exploits the Bomi Hills iron ore), but also by the many American and other agencies now in Liberia. The Liberian Government, too, has been able to build more roads now that its revenues have greatly increased. The most important road is that which runs through the country from Monrovia to Ganta and on to N'Zérékoré in Guinea. From it there are branches to Tappita and Sanniquellie. There is now quite a network of roads around Monrovia, and between it and the main Firestone plantation. In all, there are about 2,000 miles of roads, of which half are in a good state. In 1955 the U.S. Import–Export Bank made a loan of $15 million for road building.

There are international air services through Roberts Field, and from Monrovia there are services to coastal and interior towns in Liberia.

Conclusion

Until recently Liberia was undeveloped, partly because of chronic indebtedness and lack of capital for productive purposes. The price of self-government has been isolation, exposure to pressure and intermittent bullying from the great powers, and the lack of true economic assistance.

Since the 'thirties and particularly since 1942 there has been a great quickening of the economy of the country, almost exclusively as the result of the drive of various American companies and official agencies, and of President Tubman. Economic development is restricted in two main ways. The first is that this rice growing country must still import large quantities of that food. The second problem is that the population is very much less than was usually supposed, and thus the numerous firms which have been granted concessions in recent years are competing for manpower. It will be impossible for all of these to develop fully without the importation of labour.

Liberia was for long very dependent upon the United States, and exports resulted mainly from the work of large American companies, not from African farmers, as in most West African countries. Now there are many non-American companies but the ordinary Liberian contributes little to either export or internal trade.

BIBLIOGRAPHY

See books and articles mentioned in the text. Also:

R. EARLE ANDERSON, *Liberia, America's African Friend,* North Carolina Press, 1952.

G. W. BROWN, *The Economic History of Liberia,* Washington, 1941.

R. L. BUELL, *Liberia; a Century of Survival 1847–1947,* University of Pennsylvania Press, 1947.

R. CLOWER, *Economic Survey of Liberia,* Northwestern University Press, 1962.

J. GENEVRAY, *Eléments d'une Monographie d'une Division administrative libérienne* (*Grand Bassa County*), Mémoire de l'I.F.A.N., Dakar, 1952.

B. HOLAS and P. L. DEKEYSER, *Mission dans l'Est Libérien,* Mémoire de l'I.F.A.N., Dakar, 1952, has a 50-page bibliography of Liberia.

SIR HARRY JOHNSTON, *Liberia,* London, 1906 (for historical data).

L. A. MARINELLI, *The New Liberia,* 1964.

P. W. PORTER, ' Liberia ', *Focus,* American Geographical Society, September 1961.

MARVIN D. SOLOMON and WARREN L. D'AZEVEDO, *A general Bibliography of the Republic of Liberia,* Northwestern University Press, 1962.

CHARLES MORROW WILSON, *Liberia,* New York, 1947.

MAPS

Topographic:

1 : 125,000 United States Coast and Geodetic Survey, Washington, D.C.
1 : 500,000 ,, ,, ,, ,, ,, ,, ,, ,,

Chapter 22

THE IVORY COAST

THE ECONOMIC HEART OF THE BENIN–SAHEL ENTENTE[1]

THE Ivory Coast, with an area of 124,471 square miles (roughly that of the British Isles), is, after Nigeria, the largest country in the forest zone of West Africa and has, by reason of its varied economies and resources, a great potential. The opening of the Vridi Canal in 1950 was a vital step towards realising this potential.

The population in 1966 was 3,920,000, and there were about 30,000 non-Africans. Although one-third larger than neighbouring Ghana, the Ivory Coast has only one-half the population. To overcome the effects of this low population, great efforts have been made to encourage immigration from the over-populated Upper Volta. Indeed, from 1933 to 1947 the largest part of that territory was attached to the Ivory Coast, essentially for this reason and for economy.

Among many other contrasts, the Ivory Coast also differs from Ghana in having non-African planters who produce most of the bananas, many of the pineapples, and some of the coffee and cocoa exported. The Ivory Coast has also comparatively few mineral workings. Any student of West Africa will find stimulating contrasts and comparisons between these neighbouring lands.

HISTORICAL OUTLINE

Within the confines of the present Ivory Coast the once famous city of Kong was founded by the Senoufo people in the

---

[1] I record with deep thanks the help of Professor Gabriel Rougerie, formerly of the Institut Français d'Afrique Noire at Abidjan, who guided me in and around that town, and who has made valuable comments upon this chapter.

eleventh century. After considerably extending their domain, they were inter-penetrated in the sixteenth century by the Dioula, who came southward from Ségou when the Mande Empire broke up, and ultimately became the overlords. By predilection they were and are itinerant traders. Kong became famous as a caravan centre, where kola nuts from the south were bartered against cattle and salt from the north. When Binger, the great French explorer, visited Kong in 1888 there were some 15,000 inhabitants, but it was destroyed in 1895.

In the eighteenth century the Ashanti extended their control to the Bondoukou area, which they held until 1874. Moreover, the Agni of the south-east Ivory Coast and, to a lesser extent, the Baoulé of the south-centre, resemble the Ashanti in their social and political organisation. These groups comprise a quarter of the present Ivory Coast population.

By contrast, west of the Bandama River, in the western Ivory Coast, the tribes have always been highly fragmented in their geographical distribution, social and political organisation. So bad was their reputation, that in the past the western coast was marked on maps as *La Côte des Mal Gens*, in contrast to that of *La Côte des Bons Gens* in the east.

Along all the coast there was heavy surf, a lack of harbours, dense forest, a sparse population and little or no gold. Thus the attention of mariners seeking gold and slaves was directed earlier and more intensively to the favoured Gold Coast.

French contacts were in three phases. The first was from 1637 until 1704, when there were rare visits by ships of several companies and by missionaries to Assinie, a town near the Ghana boundary destroyed by the sea in 1942.

From 1843 until the Franco-Prussian War, forts were established at Assinie, Grand Bassam and Dabou, whilst French rights were fairly vigorously proclaimed along all the coast. Northward from Assinie, the town of Aboisso became an important trading post, at the head of water navigation and on the caravan route to Ashanti. Both caravan route and market have ceased with the erection of the highly artifical boundary with the ex-Gold Coast. As in other parts of the world, the French withdrew at the time of the Franco-Prussian War. Nevertheless, her interests were looked after by Verdier and

Treich-Laplène, just as British ones had earlier been kept alive on the Gold Coast by Maclean.

The next phase opens with the enunciation of the principle that title to territory could be legally sustained only by effective occupancy. Treich-Laplène spent two energetic years from 1887 to 1889 making treaties with chiefs in the interior, and in the latter year the name ' Ivory Coast ' was given to all the French part of the coast. The colony was proclaimed in 1893, with its capital at Grand Bassam. After terrible epidemics of yellow fever, the capital was moved to Bingerville from 1900 to 1934, since when it has been at Abidjan. The deep water port, opened in 1950, heralded an economic upsurge of considerable magnitude.

CLIMATE

There is the usual system, common to all Gulf of Guinea territories, with two clear rainfall maxima on the coast, merging into one maximum at approximately 8° N.

There are, however, in the Ivory Coast two special features. First, the mountainous area of the west around Man is wetter than other places in the Ivory Coast in the same latitude. Its rather heavy rainfall of some 80 inches comes in one season, which builds up evenly to a maximum in September and diminishes again in the same way. This area has a Monsoonal climate of the Guinea Highland type.

Secondly, although all the southern part of the Ivory Coast has an Equatorial regime (locally spoken of as *Attiéen*), there are marked variations in rainfall along the seaboard, which bring to mind much sharper contrasts along that of the Ghana Coast. In the Ivory Coast, the south-western and south-eastern extremities are wettest; the central part of the coast between Sassandra and Lahou is less wet. Tabou, at the extreme south-western end of the coast, averages over 92 inches (2,348 mm.) of rainfall, falling in 130 days; Sassandra has under 60 inches (1,508 mm.) falling in seventy-five days. Abidjan to its east, is wetter with 77 inches (1,959 mm.) in 150 days.

Although the central coastline, the centre, north-centre and north-east of the Ivory Coast all have less than 60 inches of rainfall, there is no area so dry as around Accra, on the Ghana coast, where the rainfall is only some 25–30 inches.

Consequently, despite the considerable rainfall variations, the Equatorial belt is exceptionally well developed in the Ivory Coast. The Rain Forest was so difficult to penetrate in the early days that the railway was built to force a way into the more open interior. It was built across the narrowest part of the forest, where the rainfall is least and the soils poor.

The forest is now the realm of production of the Ivory Coast's greatest cash crops and contributes the important though less valuable export of timber.

Beyond the Equatorial zone, the Semi-Seasonal Equatorial (or *Baoulé* type, to use the local name) is very well developed and typified by such stations as Séguéla, Bouaké and Bondoukou. Although the forest was originally semi-evergreen, man has converted much of it to poor grass woodland, with gallery forests.

To the west lies the Guinea Highland climatic zone, mentioned at the beginning. To the north is a narrow Seasonal Equatorial zone, typified by Bouna.

Lastly, on the northern fringes is the Southern Savannah zone, with its single rainfall maximum. Relative humidity varies between about 45% and 80%. Yet rainfall is often as high as or even higher than in the Seasonal and even Semi-Seasonal Equatorial zones, according to whether one is considering the wetter west or drier centre of any zone. Thus Odienné averages 61 inches of annual rainfall on about ninety-two days and Ferkessédougou 51 inches (1,300 mm.) on 100 days, although there are great variations from the average.

GEOLOGY, RELIEF AND MAJOR REGIONS

THE COASTAL PLAIN. Eastward to Fresco, the coast is characterised by low cliffs, averaging 200 feet in height, with rocky points and intervening sandy bays. Similar to much of the Ghana coast, it was, however, for centuries little visited because of its reputation as the home of cannibals.

Tabou is a calling point for French ships to pick up or set down Kru sailors. If it were a better roadstead more trade might develop.

Sassandra has the typical semi-circular bay which gives sheltered anchorage up to $4\frac{1}{2}$ fathoms. The town enjoys a healthy site on a rocky promontory and a wharf was opened in November 1951. This has greatly encouraged export trade from the south-west in bananas and wood, but communications need improvement in the hinterland.

East of Fresco, the coast becomes smooth and sandy, with a long and ever-increasing sand-bar. This is broken by the Bandama River at Grand-Lahou, by the Camoé at Grand Bassam, and by the Bia River and Aby Lagoon at Assinie. The sand-bar is everywhere bordered by lagoons on the landward side; on the north shore of the lagoon are Tertiary marine and estuarine deposits. There also are the presumed Tertiary shore-line and former estuaries (or rias), e.g. the Aguien and Potou Lagoons, near Bingerville. By contrast, the Aby Lagoon is probably partly of tectonic origin.

Near the Vridi Canal at Abidjan is the *trou sans fond*, a submarine trench which some[1] consider to be the former valley of the Camoé. Others consider it to be a structural feature.

The possible causes of this remarkable lagoon and sand-bar coast, which is repeated east of the Volta Delta, have been discussed in Chapter 1. Whatever they may be, it has been a great impediment to the development of the country. After the failure to keep open a canal cut across the sand-bar near Abidjan between 1904 and 1907, the Ivory Coast had to be content, until 1950, with wharfs at Grand Bassam and at Port Bouët, similar to that still used at Lomé in Togo.

The great Vridi Canal, started in 1936, was half finished when the Second World War halted it. Completion came in 1950. It is $1\frac{3}{4}$ miles long and 370 metres wide, or 300 metres wide at 10 metres depth, where it is three times the width of the Suez Canal. The western jetty is 520 metres long and the eastern one 180 metres, the extra length on the west being used to divert silt brought by coastal drift away from the canal and into the *trou sans fond*. A narrow entrance gives the requisite scour, and there are minimum depths of 10–15 metres in the canal channel, and 15 metres in the lagoon.

[1] E. F. Gautier, 'Les Côtes de l'Afrique Occidentale au Sud de Dakar', *Annales de Géographie*, 1931, pp. 163–74.

Along the east side of the canal are the petroleum wharves and depot, and a refinery lies to the east. At the north-eastern end of the canal is the manganese loader. The main wharves are at the west and north-western ends of Petit Bassam Island, connected by bridge with Abidjan. Behind the wharves are the industrial and Treichville quarters of Abidjan.

Immediately the Vridi Canal was opened, traffic handled increased by over 50% compared with that handled by the old wharves. The present capa-city is six times greater, or some 3 million tons. Per-haps the most striking result of the deep-water port is that it enabled the massive ex-port of valuable timbers (loaded in Banco Bay) and manganese, and greatly acti-vated all trade, especially in bananas. It also permitted the development of a fishing port and enabled the railway to use imported diesel oil so dispensing with wood fuel.

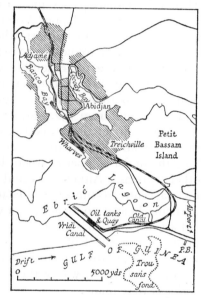

Abidjan, capital of the Ivory Coast since 1934 and terminus of the 716-mile-long railway to Ouaga-dougou in the Upper Volta, stands on the north shore of the Ebrié Lagoon, on a narrow hilly peninsula To

FIG. 67.—Abidjan and the Vridi Canal.

P.B. is the site of the former pier. A second bridge linked Abidjan with Treich-ville in 1967.

the north is the dreary African suburb of Adjamé, where some 25,000 people live. South of Abidjan is Petit Bassam Island with the superior African suburb of Treichville, with an estimated population of some 140,000. This adjoins the industrial quarter where the processing of local produce is undertaken in a coffee mill capable of treating 15,000 tons of raw coffee per annum, in factories making soluble coffee and cocoa butter, in saw mills and a plywood factory, and in fruit canneries.   There are also industries serving local needs such as soap and brick works, large bakeries, a brewery, a mineral waters factory, several printing works and engineering shops. This industrial quarter developed enormously after 1946, and especially after the opening of the Vridi Canal in 1950.

The buoyant economy and inflationary tendencies at Abidjan are reflected in the following population figures: 1937—17,143 (1,478 non-African); 1946—46,000; 1955—125,153 (7,857 non-African); 1959—185,000.   The annual growth is 12,000. Through Abidjan passes most of the external trade of the Ivory Coast, of the Upper Volta and, since 1963, of Niger. On the sand-bar is the airport, with services to Paris, and local services each way round the coast and with the interior.

Grand Bassam, 21 miles south-east of Abidjan, dates from the earliest days of French contact in 1700, and was the capital from 1893 to 1900.   The first wharf operated from 1901–22 and the second from 1922–50;   between 1908 and 1931 it was the sole wharf of the Ivory Coast.   Grand Bassam has now been supplanted by Abidjan's deep-water harbour, but was for long the major shipper of wood, brought along the Ebrié and other lagoons.   Although Grand Bassam is an ancient commercial centre, its site is unsatisfactory, and the town may decay, particularly as it no longer has a wharf.

East of Grand Bassam the smooth sand-bar coast has been built up in front of the estuary of the Bia River, now represented by the Aby Lagoon, which penetrates farther inland than any other.   It was in this region that the earliest French contacts were made.

The fact that Miocene and Pliocene rocks fringe the north side of lagoons east of Fresco, but not west of that point, may be allied with the existence of an off-shore hinge line. In any case, 10–12 miles offshore the continental shelf ends abruptly.

Dense forest extends to the lagoons, except from Fresco to the Ghana boundary, where patches of Derived Scrub Savannah occur.   These result either from early timber cutting on sandy soils and over-intensive farming, or from slight climatic variation.   Jacqueville, on the sand-bar, was a former timber exporting point, protected by Fort Faidherbe, now Dabou, on the north shore of the lagoon.   These poor areas, reminiscent of sandy heaths in temperate lands, are being gradually re-colonised by trees.[1]

THE INTERIOR PLAINS AND PLATEAUX. These comprise most of the Ivory Coast and are underlain almost entirely by Pre-

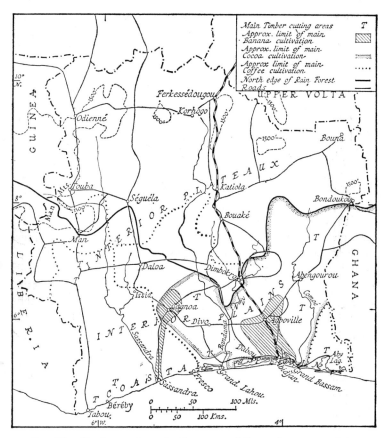

FIG. 68.—Regions and production areas of the main exports of the Ivory Coast.

Cambrian rocks. The most extensive, especially in the west, is granite. Domes are frequent, especially in the north-west, and around them the soil is often more fertile and water occurs

[1] J. Miège, 'Relations entre Savanes et Forêts en Basse Côte d'Ivoire', *Compte Rendu 5ᵉ Conférence Internationale des Africanistes de l'Ouest*, Abidjan, 1953, pp. 27–9.

readily. Pronounced north-east to south-west warpings are responsible for the gentle undulations.

There are also a number of low hills, composed of the Birrimian Series, e.g. the Grabo Chain crossed by the Cavally River north-north-west of Tabou, the Baoulé Hills and the Korhogo Hills. These are usually 650–1,400 feet high and do not upset the generally low plain and plateau character of most of the country. Birrimian metamorphic schists are found in many places, especially in the east.

It might appear from the foregoing that there is some physical variety in the Ivory Coast, but this is not so. The landscape is remarkably monotonous, the more so through severe laterisation north of 9° N. Some of the laterite has itself undergone surface decomposition to a red clay and is covered by acid (i.e. leached) but organic soil.

The greatest distinguishing factor within the Interior Plain is the occurrence of Rain Forest in the south. There, are produced the most significant cash crops—coffee and cocoa (which together account for two-thirds of the exports by value), bananas, other fruits and oil palm produce. With timber, these account for almost all exports.

Beyond the Rain Forest are generally lateritic or sandy soils with Guinea Derived Savannah, broken only by occasional gallery forest or granite domes. Large cattle cannot be kept because of the tsetse fly, there are few cash crops, and the people are poor. This is part of the poor Middle Belt of West Africa and covers fully one-half of the Ivory Coast.

Significant towns of the forest are Daloa, Gagnoa, Divo, Agboville and Abengourou (the Agni Capital). Man, at the foot of the great Man Mountains (see below), Dimbokro and Bondoukou are on the fringes of the forest. In the Derived Savannah are Séguéla and Bouaké.

Bouaké, population 75,000 (2,000 non-African) is the second largest town of the Ivory Coast, a great market and route centre, and is served by air, roads and the railway. Northwest of it is a cotton spinning and weaving factory employing over 1,800 people and using some 1,800 tons per annum of local cotton. In Bouaké itself are cigarette and rope factories.

Korhogo is an ancient focus at the edge of several food crop belts. It is a cotton and sisal market and an older centre than

Ferkessédougou, on the railway, which has rather supplanted Korhogo.

THE MAN MOUNTAINS, which rise to 4,000 feet, lie between Man and Odienné, in the north-west, and are the eastern extremity of the Guinea Highlands. Upland rice, maize, guinea corn and cassava are the staple food crops grown in a four to seven year rotation, followed by four to ten years fallow.[1]

ECONOMIC RESOURCES

AGRICULTURE

There are the usual subsistence and export crops, and also non-African (mainly French) plantations of bananas and other crops. They are most numerous around Gagnoa, Divo, Agboville, Abidjan, Lahou, Daloa, Man, Aboisso and Sassandra.

Not only are there these varied techniques of production, but also a greater crop variety than usual. The Ivory Coast includes in the west the Rice Zone of West Africa, i.e. in western Séguéla, Touba, Daloa, Gagnoa, Man, Grand Lahou and Sassandra Districts. Eastward yams become more significant, e.g. around Bouaké. Cassava and plantains are also grown there, together with maize and guinea corn in the centre and north.[2]

Coffee is a forest crop, particularly in the east and centre, and its cultivation is expanding westwards. The *liberica* variety was first grown by Verdier in 1891 at Elima, by the Aby Lagoon. Soon after 1900 the *robusta* and *kouilou* varieties of *C. canephora* were tried, especially near Agboville and Gagnoa. After trouble with a parasite in 1925 the *gros indénié* was widely distributed to African farmers, as being more easily grown. There has been much root disease in coffee trees, particularly those of the *indénié* and *kouilou* varieties, so that *robusta* is now most favoured.

Most coffee is produced in the Dimbokro, Daloa, Abidjan, Gagnoa, Agboville, Abengourou, and Man areas. There are

---

[1] For details see H. Labouret, *Les Paysans d'Afrique Occidentale,* p. 167.
[2] See further in J. Miège, ' Les Cultures Vivrières en Afrique Occidentale ', *Les Cahiers d'Outre-Mer,* 1954, pp. 25–50.

N

some 1½ million acres under coffee, of which all but 6,250 acres are African owned.

Extension of cultivation and an increase of exports were rapid after 1930, and again in the fifties when a guaranteed market at very high prices was available for large quantities of coffee in France.   In consequence, coffee was planted far beyond its ideal areas, and the Ivory Coast became the main African producer and the world's third supplier.   An international quota limited sales in the sixties, and the Ivory Coast also lost the high prices for large fixed amounts of coffee in France.   On the other hand, she gained preferential entry to the markets of the other five countries of the European Economic Community.   Also nearly one-third of the crop is sold to the U.S.A. and other countries.   Coffee has fallen from occupying a peak of one-half of Ivory Coast exports in 1960 to about two-fifths.

Cocoa comprises about one-quarter of all exports by value, though before the Second World War it was the leading export. The country is the only important cocoa producer among the successor states of former French West Africa.

Cocoa was introduced from the Gold Coast in 1895, sixteen years after it had arrived there.   Cropping was begun in the east by Europeans, but the Forced Agriculture Policy (1912 onwards) of Governor Angoulvant, whereby Africans were compelled to plant specified amounts of cocoa (and other crops) did much more to extend it.   Exports mounted rapidly, only 1,023 metric tons being exported in 1920, but 14,515 in 1928, 55,185 in 1939, and 99,728 tons in 1963.

The south-eastern districts together produce about half the crop, and lie west of the Ghana cocoa belt.   African production accounts for almost all of the total, the very small non-African production being from some 4,500 acres on the western and southern fringes of the African areas, which occupy about 600,000 acres.   Compared with coffee, more cocoa is grown on African farms and in the east, where there are good soils derived from granite and schists.   Production is about one-fifth that of Ghana, though the average quality is inferior. Sales are about equal to the Franc Zone, the other countries of the European Economic Community, and the U.S.A. and other countries.

Bananas, first grown for export in 1931, are produced mainly by French planters or companies on concessions totalling about 113,000 acres, of which about two-thirds are regularly cultivated. Because of the fragile and perishable nature of the product, concessions are mostly near the railway, roads or lagoons in the Abidjan area and the Agboville District, from which the distance to the port of Abidjan is small. However, there are developing areas around Sassandra, served by the wharf at the latter. (See Fig. 68.)

Production has increased remarkably since the opening of Abidjan as a deep-water port in 1950, the introduction in 1956 of the Giant Cavendish or Poyo variety to replace the small Chinese or Canary type (so eliminating costly packing), and the cessation since 1959 of competition from Guinea in the French market. Although, compared with Guinea, the Ivory Coast has a longer sea haul to Europe, its advantages are richer soils, more uniform temperatures and relative humidity, less violent rainfall, more flat damp land, better opportunities for supplementary overhead irrigation, fewer pests, and a more even monthly production.[1] The use of mulching, overhead irrigation, fungicides and fertilisers is widespread, and there is an excellent co-operative organisation for advice, buying supplies in bulk, and marketing. Banana exports comprise some 6 per cent of exports.

Pineapples. Some 2,000 acres are devoted to pineapples of which over 33,000 tons are produced, mostly for canning as fruit or juice. About one-tenth the crop is exported fresh, mainly from the European estates. The main areas are near Divo, Abidjan, Tiassalé, and Grand Bassam. There are co-operatives and canning factories at the latter three towns, the last two having plantations.

Oil palm. It has been estimated[2] that there are some 35 million oil palm trees in the Ivory Coast, mainly semi-wild, though there are also some 15,000 acres of systematic plantations. Production has suffered by competition from the more remunerative and more easily cultivated crops discussed above.

---

[1] For a study of banana cultivation in the Ivory Coast, see C.-R. Hiernaux, ' Les Aspects géographiques de la Production Bananière de la Côte d'Ivoire ', *Les Cahiers d'Outre-Mer*, 1948, pp. 68–84.

[2] Emm. Avice, *La Côte d'Ivoire*, 1951, p. 62.

The Man area is the main producer, not because it has the densest stands, but because relative isolation has restricted the export of many of the more rewarding crops. Likewise, most of the few non-African plantations are in the Man and Sassandra Districts. Lesser African production areas are Abidjan and Aboisso.

Palm oil and kernels are a minor export, but the government is interesting Africans and Europeans in replanting, systematic cultivation and the establishment of large estates, so as to cover increased home needs and sustain exports. There has been a small estate-type oil mill at Dabou since 1920. In recent years a larger one there (capacity 4,000 tons yearly) and another at Abidjan treating palm kernels, cocoa beans and shea butter nuts, obtain 6,000 tons per annum. The produce is partly exported and partly used in soap manufacture (4,000 tons per annum). Indeed, some oil for soap manufacture is imported from Dahomey and the Congo.

Minor Cash Crops. Coffee and cocoa so dominate the economy that the government has instituted a diversification policy by encouraging the pineapple and other fruits, and the oil palm. Coconut plantations are being developed along the coast, with good prospects. Rubber plantations were started in 1953 and, although exports began in 1961, rubber may later be used in local manufacture. It is intended to have 15,000 acres under the crop by 1970. There are many kola nut trees in the forest area, and there is an important trade in kola with Mali and Upper Volta.

Cotton is significant in the drier areas of the centre and north, and is grown for hand weaving and for the mill north of Bouaké. Groundnuts are often intercropped with cotton, and as imports of these crops are also necessary, both are being increasingly grown. Like most West African countries, the Ivory Coast also imports substantial quantities of rice and sugar, and the local cultivation of these and tobacco is likewise encouraged.

FORESTRY

There were probably greater stands of useful timber in the Ivory Coast than in any other West African country, and they are the nearest to Europe. The Ivory Coast is Africa's leading timber exporter, surpassing Ghana and Nigeria combined in weight and value of timber, which comprises about a fifth of Ivory Coast exports. The forest is a high and dense evergreen one on the seaward side, and is best developed in the rainy south-east and south-west. It is more deciduous in character on the drier inward margins, including the drier centre, where the forest narrows south of Dimbokro. The best stands are in thinly populated and rainy country between Man and Sassandra.

In the early years of this century the forced labour policy brought some 15,000 men to timber cutting along the lowest navigable reaches of the rivers and along the lagoons. Logs were floated to Assinie, Grand Lahou and to Grand Bassam, which remained the chief exporters until the Vridi Canal was opened in 1950, when much of the timber came to be floated to Abidjan by rivers and the lagoon. This facility, the deepwater port there, the wharf at Sassandra, and three roadsteads have helped to achieve a massive increase in exports, especially from western areas around Daloa, Gagnoa, Issia, Sassandra, Béréby and Tabou.

The most important timber, both for logs and sawn wood, is Sipo or Utile (*Entandrophragma utile*), which comprises nearly half the sawn timber by value and weight, and it and Samba or Obeche (*Triplochiton scleroxylon*) account for half the logs by weight and nearly that proportionate value. There are some 35 sawmills, of which ten are large, and several plywood, veneer, furniture, box and match factories. On the other hand, a factory using wood from the Umbrella and Silk Cotton trees to make packing paper soon proved uneconomic. About 13,000 are employed in the timber and wood industries.

The area of Rain Forests has been halved since 1900 and the 1963 exports of logs alone equalled one-third of all timber exported in the first half of the century. Replantings in 1963 amount to only 0·2% of areas cut, so that the forest will disappear in 25 years if present trends continue.

MINERALS AND POWER

There is an exploitation of alluvial diamonds on the Bou tributary of the Bandama River, 60 miles south of Korhogo at

Tortiya. Smaller workings are north and south-east of Séguéla. Manganese is quarried near Grand Lahou, and sent by barge along the lagoons for export from the Vridi Canal. Much prospecting is going on, especially for diamonds, gold (of which there are good indications) and oil. Some hydro-electric power is produced on the Bia River at Ayamé.

Communications

Lagoons were the only natural means of communication, and in 1923 the Asagny Canal was opened to link the Ebrié and Lahou Lagoons. Barge traffic is quite considerable, the object being to bring logs, manganese and other produce toward Abidjan and to distribute bulky imports, such as constructional material.

All other means of communication have been built in the face of great difficulties. The rivers are practically useless and the great struggles and final triumph in building a deep-water port at Abidjan have been described. The Rain Forest, another great obstacle, was overcome only by the opening of the railway as far as Dimbokro in 1909, and Bouaké in 1912. Bobo Dioulasso became the terminus in 1934, so making a line of 505 miles. In 1954 a further extension to Ouagadougou was opened, making a grand total of 711 miles of rail artery from Abidjan through the Ivory Coast and Upper Volta. Fast diesel rail-cars operate between Abidjan and Bouaké, and most of the passenger and goods traffic originates between these towns.

Roads were first built during the First World War, and the country is now fairly well provided with them. Those serving the timber concessions, others from Man and Séguéla to the railway, and the international roads have been much improved in recent years, especially into the Upper Volta, Mali and Guinea.

Abidjan has air services to Europe, and local ones along the coast and inland to five centres. Few, if any, countries in West Africa were so isolated by hostile coast, useless rivers and dense forest. Even the lagoons could not be used to reach the interior. Yet no land has been so much changed by man's communications; the Vridi Canal and Abidjan's first road and rail bridge rank among the engineering marvels of Africa.

Conclusion

The Ivory Coast should have a great economic future. Already its resources are reasonably varied, and the variety can be increased by extending the range of raw products (especially if more minerals could be developed) and through more industries. Treichville is an important industrial centre. Though Dakar has a superb strategic site, Abidjan has the richer hinterland, and is the political and economic heart of the Benin–Sahel Entente grouping Togo, Dahomey, Niger and the Upper Volta with the Ivory Coast.

The Ivory Coast is a major world producer of coffee, and the leading one in Africa. It is the fourth world producer of cocoa, and a leading African producer of timber. The advent of diamond and manganese working has greatly diversified its economy, and there are many prosperous industries.

BIBLIOGRAPHY

See references cited in footnotes. Also:

S. Coulibaly, ‘Les Paysans Senoufo de Korhogo’, *Travaux du Dépt. de Géographie de l'Université de Dakar*, No. 8, n.d.

Dominique Desanti, *Côte d'Ivoire*, Lausanne, 1962.

Mohamed Tiekoura Diawara, ‘The Ivory Coast—birth of a modern state’, *Progress*, 1967, pp. 66–70.

René Dumont, *Afrique Noire: Développement Agricole. Réconversion de l'économie agricole: Guinée, Côte d'Ivoire, Mali*, 1962.

T. E. Hilton, ‘The Changing Ivory Coast’, *Geography*, 1965, pp. 291–295.

B. Holas, *La Côte d'Ivoire*, Abidjan, 1963.

G. Rougerie, *La Côte d'Ivoire*, Paris, *Que sais-Je*, 1964.

John de Wilde and others, *Agricultural Development in Tropical Africa*, 2 Vols., Johns Hopkins Press, 1967.

Etudes Eburnéennes, Centre I.F.A.N., Abijan.

MAPS

See p. 183. Also:

1 : 3 million. Michelin.

1 : 2½ million. Institut Géographique National.

1 : 50,000 Main towns. Institut Géographique National.

1 : 10,000 Abidjan et environs. Institut Géographique National.

Chapter 23

GHANA

Land of Cocoa and Minerals[1]

GHANA is, without doubt, one of the most developed countries of Tropical Africa. Gold has been won for many centuries, it is the world's largest producer of cocoa, the third world producer of diamonds by weight and the seventh of manganese, all of which help to explain its relatively high standard of living, national revenue and expenditure. The value of its foreign trade was nearly two-thirds that of the pre-independence Congo, generally considered a rich country and almost ten times larger in area than Ghana. Furthermore, government revenue and expenditure in Ghana were about one-half those of the Congo.

These material advantages, combined with an older and more developed educational system than that of any other similar country in Africa, quickened Ghana's path to independence. This is a fine achievement for a country ravished in the past by slave raiders and by inter-African state wars. Moreover, it is a relatively small country of only 92,100 square miles, approximately the equivalent of Great Britain, and with only just about 8 million people. Within this relatively small area almost all the wealth and revenue derives from Ashanti, the Western, Central and Eastern Regions, which comprise only about one-third the total area.

Historical Outline[2]

The original inhabitants may have been pygmies who used stone implements, made pottery and lived on elevated sites in

[1] I am most grateful to Mr. H. P. White and Professor E. A. Boateng for their help and criticism.

[2] For the history see F. M. Bourret, *Ghana, The Road to Independence*, 1960; W. W. Claridge, *A History of the Gold Coast and Ashanti*, 2 volumes, 1964; J. D. Fage, *Ghana—A Historical Interpretation*, 1959; W. E. F. Ward, *A History of Ghana*, 1966.

the forests. The ancestors of the present Akan peoples probably arrived in the thirteenth to seventeenth centuries, after the successive decline of the Ghana, Mande and Songhaï Empires. It is likely that they came in periodic invasions from the northwest, as well as by a much smaller movement along the coast from the east. Some or all of them came with knowledge of metal smelting, since traces of old iron smelting ovens are widespread, brass was in common use, and gold dust served as currency until the introduction of coins by Europeans.

The first completely authenticated landing by Europeans upon the coast was in 1470–1 by a Portuguese. By the papal award under the Treaty of Tordesillas, 1494, the Portuguese were granted a monopoly of trade in Africa. But other nations and traders disregarded this monopoly and the first known English voyage was in 1553. The Dutch came by 1595, the Swedes about 1640 (just before the Dutch expelled the Portuguese in 1642), the Danes soon after and the Brandenburgers in 1683.

Castles were built as quarters, the first being that constructed at Elmina in 1481–2 by the Portuguese. It must be one of the world's first pre-fabricated buildings, since hundreds if not thousands of stone blocks were previously numbered in Portugal and taken out in convoy. This magnificent structure is excellently preserved and is a police training depot.

Most castles were, however, built in the seventeenth century at the height of the slave trade. Slaves were kept in the castle dungeons, later to be led out on to the beaches to start their tragic journeys to the New World. In the castles were also stored other articles of trade—exports of gold, ivory and spices and imports of guns, cloths and ornaments. Merchants lived on upper floors.

Until about the mid-nineteenth century Europeans scarcely penetrated the interior, contenting themselves with trading through their forts. The English companies traded from 1618 to 1820 under Charter or Act of Parliament and sometimes with financial grants from the British Government. Founded in 1750 with a government subsidy of £13,000, the African Company of Merchants, open to all British traders, was the governing body until 1820 and had its headquarters at Cape Coast Castle.

By 1820 the trading position of the company had weakened through the suppression of the slave trade and by attacks from the Ashanti. It was, therefore, dissolved and all assets and administration passed to the Crown, exercised by the Governor of Sierra Leone. This distant arrangement continued until 1874, with two breaks. From 1828 to 1843 an arrangement rather similar to the earlier one prevailed, whereby the Committee of African Merchants was responsible, through their celebrated Governor George Maclean. After another period of Crown rule from Sierra Leone for seven years, the Gold Coast became a distinct dependency between 1850 and 1866. Thereafter Sierra Leone was again the headquarters for eight years, the Gold Coast finally becoming a separate colony in 1874.

There were seven Ashanti attacks on coastal peoples and their British allies in the nineteenth century and ultimately Ashanti was annexed in 1901. In the same year the Northern Territories became a Protectorate, having come under British influence in 1897.

Only the English, Danes and Dutch survived into the eighteenth and nineteenth centuries. During the nineteenth century, especially in the first three-quarters, the trading outlook was bleak. The African Company of Merchants was wound up in 1820, the Danes withdrew in 1850 and the Dutch in 1872; British withdrawal nearly occurred. The cruel but lucrative slave trade had gone. Palm oil did not become important until the last quarter, when modern methods of gold mining also encouraged new hopes. Cocoa, introduced in 1879, did not become the leading export until 1924.

Although gold and cocoa so largely sustain the modern economy, diamonds, manganese, bauxite, timber and kola nuts are significant items. There is thus a more diversified economy than is often the case in Africa, though the production of other vegetable produce should be encouraged.

In 1922 a landlocked portion of former German Togoland was put under British Mandate, which became a Trusteeship in 1946. In consequence of a plebiscite in 1956 it became an integral part of Ghana when the latter became independent in 1957.

Ghana owes much to Sir Gordon Guggisberg, Governor from 1919 to 1927. It was he who had the eastern railway completed, the central line begun, the magnificent Achimota School established, the great port of Takoradi constructed and much else. An appropriately placed memorial to him stands at Takoradi but his greatest epitaph is the present development of the country.

Recent advance has been stimulated not only by high prices for exports, especially cocoa, but also by the spirit of initiative engendered by independence. The Volta River Scheme may also lead to an economic upsurge, since Ghana should become the world's third or fourth producer of aluminium. Power from the Volta Dam is used in industries in Tema, Accra, Takoradi and Kumasi. It is likewise available to most mines.

Population Distribution[1]

The provisional results of the census of 1960 showed the following population composition:

Region	Area in sq. miles	Per cent. of Ghana	Population	Per cent. of Population	Population per sq. mile
Western . . .	9,494	10·3	626,000	9·3	65·6
Central . . .	3,656	4·0	751,000	11·2	198·6
Accra Capital Dist.	990	1·1	492,000	7·3	496·0
Eastern . . .	7,760	8·4	1,094,000	16·3	140·3
Volta . . .	8,000	8·7	777,000	11·6	97·8
Ashanti . . .	9,700	10·5	1,109,000	16·5	114·3
Brong-Ahafo . .	14,900	16·2	588,000	8·7	39·5
Northern . .	27,122	29·4	532,000	7·9	19·6
Upper . . .	10,478	11·4	757,000	11·3	71·7
Total Ghana . .	92,100	100·0	6,727,000	100·0	72·6

The Eastern and Western Regions were created before independence, and the Central Region afterwards. Small areas on the eastern side of the Eastern Region and west of the Volta River have been incorporated in the Volta Region. The Ashanti Region comprises the southern half of the Ashanti of the Gold Coast, and is the historic core of the Ashanti peoples' lands. Brong-Ahafo Region, created in 1959, incorporates lands conquered in the past by the Ashanti in the Wenchi, Sunyani and Goaso Districts, together with the Yeji and Prang areas of the former Northern Territories. The Northern and Upper Regions are otherwise the successors of these. The Volta Region, which from 1957–9 was known as

[1] See J. M. Hunter, 'Regional Patterns of population growth in Ghana, 1948–60', in J. B. Whittow and P. D. Wood (eds.), *Essays in Geography for Austin Miller,* 1965.

Trans–Volta–Togoland, includes all areas of the former United Kingdom Trusteeship of Togoland from the Krachi District southwards, plus certain areas inhabited by Ewe people around the Volta Delta formerly in the Eastern Region.

Over two-fifths of the population of Ghana live in the

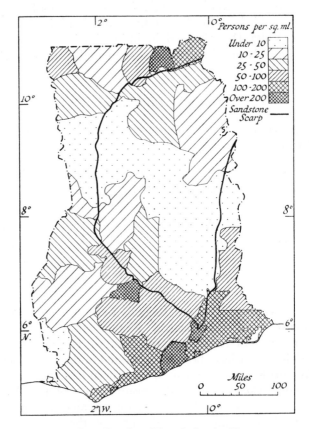

FIG. 69.—Density of Population in Ghana.

southern quarter of the country in the Western, Central and Eastern Regions, and the Accra Capital District. If these be added to well-populated Ashanti, then over three-fifths the population of Ghana lives in one-third its area.

By contrast, in the Northern and Upper Regions, two-fifths of the country, live only a fifth of Ghana's peoples, despite the existence of dense clusters of rather poor people in the extreme north-east.

The Volta Region has both the characteristics of the well populated south in its southern districts, and those of thinly populated central Ghana in its north, whilst Brong-Ahafo is thinly populated especially in the centre and east.

The greater concentration of population in the south may be explained as follows:

(a) Many areas are suitable for cocoa cultivation and it was here that cocoa cultivation commenced.

(b) Most mining is carried on here.

(c) This area has been longest in contact with the outside world.

(d) It contains Accra (the capital and by far the largest town), Takoradi-Sekondi, and the densest network of communications.

By contrast, the low density of population in central and eastern Brong-Ahafo and in the Northern Region is largely caused by the occurrence of the infertile Voltaian Sandstone. Water is scarce in the dry season, floods abound in the wet one, tsetse is rife, few minerals occur and none are exploited, cocoa can rarely be grown except on the southern fringes, and the area is rather isolated.

Yet remoteness does not necessarily exclude high population densities. The extreme north of the Upper Region lies beyond the infertile Voltaian Sandstone and has better soils derived from crystalline rocks. Water is more easily found, though there are only 40–50 inches of rainfall annually in one season. Population pressure is acute in most of Zuarungu, and many Fra-Fra males must seek work in the south on cocoa farms, or in mines. These areas of high population density and poverty are extensions into Ghana of similar areas in the Upper Volta, where these problems are even more acute.

Although the soils of the far north of the Upper Region are fairly fertile, they are thin and much eroded where there are great population densities, as in Mamprusi. The Tumu sub-district of the Upper Region and the Bole sub-district of the Northern are less densely peopled. Bole district was de-populated by Ashanti warfare and slave raiding, and then emptied by the tsetse fly. Given control of tsetse it is an area of potential resettlement, along the lines of the Anchau Scheme of northern Nigeria (see p. 479).

Areas for potential settlement lie mainly in the west of the Brong-Ahafo and Western Regions, towards which cocoa cultivation and settlement are extending. On the other hand, the rapid development of Tema and especially its industries— particularly that of aluminium—may arrest or reverse that tendency, by bringing people into the sparsely populated Lower Volta Plains. The great Lake Volta behind the Akosombo Dam has required the resettlement of some 78,000 people from poor areas of the Voltaian Basin to rather better districts on the lake margins. The west of the Northern and Upper Regions are areas of modest potential for resettlement.

Independence, prosperous cocoa-farming, mining, power development, a developing aluminium industry and a second port all continue to increase the attraction of population from the over-populated districts of the Upper and Northern Regions, the Upper Volta and beyond. The new port of Tema has attracted far more people than expected, and is growing very rapidly indeed.

CLIMATE [1]

There is greater variety of climate in Ghana than in most West African countries. Rainfall diminishes from the very wet south-west, where there are two rainfall maxima, towards the north-east, where there is only one. But there is also an extremely dry area in the south-east which, nevertheless, has two rainfall maxima.

Five climatic regions are commonly distinguished.[2]

South-Western Equatorial. Annual rainfall varies from over 80 inches in the extreme south-west to 55–60 inches on the

---

[1] See also Chapter 3 and *Portfolio of Ghana maps*, 1961, Map 8.
[2] For map see Chapter 3, p. 47. For the Accra–Togo Dry Coastal region see pp. 54–5.

other margins. Most places have about 120 rain days. Rainfall is least variable behind Axim, and wherever there is over 70 inches Rain Forest predominates. This is an important timber producing area, also well suited to rice cultivation.

In the rest of the area, where annual rainfall is approximately 55–70 inches, it is the ideal habitat not only for valuable forest trees but also for cocoa, especially where the rainfall is over sixty inches.

Semi-Seasonal Equatorial. Although rainfall may be greater (e.g. Kintampo 69 inches) than at many places in the previous zone, there are normally two relatively dry months when vegetative growth may be halted. Such is the case at Wenchi, Sunyani, Kete Krachi, Kintampo and Ejura. The forest was, therefore, less vigorous and dense, especially as the north-eastern part is on poor Voltaian Sandstone soils.

Seasonal Equatorial. Rainfall is under 50 inches north of a line roughly through Techiman and Yeji. Bole and Salaga both have just over 41 inches of rain on about 70 days, with two maxima and four relatively dry months.

Southern Savannah. All stations, north of approximately the latitude of Tamale, have a single rainfall maximum and a drought of four to six months. Yet, as in the Ivory Coast, rainfall totals may be rather higher than a little farther south, i.e. Tamale 41·2 inches on ninety days, Pong Tamale 44·7 inches on eighty-seven days and Navrongo 44·3 inches on sixty-three days. As one would expect from the direction of the rain-bearing winds and the higher relief, stations along much of the north-western border are a little wetter, i.e. Lawra with 49·9 inches on seventy-three days and Wa with 45·6 inches. This wetter area extends across the border into the Upper Volta around Gaoua.

Not only is the actual rainfall less, effective rainfall far less and variability much greater than in the Equatorial zone, but also, wherever sandstone occurs, percolation is usually rapid.[1]

[1] N. R. Junner and T. Hirst, 'The Geology and Hydrology of the Voltaian Basin', *Geological Survey Memoir No. 8*, 1946, p. 8, say, 'The value of the rainfall . . . is much less than the rainfall figures suggest; run-off during the rainy season is high and the desiccating effect of the harmattan, which starts shortly after the end of the rains and lasts for two or three months . . . is high. Evaporation is at a maximum at this time of the year and from measurements at Tamale dam . . . it would appear to average 9–12 inches per month during January to

Water is almost everywhere a problem and relative humidity may drop to under ten per cent in dry season afternoons at Tamale. It is understandable, therefore, that population densities tend to be greater on the more impermeable ' granite soils ' of northern Mamprusi and Lawra.

GEOLOGY, RELIEF AND NATURAL REGIONS [1]

Ghana is divisible geologically and geographically into contrasted regions. The northern and western fringes, together with the south-western third of the country, consist of Pre-Cambrian rocks with granite and other intrusive formations. Their trend lines are predominantly north-east to south-west, except in the far north-west, where they are north–south. In all cases the relief is in close accord with these trends.

Along the northern and north-western borders, and as far south as beyond Bole, the country is floored mainly by granite, with Birrimian Series occurring along the boundary with the Voltaian Basin and in the Bolgatanga–Zuarungu district. West and north-west of Wa and through Lawra to the northern boundary, Upper Birrimian (Greenstones) occurs.

South of Bole, in Ashanti and in the Western, Central and Eastern Regions, Upper and Lower Birrimian, the Tarkwaian, Granite and other intrusives occur frequently. In the south-east and on the east-centre boundary are found the Akwapimian (or Togo-Atacora) and Buem Series of the Akwapim Hills and Togo Mountains.

North-west of these is the largest feature of all—the Voltaian Basin, filled with Primary sandstones. It occupies northern Ashanti and the southern and central Northern Region. Except on the southern edge, it is infertile, has no important minerals and yields little water. It is also rather featureless, except where its upturned edges form the magnificent Kwahu Mampong, Wenchi and Gambaga scarps.

There are small survivals of marine-Devonian rocks at

April, compared with about 4 inches per month during August to October. The total annual evaporation at Tamale dam is approximately 7–8 feet.' This is over double the rainfall.

[1] See geological map in *Portfolio of Ghana maps*.

Accra, of Carboniferous or Devonian ones east of Axim, while Upper Cretaceous rocks occur westward from Axim.

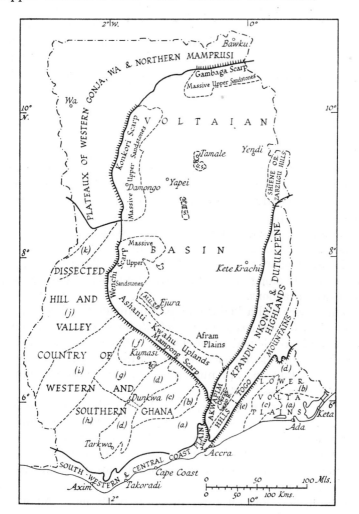

FIG. 70.—Natural regions of Ghana.
The italic letters of sub-regions refer to names in the text.

South-east of the Akwapim and Togo Mountains are Archæan and Granite rocks, deeply covered south-eastwards by Tertiary and Quaternary sands in the Volta Delta.

The explosive caldera or meteoric scar of Lake Bosumtwi probably dates from early Pleistocene times.

LOWER VOLTA PLAINS. South-east of the Akwapim–Togo Mountains are plains floored by Archæan gneisses and schists, with granite intrusions. This area was partially drowned by Tertiary and Quaternary seas. Thus crystalline rocks which floor the plains are masked seaward by up to 60 feet of marine and fluviatile sands, gravels, silts and clays. Raised beaches are further evidence of the progressive retreat of the sea and the Volta Delta is a good example of deltaic formations.

Accra may be taken as nearly the western limit of these plains which, as the ' Terre de Barre ', extend eastward into the Republics of Togo and Dahomey. The Lower Volta Plains are gently undulating and by no means uniform. According to Junner, there is evidence of several peneplanations in numerous inselbergs and ridges.[1] Wide and rather ill-defined valleys of seasonal rivers also interrupt the plains.

Soils are poor, except for the ' Terre de Barre ' clays, the alluvial soils along the Volta River and loamy soils around fresh-water lagoons.

The Lower Volta Plains may be sub-divided as follows.[2]

(a) *The Coastal and Lagoon Lowlands* have loose Quaternary sands and are devoid of inselbergs. Bluffs end eastward at Old Nugo, east of which former exits of the Volta River may be deduced. Lagoons are numerous, the Avu and Ke almost alone having fresh water.

Rainfall averages only 25–30 inches on about forty to fifty days. Along the sea-shore sedges, herbs, creepers and grasses occur with planted coconuts. Nutritious grasses grow best around the fresh-water lagoons and provide fairly good pasture. Around the saline lagoons, and for a mile up the Volta River, are stunted mangroves.

Fishing here and on adjacent coasts is the most important occupation. Herrings, horse mackerel and other fish are

[1] N. R. Junner, ' The Geology of the Gold Coast and Western Togoland ', *Gold Coast Survey Bulletin No. 11*, 1940, p. 8.

[2] See also H. P. White, ' Environment and Land Utilisation on the Accra Plains ', *Journal of the West African Science Association*, 1954, pp. 46–62, and T. E. Hilton, ' The Economic Development of the South-Eastern Coastal Plains of Ghana ', *Journal of Tropical Geography*, 1962, pp. 18–31.

smoked by women, who find a good market for them in Accra and inland. There is also some lagoon and river fishing. Salt is obtained by evaporation in the Songaw and Keta lagoons, for local use and for sale far away.

Other than fishing, cattle rearing is most important. Again there is a ready market in Accra, the country is predominantly grassland and the tsetse fly is almost absent. Nevertheless small West African Shorthorns are kept because they are very resistant to disease and because of sheer tradition. There are over 50,000 cattle; they are most numerous north-west and north-east of the Keta lagoon and around the small fresh-water lagoons. Sheep are found mainly east of the Volta. Goats, pigs and poultry are common near the lagoons, where they are kept under coconut trees. There is no mixed farming.

The Coastal and Lagoon Lowlands are fairly productive, especially round the Keta lagoon, and their economy is more varied than that of most of the Lower Volta Plains. Other than fishing and stock-keeping, there is quite intensive cropping of vegetables, cassava and maize, the latter despite the sandy soils and dry climate. The chief producing areas are between the sea and the Keta lagoon, where porous sandy marine soils meet the heavier ones of the lagoon, and the grasslands north of the lagoons, again with loamy soils and with over 35 inches of rain annually.

When cassava is grown in light sandy soils, the product is tough and reddish in colour, starchy and sticky when boiled. Hence it is fed to animals, used as fish bait or converted into garri, starch and tapioca. The best cooking cassava and sweet potatoes are grown in deeper loamy soils around the fresh-water lagoons.

Vegetables are grown for sale in Accra and Lomé. Onions are intensively grown in great numbers on some 800 acres on the edge of the lagoon between Anloga and Keta. Maize, tomatoes and okro are also planted here, and groundnuts and lima beans in drier sandy areas.

Keta, population 17,000 in 1960, is an important market, especially for cotton cloth woven around Keta lagoon, for fish, salt and onions. There is much traffic to and from Lomé. The town has suffered severely in the past from wars and from sea erosion. Much of it is now built on land reclaimed from the lagoon.

Ada, or *Ada Fua*, lies west of the Volta mouth and was established by Europeans as a commercial centre near the Chief's town of *Big Ada*, now much smaller in size. When trade up and down the Volta was important, Ada Fua was far more significant. *Otropwe*, a village just to the west, with a normal population of some 350, sometimes shelters several thousand fishermen at the height of the season.

(b) *The Terre de Barre*, north-east of the Keta Lagoon, has red clays derived from Eocene formations. These extend towards the Volta River from the Republics of Togo and Dahomey (*q.v.*). As in those territories, they are well planted with oil palm and maize, and are more densely settled than other parts of the Lower Volta Plains.

(c) *The Black Clay Belt* results from the weathering of gneiss. Extending north-east from Prampram to beyond the Volta, this area has very poor vegetation and is virtually empty. ' Shortage of water prevents settlement or stock raising and the cultivators, with their present equipment, are unable to till the intractable clays. . . . Communications are unusually bad, as only a slight shower will render the motor tracks impassable.'[1]

(d) *The Southern Volta and Trans-Volta Plains* are geologically akin to the Accra Plains, but have about 50 inches annual rainfall on 100 rain days. Rainfall is also more reliable, grass is taller, Borassus and oil palms and even forest trees occur in valleys and along the edge of the Togo Hills. Yet the soils are thin and cultivation is confined to broad basins with deeper soils. Yams and cotton, formerly much more important for the weaving of ' Kente ' or ' Keta Cloth ', are still significant in a belt of country 5–10 miles wide, extending 50 miles from west to east in the centre. Forest crops are grown on the northern fringes. The tsetse occurs and few animals are kept.

(e) *The Accra Plain*[2] lies west and south-east of the Black Clay Belt. The plain is low and has long spurs and outliers of the Akwapim Hills.

---

[1] White, op. cit., p. 61.

[2] Used in a more restricted sense than White's (op. cit.) *Accra Plains* which comprise those parts of (*a*), (*c*) and (*e*) which lie west of the Volta River.

Rainfall is only about 30–45 inches annually, on some seventy rain days. With such low and often erratic rainfall, and with mainly porous sandy soils, the vegetation is Scrub and Grassland. Low deciduous trees and bushes occur along intermittent streams. *Elaeophorbia drupifera*, *Antiaris africana* and Baobabs (*Adansonia digitata*), are common. Grazing is poor, except near Achimota, and yields of cassava, maize and vegetables are low.

Dodowa, an old half-way halt on the overland route from Akuse to Accra, is a market between the forested Akwapim Hills and the dry Plains. It was previously the collector of palm produce for export through Prampram.

Tema, is Ghana's most modern port, specially equipped for the rapid handling of cocoa, but also important for general cargo, and it has a developing fishing fleet. There are numerous and diverse industries, especially an aluminium smelter, oil refinery, a small steel works, cocoa processing and many consumer-good industries. The town is planned on garden city lines, and has notable public buildings and social facilities.

Almost everywhere in the Lower Volta Plains water is scarce and restricts settlement, stock keeping and crop farming.[1] Water is generally about 40–120 feet down, but nearer the surface near the Akwapim–Togo Mountains, and around outliers and inselbergs. Settlements tend to concentrate in these places, around fresh-water lagoons, along the Volta and other (mainly intermittent) rivers, along the Accra water pipelines, roads and the sea. In the latter case the villages may be only temporary. Permanent villages rarely have over 500 inhabitants.

The Lower Volta Plains are a fascinating field for the historical geographer and economic historian. The Danes took Christiansborg from the Swedes in 1659 and built subsidiary forts at Ningo, Ada and Keta in 1784, and at Teshi in 1787. Slaves were brought down the Volta River from the collecting centres of Yapei (Tamale Port), Kete Krachi and Yendi.

But the Danes were the first nation to abolish the slave trade, doing so in 1792. This undermined Danish trade, as other

[1] See N. R. Junner and D. A. Bates, ' Reports on the Geology and Hydrology of the Coastal Area, east of the Akwapim Range ', *Gold Coast Geological Survey*, *Memoir No. 7*, 1945, and H. P. White, ' Environment and Land Utilisation on the Accra Plains ', *Journal of the West African Science Association*, 1954, pp. 46–62.

nations continued the traffic. Moreover, Danish trade in palm oil from the forests, ivory from Kete Krachi, hides and skins from Yapei down the Volta to the forts was less than that of other merchants farther west. The Danes sold their forts to the British in 1850 and their economic significance continued to diminish.

Trade down the Volta and through this coast declined even more sharply when cocoa cultivation further activated areas to the west. The opening of the Accra–Kumasi Railway in stages between 1910 and 1924 channelled cocoa export by rail first through Accra and later through Takoradi. Akuse-Amedica, Dodowa, Ada and Prampram all stagnated.

A revival is now at hand. The new port of Tema will create a vast new market for meat, fish and vegetables, and another will be created by the aluminium smelter. Port and smelter will bring in another 100,000 people. With Accra, there will be an almost continuous conurbation of 500,000. Vast new demands for water will have to be satisfied, presumably from the Volta. If irrigation is also brought to these plains agriculture should be more productive, but the Accra Plains are exceedingly poor and may not be worth costly or extensive irrigation, which might be more advantageously directed to the Coastal and Lagoon Lowlands.

Accra,[1] capital of Ghana, lies in a very small basin of the Akwapimian Series which has been infilled with sandstone, grits, mudstones and shales of mid-Devonian age.

Fairly frequent earthquakes make this site unfortunate for a capital. Major shocks since 1858 have occurred in 1862, 1906 and 1939; and lesser ones in 1863, 1883, 1907, 1911, 1918–19, 1923, 1925, 1930, 1933–35 and 1953.[2] The tremor of 1862 almost completely destroyed Accra and was severe to the east of Accra, a fact which should concern those responsible for Tema harbour. Every stone building in Accra was razed to the ground and Christiansborg Castle and the Accra forts were rendered uninhabitable. African quarters of the town were almost completely ruined. In 1906 many government buildings were cracked and the castles and forts again damaged.

---

[1] See map in *Portfolio of Ghana maps*.
[2] N. R. Junner, D. A. Bates, E. Tillofson and C. S. Deakin, ' The Accra Earthquake of 22nd June, 1939 ', *Gold Coast Geological Survey Bulletin*, No. 13, 1941.

In 1911 the Lomé wharf was destroyed by a tidal wave occasioned by a sea earthquake. In 1939 sixteen people were killed, 133 injured and hundreds of thousands of pounds worth of damage was done to buildings. These earthquake shocks probably come from the base of long steep slopes of an off-shore deep. There is also an unstable zone along the Akwapim–Togo range as far as Atakpamé.

The Ga people came here by canoe or along the beach from Nigeria in the sixteenth century, making their first capital at Ayawaso, on an outlier of the Akwapim Hills, 8 miles north-west of Accra.[1] In the first part of the seventeenth century a settlement was started east of Korle Lagoon and towards the sea, where there were better possibilities for trade with the Portuguese. The Dutch later became supreme, and in 1650 built Fort Crèvecœur (now Ussher Fort) to replace an earlier lodge. In 1673 the English built Fort James, by the present breakwater. Both forts are now used as prisons.

The seventeenth century town was between these forts (only 500 yards from each other) and the lagoon. Sites of the slave markets may still be seen, and Ussher Town and James Town are the modern names of these oldest and most overcrowded parts of Accra. Three miles to the east was Christiansborg (Osu), the Danish headquarters from 1659. Walls of its slave market still remain and the castle is now a residence of the Prime Minister.

Although Accra was (and still is) the capital of the Ga people, the economic significance of its three forts—Dutch, English and Danish—was not quite so great as of forts to the west, where gold and slaves were more readily traded in; or of Ada farther east, near the Volta River route. Nevertheless, in the latter half of the eighteenth century the Fanti introduced the art of sea fishing and this increased local trade.

When the slave trade was abolished, ' legitimate ' trade through Accra was maintained, as forest products were brought there more easily than to the Volta mouth. In 1850 the Danes sold Christiansborg and their other castles to the British. The Dutch sold Crèvecœur in 1867 and remaining

---

[1] W. E. F. Ward, *A History of Ghana*, 1958, p. 57. An outstanding work is Ioné Acquah, *Accra Survey*, 1958.

castles in 1872.   In 1876 the capital was transferred here from Cape Coast Castle, which had, until then, been the chief British fort.   With the Danes and Dutch eliminated at both towns, Accra was felt to be more suitable as a capital, because animals could be used in and around it for transport.

Victoriaborg, between Ussher Town and Christiansborg and behind cliffs where there is always a breeze, was begun as a European residential quarter.   Until the era of cars it retained this character, which it has now lost to that of government. The Ridge and the Cantonments, north-east of Victoriaborg, are now better residential areas.

The railway from Accra was begun in 1909 and opened in Nsawam in 1910, Pakro in 1911, Koforidua in 1912, Tafo in 1917 and Kumasi in 1923.   Until Takoradi was opened in 1928, Accra was the chief exporter of cocoa, and this more than anything else led to rapid growth at the expense of Prampram, Ada, Akuse, Kpong and Dodowa.   In 1891 the population was 16,267, in 1901 26,622, in 1911 29,602 and in 1921 42,803, a figure raised by the inclusion for the first time of Labadi and twenty-six villages.   These villages were included in and after 1921 because they were served by piped water, first provided in Accra in 1915, and another powerful attractor of population to Accra.

The governorship of Sir Frederick Gordon Guggisberg saw the opening of Korle Bu Hospital and the bridging of Korle Bu Lagoon in 1923, so enabling suburbs to be built west of it. In 1925 Achimota School, 7 miles north of Accra, was opened. Construction of hospital and school brought in workers and Korle Gono was planned and settled south-west of the bridged lagoon.   Houses also spread northward along the road to Achimota, taking in Adabraka, formerly a separate Muslim village.   In 1931 the population was 60,726 and in 1948 135,926, of which only 54% were born there.   The town then occupied 40 square miles, giving a density of 3,398 per square mile.   The 1966 population was 521,900.

Development since 1931 has been more the consequence of the general development of Ghana, as Takoradi and Tema now ship all the cocoa.   Yet Accra is the greatest administrative, commercial and industrial centre, having a higher percentage of skilled workmen than anywhere else.   It has an excellent airport, served by many airlines. Although ocean vessels had to anchor half a mile out, it was Ghana's second port until 1962, handling some 400,000 tons annually through its jetty (protected to the west by a breakwater) and surf boats. There is still a submarine pipeline, which enables tankers anchored off-shore to discharge oil into tanks in Accra. Many men are still engaged in fishing.

Nevertheless, the overwhelming importance of Accra is somewhat remarkable, as Takoradi might have been expected to rival it in size. Such is the case in Dahomey, with Cotonou the port and Porto-Novo the capital. Kumasi might also have been expected to become more of a competitor with Accra; it may yet do so.

Tema, a fourteen-berth industrial port for eastern Ghana and one of the largest artificial harbours in Africa, has supplanted Accra as a port. Industrial and commercial functions may also be restricted, but the administrative and cultural rôles will presumably remain. Accra will form part of an urban area of some 500,000, so rivalling Dakar and Ibadan. Like the latter, and so many other West African cities, it lacks cohesion and has suffered from unco-ordinated though impressive development.

THE AKWAPIM–TOGO MOUNTAINS.[1] These mountains begin as prominent hills west and north-west of Accra; a fault near Senya Beraku on the coast is believed to have caused their termination there. They trend north-eastward across Togo and northern Dahomey, where they straddle the Niger River. In northern Togo and Dahomey they are known as the Atacora Mountains.

Over-folding and thrusting from the south-east, with consequential thrust-faulting and shearing, have caused the very abrupt edges to these ranges which average only 1,000–1,500 feet in height. Synclines and anticlines correspond closely with downfolds and upfolds, the regional dip of the rocks being south-eastward. Earthquake shocks were recorded in 1906, 1930, 1933 and 1939 and, as the Volta dam and hydro-electric power station are in the Volta Gorge, it is obvious that earth-tremors from fault-slipping are a menace. The gorge separates

[1] Although now out of print, the most effective map of the Akwapim Hills is the 1 : 250,000 layer coloured Accra sheet of the First Edition, 1925.

the Akwapim Hills to the south-west from the Togo (or Ewe) Mountains to the north-east.

These ranges are composed of the Akwapimian (or Togo-Atacora) Series on the east and the Buem Series on the west, both of younger Pre-Cambrian age. In the Akwapimian series, schists are very common; metamorphism has converted some sandstones into quartzites and silicified limestone occurs. Yet unaltered sandstone is widespread. There are also intrusive rocks, although granite is only locally important in the south-east. The quartzite series occur in long, narrow, tightly folded ranges adjacent to the Archæan shield rocks to the south-east. On the west, the Buem group consist of calcareous, argillaceous, sandy and ferruginous shales much more easily weathered.

(a) *Akwapim Hills.* These hills or low mountains, begin south-west of Accra as two simple masses. The higher rises only to 585 feet and is separated from the other by the Densu Gap, which shows evidence of drainage diversion.

North of the Kokoasi Gap, used by the Accra–Kumasi Railway, are two parallel ranges. On the east is a continuous, narrow, steep-edged range, preserved because it is composed of resistant white quartzite and of a band of granite on its eastern edge, from the gap to near the Volta. This eastern range is also sheltered from the full force of the rain-bearing winds and has very narrow valleys. By contrast, to the west is a lower, more dissected but wider belt of rounded hills of the Buem shales. Many hills have been isolated in the west but very few in the east.

North-east of Adawso, on the Akrapong-Mangoasi road, erosion has proceeded so far in the western range and between it and the eastern one, as to produce what Chapman [1] has called the Okrakwajo Basin. In all probability, the many headwaters of the Pawmpawm have worked on faults and flexures in this zone, near the Voltaian Series on the north-west.

(b) *The Togo or Ewe Mountains.* These are higher than the Akwapim Hills and have wider valleys, such as the Tsawe and the marshy Dayi; indeed, the Tsawe and its tributaries have cut down to the underlying Archæan rocks. To the

[1] Chapman, op. cit., pp. 7–8.

west of the Togo Mountains are the north–south trending Kpandu, Nkonya and Dutukpene Highlands.

Annual rainfall, which in the Akwapim Hills averages 55 inches on the western range and 45 inches on the eastern, reaches 55–70 inches in the Togo Mountains and on the ranges to the west. They are more forested and cocoa is grown, but the broad Dayi and Tsawe valleys have some 10 inches less rain, which is also more variable.

In both parts of the Akwapim–Togo Mountains, the usual forest food crops and yams are grown. Upland rice is significant towards and across the border between Ghana and Togo. North of Ho, much rice is grown on steep hill slopes. The Krobo,[1] who tend to migrate westward, are well-known growers of food crops for cash in the Akwapim Hill and the Okrakwajo Basin.

It was in the Akwapim Hills that cocoa was first planted in the then Gold Coast in 1879. But soils are thin and there has been much soil deterioration, as well as severe Swollen Shoot. Cocoa is now important only some 30 miles due east of Kete Krachi; it is most easily exported by road to Atakpamé and so by rail to Lomé. Lesser quantities go across the boundary farther south to Palimé and on by rail to Lomé. A little coffee is also grown in the Akwapim–Togo Mountains.

In the Akwapim Hills cocoa replaced the oil palm as the chief crop. Both are now tending to give way to food crops and citrus fruits. In the Togo Mountains crops are cocoa, rice, other food crops and coffee. Cotton is most important in the wide valleys.

The Akwapim Hills include the districts of Akwapim and New Juaben. The latter is one of the smallest districts in Ghana, but one of the most populated (1,416 per square mile). New Juaben, founded by Ashanti in 1875, is the smallest state and its density is easily the highest of any rural area in Ghana. The high density in New Juaben results from the desire of Ashanti people to live within its borders despite its small size. The other cause was the development of cocoa cultivation and, although Swollen Shoot has so reduced production

[1] See M. J. Field, ' The Agricultural System of the Manya Krobo ', *Africa*, Vol. XIV (1934), pp. 54–65.

here and in Akwapim 'that the proportion of population growing cocoa is now much less than in many other areas, Kofuridua is still one of the main centres of trade in beans which come to it from Birim, as well as Akwapim–New Juaben'.[1]

Koforidua belongs geographically to the foot of the Kwahu Uplands and the edge of the Densu Basin but belongs administratively to New Juaben. Apart from its cocoa trade, it is a political centre. Two-thirds of the population of New Juaben live in Koforidua.

Nsawam is one of the greatest route centres in Ghana. It lies near the edge of cocoa country and at the meeting place of the Akwapim Hills, the Coastal Plain and the Densu Basin.

Aburi became a European hill station for Accra and has a fine Botanical Garden. *Akropong* is, with Cape Coast, the oldest educational centre in Ghana. These with Mampong, Adawso, Pakro, Mangoasi and Adukrom are Akwapim centres.

The Togo Mountains lie mainly within the Ho District of the Volta Region. *Ho* lies at the foot of the Togo Mountains where they adjoin the Southern Volta Plains of the Lower Volta. It is a notable route centre and collecting point for cocoa. *Hohoe* and *Kpandu* are other centres. The fact that there are significantly more males than females tends to substantiate the westward movement of Ewe from Togo, at least in the past.

THE VOLTAIAN BASIN. This great syncline infilled with Ordovician, Silurian or Devonian flat bedded sandstone series, is mostly 300–600 feet in elevation, except on its upturned edges. Of these, the southern or Mampong Scarp is the most striking, rising to 1,500 feet above the adjoining country, and averaging 2,000–2,200 feet high between Koforidua and Mampong. There are also flat-topped residuals of 2,500–2,730 feet near Begoro, Mpraeso (Mount Ejuanema) and Akwaseho.[2] Between Mampong and Techiman, the edge averages 1,200–1,400 feet above sea level, but near Wenchi it is

---

[1] *Gold Coast Census of Population 1948: Report and Tables*, p. 27.
[2] N. R. Junner and T. Hirst, 'The Geology and Hydrology of the Voltaian Basin', *Gold Coast Geological Survey Memoir No. 8*, 1946, p. 9.

1,700–1,800 feet high. The highest points on the western or Konkori Scarp, on the northern or Gambaga Scarp, and in the Shiene (Zabzugu) Hills in the north-east reach 1,700 feet.

These vivid edges are composed of the Massive Upper Sandstone Series of mudstone, shale and arkose, with beds of conglomerate and sandstone. The series is at least 400 feet thick, is more fertile, and has better water supplies than most of the Voltaian Series. On the south-east is the westward or inward-facing scarp of the Buem Series of the Akwapim–Togo Mountains.

The Voltaian Basin occupies some 40,000 square miles in Ghana but is drained by only part of the Volta rivers.[1] The basin extends, as an equally poor zone, into northern Togo, along the boundary of Dahomey with the Upper Volta and just enters the Niger Republic. It covers about 45% of the area of Ghana, yet it has only approximately one-sixth the population. If the well-watered Ashanti–Kwahu Uplands on the southern margin of the basin are excluded, which have a population density exceeding 50 per square mile, the rest of the area, which covers four-tenths the area of Ghana, has only one-tenth the population.

Outside the Ashanti–Kwahu Uplands, the highest population densities on Voltaian rocks are in Western Dagomba (especially around Tamale) with thirty-six per square mile and southern Mamprusi with twenty-eight. The north-west, centre and south-east of the basin (including the Afram Plains) have well under eleven and the average for the Voltaian Basin within the Northern Region is fifteen per square mile.[2]

There are simple reasons for these low figures and for the poverty of the people in northern Ashanti and the central Northern Region. The desiccating Harmattan is at full strength and the vegetation is poor Guinea Savannah. The

---

[1] Junner and Hirst, op. cit., incidentally give details on p. 9 of 25–40 feet, 60–75 feet, 100–120 and 250–300 feet terraces on the rivers and elsewhere. The 100–120 feet terrace probably results from conditions common to all of Ghana, e.g. increased rainfall and erosion. The 250–300 feet terrace is part of a widespread erosion surface, probably of mid- or late-Tertiary age. Plateau remnants at 1,400–1,700 feet are part of an older highly dissected plain, probably of early Tertiary age.

[2] John R. Raeburn, *Report on a Preliminary Economic Survey of the Northern Territories of the Gold Coast*, Colonial Office, 1950, p. 25.

soils are generally shallow and infertile, floods occurred rapidly in the wet season before the Volta Dam was built, yet water is deficient in the dry season. Fly-borne human diseases such as malaria, sleeping sickness and river blindness are prevalent, as is trypanosomiasis (nagana) in cattle.

Consequently, there has been little incentive to provide roads in the Voltaian Basin. Their paucity has hindered development of the richer northern and western granite fringes beyond the Voltaian basin, rather than that of the poor basin itself.

In the past some areas may have been over-farmed, but vast areas were certainly decimated by warfare and by slave raiding. Tsetse killed off the survivors. If tsetse and other disease carriers could be cheaply and quickly eliminated and when the Volta Waterway is equipped with piers a cheap navigable waterway will exist through most of the basin (see Fig. 72) and will provide new income from fishing in this region the size of England.

Unfortunately, however, improvement does not depend only upon such things. No important minerals are exploited, though bauxite (Mount Ejuanema), limestones, clays and other building materials, salt, barite, alluvial diamonds and gold occur.

Nor can the poor soils be easily or readily improved. There are practically no cash crops except for cocoa, kola, the oil palm and yams on the wholly untypical Ashanti–Kwahu Uplands. Elsewhere, poor crops of groundnuts, guinea corn, maize, millet and cotton are insufficient even for adequate subsistence. The main prospects are for irrigated rice and vegetable cultivation near the waterway.

The new lake (Fig. 72, p. 410) occupies 3,250 square miles (or 3·5% of the area of Ghana), and vies with that behind the Kariba Dam on the Zambezi River between Zambia and Rhodesia as the largest artificial lake in the world. The Volta lake has necessitated the resettlement of some 78,000 people from 15,000 homes and 740 villages. These have been regrouped in over 50 new settlements, varying in size from a few hundred people to several thousand, but mostly larger than the abandoned ones. Thus New Ajena, near the dam and some 13 miles from the original village, has absorbed 21 villages. The only town much affected was Kete Krachi, which has been partly rebuilt and may become a waterway port.

Each new settlement has a planned location and layout, sewage disposal and piped water, although water supplies have been understandably difficult. Great care was taken to ensure that people were grouped with those with whom they had some affinity. There are new main and access roads and, for some of the settlements, the prospect of irrigated farming, fishing and trade on the waterway. For all there are better homes, with the chance to enlarge those provided free by the government, land initially prepared for their farms, advice on methods of cultivation and the crops to be grown. Although some mistakes were made, partly because of the short time available for resettlement, the long-term prospects are plainly far better than they were for people in this hitherto poor and secluded region.

It will be interesting to compare the evolution of reformed traditional farming in the new settlements with an older scheme of a different character but still within the Voltaian Basin.

At Damongo, in Western Gonja, near the scarp, the Gonja Development Company began operations in May 1950. Its aims were to test the mechanical cultivation of oil seeds and other crops on a large scale, to open new lands to grow food crops for all of Ghana, and to resettle people from overcrowded areas outside the Voltaian Basin.

At first 50,000 acres were to be taken over for mechanical cultivation, but this amount was reduced to 32,000. By 1955 3,438 acres were cultivated. Contour ploughing and farming were carried out, with intervening wide untilled strips to hold the soil. Each ploughed belt was planted with a different crop and farms extended up the hills. The company did the clearing, ploughing, fertilising and seed planting by machines and it was intended that farmers should look after 30 acres each, doing weeding and harvesting themselves. Eighteen acres were under mechanical tillage, ten under fallow, and two under food or compound crops. The company took two-thirds of the harvest of mechanically tilled crops and the farmer one-third. When yams were grown, however, the farmer took two-thirds and the company one-third, as the farmer also prepared and maintained the yam mounds.

Although by 1953 there were only some thirty settler families, it was hoped that ultimately there would be 250, each with a two-roomed house and 30-acre farm. Incomes were to be partly from wages for helping with mechanical cultivation, partly from shares of the crops so cultivated, and partly from the two-acre vegetable plots.

However, oil seeds were unsuccessful, and the yields of most crops poor. Costs were high because of the construction of a new road and the long haul of costly imported machinery. The scheme was abandoned, although farmers continued to be given advice. If mechanical cultivation required testing, better soils to the west of Damongo would have been more suitable. Alternatively, these vast sums might have been more profitably injected into existing farmed areas on better soils.

Tamale is by far the largest town of the Voltaian Basin and lies in a peopled but poor area. Around the town there are signs of soil exhaustion and population pressure, not found elsewhere in the basin. Tamale is the headquarters of the Northern Region and a significant commercial and transport centre.

In conclusion, more detailed reference may be made to two contrasted sub-divisions of the Voltaian Basin.

(a) *The Ashanti and Kwahu Uplands.* As already mentioned, these are the uplands of the southern edge of the basin. They terminate south and west in the impressive Mampong and Wenchi scarps, the main watershed of Ghana. These uplands have 55–60 inches rainfall, groundwater is readily available in the Massive Sandstones and they are forested. Cocoa may be grown and in every way the uplands are different from the rest of the basin and more akin (except geologically) with the regions to the south. Moreover, in the Mpraeso area population density is about ninety-one per square mile. These uplands are wide in the east, narrower near the Ashanti Colony boundary and widen again in the west where, near Wenchi, the scarp runs northward.

In the south-east the Kwahu occupy these uplands and came originally from Ashanti, making their first capital at *Abene* in a bay of lowland on the north, well protected by the southern

scarp edge from sudden attack. Their modern capital is at
Abetifi; the administrative headquarters of European origin is
Mpraeso, near which are the bauxite deposits of Mount
Ejuanema. The commercial centres are *Nkawkaw*, below the
Voltaian edge, on the railway, and *Begoro* above and beyond
the scarp.

Agogo was the subject of special study by the Ashanti Social
Survey which produced a land use map of it,[1] showing the
typical arrangement of food farms near the town and cocoa
farms farther away. It grows food for the Konongo mine and
is also in contact with the Afram plains.

Mampong is a frequent halting place for lorries and migrant
labourers at the top of the scarp on the Kumasi–Tamale road.
Wenchi, *Ejura* and *Kintampo* are small towns outside the main
cocoa zone. They all send yams and other food crops to
Kumasi.

(b) *The Afram Plains.* These have an average elevation of
about 100 feet near their ill-defined valleys and of 300 feet on
the interfluves. Guinea Savannah is dominant, except for
fringing or watershed forests. These tend to attract settlements, as cultivation of cocoa and yams may be attempted.
Otherwise, the tsetse, poor soils, floods alternating with extreme
droughts, and few roads inhibit settlement, which is often of a
temporary character. That part of Birim District north of the
Afram River and eastern Mampong have under three people
per square mile, and are typical of the very thinly peopled
areas of the central Voltaian Basin.[2]

THE MAINLY GRANITE PLATEAUX OF WESTERN GONJA, WA
AND NORTHERN MAMPRUSI. This area corresponds to the
Interior Plateaux of the Ivory Coast. Apart from predominant
granite, these areas have Birrimian rocks in central Mamprusi
along the fringes of the Voltaian Basin, and along the western
border in Wa. The country averages 600–1,200 feet in
elevation, is gently rolling with north–south trending hills in
the west through Wa to Bole and south from Tumu. Residual
granite domes and bare rock are frequent, as they are across
the border in the Upper Volta.

---

[1] M. Fortes, R. W. Steel and P. Ady, ' Ashanti Survey 1945–6: An Experiment
in Social Research ', *Geographical Journal*, CX, pp. 149–79.
[2] See Africa 1 : 125,000 Afram and Abetifi Sheets.

O

Granite and the other rocks wear down to better (though still thin) soils than do the Voltaian Sandstones. Rainfall is rather higher than farther south (see p. 367) and this, combined with the greater impermeability of the rocks and more fertile soils, makes for rather better conditions for farming.

Population is, in fact, generally far greater on the ' granite soils ' than on the sandstone ones, though slave raiding, warfare and tsetse have depopulated some relatively fertile areas, such as Bole in western Gonja. Raeburn[1] provides the following statistical contrasts in the Northern Region (of 1950):

MAINLY ON GRANITE ROCKS	Density per sq. mile	MAINLY ON VOLTAIAN SANDSTONES	Density per sq. mile
Kusasi (i.e. Bawku environs) . . .	122		
Zuarungu (Fra Fra) .	209		
Navrongo . . .	94		
Average northern Mamprusi granite areas .	142	Southern Mamprusi . .	27
Wa			
Tumu . . .	12	Other areas entirely on Voltaian rocks (W. and E. Dagomba and Krachi) .	21
Lawra . . .	71		
Wa (Greenstone area in W.) . . .	67		
„ (Granite area in E.)	10		
Western Gonja			
Bole area, mainly on granite . . .	5	Eastern Gonja on Voltaian rocks	6
Average on mainly granite rocks	46	Average on Voltaian sandstones	15

It is possible that there is population pressure in Zuarungu, where there is much poverty and over 600 people per square mile. But with tsetse and simulium fly control, less erosion of populated watersheds and more all-season roads, there should be good prospects for settlement in eastern Wa and Bole. Population is mainly in the east; potential areas for resettlement are in the west.

Meanwhile there is a regular exodus of males from the more populated districts for temporary work in mines and on cocoa

[1] J. R. Raeburn, op. cit., p. 25. His figures differ slightly from those quoted in the Gold Coast census, 1948, because census districts do not quite coincide with geological boundaries.

farms in southern Ghana. In 1943–50, 732,126 Ghana labourers passed over the five Volta ferries bound for the south and 674,866 returned. The corresponding numbers from Upper Volta and Mali were 499,278 and 446,564. Since 1945 the number of Ghana labourers seeking work in the south has about doubled and the number of ' French ' labourers has trebled.[1] Absence of many males has led (as in Central and South Africa) to poorer farming methods (e.g. in Tumu Division) and, together with general pressure of population and consequent overcropping, to soil erosion in Zuarungu and other areas. These problems are being met by contour cropping, mixed farming, afforestation of river sources and of steep slopes.

' Despite the comparatively high density of human populations, only about 14% of the total area of North Mamprusi (10% in Lobi and Dagarti areas of Lawra) is tilled for crops in any one year. Since the fallow period is short or non-existent in some localities, this means that though some land is overcropped, much is never cropped. It supplies only fuel, building materials and other bush products and it maintains at a very low level of productivity a small number of cattle— three to four per 100 acres.

' A considerable part of the uncropped 86% of land area (90% in Lobi and Dagarti areas of Lawra) is, of course, needed as restorative fallow and to provide bush products and grazing. A further part is rock and boulder strewn and unplantable. But the remainder is:

(i) Wet season swamps and areas liable to water logging, which could be used if minor water-control arrangements were made[2]

(ii) Better-drained areas near rivers not now used because sufficient labour is not available for hoe cultivation

(iii) Swampy and waterlogged areas that would not be used unless major water control arrangements requiring much capital were made

(iv) Areas near rivers not now used for medical reasons

(v) Areas where soils have been badly depleted.

[1] *Annual Report of the Gold Coast Department of Agriculture*, 1950–1, Appendix.
[2] Since this report was made, some of these swamps have been developed in northern Mamprusi for rice farming. The rice is sold in southern Ghana.

' The limitations on the use of these areas are such that over-cropping of other areas will continue and become more serious as the human population increases.   This overcropping would be aggravated by any cheapening of transport charges that raised net returns for cash crops substantially.'[1]   The need to find alternative employment to farming is emphasised by census returns showing Mamprusi and Wa as having the highest and second highest proportions respectively of farmers of all Ghana administrative districts.

Northern Mamprusi exhibits an unusual settlement pattern. Very numerous farm compounds are found scattered over the countryside but, because of fly, tend to avoid the rivers. *Bawku*, an important point of transit for cattle coming from the Upper Volta and Niger, and *Bolgatanga* are the only true towns.   Zuarungu and Navrongo Districts have only administrative nuclei.   To the west, however, other towns reappear, e.g. Wa and Lawra.

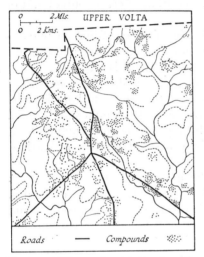

FIG. 71.—Dispersed compound settlement in Kusasi country of Navrongo District.
Streams are generally avoided because of the danger from tsetse and simulium flies. Watersheds are often eroded, so that the middle slopes of interfluves are most favoured.   Roads converge on Navrongo.
(From the 1 : 125,000 Navrongo sheet, Ghana Survey.)

Although inherently richer than the Voltaian sandstone areas, over-population of some granite areas has lowered their productivity and caused erosion. Population re-distribution within the granite areas is highly desirable.   Both granite and sandstone areas of the Northern and Upper Region have suffered from low incomes, poor and costly communications, so that there is little variety of foodstuffs or of other necessities.   Diets are almost always poor and disease rampant. The Regions, although divided into two major contrasted

[1] Raeburn, op. cit., pp. 15–16 and 35.

natural regions of granite and sandstone, are throughout the poor relation of Ghana, neglected in the past because they could neither produce exports nor offer a market.

DISSECTED HILL AND VALLEY COUNTRY OF WESTERN AND SOUTHERN GHANA. Corresponding to the Interior Plains of the Ivory Coast, this region consists ' of highly dissected plain residuals and ranges of hills, separated by wide flat-bottomed valleys. The country has a steady fall to the south; the general level is well below 1,000 feet, but the higher hills and ranges rise to 1,500–2,500 feet above sea level '.[1] It has north-east to south-west bands of the Lower and Upper (Greenstone) Birrimian and Tarkwaian Series, with granite and small occurrences of basic intrusives.

The Birrimian predominates in the Western Region and western Brong. Either it forms steep-sided, flat-bottomed, swampy valleys where the rock has weathered to clay, or irregular isolated hills and ridges where lateritic cappings survive. It is by far the most important mineral-bearing series in Ghana, yielding lode gold, manganese and other minerals.

The Tarkwaian Series, practically confined to Ghana, has been an important source of gold from south of Tarkwa to Konongo. Other occurrences of the Tarkwaian, not important for minerals, are south-west to north-east of Bamboi on the Black Volta, in the Kibi Hills, and just west of Apam. Granite and gneiss predominate south of 6° N., the granite as usual forming rounded hills and isolated domes.

This area of varying relief has at least 50 inches annual rainfall, which is more reliable than farther north. Even more important, the Wenchi and Mampong scarps shield most of western and southern Ghana from the Harmattan, so that the forest survives. Here is grown the cocoa, which is the country's chief export; subsidiary crops are kola, oil palm, citrus fruits and many food crops. Valuable timber is cut. Almost all the minerals are won here, so that this region has most of the revenue-earning resources of Ghana. Two-thirds of the people of Ghana also live in this region, which covers

[1] N. R. Junner, ' The Geology of the Gold Coast and Western Togoland ', *Gold Coast Survey Bulletin No. 11*, 1940, p. 47.

only one-third of the area. Yet, despite this higher density of population, there are still lands in the south-west, west and north-west where land is available for cropping and settlement, though these will be at the expense of the forest and of the timber industry.

This large region may be subdivided into the following smaller ones:

(a) *The Densu and Pra Basins*. The basins are floored by granite of which their scenery is typical. Cocoa has been important here from the earliest days but has suffered severely from Swollen Shoot and from soil deterioration. Some cocoa has been replaced by kola, citrus fruits and food crops, the latter much grown by Krobo immigrants. Population density is over 100 per square mile.

New Tafo, headquarters of the Cocoa Research Institute is a typical cocoa collecting centre. *Koforidua* in New Juaben (p. 380) and *Nsawam* (p. 380) are more important centres.

(b) *The Kibi Hills* are composed of Birrimian and Tark-waian rocks, have good reserves of bauxite, and are well forested. They are abrupt, rise quickly to a maximum height of 2,505 feet, and extend south-westward some 33 miles and are 8 miles in width. Between them and the Mampong Scarp of the Voltaian Series is the Osino Gap, barely 2 miles wide, used by the Accra–Kumasi Railway and road. At the south-western end of the hills is *Asamankese*, a lively town of 17,000 inhabitants in 1960, where there are diamond mines.

(c) *The Birim Plains*, west of the Kibi Hills, are higher than the Densu Basin and are floored by Lower Birrimian rocks. The typical wide, flat-bottomed valleys have an annual rainfall of over 65 inches. This is another important but younger cocoa-producing region,[1] where cocoa mainly developed after the opening of the Accra–Kumasi Railway in 1923 and of roads to Winneba, Saltpond and Cape Coast. Fully one-third of the men are engaged in growing cocoa and about one-fifth of the women, whilst land is still available for cultivation and settlement.

Most of Ghana's diamonds are produced in this basin and the largest workings are at Akwatia. The Central Railway,

---

[1] See W. H. Beckett, *Akokoaso: A Survey of a Gold Coast Village*, London School of Economics and Political Science Monographs on Social Anthropology, 1944.

opened in 1927, stimulated diamond and timber production. Population density is about ninety per square mile and is increasing.

Oda, population 20,000, is a flourishing route centre near diamond mining, timber cutting and rice growing areas, the latter lying along the marshy Birim River.

(d) *The Tarkwaian Hill Country* consists of narrow elongated and parallel strike ridges and valleys, showing a fold and fault structure. Faults have given rise to many transverse valleys and gaps. The region begins mid-way between Tarkwa and the sea and extends north-eastward to Konongo, where Tarkwaian rocks disappear under the Voltaian Sandstones. The Tarkwaian sediments form part of a long and narrow north-east trending geosyncline. The total thickness of the rocks is roughly 8,000 feet. Near Tarkwa the folding is open, but elsewhere closely packed folds are the rule. In general, metamorphism is much less than in the Birrimian, although there are some basic intrusives.

These mountains are wooded, and through their narrow valleys the Takoradi–Kumasi railway winds its way from south of Nsuta to Obuasi. On the other hand, main roads rather skirt the region, except at Tarkwa, Dunkwa (Ofin Gap), Obuasi and Konongo.

If the Birrimian rocks along the margins are included, this area accounts for almost all the gold and manganese mining in Ghana. The gold-bearing banket conglomerates of the Tarkwaian are akin to the banket reefs of the South African Witwatersrand. They are auriferous between Eduapriem and Damang but have been mined on the eastern edge from Tamsu through Tarkwa and Abosso to Cinnamon Bippo. The other gold-mining areas within the ' gold channel ' but in the adjacent Birrimian are Prestea, Obuasi, Bibiani and Konongo. The Nsuta manganese deposits are also in the Birrimian.

The mining towns have European and African quarters often provided and maintained by mining companies. The principal towns and populations are Obuasi, 23,000; Tarkwa, 14,000; Konongo, 11,00; and Prestea, 13,000. The five former or still active mining towns of Abontiakoon, Aboso, Nsuta, Tamsu and Tarkwa form an almost contiguous urban area.

In the south, mining is the dominant economic activity and cocoa is relatively little grown, food crops for the miners and timber for fuel being more significant.   In the north, however, cocoa is far more important, Konongo also being a great cocoa collecting point.

The average density of population is low because of rugged terrain and poor, thin soils, but urbanisation is high and there are some 25,000 immigrants from northern Ghana, the Upper Volta, Mali, Niger, Nigeria and Liberia, all attracted by mining employment.

(e) *Lake Bosumtwi*, 13 miles south-east of Kumasi, is either a meteoric scar or an explosive caldera.   A lake 6 miles across lies within a possible crater 40 square miles in area.   If a crater it was probably formed in early Pleistocene times by explosions followed by subsidence, and has an unbroken rim rising 1,450 feet above the lake, which is 260 feet deep.[1]

Much lore and superstition are connected with this remarkable natural phenomenon.   Lake fishermen are forbidden to use boats, so they go fishing astride planks.   The ' name for the country round the lake is Amanse, " the beginning of nations " . . . Most of the important divisions of Ashanti say that they " came out of a hole in the ground " ',[2] which might refer to this lake.

(f) *The Kumasi Plateau*, dissected, and averaging 800–900 feet in elevation, is in the heart of Ashanti.   Towards the Mampong Scarp it is over 1,100 feet high and to the east about 700 feet. The plateau is closely settled, with over 230 people per square mile (excluding Kumasi).   There is a remarkable radial network of roads, as well as the railways to Takoradi and Accra.

Composed mainly of granite rocks, the plateau is probably more intensively planted with cocoa than any other area in Ghana, about one-half of the male population over fifteen years of age and one-fifth of the women being cocoa farmers. Within about 10 miles of Kumasi, however, the villages are also concerned with growing food crops (especially maize and cassava) for sale in the city.   In the upper Ofin country on the west, kola is also much grown for sale to the north; this

---

[1] Junner, op. cit., p. 53 and ' The Geology of the Bosumtwi Caldera ', *Gold Coast Geological Survey Bulletin No. 8*, 1937.

[2] W. E. F. Ward, op. cit., pp. 54–5.

crop may spread east of Kumasi, where there has been some soil exhaustion, especially near the city.

Kumasi is the Ashanti capital and a great political, cultural and commercial centre. When described by Bowdich,[1] it lay on the side of a hill ' insulated by a marsh close to the town northwards and by a narrow stream '. He put the population at 12–15,000. The 1901 census revealed it as reduced to about 3,000 by the Ashanti Wars.

In 1903, two years after the end of the last of those wars, the railway from Sekondi reached Kumasi, where the station was then along the West Nsuben River. By 1911 the population was 18,853 and in 1921 23,694.

In 1923 the railway from Accra was completed and a new central station was built by draining the marsh of the East Nsuben River. Henceforth served by two railways, Kumasi was further assisted in 1928 by the opening of the deep water harbour at Takoradi. Radial roads were also built and these confirmed its commercial supremacy as a cocoa collector, a market for cattle, yams and maize from the north, and as an imports distributor for Ashanti and the north.

By 1931 the population was 35,829, in 1948 53,626, and in 1960 180,600. The city is now fairly clearly separated into separate functional areas, each on a ridge separated by a valley. In the north-east is Menhyia, with the Asantehene's Palace and other notables' houses. In several outer areas there are impressive housing estates. Mainly across the valley occupied by the Accra railway is the Zongo or northerners' town, as well as many schools. West of both these sectors was the swamp now occupied by the lorry park, station and a park. On a hill immediately to the west is old commercial Kumasi, beyond which is the original European military and official quarter around the fort. Offices of technical departments are located here, west of which are barracks, fine hospitals and the old Ashanti Royal Mausoleum at Bantama. Across the West

---

[1] T. E. Bowdich, *Mission from Cape Coast Castle to Ashantee*, 1817, and quoted by R. W. Steel, ' The Towns of Ashanti: A Geographical Study ', *Comptes Rendus du Congrès International de Géographie*, 1949, pp. 81–93. See also K. A. J. Nyarko, ' The Development of Kumasi ', *Bulletin of the Ghana Geographical Association*, Vol. 4, No. 1, 1959, pp. 3–8, and W. Manshard, ' Die Stadt Kumasi ', *Erdkunde*, Band XV, fig. 3, 1961, pp. 161–180. For maps of Kumasi see *Portfolio of Ghana maps* and *Geographical Journal*, 110, p. 162.

Nsuben valley to the south-west is the formerly exclusively European and newer ' political Kumasi '. On the south-east side are many industries, notably timber mills.

The city is growing fast, partly as the result of the advent in 1953 of the College of Technology, now a University, and of industries. Replanning is needed, and the railway goods station is to be removed to the north-east part of the city.

(g) *The Lower Oda and Ofin Basins* (*Denyiasi*) roughly correspond with Bekwai District. Lower Birrimian rocks underlie this region of gentler relief and lesser population density than the Kumasi Plateau, having just over seventy per square mile. Cocoa growing is again important, especially in the north and east, where communications are good, and more than a fifth of the available male population is employed in cocoa cultivation. The rivers were previously significant for alluvial gold.

Bekwai is an old Ashanti political centre and a cocoa and foodstuffs market made possible by numerous roads and the railway.

(h) *The Wasaw Lowlands* may be defined as the country south of the Ofin River, south-east of the Greenstone ridges and behind the Coastal Plain. Like the Lower Oda and Ofin Basins, they have mainly Lower Birrimian rocks, but also some granite west of the lower Ankobra River. Moreover, they have at least 60–70 inches annual rainfall and have the low population density of under ten per square mile. They constitute the main forested area of Ghana. As the timber is cut, so land is being put under oil palm or cocoa, and population will increase in this ' pioneer fringe ' of the Western Region.

(i) *The Birrimian Greenstone Ridges of the Upper Tano.* These hills, formed mainly of volcanic and pyroclastic rocks with igneous intrusions, extend from the Ivory Coast through Enchi, Yenahin and Wiawso. Their narrow, densely forested ridges tend to hamper communications between the east (e.g. Kumasi) and west.

Gold occurs at intervals along the eastern edge and is mined at Bibiani, population 13,000, where about 4,000 men are so employed. Bauxite mines near Awaso and Kanayerebo employ about another thousand but the vast reserves at Yenahin await the second stage of the Volta River Aluminium Scheme.

Meanwhile, the Dunkwa–Awaso railway, opened in 1944, has not only made possible the export of bauxite from Awaso, but has greatly increased timber exploitation and helped the Bibiani gold mines.

(j) *Western Brong-Ahafo* comprises Birrimian and granite country of those parts of Wenchi and Sunyani Districts west of the Voltaian Sandstones. Within north-western Brong-Ahafo the sharp Banda Hills (*k* on Fig. 70), extending north-eastward across the Black Volta into the Northern Region, form a marked sub-region. A second Volta dam has been suggested at Bui.

The whole area is a ' pioneer fringe ' and cocoa cultivation has spread rapidly. About one-fifth of the men and many women are already engaged in it, yet kola, yam and sub-sistence farming, as well as timber cutting, are probably more important.

Population density is only about forty per square mile, and towns such as *Berekum*, 11,000, *Sunyani*, 12,000, and *Wenchi* 11,000 (an old town) are small. As communications improve, these districts should become more productive and more closely settled.

SOUTH-WESTERN AND CENTRAL COAST PLAIN. Under about 200 feet, this extends inland irregularly, up to 20 miles north-west of Accra. The Lower Volta Plains, east of the Akwapim–Togo Mountains, have been considered separately, because of their young deposits and greater aridity.

Continuing from the Ivory Coast and as far as Axim, the coast remains smooth. At first there is a sand-bar backed by the Ehy and Tendo Lagoons, into which the Tano River empties and along which the boundary runs for some 12 miles. Cretaceous–Eocene marine sands, with thin pebble beds and some limestone, lie behind the lagoons up to ten miles inland. As in the Ivory Coast, oil and gas seepages are known and the limestone is to be used for cement making. There is also a chance that coal might be found, as it was in similar series in Nigeria.

Coconuts are grown along the strand; inland, food crops and the oil palm are most important. As the south-western coast has over 80 inches annual rainfall and swamps are frequent, rice is also a very important food crop. Timber cutting is also significant and, as the forest is cut, oil palms are planted. On the drier central coast, however, cattle survive around Cape Coast and Winneba (as well as east of Accra). There are under fifty people per square mile on the south-western coast but on the central coast over 100, because of better communications and trading possibilities.

From Axim to Accra, Pre-Cambrian and Primary rocks alternate frequently. There are many small promontories upon which slaving and trading castles were erected. These sites were good for defence from land attack, and forts could afford protection for ships anchored in a sheltered bay to the leeward. Most points also offered fresh water and were near a river estuary.

Sekondi, was the first railway terminus in Ghana and until 1923 most trade passed through its piers. The town is still an important residential and commercial centre having close connexions with Takoradi.

Takoradi, 4 miles west of Sekondi and with a population in 1960 of 41,000, was Ghana's first deep-water harbour. It took five years to build, in the face of great difficulties. Takoradi was from the first recognised as a superior site to Sekondi, where the first wharf was built and the railway was based for economy.

Takoradi harbour consists of a mile-and-a-quarter-long southern breakwater, which turns north seaward to give a narrow entrance between it and the shorter direct northern breakwater quay. The narrow entrance at the north-east is thus kept clear of silt brought by west to east drift. Takoradi greatly cheapened and simplified the export of cocoa and even more so that of manganese and timber. During the Second World War it was an important reception and assembly point for American aircraft and other supplies. The airport now deals with internal traffic.

In 1953 new quays and docks for timber, a larger main wharf with three new berths, and better loading facilities for bauxite were completed. The 80 feet high Cox's Fort Hill was removed, so levelling 24 acres, clearing $1\frac{3}{4}$ million tons of rock and reclaiming 49 acres from the sea for marshalling yards. The port is now fully mechanised and is dealing with about two million tons of cargo annually.

Takoradi has two cocoa-processing factories; the most modern makes cocoa butter and powder, while the other makes ' neats ' (a half-way stage between cocoa and chocolate) and ' couverture ' (biscuit and cake chocolate). There are also timber, plywood and veneer mills, a factory making paper goods from imported tissues, cigarette, hardware, aluminium sheeting and furniture works, and a boatyard.

Cape Coast, has long been an important centre and three of its four forts survive. The Castle, which was the British capital before Accra, is now used as government offices. Another castle is the lighthouse. Cape Coast is a famous educational centre, and has a university. Lime juice is produced from plantations in the neighbourhood for a famous firm. Around both Cape Coast and Saltpond are quite intensive citrus growing and food cropping areas.

Winneba, like Cape Coast, has many fishermen. For Accra and the coast plain to its east, see pp. 370–7.

ECONOMIC RESOURCES

AGRICULTURE

Cocoa more than any other resource dominates Ghana's economy. Whilst mining, forestry and commerce are partly in the hands of external companies, all cocoa is grown by Africans, mainly on small farms.

The tree was planted unsuccessfully early in the nineteenth century but was properly established by Tetteh Quarshie of Mampong, Akwapim, who in 1879 returned from a Fernando Po plantation with some beans. Some germinated and the young trees grew so well that the Governor visited them. In 1887 there was an official distribution of seedlings raised from seed imported from São Tomé.

Export began in 1891. Thereafter plantings were made with immense rapidity, rubber-tapping and palm fruit collecting being forsaken. The almost empty countryside was re-peopled with small villages and the Accra–Kumasi Railway was built in stages between 1908 and 1923 to facilitate exports. So also were many roads. Ghana became the leading world producer in 1913 and has remained so. Cocoa became the largest export of the country in 1924 and continued so thereafter. Record exports of over 400,000 tons have occurred in recent years, a grand reward for a long and hard struggle against Swollen Shoot and other diseases. This has involved cutting down many millions of trees, replanting as many, spraying, and careful extension work with farmers.

Cocoa still accounts for about two-thirds of Ghana exports by value, partly because, until recently, of the good fortune of high prices. The value of cocoa exports rose fourteen-fold between 1938 and 1964 to over £72 million. Ghana produces over one-third of the world's cocoa, but competition is increasing from, e.g. the Ivory Coast and Cameroon, which have preferential entry to the European Economic Community, and from other countries.

The price obtained for cocoa determines more than anything else the prosperity of Ghana peoples. The non-cocoa areas (except the coastal towns) are almost always poorer than the flourishing cocoa districts. From profits and taxes on cocoa have come many impressive developments.

In Brong-Ahafo over two-fifths, in Ashanti nearly two-fifths, and in the Eastern Region one-quarter of all males 15 years of age and over are growing cocoa. The greatest number engaged and the highest proportion are to be found in Birim.[1] The crop is responsible for making the Kumasi Plateau one of the most thickly populated parts of Ghana.

The physical conditions required for cocoa and the relative place of Ghana production are discussed on pages 109–13. Cocoa has spread west and north-west from the Akwapim Hills, so that it is now found in Ashanti, in Western Brong-Ahafo, and in the Western, Central and Eastern Regions, except near the coast.[2] The first area of maximum production was in the Densu and Birim Basins between Koforidua, Begoro, Kibi, Kade, Oda, Swedru and Nsawam. This area declined to insignificance as the result of endemic Swollen Shoot. Newer and less heavily infected areas are south-west and north-east of Nkawkaw; within a circle around Kumasi limited by

---

[1] *1960 Census of Ghana, Advance Report of Volumes III and IV*, pp. 42 and 46; also P. Hill, *The Gold Coast Cocoa Farmer*, 1956. The distribution of cocoa in Ashanti is shown in *The Geographical Journal*, 110, p. 157.

[2] See map of Agricultural Products in *Portfolio of Ghana maps*.

Bekwai, Abori, Mampong, Konongo; between Berekum, Techiman, Kukoum and Tanoso; and well to the east of Kete Krachi. There are probably 4–5 million acres under cocoa.

Although Swollen Shoot has not been cured, it has been countered, and cocoa remains dominant in the Ghana economy. It is, however, too dominant, and when prices fall the whole economy of the country is imperilled and thousands of people are impoverished. Nor can power from the Volta River Scheme provide equivalent employment.

Minor crops. Kola trees are grown with cocoa in the upper Densu-Birim valleys, where they are largely replacing cocoa, as well as from north-west of Kumasi towards Sunyani. The nuts are sent to the Northern Region, the Upper Volta, Mali and Niger. The official figure for annual exports is about £1 million, but the real one is higher. Coffee is developing in the Volta Region. Coconuts occupy 30,000 acres and provide extra cash for coastal fishermen, especially west of Axim. Palm oil and kernels do the same for farmers between the coast and the cocoa areas. Sugar is developing at Komenda, east of Sekondi, and tobacco in many drier areas. Bananas are being encouraged and rubber is produced on state and ordinary farms by co-operative methods. There are also 3,000 acres of lime orchards near Cape Coast. All these crops together represent only about 3% of the value of cocoa exports.

The usual food crops are grown, yams being more than usually important, especially in north-western Ashanti. Approximate figures for food crops are:[1]

	Production in thousand tons	Area in thousand acres
Plantain . . .	1,300	314
Cocoyam . . .	500	199
Cassava . . .	1,250	400
Yams	1,200	422
Maize	180	496
Millet . . .	100	432
Guinea Corn . .	80	332
Cowpeas and Pulses .	30	39
Groundnuts . . .	50	166
Rice	41	107

[1] See also H. P. White, ' Provisional Agricultural Regions of Ghana ', *The Journal of Tropical Geography*, Vol. 11, 1958, pp. 90–9.

LIVESTOCK[1]

About two-thirds of Ghana's relatively high consumption of meat (see Chapter 7) is imported from Mali and Niger. The vast majority of cattle pass through Mogonori and Pusiga but substantial and increasing numbers enter near Navrongo. There is a meat-packing plant nearby at Zuarungu, but many animals are driven south along well-marked but badly equipped routes to converge on Prang for Kumasi and Accra. The condition of the cattle is much impaired, and urgent provision is required of pastures, kraals and water, especially as there is increasing competing demand in the Ivory Coast for cattle.

Ghana herds number 528,000 (1966), a number which could be increased if the measures suggested were taken. Although most are in the Northern Region, some are kept around Cape Coast, Winneba, and especially in the Lower Volta Plains.

FISHING[2]

Fanti fishermen are especially adept and are often found far away from Ghana. In 1960 there were 48,000 fishermen along the coast, and in most coastal towns fishing is the principal occupation. Many women are fish-sellers and fish is an important item of internal commerce. Efforts are being made to improve catches (now about 85,000 tons annually) by using power-driven canoes. Some twenty large refrigerated trawlers, capable of staying at sea for several weeks, as well as over a dozen smaller trawlers, are also coming into service. Their cost and the price of fish landed have been high.

FORESTRY[3]

As in the neighbouring Ivory Coast and in Nigeria, forestry is an important part of the economy. The productive and

[1] See map of Cattle Areas and Routes in *Atlas of the Gold Coast*, p. 15. Also W. C. Miller, *Report on Animal Health and Husbandry in the Gold Coast Colony*, 1947, and J. L. Stewart, *The Cattle of the Gold Coast*, 1937.

[2] See T. E. Hilton, ' The Coastal Fisheries of Ghana ', *Bulletin of the Ghana Geographical Association*, July 1964, pp. 34–51; ' Ghana Fisheries ', *The Economist*, 25 February 1967, pp. 742–3.

[3] See *Portfolio of Ghana maps*, Maps 3 and 8.

potentially useful forest area is approximately 9,425 square miles.

This includes 5,855 square miles of forest reserves permanently dedicated to forestry, of which under one-half are capable of timber production. These reserves are sufficient to protect water supplies, maintain a climate favourable to the growth of the principal agricultural crops, control erosion and to provide a permanent supply of timber, with a surplus for export. With an expanding population, however, further reservation is desirable, if Ghana wishes to continue as a large exporter.

Some of the timber output comes, however, from the unreserved forest, which is being cut by farmers at the rate of about 700 square miles a year. As the timber will, in any case, be removed by them, the aim is to cut and market it in a systematic way before it is ruined. Most felling is done where farming needs will require the forested area within the next ten years. Most timber concessions are for three years per plot of three square miles, although concessions of up to 32 years are granted over areas reaching 40 square miles.

Rain forest is largely confined to Ashanti, south-western Brong-Ahafo, the Western and Eastern Regions. It is found on the western boundary as far north as 7° 30′ N. and extends over the Ashanti–Kwahu Uplands and into the Togo Mountains, wherever the rainfall is at least 50 inches. There are more used but less valuable trees in the drier parts of the forest than in the wetter ones.[1] Timber exploitation is mainly in the thinly peopled parts of Ashanti, Brong-Ahafo and the Western Region, and there is also a large area to the west of the Cape Coast–Fosu road.

Woods from the wetter forests include various mahoganies (*Khaya ivorensis* and *anthotheca*), Makore (*Mimusops heckelii*), Scented Guarea (*G. cedrata*), African Walnut (*Lovoa trichilioides*) and Sapele (*Entandophragma cyclindricum*). Attractive veneers may also be obtained from these. A very heavy evergreen tree is Dahoma (*Piptadeniastrum africanum*). Among semi-deciduous trees from the drier forest are Odum—better known by its

---

[1] 'Timber in West Africa', *Statistical and Economic Review of the United Africa Co. Ltd.*, September 1952, p. 11. See also *Gold Coast Timbers*, Gold Coast Forestry Department, and *Timber Industry—Report of a Fact Finding Committee*, Government Printer, Accra, 1951.

Nigerian name of Iroko (*Chlorophora excelsa*), a superb wood of many uses. As it is the traditional building timber of Ghana, its export is prohibited. Wawa (*Triplochiton scleroxylon*) is soft and relatively light; it is used in West Africa for canoes and is exported for commercial plywood and corestock for cheap furniture, shuttering and box-making. Kokorodua (*Afrormosia elata*), Utile (*Entandrophragma utile*), Mansonia (*M. altissima*), Albizzia (*A. ferruginea*) and Danta (*Nesogordonia papaverifera*) are others, the latter being an excellent wood for axe and tool handles.

Unlike Nigeria, most Ghana logs must be moved at high cost on roads (often specially constructed) and by rail. Important railing points are Nkawkaw, Konongo, Ejisu, Kumasi, Bekwai, Dunkwa, Awaso, Prestea, Foso and Oda. Timber is shipped exclusively at Takoradi, where new timber wharves were opened in 1953.

The expansion in volume and value, variety of timber marketed, and in its processing is one of the most remarkable features of Ghana, as the following figures illustrate:

Exports	1938	1965
Logs in cubic feet	667,000	10,301,000
Logs by value	£69,000	£7,953,000
Sawn Timber (cu. ft.) . . .	39,000	8,170,000
Sawn Timber by value . . .	£7,800	£6,859,000
Veneers (cu. ft.)	Nil	429,000
Veneers by value	Nil	£864,500

Substantial quantities have also been sold in Ghana.

In early years 95–99% of timber exports were of mahogany; that wood now represents a very small part of exports. Other popular woods are wawa, makore, sapele and utile; much more may yet be achieved in diversifying demand and so using forests more fully.

Lastly, there is the vast increase in local processing. Previously, almost all exports were in log form and until 1945 there were only six small saw mills. There are now some fifty saw mills whose capacity is vastly greater. Sawn timber output (as distinct from export) has exceeded log export since 1952, and over one-half the sawn timber is exported. Local manufacture of veneers started in 1950.

Timber shipments have fallen by well over one-half since 1960 because of Ivory Coast competition, and political and economic difficulties in Ghana. Total annual timber exports are now valued at about £11 million, or about 10% of all Ghana exports. Most go to the U.S.A. and Europe; much capital is invested in the industry, which provides employment for some 10,000 men, as well as many more contractors and sub-contractors.

MINING[1]

Although cocoa is by far the greatest present resource of Ghana, it was gold which gave the first name to the country and lured Europeans there. Yet at the beginning of the present century the average annual value of minerals won was only £38,000. In 1914 it was £1,744,500 but in 1928–9 only £710,000. In 1965 it reached £27 million. The total value of mineral production from 1880 to March 31st, 1945 was approximately £120 million, of which gold accounted for £90 million.[2]

As with cocoa cultivation, all major minerals occur in the Western Region and Ashanti. Indeed, almost all minerals are obtained from within a radius of 60 miles from Dunkwa, on the Takoradi–Kumasi railway. This was one of the world's richest concentrations of minerals, and around the Obuasi mine is probably the richest square mile in the world.

Factors which have helped this remarkable concentration are:

(a) The wide and deep geosyncline of slightly metamorphosed Birrimian and Tarkwaian rocks in the Western Region and Ashanti.

(b) Deep-seated faults and shear zones formed during the folding of the Birrimian rocks, and during their intrusion by granitic rocks.

(c) The intense pre-Tarkwaian and Tertiary to Recent erosions of the Birrimian. The first erosion probably concentrated gold in the Tarkwaian banket reef and

[1] See map of ' Mineral Deposits ' in *Portfolio of Ghana maps*.
[2] N. R. Junner, ' Progress in Geological Investigations and Mineral Developments in the Gold Coast ', *Bulletin of the Imperial Institute*, 1946, pp. 44–62 (also *Gold Coast Geological Survey Bulletin No. 16*).

diamonds in the Tarkwaian basal conglomerates, while it enriched the manganese oxide concentrations. The latter erosions also enriched bauxite and oxidised auriferous ores.

Several Ghana ore deposits were exceptionally large and rich. Thus the Obuasi mine of the Ashanti Goldfields Corporation has the best grade ore of any large gold mine in the world. In fifty-six years up to 1953 it produced over $6\frac{1}{2}$-million ounces of gold from about the same number of tons of ore, or over one-third of all gold produced in Ghana.

Then there is a prodigious concentration of alluvial diamonds near Akwatia and Atiankama (Birim Valley), which has yielded more than 21 million carats, over 4 million carats of which have come from an area of less than a quarter of a square mile at Esuboni.

Again, there are substantial amounts of high-grade manganese ore at Nsuta, alongside the pre-existing railway line. The single open-cast mine there is the largest individual producer of high-grade manganese ore in the world and probably the largest producer of crystalline manganese dioxide (for batteries). Lastly, the vast and concentrated bauxite deposits at Kibi and Yenahin may be used in the second phase of the Volta River Project.

Mining employs many men and is an attractor of labour from northern Ghana, Upper Volta, Mali and Niger. There are some 23,000 miners employed by companies or the state, of whom about 17,000 are employed in gold-mines, 3,600 in diamond workings, 2,000 in manganese and 450 in bauxite. Previously thousands more panned diamonds; they now work for the State Diamond Mining Corporation. There are some 700 non-Africans in mining, of whom about 450 are in gold workings. The gold-mines employ nearly forty Africans to each European, whereas in similar South African mines the proportion is only ten to one.

Gold.[1] It is probable that the Mali, Ghana and Songhaï

---

[1] See for further information, *Gold from the Gold Coast*, The Gold Coast Chamber of Mines, 1950; G. W. Eaton Turner, *A Short History of Ashanti Goldfields Corporation Ltd., 1897–1947*; N. R. Junner, op. cit.; N. R. Junner, ' Gold in the Gold Coast ', *Gold Coast Geological Survey Memoir No. 4*, 1935; T. Hirst, ' The Geology of the Konongo Gold Belt and Surrounding Country ', *Gold Coast Geological Survey*

Empires obtained gold from what is now modern Ghana and traded it overland to North Africa and Europe. Portuguese, Spanish and Italian coins may have been made from West African gold. The first European to be recorded as getting it direct was a Portuguese, who first traded in gold dust at the mouth of the Pra River in 1471; the first Englishman did so in 1552–3. The slave trade later became more profitable than that in gold, yet in the early part of the eighteenth century annual shipments of gold to Europe in peace years were worth about £250,000. Meanwhile, gold was highly appreciated among the Ashanti and Baoulé (Ivory Coast) peoples.

British soldiers returning home after the Ashanti War of 1873 made known the occurrence of gold. Due largely to the initiative of Pierre Bonnat, a French trader and explorer, large scale methods were begun in 1878. Exclusive concessions caused the decline of the very narrow shaft or pit mining by Africans, such as is still carried on in the Siguiri area of Guinea (pp. 294–5).

The railway from Sekondi reached Tarkwa in 1901 and Obuasi in 1902. Publicised comparisons with the Johannesburg Rand caused a bubble of speculation, some 400 companies being formed in 1901. None of them survives. There are now only one company and a few state mines exporting annually 700,000 ounces of gold worth about £8½ million. The country produces 2% of the world's gold.

Gold occurrences and workings may be classified as follows:

(a) *Ores in Birrimian Rocks.* About 70% of the gold worked since the advent of European companies has come from quartz reef lodes and sheared rocks, as mined at Obuasi, Prestea, Bibiani, Bondaye and Konongo. The lodes are found mainly in 2–4 feet wide veins of quartz, deposited in fissures on the flanks of synclinal depressions. These depressions occur

Bulletin No. 14, 1942 (also *Bulletin of Imperial Institute*, 1942); T. Hirst and N. R. Junner, 'Reports on the Bibiani Goldfield', *Gold Coast Geological Survey Memoir No. 9*, 1946; N. R. Junner, 'The Geology of the Obuasi Goldfield', *Gold Coast Geological Survey Memoir No. 2*, 1932; N. R. Junner, T. Hirst and H. Service, 'The Tarkwa Goldfield', *Gold Coast Geological Survey Memoir No. 6*, 1942; W. G. G. Cooper, 'The Geology of the Prestea Goldfield', *Gold Coast Geological Survey Memoir No. 3*, 1934. Also the following maps: 1 : 500,000 Geological Map of the Gold Coast (Southern Sheet); 1 : 25,000 Geological Map of the Tarkwa Goldfield and the Nsuta Manganese Deposits and 1 : 25,000 Tarkwa Goldfield Area showing Concessions.

especially near the boundary between the Upper and Lower Birrimian, and between the Upper Birrimian and Tarkwaian on the western edge of the Tarkwaian geosyncline. Occurrences are also close to intrusions of younger (Dixcove) granite and porphyry. The largest ore bodies are in deep-seated shear zones, faults or fractures.

Birrimian gold was extensively worked along outcrops by Africans, e.g. at Bibiani, where, in 1891, there were some 3,000 feet of workings with some pits up to 100 feet deep. Much the same was true at Obuasi in 1895 when it was visited by E. A. Cade and he obtained his rich 100-square-mile concession which led to the establishment of the Ashanti Goldfields Corporation.

(b) *Ores in Tarkwaian Rocks*. Banket or conglomerate reef lodes have been mined at Tamsu, Abbontiakoon and Fanti, all near Tarkwa. Small amounts have also been obtained at Ntronang, south-east of Kumasi. Nearly 30% of gold obtained since the advent of European companies has come from the Tarkwaian series. They were also previously worked by Africans, especially the surface oxidised ores.

(c) *Placer deposits*. These have been formed by past or present rivers draining gold-bearing areas, but workings are confined to present-day rivers. There has been extensive exploitation of gravels and sands on valley flats and low terraces of the Ofin, Pra, Ankobra, Tano, Fura and Birim rivers in the past by Africans and, after 1897, by European companies which have produced about 400,000 ounces or around 2% of the total. Most is obtained from the Ofin, Jimi and Ankobra rivers. Gold content is very low, being only about $2\frac{1}{2}$ grains per cubic yard, and the production small.

(d) *Ores in acid igneous rocks intrusive to the Birrimian*. These were extensively worked by Africans, but have never been worked by Europeans.

Most mining is now done from shafts of up to 3,700 feet in depth. But low-grade, weathered (oxidised) Birrimian and Tarkwaian ores, occurring near the surface, have been worked in the past by large draglines, e.g. at Bogoso and at Pepe. Placer, or alluvial deposits, were worked by dredges. Africans now do only insignificant panning. This is partly because of the concession system, but mainly because of the vast capital needed.

About 15 million ounces were produced by Africans before the advent of European mining, and over 30 million ounces have been produced by European companies. Formerly gold was a major export, but it declined relatively during the First and Second World Wars. There was a recovery from 1931 to 1941 and again in the fifties, but there has been a decline since then because of labour difficulties and high costs. Many mines have remained closed and there has been much concentration in capital and mining. Gold now represents between 8% and 10% of Ghana exports.

Manganese.[1] Occurrences of manganese ore are widespread, but those of economic importance are large deposits in the Upper Birrimian at Nsuta, 39 miles by railway from Takoradi, smaller ones at Hotopo, 12 miles from Takoradi on the Sekondi–Axim road, and at Yakau near Dixcove.

The Nsuta ores form five prominent hills on two parallel ridges $2\frac{1}{4}$ miles long, running in a north or north-north-east direction and up to 400 feet above surrounding streams. There is a capping of detrital ore over large lenticular high-grade ore bodies. Together they are about 100 feet thick.

These ores were discovered in 1914 and mining began two years later. Workings are of the simpler, though highly mechanised, opencast type. The ore is cut away in terraces on the hill by power shovels and loaded into railway trucks.

Most of the ore is used in steel making and some in paint, varnish and dry battery manufacture. The mine is one of the largest in the world, and Ghana is normally the seventh world producer after the U.S.S.R., India, South Africa and Brazil. Manganese exports are below those of gold in value, being about 5% of total exports.

Diamonds.[2] Ghana diamonds are probably derived from Upper Birrimian rocks, are alluvial in occurrence and mostly of the smallest industrial type. They were discovered in the

[1] See also H. Service, ' The Geology of the Nsuta Manganese Ore Deposits ', *Gold Coast Geological Survey Memoir No. 5,* 1943, and 1 : 25,000 Geological Map cited above under Gold (footnote).

[2] See also N. R. Junner, ' The Diamond Deposits of the Gold Coast ', *Gold Coast Geological Survey Bulletin No. 12,* 1943.

Birim Valley in 1919 and in the Bonsa Valley (south-west of Tarkwa) in 1922.

In the former area they are worked by three European companies and a state corporation at Akwatia, Oda and Kade. The diamonds, which occur profusely in terraces and in the very shallow stream beds, are concealed by 2–20 feet of silt overburden. The companies excavate, wash and screen mechanically, and the diamonds are then collected on greased tables.

The Bonsa deposits, worked by Africans, are much more restricted in area and thickness, and were not worked until 1933. The diggers work singly or in family groups, washing the gravel in calabashes. Unfortunately, about a quarter of the diamonds in the gravel are lost and 20–30% of the gravel is never treated because of haphazard digging.

The proportion of diamonds won by African diggers is now small. The number of persons engaged in the African industry amounted to some 8,000 at the end of 1964. The average income per licensed digger in 1954 was over £6,300, but the average tributing labourer, who earned on every carat which he found, got about £125 per annum. Other members of his family were earning, but the conditions of work are exceedingly bad.

Ghana is generally the third world producer by quantity, but produces only 5–10% of world output by value. Diamonds represent about 8% of Ghana exports.

Bauxite.[1] The largest deposits are at Yenahin, 40 miles west of Kumasi. Smaller but still very significant ones are at Atwiredu—near Kibi and the Eastern Railway, at Awaso, 55 miles north-west of Dunkwa, and at Mount Ejuanema on the Mampong Scarp above Nkawkaw. There are some 200 million tons at Yenahin on the flat tops of high hills over a distance of some 20 miles, the bauxite being 20–50 feet thick. The Atwiredu and Awaso deposits, with 30 million tons each, are up to 70 feet thick; those at Mount Ejuanema are about 20 feet thick and contain about 4 million tons. The first three deposits rest on Birrimian rocks and the last on Voltaian Sandstones.

[1] See also W. G. G. Cooper, ' The Bauxite Deposits of the Gold Coast ', *Gold Coast Geological Survey Bulletin No. 7*, 1936.

The last two deposits were first worked in 1942. To work the Awaso deposit the Dunkwa–Awaso branch railway was hurriedly built, with a road from it up Kanayerebo Hill. Likewise, a road was built up the exceedingly steep scarp from Nkawkaw, on the Accra–Kumasi Railway, to Mount Ejuanema. Until the second phase of the Volta River Project is reached, only the Awaso deposit is being exploited and the bauxite is shipped through Takoradi.

THE VOLTA RIVER PROJECT [1]

The 370 feet high dam, begun in 1961 at Akosombo, in the Volta gorge of the Akwapim–Togo Mountains, 70 miles from the sea, was completed in 1965. It has created a 200 mile long lake, flooding over 3·5% (3,250 square miles) of the country, fortunately land of little use, and creating the largest artificial lake in the world. Generating capacity will ultimately be 768,000 kw. By far the greater part will be used to make up to 210,000 tons of aluminium annually, and Ghana will then become the third or fourth world producer. Power is also available for the existing gold and other mines (so lowering their costs and improving their outputs), and for coastal, mining and other towns. Irrigation water might be made available to the Lower Volta Plains.

Power became available in 1965, and full aluminium capacity will be reached within twenty years of opening the smelter. At first alumina will be imported, but later local bauxite will be used, when new railways will be necessary from Yenahin to Kumasi. Initial expenditure will be quite £170 million and about £300 million for the full scheme, the money being loaned by the Ghana and other governments, banks and aluminium companies.

This is the greatest project West Africa has ever known. The giant lake has changed some of the landscape of the country, provides a great navigable waterway, water supplies and fresh water fisheries. It may even make very local rainfall more reliable and uniform. It will lead to increased urban concentration and encourage industrial skills. Construction was

[1] See also D. Hilling, 'The Volta River Project', *The Geographical Magazine*, March 1965, pp. 830–41.

achieved in less than the time envisaged and did not create labour shortages.   However, re-settlement of 78,000 people had to be done hurriedly and there are still some problems (see

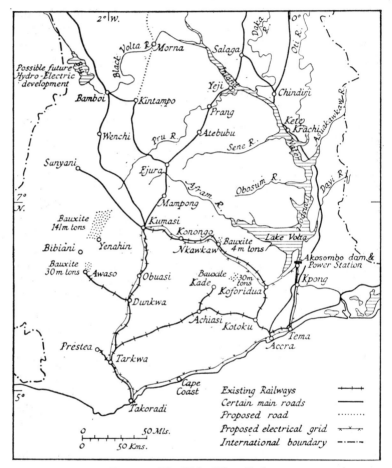

FIG. 72.—The Volta River Project.

pp. 382–3).   Widespread anti-malarial measures round the huge lake have been necessary.   There is also the possibility of danger to the dam and power-station at Akosombo, and to the smelter and port at Tema from earthquakes.

The scheme will increase the taxable capacity of the country to offset the service of the necessary new loans, and broaden its economy. The project will be of immense consequence to Ghana's standard of living, to world aluminium output, and to the Sterling Area. The implementation of the project owes much to the persistence of Dr. Nkrumah, and to the prior construction nearby of Ghana's second deep water harbour at Tema.

COMMUNICATIONS

The original impetus to railway construction came from the gold mining companies at Tarkwa, to which the railway from Sekondi was opened in 1901. By offering a financial guarantee the Ashanti Goldfields Corporation secured the extension of the railway to Obuasi in 1902 and it was completed to Kumasi in 1903 for political reasons. Gold mining companies were also the cause of the construction of the Tarkwa–Prestea branch opened in 1912 and urgent needs of bauxite for aluminium caused that from Dunkwa to Awaso to be built in 1943–4.

If gold was the main reason for building railways in the west, it was cocoa in the east, where the line from Accra was built in easy stages from 1909 and completed to Kumasi in 1923 after war delays.

The Central line, opened in 1928 from Huni Valley to Kade, was for long a liability, as it runs into an area well served by more direct roads. A branch from Achiasi to Kotoku (on the Accra–Kumasi line), opened in 1956, provides a direct line from Takoradi to Accra. A shorter rail route than the devious one through Kumasi was long needed, but the newer line competes with an even shorter road. After the contractors' needs at Tema harbour have passed and now that Tema serves the eastern Ghana coast, it is difficult to envisage much rail or road traffic passing between Accra and Takoradi. A branch—the first from the Accra–Kumasi line—was opened in 1954 from Achimota to Tema. Other branches may be built in the 'seventies to open bauxite deposits for Phase Two of the Volta River Project.

Kumasi, the inland terminus, is only 168 miles from the coast and beyond lie northern Ashanti and over half of Ghana. A rail extension beyond Kumasi has been much discussed, but it is difficult to see how it could develop traffic that could not be more economically developed by road transport. Moreover the Volta River Project will provide an excellent waterway as far as Yeji for very cheap all-season bulk transport for non-perishable goods. Finally, the Abidjan (Ivory Coast) to Ouagadougou (Upper Volta) line, completed in 1954, is a competitor for traffic to and from the Upper Volta. Exports from and imports to the far north of Ghana might, by improved trans-frontier feeder roads, use more economically the Ouagadougou–Abidjan line.

Without the existing railways mining could never have been developed to its present scale, nor could cocoa cultivation until about the mid-twenties when lorry competition appeared. On the whole, the relatively short railway lines have been confined to the most productive areas of the country.

The railway has long been used to capacity for goods traffic, especially timber-haulage. Consequently, the track was doubled from Takoradi to Tarkwa in 1953. Despite intense lorry competition for cocoa and passenger traffic, and from air services for passengers between Accra and Kumasi, the railway carries more goods and passengers than all the ex-French West African lines and about two-thirds that of the much larger Nigerian system.

Road competition became acute in the 'thirties, and until the Second World War it was legally restricted in certain areas. There is a fairly good network of roads in the well populated areas of southern Ghana; and one of the outstanding characteristics of the country has been the very extensive African and Lebanese ownership and operation of lorries. One African company operates services to Khartoum (3,400 miles) en route for Mecca, and to Lagos.

Air services between Accra, Takoradi, Kumasi and Tamale provide over thirty flights a week. The country is also served by Nigerian and other West African services and by British, American, Italian and other inter-continental services through Accra.

(For Ports see under Lower Volta Plains and the Southwestern and Central Coastal Plain. Also H. P. White, ' Port Developments in the Gold Coast ', *Scottish Geographical Magazine*, 71, pp. 170–3.)

Conclusion

Until the end of the Second World War, prices for cocoa were low and, in consequence, the country had limited funds for development. After the war, however, high world prices prevailed for cocoa, although a lower price was paid to farmers so that a support fund might be created for use in periods of low prices. However, these came much later and were of shorter duration than many people had feared, so that vast sums accumulated, and some of these were employed in general economic and social development. This was also fostered by Colonial Development and Welfare Fund grants and loans, by grants from international bodies, and by a buoyant national revenue which could be used to finance many useful projects. Consequently, the country developed rapidly economically, as well as making headlong progress politically.

Before the Gold Coast became independent, a plebiscite was held in the then United Kingdom Trusteeship of Togoland to decide upon its future. Out of the 160,587 votes cast, 93,095 were for union with the Gold Coast and 67,492 were for continuation under United Kingdom Trusteeship. Union was favoured by peoples in the north and centre who were akin to those in the Gold Coast; but in the south, the divided Ewe (see pages 417–19) provided most of the opposition, particularly in the Kpandu and Ho Districts, the most southerly of the former Trusteeship, where over two-thirds of the votes were for continuing Trusteeship. The Gold Coast became independent on March 6 1957 as Ghana, and incorporated all the former United Kingdom Trusteeship of Togoland of 13,041 square miles and 382,768 people as an integral part of the country, which then totalled 91,843 square miles and 4,118,450 people. Significantly, it was in the Kpandu and Ho Districts that some dissatisfaction was shown.

The economic integration of Togoland with Ghana has been facilitated by the fine Adomi bridge over the Volta River, so speeding up travel not only between Accra and Ho, but also providing a third through road to the north. Cocoa and yams are the chief sources of wealth in the former Trusteeship. Mineral deposits of potential importance are iron ores in the Shiene Hills between Shiene and Kubalem, about 40 miles south-east of Yendi. Similar deposits lie 22 miles to the north-east, where are large deposits of siliceous hæmatitic replacements of shales and tillite, variable in quality and remote from cheap transport, but these might be worth working now that the Volta River Project provides a cheap means of transport by water, and of electric power for smelting.

The Volta River Project has been described as the greatest hope of the country. Its implementation was delayed by long investigations during which time other projects at Edea (Cameroon) and in Canada got under way. At the same time, the market for aluminium became less buoyant, so that the aluminium companies feared excess capacity if they went forward in Ghana. The creation of the Ghana–Guinea Union, and the completion of the alumina plant at Fria in the latter country, opened up the possibility of co-operation by Ghana using its power to convert Guinea alumina into aluminium. Furthermore, these two countries produce rather dissimilar exports and tend to sell in different markets, so that they do not compete seriously against each other. On the other hand, the economic development of this Union (later joined by Mali) has been abortive in view of the different currency and tariff zones to which its members belong.

Independence has encouraged many new economic developments, partly as the natural consequence of the new feelings of pride and initiative which freedom has encouraged. Thus, many fine buildings have been erected in Accra and, indeed, in other major towns such as Kumasi, while the Black Star Shipping Line and Ghana Airways are other evidences of the same thing.

More important still are the great educational, industrial and agricultural developments which are transforming the country socially and economically. Thus at Tema, Ghana's large new port in the east, 800 acres have been set aside for a model industrial estate. Industries already established include a chemical one making an insecticide used in spraying cocoa trees against capsid pests, one manufacturing aluminium corrugated sheets, a motor assembly works, a firm making storage tanks and pipes from imported flat metal sheets, another making sandcrete blocks, a fish freezing plant, and others.

Industrial development is also proceeding apace in the older towns such as Accra, Kumasi, Takoradi and Kade.

Some experts have maintained that agricultural development is the surest path to proper industrial growth. On the one hand, it is cocoa that has made Ghana economically, and, on the other hand, there are grave dangers in over-reliance upon the production entirely for export of a semi-luxury commodity like cocoa, subject as it also is to attacks by many vigorous pests. Consequently, it is welcome that timber and its products have become more important, and efforts are being directed to developing rubber and banana exports, to growing more cereals and raising better cattle in northern Ghana, to irrigation in the lower Volta River plain and, by the improvement of methods and the application of fertilisers, to raising the output of all crops.

Apart from cocoa, most other revenue comes from four minerals. There is a far more varied mineral production than in any other West African country. The Volta River Project will support a local industry of world importance. Aluminium production may provide some re-insurance against decline in cocoa and timber exports, but it can hardly compare with cocoa in putting so much money into so many pockets.

BIBLIOGRAPHY

See references cited in footnotes. Also:

Bulletin of the Ghana Geographical Association.
E. A. BOATENG, *A Geography of Ghana,* 1965.
T. E. HILTON, *Ghana Population Atlas,* 1960.
S. LA ANYANE, *Ghana Agriculture,* 1963.
WALTHER MANSHARD, *Die geographischen Grundlagen der Wirtschaft Ghanas,* Wiesbaden, 1961.
JANE ROUCH, *Ghana,* Lausanne, 1964.
W. J. VARLEY and H. P. WHITE, *The Geography of Ghana,* 1958.
J. B. WILLS, *Agriculture and Land Use in Ghana,* 1962.
Economic Survey, Central Bureau of Statistics, Accra. Annual.

MAPS

Portfolio of Ghana maps. Survey Department, 1961.

Topographic:
  1 : 50,000 Directorate of Overseas Surveys.
  1 : 62,500 Ghana Survey Department.
  1 : 125,000 and 1 : 250,000 Ghana Survey Department.

1 : 400,000 General Wall Map.   Ghana Survey Department.

1 : 500,000 Road Map.   Also Forest Reserves Map.   Ghana Survey Department.

1 : 750,000 Historical Map.   Colony and Ashanti since A.D. 1400. Ghana Survey Department.

1 : 1 Million Layer Coloured General Map.   Ghana Survey Department.

1 : 1 Million Native States.   Ghana Survey Department.

Special and Cadastral:

1 : 5,000 Volta Delta and Volta Dam Site.   Directorate of Colonial Surveys.

1 : 1,250, 1 : 6,250 and 1 : 12,500 Town Plans.   Ghana Survey Department.

1 : 1 Million Geological Map.   Ghana Geological Survey.   See also footnotes pp. 403–8.

80. Christiansborg Castle built 1657 for the overseas slave trade and, until 1850, the Danish H.Q., is now Government House. Behind the first promontory, at the other end of the bay, lies Ussher Fort, built about 1650 by the Dutch. Near the lighthouse and breakwater is James Fort built by the English in 1673. Between these last two forts is the old town. In the distance are the seaward extremities of the Akwapim Hills.

GHANA

81. Takoradi Harbour. Manganese and bauxite are loaded on the right of the pier, passengers and general cargo on the left. Timber wharves are on the left inner side of the harbour.

82. The Volta Dam in the gorge of the Akwapim-Togo Mountains.

83. Obuasi, the major gol
mining centre.

84. A compressed air drill making a hole for an explosive charge to loosen hard gold-bearing rock

85. Haulage in a gold min

86. After hard gold-bearing rock has been crushed to fine gravel, it is washed to separate gold and gold-bearing gravels from waste. Both the former are then mixed with water and run over corduroy mats, which collect free gold grains (*left*). Remaining gold-bearing gravels must be treated with cyanide, which combines with the gold, and the two are later separated.

87. Nsuta Manganese Quarry

Chapter 24

TOGO[1]

Diversity in Miniature

With an area of only 22,002 square miles and a population (1966) of 1,680,000, Togo is the larger and eastern part of former German Togo, and includes all the coastline, the capital and railways of that colony.

The boundary between the British Gold Coast and former German Togo, agreed in 1904, divided the Dagomba people of the north between the British and the Germans. The Dagomba capital at Yendi became German; to govern his divided people, the paramount chief delegated authority in the Gold Coast to a sub-chief at Savelugu. On the other hand, in the south, the same boundary put four-fifths of the Ewe people under German administration, only about one-fifth of them being in the Gold Coast, east of the Volta River.

After the First World War, the effect of the present boundary was to reunite the Mamprusi, Dagomba and Gonja but to divide the Ewe completely, so that some three-fifths were under British administration and two-fifths under French. The Ewe protested, but only under the Trusteeships were they able to make oral representations. Thus their division has received most publicity since 1946.

The problem arose not merely from division by a boundary but also from the contrasting principles and practice of British and French rule. Thus, the British encouraged the use of the Ewe language; the French favoured French. The British developed elected local government in villages and districts, but the French very little. Togoland under United Kingdom

---

[1] M. Gérard Brasseur, formerly Director of the Institut Français d'Afrique Noire at Bamako, and once stationed at Lomé, and Mr. E. A. Smith, British Chargé d'Affaires at Lomé 1964, have given me most useful criticism of this chapter.

Trusteeship had African representatives in the Gold Coast Legislative Assembly and an African Minister in the all-African Executive Council, with its African Prime Minister. Togo under French Trusteeship had an Assembly only

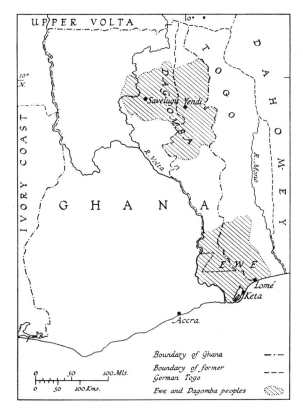

FIG. 73.—Past and present boundaries of Togo and the distribution of the Ewe and Dagomba peoples.

from 1946, and its powers, compared with that of the then Gold Coast, were small.

In 1956 universal suffrage was introduced, the Assembly was given legislative powers on all internal matters, and a ministerial system was established. A referendum taken in October showed wide support for these changes, for the termination of the Trusteeship, and for its replacement by an autonomous republic, which was proclaimed shortly after. It became independent in 1960; but the Ewe will not be reunited unless Togo decides to join or federate with Ghana.[1]

History

Little is known of the origins of the people of the centre and north, but the Ewe in the south came to their present home from the Niger Valley, under pressure from the east, five or six hundred years ago.

The Portuguese visited this coast in the fifteenth and sixteenth centuries, from their headquarters at Elmina, and from its successor at Ouidah. They probably shipped slaves locally from Grand Popo, Petit Popo (Anécho) and Porto-Ségouro, whose names are somewhat Portuguese. They introduced coconuts, cassava, maize and other crops to provision the slave ships, and the intensive cultivation of these along this coast and in Dahomey is partly their legacy.[2]

The French established a trading-post at Anécho in 1626 and in 1787, but on both occasions it was short lived.

German contacts probably originated with the arrival of traders at Grand Popo in 1856, but from 1865 to 1883 the French were again active politically and commercially at Anécho and at Porto-Ségouro. In 1880 more German traders arrived and acute rivalry ensued. Finally, in 1884 a German Protectorate was declared along the coast, so creating the first German territory in Africa. Dr. Nachtigal had made a treaty with the chief of Togo Village, on the north side of a lagoon behind Porto-Ségouro, east of Lomé. The village name, an Ewe word meaning ' behind the sea ', was taken for that of the whole territory. The Germans had their first capital at Baguida, then at Zébé, and in and after 1897 at Lomé.

---

[1] On the subject of the divided Ewe see the present author's *Modern Colonization*, 1951, pp. 118–21 and for a study of the Ewe see Madeline Manoukian, *The Ewe-speaking People of Togoland and the Gold Coast*, International African Institute, 1952.

[2] For cassava cultivation see W. O. Jones, ' A Map of Manioc in Africa ', *Geographical Review*, 1953, pp. 112–14.

German Togo was conquered in August 1914 by French and British units from neighbouring territories. The country was divided, so that the British held all the coast and railways, and the French the interior.

In 1919 the situation was reversed. The Mandates were made definitive in 1922 and became Trusteeships in 1946, the British one being terminated in 1957 when Ghana achieved independence, and the French one in 1960 when the Republic of Togo attained it.

CLIMATE

The coastal belt of Togo has the exceptionally dry Accra–Togo Dry Coastal climate. Lomé averages 29·1 inches annual rainfall, with an average of sixty rain days. Anécho has two inches more per annum but only forty-eight rain days, and Grand Popo, just inside Dahomey, has 32 inches. Although relative humidity is high, Lomé and Anécho have by far the lowest rainfall and fewest days of rain in all Togo. Baobab trees are common up to about 6 miles inland.

Between Tsévié and Nuatja, on the central railway, and to the west and east, the Semi-Seasonal Equatorial climate prevails, in which there is rather more rain than on the coast. Thus Tsévié has 39·8 inches on seventy-three days and Nuatja 42·4 inches on eighty-one days.

Only in and near the Togo Mountains are conditions found which are typically Equatorial. Palimé has 59·2 inches on 100 rain days. Klouto, nearby, with 69·5 inches on 199 days, is probably the wettest settlement in Togo.

Atakpamé lies in the Seasonal Equatorial climatic zone, near where the Equatorial climate makes its most north-easterly projection inland.

All Togo north of a line south of Blitta has the Southern Savannah climate. At first there is rather heavier rainfall than for comparable stations in Ghana. Thus Blitta has 51·7 inches on eighty-four days, Sokodé 53·4 inches on ninety-

eight days, and Bassari 50·7 inches on 102 days. In the far
north, however, Sansanné Mango with 41·1 inches on seventy-
three days and Dapango with 42·7 inches on sixty-nine days
are rather drier than similar places to the west.

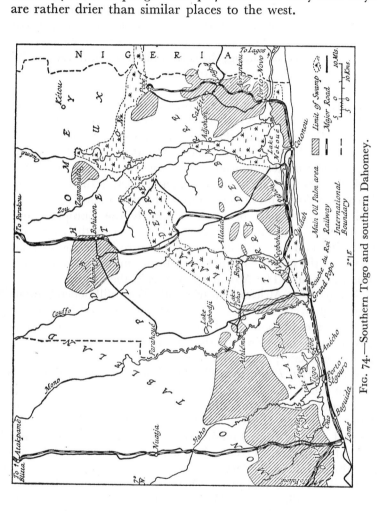

FIG. 74.—Southern Togo and southern Dahomey.

GEOLOGY, RELIEF AND MAJOR REGIONS

SAND-BAR COAST AND LAGOONS. As in Dahomey, the
smooth sand-bar is backed by lagoons, which in the Republic
of Togo extend deeply inland as Lakes Togo and Ouo.

These lakes are the former estuaries of the Chio, Joto and other rivers.

Beginning in 1886, the sand-bar has been closely planted with nearly a million coconut palms, covering some 14,000 acres, but are now heavily diseased. Under the palms small Lagoon cattle are grazed. Lagoon and sand-bar villages are mainly engaged in fishing, the collection of coconuts and in the preparation and marketing of these products which are important in internal trade.

Lomé, the capital, with a population of some 87,000, adjoins the Ghana boundary. Served by railways terminating at Palimé, Blitta and Anécho, by several roads, by inter-continental and West African air services, and by a wharf, it is also the commercial headquarters. There is normally a great deal of traffic across the boundary to Keta and Accra (Ghana), mostly in cassava flour and tapioca, and in dried fish and lagoon fish.

The western part of Lomé is largely the European and administrative quarter. It was well laid out by the Germans, is shaded and very attractive. The centre is the commercial quarter; the east is envisaged as a future industrial zone, with a new station. The African quarter is in the north.

Among West African countries only Togo still depends upon a pier for overseas trade. The pier was replaced in 1968 by a deep-water harbour 4 miles east of Lomé. The initial capacity is only one-third greater than that of the wharf, but handling is safer, easier and cheaper.

Anécho (*Petit Popo*), near the Dahomey boundary, lies more on the southern shore of the lagoon than on the coast. It is much older than Lomé and, as well as being on the Ghana–Togo–Dahomey–Nigeria road, is also the terminus of the coastal railway from Lomé. It is an important cassava and dried fish market. Cassava is much grown nearby and fish are caught mainly in the lagoons.

LA TERRE DE BARRE OR OUATCHI PLATEAU. This corresponds to similar country behind the lagoons in Dahomey. As there, ' la Terre de Barre ' is limited by a clear northern edge and divided by rivers. Where there is adequate water, it is well cultivated and settled, with up to one hundred and fifty persons per square mile. Compared with the Dahomey sector, the oil palm is slightly less densely planted. Maize, yams and cassava are rather more important and are traded to Ghana, especially Accra. Indeed, Togo produced about 6% of the cassava and exported some 50% of the tapioca of the French Union before independence.

MONO TABLELAND. Beyond the northern edge of the Terre de Barre, some 30 or 40 miles inland, comes the usual monotonous and silicious clay-covered tableland. Because of the low rainfall, baobabs occur widely along the southern edge, and poor Southern Guinea Savannah is dominant up to the northwestern limit along the Togo–Atacora Mountains near Palimé, Atakpamé, Sokodé and Lama-Kara.

Villages are rare, except along the railway and north road, and cultivation is restricted to areas round them. Yams and maize are dominant, the oil palm is important around Atakpamé, the shea butter tree towards Blitta and Sokodé, with groundnuts also around the latter. Cotton is sometimes grown for sale. Nuatja is the most important local market for all crops.

In the Atakpamé District a three-year rotation is common, with crops grown on yam mounds to prevent erosion. In the first year yams and cotton are grown, in the second, maize and cotton or guinea corn and, in the third year, cassava with groundnuts, beans, etc. Rice is grown dry with yams, or wet in the Mono Valley. Fallow periods are from eight to fifteen years.

In the extreme north-east of this area, in the Kabrai Massif, south-east of the Atacora Mountains, there is a very dense population in the Lama–Kara Division and across the border in Dahomey. The average population, over more than 1,000 square miles, and embracing between 200,000 and 235,000 people with a yearly increase of 5,000–6,000, is 180 per square mile. Yet the environment is so rugged that only one-third of the land is cultivable. Thus the effective average population density is about 500 per square mile, but reaches 1,500 per square mile in some mountainous cantons. This is possible only because of the relative fertility of soils derived from granites, gneiss and basic green diorite, and because of intensive cultivation. Tiny terraces are laboriously built by the Kabrai and, to a lesser extent, by the Naoudemba and Lamba, and are manured and irrigated.

Resettlement has been going on since 1926 between

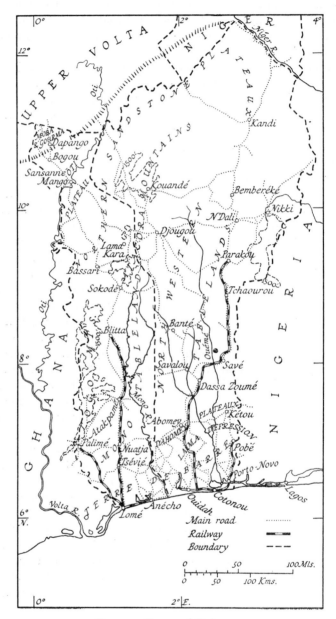

FIG. 75.—Togo and Dahomey.

Atakpamé and Sokodé, where some 30,000 people now live. People moved from over-populated areas are allotted new villages, farming equipment, seeds (especially cotton), animals, some money until the first harvest and freedom from taxation for two years.[1] Individual emigrants also go to the Bassari District and to southern Togo and Dahomey. Unfortunately, the farming methods of the Kabrai sometimes deteriorate in a lowland environment.

Palimé lies in a hollow near Mount Agou. It collects local cocoa and from Ghana when prices are higher in Togo. Railway and road link it with Lomé.

Atakpamé, in a narrow valley and on adjacent hills, is likewise a regional market, collecting palm oil, kernels and cotton, there being ginneries in the town.

Sokodé is the northern administrative centre and market.

Lama-Kara, the Kabrai administrative centre, is situated at the outlet from the only point where the Kara River may be crossed easily in all seasons.

TOGO–ATACORA MOUNTAINS. These denuded thrust-fold ranges are highest (Mount Agou 3,366 feet) and widest (45 miles at Atakpamé) in the Republic of Togo. This massive and rugged double range, with deep valleys and abrupt-edged plateaux, begins near Accra as the Akwapim Hills, and is aligned north-eastwards across Togo into Dahomey, where it obstructs the Niger River in the famous double V.

The south-eastern range is composed of the Akwapimian–Togo–Atacora Series (probably Middle Pre-Cambrian), and the north-western wider one of the highly folded, contorted and faulted Buem Series (Upper Pre-Cambrian). The double range is usually called the Atacora Mountains in the north-east. Around Sokodé is a low saddle, which divides

[1] *Report by First Visiting Mission of United Nations to French Togoland*, 1950; J. C. Froelich, 'Densité de la population et méthodes de culture chez le Kabré du Nord-Togo', *Comptes Rendus du Congrès International de Géographie*, Lisbon, 1949, Tome IV, pp. 168–80, and 'Généralités sur les Kabré du Nord-Togo', *Bulletin*, I.F.A.N., 1949, pp. 77–106; H. Enjalbert, 'Paysans noirs: Les Kabré du Nord-Togo', *Les Cahiers d'Outre-Mer*, 1956, pp. 137–80; D. V. Sassoon, 'The Cabrais of Togoland', *Geographical Magazine*, 1950, pp. 339–41; E. Guernier, *Cameroun-Togo* (*Encyclopédie de l'Afrique française*), 1951, p. 428, has a map of the new villages, on p. 426 a general population map of Togo and, on p. 431, an ethnic map.

these from the Togo Mountains in the south-west. Before the arrival of Europeans the whole range kept apart Islamic and animist peoples in this area.

The Atacora Mountains are, by reason of their more north-easterly position, drier and poorer, with thinner soils and poor vegetation. Millet is the dominant food crop; groundnuts, tobacco and kapok are almost the only cash crops.

In the Togo Mountains rainfall is heavier (1,200–1,500 mm.) than elsewhere in the Republic of Togo, and this is the only mainly forested area. Temperatures are lower than on the coast, and it was here, around Klouto and Palimé, that some German plantations were early established for cocoa, coffee and rubber. Cocoa is still grown on some plantations with Kabrai labourers, as well as on African-owned farms. Coffee is now entirely grown by Africans, and is Togo's first or second most important export, or about 20% by value of all exports. Upland dry rice, maize and millet are the main food crops.

ŌTI SANDSTONE PLATEAU. This is the eastern part of the Voltaian Sandstone Basin, continued from Ghana and extending into northern Dahomey. As in the other areas, this plateau is very infertile, and subject to alternation of flooded and baked-out soils. Consequently, population is slight and the crops of groundnuts and millet are, like the people, poor. The Bogou Scarp is the lower eastern continuation of the more impressive Gambaga Scarp of Ghana's Upper Region. *Sansanné Mango* is the main market.

MOBA AND GOURMA GRANITE LANDS. North of the Bogou Scarp granite occurs. There is here, as in the extreme dry north of the Ghana Upper Region, a denser but poor and isolated population. The Moba and Gourma cultivate ground-nuts, cotton, irrigated rice, and millet, and take to keeping livestock fairly well. *Dapango* is the local market.

ECONOMIC RESOURCES

AGRICULTURE

Until 1960 the Republic of Togo found its resources exclusively in agriculture, and about 40% of the country is cultivated.

In the south the main food crops are maize, cassava, the oil palm and yams, the first three being grown in surplus. Cassava is normally sold to Ghana traders, mainly from Keta; palm oil and kernels go overseas. There is a palm oil factory at Alokouégbé (2,000 tons capacity), one at Ganavé for cassava starch, and another for desiccated coconut at Lomé.

In the east-centre, cassava, yams and maize remain basic food crops, but cotton (intercropped with yams) becomes the main cash crop south-east of Atakpamé. A modern spinning and weaving mill at Dadja is using much of the cotton crop.

The south-eastern lower slopes of the Togo Mountains produce cocoa and coffee, with rice for local food. A little coffee is also grown nearer the coast in la Terre de Barre.

In the centre and north, millet and beans are the basic foods. Yams and rice are locally important, e.g. north of Bassari and Sokodé. Groundnuts and cotton are grown both for subsistence and export. Shea butter nuts are collected in most areas and kapok north of Bassari.

The main exports by value are, approximately, phosphates (30% and increasing), cocoa (25%), coffee (20%), palm kernels and cotton (each 5–10%). Although it is generally the major crop export, the amount of cocoa varies greatly according to relative prices on either side of the boundary with Ghana. Cassava flour is sent over land boundaries in quantities difficult to determine.

MINERALS AND POWER

Calcium phosphate deposits north-east of Lake Togo have been worked since 1960. They occur mixed with clay in a layer 18–28 feet thick, covered by 20–80 feet of soft overburden. A 14-mile railway takes the phosphate to a concentrator and wharf east of Porto-Segouro (Fig. 74, p. 421). Annual exports are $1\frac{1}{4}$ million tons of 80% phosphate.

Chromite occurs at Mount Ahito near Chra, and bauxite and other minerals are known in various places, but none is exported because of inaccessibility and present poor port facilities.

A little hydro-electric power is produced at Kpimé near Palimé, and negotiations have taken place to bring in power from Ghana's Volta Dam.

Conclusion

The resources of this small though regionally varied territory are few, and it has the acute political problems of the divided Ewe.

BIBLIOGRAPHY

See references in footnotes. Also:

Rapports Annuels du Gouvernement français a l'Assemblée Générale des Nations Unies sur l'Administration du Togo placé sous la tutelle de la France.
Reports by Visiting Missions of the United Nations to the Trusteeship Council. (Include maps.)
R. R. KUCZYNSKI, *The Cameroons and Togoland*, Oxford, 1939.

MAPS

See p. 183. Also:

1 : 5,000 Lomé. Institut Géographique National, 1949.
1 : 50,000 Togo. Institut Géographique National, in progress.
1 : 100,000 Southern Togo. Service Géographique de l'Afrique Occidentale Française, 1924–42.
1 : 500,000. Institut Géographique National, 1960. Carte de la Republique du Togo—Physique, Administrative, Routière et Touristique.

Chapter 25

DAHOMEY—ANCESTRAL HOME OF MANY AMERICANS[1]

DAHOMEY, one-fifth the size of France, has an area of only 44,684 square miles, but a population in 1966 of 2,410,000, and an average density of 54 per square mile.

This higher-than-average population is explained by concentrations in the south, continuing from the days of the famous Dahomey kingdom. Like Ashanti, Yorubaland and Benin, this was a powerful well-organised state, famous for the women's battalions of its army, which were first raised in 1729. It was notorious for its 'customs' or human sacrifices, and for its vast part in the slave trade up to their eventual suppression after the mid-nineteenth century.

Ouidah (Ajuda in Portuguese and sometimes Whydah in English) was for long probably the greatest slave exporter of the Gulf of Guinea. Vivid accounts have been left by Bosman, Dalzel, Burton and others. The Portuguese established themselves in 1580 at this town, which later became their headquarters after the Dutch evicted them from the Gold Coast between 1637 and 1642. Eleven acres of Portuguese territory survived until 1961 at Ouidah, with military and civil governors but no population! A French fort was founded in 1671, and the English and Danish also established forts, the buildings of which are still in use. These forts did not originally have political rights, as did such establishments elsewhere in West Africa; instead, they were subject to the Dahomeans (who occupied the town in 1741) through a local representative, the Yevogan or 'Resident Minister for White Affairs'.

At the end of the seventeenth century 20,000 slaves were

[1] M. and Mme. Brasseur, formerly resident in Dahomey, who gave me great help in that territory, have made me further indebted to them for their comments on this chapter.

exported annually, but in the early nineteenth century the number had fallen to 10,000–12,000 per annum, because of excessive human sacrifices of potential slaves. So in 1810 a famous Brazilian mulatto, Francisco de Souza, himself the descendant of ex-slaves, stepped in to depose the Dahomey Regent, reduce the sacrifices and so revive the slave trade. In this he and his descendants succeeded until 1885, despite the desperate efforts of the British Navy. In that year the last Portuguese slave ship left Ouidah.

In 1847 the Governor of the Gold Coast visited Guezo, the Dahomey King, but, as he had already limited the annual sacrifices, he could not easily also stop the supply of at least 8,000 prisoners, then exported annually as slaves. Fearing British intervention, Guezo made a treaty with France in 1851. By Franco-British efforts the slave trade through Ouidah, Lagos and Badagry mainly ended about 1863. France finally took political control of Cotonou in 1878 and of Porto-Novo in 1883. Portugal declared a protectorate over all the coast in 1885, but withdrew it in 1887.

Behanzin, the last real monarch, who began his reign in 1889, soon attacked the French. His state was conquered in 1892 and he was deported in 1894. Thereafter, the lands north of African Dahomey were occupied, and the present boundaries were achieved by treaties with German Togo in 1897 and with Nigeria in 1898.

The former state of Dahomey and the late survival of the slave trade have left their mark. In the former capital at Abomey are the old royal residences (one with the tomb of Behanzin), where many descendants of the royal families live. Around Abomey are the extensive oil palm plantations, established by prisoners when these could no longer be exported as slaves. Former slave merchants advised the establishment of these plantations as an alternative income. To-day they provide Dahomey's chief export and are among the few extensive African-owned plantations in West Africa.

The capital is at Porto-Novo, in the extreme south-east, once a rival and later a vassal state to Dahomey. It was the first to ask for French protection and has remained the capital, despite the rise of Cotonou as the commercial centre. Ouidah, the former slave roadstead, is the headquarters both of Roman

Catholic Missions and of the local Fetish, whose buildings face each other.

CLIMATE [1]

Along the Dahomey coast, between Ouidah and Cotonou, the extremely dry Accra–Togo Dry Coastal climatic zone comes to an end. On the Togo border, Grand Popo has only 32·4 inches. Occasional baobabs may still be seen and, were it not for swamps in the neighbourhood, they would be even more evident and scrub general. Eastward, Ouidah has 41·7 inches, Cotonou—where the Equatorial climate recurs—49·8 inches and Porto-Novo 50·6 inches; the rain days also increase from only 50 at Grand Popo to 100 at Porto-Novo.

Rainfall inland from the coast in the Semi-Seasonal and Seasonal Equatorial climatic zones remains low, as in the Republic of Togo, being 38–50 inches per annum on about seventy rain days. The amount of rain is thus much the same as on the coast, though it is progressively less effective. Were it not for the fertile soils of the Terre de Barre and high humidity, oil palms could not survive with as little as 37 inches of rain.

North of the Savalou–Tchaourou line the Southern Savannah climate occurs. The heaviest rainfall in the whole territory is at Djougou, in the Atacora Mountains, which averages 53 inches annually. Kouandé, Natitingou, Nikki and Bembéréké, in about latitude 10° N. and on high ground, get about 50 inches annually and this area was originally covered with Rain Forest.

North of the Atacora Mountains rainfall diminishes sharply to about 38 inches annually, and is highly variable. This low average, combined with the widespread occurrence of lateritic crusts, accounts for exceptionally poor Sudan Savannah vegetation.

GEOLOGY, RELIEF AND MAJOR REGIONS

SAND-BAR COAST AND LAGOONS. In Dahomey this type of coastline is well developed, lagoons being continuous from the Republic of Togo into Nigeria. In the west they

---

[1] For this and succeeding sections, see Figs. 74 and 75.

are narrow, the first being very near the sea; in the east they are broader and deeper. The Porto-Novo lagoon provides an excellent waterway to Lagos, but is impaired economically by the international boundary which crosses it.

As in the Republic of Togo, the coastline was built off-shore from river estuaries. Relics of these are represented by Lake Ahémé, fed by the River Cuffo whose old estuary is now the lake, and Lake Nokoué, formerly part of the estuary of the Ouémé River. In this latter case, however, there has been great siltation, and above the former estuary or present lake the river has divided into two parts, the Zou and the Ouémé proper. Between them is the well-populated delta, which may be improved for palm cultivation on the northern fringes, and on the southern side for rice in the wet and maize in the dry season.

There are two outlets to the sea. One is the *Bouche du Roi*, east of Grand Popo, where erosion is going on, and the other from Lake Nokoué at Cotonou, where deposition is occurring. Meanwhile, about 100 yards out to sea another sand ridge and future coastline is being built.

On the seaward half of the sand-bar are considerable coconut plantations, mostly owned by non-Africans, in contrast to the predominantly African-owned ones of the Republic of Togo. The railway from Segbohoué via Ouidah, Pahou and Cotonou to Porto-Novo runs along this sand-bar. Beyond the railway, on the lagoon side, the sand is less consolidated and is heavily laden with fresh water. Here oil palms flourish, in contrast to the seaward side, and there is an oil mill at Ahozan, near Ouidah.

Many former lagoons have become partly silted, especially west of Cotonou. In these marshes, and on those along obstructed rivers, patches are cleared for cocoyams, maize, cassava and vegetables. As mentioned above, rice could be added if the technique were taught.

In the lagoons and lakes, fish are caught in elaborate wicker traps. Great amounts of smoked fish are produced annually. The trade in fish and vegetables extends as far north as Bohicon, westward into Togo, eastward to Lagos, and is very important.

Porto-Novo, population (1964) 69,500, is the capital and an old

African centre. It lies on a slight eminence on the north side of the Ouémé Lagoon, which communicates eastward with the sea at Lagos and, with difficulty, westward with Lake Nokoué and Cotonou. Originally, much external trade passed via Lagos until the deep-water port at Cotonou was opened in 1965. The railway north to Pobé serves the rich palm-belt, but Porto-Novo lacks roads to central and northern Dahomey. Most trade, almost all foreign missions, and the technical departments of the government have moved to Cotonou.[1]

Cotonou, population (1951) 21,300, including over a thousand non-Africans, is the commercial headquarters of Dahomey and a European creation. It has Dahomey's deep-water port and lies immediately west of the intermittent sea outlet of Lake Nokoué. There is an industrial suburb 2 miles to the east of the outlet, with a modern palm kernel oil mill, soap and perfume works, nail and furniture factories, a brewery, and soft drink manufacturer. Cotonou is served by railways to Porto-Novo and Pobé, to Parakou, to Ouidah and Segbohoué, and by many roads. There are air services in each direction along the coast, and to other countries.

Ouidah, 15,000 inhabitants, is some 3 miles from the coast, on the north bluff of a reed-obstructed lagoon. On the coast there remain only ruined buildings to remind one that from here hundreds of thousands of slaves were shipped to the New World in the course of several centuries. In the town the old Danish and English forts are still used as commercial houses, and the Portuguese retained symbolic territorial rights until 1961. Ouidah is the military and religious headquarters of Dahomey.

LA TERRE DE BARRE. ' *Barre* ' is a French corruption of the Portuguese *barro*, meaning clay. This region, sub-divided by the Cuffo and Ouémé Rivers, lies north of the lagoons, and averages 300 feet in elevation. Its loams and clayey sands are formed from Miocene and Pliocene rocks, and there are occasional outcrops of ferruginous sandstones or lateritic sands and clays. The soil is light red in colour and very sandy. Fertility has been increased by the use of night-soil and the land is continually cropped.

[1] For a very full study see P. Brasseur-Marion, ' Porto-Novo ' in *Porto-Novo et sa Palmeraie*, I.F.A.N., Dakar, 1953, pp. 7–47.

It is densely planted with the oil palm for cash; maize, cassava, sweet potatoes and beans are grown for food, maize being by far the most important annual crop. Cultivation is most intensive near the towns, near which small Lagoon cattle are tethered in the fields and sold for meat. There are factory oil mills at Avrankou and Gbada, north of Porto-Novo, with annual oil extraction capacities respectively of 4,000 and 2,000 tons.

Population is rather less dense in the central (Allada) sector, mainly because it was on the slave route between the Daho-mean capital at Abomey and the sea at Ouidah, and also because water is usually found only at 160 feet.[1]

THE LAMA DEPRESSION. This arc-shaped clay swamp is less than 100 feet above sea level, is limited by clear bluffs, and has fertile peaty soils and patches of Rain Forest. Because of annual flooding it is little used, though it could support rice. The Lama was the southern boundary of the Dahomey State and was a major obstacle to the central railway.

THE DAHOMEY PLATEAUX. There are four plateaux, around respectively Parahoué, Abomey, Zagnanado and Kétou. These are akin to the three plateaux of the Terre de Barre, but water is even deeper. All are planted with the oil palm and there is another large oil mill near Bohicon (capacity 2,000 tons). Oranges are another important cash crop near Abomey, some being sent by lorries annually to the coast and to the north. Of all these plateaux, population is densest on the first two. *Abomey*, the old Dahomey capital, is now mainly of historical interest, but remains an important market and crafts centre.

Zagnanado was the Dahomey war base against the Egba and other Yoruba peoples.

Kétou is mostly inhabited by Yoruba.

NORTH-WESTERN TABLELANDS. Bare domes and lateritic cappings are frequent, and soils are poor and thin. A few forests survive here, e.g. at Banté beyond the limits of the old Dahomey state. To the north, however, vegetation generally becomes poorer, though around N'Dali are fine forests.

As far as Savé, the railway is mainly within fertile country;

---

[1] On the Porto-Novo oil palm country see G. Brasseur, ' La Palmeraie de Porto-Novo ' in *Porto-Novo et sa Palmeraie*, op. cit.

thereafter its traffic is slight, since much of the upper Ouémé basin is thinly peopled. The main cash crop is cotton and at towns served by the railway there are ginneries.

ATACORA MOUNTAINS. These extend from the Republic of Togo and, as in that country, are well peopled. These mountains have the heaviest rainfall in Dahomey—over 50 inches. With the removal of the original forest cover, there has been severe erosion around the headwaters of the Ouémé River.

Djougou has cotton ginneries, is an important route centre and has a much greater population than any other town in central or northern Dahomey.

NORTHERN SANDSTONE PLATEAUX. These slope in gentle undulations to the Niger River. In the north-east, Pre-Cambrian rocks are covered by Pliocene clayey sandstones, which are themselves capped by ferruginous lateritic crusts. In the extreme north-west, Primary Voltaian sandstones lie along the border and are also infertile.

Everywhere the vegetation is very poor Sudan Savannah. Many areas are unpeopled, except by Fulani nomads. Where cultivation is possible and there are people to do it, millet, guinea corn and cotton are grown, and shea butter and kapok trees are protected.

ECONOMIC RESOURCES

AGRICULTURE

The peoples of the south are alert and vigorous, and have long been in contact with Europeans. Their elaborate political organisation encouraged early specialisation, so that many people could not grow their own food. Furthermore, large quantities of food had to be grown for provisioning slave ships on their long voyages, as well as for slave merchants and their employees. Thus there was, early on, much specialised agriculture, especially in growing cassava, yams, sweet potatoes, maize, peas, chillies, beans and groundnuts, which would keep well on slave ships. These crops (especially maize and vegetables) are still overwhelmingly the most important in the south, and are mainly grown under oil palms. Comé, near Grand Popo, has a factory for making cassava flour and tapioca.

Crops of the north are yams, rice, millet, beans, peas and vegetables. Cassava and groundnuts are grown almost everywhere.

Nature has also been kind to intensive food cropping in southern Dahomey. The rainfall of some 40 inches is admirable in amount and distribution, and the territory has more alluvial soils than many. The Tertiary Terre de Barre is easily worked and retentive of moisture, though the actual water-table is deep and the soils mediocre.

On the other hand, rainfall and vegetation conditions have not favoured cultivation of the more lucrative cocoa or kola crops.

Oil palm.[1] Oil palms were planted by prisoners of the Dahomey and Porto-Novo kings, after 1839, and especially after 1848 (when France abolished the slave trade), as they could no longer all be sold as slaves. The plantations were well laid out, the seeds selected and the trees tended, probably under the guidance of ex-slave merchants. There are some 30 million trees, occupying nearly 1,600 square miles as far as $7\frac{1}{2}°$ N. Oil palm produce is Dahomey's main export by far. The oil is notable for its high carotene content—1·7–2%.

Since 1924 a research station at Pobé has distributed several million seedlings of improved varieties. These are the more necessary, as the annual rainfall of under 40 inches and the low water table are considerable disadvantages. Against these may be set the constantly high humidity and clay soils. The most suitable districts are Porto-Novo, Ouidah, Abomey, Parahoué and Allada.

Large oil mills, capable of extracting 90% of the oil, are possible in these plantations. There are now four—at Avran-kou, just north of Porto-Novo, with a capacity of 4,000 tons per annum, and nearby at Gbada, at Bohicon (near Abomey) and at Ahozon (near Ouidah) all with annual capacities of 2,000 tons, but with uncertain futures because of irregular and insufficient supplies of fruit. Much of the latter is kept back for primitive methods of treatment to secure oil for domestic use by the rapidly increasing population. Factory-expressed oil is also used in soap works at Porto-Novo and Cotonou, which each have a capacity of about 1,000 tons a year.

[1] See also G. Brasseur, op. cit.

Coconuts are grown on mainly non-African plantations along the sand-bar; and by Africans there, near lagoons, and between Grand Popo and Athiémé. It is mostly more profitable and far less trouble to sell the fresh nuts as fruit or for local soap production, than to undertake the expensive preparation of copra for export. One ton of copra requires some 7,000 nuts.

Cotton is mainly grown for the local market. Peruvian and Allen are grown in the north and *G. hirsutum* (Ishan) between Savé and Savalou. *G. arboreum* is grown for a black dye from the flowers, a red one from the leaves and twigs, and the leaves are used medicinally.

Cotton cultivation is rather more careful than in most African lands, so that yields and qualities are above average. Annual sales are over 4,000 tons (mostly from Savalou and Abomey Districts). Most of the cotton sold is used within the country, especially in the north.

Groundnuts are important in the Abomey, Savalou and Natitingou Districts. The first crop is kept as food and the second crop in the north is exported. In all, some three-quarters of the crop are retained within Dahomey and about 5,000 tons of shelled nuts are normally exported annually, mainly from the drier and less peopled northern districts.

Shea butter trees are widespread in the centre and north, but particularly localised in Natitingou, Abomey, Kandi, Nikki and Parakou Districts. Internal trade in shea butter nearly equals that in cotton, and some kernels are generally exported.

MINERALS

There has been a little washing of gold from the River Perma near Natitingou, but no deep workings. Relatively rich oolitic and hæmatite iron and chrome ores exist, while rutile, phosphates, mineral oil and limestone may be worked later.

CONCLUSION

Old Dahomey was famed as an African state but notorious for its human sacrifices and as the last great exporter of slaves to the Brazilian and European slave merchants. Its oil palm plantations, established by prisoners for legitimate trade, survive and are unique in Africa. Also exceptional is the intensive cultivation of food crops from the oil palm plantations, and from the unusually extensive alluvial areas. But Dahomey is also over-dependent upon vegetable oil exports, and should diversify its economy.

Like Togo, Dahomey has suffered from its small size, the poverty of the north, and from the lack of a deep water port until 1965. This port is normally also a main inlet and outlet for Niger's overseas trade.

BIBLIOGRAPHY

See footnotes cited above. Also:

Dr. AKINDELE and C. AGUESSY, *Le Dahomey*, Paris, 1955.
G. BRASSEUR, *Le Bas Ouémé*, 1962.
M. J. HERSKOVITS, *Dahomey*, New York, 1938.
P. PÉLISSIER, ' Les Pays du Bas-Ouémé ', *Travaux du Dépt. de Géog.*, No. 10, Univ. de Dakar.
H. P. WHITE, ' Dahomey—the geographical basis of an African State ', *Tijdschrift voor Economische en Sociale Geografie*, 1966, pp. 61–8.
Etudes Dahoméennes, Centre I.F.A.N., Porto-Novo.

MAPS

See p. 183. Also:

Topographic:
    1 : 50,000 Dahomey. I.G.N. 1952–.
    1 : 100,000 Southern Dahomey. S.G./A.O.F. 1924–42.

Soils:
    1 : 100,000 Ouémé Delta. R. Maignien, 1947.

Vegetation:
    1 : 50,000 Dassa Zoumé. S.G./A.O.F. 1951.

Chapter 26

THE FEDERATION OF NIGERIA—AN EPITOME OF WEST AFRICA[1]

WITH an area of 356,669 square miles and a population in 1966 of 58,600,000, Nigeria is the most populated country in all Africa. Its area is four times that of the United Kingdom, or three times that of Ghana and Sierra Leone together. Although it occupies only about one-seventh of the settled and productive area of West Africa, it contains much over one-half of the population. Indeed, Nigeria has at least three areas of exceptionally high population density.

Because of its latitudinal extent from approximately 4° to 14° N., Nigeria has exceptionally varied physical conditions, human types and economy. Rainfall varies from some 120 inches at Calabar, to not much more than one-fifth of that figure in the Chad Basin. In the south-east there is an excess of rain all the year; in the north there is adequate rain only in two or three months. There is a corresponding vegetational range, though a characteristic of Nigeria is the exceptional width of the Guinea Savannah.

Relief is likewise varied, and there is higher land here than anywhere else in West Africa. The south-eastern boundary extends along the fringes of the Cameroon and Bamenda Highlands, most of which average 4,000–5,000 feet. Most of the Jos Plateau lies at 4,000–6,000 feet. The geology is also unusually varied because, apart from Pre-Cambrian rocks, Cretaceous to Recent sedimentary series and volcanic rocks are fairly widespread.

[1] I am indebted to Dr. W. B. Morgan, M.A., and to Professor J. C. Pugh, formerly of University College, Ibadan, for most helpful criticism of this chapter.

Human variety is likewise great. Between the four main groups—Hausa and Fulani in the north, Yoruba in the south-west, and Ibo in the south-east—there are great differences of outlook and organisation.

The size and variety of Nigeria are likewise reflected in its varied economy, though this is perhaps less than one expects. There are only a few outstanding exports—cocoa from the south-west, mineral oil from the south-east, as well as palm oil and kernels mostly from there, groundnuts, cotton, hides and skins, and tin from the north. Moreover, these exports come from relatively restricted areas. On the other hand, food crops are well represented (as one would expect in such a densely populated country), and there is a large internal commerce in them, as well as in kola nuts and livestock. Nigeria is, indeed, the only West African country producing forest crops in the south, as well as possessing great numbers of the humped livestock in the north. She is also one of the few large timber exporting countries of West Africa, and has other unusual resources such as tin, coal, oil and gas.

There is perhaps more of a network of communications in Nigeria than elsewhere in West Africa. The Niger, Benue and Cross Rivers, the various streams of the Niger Delta, and the many lagoons are all important waterways. There are 2,172 miles of railway and 55,000 miles of road, with marked concentration in the main cash crop areas. There is also a network of air services.

Because of its human variety and differing outlooks, it has a federal constitution with varying constitutional arrangements in its twelve States.

HISTORICAL OUTLINE [1]

The establishment of the Hausa in the north goes back to at least the tenth century. Their political and social organisation were much influenced by the penetration of Islam in the thirteenth century, when the Fulani were also spreading eastward. For centuries the crop-growing Hausa, and the pastoral or aristocratic Fulani, lived in peace, but in 1802 Othman dan

---

[1] For further details see M. Crowder, *The Story of Nigeria*, 2nd edit., 1966, and Sir Alan Burns, *History of Nigeria*.

Fodio quarrelled with the King of Gobir and, in a religious war, rallied Muslims and Fulani rule was extended over most of the Hausa kingdoms.

Some consider that the Yoruba originated in north-eastern Africa and, having come early into West Africa, acquired negro characteristics by intermarriage. Yorubaland once extended farther westward, and Yoruba peoples are still found in Dahomey. Southward penetration by the Fulani to Abeo-kuta [1] much affected the Yoruba, as did slave raiding from north and south. Benin was independent but was influenced by barbaric fetish-priest domination and by the slave trade. Less is known of the early history of the Ibo and other peoples of the east.

The earliest documented European contact was by the Portuguese in 1472. As the overseas slave trade developed they were followed by other nations. Geographically, the Nigerian coast was well suited to the trade, and to its late survival, by reason of the many creeks of the Niger Delta. The Yoruba civil and other wars provided slaves, who were also easily captured by African intermediaries from the socially fragmented Ibo, and from as far north as Nupe country around the middle Benue Valley. Slave-raiding was, of course, for much longer a feature of the north, though the slaves were generally used locally.

After the British abolition of the slave trade in 1807, the penetration of the interior of Nigeria was due to Buxton's thesis that legitimate trade rather than armed force was the best way to stop slave-holding. Penetration was made easier by the discovery in 1830 of the true course of the Niger; though there were fearful losses from disease by expeditions until 1854, when Baikie showed that these could be avoided by doses of quinine. During much of the century, especially during Gladstone's administrations, there was either indifference or even hostility to British political expansion in Africa.

Lagos was taken in 1861 in order to suppress its illegal slave trade. In 1879 the United African Company (later the National African Company and, finally, in 1886 the Royal Niger Company) eventually opened up the Niger River and

---

[1] This was the extreme southern limit of the Fulani. Tsetse fly made this advance very dangerous to Fulani cavalry; further penetration was impossible.

undertook the government of the interior. Meanwhile, in 1885 the Oil Rivers Protectorate was proclaimed over most coastal territory from Lagos towards the Cameroons, but no administration was created for it until 1891. In 1893 the protectorate was enlarged over the hinterland, and the name changed to the Niger Coast Protectorate. Benin was occupied in 1897, and appalling human sacrifices there were stopped.

By 1897, therefore, Lagos was under the Colonial Office, the interior under a private company, and the coast under the Foreign Office. But in April 1899 the Colonial Office took over the Niger Coast Protectorate from the Foreign Office, and in January 1900 the Charter of the Royal Niger Company was revoked. In their places, respectively, the Protectorates of Southern and of Northern Nigeria were proclaimed. The Fulani and other emirates of Northern Nigeria were brought under British control by 1903. Lugard introduced Indirect Rule through the emirs, on condition that they prohibited slave raiding and trading. Islam was to be respected and the entry of Christian missions subject to permission from the emirs—a fact which has caused the educational retardation of the North.

In 1906 Southern Nigeria and Lagos were merged. In 1912 the through railway from Lagos to Kano was opened and also the then main line from Kano to Baro on the navigable Niger. With such improved communications it was possible to proclaim a unified Nigeria in 1914. Sir Frederick Lugard, who served the Royal Niger Company in the nineties, was later first High Commissioner for the Protectorate of Northern Nigeria, then Governor of both Southern and Northern Protectorates in 1912, became first Governor of Nigeria in 1914.

In 1939 the Southern Provinces were divided into Western and Eastern Provinces, and in 1946 Regional Houses of Assembly were created in Ibadan for the Western Region, at Enugu for the Eastern and at Kaduna for the Northern Region.

Under the 1951 Constitution, far greater powers were given to these Regions. In 1953-4, however, at the wish of Nigerians amendments were agreed whereby regionalisation and home rule were increased. Western and Eastern Nigeria became self-governing in 1957, Northern Nigeria in 1959, and the whole

Federation achieved independence in 1960.   A fourth Region
—the Mid-West—was created in 1963.

The Cameroons and Bamenda Provinces of the Cameroons

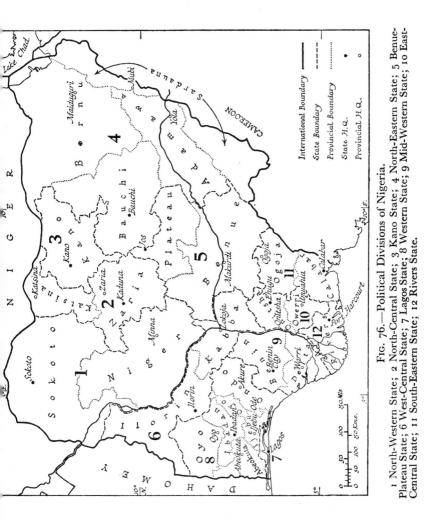

FIG. 76.—Political Divisions of Nigeria.

1 North-Western State; 2 North-Central State; 3 Kano State; 4 North-Eastern State; 5 Benue-Plateau State; 6 West-Central State; 7 Lagos State; 8 Western State; 9 Mid-Western State; 10 East-Central State; 11 South-Eastern State; 12 Rivers State.

under United Kingdom Trusteeship, dissatisfied with rep-
resentation in the Eastern Regional Assembly, secured a
legislative and executive council and became the Southern
Cameroons in 1954.   Responsible Government came in 1958,

and detachment from Nigeria in 1960 to remain awhile under trusteeship. In 1961 it joined the Republic of Cameroon as Western Cameroon.

The Northern Region dominated (or was thought to dominate) the rest of Nigeria by its size, population and voting strength. It became clear that to save the federation more nearly-equal component areas were essential. So in 1967 twelve states were substituted for the four regions. Northern Nigeria was sub-divided into six states, Eastern Nigeria into three, the already small Mid-West Region was merely renamed, Lagos Federal Territory was enlarged by appropriate additions from Western Nigeria, the rest of which became the Western State (Fig. 76). Meanwhile, the Eastern Region attempted to secede as Biafra.

POPULATION[1]

Fig. 32 (p. 166) shows that there is an exceptional range of population density in Nigeria, from many almost uninhabited areas to those with about 1,400 persons per square mile in small areas of Owerri and Onitsha Provinces. Because of the varied physical character of the country and the diverse antecedents and character of its peoples, there is no simple explanation of this wide variation. Nevertheless, the factors discussed in Chapter 10 are well exemplified in Nigeria.

The very densely peopled Ibo lands lie mainly east of the Niger River, from north and south of Onitsha, eastward nearly to 8° E., northward to a little north of 7° N. and southward to 5° N. Although there is a dense population, there were almost no true towns until the Europeans came. The Ibo live in numerous clusters of mud houses. They maintained themselves because the tsetse fly isolated them from Fulani attack,

[1] For population figures of each Region see p. 178. See also 1 : 3,000,000 Population Map, Survey Dept., Lagos; Provincial and Regional reports of the 1963 Population Census; Articles by N. C. Mitchel and W. B. Morgan in *Research Notes*, No. 7, Dept. of Geog., Univ. Coll., Ibadan, 1955; Chapter 10 in this present book, and C. R. Niven, ' Some Nigerian Population Problems ', *Geographical Journal*, 85, pp. 54–8. On the ethnographic side, see Daryll Forde, *The Ibo and Ibibio-Speaking Peoples of South-Eastern Nigeria*, *The Yoruba-Speaking Peoples of South-Western Nigeria* and *Peoples of the Niger–Benue Confluence*; Laura and Paul Bohannan, *The Tiv of Central Nigeria*; H. D. Gunn, *Peoples of the Plateau Area of Northern Nigeria*; F. St. Croix, *The Fulani of Northern Nigeria*; S. F. Nadel, *The Nupe—A Black Byzantium*.

and the forest prevented their complete annihilation by slave raiders from the coast or the interior.

The numerous Ibo nourished themselves on a basically vegetarian diet in which palm oil, yams and cocoyams were and are very important. Although present conditions are not as ideal for the oil palm as in parts of the Congo or Indonesia, it tolerates the light soils, as cocoa will not, so that palm products and garri (from cassava) are the main cash products of Ibo country.

There is now almost certainly over-population in Owerri and Onitsha Provinces. Ibo are found in temporary work all over Nigeria and some 20,000 are employed on Fernando Po.

The Yoruba concentration, between Lagos and Ilorin, contrasts in most ways with conditions in Ibo country. The soils are derived from Pre-Cambrian rocks (not sandstones), rainfall is lower and less continuous, and fallow periods are longer. Water is generally freely available in Central Yorubaland.

The Yoruba maintained themselves despite constant attacks. The low population density in northern Oyo Province results from Fulani attacks, from this area being a no-man's land between Yorubaland and Dahomey, and from the lower rainfall, poorer soils and cropping possibilities. But political organisation and military power enabled most of the Yoruba concentration to survive.

Large towns are an outstanding characteristic of Yorubaland, many old cities having over 50,000 people. Ibadan, the largest city of Tropical Africa, now has 627,379 inhabitants. One half at least of the urban population of Nigeria is Yoruba (see Fig. 34) and, whereas over half of the population of Western Nigeria is urban, only 14% is so in the eastern states, and 9% in the northern ones. In Ibadan and Oyo Provinces two-thirds of the people are urban. This urbanisation came about by the concentration of farmers in protected towns by night, while still farming several miles away by day.[1]

The railway runs through the heart of Yorubaland, serving its main centres. Railway and roads have helped to confirm and extend urban concentration and have made more profitable

[1] See W. Bascom, ' Urbanization among the Yoruba ', *The American Journal of Sociology*, 60, 1955, pp. 446–54.

the cultivation of cocoa for export, and of kola nuts and yams for internal sale, all on a large scale.

Ondo, Benin and Warri lie between the Yoruba and Ibo concentrations. In northern Ondo and Benin the population of about 100 per square mile survived Fulani raids because of the rugged terrain of the Niger–Bight of Benin watershed. Southern Ondo and Benin are thinly populated or even unpopulated because of Yoruba civil wars, slave raiding and Benin human sacrifices in the late nineteenth century, depth of water table (sometimes over 600 feet), thin, poor and dry soils and, in parts, because of dense forest. Yet in Ibo country these physical factors were no impediment to dense population. The population is denser nearer the sea.

The generally thinly peopled Middle Belt comprises two-fifths the area of Nigeria but has only one-fifth the population. This low density results from slave raiding from south and north, and from the consequentially greater infestation by tsetse and other pests. It is also a ' shatter zone ' or ' no-man's land ' between the contrasting northern and southern peoples, and has few large tribes. Physically, many of its soils are poor, water is scarce and rainfall variable. Indeed, it seems to have the disadvantages of the south and north, with none of their advantages. There are no large towns of the Middle Belt peoples themselves. Such towns as exist are either mainly Yoruba, such as Ilorin; rare capitals such as Bida and Yola; or European in origin, such as Kaduna, Minna and Jos. Except round the latter town, communications are also rather poor in the Middle Belt.

A few islands of greater than average density (thirty-three per square mile) in the Middle Belt should, however, be noted. Broken country around Abuja, the Jos Plateau and on the eastern boundary north of the Benue River saved so called ' pagan ' (non-Muslim) peoples from extinction. European influence has tended to spread them out on to new lands, e.g. by the Shendam Scheme (see below). Tin mining on the Jos Plateau has, however, brought in far more people.

Where the Fulani settled, they often added notably to the population density, e.g. in Nupeland east of the Kaduna (Bida Emirate) River, and around Yola.

Notable Middle Belt peoples are the Nupe and the Tiv, who live in the Niger–Benue Plains. The Tiv went there in the eighteenth century, settling at first in the southern districts on the margin of the Benue Plains, rather as emigrants to the United States tended at first to congregate in New York. Thus Tiv country south-east of Makurdi has over 200 people per square mile and locally severe over-population; but across the Benue River, in the north-west of Tiv country, there are much lower densities.

The Northern clusters attain their highest densities along the Sokoto Valley, around Katsina, Kano and Zaria and, to a lesser extent, in the heart of all emirates. Settlement was facilitated by light soils and relative freedom from the tsetse fly, but limited by water, e.g. north-west and south-east of Sokoto and east of a line through Nguru and Potiskum.

Wherever there was water, other factors caused particular concentrations. Sokoto is a religious centre of the North. Sokoto, Katsina, Kano and Zaria were on trans-Saharan caravan routes, but their survival was due to superior political and military organisation. Soils are easily tilled, but no more so than those of many thinly peopled areas in Nigeria. Much of the explanation lies in the intensive cropping methods of the Hausa, their use of night soil and of animal manure. Railways have provided an outlet to markets for their groundnuts, cotton and surplus foodcrops, as well as for Fulani cattle.

Over-populated areas. Stamp made certain calculations in 1938,[1] but his figures and conclusions have not been accepted. He did not allow for differences in soil fertility, farming method and social custom, which much affect productivity. His assumed need of seven years of fallow to one of cultivation implied no attempt at crop rotation, and is unduly long for regeneration. Nor do people live exclusively from farm crops; there is also much wild produce, such as fruits, firewood and game. Many are supported by part or whole-time non-agricultural work, such as commerce, transport and crafts. Nevertheless, there is probably over-population in parts of Ibo and Tiv countries.

Conversely, about one-half of Nigeria, mainly in the Middle

[1] L. D. Stamp, 'Land Utilisation and Soil Erosion in Nigeria', *Geographical Review*, 1938, pp. 32–45.

Belt, might take more people, even with present farming techniques, so long as tsetse flies are controlled and clean water supplies assured. The Anchau Scheme, by which people were resettled in an area cleared of tsetse lying between Zaria and Jos, showed that at least seventy people per square mile are needed to keep the tsetse at bay, and so keep the area peopled at all. In practically tsetse-free Bornu, resettlement depends upon the provision of wells, as the rainfall is too borderline for farming development without expensive irrigation.

The Government has undertaken other resettlement schemes,[1] such as that at Shendam on the southern edge of the Jos Plateau, to receive people from the plateau whose soils are ruined by over-farming or by tin mining. More elaborate but unsuccessful schemes were undertaken by the Kontagora Native Authority and by the Colonial Development Corporation in association with the Nigerian Government at Mokwa, and by the Eastern Nigeria Development Corporation in the Cross River–Calabar Project. The solution of social problems and the development of initiative have proved difficult.

CLIMATE [2]

Nigeria has a greater variety of climate than any other West African country; the Cameroon, Equatorial, Semi-seasonal Equatorial, Seasonal Equatorial, Southern Savannah, Jos Plateau, Savannah and Sahel types of climate being found. Apart from latitudinal extent, the wide range of relief increases the variety.

There seems to be a rain-shadow effect in the lower Niger–Benue Valleys and, possibly, towards Lake Chad. In general, however, rainfall diminishes from the south-east and south, towards the north and north-east.

An outstanding contrast exists between western and eastern Nigeria. In the former, rainfall averages 40–60 inches and there is a ' little dry season ' from about mid-July to the middle

---

[1] J. T. Coppock, ' Agricultural Developments in Nigeria ', *The Journal of Tropical Geography*, 23, 1966, pp. 1–18.

[2] B. J. Garnier, *Weather Conditions in Nigeria*, Climatological Research Series, No. 2, Department of Geography, McGill University, Canada, 1967; R. Miller, ' The Climate of Nigeria ', *Geography*, 1953, pp. 198–213; R. Hamilton and J. Archbold, ' Meteorology of Nigeria and adjacent territory ', *Q. Journal of the Royal Meteorological Society*, 1945, pp. 231–64, and D. Shove, *Idem*, 1946, p. 105.

88. Phosphate mine near Porto-Segouro. Overburden is being cut away at rear (*right*) and stocked cn the *left*, from where phosphate has been removed. The white phosphatic layer is being cut in the centre.

9. Fish traps in the lagoon Lake Ahémé.

90. Ovens for drying and smoking fish for the considerable market in dried fish which exists here and in other countries along the Gulf of Guinea.

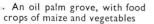

. An oil palm grove, with food crops of maize and vegetables

92. Bas-reliefs on the exterior wall of the audience chamber of the palace of King Glélé (1858–89), Abomey. The lion was his symbol.

NIGERIA

93. Part of Ibadan from
    Mapo Hall.

94. Lokoja waterfront, the co
    fluence of the Benue and Nig
    rivers, and the north-eastern e
    of the Udi Plateau

95. Jos Plateau at Bukuru.
Note the lack of spontaneous trees, a dragline working for tin gravels and
creating extensive spoil
dumps and old flooded
quarries, which obstruct
cultivation of adjacent
fields. Note also the high
granite masses and the Jos-
Kafanchan railway and road.

96. Kano from Dalla
On the right is a bor
pit, from which mud
been taken for hou
Houses of richer pe
are often whitewas
The white mosque is in
distant left centre.

of September. It enables a greater variety of crops to be grown and two harvests to be secured. Eastern Nigeria however, where the Equatorial and Cameroon climates are extensive, and which lies generally farther south than western Nigeria, has heavier rainfall, in a longer season and, normally, no ' little dry season '. Consequently, soils are more leached, crops are perforce less varied than in the west, harvesting is more difficult, and dry storage of crops is a problem. The oil palm, tolerant of poor soils and preferring the greater rainfall, is the main cash crop and the moisture loving cocoyam is often found.

In the Middle Belt, although rainfall may be as high as in the south-west, it is far more variable from year to year in amount, times of onset and cessation, and distribution. The north has less rain than the Middle Belt, but the fall is often more regular and reliable.

VEGETATION [1]

As one would expect from the climatic and altitude range, there is vegetational variety in Nigeria. Mangrove vegetation is well represented around Lagos, west of Warri, south of Degema and Port Harcourt, and around Calabar. Inland lies much Fresh-water Swamp, continuous from the eastern boundary to Port Harcourt, and extending up the Niger to north of Aboh.

Inland again is Rain Forest to an approximate northern limit through Ilaro, Abeokuta, Offa, Owo, Onitsha, Okigwi, Obubra, Ogoja and Obudu. Thus forest is poorly represented in much of Yoruba country but is still well seen in Ondo, Benin and eastern Calabar provinces. In Owerri Province it is mostly Secondary Forest with planted oil palms, and in south-eastern Oyo and Ibadan provinces Secondary Forest with cocoa.

Northward of the Rain Forest is an ever-widening belt of

[1] See D. R. Rosevear, ' Checklist of Nigerian Mammals ' and chapter on ' Vegetation ' in *The Nigerian Handbook*, 1953, pp. 139–73, and R. W. J. Keay, *An Outline of Nigerian Vegetation*, Lagos, 1953, which contains a bibliography and map. Also Chapter 4 of the present book.

Q

Derived Savannah, the northern limit of which runs approximately through Iseyin, Ilorin, Kabba, Oturkpo, near Obudu, and then north-eastward. This line approximately represents the former limit of Rain Forest.

Beyond lies a broad wedge of Guinea Savannah. According to Keay, its northern edge lies near Bussa, Gusau, Ningi, thence south to east of Shendam, north of Jalingo, and south of Yola. This zone was formerly occupied by Open Woodland which has suffered severely from cutting and burning by man and has been replaced by Savannah. This vegetation is especially typical of much of Nigeria, because the belt is wide and occupies quite half the country, coinciding roughly with the Middle Belt. Within it lies the Jos Plateau (see pp. 479–481), which now has exceedingly poor short grass.

Most of the rest of Northern Nigeria is occupied by Sudan Savannah, except that Sahel Savannah occurs north of a line through Geidam to the southern edge of Lake Chad.

GEOLOGY [1]

Pre-Cambrian igneous and metamorphic rocks (gneisses, migmatites, granites, schists, phyllites, quartzites and marbles), occupy four large areas. The largest of these—the High Plains of Hausaland—lies north of the Benue and Niger Rivers. This area is connected by a narrow neck to the second large area, which extends over most of Ilorin, Kabba, Oyo and Ondo Provinces. The third area mainly occupies Ogoja, Benue and Adamawa provinces. The fourth area lies north of the Benue, largely in Adamawa Province. These areas occupy nearly two-thirds of the country. The older of the granites give rise to numerous smooth-domed inselbergs. Younger Granites, which are more resistant, form rugged hills, e.g. near Jos. The weathering of these Younger Granites has given tinstone, columbite, wolfram and pyrochlore, and these have been concentrated in ancient stream beds mainly on or near the Jos Plateau.

[1] See Chapter 1 and Fig. 2; 1 : 2,000,000, *Geological Map of Nigeria*, Land and Survey Dept., Lagos; F. Dixey, ' Nigerian Geology and Mineral Resources ', *Bulletin of the Imperial Institute*, Vol. 43, No. 4.

If severance of South America and Africa is accepted, it is thought [1] to have taken place in Cretaceous (Albian) times, first along a rift now occupied by the Benue River west of Yola, and extending off the Guinea Coast to beyond Cape Palmas (see also p. 15) ; and then along a down-warped trough now followed by the Niger south of Bourem (Mali) and extending seaward towards Angola.

The Benue Valley and central Sokoto have early Cretaceous marine rocks and late Cretaceous terrestrial formations (including poor coal). The Niger Valley has only the later Cretaceous formations, which also occur around the Gongola tributary of the Benue. In eastern Nigeria Cretaceous deposits are up to 15,000 feet thick.

It is in the oldest Cretaceous rocks that the lead and zinc ores of Abakaliki Division are found. Also in Ogoja Province, at Nkalagu, younger Cretaceous limestones are being used for cement manufacture. In late Cretaceous times the sea became shallower and the vegetation of its fringing swamps and lagoons decayed to form the coals now found in Onitsha, Kabba, Benue and eastern Bauchi Provinces. That worked at Udi is the only coal exploited in West Africa and is poorer than most coals worked in the world. As well as the limestone and coal seams, the Cretaceous series consists of shales, sandstones, sands and clays. Oil is being worked at many places in southern Nigeria.

The early Cretaceous rocks of eastern Nigeria and the Benue were strongly folded before the accumulation of later series, which are unconformable and only slightly folded.

At the end of Cretaceous times, the land sank and the sea advanced again, so that Tertiary (Eocene) marine clays, shales and sandstones overlie Cretaceous rocks across the southern edge of the country, as well as in north-western Nigeria where there was another Eocene sea.

Above these deposits are deep beds of sand and clay, with lignite seams. The latter occur in Benin, Owerri and Onitsha Provinces. Lignite indicates that the Tertiary sea was withdrawing, leaving lagoons and swamps on the coastlines. In the south, Cretaceous and Tertiary sediments break down into

[1] J. C. Pugh and Lester King, ' Outline of the Geomorphology of Nigeria ', *South African Geographical Journal*, 1952, pp. 30-7.

the acidic and easily eroded formations often loosely and erroneously called the Benin Sands.[1]

There are upper erosion surfaces at 4,000–4,600 feet on the Jos Plateau and on the Eastern Highlands from 3,000–6,000 feet. Lower surfaces are at 2,000–2,500, 1,500–2,000, 1,200, 700 and 300 feet, on an average.[2]

Erosion surfaces have been used by Dixey [3] to suggest that the Fluvio-Volcanic Series, found widely on the Jos Plateau, is of early Tertiary age. The Fluvial sands on the Jos Plateau include tin bearing sands and gravels, above which are thin beds of clays and sometimes more sands or partly decomposed basalts, which are also usually weathered to clays.

Younger unweathered basalts overlie some tin bearing gravels and have also overflowed the edge of the plateau. Volcanic cones may still be seen. In Cameroon and the isles of the Bight of Biafra, the basalts and volcanic cones are likewise of two periods. Mount Cameroon has erupted recently.

In Pleistocene times, down-warping in north-eastern Nigeria formed the Chad Basin, in which were deposited terrestrial and lacustrine sands and clays of Pliocene to Pleistocene age.

Pronounced outward monoclinal tilting of the coastline is shown by the linear outcrop of the Eocene rocks, upon which rests the base of the Pleistocene–Recent delta. Later outward tilting is indicated by the drowned lower courses of all the rivers, though these are masked seaward by sand-bars and spits. Easy excavation of the soft sediments of the Benue and Niger Valleys has supplied abundant material for the Niger Delta.

MAJOR DIVISIONS
LAGOS STATE

SAND-SPIT COAST.[4] This lies south of the Porto-Novo Creek or Victoria Lagoon, from east of Lagos to Porto-Novo, which varies in depth from 9 to 30 feet and is an excellent waterway.

[1] On soils see *The Nigerian Handbook*, 1953, pp. 130–33 (with map) and H. Vine, *Notes on the Main Types of Nigerian Soils*, Agricultural Dept., 1953.

[2] J. C. Pugh, ' High-level Surfaces in the Eastern Highlands of Nigeria ', *South African Geographical Journal*, 1954.

[3] Dixey, op. cit., pp. 301–2.

[4] See J. C. Pugh, ' The Porto-Novo–Badagri Sand Ridge Complex ', *Research Notes*, Dept. of Geography, Univ. Coll., Ibadan, No. 3, pp. 3–14, and ' A Classification of the Nigerian Coastline ', *Journal of the West African Science Association*, Vol. I, Oct. 1954, No. 1, pp. 3–12.

Were there no political boundary to restrict traffic, it could be much more used.

South of the lagoon are recurved spit ends, shaped by eastward-moving material. South of the recurves are sub-parallel sand ridges, separated by strips of former swamp mud. Vegetation is always greater on the sand ridges. In the west these are relatively few, close together and clear; eastward they diverge, and breaks in continuity are more frequent. Between these sub-parallel sand ridges and the sea is a broad belt of sand, terminating in the surf beach. The sand-belt has fishing villages and large coconut palm plantations, as in Dahomey.

Just west of Badagry the sub-parallel sand ridges end abruptly marking a former break-through between creek and coast. Consequently in the Badagry area the outer sand belt is backed immediately by recurved spit ends.

Badagry, on the mainland, is an old European point of contact and missionary headquarters, now reviving somewhat. Behind it lies a system of east–west trending belts of sand and mud, indicating former open creeks between islands and mainland. Three miles east of Badagry the recurved spit ends also cease, and, consequently, as far as Lagos there is only a comparatively narrow and geologically recent sand belt.

Lagos,[1] with a population in 1963 in the federal district of 665,246, is the capital of Nigeria, its most important and best equipped port, and the largest town.

The broad and calm Lagos lagoon, with several islands, a permanently open outlet to the sea fed by the Ogun River and fringing mangroves afforded unusual possibilities for defence and trade. Lagos Island was first settled by Yoruba who began by establishing themselves at Isheri, 12 miles north of Lagos, moved later to Ebute Metta and subsequently to Iddo Island. From the latter they began to cultivate on Lagos Island (then called Eko = farm), though they made few settlements. However, peaceful penetration of Benin people became intense, and by the end of the fifteenth century they predominated, Lagos falling under their overlordship.

[1] See *Map of Lagos and Environs*, 1 : 12,500 or 1 : 30,000, Federal Surveys. Also Akin L. Mabogunje, ' The Evolution and Analysis of the Retail Structure of Lagos ', *Economic Geography*, 1964, pp. 304–23; and *Report on the Redevelopment of Metropolitan Lagos*, United Nations, 1964.

About the time this happened, the Portuguese appeared and applied the name Lago de Curamo. Later they called it Onin and, finally, Lagos, after one of their home towns. The site was unhealthy because of its low elevation and bad drainage encouraging bubonic and other plagues, and because of malarial mosquitoes bred in the occasionally flooded areas. Nevertheless, it was an excellent lair for slave-traders, near the sea, yet easily protected from sea attack. To it slaves could be sent by inland waterways from the Dahomey, Yoruba and Benin kingdoms, which were willing to sell their military and political captives.

Because of these physical advantages, and the exceptionally heavy supply of slaves from the Yoruba civil wars of the nineteenth century, Lagos remained one of the last great centres of the illegal slave trade. To stop it, the British occupied Lagos in 1851 and installed a new king and a vice-consul, but Portuguese merchants restarted the trade. So in 1861 Lagos was taken to suppress it, restrict the sources of supply, and develop legal commerce.

The island of Lagos became a Colony or Settlement in 1862, was added to in 1863, and between 1883 and 1895. In 1866 it was included (rather as a necessary encumbrance) in the ' West African Settlements ' under the Governor resident in Freetown, Sierra Leone. In 1874 Lagos came under the Governor of the Gold Coast, and in 1886 it regained independent administration as the ' Colony and Protectorate of Lagos '.

The oldest and most densely peopled part of Lagos Island is the north-north-western part. After 1861 the south-western corner became the commercial quarter and many firms established their own wharves. The south-eastern part came to be occupied by Government, missions, schools, hospitals and major European residences. Behind it, in the centre of the island, ex-slaves from Brazil had settled earlier in the area then called the Brazilian quarter. Beyond this, on the north-east, are late nineteenth and early twentieth century African houses. The eastern extremity of the island was at first the European quarter.

The Governorship of Sir William MacGregor (1899–1904) saw much development and improvement. The MacGregor canal was dug along the then eastern limit of the town, so creating Ikoyi Island. This was partly used for the cemetery and farther east for the later European (now Senior Service) residential quarters. The railway was opened to Ibadan in 1901 and, at the same time, the Denton railway bridge between Iddo Island and the mainland, and the Carter road bridge

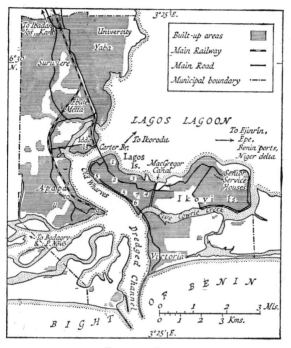

FIG. 77.—Lagos.

1 Old Town; 2 Old Brazilian Quarter; 3 Newer Town; 4 Early European Quarter, now offices; 5 Commercial Sectors; 6 Government House; 7 Racecourse; 8 Apapa Wharves; 9 1955 and 1965 Extensions; 10 Apapa Industrial Area; 11 Apapa Housing Estate.

from Iddo Island to Lagos. The latter was rebuilt in 1931, when the former was transformed into a causeway.

The fusion in 1906 of the Colony of Lagos and the Protectorate of Southern Nigeria eliminated the danger of a railway being built from a rival port west of the Niger. It also concentrated the trade of a larger political unit at Lagos.

Ocean steamers were still unable to enter Lagos. Passengers were transferred by ' mammy chair ' to surf boats or tenders off-shore, while cargo was transhipped at Forcados to 'branch boats' of 900–1,200 tons which could enter Lagos.

With rapidly increasing trade this became intolerable, so that dredging and the construction of moles and training banks on either side of the entrance were begun in 1906. Ocean vessels first entered in 1914, just as the opening of the Lagos–Kano Railway in 1912 and the unification of Nigeria in 1914 (with its capital at Lagos) were concentrating ever more trade upon it.

The inauguration of the Apapa wharves on the mainland west of Lagos, in 1926, greatly increased port capacity, though lighterage was sometimes necessary to Lagos Island wharves. Some smaller ocean vessels still anchor in the intervening channel, off these private wharves. Government Wharf at Apapa was extended south-eastward in 1955 to 2,565 feet to berth five additional ships. A lighter berth 370 feet long was also provided. Apapa Wharf was again extended in 1965.

South-west of the Apapa berths are the larger and newer industries, well planned on a 'trading' (industrial) estate. These include the Nigerian Brewery, employing 500 people and using empty bottles from competing imported beers, a motor vehicle assembly and repair plant, metal drum manufacture and conditioning, soap and margarine works, a bulk palm oil installation, a mineral oil depot and an oxygen works. Some deep-sea trawlers operate from Lagos.

Farther to the south-west are the new housing estates of the Lagos Executive Development Board. This is encouraging industry to move to sites adjacent to the Apapa wharves, and Lagos Island slum dwellers to new houses at Apapa. It thus hopes to reduce congestion on Lagos Island, to concentrate commerce and larger industries at Apapa, and so reduce lighterage and passenger ferrying between Apapa and Lagos Island. This should improve industrial efficiency and raise the standard of living.

North of Apapa and of Iddo Island (now the site of West Africa's largest power station) is the mainland African suburb of Ebute Metta, which is also the site of the large railway workshops and railway administration. North-west again is Yaba, with many newer missions, hospitals and an industrial estate for small firms. The University of Lagos is nearby.

Ikeja, twelve miles north of Lagos, and near its airport, has an impressive industrial estate with many factories making a variety of consumer goods such as textiles, shoes, drugs, beer and hardwear, as well as paints and asbestos cement, etc. The area benefits from proximity to the port of Lagos, yet it avoids its disadvantages, such as congestion.

WESTERN STATE

SOUTHERN ABEOKUTA AND WESTERN IJEBU.[1] These have the same Eocene clays, sand and sandstones as the Togo and Dahomey ' Terre de Barre ' and Dahomey plateaux. Similar food crops are grown, vegetables being especially important west of Ilaro and rice in swampy valleys. Lagos and Ibadan offer excellent markets.

Previously this area was extensively planted with cocoa, but the soils are too light, poor and quick draining. There has been considerable replanting with kolas, citrus, bananas and pineapples. The value of kola nuts sent north by rail and road is between £7 and £10 million per annum. Citrus fruits and pineapples are canned at Agege, Abeokuta and Ibadan. There is a small export of bananas.

At Apoje, on the Oshun River, the Western Nigeria Development Corporation is experimenting with the 20 square mile Ijebu Farm Project, begun in 1950. The aim is to establish cocoa, citrus, palm plantations, food crops, a model village, and to experiment with cultivating the Awusa nut (*Tetracarpidium conophorum*).

CENTRAL YORUBALAND. This includes northern Abeokuta, Ibadan, Ife–Ilesha Division of Oyo and western Ondo. It lies on the southern side of the Niger River–Gulf of Guinea watershed, the relief of which is higher and more broken in the east, e.g. around Ilesha and Akure. Central Yorubaland is the fortunate possessor of fairly fertile loamy

---

[1] For this and succeeding divisions of Western Nigeria, I have drawn upon K. M. Buchanan, 'An Outline of the Geography of the Western Region of Nigeria ', *The Malayan Journal of Tropical Geography,* 1953, pp. 9–24 and ' The Delimitation of Land Use Regions in a Tropical Environment—An Example from the Western Region of Nigeria.' *Geography,* 1953, pp. 303–7.

soils, derived mainly from Pre-Cambrian hornblende–biotite gneiss.

The Yoruba has generally been a careful and fairly intensive

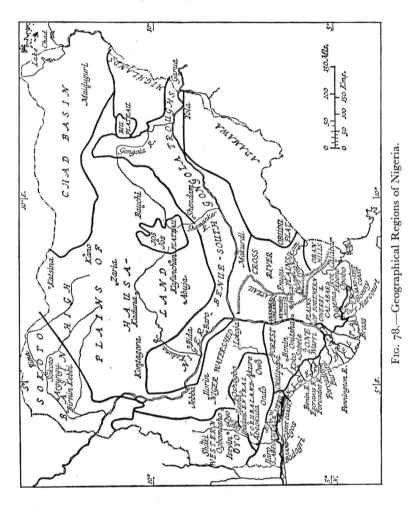

FIG. 78.—Geographical Regions of Nigeria.

farmer. Yams, cassava, maize, plantains and palm produce are important food crops, but there is no surplus for sale because of the dense population. The Yoruba farmer still tends to live partly in towns, so that large cities such as Ibadan and Abeo-kuta are an outstanding feature of Yorubaland. Population density is everywhere over two hundred per square mile, and often over 300. The area is well served by communications.

This is probably the most productive area in Nigeria, deriving its wealth from cocoa farming, commerce and craft industries. Cocoa production is limited by insufficient humidity on the north-west and north and by leached sandy soils on the south and east. There are about 900,000 acres under cocoa, cultivated by some 275,000 farmers, so that three-fifths of the Yoruba are directly dependent upon the crop as their major source of income. Farms vary from half an acre to over sixty acres, one or two acres being the most common. The area is affected by Swollen Shoot, especially east of Ibadan, but less so than in Ghana. The main cocoa belt extends east-north-east from Abeokuta for some 200 miles and is about 40 miles from north–south. In area about 10,000 square miles, it includes Ilaro, Abeokuta, Ibadan, Oshogbo, Ondo, Akure, Owo and Ikare. The last two lie near its eastern boundary, while the first lies on unsuitable Tertiary-derived soils. In the centre of the cocoa belt over half the farm lands have been planted with cocoa, often now old. Cultivation is less intensive and more recent in Ondo Province.

Commerce is largely in cocoa, yams from northern Oyo and northern Ondo, cassava from Ijebu (as Central Yorubaland no longer produces sufficient food crops itself), kola nuts from southern Abeokuta and Ijebu going north, fruit for canning or for despatch to the north, and in local craft goods and imports for the massive urban populations.

Abeokuta, centre of the Egba people, like Ibadan owed its foundation about 1830 to the disintegration of the Oyo–Yoruba Kingdom. Abeokuta is near contrasting soils and cash crops—mainly cocoa and yams to the north; kola, citrus, pineapple and cassava to the south. There is some fruit canning and juice production in the town, which is also an important market and collector of these crops.

Ibadan,[1] population (1963) 627,379, is the largest truly indigenous city in Tropical Africa. It is also the capital of

---

[1] See N. C. Mitchel, ' Some Comments on the Growth and Character of Ibadan's Population ', *Research Notes*, No. 4, 1953, Dept. of Geog., Univ. Coll., Ibadan; *Ibadan*, Univ. Coll., Ibadan, 1949; and A. Mabogunje, ' The Growth of Residential Districts in Ibadan ', *Geographical Review*, 1962, pp. 56–77.

Western Nigeria, the site of two universities, the major collecting point for farm produce, and a great centre of commerce, crafts and industries. Despite all this and its size, about one-fifth of its population is engaged in farming, so that Ibadan is often described as a gigantic village. Farmers may reside partly in a village and partly in Ibadan. Within 20 miles there is a rural population of 300,000.

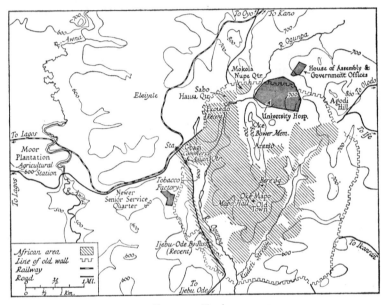

FIG. 79.—Ibadan.

Ibadan was founded near the end of the eighteenth century as a camp of outlaws. The modern settlement dates from about 1829, when it became a rallying point and Yoruba military headquarters after the Owu Wars (1821–5), which had disrupted Yorubaland. It also sheltered refugees from the Fulani conquest of northern Oyo.

By 1851 the town had 11 miles of walls, which, in time of civil war, provided protection by night for farmers who by day cultivated land up to 6 miles away. Successful protection for a population of about 60,000 accounted for the survival and growth of Ibadan. When it came under British rule in 1893, the population had risen to about 120,000. Commercial and European quarters were soon built and the railway came in 1901.

In the centre of the town are narrow north–south quartzite hills, the highest and most northerly one being Oke Aremo, 892 feet above sea level and some 200 feet above the surrounding country, so commanding an excellent view of possible attackers and aiding defence. The southern hill is Oke Mapo, on whose eastern and southern slopes the original war camp was established. It has Ibadan's oldest houses, largely inhabited by descendants of the original settlers.

On either side of these hills streams flow, but disease kept early settlement on the hill slopes or on adjacent pediments. Draining of the marshes has brought settlement nearer the streams, along which vegetables and sugar cane are still grown. On the north-eastern Agodi Hill are Government offices.

Within the $8\frac{1}{2}$ square miles inside the old walls, the population density is about 54,000 per square mile, averaging 24 per house and up to 100 per compound.

There are three exceptionally large markets. The major traditional crafts are weaving, dyeing and metal work, mostly found in compounds in the oldest quarters. Tailoring (the most common undertaking), cycle and car repairing, and woodworking are more modern and scattered, and are now more important than the traditional crafts.

Industry is, for example, represented by a very modern tobacco factory, by a cannery dealing with grapefruit and pineapple, and by a tyre-retreading works.

Other major towns of Central Yorubaland are Ife (the spiritual centre of the nation), Ilesha, Iwo and Oshogbo. Most of those developed, like Abeokuta and Ibadan, to house farmers whose fields might lie up to 6 miles from the town. They had double wall systems, with farmlands between inner and outer walls to withstand siege. Protected town dwelling by night was the Yoruba answer to war and civil war. It was not urbanisation as found in Europe.

WESTERN OYO. This is distinguished from the former area by shallow and sandy soils which are far less fertile, lesser rain of the Seasonal Equatorial type, poorer vegetation and eccentric position. For these reasons, those of history and of forest reservation, population density drops sharply to under 100 per square mile in the west and to under 50 in the north-west. There are few towns, Ogbomosho, a marginal town, being the largest.   Low population density and few towns result from this having been a no-man's land between the Yoruba and Dahomey peoples, and from Fulani attacks.   Cocoa and the oil palm cannot be grown economically, and although crops are more varied there are no very valuable ones grown over extensive areas.

As the annual rainfall is under 45 inches and the population sparser, there is a surplus of yams and cassava for sale, and guinea corn and millets are grown for local subsistence.   Other cash crops are tobacco (grown for the Ibadan factory) around Shaki, Ogbomosho, Oyo and Ipetu-Ijesha, the last three producing darker air-cured varieties.   There is a large flue curing installation near Shaki.   Cotton, indigo (much used in dyeing at Oyo and Iseyin) and chillies are also grown for sale. Zebu cattle are even kept in the north of Oyo Province.   There is an interesting goat- and sheep-skin leather craft industry at Oyo, as well as cloth weaving and dyeing.

This area, undoubtedly impoverished in the past, is capable of some development, although it can never be as productive as Central Yorubaland.

CONCLUSION—WESTERN STATE.   The country has considerable physical and human variety.   Cocoa, timber and palm kernels are important exports; kola nuts and palm oil are major cash crops for internal marketing.

Some richer soils and lower rainfall than are usual in eastern Nigeria have enabled the careful Yoruba farmer to find in cocoa an outstandingly valuable crop, though it is one of possible danger in view of Swollen Shoot and new competitors.

MID-WESTERN STATE

THE NIGER DELTA.   This magnificent example of a delta may be taken to begin 5 miles east of Ajumo, 62 miles east of Lagos.   Surf, sand, palms and undergrowth give way to smooth water running over a wide mudflat with mangrove and swamp.   This great change coincides with a south-eastward turn in the direction of the coast.

Instead of an easterly longshore drift there is a north-westerly one on the west side of the delta. The rivers Benin, Escravos and Forcados, unobstructed by sandspits, are never-theless increasingly impaired by large submerged bars, that in the Forcados mouth being over 3 miles wide, seven times wider than in 1899. The depth of the navigable channel over that bar decreased from 21 feet to 13 feet between 1899 and 1947, but deepened by two feet in the next two years. Until 1914 goods for Lagos were transhipped at Forcados but now, partly because of the state of this bar, Forcados is a dead port. In-stead, the narrow Escravos entrance was opened in 1940 (minimum depth now of 22 feet). It soon became to be preferred to the Forcados entrance, as giving deeper water and being easier to navigate. Yet the Escravos entrance re-quires a longer journey for ships using Burutu and Warri, though a shorter one for those using Koko and Sapele. It has been dredged, and maintained by a breakwater to the south.

Warri and Burutu export groundnuts, cotton, cotton seed and cake brought down the Benue River from Cameroon and Chad; groundnuts from regions along the Benue, and from northern Nigeria brought by rail to Baro and thence down the Niger River; and cocoa, palm oil, kernels, rubber and timber from those parts of southern Nigeria near the Niger River. Imports are distributed to the same areas. Some 150,000 tons are exported from these ports.

Burutu is a nineteenth-century creation of the Niger River Transport Company, and has two ocean berths. Here goods are transhipped to and from river vessels, which include petro-leum barges. The port is also a base for offshore petroleum exploration and production.

Warri performs a similar function for John Holt and Com-pany and the French Niger–Benue Transport Company, and is a general port as well. It is an old settlement, which in the fifteenth and later centuries saw Portuguese missionaries and Portuguese and Dutch slave traders.

Sapele, 70 miles up the Benin River, is the site of the U.A.C. timber mill, plywood and veneer factory (see p. 500), as well as of the same company's Cowan oil palm estate and mill. Up-river are two of its rubber estates.

Koko has bulk palm oil plants, and is being developed as a general port.

The delta mouths offered shelter to the early slave traders and easy concealment in the last days of the illegal trade. In addition to the many mouths, there is a continuous line of creeks and lagoons from the Pennington River north-westward via Forcados, Epe and Lagos to Porto-Novo in Dahomey. This provides an increasingly important, calm inland waterway for vessels of up to 4 feet 6 inches draught and, in places, more.

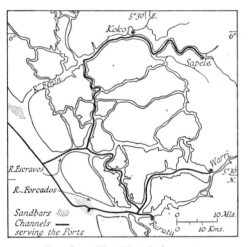

FIG. 80.—The West Delta ports.

On the landward or inner side of this waterway, Fresh-water Swamp Vegetation is found from which Raphia is obtained, and Sudd obstruction occurs in some parts of the creek-lagoon waterway. On the seaward side, mangrove is cut for tanning material, constructional timber and fuel. Swamp rice cultivation is developing where salt content of the soil is low.

THE FOREST ZONE OF E. IJEBU, S. ONDO, N. BENIN AND N. DELTA PROVINCES. Soils of this zone are derived from post-Middle Eocene sands which drain rapidly. As the rainfall is 90–120 inches in an Equatorial régime, and the soils were originally poor, they are now severely leached and acidic. Water is generally found at great depth, so that settlement was probably always sparse in southern Ondo and western

Benin. As this area was also a frontier zone between the Yoruba and Edo (Bini) peoples and was raided for slaves, its sparse population was reduced still further. Nigeria's best and most accessible timber reserves are being developed here, mainly in the Mid-Western State.

In the south and south-east, where the rainfall is highest, the oil palm, rubber and rice are significant crops. Rubber comes mainly from the Warri–Sapele–Kwale–Benin areas, and rice from along the many rivers. In southern Benin, the Sobo Grasslands were probably caused by over-farming and forest regeneration is prevented by annual burning.

In eastern Benin, westward from the Niger River, where the annual rainfall is still over 90 inches, is an extension of the main palm belt from eastern Nigeria. There is the same oil palm bush, with associated cocoyam, cassava and maize as food crops. Moreover, this has scattered houses of the Ibo, unlike the usually linear villages of the Bini, or the compact large villages or once walled towns of the Yoruba.

Population density exceeds 180 per square mile in Asaba Division. Consequently, although palm oil production is high, so much is consumed locally that the amount available for export is smaller than farther south or west, where the population is less. Palm oil is bulked and exported through Koko. Export of kernels is much higher than that of oil. (See also under Eastern States.)

North-eastern Benin, being drier and less populated, produces less palm oil and kernels, but is a significant producer of rice, yams and of the local Ishan cotton. As it is rather remote from communications and markets, the economy is essentially a subsistence one.

Benin, population (1963) 100,694 is the capital of the Mid-Western State and the centre of the Bini people. Benin was visited by the Portuguese in 1485, when it was a powerful independent kingdom. It soon engaged fully in the pepper, ivory and slave trades, and later fell under a tyranny of fetish priests who made huge annual human sacrifices. The famous brass figures, and the less well-known wood and ivory articles are still made.

CONCLUSION—MID-WESTERN STATE. At first sight the Mid-Western State—less developed and with only one-quarter the population of the Western State, and with no railway, would seem to have poor prospects. However, it has important resources of mineral oil and gas, timber, rubber and palm oil. Although the oil is piped to Bonny in Rivers State, it earns royalties for the Mid-West, and the natural gas is being used in industry and electrical generation. Rubber cultivation by ordinary farmers leaves much to be desired but could be improved. The delta ports have improved access, and are of increasing importance for local commerce as well as serving mainly as inlets and outlets for transit traffic to and from northern Nigeria and beyond, in successful competition with congested Lagos and Port Harcourt. Given good government and sensible policies the Mid-West could be quite prosperous.

RIVERS, EAST-CENTRAL, AND SOUTH-EASTERN STATES

THE NIGER DELTA. The western part of this occurs in the Mid-Western State. Rainfall often exceeds 140 inches per annum, mangrove vegetation is luxuriant and swamps widespread.

As permanently dry points are rare, roads are few. The infrequent villages are on or near waterways which alone provide constant access. With such difficulties and the unhealthy character of the country, the population density is no more than forty per square mile in Brass Division. Population may also have been lowered by slave raiding, for here were the slave and oil trade ports of the Oil Rivers, such as Akassa, Brass, Degema and Bonny. Most of these have declined, though Opobo and Abonnema have palm oil bulking plants, and Bonny has a mineral oil export terminal.

Port Harcourt, population (1963) 95,768 and growing fast, lies 41 miles up the Bonny River, at the limit of Mangrove, where there are depths in the river of 24 feet at high-water and firm dry land. These advantages were noticed by Sir Frederick (later Lord) Lugard in 1913, when he was seeking a terminus for a railway to serve the coalfield at Enugu. The railway between the two was opened in 1916, and Port Harcourt became a distributor of coal by sea to other ports, the rest of Nigeria and, on occasion, other countries in and even outside West Africa. It also immediately became an exporter of palm oil and kernels from the nearby oil palm belt and now has a large bulk palm oil plant.

The railway was extended to Kaduna and Jos in 1927. After this, and especially after 1932, when the Benue bridge was completed, Port Harcourt also became the port for the Jos tinfields and for some of the produce of northern Nigeria, especially groundnuts.

The town is built above and east of the Bonny River, between it and Almadi Creek on the east and Dockyard Creek on the south.[1] It is Nigeria's second port, the main one of eastern Nigeria and has road, rail, river and air connections.

Port Harcourt is the centre for the nearby oilfield and has a refinery. Natural gas is piped to the Trans-Amadi Industrial Estate where tyres, aluminium sheets, bottles and other goods are made. Port Harcourt could become a major Nigerian town, and the leading industrial centre of the Federation.

SAND-SPIT COAST. This occurs east of the delta, but lagoons are ill-developed and creeks take their place.

Calabar, once known as Old Calabar, lies 48 miles up the Calabar River, a tributary of the Cross River. It was a notorious slave port, the last illegal ship leaving only in 1839. It was also the centre of the subsequent palm oil trade and of the famous ' ruffians ', or masters of trading hulks moored in the rivers. Trading houses were not built ashore until the 'seventies.

The Oil Rivers Protectorate was proclaimed in 1885, and Calabar became its headquarters until, in 1906, the Protectorate (by then called Southern Nigeria) was amalgamated with Lagos Colony.

A Presbyterian Mission was founded in 1846, and Calabar remained the headquarters of that church. The palm oil trade and the mission are still dominant in the town, but Calabar has suffered much relative economic decline compared with Port Harcourt. Calabar is, however, served by air, by a few roads, and by the Cross River. This is navigable in the wet season to Mamfe in Cameroon, for which Calabar acts as a trade centre. A new road connects these towns, and Calabar may become an outlet for more of eastern Nigeria.

After declining in competition with Enugu and Port Harcourt, Calabar may have a new lease of life as the capital of the

[1] *Port Harcourt*, 400 feet to 1 inch, Land and Survey Dept., Lagos.

South-Eastern State.   Calabar people are important in fishing
and commerce in all the Bight of Biafra.

PLAINS OF SOUTHERN OWERRI AND CALABAR.[1]   These lie
inland from the previous region and south of a north facing
Eocene sandstone scarp.   This begins near Awka (near
Onitsha, see Figs. 81–2) and extends south-eastward as the edge
of the Awka–Orlu Uplands to just north of Calabar, and so into
Cameroon.   In the north-west this scarp is some 400 feet high
and severely gullied, but it is lower in the south-east.   Other
than the fringing scarp, the deposits are clays, sandstones and
lignites of post-Middle Eocene age.

Acid sandy soils are again found, similar to those dominant
in the Forest Zone of the Western State (see p. 461).   They are
even more leached in the east, by very heavy rainfall of at
least 70 inches.   Severe leaching is not only a function of the
heavier rainfall, but also of the generally uninterrupted rainy
season of the Cameroon type.   In Southern Owerri and Calabar, heavy lateritic soils occur in lower lying and ill-drained
areas, which are also less peopled and unhealthy.

In place of the original Rain Forest, oil palms now predominate.   The climate for the oil palm is ideal and, although
the soils are poor, it tolerates them.   There has been much replanting under the Palm Grove Rehabilitation Scheme.   This is
the heart of the oil palm belt and from here the bulk of the production comes.   Pioneer mills and hand presses have been introduced to increase the extraction of oil and its quality.   Cassava
is the main food crop, followed by yams, cocoyams, maize and
vegetables.   Production of palm oil for the large local population and for export (as well as kernel export) dominates the
economy.   There are also some oil palm and rubber estates
east of Calabar.

The density of oil palms is closely allied with that of human
population—this despite the most unfavourable conditions of
sandy soils and elusive water supplies.   Settlements are compounds, rather than villages or towns.   Though the area is
intensively farmed, the pattern of settlement contrasts strongly
with the urban clusters of Yorubaland.

[1] See also J. T. Coppock, op. cit.; W. B. Morgan, 'Farming Practice, Settle-
ment Pattern and Population Density in South-Eastern Nigeria', *Geographical
Journal*, 121, pp. 320–33, and R. Mansell Prothero, 'The Population of Eastern
Nigeria', *Scottish Geographical Magazine*, 71, pp. 165–70.

Population densities here are the highest in Nigeria. There are, almost everywhere, over 250 persons per square mile and in Owerri 537 as an average; with local densities of up to about 1,350 per square mile in the southern part of Onitsha Province and northern Owerri. There is certainly severe pressure of population here, the visible consequences of which are the renting of farm lands outside the area and temporary migration of labourers to other parts of Nigeria, to Fernando Po and Gabon. (See also Chapter 10.) Mineral oil production near Port Harcourt normally provides much employment locally.

Road density here is also the highest in Nigeria, a reflection of the export possibilities for palm oil and of the dense population relatively near the coast.

Onitsha lies on the higher east bank of the Niger, at the edge of the Nkwele Hills and at the confluence of the Anambra River. It has long had a huge market for goods originally brought or despatched mainly by canoe. The importance of this route has been maintained by the fact that Onitsha can be reached by Niger steamers at all seasons and that it has a bridge across the river. European traders were established here as early as 1860. Its modern importance as a market is enhanced by the great concentration of roads upon it. Like the lesser markets of Orlu, Owerri and Umuahia, it is a major collector of palm oil.

THE CRETACEOUS COUNTRY OF THE ANAMBRA LOWLANDS, UDI PLATEAU AND CROSS RIVER PLAINS.[1] The constituent regions are:

(a) *The Cross River Plains* in the south-east and east are drained by the Cross River and its tributaries, and vary in altitude from 700 feet in the north-west to less than 200 feet in the south. Beneath them are intensely folded Middle Cretaceous shales, sandstones and limestones.

(b) *The Udi Plateau or Donga Ridge*, running north–south, is bounded on the east and north by a bold escarpment.

---

[1] I acknowledge my indebtedness here to A. T. Grove, *Land Use and Soil Conservation in Parts of Onitsha and Owerri Provinces*, Bulletin No. 21 of the Geological Survey of Nigeria, 1951 and ' Soil Erosion and Population Problems in South-East Nigeria ', *Geographical Journal*, 117, pp. 291–306.

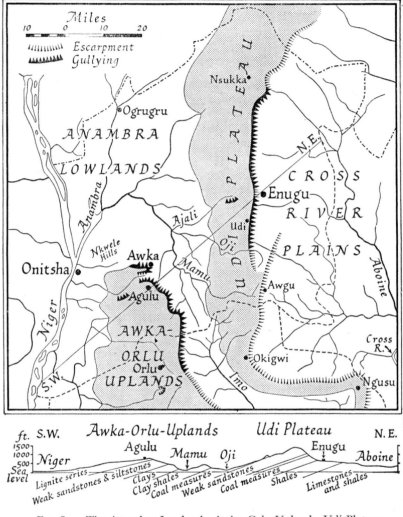

FIG. 81.—The Anambra Lowlands, Awka–Orlu Uplands, Udi Plateau and Cross River Plains.

(From A. T. Grove, ‘ Soil Erosion and Population Problems in South-East Nigeria ’, *Geographical Journal*, Vol. CXVII, Part 3, Sept. 1951, p. 295, by kind permission of the author and editor.)

The surface rises in places to over 1,500 feet above sea level and slopes south-westward into the syncline of the Anambra Lowlands.   These several features result from the sub-aerial denudation of an anticline, whose eastern limb has been eroded.

The cuesta is composed of Upper Cretaceous Coal

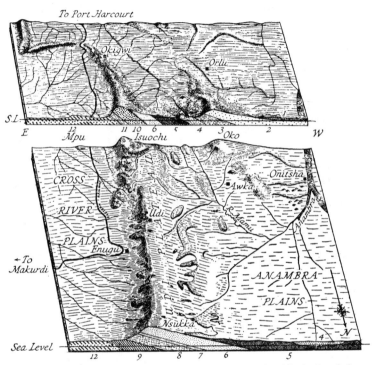

FIG. 82.—Block Diagram of Anambra Plains (Lowlands), Awka–Orlu Uplands, Udi Plateau and Cross River Plains.

(From A. T. Grove, *Land Use and Soil Conservation*, Bulletin No. 21 of Geological Survey of Nigeria, 1951, p. 2, by kind permission of the author and director.)

Measures, hard sandstones and shales; the dip slope has false-bedded sandstones.   These are also exposed in the northern sector of the scarp (north of the Oji River—south of Udi), and it is these sandstones which have been easily eroded in gigantic gullies.   South of the river another scarp, formed of far more resistant Awgu sandstone, overlaps the northern section and gullying is absent.

The cuesta runs southward to near Okigwi, where it swings eastward as a three to four mile wide hog's back to within 10 miles of the Cross River, and then turns south and south-east[1] to Cameroon. Ten to twenty miles separate it from the Eocene scarp of the Plains of Southern Owerri and Calabar.

(c) *The Anambra Lowlands* (or Plains), in the north-west, between the Niger River and the Udi Plateau, are floored by sandstones and shales of the Upper Cretaceous Coal Measures. On the southern edge is the Eocene scarp of the Awka–Orlu Uplands and the post-Middle Eocene Nkwele Hills very near Onitsha.

Rainfall varies between 60 inches in the north and 85 inches in the south. The Udi Plateau also has a generally higher rainfall than the Anambra Lowlands or Cross River Plains. Rainfall is of the Seasonal or Semi-seasonal Equatorial type, and the original vegetation was probably Rain Forest. On the uplands, economically useful trees survive only on steep slopes and around villages—' cool green islands set in poor grassland where fire resistant species . . . become more numerous as the distance from the nearest village increases. The barren appearance of this outside farm-land is surprising in a region with such a high annual rainfall '.[2] Grassland also covers wide areas below the Udi escarpment and in the Anambra Lowlands.

The Udi Plateau has poor and acidic soils. Those of the Anambra Lowlands and Cross River Plains are often lateritic but are less peopled. In the Anambra Lowlands water is found only at 250 feet or more. It is often insufficient or distant on the Udi Plateau, though on the scarp there are numerous springs.

On the plateau population density averages 300 or more per square mile and population pressure exists. Alleviation is secured by temporary migration or by renting farm land in nearby lowlands, in Benin, Ahoada (Rivers State) and Calabar Divisions.

The main income is from the oil palm, supplemented by food

---

[1] C. Daryll Forde, ' Land and Labour in a Cross River Village, Southern Nigeria ', *Geographical Journal*, 90, pp. 24–51, describes a village athwart the ridge east of Afikpo.

[2] Grove, op. cit., *Geographical Journal*, pp. 293–5.

crop sales in the less populated lowlands and by employment in the coal mines, and the cement works at Nkalagu east of Enugu. Further employment might be provided by the exploitation of clays for brick-making, of iron ore found near the (unfortunately poorly-coking) coal, of lead and zinc at Abakaliki and Ameka–Nyeba also east of Enugu, and by the development of a fertiliser industry based on the sulphur fumes from refining the latter minerals.[1]

Enugu, population (1963) 138,457, lies at the foot of the Udi scarp, where coal-mining began in 1915. Enugu owes its origin and development to mining, to being a capital, and to asbestos–cement and steel factories.

THE OBAN HILLS. Lying north-east of Calabar, these are a north-westerly projection of the Cameroon Highlands and consist of Pre-Cambrian basement rocks. Rainfall is between 100 and 140 inches annually, population is sparse, and the hills are still thickly covered with Rain Forest. On the southern edge are rubber estates.

THE OBUDU PLATEAU AND SONKWALA HILLS. Also Pre-Cambrian, these are north-western projections of the Bamenda Highlands extending into Ogoja Province, and drained by the Katsina Ala tributary of the Benue and mainly covered by grassland.

A project has been developed for cattle ranching on 20,000 acres. Population is sparse.

CONCLUSION—RIVERS STATE, EAST-CENTRAL STATE AND SOUTH-EASTERN STATE. These States are the successors of the Eastern Region, the poorest Region until 1962. Yet in some four years the mounting development of mineral oil and gas transformed it into the most productive Region.

Yet agriculturally there are severe problems. There is excessive dependence upon the oil palm. The States have an unusual proportion of Secondary, Tertiary and Quaternary rocks, which weather to mediocre soils. In turn these are rapidly leached by the rather long and continuous rainy season in the south. On the Secondary and Tertiary escarpments there is locally severe gullying.

---

[1] For these and the lignite found in the Eocene series to the west, see under Minerals.

The East-Central State, the Ibo homeland, is the most densely peopled state of Nigeria, and was the centre of resistance to federal troops in 1967. Large numbers of Ibo had to return to the state, and their re-settlement in an already heavily peopled and impoverished country poses great problems.

NORTH-WESTERN, NORTH-CENTRAL, KANO, NORTH-EASTERN, BENUE-PLATEAU AND WEST-CENTRAL STATES

I. THE MIDDLE BELT

The Middle Belt roughly coincides with Ilorin, Niger, Zaria (southern part), Kabba, Benue, Plateau and Adamawa Provinces. One of the most distinctive divisions of

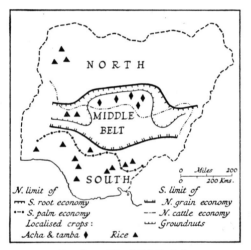

FIG. 83.—The Middle Belt.

(From K. M. Buchanan, ' Nigeria—Largest Remaining British Colony ', *Economic Geography*, 1952, p. 308, by kind permission of the author and editor.)

Nigeria, as indeed of all West Africa, the Middle Belt lies between about 8 and $10\frac{1}{2}°$ N. It is particularly clear in Nigeria, because of the size of that country, and because the belt separates the ' Nigerian Sudan ' from the forest lands.

Geologically and physiographically the belt has no unity, but climatically it roughly corresponds to the realm of the

[1] I have drawn partly on K. M. Buchanan, ' The Northern Region of Nigeria ', *Geographical Review*, 1953, pp. 451–73.

Southern Savannah climate. There is even closer correspondence to the fire scarred Southern Guinea Vegetation zone.

Although the Middle Belt produces both the grains of the north and the root crops of the south, tsetse fly prevents the keeping of humped cattle (except on the Jos Plateau and in the Adamawa Highlands), and the oil palm and cocoa do not thrive. Thus the advantage of the Middle Belt in combining some northern and southern crops is much diminished, and it has no equivalent compensation. The population pattern and its causes are discussed on pp. 446–7.

The consequences of all this are that, although the Middle Belt covers at least one-quarter of Nigeria, it is very unproductive, as it is elsewhere in West Africa, and contributes little to exports and not much to internal trade. Economic development requires reduction or elimination of the tsetse fly to permit the keeping of Zebu cattle and to prevent sleeping sickness. A greater population could then develop the country with such crops as benniseed, now so successfully grown by the Tiv. Pig rearing might be developed by these non-Muslim peoples, using both root and grain crops. Hydro-electric power from the Jos Plateau might be used for the development of industries. Meanwhile, the main significance of the Middle Belt is in the production of food crops for deficient areas in Nigeria. It may be divided into the following regions:

THE NIGER WATERSHED. This is the divide through which ran the boundary between Northern and Western Nigeria, following the main limit of Fulani conquest, rather than the precise water-parting. It leaves within the West-Central State a Yoruba majority in the Ilorin Emirate.

The watershed has Pre-Cambrian rocks, its soils are thin and the vegetation poor Guinea Savannah. Yams, beans, onions and rice are the main cash crops, mostly sold in the cocoa lands.

Ilorin, population (1952) 40,994, the seat of a Fulani but Yoruba-speaking Emir, has a tobacco factory and produces pottery mainly sold in the Western State.

THE NIGER–BENUE–SOUTH GONGOLA TROUGHS. Probably of tectonic origin, these troughs have Cretaceous deposits, which weather into sandy but fairly productive soils, used for benniseed cash cropping in Benue Province and for cotton in

Kabba Province. Alluvial soils along the rivers are being used for rice and for irrigated sugar, as at Bacita (see page 488).

The Benue is navigable to *Garua* (Cameroon) for two months and *Makurdi* is the flood season headquarters of Benue steamers. *Jebba* is the absolute limit of navigation on the Niger in Nigeria but *Baro* is the usual limit, mainly because it is the point of transhipment to the railway ' feeder ' branch line. The Kainji dam is being built 64 miles upstream from Jebba. *Bida* is the Nupe capital, famous for brass, silver, glass and mat craftsmen.

Lokoja, at the confluence of the Niger and Benue Rivers, had its origin on Mount Patti, where iron has been located and will be smelted locally. The modern town is by the river, since it is an important calling point for steamers and a trade centre for local foodstuffs, cotton and cotton goods, leather from the north, kola nuts from the south, and for imported goods.

THE SOUTHERN HIGH PLAINS OF HAUSALAND. These consist of Pre-Cambrian schists and quartzites. Elevation varies between about 1,000 feet in Kontagora and nearly 3,000 feet south-east of Kaduna. It includes most of Niger and the southern part of Zaria Provinces.

Kontagora Division of Niger Province is very thinly peopled because of past slave raiding. By contrast, broken country around Abuja kept the people freer from attack and there is a pocket of denser population. Various efforts have been made to re-people more or less empty areas; thus a fly-free corridor has been made for settlers at Anchau, south-east of Zaria. In Kontagora the local authority tried land settlement with mixed farms, but this and the Mokwa Scheme run by the Colonial Development Corporation failed. The only considerable cash crops are cotton, tobacco and ginger.

Kaduna, population (1963) 149,910, was made headquarters of the Northern Provinces in 1917, later became the capital of Northern Nigeria, and then that of the North-Central State. Kaduna is a substantial industrial (especially textile) centre.

THE JOS PLATEAU.[1] This is often misnamed the Bauchi

---

[1] I have drawn on F. Dixey, ' The Morphology of the Jos Plateau ', in R. A. Mackay, R. Greenwood and J. E. Rockingham, *The Geology of the Plateau Tinfields—Resurvey 1945–8*, Bulletin No. 19 Geological Survey of Nigeria, Kaduna, 1949.

Plateau, but Bauchi town is beyond the plateau and much of Bauchi Province lies beyond its confines.

The plateau extends some 65 miles from south to north and 50 miles from east to west, with an average height of about 4,300 feet. Granite masses, some reaching about 6,000 feet, have formed a resistant core throughout many erosion cycles, compared with less resistant surrounding gneisses. The plateau surface has very gently undulating grassy plains, with occasional granite tors, some flat-topped hills of the Fluvio-Volcanic Series, and clusters of small recently extinct volcanic cones with basalt flows. An important erosion surface is found at 4,000–4,600 feet.

The edges of the plateau are much indented, the granites causing bold or rocky scarps and buttresses. Between these are embayments, with gently sloping floors, eroded on less resistant gneiss. With larger outcrops, the embayment floors continue to rise inward toward the plateau centre, thus somewhat facilitating rail and road access, e.g. the Kaduna–Jos road and the Kafanchan–Jos railway past the Assob basalts.

West and east, the plateau scarps are frequently 1,500–2,000 feet high. On the south, they are 3,000 feet or more; the structure is complex and the relief rugged. In places two or three bevels, with sharp scarps, intervene between plateau surface and the plains. Falls, developed for hydro-electric power, are caused by these intervening scarps.

Whereas the Fulani penetrated and settled in the Fouta Djallon in Guinea, despite its abrupt edges and many deep gorges, they did not do so until recently on the Jos Plateau. This is higher, but it has the advantage over the Fouta Djallon of being free of tsetse fly and of being less divided by gorges.

Instead, the Jos Plateau was the refuge for ' pagan ' peoples who had been attacked by the Fulani, and it is still almost surrounded by Islamic peoples. The inhabitants of the plateau have been retarded by their isolation, the poverty of their soils, and the limited cropping possibilities offered by these in conjunction with the cooler rainy climate. Their main cereals have been the poor Acha (*Digitaria exilis*) and Tamba (*Eleusine coracana*). Temperate vegetables are also produced for sale.

Cattle keeping has been encouraged from the veterinary

headquarters at Vom, south-west of Jos. Butter, cheese and clarified butterfat are made here, for sale.

Tin mining (see pp. 501–5) has been the greatest economic activity on the Jos Plateau since about 1903. Although this mining has benefited Nigeria as a whole, it has ruined some of the plateau farm land and, in the past at any rate, discouraged its peoples.

For this and other reasons, there is local land pressure, which the Shendam Agricultural Development and Resettlement Scheme has sought to alleviate. Many farmers and their families have been resettled in the thinly populated Shendam district, where rice can be grown in the Shemankar valley.[1]

Mining has had other more wholly beneficial results. It has led to the development of hydro-electric power on the plateau edges and to the construction of many roads. But if the several minerals become unprofitable to work, the Jos Plateau might become a problem area.

Jos, population (1952) 32,105, is a European creation. It is the headquarters of Benue–Plateau State and the organising centre for the tinfields. By reason of its Hill Station, museum, healthier climate and pleasant surroundings, Jos has some tourist trade, which might be fostered. It could be an ideal place for multi-racial schools. Jos is well served by road, air and rail.

THE ADAMAWA HIGHLANDS. These rise sharply on the eastern borders of Nigeria and Cameroon. They lie between about $7\frac{1}{2}°$ and $11\frac{1}{4}°$ N., mainly in Cameroon.

The Adamawa Highlands, unlike the Bamenda Highlands farther south, are almost devoid of volcanic outcrops and so the soils are poorer. The highlands average 2,500 feet in elevation, but in places reach about 6,700 feet. Divided by the Benue Trough, they rise steeply but their summits are mostly smooth. Vegetation is Sudan Savannah, the original Woodland having been degraded.

South of the Benue River, the population is exceedingly sparse, communications poor and the country under-developed.

---

[1] For this and other settlement schemes, see J. T. Coppock, op. cit. at pp. 11–12, and K. M. Buchanan, 'Internal Colonization in Nigeria', *Geographical Review*, 1953, pp. 416–18.

Though primitive, the pagans are often careful farmers, terracing their land, using manure, rotating crops, planting trees and keeping animals. Some have moved to the plains on the west (previously the domain of Hausa and Fulani), but they often farm badly and wastefully there, so creating a ' dust bowl '. Their crops are guinea corn, millet, peppers, okro, yams, potatoes and cotton, and they collect wild produce. Small cattle are kept in the highlands, and Shuwa, Red Longhorn and White Fulani Zebu in the plains—probably 250,000 head in all.

Those parts of the former United Kingdom Trusteeship of the Cameroons which opted to join Northern Nigeria in 1961 were far more closely identified with Nigeria than with Cameroon. This is because of kinship ties, closer economic relations and means of communications. Distances from the outside world are the main problem, and roads are especially necessary in the southern districts.

2. The ' Nigerian Sudan '

The ' Nigerian Sudan ' comprises almost all Sokoto, Katsina, Kano, the northern third of Zaria, northern Bauchi and Bornu Provinces.

Like the Middle Belt, the Nigerian Sudan has no geological or physiographic unity, but climatically it belongs mainly to the Savannah type and its vegetation is that of the Sudan Savannah.

The Nigerian Sudan stands in sharp contrast to the Middle Belt, not only in its climate and vegetation, but also in its cereal food and groundnut cash crops, rarity of tsetse fly and the importance of livestock. It provides most of the revenue of the northern states; here also are great and sometimes extensive clusters of population, analysed on p. 447. The restrictions upon development are the availability of water and roads. The Nigerian Sudan may be divided into the following regions:

NORTHERN HIGH PLAINS OF HAUSALAND. These are the continuation of the southern High Plains of Hausaland, which they resemble geologically, except that some Cretaceous deposits occur on the boundary between Katsina and Daura. In the northern part of Zaria Province the average altitude is 2,000–2,500 feet, in Kano Province it is 1,500–2,500 feet, and in Katsina Province between 1,000 and 2,000 feet. In the south there are more granite domes and rock masses than in the north, where the surface is very flat because of masking by recent sands. The Niger–Chad watershed is tilted towards the north and east. The rivers, dry for seven to eight months, flow seasonally in broad and shallow trenches.

Soils are light, sandy but water-holding in Kano and Katsina Provinces, where they are ideal for groundnuts. In northern Zaria, eastern Sokoto and southern Katsina they are heavier, and more suitable for Allen cotton. Nevertheless, these crops are often either inter-cropped or rotated. Tobacco is the subsidiary cash crop to cotton in Zaria Province, where it has gained on sugar cane which suffers here from red rot disease. Tobacco follows groundnuts and cotton in importance in Gusau District (eastern Sokoto). The main food crops are guinea corn, bulrush millet, beans, peas and a rapidly increasing amount of cassava. In town gardens and in the *fadamas* (flood plains) of all provinces, where darker alluvial soils occur, maize, rice, sweet potatoes, sugar cane, onions, tomatoes, indigo, tobacco, wheat and henna are grown, often in tiny irrigated fields. The protected shea butter tree provides oil and the locust bean fruit a kind of edible cake and a hardening material. Baobab leaves are used in soup and as spinach, the fruit is edible and used in dyeing, and the bark is used for ropes. These are also made from the fibre of the dum palm.

Around large towns there is extremely 'close farming', sustaining dense populations by permanent and intensive cropping, fertility being maintained with night soil brought from the towns on donkeys. Up to about 10 miles from Kano there are 1,000 persons per square mile, and up to 30 miles there are approximately 400 per square mile. In all there are about 1 million people, and some forty walled towns. Most farms are under an acre in area, every piece of ground is or has been used, and the intensity of cultivation recalls Flanders. During the dry season, when food may be insufficient, some farmers engage in petty trading or labouring.

These are among the few areas in Africa where Africans have, to use a French term, 'humanised' the countryside.

In the wet season the impression is that man is dominant, rather than nature.

Zaria, population (1952) 61,670, lies near the southern edge of this region, on a strong defensive site. It was the capital of the ancient Hausa kingdom of Zazau and was probably founded about 1536. It is a walled town with tanning, weaving, dyeing and basket-making crafts. Outside, on the north around the railway station (junction for a branch to Kaura Namoda), are important railway workshops, a large cotton ginnery, cigarette

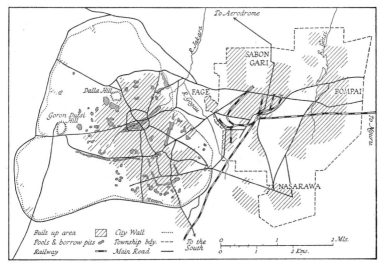

FIG. 84.—Kano.

factory and the Gaskiya Corporation printing press. The corporation publishes newspapers, pamphlets on such matters as hygiene, farming and housing, and books, all mainly in the Hausa and Tiv languages. Near Zaria are the buildings of the Ahmadu Bello University, incorporating the former branch of the Nigerian College of Arts, Science and Technology.

Kano, population (1963) 147,841, is one of the most interesting cities of West Africa, and the principal commercial centre of northern Nigeria. Neolithic stone implements prove early occupation, and these and local legend point to the probable importance of Dalla Hill as a source of ironstone, attractive to blacksmith settlers. Certain it is that there was an influx in

R

the tenth century.   Dalla and Goron Dutsi Hills may also
have been valued as guides to trans-Saharan caravans at the
end of their journey; the hills undoubtedly served as watch-
towers, like those in Ibadan.   Kano was at the height of its
glory and prosperity from 1463 to 1499, when trans-Saharan
trade was considerable, Kano then receiving European goods
in exchange for leather.

The wall is 13 miles long, enclosing an area of 14 square miles.
Within are the two hills, the Jakara stream and grazing and
agricultural land to help withstand siege.   There are also many
' borrow pits ' from which earth has been taken to build the
flat-roofed and interestingly patterned houses.   The central
market, astride the Jakara rivulet, is a particularly busy one.
Also in the walled city are many brass and silversmiths, leather
tanning and ornamental leather workers, makers of mats and
rope, indigo blue and purple dyers (in the Dalla quarter),
weavers, blacksmiths and potters.   Tailors are now, however,
the most numerous workers.   Fulani dominate the southern
quarters and Hausa the northern ones.

The British occupied Kano in 1903.   At first Europeans lived
in Nasarawa, in and around the Emir's suburban house.   In
1905 government headquarters were developed at Bompai,
where more water was available, and which commands roads
to north and east.   But between 1909 and 1926 all but the
Police, Judicial and Military Departments moved back to
Nasarawa.   In 1912, on the arrival of the railway, the Commercial Township (where the Asiatic community lives) was
begun.   Between it and the east wall of Kano is Fage, the
settlement for Hausa strangers.   North-east of Fage is Sabon
Gari, for people from the south.   Away to the north, is the
intercontinental airport, served by many corporations and
with direct services to Europe, many parts of Africa and most
towns in Nigeria.

Modern industries are also outside the walled city.   They
include soft drink, cosmetic, confectionery, tile, furniture and
soap factories, groundnut oil and flour mills, cotton weaving, the
making of hollow ware and rubber shoes, tyre re-treading,
tanneries, a cannery, and a bone-crushing plant.   There is also
a huge piggery, managed by non-Muslims.

Kano lives a great deal by commerce.   Its largest market has been mentioned. Camels and lorries also bring in much produce from the Niger Republic, especially groundnuts, hides, skins, gum, salt and natron. Kano is the largest centre of the groundnut, cattle, hides and skin (especially goat) trades in Nigeria.[1]

Katsina was founded about 1100 and has a population (1952) of 55,672.. It is smaller than Kano, but was a successful commercial rival to it until the Fulani Jihad in the early nineteenth century. Although Katsina does much trade, it is more interesting as the Hausa cultural centre. There are 7 miles of wall enclosing $2\frac{1}{2}$ square miles. Building, metal and leather working, pottery, embroidery, calabash carving and tailoring are the main crafts.[2]

Katsina lies where Cretaceous rocks extend into a hollow of the impervious Pre-Cambrian series, forming a semi-artesian basin. Water is rarely more than 30 feet down, though three-quarters of the 28 inches of average annual rainfall are concentrated between July and September.

THE SOKOTO BASIN. The south-eastern part of Sokoto Province belongs to the Northern High Plains of Hausaland just described. By contrast, Pre-Cambrian rocks are covered in the centre by Cretaceous series and in the west by Tertiary ones, which together occupy two-thirds of the Province. This part, the Sokoto Basin, ' is characterised by gently undulating plains broken at intervals on the north-west by ranges and isolated groups of steep-sided, flat-topped hills capped with ironstone and scored by numberless gullies. The natural vegetation consists mainly of thorn scrub.'[3]

The gently undulating plains have light, dry, coarse soils which, because of water scarcity and low population, are only intermittently cultivated for groundnuts and millet. The low density of population is, in places, the consequence of past strife between the Emirates of Katsina and Sokoto.

However, the Sokoto and Rima Dallols are well populated

---

[1] See also D. Whittlesey, ' Kano: A Sudanese Metropolis ', *Geographical Review*, 1927, pp. 177–99; B. H. Sharwood Smith, *Kano Survey*, Gaskiya Press, Zaria, 1950; and articles in *West Africa*, 8 Sept. 1962 and June 1963.

[2] R. Miller, ' Katsina, A City of the Desert Border ', *Geography*, 1937, pp. 283–92. Also ' Katsina, A Region of Hausaland ', *Scottish Geographical Magazine*, 1938, pp. 203–19.

[3] B. E. Sharwood Smith, *Sokoto Survey 1948*, Gaskiya Corporation, Zaria.

and cultivated with rice, sugar, cotton and onions. Mechanical cultivation, mainly for rice, has not been very successful. The only surplus commodities from these areas are hides, skins, onions and fish.

Sokoto is the spiritual headquarters and first capital of the Fulani. *Gusau*, east of the basin and on a railway line from Zaria opened in 1927, is the second commercial centre of the north after Kano. Both have developing industries.

THE BIU PLATEAU. This small but distinctive region, averaging 2,300 feet in altitude, is composed of Tertiary (or younger) volcanic rocks overlying the Pre-Cambrian series. It lies, rather inaccessibly, east of the Gongola tributary of the Benue and west of Biu. Its volcanic rocks are probably associated with faults in the Gongola Valley. Biu Plateau soils are thin.

THE CHAD BASIN. There was a gentle down-warping of the Chad Basin in Pleistocene times, and Tertiary and Quaternary rocks mask the Pre-Cambrian rocks in eastern Kano, northern Bauchi and northern Bornu provinces.

The Basin is under 1,600 feet in elevation and has light sandy soils with patches of black cotton or ' firki ' soils, especially in the north-east. Southern Sahel conditions prevail over the north of the basin, except for marshes near Lake Chad, but otherwise the basin has Sudan characteristics. Aridity alternating with floods, and poor communications, have hindered settlement, which was also obstructed when the centre of the basin was the shatter zone between the Fulani and Bornu Empires.

In the environs of Lake Chad rice is grown in fadamas and a dry season guinea corn is planted as the floods recede, but livestock and groundnuts are the main resources. There is a large trade in salt, potash and fish from Lake Chad.

Maiduguri is the headquarters of Bornu Province, the centre of a small intensively farmed area, and is growing fast.

CONCLUSION—NORTH-WESTERN STATE, NORTH-CENTRAL STATE, KANO STATE, NORTH-EASTERN STATE, BENUE-PLATEAU STATE and WEST-CENTRAL STATE. The creation of these six states in 1967 ended the long dominance of the North in Nigeria. There is great diversity of physical and human conditions; outstanding are the contrasts between the Middle Belt and the Nigerian Sudan. Within each of these are such physical contrasts as that between the Niger–Benue–Gongola troughs and the Jos Plateau in the Middle Belt; and such human contrasts as that between the craftsmen and dealers of the cities, with their intensive suburban farmers, and the nomadic Cow Fulani.

Development is, like the population distribution, uneven. The outcrop of cash crops is almost restricted to Kano, Katsina, eastern Sokoto and northern Zaria provinces, but livestock are more widely important. The future of mining on the Jos Plateau is uncertain. These northern states are hampered by the length of communications with the outside world. More roads and water, and effective tsetse fly control, are probably their greatest economic needs.

ECONOMIC RESOURCES

AGRICULTURE [1]

GENERAL CONSIDERATIONS. Of all West African lands, Nigeria is alone able to produce the complete range of food-stuffs described in Chapter 6. Range of latitude, the varied relief, climate, vegetation and soils, differing peoples with their contrasted methods and crops, and the existence of a few plantations, make this possible.

Nevertheless, the Government of Nigeria has been opposed to the general grant of plantations to non-Africans. A few were granted in early days, and two or three permitted in depression years for demonstration purposes. Collectively, they cover no more than some 16,000 acres and are of little account in total production. More important are plantations now being made by the several Development Corporations, often in collaboration with foreign companies.

As elsewhere in West Africa, subsistence farming is general, especially in the Middle Belt and in other more remote areas. However, as in Senegal and Ghana, ordinary African farmers produce massive quantities of surplus crops. These are especially yams, cotton and kola nuts for the internal market and

[1] Mr. T. A. Russell, formerly Senior Botanist with the Department of Agriculture, Nigeria, and now at the Royal Botanic Gardens, Kew, has also kindly criticised this section.

palm produce, cocoa, rubber and groundnuts for export. Plantations produce a relatively small part of the palm produce and rubber exported.

Although less than one-third of Nigeria as a whole is uncultivated,[1] the Western State is exceptional in having only 7% of uncultivated bush and waste. There, about one-third is under arable crops, another third is resting, and about 18% is under tree crops. The remainder consists of valuable Forest Reserves.

The Sample Census of Agriculture estimated the areas and production of principal farm crops (excluding trees) in 1950–1 as follows (including the then British Cameroons):

	Area Thousand acres	Production Thousand tons
Cassava (roots) . . .	2,467	10,581
Yams (tubers)	3,047	9,341
Guinea corn (threshed) . .	4,252	1,833
Millet (threshed) . . .	3,072	958
Cocoyams (roots) . . .	777	965
Maize (shelled) . . .	1,997	744
Sugar cane (fresh) . . .	24	555
Sweet Potatoes (roots) . .	179	475
Rice (paddy)	422	246
Groundnuts (shelled) . .	1,018	299
Cow peas (shelled) . . .	1,331	237
Cotton (seeded) . . .	931	136

The average acreage per cultivator was 3·5 acres in the Northern, 2·8 in Western and 4·0 in Eastern Nigeria.

AGRICULTURAL ZONES. The following agricultural zones are based on those used in the Census.[2]

1. Low-lying oil palm belt. Cassava, yams and maize grown for subsistence only.
2. Cocoa zone, with kola in the south-west.
3. Food crops, with subsidiary cocoa and oil palm. Yams are the main crop, followed by cassava, maize and cow peas.
3A. Udi Plateau and environs. Subsistence farming, mainly for yams.
4. Yam zone, with maize in the south, and guinea corn and millet in the north. Food crops are sold mainly to

[1] *Report on the Sample Census of Agriculture, 1950–1*, Lagos, 1952.
[2] Op. cit., pp. 79–80 and end-map. See also R. Mansell Prothero, 'The Sample Census of Agriculture, 1950–1 ', *Geographical Journal*, 121, pp. 197–206.

southern towns. Rice is important on the Niger flood plain and in Ogoja Province, and benniseed in Tiv country.

5. Subsistence Grain zone (millet and guinea corn). Rice is important in swamp areas of Bida Division, and groundnuts elsewhere.

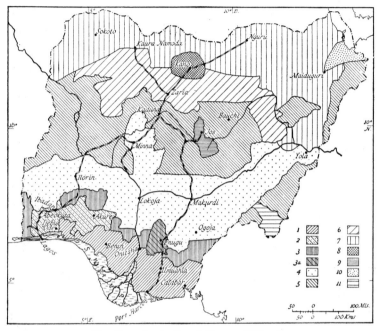

FIG. 85.—Agricultural Zones of Nigeria.

(After map in *Sample Census of Agriculture* 1950–1, Department of Statistics, Lagos. See also W. B. Morgan, 'Agriculture in Southern Nigeria', *Economic Geography*, 1959.)

6. Cotton zone, with subsidiary groundnuts. Guinea corn, millet and cow peas are the principal food crops. Fadamas are cultivated for vegetables.

7. Groundnut zone, with greatest production in northern part of Kano Province. Food crops as in Zone 6.

8. Permanent cropping of Kano country districts, with market gardening by irrigation adjacent to the city. Otherwise, crops as in 7, except that millet is the leading food crop.

9. Jos Plateau. Acha the main food crop, with Durra, Tamba and yams. Temperate vegetables are grown for cash.

10. Dry-Season Guinea Corn zone of Lake Chad black cotton soils (Firki). The crop is planted at the end of the rains, when most of the land is flooded. It ripens as the floods recede during the dry season.

11. High Grassland zone. Some Fulani herdsmen have settled. Varied crops, especially cocoyams, cassava, maize, sweet potatoes, bambarra groundnuts, African and European vegetables.

CROPS

Cassava is certainly the most widely grown crop. It is increasing rapidly in northern and eastern Nigeria, in the latter at the expense of yams. Cassava is a very tolerant crop, easy to grow, but impoverishes soils. (See Chapter 6.)

Yams are a much appreciated food but rarely one which farmers will grow in competition with lucrative cash crops like cocoa. Hence cash cropping of yams tends to be restricted to the Middle Belt, where there are few competing cash crops, and to land near the railway or roads leading to the best markets in the prosperous cocoa country of the Western State.

Guinea Corn, Millet, Sugar cane and Cow peas, all grown mainly in the north, give rise only to commerce for home consumption. Sugar cane is grown with irrigation on 6,380 acres at Bacita, 12 miles east of Jebba, on the Niger alluvial plain. Eventually, some 230,000 tons of cane should yield 27,000 tons of sugar annually. Sugar cane is also grown on small plots in most alluvial valleys in the North.

Rice cultivation has vastly increased in recent years in area, as have yields. Thus the area under rice in Eastern Nigeria expanded from 100 to 60,000 acres between 1938 and 1954. In the whole country there are now about 422,000 acres under the crop. In the northern states it is grown in fadamas where mechanical cultivation has achieved only modest success in face of formidable troubles. New areas are being developed along the Sokoto, Rima, Niger, Benue, Gbako (near Bida) and other rivers. Inland and coastal swamps are also being brought into cultivation for swamp rice, to take the place of upland rice. Nevertheless, coastal swamps are less suitable in Nigeria than in Sierra Leone. Nigeria's main rice potential is probably along its rivers, especially the Niger and Cross.

Oil palm Produce. The oil palm not only provides a considerable range of produce for local needs, such as building material, fibre for mats, wine, oil for cooking, cleaning and illumination, but it also provides about one-eighth by value of all Nigerian exports.

About one-half the oil is consumed in Nigeria, but almost all kernels are exported. Export of palm oil goes back to the earliest days of trade with Europe. Nigeria is still the leading world exporter, though this may be due to unsettled conditions in South-east Asia and Congo (Kinshasa). Nevertheless, Nigeria produces two-thirds of all palm kernels entering world trade and over one-quarter of the palm oil.

In 1965 the various marketing boards exported 152,400 tons of oil for export and 422,200 tons of kernels. This palm oil is sufficient to make about 235,000 tons of high quality soap. Oil from the palm kernels, and from Nigeria's groundnuts, could produce over 330,000 tons of margarine. Nigeria exports enough palm oil and kernels, groundnuts, cotton seed and benniseed to meet a weekly demand for 60 million 3 oz. tablets of soap and 35 million half-pound packets of margarine. Vegetable oils and oil seeds exported from Nigeria to the United Kingdom constitute about 40% of the United Kingdom's requirements of oils and fats.[1]

In the south-west or Yoruba country, the oil palm reacts badly to the marked dry season, the pericarp is very thin, and cocoa cropping is far more profitable. The small amount of oil produced is mainly used locally or sent north, but there is an appreciable export of kernels.

In the Mid-West, East-Central and South-Eastern States the economy is based on the oil palm. Stands are densest here because rainfall is generally over 60 inches annually, the density of population is high, and the palm will tolerate

[1] Based upon *Statistical and Economic Review*, United Africa Company, March 1949, p. 1, with adjustments for later figures.

mediocre soils. There is an appreciable surplus of oil and kernels for export, the oil being of average quality.

At Sapele and Calabar are plantations which produce very high quality oil and kernels. All plantations account for about 6% of the oil exported. The quality of oil from African-owned trees improves eastward, and is especially good around Port Harcourt, the most prolific area for the export of oil and kernels. The following table shows the sale for export in thousand tons of oil and kernels from Produce Inspection Districts, in 1963, including plantation production.[1]

District	Oil	Kernels
WEST Lagos, Ibadan, Ilesha, Ijebu-Ode, Abeokuta, Ondo and Ubiaja	9·6	197·7
EAST Warri, Port Harcourt, Onitsha and Calabar .	139·4	197·0

One of the most notable economic changes in Nigeria has been the remarkable improvement in the quality of oil, lifting much of it from the non-edible grades into the higher-priced edible category. This has been done by bonuses for the best qualities, and by encouraging the use of hand presses and pioneer oil mills. These have also enabled much more oil to be extracted. Most pioneer mills (mostly publicly owned) and presses (privately owned) are found in the hinterland of Port Harcourt, i.e. Aba, Opobo, Abonnema, and as far north as Oguta. The table below shows these facts in statistical form. Comparable figures for later years are not available.

Year	Premium in £ per ton for Special Oil (under 4½% f.f.a.)	Hand Presses		Pioneer Mills			Special Oil as % of Oil Exports
		Nos.	Potential annual output in tons	Nos. in pro-duction	Pro-duction of oil in tons	Quality	
1949	None	2,671	36,000	5	830	Grade 1 (4–9½% f.f.a.)	Nil
1950	10·25	3,772	48,000	8	1,263	25% Special	0·2
1951	16·00	4,481	61,500	34	2,089	34% ,,	6·3
1952	19·00	4,587	67,500	50	5,595	71% ,,	29·6
1953	17·50	5,333	75,000	53	7,508	97% ,,	50·4

[1] *Statistical and Economic Review*, United Africa Company, March 1954, p. 9. From this the succeeding material on palm produce is also mostly drawn.

The next necessity is more widespread planting of new and better palms, greater care in their cultivation and in gathering and bringing in fresh fruit. The oil also needs quick bulk-carrying facilities. Bulking plants remove dirt and water, thus slowing down the formation of free-fatty-acid (f.f.a.), store the oil in clean and safe conditions prior to shipment and pump it into coastal or ocean vessels.

Rubber is produced in much the same areas as the oil palm but most of the output comes from the Warri–Sapele–Kwale–Benin areas and from near Calabar.

In the nineteenth century wild rubber was obtained. Then before the First World War plantings were made, especially in Benin Province, of *Funtumia elastica*. *Hevea brasiliensis* was planted near Sapele and that species is alone important. *Landolphia owariensis* is the indigenous species and provides good rubber.

Rubber, like the oil palm, tolerates the poor soils of much of Ondo Province, Mid-West and South-Eastern States. Most of the production is by Africans but leaves much to be desired. The trees are rarely well spaced, are tapped with insufficient care, and not according to a proper rhythm, while the rubber is badly processed and is often dirty, so that it fetches a low price. Farms are not properly tended, are often overgrown, and only semi-productive. Most African-produced rubber has been of B_2 quality used for tyres.

There are also some large plantations, belonging to foreign companies, government boards, Nigerian companies or individuals, at Ilushin, east of Ijebu Ode, near Sapele, Calabar and Oban. These have their own processing plants and produce the highest grade rubber.

No crop has been more subject to price fluctuations than rubber, so that exports have varied enormously; and rubber has rarely been a profitable crop for ordinary farmers. However, some believe that Malayan and Indonesian production will decline because of high costs, and that Nigeria can better withstand low prices. Nigerian farmers' rubber, properly processed and graded, can command high prices. Crepe and sheet-rubber factories have been built for farmer-produced rubber, especially near Benin and Warri. Moreover, rubber is used in tyre manufacture at Port Harcourt and Ikeja (near Lagos) and, in small amounts in other local manufactures.

Cocoa. High prices for cocoa in world markets after the Second World War, made this a most profitable crop to grow. Probably introduced from Fernando Po by Squiss Bamego in 1874, it thus antedates by five years its final establishment in the Gold Coast. Nigeria also began exporting before the then Gold Coast.

Yet Nigeria has never come near to achieving the Ghana export figures. Favourable conditions are much more restricted in Nigeria, where cocoa must be grown in areas with the rather low annual rainfall of 45–60 inches, and with a distinct dry season from December to March. Cultivation is made possible, however, by moisture-holding soils. It is limited on the west and north by insufficient rain, and on the east and south by unsuitable light sandy soils. Early plantings near Bonny and Calabar failed for this reason and, more recently, cocoa has given way to kola, the oil palm, citrus and food crops in southern Abeokuta. Cocoa growers were also troubled by exceptionally low rainfall in the Ibadan area after 1941, especially during the critical drier months.

Cocoa is the leading cash crop in Ibadan, and adjacent parts of Oyo, Ondo and Abeokuta Provinces. It is reckoned to cover 591,000 acres, with 175,000 growers, so averaging under $3\frac{1}{2}$ acres each. The western area has an unduly high percentage of old trees, and much replanting is required. Swollen Shoot is also most severe here, particularly between Ibadan and Badeku, 13 miles to the east. In this zone of 250 square miles are one-ninth of the cocoa trees, producing nearly 30% of the crop but often from infected and old trees. Capsid infestation is general throughout the cocoa area; Blackpod is worst in the wetter areas of Ondo and Ijebu but much less so round Ibadan.

Cocoa accounts for one-tenth of all exports by value. The tonnage exported varies between about 80,000 and 150,000 tons and may decline. It accounts for most of the Western State's exports. Cocoa cultivation, trade and transport (by road and by lagoon) support quite one-half the people of that State.

Kola cultivation has developed greatly north of Lagos,

in Southern Ijebu and Abeokuta on soils unsuitable for cocoa, but also in Ibadan and Oyo, wherever there is ready access to the railway line to the north.   Ibadan is an important market for the nuts, which are sent north, especially to Kano.

Benniseed is an oilseed and almost a Tiv monopoly.   It is the only significant export crop of the Middle Belt, whose poor soils it tolerates.   India is the main producer, compared with whose production that of Nigeria is insignificant.   Nevertheless, India exports little and Nigeria is often the main exporter.

Tobacco[1] is grown in almost all parts of Nigeria, but types used in the cigarette factories are grown only in the west and north.   There are some 150,000 farmers who produce tobacco on about a third of an acre, in addition to other and often much more important crops.

About $5\frac{1}{2}$ million pounds of cigarette tobacco are produced. Most of this is of the bright air-cured variety, which does well mainly in Zaria, Sokoto, Kano, Katsina, Bornu and Bauchi Provinces.   One-quarter of the production is from fadamas. The great advantage of this tobacco is that it does not require expensive flue curing.

In the Western State cigarette tobacco cultivation is important around Ogbomosho, Oyo and Ipetu-Ibokun in Oyo Province.   Of its somewhat smaller production, four-fifths are dark air-cured and one-fifth is flue-cured.   Production of Nigerian flue-cured tobacco began in Oyo Province near Shaki in 1950, where the Nigerian Tobacco Company has curing stations.

Cotton[2] cultivation is widespread in Nigeria because it is needed for the very considerable local artisan and factory weaving of cloth, and because several varieties have been selected to suit differing climatic and other conditions.

Ishan is one variety grown in the forested south, especially from a little south of Abeokuta to about Oshogbo, in losing competition with cocoa.   *Ishan* was developed by selection from cotton found in the Ishan Division of Benin, derived from the *Vitifolium* sub-variety of *Gossypium barbadense*, probably

[1] J. T. Coppock, 'Tobacco growing in Nigeria', *Erdkunde*, 1965, pp. 297–306.

[2] *Statistical and Economic Review*, United Africa Company, March 1951, and H. B. Leonard, ' The Development of Cotton Production in the Northern Region of Nigeria 1949–52 ', *Empire Cotton Growing Review*, 1954, pp. 12–26.

originally introduced by the Spanish. The product is coarse and mainly used inside Nigeria, but the staple is $1\frac{1}{8}$ inch.

Another sub-variety, *Peruvianum*, which grows best in the drier south, was the source of the cotton first developed and exported from the Abeokuta region, and was probably introduced by the Portuguese. Selection and breeding of a plant of this variety, taken from a field at Meko, have given rise to the *Meko* variety, widespread in southern Nigeria. But its product is short, rough and dark, and is not exported.

Cotton grown in the Lokoja District of the Middle Belt developed from a mixture of various American and *G. barbadense* varieties. They are now being replaced by an Allen variety.

In the north, *North American Allen* is grown, first imported in 1909. It thrives in the clay loams or deep loams of the black soil regions of southern Katsina, south-eastern Sokoto and northern Zaria, which are, in that order, the main producers of cotton for export. Minor areas are Gombe Division of Bauchi Province, Kontagora Division of Niger, and Benue Province. Ideal rainfall is 35–50 inches annually but 20–55 inches may be tolerated. The ideal altitude seems to be between 1,200 and 3,000 feet.

The cultivation of *Allen* cotton in northern Nigeria results from the initial efforts of an industrial missionary of the Church Missionary Society, the British Cotton Growing Association, and the first Director of Agriculture in Nigeria. It was also much encouraged by the arrival of the railway in Kano in 1912 and, since 1949, by the Northern Nigeria Development Corporation. Strict control of the crop is effected by the distribution of selected seed. The staple is consistently $1-1\frac{1}{16}$ inch in length. Ginning out-turn is at least 34% and the colour very white. The grade is ' Good Middling ' or ' Strict Good Middling ' and so commands a higher price than ' American Middling '. There are 13 ginneries, 9 being in the major producing districts.

According to the Sample Census, there were probably 931,000 acres under cotton in Nigeria and the Cameroons under United Kingdom Trusteeship in 1950–1, when production was about 136,000 tons. Exports were about 15,000 tons, so that most was used locally. The poorer types are taken by hand spinners and weavers, the better ones by mills at Kaduna, Kano, Ikeja and Mushin (Lagos). So important have these and other mills become that most Nigerian grown cotton is used by them, and little is exported.

Groundnuts are the major crop of the northernmost states of Nigeria. Although Senegal is the leading West African processor, Nigeria is the greatest exporter of groundnuts in the world. They normally represent about one-fifth of Nigerian exports by value, and about two-fifths of the world trade in this commodity. An export of 600,000 tons yields at least 250,000 tons of groundnut oil, sufficient to manufacture 300,000 tons of margarine—enough to supply 1 pound a week throughout the year to 13 million persons.[1]

The massive production of northern Nigeria is a consequence partly of the use of groundnut oil in margarine manufacture since 1903, and partly of the arrival of the railway at Kano in 1912. Up to 1911 export had never exceeded 1,936 tons (1907). In 1913 it was 19,288 tons. Exports increased fairly steadily until the Second World War and are now often over 600,000 tons. Groundnuts are also crushed locally, and are an important source of local edible oil and food.

The crop is well suited to the sandy ' drift ' soils of northern Nigeria, though they benefit from dressings of lime, phosphorus and magnesium. About nine-tenths of the export crop comes from an area enclosed by a line from west of Kaura Namoda south to Zaria and north-east to beyond Nguru. In the southern part of this area the soils are heavier and cotton is more profitable, but groundnuts are useful as the last crop in the rotation. The ' Upright ' variety is grown, which is better suited to heavier soils, but its yield is only two-thirds that of the ' Spreading ' variety used farther north. There, e.g. around Kano, the soils are lighter and the rainfall of 30–40 inches is ideal. Farther north still, e.g. around Katsina (and in the Niger Republic), the soils are even lighter and poorer, and the rainfall only 20–30 inches. Yields are lower, but the crop is the most profitable export one. Over one-half of the groundnuts come from Kano Province and most of the rest from Katsina, Sokoto and Bornu Provinces. The crop is

---

[1] *Statistical and Economic Review*, U.A.C., Sept. 1949, p. 4. Some of the succeeding material on groundnuts is also drawn from this source.

generally produced for export near the railway or roads. Kano is by far the most important railing point.

According to the Sample Census of Agriculture 1950–1, there were 1,018,000 acres under groundnuts. In 1966 there were about 2 million acres. Almost all these have been brought into cultivation for this crop since 1911. The average farm of $3\frac{1}{2}$ acres may have one acre devoted to the crop, grown alone or intercropped with millet. Some three-fifths of the people of Sokoto, Katsina, Kano and Bornu Provinces depend upon the crop for cash.

Groundnut oil mills were established in Nigeria only in the later 'fifties. Unlike Senegal, which had a protected market for the oil in North Africa, Nigeria had no such market and only small amounts of oil and cake can be sold in Nigeria. Moderate sized mills in Kano and elsewhere had had their groundnut purchases restricted by the former Northern Nigeria Government, anxious to retain its place in world nut markets.[1]

Improved means of communication are required to enable the crop area to be extended, e.g. in Adamawa, Bornu and Sokoto Provinces. More research on the crop and cheap fertilisers are other needs.[2]

LIVESTOCK

(See also Chapter 7)

Trans-Saharan trade in Nigerian red goat skins goes back many centuries. They were carried by camel to Morocco, and on to Europe, where their high quality made them world famous as ' Morocco ' leather.

Livestock are to-day of outstanding importance in Nigeria. Numbers are not known exactly, but there are probably about $7\frac{1}{2}$ million cattle. Most authorities consider that this represents about ten times those slaughtered annually.

The goat population is about 20 million and the sheep (all hairy and thin-tailed) about 8 million.

Livestock are important for the internal trade in meat and

[1] J. C. Gardiner, *Oilseed Processing in Nigeria*, Lagos, 1953, and *Oilseed Processing in Nigeria—A Statement of Policy*, Lagos, 1954.
[2] *The Cultivation of Groundnuts in West Africa*, O.E.E.C., Paris, 1953, pp. 34–8.

97. Hides and skins are stretched and left to dry before being processed in northern Nigeria.

98. Peeling and preparing veneer

99. The African Timber and Plywood Factory, Sapele.

100. Bomo-Bonny mineral oil pipeline in mangrove, Nigeria.

101. The Obwetti adit coal mine in an embayment of the cuesta of the Udi Plateau at Enugu. The working entrance is in the highest building. Below is the covered lorry and rail wagon loader. Note also the outcrop of resistant sandstones and shales, the paucity of vegetation, and yam mounds on cultivated patches

102. The simplest form of tin mining. Water loosens the over burden, which is dug away by men and carried by women.

103. Tin-bearing gravels ar separated by washing in bowl

TIN MINING, JOS PLATEAU

NIGERIA

104. Excavation by a walking or mobile dragline. Giant shovels, and other modern earth-moving machinery is also used. Note the African huts and granite hills in the background.

105. Tin-bearing gravels being washed out by a powerful water jet (back centre of quarry). They are pumped up the slope to the right, and then concentrated in sluice boxes (parallel with road). Waste is then put back in the quarry (right). Note the competition for land by farms, divided by euphorbia hedges.

106. After mechanical excava tion, tin-bearing gravels an water are sent through sluic boxes. Tin and columbit collect below each step (Centre group being cleared

FERNANDO PO

107. A street in Santa Isabel. Note the Spanish style of arcades.

108. Pasture lands near Moka, 4,600 feet

9. Giant lobelia with grass-
d and extinct volcanic cones
ove Moka. Crater lakes are
also numerous.

110. Volcanic phonolithic needle on São Tomé

111 Coconut plantation on Príncipe

SÃO TOMÉ AND PRÍNCIPE

112. Coprah drying floors on a São Tomé estate

113. Views of a São Tomé cocoa estate or "roça" (a) Courtyard and warehouses, with forest beyond

114. (b) Large mechanical cocoa-bean driers. Above and to the right is the administrative block. Note the mountainous terrain.

dairy produce, and for the valuable home and export trade in hides and skins.   Animals in the north are an important source of fertiliser.   Despite all this, however, most livestock are kept as a sign of wealth and often slaughtered for ritual purposes.

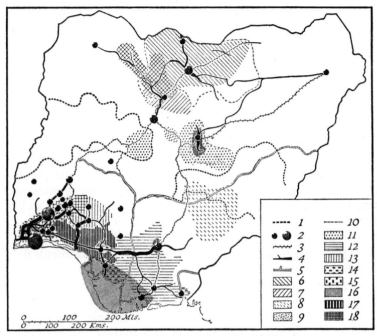

FIG. 86.—The economic geography of Nigeria.

Numbers refer as follows: 1, areas of very low population density; 2, major towns; 3, railways; 4, traffic flow on major roads; 5, navigable waterways (wet season); 6, major groundnut producing area; 7, export cotton region; 8, benni-seed (sesame) area of Benue Province; 9, commercial ginger production; 10, major cattle areas; 11, dairying regions of Middle Belt; 12, major oil palm regions; 13, cacao belt; 14, plantation rubber production; 15, commercial kola production; 16, mineral oilfields (oil is also produced on- and off-shore in the Mid-West State); 17, major commercial lumber region; 18, major mining areas.

(From K. M. Buchanan, ' Nigeria ', *Economic Geography*, Vol. 28, No. 4, October 1952, p. 320, by kind permission of the author and editor.   Subsequent changes have been added.)

About nine-tenths of the cattle are in northern Nigeria, mainly in Sokoto, Katsina, Kano and Bornu Provinces.   No-madic Fulani keep the humped non-resistant Zebu cattle in tsetse-free areas.   The main breeds are the widespread *White Fulani*, the less common *Gudale* or *Sokoto*, and the red *Rahaja* (or *Bororo*). There is also the humpless *Kuri* or *Chad*, kept by the Kanuri, and found near the lake.[1]

In the Middle Belt are some humpless crosses of Zebu and humpless cattle, but they are not resistant to the tsetse, which infests the belt. Hence cattle keeping is unimportant there, except on the Jos Plateau, though if the tsetse could be eradicated, cattle should increase, as the belt has good pasture and fodder crops.

In the south the small humpless *Muturu* is tolerant of trypanosomes. In aspect like the European *Shorthorn*, they number about 200,000; but they are so small as to be of little value and are usually less well cared for than the Zebu of the north.

To supply meat to the southern peoples, cattle are sent south mainly from Sokoto and Bornu Provinces, and from the Niger Republic. Kano is by far the most important railing point; meat cannot be carried, as refrigerator cars are considered uneconomic. But most cattle go south ' on the hoof' by well-recognised cattle routes (see Fig. 27), of which there are some 13,000 miles. There is a heavy loss in weight and quality on treks of between twenty and sixty days, and many animals die or become diseased.[2]

Improvements in Nigerian cattle keeping depend upon eradicating the tsetse fly, growing and making available more feeding stuffs (especially guinea corn), getting more crop farmers to become mixed farmers and settling the nomadic Fulani. ' The Fulani have already shown a readiness to abandon the nomadic life when unchallenged rights to land and adequate water and fodder for their cattle can be assured to them.'[3]

Sheep are kept widely in the north and goats everywhere in Nigeria, but the *Sokoto Red* and *Kano Brown* goats are kept essentially for their skins. About 8,000 tons of cattle hides, sheep and goat skins are exported annually, an export initially encouraged by the arrival of the railway in Kano in 1912. There has been much decline in exports in recent years, and

[1] For further details of breeds, see several articles in *Farm and Forest*.
[2] *Report of the Nigerian Livestock Mission*, Colonial No. 266, 1951, and G. I. Jones, ' The Beef Cattle Trade in Nigeria ', *Africa*, 1946, pp. 29–38.
[3] *Proceedings of a Conference called to consider the Report of the Nigerian Livestock Mission*, Lagos, 1953.

hides and skins represent no more than about 3% of Nigerian exports by value. To this must be added the greater value of the meat trade inside Nigeria.

About one-sixth of the hides and skins originate from the Niger Republic, and about one-sixth of the Nigerian output is retained for local use. Both these categories are of low grade, though most of the Nigerian output is of better quality than is usual in West Africa. The quality of Sokoto Red and Kano Brown goat skins is world-renowned as glacé kid leather, achieved partly by careful killing and preparation.[1]

Dairy produce is made haphazardly by the Fulani. Far more significant is production on modern lines at Vom, Jos, Kano and a little elsewhere, with milk mostly purchased from the Fulani. Clarified butter fat is more widely produced, again on the Jos Plateau.

The plateau has fly-free and well-watered pastures, numerous cattle, cooler conditions, and a good network of roads. This combination of favourable factors is found nowhere else in West Africa, though with roads the Bamenda Highlands might be so developed.

Yorkshire and Berkshire pigs are kept increasingly by Lebanese to satisfy the domestic demand for bacon and ham. Poor chickens are found everywhere. They are sent south in considerable numbers from Kano, Maidobi, Kwakwanso, Zaria and Gusau. The Fashola experimental poultry farm, between Oyo and Iseyin, is endeavouring to improve the breed of fowl.

FORESTRY

Although Nigerian timber exports are surpassed in Africa by those from the Ivory Coast, Gabon and Ghana, Nigerian reserves are far greater than those of her West African competitors, she is making more resolute attempts to replant, and is more fully aware of the dangers of illegal and over-felling.

The country is pursuing a cyclical felling policy, whereby part of a reserve or estate is felled and then allowed to regenerate. Thereby, forest reserves will be at least maintained, as well as providing sustained annual yields of timber. Intensive rather than selective felling is also the rule, so that full natural

[1] *Statistical and Economic Review*, U.A.C., September 1951, pp. 27–48.

regeneration can be effected. All this contrasts with much 'salvage felling' of timber in Ghana, most of whose forests are destined for agriculture in the near future. Commercial trends are, however, similar in both countries, with increasing variety of species cut, more local processing and rising local timber demands.

About 9% of Nigeria is covered by official forest reserves, but in the Mid-West State the proportion is much higher. There is also nearly twice as much Unreserved Forest in that State, where about half the area is occupied by High Forest. The Mid-West produces 70% of Nigeria's sawn timber, almost all the logs, 80% of the total output by value, and almost all the exported timber.

The main producing areas are Ijebu, southern Ondo and south-western Benin provinces (three-fifths of all trees felled and four-fifths of exports), all in former no-man's lands between towns. Minor producing areas are in the South-Eastern State east of the Cross River and in eastern Ogoja. Here access is difficult, but in the Mid-West State the many streams make floating easy. Thus Nigeria (and the Ivory Coast) are at a great advantage compared with Ghana, where much timber has to be carried by rail, and where rivers can rarely be used.

Despite the pronounced tendency to the exploitation of more species, Obeche (*Triplochiton scleroxylon*) still accounts for over one-half the volume and value of logs exported, and about one-third the volume and value of sawn timber. Timber and wood products account for about 3% by value of Nigerian exports.

The United Africa Company, apart from operating important timber concessions, has a large sawmill and an adjacent larger plywood mill at Sapele. About 3,300 Africans work in these establishments. The mill is one of the largest and most up-to-date plywood and veneer factories in the world.

MINING[1]

Although Nigeria is about four times the size of Ghana, Nigerian mineral production was much less important until

[1] See also section on Geology.

the opening of the oilfield in the late nineteen-fifties. The output of oil developed so fast that it quickly overtook tin in value, and Nigeria's total mineral output far exceeds Ghana's. Mineral exports are proportionately much more important to Nigeria than they are to Ghana, and this difference is rapidly widening, as mineral exports from Ghana are somewhat static. Nigerian mines employ about 50,000 Africans and 650 non-Africans. Of these, 40,000 Africans and 250 non-Africans are in tin workings, 5,000 Nigerians and 350 expatriates in oil production, and almost all the rest in coal mining. Mining in Nigeria provides many millions of pounds of revenue to the Federal and State Governments and the companies spend large amounts in the country.

Mineral oil and natural gas. The search for oil lasted from 1937–41 and from 1946–56, when commercial quantities were proved west of Port Harcourt at Oloibiri. Some £15 million had then been spent on exploration, mostly in mangrove or fresh-water swamps of the Niger Delta, probably the most arduous area in the world, and further complicated by seasonal rain and flooding. Furthermore, transport of oil is possible only by costly laid and maintained pipelines. Export began in 1958, and progress has been so rapid that this is the most significant recent development in Nigerian economic history.

Oil is produced from some 70 wells by several companies, on and off-shore. Other companies are prospecting. Over 20 million tons are normally produced annually. Oil has become Nigeria's leading export, as well as saving her costly imports. The producing areas (Fig. 87) are east and west of Port Harcourt and on the Nun River (both in Rivers State); and at Ughelli and Kokori, near Warri (Mid-West State). They are linked by pipelines to the Bonny export terminal, that from Ughelli crossing the Niger River. The channel into Bonny has been deepened to 35 feet, to accommodate 33,000 ton tankers. A refinery near Port Harcourt has an annual capacity of 1·9 million tons, mainly for the Nigerian market. The first off-shore producing well is off the north west corner of the delta, seven miles out to sea, in 30 feet of water. Here oil is pumped to a shore terminal from which sea tankers are loaded. Somewhat off-setting the formidable difficulties of exploration, production and transport, Nigerian oil benefits from having little sulphur, and being relatively near Europe as well as African markets.

Gas has been found in far greater quantities than can be used.

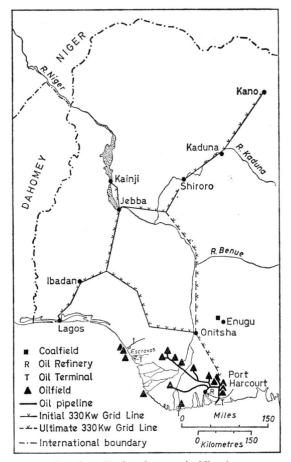

FIG. 87.—Fuel and power in Nigeria.

A little is employed in electrical generation near Port Harcourt and at Ughelli, and in industry at these places and at Aba. It may later be exported in liquid form, as well as being taken by pipeline to other centres in Nigeria. If it were sold cheaply in bottles, it could displace costly wood for domestic cooking in

Nigeria and beyond. It could be the base for fertiliser, polyethylene, and diverse chemical production. For gas, as for oil, the prospects are bright, although Nigeria is unlikely to become a major world producer nor, fortunately, will oil and gas ever be so dominant in Nigeria as in Libya.

Tin. In 1884, when the Benue Valley was being opened for trade by the Royal Niger Company, Sir William Wallace found that the tin used locally was produced by Africans at Naraguta on the Jos Plateau. It was smelted nearby at Liruein Delma, from where it was distributed in the form of thin rods or ' straws '. Previously it had been thought that the tin was obtained from across the Sahara.

In 1902 Wallace took back to England a trial 28 pounds of tin concentrate from the Delimi stream. As a result, a prospecting party went out in the same year, and in 1903 rational mining was begun. Development was necessarily very slow, because transport had to be by porterage to and from the Benue River at Loko and then by canoe on that river.

Public attention was drawn to the deposits in 1909, and from 1911 transport was by porterage to Rigachikun (north of Kaduna) on the Lagos–Kano Railway. This and the increased number of operating companies greatly stimulated exports, until there was a minor recession in 1913. In 1914 the Bauchi Light Railway from Zaria to Bukuru was opened, just as there was a prodigious demand for tin during the First World War and consequent expansion of production. After that war there was a slump from 1921 to 1923. The building of a branch of the Eastern Railway to Bukuru and Jos in 1927 reduced costs of transport in Nigeria by one-third.

Under the Tin Production and Export Restriction Scheme of 1931, Nigeria agreed to limit production to 7,750 tons annually, and prices went up. In the Second World War, after the loss of Malaya in 1942, Nigeria and Bolivia were the main producers of tin for the Allies.

Pegmatite, associated with some of the Older Granites, contains workable tinstone and columbite-tantalite in certain places. But the principal deposits of Nigerian tinstone and columbite have been formed from the weathering of tin veins and lodes in the Younger Granites emplaced into a region of Pre-Cambrian rocks. The minerals have been concentrated in former and present stream beds and, in many places, covered not only with soft overburden but by Tertiary or Quaternary volcanic basalt as well.

So far it is alluvial tin which has been obtained almost exclusively in Nigeria. African and early European workings were in the existing rivers. Since approximately 1936 more and more attention has been directed to former stream beds obscured by considerable soft overburden. There was once concern whether the tin (but not the columbite-tantalite) of these thick alluvial deposits may be exhausted as well. Consequently, the larger companies envisaged underground exploitation of tin gravels in old stream beds covered by basalt. But this would be an expensive operation and possible only if tin prices were sufficiently high. Colonial mining leases did not insist upon prospection as well as mining, but this is now required, and has revealed new surface deposits.

Meanwhile, four-fifths of the present output is from Plateau Province, especially south of Jos. Most of the rest is from Bauchi Province. Production was again restricted by international quota from 1957–60 but is now around 11,000 tons, or 5% of the world total. Nearly half the output comes from one company, and much of the rest from many small ones.

In the past most mining was by very simple methods. Water was and still is used to loosen the overburden, which is often dug out by men and carried away by women, here the traditional porters. The tin-bearing gravels below are then washed in calabashes, until the heavier black tin oxide remains. This method is still used by the numerous small companies, private operators (African, European and Lebanese) and by individual African ' tributors ', of whom there are now only some 1,500, and who work for the companies or operators.

About one-half of Nigerian tin is produced by mechanical means, operated by large companies. The simplest method is to direct a powerful water-jet (rather like a fire-hose) to wash out the tin-bearing gravels. These are then pumped up for concentration at the lower end of a range of sluice-boxes, down and through which the water and gravels pass. Quicker excavation is by a drag-line which cuts large blocks of earth at each ' dig ' and can move by mechanical ' legs ' to new ground. The material it excavates is washed as described above.

Mechanical shovels and dredges are also used. (See photographs, pp. 496–7.)

As so much water is used, reservoirs have been built to store it; nevertheless, water shortage through variable rainfall often restricts output. The industry also has need of much motive power and, when the Enugu coal deposits were opened in 1915, it looked forward to a railway between the Jos Plateau and Enugu to bring in coal supplies. But as the railway did not reach Jos until 1927, the companies had meanwhile developed hydro-electric power sites at the Kurra, Kwall, Jekko and Ankwill falls on the plateau's southern edge. Tin smelting began near Jos in 1961.

Early tin mining caused much of the present severe deforestation on the plateau. Excavation and spoil dumps have degraded the soils, destroyed farm land (though compensation was paid) and silted the rivers. Some farmers have become discouraged in the face of increased quarrying and creation of spoil dumps, though mining leases now contain a restoration clause.[1]

Columbite, the main ore of the metal niobium, has come into prominence because of its use as an alloy in making heat-resisting steels for gas turbines, jet engines and rockets. Almost all the world's supply comes from Nigeria, where the mineral occurs in association with tin and tantalite, with uranium in the radio-active granites of the Liruein–Kano Hills, and as a primary constituent of the Younger Granites, all on the Jos Plateau.

Three-quarters of the exports come from Plateau Province, and most of the rest from Bauchi and Kano Provinces. Production of columbite is more dispersed than tin mining, largely because it was for long rejected as a waste product and is now being recovered from dumps of abandoned, as well as from active, tin workings. Small amounts of tantalite are also mined on and around the Jos Plateau.

Coal was first found in the Ofam River at Udi in 1909; production began in 1915, when the railway was built from

---

[1] See also *The Geology of the Plateau Tinfields—Resurvey 1945–8*, Kaduna, 1949; B. W. Hodder, ' Tin Mining on the Jos Plateau of Nigeria ', *Economic Geography*, Vol. 35, pp. 109–22; and articles by H. Hake, *West Africa* 23 and 30 January and 6 February, 1965.

Port Harcourt to Enugu to make this possible. Coal occurs in places as far apart as Ankpa and Gombe in the north-east, and Benin Province in the south-west, but is mined only at Enugu, where there are open adit mines and surface workings. Five workable seams occur in the Upper Cretaceous rocks of the Udi Plateau or Donga Ridge. The coal yields much gas and tar oils on distillation, and would best be used for gas or chemical by-product manufacture. Nevertheless, it is mainly used in electric power generation. The combustible character of the coal, resulting from high gas content, makes it dangerous to transport by sea; and its poor coking character and very small output (*ca.* 500,000 tons annually) makes its use in local heavy industry difficult, even though iron ore of 45% content occurs nearby. It might well prove more useful to build another electricity station near the mines and distribute electricity from Enugu by grid, to make coal by-products and, with other local materials, use coal to make glass, bricks, tiles, pottery and cement. Coal production is by a Government Corporation and has been restricted by strikes, low output per man, by shortage of rail wagons and locomotives and, more recently, by dieselisation of Nigerian and Ghana railways.

Limestone is being used for cement manufacture at Nkalagu, 25 miles east of Enugu's coal mines, at Port Harcourt, Calabar, Ukpilla (near Auchi) in the Mid-West State, Ewekoro (near Abeokuta), Lagos and Sokoto. The first has a capacity of some 250,000 tons of cement a year, about one-quarter of present Nigerian needs. A branch railway has been built from Ogbaho to Nkalagu, and a power station for the factory at Oji River. Some of the other works are less well-sited or efficient.

Minor Minerals

Lignite occurs in the Eocene series west and south of the Enugu coalfield, over a wider area than the coal, from Benin in the west to Onitsha in the east, and from Ubiaja in the north to Newi in the south. Seams are from 6 to over 20 feet thick, the thickest being near Asaba and Onitsha.

Lead–Zinc. At Abakaliki and Ameri-Nyeba, about 40 and 50 miles respectively east of Enugu, are slag heaps of former lead smelters, either Portuguese or African. The zinc, however, could not be extracted from these ores of Lower Cretaceous rocks.

After the Second World War prospecting was intense, but water difficulties delayed re-development at the above sites, at Wukari near the Benue River, at Zurak north of the Benue, and near Abuja south-east of Minna. A false start was made at Ameri in 1955, and a new effort in 1965.

THE NIGER DAMS PROJECT (Fig. 87, page 502)

The first dam in this scheme is due for completion in 1968 at Kainji, 64 miles above Jebba. The power station will have a capacity of 320,000 kw., and additional generators will raise this to 960,000 kw. Power will be distributed to Kaduna, Lagos, Benin and the Onitsha areas, thereby greatly encouraging industrial and general development. By about 1980 another dam and power house will be constructed at Jebba, with an ultimate capacity of 500,000 kw., and by 1984, a third will be needed in the Shiroro Gorge of the Kaduna tributary with a capacity of 480,000 kw.

Jebba will be the base-load station, as it will have the most even flow, being backed by its own and the Kanji lake, and by the middle and upper Niger. Jebba and Kainji will be further helped by high water from local rains from June to September, and by another peak from December to March from the same rains in the upper Niger basin, the effects of which are brought to Nigeria months later through the tortuous channels of the Niger's middle reaches. The local flood of the Kaduna will immediately generate power, because of limited storage capacity. Meanwhile, the Jebba and Kainji lakes will be filling again to be ready for operation when the Kaduna is low. When all are at a minimum in March or April, the Kainji and Jebba reservoirs will be lowered until the first flood occurs—that of the Kaduna.

The scheme is a fine example of using different river regimes, as well as being part of a national scheme also incorporating electrical generation using oil, gas and coal. The relative merits of hydro-electric power versus gas or oil-generated electricity were investigated in 1960–61. The first is an inexhaustible source while at that time, when a decision had to be taken, oil and gas resources were less well known.

CRAFTS AND INDUSTRIES

Most countries still have certain traditional crafts, and at least some modern industrial units. But Nigeria is unique in the survival of so many varied and vigorous crafts, alongside the emergence of diverse modern industries.

Among its many traditional crafts, the narrow cloth weaving and dyeing trades are well represented in the north and west of Nigeria. In the latter, women produce fine patterns either by sewing stones and pieces of wood in the material before dyeing, or by making a pattern with starch on the undyed cloth, the starch hardening before immersion in the dye vat. In the former process, the pattern is revealed after dyeing by undoing the stones and sticks. In the latter method, the pattern is seen after scraping off the hardened starch, so revealing undyed spaces. Indigo and other vegetable or local dyes are used, as well as imported synthetic ones. Indigo is most used in the Western State. At Akwete, in East-Central State, vivid coloured embroidery in parallel geometric patterns is worked on black cloth.

Raffia and fibre mats, baskets, etc., are made at Ikot Ekpene (South-Eastern State), Kano, Bida and elsewhere. At Benin woodworking in ebony has a long history. Wooden goods with Ibo patterns are made at Akwa, near Enugu. Calabashes are much carved in Oyo and Kano.

Leather working is a major craft in the North. Dyed goat and sheep skins are used for cushions, bags and saddlery. Kano is the main centre. Oyo produces black-and-white cushions.

Gold and silversmiths work in most towns, but they are renowned at Bida and Kano. Benin brass figures have been famous for centuries. The making of domestic and agricultural iron goods is widespread. Pottery is important at Ikot Ekpene, Abuja and Ilorin. Glass articles of personal adornment from Bida are well known.

Kano, Bida, Benin, Ikot Ekpene and Bamenda are centres of several crafts. From Kano, Bida and other towns, Hausa traders peddle goods through many Guinea lands.

To these traditional crafts have been added the often far more important ones of tailoring, broad-loom weaving, mechanical repairing and carpentry.

Capitalist enterprise, as elsewhere, was first directed to the processing of local materials, such as palm oil, timber, groundnuts, fruit, rubber and cotton.

Factories making consumer and other goods for the Nigerian market have mostly been established since the Second World War. Nigeria is virtually self-sufficient in refined petroleum products, the simplest cloths and some garments, cement and asbestos-cement, tyres, plastic goods (including sandals), furniture, soap, paints and steel rods; while she also produces substantial proportions of canned or bottled drinks and certain foods, cigarettes and hardware. Radio sets, cycles and trucks are also mostly assembled in the country.

Most works have been concentrated on industrial estates at Lagos and environs, Ibadan, Sapele, Port Harcourt, Enugu, Kaduna and Kano. Financing has been commonly in the form of a partnership between foreign companies, partly local ones, regional government funds and, to a small extent, Nigerian investors.

Regional rivalry has played a great part in industrial development, but has also led to some wasteful duplication and consequent narrowing of the market for each factory. This is especially noticeable in the establishment of regional textile mills, cigarette factories and cement works, as well as in the negotiations for an iron and steel industry. The latter may be established with blast furnaces in one state and the steel furnaces in another!

Communications [1]

Nigeria is unique in West Africa in the diversity and extent of its means of transport. In view of the size and variety of the country, communications have probably done more than anything else either to encourage or, where lacking, to restrict economic development.

Waterways. In its provision of natural waterways, Nature was kinder to Nigeria than to most West African lands. There

[1] See Figs. 29 and 86.

are some 4,000 miles of waterways permitting cheap transport at high water.

The Niger River was the first means of export from northern Nigeria and, in conjunction with the Minna–Baro branch railway, still carries a great deal of seasonal traffic to and from that Region. Likewise, the Benue River is important to much of eastern Nigeria and, via Garua, to the northern part of Cameroon. The Cross River permits seasonal traffic between Calabar and Mamfe, in Cameroon.

Parallel with the coast is an excellent calm lagoon waterway, from west of Lagos to the many streams of the Niger Delta. There is also much coastal traffic, especially in the transhipment of oil and other produce between Port Harcourt, the West Delta ports and Lagos.

Port facilities at Lagos and Port Harcourt have been severely over-loaded, but extensions at both have changed this. Entry has been much improved to the Delta ports by a breakwater at the Escravos mouth, and by the dredging of the river.

Railways. The Nigerian Railway was the second longest in the British Colonial Empire and comprises 2,172 route miles.

The line from Lagos to Ibadan was opened in 1901, to develop trade and improve living conditions in Lagos. As Lagos was not then a deep-water port, it was far from clear whether the railway should be extended, or a new one built from some other port. Moreover, Lugard favoured a railway from the highest point of navigation on the Niger River. In 1907 it was decided to build a railway from Baro on the Niger to Kano, and to extend the Lagos Railway to meet it. Both were opened in 1912. The through line to Lagos soon became the main line, and the export of groundnuts, cotton, hides and skins increased enormously. However, the Minna–Baro branch is vital to the maintenance of the Niger–Benue river fleet. The main line was extended from Kano to Nguru in 1927, and the branch from Zaria to Kaura Namoda was built in 1929.

In 1914 the Bauchi Light Railway of 2 feet 6 inches gauge was opened from Zaria to Bukuru, to facilitate development of the tinfields. It was closed in 1957.

The line from Port Harcourt was opened to Enugu in 1916,

primarily to distribute coal. Extensions were made to Kaduna and Jos in 1927, and to Maiduguri in 1964.

Although the railway serves the main cash crop areas and population clusters, its western and eastern lines have long traverses of the unprofitable Middle Belt, and there is no direct west–east line.

Roads. The first road, from Oyo to Ibadan, was built as early as 1906. There are now about 55,000 miles of roads, of which 35,000 are all-season and 10,000 tarred, including the North Road from Lagos. Often the main form of transport is by road and it is estimated that road traffic exceeds a thousand million ton-miles. The densest road networks are in the palm and cocoa belts, the tinfields, and around Kano, Katsina and Lagos. Better roads are required from Lagos to northern Nigeria; more roads are needed almost everywhere, but especially in northern Nigeria.[1]

Air Services. Some twelve towns are served by scheduled air services at least once a week, often several times weekly. Kano is a major inter-continental airport, served by many air lines, and is one of the major nodal points of air traffic in Africa. Lagos (Ikeja) is also a major West African airport. Air transport has done a very great deal for Nigeria, especially in facilitating movements between west and east.[2]

CONCLUSION

With its great physical, social and economic diversity it is appropriate that Nigeria should be a federation. Size and diversity have encouraged a more varied internal economy and a wider range of exports than is usual in West Africa. No one commodity is supremely important. Local foodstuffs are diverse and are the basis of an important internal trade. State exports (cocoa from the West; mineral and palm oil, rubber and timber from the Mid-West; palm produce, rubber and mineral oil from eastern states; groundnuts, cotton, hides, skins, tin and columbite from northern states) are varied.

Only nine countries in the world (including four in the

[1] See also E. K. Hawkins, *Road Transport in Nigeria,* 1958.
[2] Peter M. Gould, ' Air traffic in Nigeria ', *African Studies Bulletin,* Vol. 4, 1961, p. 21.

Commonwealth) normally export more to the United Kingdom than Nigeria. It produces about one-third of the United Kingdom's requirements of vegetable oil and oil seeds, and of cocoa; one-quarter of the imports of tin and of hides, and a tenth of the hardwoods.

Yet its very diversity presents difficulties. In particular, its peoples seem less united than those of some other countries. It also has its special economic problems. Among these are the uncertain future for coal mining, and the need for profitable alternatives to cocoa and the oil palm. Soil conservation is a pressing need, especially in densely peopled Ibo country.

The Middle Belt is a vast poor area in the centre of the country, impeding exchange between north and south, and contributing little. Many other areas await development, such as the thinly peopled lands between Kaura Namoda and Sokoto, between Maiduguri and Kano, the southern Adamawa Highlands, eastern Calabar, eastern Ogoja, and much of Benin, Ondo and Oyo provinces.

If the tsetse fly could be eradicated, water made available cheaply and widely, and social resistance to resettlement overcome, then there are many areas in Nigeria capable of development.

Industrial development has better prospects in Nigeria than elsewhere in West Africa, mainly because of the potentially large market. Over one of every two West Africans is a Nigerian, as is one in five of all Africans. Nigeria is, furthermore, the fourth most populated country of the Commonwealth, and is ninth among world states. Factories such as the very modern Kaduna textile mills, the other numerous textile and cement works, and the oil refinery are very much oriented to the large market. Industries are also being encouraged by varied resources, such as the natural gas at Port Harcourt. This gas, with coal, lignite and oil, could activate a whole complex of industries.

BIBLIOGRAPHY

In addition to books cited in the footnotes, see:

K. M. BUCHANAN and J. C. PUGH, *Land and People in Nigeria*, 1959.
Economic Survey of Nigeria, Lagos, 1959.
G. BRIAN STAPLETON, *The Wealth of Nigeria*, 1958.

The Economic Development of Nigeria—Report of a Mission organised by the International Bank for Reconstruction and Development, 1955.
The Nigeria Hand Book, 1953. (Includes a bibliography.)
Nigeria (Quarterly), Lagos.
Farm and Forest (Quarterly), Ibadan.
Annual Reports of the Regional Production Development Corporations; of the Marketing Boards; and of the Ministries of Agriculture, Commerce and Industries, Marketing and Exports, etc.
Nigerian Trade Journal.
Statistical Digest for Nigeria (Quarterly).
Nigerian Geographical Journal.

MAPS
(Survey Departments, Lagos, Ibadan, Benin, Enugu and Kaduna)
Topographic (all Federal Surveys):

1 : 50,000.
1 : 62,500.
1 : 100,000.
1 : 125,000.
1 : 250,000.
1 : 500,000.
1 : 1,000,000 Layer coloured.

Town Plans:

1 : 1,200, 1 : 2,400, 1 : 4,800 and 1 : 12,500 for most towns.
Also 1 : 30,000 Street map of Lagos.

Geological:

1 : 100,000, 1 : 125,000 and 250,000. A few sheets available.
1 : 2,000,000 Nigeria.

Population:

1 : 500,000 Eastern Region.
1 : 1,000,000 Federation of Nigeria.
1 : 1,000,000 and 1 : 2,000,000 Northern Region.

Various:

1 : 3,000,000 Agriculture, Agricultural Zones, Administration, Rail, Road and River Communications, Domestic Trade, Forest Reserves, Geology, Languages, Physical, Population, Mean Annual Rainfall, Tribal, Vegetation, Mean Maximum Temperature, Mean Minimum Temperature, Isothermal, Boundaries, Tsetse areas, Industries and main Agricultural Exports, and Mineral Deposits.
25 miles to one Inch. Road map of Nigeria.
1 : 750,000. Road map of Western Nigeria.
1 : 1,750,000. Road mileage map of Northern Nigeria.

S

Chapter 27

THE PROVINCE OF FERNANDO PO—
SPAIN'S PLANTATION ISLES

ALONG south-west trending faults, which continue seaward
beyond Mount Cameroon, are located the islands of Fernando
Po (Spanish), Príncipe and São Tomé (Portuguese), and
Annobon (Spanish). Like Mount Cameroon and the Cameroon
and Bamenda Highlands, these result from Tertiary and
Quaternary volcanism.

They were probably discovered by the Portuguese explorer
Fernão de Po in 1471–2. Fernando Po was then named
'Formoso' ('beautiful'); Annobon was so called as it was
discovered on New Year's Day.

In 1494 the remarkable Treaty of Tordesillas awarded new
lands west of 50° W. to the Spanish, and those east of that line
to the Portuguese. The Portuguese were thus confirmed in
Africa and Asia; South America was unequally divided, most
being Spanish. As the slave trade developed, the Portuguese
had the legal monopoly of supply from Africa to both their own
and Spanish possessions in America. This caused increasing
Spanish resentment, and a claim for their own source of supply
in Africa.

In 1778 the Portuguese agreed to cede to Spain the terminal
islands, as well as rights along the mainland between the
Ogowe and Niger Rivers. In exchange, the Portuguese
were confirmed in areas into which they had already spread
beyond the 50° W. line in what is now Brazil. The Spanish
landed on Formoso in 1778 and renamed it Fernando Po after
its discoverer, but yellow fever so decimated their numbers
that they evacuated the island again in 1781. No occupation
was made of the mainland.

The British abolished the slave trade in 1807. To make
this effective, the British Navy required more bases, from

which to watch the Niger mouths and the Slave Coast of what is now Nigeria and Dahomey. The Spanish agreed in 1827 to lease land on Fernando Po to the British for anti-slavery naval bases at Port Clarence (now Santa Isabel) and in San Carlos Bay. The administration of the island also became effectively British.

During the next sixteen years the British Navy landed many freed slaves from captured slave ships. Many Sierra Leone Creoles and West Indian Maroons also settled, and Creole English is still spoken in and around Santa Isabel and San Carlos. From 1879 Spain used the island as a Cuban penal settlement and there are a few descendants of Cubans who remained here after serving their sentences.

As the island was so attractive, and as Spain exercised little or no control, Britain made several proposals for its purchase, £50,000 being offered in 1839. After two years' delay, Spain agreed to sell at £60,000. When, however, this figure was accepted by Britain, Spain withdrew her offer to sell. By 1843 the British Navy was able to concentrate its work at Freetown (Sierra Leone), as the slave trade was dying, and sold its buildings to Baptist missionaries who were, however, ejected by the Spanish in 1858. From 1844 more effective occupation of Fernando Po was made by Spain. On the mainland around the estuary of the Rio Muni treaties were concluded with local chiefs in 1845. The explorers Iradier and Ossorio also travelled on the mainland in the twenty years ending in 1877.

In 1898 Spain was defeated by the United States, and had to surrender all her American tropical possessions. France, profiting from Spain's weakness and in a bellicose mood herself after the Fashoda Incident, was able to constrict Spain's mainland territory of Rio Muni to 10,163 square miles surrounded by Cameroon and Gabon. Development of Fernando Po may be said to date from this time. Rio Muni has been developed by the Spanish only since the Spanish Civil War of 1936–9.

The Province of Rio Muni includes the nearby islands of Corisco, Great and Little Elobey, but lies outside the scope of this book. The Province of Fernando Po includes the islands of Fernando Po (779 square miles) and Annobon (7 square miles). These two overseas provinces of Spain, each with a Governor, constitute her Equatorial Region.

FERNANDO PO

This beautiful island, the largest of the four volcanic islands, lies on a continental shelf with depths of only 330 feet separating

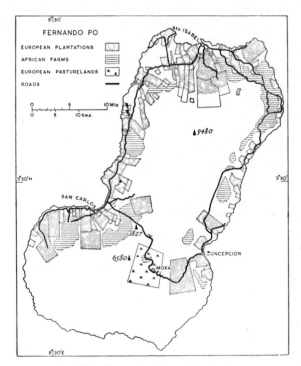

FIG. 88.—Fernando Po and its land use.
(By kind permission of the Editor of *West Africa*.)

it from the mainland. It has a typical north-east to south-west trend, is about 44 miles long, and 22 miles wide. In the north-centre is the Santa Isabel peak (9,480 feet), and in the centre the San Carlos peak (6,580 feet). There is evidence of a transverse fault running west–north–west to east–south–east across the island; this may explain the bays of San Carlos and Concepcion, and the west–east cordillera of the southern part of the island. In that area are valleys several hundreds of feet deep, but the area is little known and is virtually uninhabited and uncultivated. Yet the southern coast has a monsoonal rainfall of some 400 inches annually and, if the valleys could be dammed, the hydro-electric power potential should be high.

With an area of 779 square miles, only about half of which are productive, the indigenous population numbered 33,497 in 1960. Of these, most are more or less pure Bubi people, of Bantu stock. Once declining in numbers, they are now increasing slightly. Their ancient centre was at Moka, 4,600 feet, but they now live mainly at lower altitudes.

The ex-slave community, with its varied origins described above, is included in the above figure. Together with people of mixed indigenous Bubi and Spanish or Portuguese blood, these several groups constitute an exceedingly varied Creole community, akin to that at Freetown, and known to the Bubi as ' Portos ' (a corruption of Portuguese).

Additional to the indigenous Africans there were, in 1960, 23,485 temporary immigrant Africans employed on plantations. Most of them are Ibo from Nigeria, together with others from Rio Muni, Cameroon and Gabon, all to work on the plantations. In the past, most labourers came from the Gold Coast, Liberia, Rio Muni and Cameroon—roughly in that order chronologically. Four-fifths are men, and African men outnumber women on the island by over two to one. There is also a small group of fishermen from Annobon.

In 1960 there were 4,215 white non-Africans, largely made up of officials and the planter community, and living mainly in the three towns. The planter, or plantation manager, his elegant wife and beautiful daughters are very much a part of Fernando Po.

Most settlement and economic activities are concentrated north of the presumed fault. On the western, northern and eastern coasts, from west of San Carlos through Santa Isabel to Concepcion, runs a good road, around which are plantations on fertile volcanic soils. Cocoa, overwhelmingly the main crop of the island, is grown up to about 2,000 feet. Some estates also grow a little coffee, and a few grow coffee exclusively. The most cultivated kind of cocoa is *teobroma*, a variety said to be exclusive to Fernando Po. Other varieties grown are *forastero* and *amelonado dorado*. The European plantations are well cultivated and employ some 23,000 labourers. Swollen Shoot is unknown, but other diseases including Black Pod are troublesome.

Exports of cocoa are about 25,000 metric tons per annum, but vary with the availability of labour. Yields are high and quality good. Sufficient cocoa is grown for the needs of Spain, which accords preferential duties. Without these, Fernando Po could not compete with Ghana which, incidentally, received its cocoa from Fernando Po in 1879.

Coffee, found up to about 3,000 feet, is almost entirely grown on European plantations. The main variety is *liberica*. Exports are about 1,600 metric tons annually. Bananas are grown to shade the cocoa, and the fruit is being increasingly exported. Cocoa and coffee occupy over four-fifths of the cultivated area of Fernando Po, most of the rest being occupied by yams, cocoyams, bananas and rice grown by Africans.

From Fig. 88 it will be seen that non-African plantations belonging to settlers, absentee landlords, or companies, occupy most of the cultivable area. In 1940 there were 583 non-African plantations covering 81,292 acres, averaging 140 acres each, with some companies owning several plantations. In 1942 there were 3,026 African plantations, covering 37,173 acres, each averaging twelve acres, a situation recalling East, Central and South African land apportionment.

Santa Isabel is, in its centre, a well-planned and spacious town with some good buildings, especially the cathedral and mission. This may in part be due to the cheapness of volcanic rock, building stone normally being rare in West Africa. African quarters on the outer margins are less satisfactory, but are better than those normally found elsewhere in West Africa. Air services are maintained with Madrid, Bata (Rio Muni) and with Duala (Republic of Cameroon). The deep and arcuate harbour results from the sea having breached a volcanic crater. Most of the island's trade and all its overseas passengers pass through the town, whose population in 1960 was 37,237 out of 61,197 for the whole island. Non-African whites living in the town numbered 3,358, or three-fifths of all non-Africans on the island. The others can reach it easily in under an hour. Many live more or less permanently on the island, so explaining the good shops and casino.

Above the plantations much forest remains, especially on steep ground. Mainly between 4,000 and 5,300 feet are pasture lands resulting from forest clearance. Trees, including giant tree-ferns, survive in valleys and, because of the high relative humidity at this altitude, lichens often festoon the trees. Swiss, Galicia and Canary Island cattle are kept on the pasture lands of a Spanish ranching company around Moka, in the south-centre of the island. Fernando Po is self-sufficient in dairy produce, even with the considerable European population, but has to import some meat from the Cameroon Republic. At Moka there is also a co-operative of African peasant owners, who grow temperate vegetables, especially potatoes.

Above the rich Moka pasture lands is a narrow Montane Woodland on steep slopes. Where these flatten out, at about 5,500 feet, bracken occurs and the lovely *Lobelia columnaris*, which attains some seven feet. More pasture lands succeed this, and then give way to moorland up to the high peaks.

Fernando Po, though geographically in West Africa, is, like São Tomé and Príncipe, more akin in its social and economic character to the Kenya Highlands, South Africa or Caribbean Isles. There is the same dependence upon one main export crop, grown on volcanic soils, with the help of more or less landless labourers.

ANNOBON [1]

Annobon, 400 miles to the south-west of Fernando Po, and beyond Príncipe and São Tomé, is also volcanic (highest point 2,438 feet), but has an area of only 6·6 square miles. In 1960 its population was 1,415. The main exports are palm kernels and copra, cocoa and coffee; it is heavily over-populated, as much of the island is rugged and useless. Some 400 Annobonese are in Fernando Po and Rio Muni working as fishermen, and a few on plantations. Fishing is also important off Annobon.

[1] For a detailed study see Hernandez-Pacheco, 'La Isla de Annobon', *Boletin de la Real Sociedad Geográfica*, Madrid, 1942, pp. 430–46.

BIBLIOGRAPHY

Fernando Po. Circular of the Fourth C.I.A.O. (International West African Conference, 1951).

J. Nosti, *Notas Geográficas, Físicas y Económicas sobre los Territorios Españoles del Golfo de Guinea,* Instituto de Estudios Africanos, 1947.

René Pélissier, *Les Territoires Espagnols d'Afrique,* Direction de la Documentation, Paris, 1963, and *Los Territorios españoles de Africa,* C.S.I.C.— I.D.E.A., Madrid, 1964.

D. J. Bonelli y Rubio, *Notas sobre la Geografía humana des los territorios españoles del Golfo de Guinea y Geografía económica de la Guinea española,* Direccion General de Marruecos y Colonias, 1944–5.

Resumenes Estadisticos del Gobierno General de los Territorios Españoles del Golfo de Guinea, Direccion General de Marruecos y Colonias.

Atlas Histórico y Geográfico de Africa Española, Direccion General de Marruecos y Colonias, 1955.

Chapter 28

THE PROVINCE OF SÃO TOMÉ AND PRÍNCIPE—
PORTUGAL'S PLANTATION ISLES [1]

SÃO TOMÉ (approximately 330 square miles) and Príncipe (approximately 42 square miles) were probably discovered by the Portuguese in 1471. Settlement began in 1485, and in the succeeding hundred years Portuguese came from Portugal and Madeira, as well as Jews, Spanish, French and Genoese. The sugar cane was introduced, as it had been earlier in Madeira. To work the sugar plantations slaves were brought from the Guinea Coast, and from what are now the Gabon and Angola.

Portuguese royal decree permitted each Portuguese settler to take one woman slave as a mistress. Thus by 1554 there was already a large percentage of Creoles in the population, and they were free and prosperous. Sugar was extracted in sixty factories located in the lower lands of São Tomé, and the annual export of sugar reached a maximum of about 2,250 metric tons. The population of São Tomé was then over 9,000, but only the north-eastern third of the island was being occupied.

However, sugar production was soon ruined by the competition of Brazilian sugar, political instability, and by the rioting of Angolan ex-slaves. These 'Angolares' were descendants of fugitives from a slave ship which had been wrecked on the east coast of São Tomé. They established themselves high upon the island and, some fifty years after, wrecked the sugar mills. The Angolares were not pacified until three centuries later, a story akin to that of the Maroons of Jamaica in the eighteenth century.

[1] This chapter is by Francisco Tenreiro of São Tomé, a member of the Centre de Estudos Geográficos of the University of Lisbon. The material has been edited and revised by the general author.

With the ruin of the sugar plantations and trade, most Portuguese planters migrated to Brazil. In the seventeenth and eighteenth centuries the islands served merely as victualling points for Portuguese ships going to India, or to the New World with slaves. Warehousing of slaves was the main commerce. The few remaining settlers and Creoles fought for political supremacy, and the Dutch and French attacked the islands repeatedly.

Agriculture was not revived until the introduction of coffee in 1800 and of cocoa in 1822. The development of these crops attracted new landowners and, between them and the older community, there were savage struggles for land. The new coffee and cocoa plantations were, moreover, nearly ruined by the final abolition of slavery in São Tomé and Príncipe in 1869. As the Creoles would not work on the plantations, contract labourers have since been employed from Angola and Mozambique.

The islands form a Province of Overseas Portugal.

POPULATION

The 1960 census gave the population of the islands as 63,485, or 173 per square mile. The population of São Tomé is 58,880 and that of Príncipe 4,605. Men accounted for 35,259, as there are contract labourers, as on Fernando Po. On the Portuguese islands the contract labourer serves for four to five years, and is paid a minimum of 100 escudos (about £1 10s.) per month with free food, barrack lodging and medical attention.

Some of the indigenous Africans are descendants of freed slaves, somewhat similar to the 'Portos' of Fernando Po. Other Creoles, who numbered 6,632, cultivate small farms, engage in domestic and manual work, or are teachers or government officials.

The white population of 2,520 is engaged in the ways usual in West Africa, and as managers of plantations owned by wealthy absentee landlords living in Lisbon. There were very few Asians.

Although there is no colour bar, there are self-contained cultural and economic ' racial classes ', with rigid occupational and social immobility. Efforts are being made to reform the contract labour system into a fixed one by means of land grants, by extending roads to the south of São Tomé to open new country, by enlarging the scope of education, and by rural and urban betterment.

The north-eastern parts of both islands are lowest and the least healthy, but they are the most level and fertile. Hence they have, in turn, been cultivated mainly for sugar and now for cocoa and coffee. The density of population is greatest there and reaches 625 per square mile. The town of São Tomé, at the head of the fine Ana de Chaves Bay, and that of Santo António at the head of the bay of the same name on Príncipe, occupy similar lowland sites on the north-eastern parts of the islands. A narrow-gauge railway links the town of São Tomé with Trindade and many plantations.

On the south-eastern side of the island of São Tomé there are fewer plantations and people, as the soils are less fertile and the region is ill-served by roads. In the north-east, settlement regularly reaches about 2,750 feet and, occasionally, 4,000 feet where a little cinchona is grown. But in the south-east, settlements are rarely found above 1,400 feet.

CLIMATE AND VEGETATION

Equatorial conditions prevail, with strong orographic and maritime influences. Unlike the rest of West Africa, these islands and Annobon have Southern Hemisphere seasons, with the drier period (*Gravana*) and south-easterly winds from June to September.[1]

Four sub-regions may be distinguished. First come the lower lands on the north-east side of both islands, where temperatures and relative humidity are consistently high and rainfall averages 40 inches annually. Above 1,300 feet, however, temperatures are lower and more variable, there is more movement of air, and much more rain. Thirdly, there are the mountainous areas above about 2,000 feet, where temperatures are again lower, there is persistent light rain,

[1] See Chapter 3, page 53.

much mist and cold nights. Fourthly, on the south-eastern lower lands, there is rain all the year.

Rain Forest covers the mountainous centres, and much of the south and south-eastern sides of the islands. Below about 3,250 feet most of the forest has been cleared for plantations, or is Secondary Forest with *Adansonia digitata* and *Ceiba pentandra* often remaining. Red Mangrove occurs on favoured parts of the coasts.

GEOLOGY AND RELIEF

Príncipe is roughly rectangular in form and, in shape and disposition of relief, is a smaller version of Fernando Po. It is about 10 miles from south-west to north-east and 4–6 miles across. It rises to 3,110 feet and is mainly basaltic in character.

São Tomé, oval in shape, is 30 miles in length from south-west to north-east, and 20 miles across at its widest part. The Ilhéu das Rôlas, off the southern coast, lies on the Equator. There are many bays on the east and lower north-east coasts of São Tomé, and on all sides of Príncipe.

The island of São Tomé is mainly basaltic, and has many craters and lava flows, the latter being well preserved in the north-east. Andesites and trachytes also occur.

Sedimentary sandstone and clayey limestone, with indications of lignite, gas, oil and bitumen, have been found at Uba-Budo, and on Príncipe, and are probably Lower Cretaceous in age. Miocene limestones have been found in the great Santo António bay of Príncipe.[1]

São Tomé rises to 6,640 feet and, in the west-centre of the island, there are over ten peaks above 3,500 feet. These often terminate in finger-like phonoliths, which have survived after softer volcanic materials have been eroded, and are akin to similar peaks at Le Puy (France). From such impressive peaks there is an abrupt descent to the west coast, with gentler slopes in other directions. In the south the lowlands are covered by volcanic cinder and ash, and the Rôlas islet is composed of lava and basalt, and has two craters.

---

[1] C. Teixeira, 'Notas sobre a Geologia das Ilhas de São Tomé e do Príncipe', *Estudos Colonias*, I, 1948–9.

ECONOMIC RESOURCES

Almost all export crops are grown, as on Fernando Po, in large plantations, or *roças*, owned by absentee Portuguese landlords or companies, with mainly European local managers. One cocoa estate covers over 25,000 acres, or one-tenth of São Tomé.[1]

The coconut was introduced from India in the sixteenth century. It grows well round almost all the coasts. Copra and coconut exports, which are increasing, account for about 20% of all exports by value. Oil palm products account for about 5% of the exports.

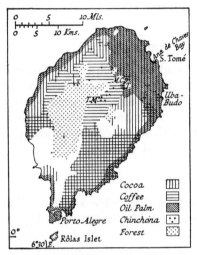

FIG. 89.—Cash Crops of São Tomé.

Coconuts are found on all coasts, except the west-south-west. T = Trindade, M.C. = Monte Café, TM = Trás-os-Montes.

Up to about 1,400 feet, however, the north-east of both islands is mainly under cocoa. Coffee is of minor importance at higher levels up to about 1,500 feet and is the main crop on Monté Café and in Trás-os-Montes. A very little cinchona is grown at higher altitudes up to about 3,000 feet.

São Tomé and Príncipe were the leading world exporters of cocoa until 1905 and the highest export was 49,945 metric tons in 1919–20. Since then exports have declined; they were only 8,850 tons in 1965 and have been lower. Reduced cocoa production results from declining fertility of the plantations and the impossibility of finding much new land in such a mountainous environment. Production methods on the plantations are very traditional, and after 1908 British chocolate firms ceased their purchases following complaints of slave-like labour conditions on the plantations. About one-quarter the cocoa export now goes to the

[1] G. Viers, ' Le Cacao dans le Monde ', *Les Cahiers d'Outre-Mer*, 1953, p. 317.

Netherlands, one-third to the United States and only one-sixth to Portugal. Cocoa exports account for two-thirds of all exports from São Tomé and Príncipe. Coffee exports comprise about 5% of exports. Livestock are of very minor importance. The usual African foodstuffs are grown, especially yams. Maize flour, soap and lime are made on the islands. Descendants of the Angolares are fishermen. Norwegian and other ships occasionally fish for sharks and small whales, the oil being extracted on the ships and on shore.

COMMUNICATIONS

Although there is a coastal road on Príncipe, São Tomé is still without one. Most plantations have beaches and use sailing canoes for transport. There is also the narrow-gauge railway on São Tomé. Three airfields have services between the towns of São Tomé and Porto Alegre, between the two islands, to Fernando Po, Angola and Portugal.

CONCLUSION

Like Fernando Po, São Tomé and Príncipe are plantation territories more akin to the Kenya Highlands or to West Indian isles than to the rest of West Africa. Their plantation economy and social organisation stand in vivid contrast to the rest of West Africa.

BIBLIOGRAPHY

H. GALVAO and C. SALVAGEM, Império Ultramarino Português, Vol. II, 1951.

C. TEIXEIRA, Geologia das ilhas de São Tomé e do Príncipe e do territorio de São, João Baptista de Ajudá, Anais da Junta das Missões Geográficas e de Investigações Coloniais, Vol. II, No. II, Lisbon, 1949.

F. TENREIRO, A Ilha de São Tomé, No. 24 de Memórias da Junta de Investigações do Ultramar, Lisbon, 1961.

F. TENREIRO, 'A Agricultura na ilha de São Tomé: suas relações com as condições geográficas, a colonização e a economia geral', Comptes Rendus du XVIe Congrès International de Géographie, Lisbon, 1949, Vol. 3, 1952, pp. 41–60.

MAPS

1 : 100,000 and 1 : 50,000 (photographic enlargement) São Tomé, 1921–2.
1 : 75,000 and 1 : 30,000 Príncipe, 1921 and 1929–30. One sheet for each island in each case. All Ministério das Colonias.
Atlas de Portugal Ultramarino, 1948.

CONCLUSION

L'Afrique—Terre qui Meurt (Title of J. P. Harroy's book, published 1944).
' Africa to-day remains a continent of uncertainties ' (*The Times*, 5 March,
1955).
' Africa is the new continent; she is a focus of twentieth century development ' (*The Times*, 1 December, 1949).

WEST AFRICA is a mosaic of many countries in which, except
for Liberia, four European powers pursued their divergent and
often contradictory aims. The nine ex-French and four ex-
British countries all became independent between 1957 and
1965, while the Spanish province has local autonomy. Only
the Portuguese provinces, still in close association with Portugal, have no democratic institutions. Liberia, for long politically independent, lives largely by concessions, which, in the
past, kept it in closer relationship with the United States of
America than most ex-colonies ever were to their metropolitan
country.

Although there is no other area of Africa with such a mosaic
of political units and contrasting policies, West Africa has, for
the most part, been saved the added social stresses of planter
communities. Even in the isles of the Bight of Biafra, the
problem is one of land alienation rather than that of white
settlement.

Three outstanding problems result from the many and varied
political units. As the territories became independent there
has been a most unfortunate tendency to break up into smaller
entities. Nigeria has accentuated its division from four
Regions and the Federal Territory of Lagos into twelve states,
and there are Nigerians who wish to create more states, although
they acknowledge the importance of the federation. The
Federation of French West Africa has given place to eight
individual countries whose policies are often at variance, and
whose boundaries have become major divides, e.g. between

Guinea and Senegal. Although new groupings such as the Ghana–Guinea–Mali Union, and the Benin–Sahel Entente of the Ivory Coast, the Upper Volta, Niger, Dahomey and Togo have been formed, West Africa is as divided politically as ever, and more so economically.

Secondly, many problems result from the quite incredible ignorance of what is going on across the artificial boundaries. Despite the work of the Organisation for African Unity, the United Nations Economic Commission for Africa, and many West African bodies, much research is pursued in ignorance of similar work across the boundary.

Lastly, the unrealistic boundaries created by the colonial powers, have been inherited, but each country seems determined to hold what it has. The new nations have contrasted legacies of language, administrative method, tax and tariff structure, currency zone allegiance, educational system, and so forth. All these are major impediments to political integration, economic development, and even simple collaboration.

Almost all means of transport have been constructed from nothing in a half-century. It is not surprising, therefore, that economic development has been patchy and largely coastal. Particularly is this so in the successor states of ex-French West Africa, where 90% of the exports by value and by tonnage come from two-fifths of the people.

Development of the interior is not only impeded by its greater dryness, water shortage and length of communications, but also by the existence of the intervening Middle Belt. Lying between approximately 8° N. and $10\frac{1}{2}°$ N., and coinciding largely with the Guinea Savannah, it contributes little to West Africa or the World.

Crucial to the development of the Middle Belt is the elimination of the tsetse; a pioneer fringe would then become available for settlement by nearby peoples. Cattle raising could also develop. Elimination of the tsetse is no less vital elsewhere, to man and beast. But so long as this fly is widespread, more attention might profitably be given to improving the small resistant cattle. The south is also in need of cheap suppressives of malaria and of yaws. Poor physique starts the vicious circle of low initiative and productivity, leading to low income and poor nutrition.

Fundamental to all life in West Africa is agriculture. While it is possibly the case that for the cultivation of food crops the optimum areas and conditions have been found by African farmers, this is not always true of export crops. These must generally be grown near lines of transport. Nor is the best use always made of the optimum areas where they are known.

There is potential danger in the apparent general decline in food crop production. Farmers' sons prefer more remunerative and less arduous occupations, and the remaining farmers, especially near the coasts, turn more and more to export crops. Moreover, certain food crops are in rapid decline, such as yams—which are tedious to cultivate—in favour of cassava, which is so easily grown. On the credit side, however, the increasing cultivation of swamp rice is admirable.

Export crops were exceedingly prosperous after the Second World War, but there has been some recession. With increasing competition from other tropical producers, especially from plantations, more is likely. The threat is grave because so much revenue depends on so few export crops. Furthermore, prosperity has resulted not only from increased production but from the good fortune of high prices for long periods, and heavy demand. On the other hand, due credit must be given for the notable improvement in the quality of Nigerian palm oil and cotton, and the great output of Ghana's cocoa.

It remains doubtful whether there will be any great increase in agricultural output, except by the development of new areas, or by a technical revolution, or both. Some alternative to the land-wasting system of bush fallowing will force itself upon West Africa as the population increases. It has already done so in certain areas of high population density, such as in the Kabrai country of northern Togo where there are tiny terraced fields and permanent rotational farming using vegetable and animal waste.

Some have seen an answer in mechanisation. Outside Africa it has not been applied to small farms, so that it is unlikely to be useful in the difficult physical conditions of West Africa, further complicated as it is by unhelpful forms of land tenure. Mechanisation is limited by the high cost of clearance, the difficulty of maintaining fertility when shifting cultivation is abandoned, low crop yields compared with more intensive cultivation, scattered and tiny cultivated patches, and the cost and difficulty of mechanical maintenance and repair. Mechanical cultivation may be valuable for rice cultivation in treeless valley bottoms, and on level dry land in thinly populated areas. It is not certain to pay even in these environments; it is almost certainly no solution elsewhere.

Publicity has been given to the dangers of soil erosion. They are real, but the extent of the disaster has been grossly exaggerated. Far more important, in area and in degree, is the loss of soil fertility. Man needs quicker, easier and cheaper means of restoring fertility than by bush fallowing. Especially is this so in cash crop areas, where plant nutrients are exported overseas, e.g. in the form of the massive crops of groundnuts from Nigeria or Senegal.

Great progress has been made in industrialisation, especially in Nigeria, Ghana, the Ivory Coast and Senegal. Socialist methods of control and development have been tried in Ghana, Guinea and Mali. However, countries such as Mauritania, Mali, Upper Volta, Niger, Gambia, Portuguese Guinea, Liberia, Togo and Dahomey have such small, poor or dispersed populations that they cannot at the moment support most types of industries. Furthermore, each country excludes most industrial produce from other African states. Industrial development also depends not only upon the possession of the requisite raw materials but upon the existence of sufficient engineering, managerial and other technical skills, the availability of capital, and of an acquisitive, rational and expansionist society. The most immediately hopeful lines for industrialisation are in the processing and grading of local materials, already grown or produced cheaply in West Africa and in great world demand, such as palm oil and other vegetable oils. There are also good prospects for most consumer-good industries and assembly plants. The future for heavy industry is mainly linked with the massive generation of cheap hydro-electric power in Ghana and Nigeria, and with the more varied use of Nigeria's oil, gas, coal and other resources.

West Africa has been in contact with North Africa for a millennium, with Europe for half that time, but with world economy for little over half a century. Intensive and generalised economic development dates only from the Second World

War. West Africa already has more than its proportionate share of Africa's population and external trade; it has also been the scene of some of the most interesting political developments.

May these be viewed in the spirit of the dedication of this book, and in recollection of the words of one of the greatest scholars of Africa

' History, looking back in retrospect on the part played by Imperial Powers in Africa, will be more concerned with the nature of the contribution which the European occupant will have made to the future of the African peoples, than with the profit or loss which the African connexion may have brought to Europe.'[1]

[1] Lord Hailey, *An African Survey*, 1945, p. XXIII.

INDEX

The numbers in heavy type refer to a more important mention of the subject. Numbers in italics refer to photographs facing, or maps on, pages not otherwise listed. Conventional abbreviations are used, e.g., R for River, etc. An asterisk indicates that further reference should be made to the same subject under the countries.